Convergence in European Consumer Sales Law

A Comparative and Numerical Approach

Cătălina Goanţă

Convergence in European Consumer Sales Law
A Comparative and Numerical Approach

intersentia

METRO

Intersentia Ltd
Sheraton House | Castle Park
Cambridge | CB3 0AX | United Kingdom
Tel.: +44 1223 370 170 | Fax: +44 1223 370 169
Email: mail@intersentia.co.uk
www.intersentia.com | www.intersentia.co.uk

Distribution for the UK and Ireland:
NBN International
Airport Business Centre, 10 Thornbury Road
Plymouth, PL6 7PP
United Kingdom
Tel.: +44 1752 202 301 | Fax: +44 1752 202 331
Email: orders@nbninternational.com

Distribution for Europe and all other countries:
Intersentia Publishing nv
Groenstraat 31
2640 Mortsel
Belgium
Tel.: +32 3 680 15 50 | Fax: 32 3 658 71 21
Email: mail@intersentia.be

Distribution for the USA and Canada:
International Specialized Book Services
920 NE 58th Ave. Suite 300
Portland, OR 97213
USA
Tel.: +1 800 944 6190 (toll free) | Fax: + 1 503 280 8832
Email: info@isbs.com

Convergence in European Consumer Sales Law
A Comparative and Numerical Approach

ISBN 978-1-78068-431-4
D/2016/7849/135
NUR 822

British Library Cataloguing in Publication Data. A catalogue record for this book is available from the British Library.

In loving memory of Grandfather

'S-a stins lumina lumii..'

ACKNOWLEDGEMENTS

The journey of writing one's first book, especially of an academic nature, is infamously difficult. The rainbow of situations and emotions that come with this experience can barely be put into words, but this preface is dedicated to just that. After all, legal scholars might not have microspectrometers or telescopes (at least private lawyers do not), but we are supposed to master the art of the written or spoken word.

I have finally managed to complete my very own PhD saga. In other words, I made it through the extreme ups and downs inherent to this process: from the early confidence and enthusiasm in a new topic, to the troubled times of working out methodological details and finding the best way to package thoughts, to the gained ownership of the final result. This journey has been overwhelming in many ways, and the engine of the entire undertaking has not been my individual perseverance, but the amazing individuals who both guided and accompanied me through this odyssey.

In a world full of people who generally could not care less, I have been blessed to be surrounded by people who could not care more, and that first and foremost applies to my supervisors, *Jan Smits* and *Caroline Cauffman*. I genuinely could not have wished for better supervisors, better academics, or better persons. The amount of time and effort that both of them have put into the development of the ideas behind this manuscript, consisting of precious feedback and endless support, has been out of this world. Our dense meetings, for which both *Jan* and *Caroline* managed to always make enough room, have constantly challenged me to look at the project from their two very different perspectives and styles, one Dutch, the other Belgian, that had, among others, an essential commonality: the strive for academic excellence. They have taught me the value of high research standards and in the light of that I was inspired to follow in their footsteps and attempt to make a meaningful contribution to European consumer law. To achieve that, my research has taken me to an empirical territory considered controversial by some; yet I have learned from my supervisors that trying to be innovative might come with risks one needs to courageously assume, instead of shy away from. I am equally eternally grateful to both *Jan* and *Caroline* for all the opportunities they have given me in terms of personal development, both in research as well as in teaching. Had it not been for Jan's endorsement and nomination, I would have never been anywhere close to the Wynand Wijnen Education Prize, and had it not been for Caroline's support and advice, I would have perhaps never become a doctoral candidate in the first place. I have listed here only a handful of reasons why I will forever be thankful to and for my supervisors; and while the complete list would probably be a self-standing novel, for now I would just like to emphasise that working under their supervision has been an amazing time that I will forever cherish, and I hope my manuscript does this experience justice.

My appreciation is also directed towards the Assessment Committee, for the time and willigness to assess my PhD manuscript. *Gerard-René de Groot* has been a constant source of wisdom on comparative law methodologies, which I have gotten glimpses of through long discussions but also through our great collaboration within the ambit of a course on this very topic. I am thus honoured that he has accepted to be the Chairperson of the Committee. I can say the same for the rest of the Committee members. *Hans Schulte-Nölke* has authored some of the most extensive studies in European consumer law to date, which have been a valuable stepping stone for this project. *Mathias Siems*' work on numerical comparative law as an empirically-oriented methodology has also been central to this study, and I am trankful for having had the opportunity to discuss this with its original author in September 2015, with the occasion of the MEPLI Conference 'Consumers Without Borders'. Lastly, but most certainly not least, I am especially indebted to *Bram Akkermans*, whose challenging questions and feedback pushed me to refine my understanding of what I wanted to achieve with this study (#bakebread), and nudged me to look into policy-making to obtain a better understanding of how harmonisation really works.

I would also like to thank *Omri Ben-Shahar* and *Richard McAdams* for their challenging yet enthusiastic comments on my research. I had the opportunity to present the findings of this study in the 2016 Summer Institute of Law and Economics organised by the Coase-Sandor Institute at the University of Chicago. The law and economics views expressed by Chicago faculty have tremendously helped me with improving the communication of my findings, as well as with endless inspiration for research spin-offs for the short-term future.

In the same vein, our own faculty members, *Marcel Schaper, Niels Philipsen* and *Mariolina Eliantonio* have played meaningful roles in the fine-tuning of my empirical ideas, either by participating in random creative brainstorming sessions, or suggesting literature from very different fields of law. Thus I am greatly indebted to their availability and feedback.

A self-standing recognition of appreciation must, without a doubt, be directed to our amazing Dean, *Hildegard Schneider*. Her constant support during the years in which I have completed my PhD has had an incredible impact in terms of my overall development in the faculty. Her passion for moot court competitions, out-of-the-box thinking, and student development have been a constant source of inspiration as well as respect.

A special thank you goes to my beloved paranymphs, *Anna Beckers* and *Lucian Mircescu. Anna* and I have bonded before through paranymphing duties, with the occasion of her outstanding PhD defense. However, her support has always gone beyond any such duty. Her kind advice helped me soldier on through writing this manuscript, and it is all the more impressive as it comes from true friendship, and not just mere colleagiality. As for *Lucian*, I am happy to have shared with him a fantastic UNU-MERIT Graduate School of Governance experience, which has been defining in my endeavour to embrace a more empirical view of the law, and to understand the importance of such a view for public policy.

Also deserving endless praise is my family: my mother, *Cornelia Goanţă*, my father, *Viorel Goanţă*, my brother *Florin Goanţă* and my sister-in-law, *Loredana Din*. Apart from being incredibly supportive, they have all been greatly helpful as well. My mother - also a lawyer - has given me priceless legal advice on procedural aspects of Romanian unfair contract terms, and my bother and sister-in-law have provided me with daily consumer experiences in the field of online sales, in the light of their online tyre business. As for my father, words are not enough to thank him for the hundreds of hours he spent helping me on a wide array of research tasks: finding case law, finding sources, double-checking bibliographic references, and so on and so forth. With this occasion I have witnessed how my father, a military engineer, has achieved outstanding legal research skills.

Moreover, I would also like to thank my Japanese brother, *Mark Kawakami*, for being an inspiration and always playing devil's advocate during our numerous formal and informal discussions. This helped me become absolutely convinced that the world needs empirical legal research. I am also grateful for Mark's delicious Juicy Lucys, and shared scifi preferences: watching Star Wars and Star Trek in good company can definitely alleviate some of the negative side-effects of PhD editing.

As part of my teaching obligations during my PhD time I have been engaged in many activities, but I hold one of them particulary dear to my heart, as its inspiring nature has most certainly changed the way in which I see legal education. My new colleague and friend, *Gwen Noteborn*, has been the mastermind behind our 2015 'Google Glass in the legal classroom' project, one of the most fun teaching activities I have ever undertaken. I am incredibly grateful to have been a part of this.

Also during my PhD time in Maastricht, our MEPLI corridor has been our home (perhaps too much so). My fantastic MEPLI colleagues *Anna Berlee, Jiangqiu Ge, William Bull, Daniel On, Nicole Kornet, Katja Zimmerman, Caroline Calomme, Pim Oosterhuis, Kate O'Reilly, Adela Ognean, Serban Vacarelu, Thera Dieleman, Agustin Parise, Lars van Vliet* as well as non-MEPLI colleagues *Matteo Bonelli, Mieke Olaerts, Sascha Hardt, Tanja van der Meer, Catherine de Rijdt, Ria Wolleswinkel*, have contributed to making Maastricht University feel like a family, and not just a workplace. I will forever treasure this.

Marina Jodogne has been my rock in the weeks leading up to the submission of this manuscript. Her eagle-eye editing, her amazing composure in front of deadlines and her wise advice have been the balancing act ensuring the successful completion of this project. *Marina*, I know you will have to review these lines, so let me say it here as well: thank you from the bottom of my heart.

Of course, no list would be complete without acknowledging some of the amazing students I have had the pleasure of getting to know and work with along the years of my PhD and beyond. I would like to explicitly mention the fantastic *Jasmine Styles, Merle Temme, Andrea Rigamonti, Olav de Wit, Luca Bücken, Anca Bliort, Stefan Cirjan, Felix Pflücke, Benedikt Schmitz, Rikke Øksnes, Simon Schneider* and *Harvey*

Davies. Moreover, *Cristiana Cozac* and *Eddie King* have spent sleepless nights during their holiday to proofread and edit my manuscript, and I could not be more grateful for that.

I would also like to thank French bands *M83* and *Daft Punk* for having created the greatest legal writing soundtracks ever known to mankind (M83's *Oblivion* sountrack and Daft Punk's *Random Access Memories* album).

I saved the most important kind of support for last. I would like to thank my absolutely one-in-a-million husband *Willem Loof* for his eternal patience as well as for his active support in the completion of my manuscript. I want to thank him for putting up with my (very) stressful deadlines, my spontaneous exhilaration with eureka moments, and my endless questions about Dutch terminology or literature. I want to also thank him for allowing me to make post-it maps of case law and to write graphic timelines and check-lists on our livingroom walls. I want to thank him for asking me more questions about my research than I have ever asked him about his, and helping me answer my own questions by using his outstanding knowledge of private law as a sounding board to fix my dead-ends. And more than anything, I want to thank him for being a researcher too, and for understanding me as well as he does. Without him by my side, I could not achieve anything.

Cătălina Goanţă
Maastricht, October 2016

CONTENTS

LIST OF ABBREVIATIONS

AG	Advocate General
Art.	Article
B2B	Business to Business
B2C	Business to Consumer
BGB	Bürgerlich Gesetzbuch (German Civil Code)
BW	Burgerlijk Wetboek
CC	French Civil Code
CCAS	Consumer Codes Approval Scheme
CESL	Common European Sales Law
CFR	Common Frame of Reference
CI	Convergence Index
CISG	United Nations Convention on Contracts for the International Sale of Goods
CJEU	Court of Justice of the European Union
CPR	Consumer Protection for Unfair Trading Regulations
CRD	Consumer Rights Directive
CSE	Comparison Shopping Engine
DCFR	Draft Common Frame of Reference
DE	Deutschland (Germany)
DG	Directorate-General
ECR	European Case Report
EEC	European Economic Community
EFTA	European Free Trade Association
ESME	European Securities Market Expert
EU	European Union
EUR	Euros
FR	France
fsQCA	fuzzy set Qualitative Comparative Analysis
MvT	Memorie van Toelichting
NCA	National Consumer Agency
NL	the Netherlands
No.	Number

OECD	Organisation for Economic Co-operation and Development
OFT	Office of Fair Trading
OHIM	Office for Harmonisation in the Internal Market (Trade Marks and Designs)
OJ	Official Journal
Para.	Paragraph
PECL	Principles on European Contract Law
PEL S	Principles of European Law of Sales
RO	Romania
SGSA	Supply of Goods and Services Act 1982 (UK)
SI	Statutory Instrument (Ireland)
SME	Small and Medium-Sized Enterprise
SoGA	Sale of Goods Act 1979 (UK)
TEC	Treaty Establishing the European Community
TEU	Treaty on the European Union
TFEU	Treaty on the Functioning of the European Union
TSI	Trading Standards Institute
UK	United Kingdom
US	United States
UWG	Gesetz gegen den unlauteren Wettbewerb (German Unfair Commercial Practices Act)

LIST OF TABLES AND FIGURES

Chapter 1

INTRODUCTION

1. Globalisation and Legal Convergence: The Background

1.1. *Introduction*

This is a study about legal convergence in European consumer sales law. It aims to offer a comparative and numerical analysis on the extent to which European directives in this field contribute to convergence. It does so by developing a comparative and numerical framework to evaluate the ambit of such convergence, as well as the factors on which it is dependent. This analysis aims to fill a clear gap in the existing literature on European harmonisation that, until now, has avoided assessing the actual converging effect of European Union (EU) legislation.

This Chapter is structured as follows. The remainder of this Section provides the background to globalisation and legal convergence. Legal convergence, as a result of globalisation, is firstly defined (Section 1.2), and subsequently explained by making an inventory of the driving forces behind it (Section 1.3). This is essential for the clarification of a concept ('convergence') that has until now been used in many different ways and contexts. Section 2 is then devoted to one specific policy behind convergence: the harmonisation of laws as practiced by the European Union. This opens the way for defining the aims and methodology of this study (Section 3). The remaining Sections of this Chapter focus on the novelty of the study (Section 4), its limitations (Section 5) and overall structure (Section 6).

Although globalisation might be nothing new,[1] the beginning of the 1990s brought another understanding of how interconnected individual economies are and how they contribute to the emergence of one new world economy.[2] This renewed understanding of globalisation coincided with the further opening of markets, technological advances, and the democratisation of finance and information.[3] Corporations openly became key players in governance, as did

1 Van Den Bossche 2005, p. 4; see also Mahbubani 2013, p. 247.
2 Fazio 2007, p. 1.
3 Van Den Bossche 2005, p. 5.

citizens.[4] Diversity seemed to be a common feature of the multiple facets of globalisation, as it not only affected the actors involved, but the essence of the internationalisation process itself. In Stiglitz' words, globalisation 'encompasses many things: the international flow of ideas and knowledge, the sharing of cultures, global civil society and the global environmental movement'.[5] Given that it touches upon so many aspects of politics, society, commerce and culture to name a few, the full impact of globalisation remains blurry. However, what becomes increasingly clear is that while globalisation can lead to economic growth and poverty alleviation, it can also have destructive effects.[6]

The pros and cons of globalisation have been intensely covered by literature, so it is highly circumstantial to claim globalisation is either (solely) detrimental or beneficial.[7] The focus of this study reflects one specific aspect of globalisation: its effect on law. The last few decades have seen a spike in this debate, including at European level (see Google Ngrams below).[8]

Figures 1 & 2: Google Ngrams for 'globalisation' & 'European harmonisation'

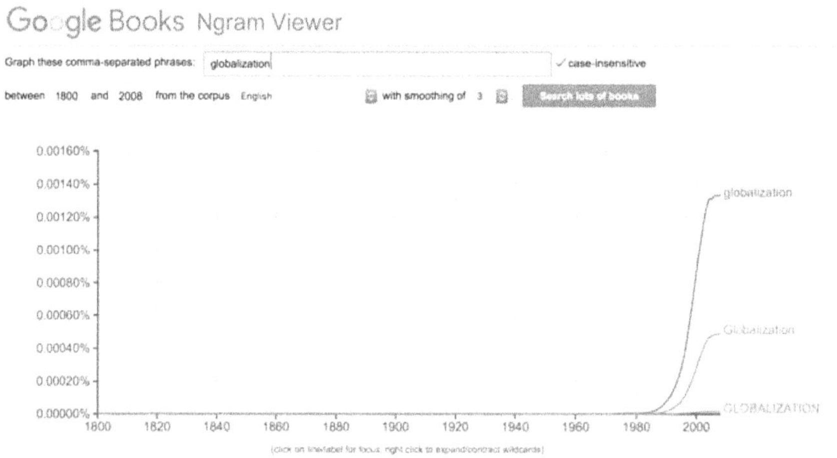

4 *Citizens United v Federal Election Commission*, 558 U.S. 08-205 (2010); Anderson 2011, p. 1.

5 Stiglitz 2006, p. 6.

6 The East Asian meltdown of 1997 with its subsequent global financial crisis, and the Great Recession of 2007-2009, called by Krugman 'the Lesser Depression' are just a few examples of a world-wide domino effect: one piece falling triggers a chain reaction: Stiglitz 2006, p. 221; Krugman 2011, available at: <www.nytimes.com/2011/07/22/opinion/22krugman.html>, last accessed on 2 January 2015.

7 See Stiglitz 2002, p. 4; Chomsky 2010, p. 35.

8 Google Ngram Viewer is a search service that shows how the popularity of chosen terminology in a given body of books.

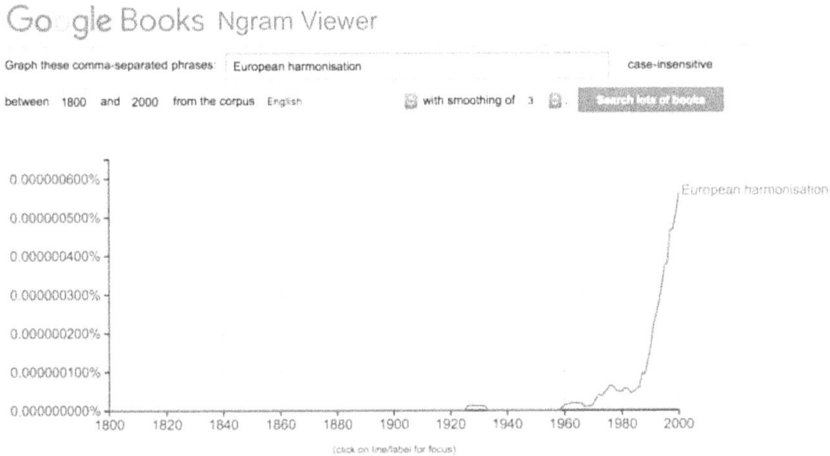

Some have said that different laws in different countries can be a burden for economic transactions,[9] whether from the perspective of businesses or consumers. This led lawmakers to plead for the development of international common standards.[10] In the case of EU governance, political institutions work with the conviction that legal harmonisation helps achieve common standards in a great variety of fields. At this point, it suffices to define such harmonisation as a *technique* used at EU level to bring national rules to similar standards, whereas legal convergence is the effect of this process.

1.2. *Defining Convergence*

Convergence, just as globalisation, is a chameleonic term. Not only can it have different meanings depending on the context, but it may also occur in various fields of governance, such as politics or economics. As mentioned above, this study focuses on *legal* convergence.[11]

Existing literature is rather unclear on what the exact meaning of convergence is. It often uses convergence as a synonym for harmonisation, unification, standardisation or coordination, adding to what Merryman calls a 'miniature Babel of terminology'.[12] Merryman's answer is that each term is relevant, but in different

9 Merryman 1981, p. 357.

10 What is more, convergence might occur between different fields of law, not just between different jurisdictions; for instance, Brand argues that the creation of fields such as international economic law entails the convergence of public and private law; see Brand 1996, p. 3. However, some opinions point out that greater connectivity does not necessarily lead to more convergence; see Ghemawat's concept of 'semiglobalisation' in Ghemawat 2011, p. 23.

11 For in-depth analysis of global or economic convergence see Fukuyama 2011.

12 Merryman 1981, p. 358; Smits 2008, p. 47.

contexts.[13] There are many authors who focus on the phenomenon of convergence; however, there are fewer who try to define it.

Considering its features, Seita looks at convergence as a globalisation-driven phenomenon that brings uniformity to values and is facilitated by procedural mechanisms and substantive principles.[14] Van Gerven takes the analysis even further and states that convergence does not only include the 'approximation of laws through institutionalised legislative and judicial processes but also the growing together of rules through voluntary or even spontaneous action'.[15] When referring to an 'Open Method of Convergence', Van Gerven coins the term 'Open Method of *Coordination*', a governance model introduced by the European Council in 2000 and described as voluntary cooperation between relevant stakeholders. On a different note, Faure and Van der Walt consider convergence to occur out of a 'higher level of governance, that is centralisation',[16] implying that multi-level governance has to be taken into account when understanding the driving forces behind the process of convergence. Glaeser and Schleifer refer to convergence as a process leading to similar court decisions in the perspective of a study focusing on substantive outcomes.[17]

In the opinion of other authors, such as Hermida:

> '[c]onvergence constitutes the evolution of the legal institutions of different legal systems where the legal institution of one system resembles the other and the legal norms, principles, and scholarly comments of both are used in equal measure and even regarded with equal authority'.[18]

For Smits, convergence is rather 'a synonym for legal integration',[19] while Mattei and Pes consider that it is a phenomenon that 'must emphasise the aspect of time, showing a process by which two or more legal systems "become", rather than "are" more alike',[20] and they 'should and would eventually reach similar "natural" results that are dictated by "reason"'.[21] In trying to determine the content of convergence, Mattei and Pes also mention Schlesinger's view that legal convergence refers to a process by which two legal systems defined by different rules to start with, meet somewhere at a middle point.[22]

Stepping outside of the field of law, other disciplines may also serve as inspirational sources for alternative meanings of convergence. A *mathematical* view of convergence can be interpreted to mean a specific property of series or sequences

13 Merryman 1981, p. 359.
14 Seita 1997, p. 429.
15 Van Gerven 2008, p. 34; see also Van Gerven 2006, p. 41-42.
16 Faure & Van Der Walt 2010, p. 463.
17 Glaeser & Schleifer 2002, p. 1224.
18 Hermida 2004, p. 340.
19 Smits 2008, p. 47.
20 Mattei & Pes 2008, p. 268.
21 *Ibid.*, p. 269.
22 *Ibid.*, p. 271.

of numbers to approach a certain point;[23] while a *technological* definition of convergence shows that unrelated industries can become similar by using the same technological processes.[24] Moreover, recent *media* developments associate convergence with 'collaboration, cooperation, combined content, changing consumption and integrated connection'.[25]

All in all, what legal as well as non-legal definitions or interpretations of convergence show is that its meaning is most certainly not set in stone. Convergence may relate to both substance and process. However one aspect I consider to be embedded in all definitions illustrated above is that when discussing convergence, the focus lies, whether directly or indirectly, on the end result. Rules and legal systems become more similar, numbers are set on a certain path, production lines operate the same way and media communication becomes more integrated. To this extent it can be said that convergence is the *effect* of a process of similarisation. Thus in my own understanding, and for the purposes of this study, legal convergence is considered as the *effect* of a process of making rules more similar.

But what pushes legal convergence more precisely? In what follows, the main driving forces behind this phenomenon are analysed for a better understanding of its implications across disciplines and jurisdictions.

1.3. *Convergence: Driving Forces and Types*

Turning back to Merryman, one of his statements stands out as a timeless observation: '[d]ifferences between legal systems have been regarded, at least from the time of Cicero, as evils or inconveniences to be overcome'.[26] With this in mind, it is not necessarily the very existence of different systems of law that was considered a flaw to be corrected, but rather their implications in legal practice.

Legal convergence did exist before modern times.[27] However, what is unprecedented at this moment in history is the pace with which legal cultures

23 Abbott 2000, p. 58.

24 Rosenberg 1976, p. 16.

25 Drucker & Gumpert 2010, p. 2.

26 Merryman 1981, p. 357.

27 It is from the times of Cicero that one can start noticing some incipient elements of legal convergence: one language spread out throughout one forcefully increasing jurisdiction, where law was primarily emanating from one power: Rome. These considerations are nevertheless limited, as it is envisaged that convergence was a farfetched concept at a time when there existed a plethora of sources of law, first of all within Roman law itself, but second of all also taking into account the fragmented customary law applied in the Roman provinces. By the time the Corpus Iuris Civilis, as a true code consisting in the collection of fundamental legal rules and jurisprudence, surfaces the legal landscape in 534, the unity of the Roman Empire was long lost, not to mention that the Middle Ages had been creeping in the territories of the former Western Roman Empire for more than half a century. Moreover, Byzantine lawyers would speak Greek and thus Justinian's work was inaccessible to them until one of the jurists working on the Institutes, Teophilus, translated the work into Greek. The same parallel can be drawn with respect to the *Ius Commune*. Indeed, the unity of the European space in terms of legal understanding was discussed in Coing: Europe was using the same source of law (Roman law), was disseminating the same legal education based on →

interact. This interaction is driven by a number of global developments signalled by different authors. Among these are:

i) *Trade internationalisation* – although not a new phenomenon, commercial convergence brought about through international cooperation reached a new level with the formal creation of the World Trade Organisation in the 90s, making it considerably easier for private actors to benefit from international trade and thus to conclude contracts;
ii) *The Internet* – lower communication costs bring more options to consumers, who might need more protection when concluding contracts outside brick-and-mortar stores;[28]
iii) *Mobility of knowledge & innovation* – the transition from primary products and manufactured goods to knowledge-based service-oriented economies is facilitated by technology, and the diffusion of technology moves innovation across borders (sharing economy start-ups like Uber are an example in this respect);[29]
iv) *Standard setting* – international voluntary consensus standards are soft law rules, created in an informal environment as opposed to the state legislative mechanism, that private law actors undertake to comply with as the standards provide a common playing field enabling healthy competition in the marketplace;[30]
v) *Shared commercial culture* – business practice continues to bring different industries/markets together, at a constantly faster pace, due to the facilitation of trade;[31]
vi) *Education internationalisation* – access to international education allows future practitioners of law or future business actors to gain access to systems that were otherwise unknown and popularise their practice in new environments;[32]

common literature and thus a 'uniform European culture' was created. However, it is also said that Roman law was not applied uniformly given the resistance of the insular legal family to continental influences. See Stein 2003, p. 35; see also Buckland 2007; Frier 1985; Tamanaha 2008, p. 377; Twigg-Flesner 2010, p. 23; Smits 2002a, p. 43; Heirbaut & Storme 2010, p. 21.

28 Rosch 2007, available at: <www.ftc.gov/speeches/rosch/0711056venice.pdf>, last accessed on 27 July 2016.

29 European Commission, 'A Single Market for 21st Century Europe', Communication from the Commission to the European Parliament, the Council, the European Economic and Social Committee and the Committee of the Regions, Brussels, COM(2007) 724 final, 20 November 2007, p. 8-9.

30 See National Research Council (US), 'Standards, conformity assessment, and trade into the 21st century' (Washington: National Academy Press, 1995), p. 48.

31 Rosett 1992, p. 693.

32 *Ibid.*

vii) *Political integration* – supra-state institutions have developed their own complex lawmaking mechanisms in the past decades, leading to more centralised decision-making.[33]

As mentioned above, these factors influence the interaction of contemporary legal cultures. However, there are those who claim the exact opposite, whereby these driving forces are not enough to trigger a process of convergence. Legrand, one of the most renowned supporter of divergence, considers that different legal origins have left deep marks in the understanding of law, marks that cannot be harmonised to achieve convergence:

> '[...] there have developed, and there exist, both a civil law and a common law *mentalité* – two different ways of thinking about the law, about what it is to have knowledge of law and about the role of law in society'.[34]

To better grasp the effects of legal convergence, it is necessary to look at the various types or ways in which law can converge. Some distinctions made in this respect are:

i) *Top-down/Bottom-up (de jure/de facto)* – these two types of convergence can only emerge where governance is a hierarchical construct: top-down convergence reflects centralided governance (e.g. EU Regulations), whereas bottom-up convergence entails initiatives that do not stem from a central authority, but which are rather driven by, for example, market needs;[35]
ii) *Formal/Substantive* – this way of convergence can best be described as on the one hand the *existence* of a single instrument applicable to multiple jurisdictions (formal, e.g. CISG, EU Directives to the extent they are taken over literally), and on the other hand the *application* of existing instruments in a uniform way (this is also referred to as conceptual convergence);[36]
iii) *Voluntary/Spontaneous* – voluntary convergence takes place when the unification of law becomes a policy goal (and policy is to be construed as a governance tool in the hands of the state), whereas spontaneous convergence is the result of developments occurring outside the influence sphere of the state (e.g. the market);[37]
iv) *Optional/Mandatory* – optional convergence deals with the existence of unifying optional instruments that private actors choose as the applicable law to their contracts (meaning that parallel divergent systems can remain in place), whereas mandatory convergence covers the situations where the unifying legal regime is exclusively applicable.

33 Friedberg 1990-1991, p. 289.
34 Legrand 1997, p. 45.
35 Chiu 2008, p. 10; Reimann & Halberstam 2011, p. 363.
36 On an opposite note, Chirico and Larouche discuss conceptual divergence which they refer to when 'the same words can mean different things to different people', in Chirico & Larouche 2013, p. 12.
37 See Smits 2006, p. 85; Hesselink 2011a, p. 140.

So far, convergence has been presented as a concept that occurs world-wide. However, this study focuses on consumer sales law as a specific field of law where convergence has taken place by virtue of the EU's harmonisation policy intervention. The following Section addresses convergence from this specific perspective.

2. Harmonisation by the European Union: The Background

2.1. *Introductory Remarks*

So far, legal convergence was discussed as a global phenomenon driven by globalisation. Section 1.2 defined legal convergence as the effect of a process of similarisation, triggered, as stated above, by the EU's harmonising measures. At this point it is necessary to ask: what does harmonisation mean, and what does it entail? In the upcoming Sections harmonisation is analysed from three perspectives: firstly, existing definitions from legal writings are consulted (Section 2.2), leading up to the view used throughout the entire study; secondly, a brief history of harmonisation by the European legislature is presented together with the various types of harmonisation (Section 2.3); and lastly, the reasons for and against harmonisation are discussed (Section 2.4).

2.2. *Defining Harmonisation*

What exactly is harmonisation? It should come as no surprise that this term is unclear.[38] As seen previously, terminological issues are not always tackled explicitly and generally opinions may differ. There is no charter, treaty, directive, law, or any other legal instrument that clearly and consistently defines the concept of 'legal harmonisation'. The most classical reference to a definition goes to the etymology of the term and its conspicuous musical roots:

> '[...] jurists seem to have forgotten that harmony is not one single boring uniform tune or sound. It is different sounds standing against each other and out of the interplay of different tunes comes a harmony. Harmony is the unity of diversities'.[39]

Looking into private law literature, a plethora of contributions have been published on the goals of harmonisation:

> '[...] harmonisation of private law has the objective of establishing an equivalent or even uniform set of rules in private law, with the effect of approximating or bringing the heterogeneous legal systems closer together in the EU'.[40]

38 See for example Lohse 2011, p. 292.

39 Thue 2000, p. 319-328; see also Boodman 1991, p. 701.

40 Sefton-Green 2010, p. 50; see also Smits 2002b, p. 79-99.

There is no shortage of authors engaged in the dissemination of harmonisation and its effects. Many pertinent voices have gone on to prove how harmonisation works,[41] or on the contrary, does not work,[42] including what nuances it has, and what its optimal parameters are.[43] This being said, just as with convergence, the volume of literature discussing terminological distinctions is not equal in size.[44] Still, this is not to say that the lack of agreement over what harmonisation is and what synonyms are used to refer to it have not been reported before.[45]

While Gomez calls it a phenomenon that has 'an initial stage of [...] a high degree of legal fragmentation, and a final stage resulting from [the process] is essentially similar in terms of a reduced level of fragmentation, even identical or similar rules in terms of content',[46] Baffi and Santella refer to it as 'a process that aligns legal rules either within a federal framework, [...] through the adoption of regulatory models agreed at a multilateral level [...] or through the unilateral adoption of a foreign sovereign state's legal system by a different sovereign state'.[47] Moreover, harmonisation can be understood to be synonymous with Europeanisation. This is a development operating on two levels: the de-territorialisation of contract law and the entrance of Europe-derived rules in national legal systems.[48]

After taking a look at some of the different proposed definitions of harmonisation, which one can be described at the most accurate? For the purposes of this study, I define harmonisation as a specific technique used by the European institutions to make national laws of Member States more similar to one another by removing barriers identified in specific sectors. Legal convergence is thus the possible effect of this technique.

41 See for instance the collection of essays in Smits 2005b.

42 See Legrand 1996, p. 52; Smits 2000a.

43 See Parisi 2008; Gomez-Pomar 2011), p. 401; Gomez & Ganuza 2011b, p. 275.

44 The official website of the European Union used to include a 'Eurojargon' page, describing harmonisation in layman's terms: '[...] may mean bringing national laws into line with one another, very often in order to remove national barriers that obstruct the free movement of workers, goods, services and capital. In other words, harmonisation means making sure that, on any particular issue for which the EU has responsibility, the rules laid down by the different EU countries impose similar obligations on citizens of all those countries and that they impose certain minimum obligations in each country'. This definition was retrieved from <http://europa.eu/abc/eurojargon/index_en.htm>, but is no longer featured on the page.

45 Lohse 2011, p. 283.

46 Gómez-Pomar 2011, p. 404.

47 Baffi & Santella 2011.

48 Miller 2011, p. 4; Lando 2000a, p. 59.

2.3. *European Private Law Harmonisation: Chronological Overview, Types and Competence*

2.3.1. Directives as Harmonisation Instruments

Having first tackled terminological clarifications, this Section aims to give a brief overview of the historical development of European private law. In doing so, it firstly explores directives as harmonising legal instruments. In what follows, the discussion centres on legal acts adopted by the European Union in different fields of private law such as product liability (contractual and non-contractual) and safety, doorstep and distance selling, financial services, unfair terms and commercial practices, and enforcement.

The Product Liability Directive of 1985[49] is typically seen as the first European directive in the field of general private law. In the years that followed, the Consumer Sales Directive addressed liability for contractual non-conformity,[50] and safety concerns regarding sold products were integrated in the Directive on Product Safety.[51]

Also starting in 1985, the sale of goods or services outside of business premises became a field that the European Union sought to harmonise through the Doorstep Selling Directive.[52] In the light of subsequent technological developments that allowed consumers to purchase goods over the phone or on the internet, rules dealing with distance selling were added. This was achieved through the Distance Selling Directive,[53] the Electronic Signatures Directive[54] and the Electronic Commerce Directive.[55] The Doorstep Selling and Distance Selling Directives were replaced in 2011, when the Consumer Rights Directive was adopted.[56]

49 Council Directive 85/374/EEC of 25 July 1985 on the approximation of the laws, regulations and administrative provisions of the Member States concerning liability for defective products, *OJ* L210 of 7 August 1985.

50 Directive 1999/44/EC of the European Parliament and of the Council of 25 May 1999 on certain aspects of the sale of consumer goods and associated guarantees, *OJ* L171 of 7 July 1999.

51 Directive 2001/95/EC of the European Parliament and of the Council of 3 December 2001 on general product safety, *OJ* L11/4 of 15 January 2002.

52 Directive on the protection of consumers in respect of contracts negotiated away from business premises 85/577/EEC, *OJ* L372 of 31 December 1985.

53 Directive 97/7/EC of the European Parliament and of the Council of 20 May 1997 on the protection of consumers in respect of distance contracts, *OJ* L144 of 4 June 1997.

54 Directive 1999/93/EC of the European Parliament and of the Council of 13 December 1999 on a Community framework for electronic signatures, *OJ* L013 of 19 January 2000.

55 Directive 2000/31/EC of the European Parliament and the Council of 8 June 2000 on certain legal aspects of information society services, in particular electronic commerce, *OJ* L178 of 17 July 2000.

56 Directive 2011/83/EU of the European Parliament and of the Council of 25 October 2011 on consumer rights, amending Council Directive 93/13/EEC and Directive 1999/44/EC of the European Parliament and of the Council and repealing Council Directive 85/577/EEC and Directive 97/7/EC of the European Parliament and of the Council, *OJ* L304/64 of 22 November 2011.

Another field where the European legislator took harmonizing measures is that of financial services, namely: the Directive on Financial Collateral Arrangements,[57] the Distance Marketing Directive[58] and the Credit Agreement Directive[59] are suitable examples.

Moreover, some of the most important developments relating to the consumer *acquis* have been shaped by the introduction of European rules on unfair terms by virtue of the Unfair Contract Terms Directive,[60] as well as unfair commercial practices by means of the Unfair Commercial Practices Directive.[61] In connection to the advertising matters included by the latter, additional rules were made available in 2006, when the Directive on Misleading Advertising was adopted.[62]

To facilitate substantive rules, directives dealing with the enforcement of various private law matters were introduced, such as: the Settlement Finality Directive,[63] the Consumer Injunctions Directive[64] as well the Late Payment Directive[65] all fall into this category.

Moreover, not necessarily directly connected to the aforementioned fields, rules were adopted also with respect to self-employed commercial agents,[66] package travel[67] and timeshare.[68]

Having made an overview of what instruments have been adopted by the European legislator to harmonise different matters of European private law, the next part of this Section looks at the policy behind these instruments.

57 Directive 2002/47/EC of the European Parliament and of the Council of 6 June 2002 on financial collateral arrangements, *OJ* L168 of 27 June 2002.

58 Directive 2002/65/EC of the European Parliament and of the Council of 23 September 2002 concerning the distance marketing of consumer financial services, *OJ* L271 of 9 October 2002.

59 Directive 2008/48/EC on credit agreements for consumers, *OJ* L133/66 of 22 May 2008.

60 Council Directive 93/13/EEC of 5 April 1993 on unfair terms in consumer contracts, *OJ* L95 of 21 April 1993.

61 Directive 2005/29/EC of the European Parliament and of the Council of 11 May 2005 concerning unfair business-to-consumer commercial practices in the internal market and amending Council Directive 84/450/EEC, Directives 97/7/EC, 98/27/EC and 2002/65/EC of the European Parliament and of the Council and Regulation (EC) No 2006/2004 of the European Parliament and of the Council, *OJ* L149/22 of 11 June 2005.

62 Directive 2006/114/EC of the European Parliament and of the Council of 12 December 2006 concerning misleading and comparative advertising, *OJ* L376/21 of 27 December 2006.

63 Directive 98/26/EC of the European Parliament and of the Council of 19 May 1998 on settlement finality in payment and securities settlement systems, *OJ* L166 of 11 June 1998.

64 Directive 98/27/EC of the European Parliament and of the Council of 19 May 1998 on injunctions for the protection of consumers' interests, *OJ* L166 of 11 June 1998.

65 Directive 2011/7/EU of the European Parliament and of the Council of 16 February 2011 on combating late payment in commercial transactions (recast), *OJ* L48/1 of 23 February 2011.

66 Council Directive 86/653/EEC of 18 December 1986 on the coordination of the laws of the Member States relating to self-employed commercial agents, *OJ* L382 of 31 December 1986.

67 Council Directive 90/314/EEC of 13 June 1990 on package travel, package holidays and package tours, *OJ* L158 of 23 June 1990.

68 Directive 2008/48/EC on credit agreements for consumers, *OJ* L133/66 of 22 May 2008. Moreover, apart from the directives mentioned in this Section, several regulations were adopted in the light of private law harmonisation; see Smits *et al.* 2014.

2.3.2. Chronological Overview of EU Policy on the Harmonisation of Private Law

As it has been shown above, European private law instruments on consumer protection started to be adopted in the 1980s.[69] These directives were accompanied by an increasing stream of European policy documents. This Section aims to offer a brief historical account of how harmonisation became the technique of tuning Member States' legal standards. In order to do so, both European primary law and policy documents relevant to European consumer contract law are consulted.[70]

Harmonisation of law, as a European policy, was not always mentioned in the treaties setting up the precursors to the European Union. For instance, the 1951 Treaty of Paris establishing the European Coal and Steel Community signed in the echoes of the Schuman Plan did not make any reference to harmonisation or legal approximation, nor did it touch upon private law as such. This changed in the 1957 Treaty of Rome establishing the European Economic Community (EEC), with the introduction of Article 100 on the approximation of laws that granted a new competence to the Commission, namely to protect Member States from trade impediments arising from different national rules.[71] To this extent, between 1965 and 1975, the EEC used approximation to identify the areas where Member States had taken individual action for the removal of non-tariff barriers, or whether the Community had by itself enacted legislation to overcome the same obstacles.[72]

What resulted from these efforts was the creation of the common market, or as it became known as of 1987, when the Single European Act came into force, the internal market: a trading area characterised by rules on the four freedoms (goods, persons, services and capital) and the control of competition, which has been the backbone of the Community.[73] The internal market gained momentum with the emergence of the 1985 White Paper on the completion of the internal market. This set out the schedule and policy conditions for the single market program, targeting the reduction of non-tariff barriers to trade (e.g. approximation of legislation, harmonisation of rules, etc.), since quantitative impediments had already been dropped.[74] Product standards and rules on competition were given a central place

69 For example, Directive 85/374/EEC or Council Directive 85/577/EEC of 20 December 1985 to protect the consumer in respect of contracts negotiated away from business premises, *OJ* L372 of 31 December 1985.

70 For a more comprehensive discussion on what European private law includes see Cafaggi 2008a, p. 289-290.

71 Sabin 1991, p. 225.

72 Executive Secretariat of the Commission, 'Community measures for the approximation of laws (1972-1974)', *Bulletin of the European Communities*, Supplement 3/75; Executive Secretariat of the Commission, 'Approximation of legislation. Work undertaken between 1 January 1958 and 31 March 1965', *Bulletin of the European Economic Community*, Supplement 8/66; Executive Secretariat of the Commission, 'Approximation of legislation. Work undertaken between 1 June 1958 and 31 March 1965', *Bulletin of the European Economic Community*, Supplement No. 8, 1966.

73 De Vries 2006, p. 12-13; see also Chalmers *et al.* 2011, p. 12.

74 Intergovernmental Committee created by the Conference of Messina, 'Report of Heads of Delegation of the Foreign Affairs Ministries (Spaak Report)', 21 April 1956; see also Gormley 2006, p. 14.

in this framework that would gradually liberalise and deregulate domestic Europe in the next two decades.[75] According to the White Paper, harmonisation - a term now regularly used by the Commission - was a technical mean to meet the goal of 'essential equivalence of the objectives of national legislation'.[76] Still, it was the Commission Programme published some months earlier that actually explained why legal harmonisation was necessary. Given the young and prosperous economic area, new common rules were needed in order to replace the abundant national ramifications.[77] At this point in time the focus was on areas such as technical standards, competition, state aid and monopolies.[78] What is more, 1985 saw the introduction of a so-called 'New Approach' to legislative harmonisation in matters dealing with the standardisation of safety requirements.[79]

More private law oriented developments took place in 1989, when the European Parliament passed a resolution targeting private law exclusively, explaining that while harmonisation had already occurred in various 'aspects', it did not cover entire 'branches'.[80] Considering private law to be such a branch eligible for further unification, the Parliament even requested 'that a start be made on the necessary preparatory work on drawing up a common European Code of Private Law [...]'. This direction was also supported by a subsequent Parliament resolution from 1994.[81]

A landmark development occurred in 2001, when the Commission released its *Communication on European contract law* and emphasised the need for the

75 Eichengreen & Boltho 2010, p. 285.

76 European Commission, 'White Paper on Completing the Internal Market', COM(85) 310, para. 63.

77 European Commission, 'Programme of the Commission for 1985 - Statement by Jacques Oelors, President of the Commission, to the European Parliament and his reply to the ensuing debate Strasbourg', *Bulletin of the European Communities,* Supplement 4/85, para. 5.

78 *Ibid.*, para. 28.

79 1985 is equally important because it marks a shift in the approach towards harmonisation for certain legislative developments. While the Old Approach focused on the harmonisation of detailed rules and specifications which made it a cumbersome political process, according to the Council's Resolution of 7 May 1985 the 'New Approach' would be based on four principles dealing with, among others, safety requirements and voluntary industrial standardisation. In other words, the New Approach to legislative harmonisation was the policy choice for directives that would aim to ensure a high level of product safety. Directive 85/374/EEC on liability for defective products is an example of a legislative act adopted under the New Approach; see also Council Resolution 85/C 136/01 of 7 May 1985 on a new approach to technical harmonisation and standards; Communication from the Commission of 7 May 2003 to the Council and the European Parliament 'Enhancing the implementation of the New Approach Directives', COM(2003) 240 final; see also Craig & De Búrca 2003, p. 1190; OECD, 'Regulatory Reform in Hungary' (Paris: OECD Publishing, 2000), p. 234.

80 European Parliament Resolution A2-157/89, Official Journal C 158/400; see also Lando 1993, p. 161; Keirse 2011, p. 35.

81 European Parliament Resolution of 6 May 1994, *OJ* C205/518. Other resolutions on the progress of a potential European Civil Code followed between 2001 and 2006: Resolution of 15 November 2001, *OJ* C140 E; Resolution of 2 September 2003, *OJ* C76 E; Resolution of 23 June 2006, 2005/2022(INI); see also Cafaggi 2008, p. 289; Staudenmayer 2002, p. 250; Smits 2002a, p. 4.

harmonisation of private law by underlining four examples of alternative measures that could be taken to address this need: (i) taking no action; (ii) developing common principles of contract law; (iii) improving existing legislation; and (iv) adopting new legislation.[82] Academic networks welcomed the increased attention given by the Commission to contract law and to the discussion surrounding the topic of harmonisation.[83] This is particularly significant given the use of a very central concept to law-making at the time: minimum harmonisation. This type of harmonisation consists in the adoption by the European legislator of standards common to all Member States but that still allow the imposition of more protective national rules. That same year, the *Green Paper* on European consumer protection was issued, and included - but was not restricted to - contract law matters arising out of consumer transactions.[84] The *Green Paper* sought to trigger an extensive consultation process on matters such as: the barriers faced by consumers and businesses due to different national rules on advertising, pre-contractual/contractual/after-sales practices; potential reforms necessary for consumer protection; the impact in terms of costs and benefits of potential reform approaches on consumers and businesses.[85] The *Green Paper* made reference to minimum harmonisation, albeit referring to it with the formulation 'minimum clauses'.[86] However, the *Consumer Policy Strategy 2002-2006* already started using the concept of 'full harmonisation', without providing any definition.[87]

Going further, in the 2003 *Action Plan* calling for the development of a Common Frame of Reference (CFR), the Commission acknowledged some of the drawbacks of the minimum harmonisation approach:

> 'While EC law has led to some degree of convergence, it is still difficult for businesses to develop distribution strategies that can be applied throughout the internal market,

82 European Commission, 'Communication from the Commission to the Council and the European Parliament on European contract law', COM(2001) 398 final, *OJ* C255 of 13 September 2001, para. 46.

83 Academic focus on European contract law had already existed since the creation of the Commission on European Contract Law that issued the Principles of European Contract Law in 2000, the Study Group on a European Civil Code as well as the Common Law of Europe casebooks project led by Walter Van Gerven; see Staudenmayer 2002, p. 251; see also Von Bar *et al.* 2002, p. 183; Howells 2002, p. 475; López-Rodríguez 2004, p. 167; Wilhelmsson 2001, p. 23; Wilhelmsson 2002, p. 541; Micklitz 2002, p. 583; Wagner 2002, p. 995; Weatherill 2002, p. 497; Gambaro 2003, p. 768.

84 European Commission, 'Green Paper on European Union Consumer Protection', COM(2001) 531 final, *OJ* C125 of 25 May 2002.

85 *Ibid.*, p. 2.

86 *Ibid.*, p. 7: '[...] consumer protection rules at EU level generally allow Member States to take more detailed or stricter measures (through the so-called 'minimum clauses') to protect consumers, or, as is more common, to maintain existing rules, provided they are stricter than the EU rules'.

87 European Commission, 'Communication from the Commission to the European Parliament, the Council, the Economic and Social Committee and the Committee of the Regions - Consumer Policy Strategy 2002-2006', COM(2002) 208 final, *OJ* C137 of 8 June 2002, p. 7.

> because the rules adopted by Member States going beyond the minimum harmonisation prescribed by EC law are necessarily divergent'.[88]

As expected, Member States had dealt with minimum standards differently, which in turn led to legal uncertainty for both individuals and businesses. To remedy this alleged shortcoming, the Commission suggested a mix of regulatory and non-regulatory measures as a way ahead.[89] These measures made reference to: (i) the creation of a common frame of reference; (ii) the promotion of self-regulation; and (iii) the introduction of optional instruments. The *Action Plan* had a consultative character and therefore one of its goals was to build on the consultations following the 2001 Communication and to gain more feedback from institutional, market and academic stakeholders.

2007 saw the Commission's *Green Paper on the review of the consumer acquis*.[90] This evaluation was launched earlier in 2004 through the *Commission Communication on European contract law and the revision of the acquis*.[91] The 2007 *Green Paper* proposed three approaches for the future of European consumer law: (i) a so-called vertical approach consisting in the review of existing directives; (ii) a so-called mixed approach reflecting a horizontal policy (adopting new directives/framework instruments) combined with vertical action; and (iii) no action. What is interesting about this *Green Paper* is that some aspects of full harmonisation are at last discussed:

> 'This would mean that no Member State could apply stricter rules than the ones laid down at Community level. Full harmonisation would not only entail the repeal of the minimum harmonisation clauses; it would also imply the elimination of the regulatory options available to Member States on specific aspects by some provisions in the directives, which could result in modifying the level of consumer protection in some Member States'.[92]

This view was also referenced in the Commission's *Policy Strategy 2007-2013*, where a new term was used at the same time: 'targeted full harmonisation'.[93] 'Targeted full harmonisation' is a concept that appeared in the *Commission Staff Working Paper on*

88 European Commission, 'Communication from the Commission to the European Parliament and the Council - A More Coherent European Contract Law - An Action Plan', COM(2003) 68 final, *OJ* C63 of 13 March 2003, para. 50; see also Schulze 2005, p. 4; Hondius 2004, p. 856; Hesselink 2004, p. 397-419; Staudenmayer 2003, p. 113; Beale 2005, p. 4; Von Bar & Swann 2003, p. 595; Blair & Brent 2004, p. 5; Editorial Comments 2005, p. 1; Calliess 2003.

89 COM(2003) 68 final, para. 52; see also Mak 2011a, p. 41-52.

90 European Commission, 'Green Paper on the Review of the Consumer Acquis', COM(2006) 744 final, *OJ* C256/27 of 27 October 2007. The Directives reviewed are: Directive 85/577/EEC; Directive 90/314/EEC; Directive 93/13/EEC; Directive 94/47/EC; Directive 97/7/EC; Directive 98/6/EC; Directive 98/27/EC; Directive 1999/44/EC.

91 European Commission, 'Communication on European Contract Law and the revision of the acquis: the way forward', COM(2004) 651 final, *OJ* C14 of 20 January 2005.

92 COM(2006) 744 final, p. 10.

93 European Commission, 'EU Consumer Policy Strategy (2007-2013) - Empowering consumers, enhancing their welfare, effectively protecting them', COM(2007) 99 final, *OJ* C181 of 3 August 2007, p. 7; see also Micklitz 2009b, p. 47-86; Whittaker 2009, p. 223; Smits 2010b, p. 5.

the Review of the Consumer Acquis, which specified that it was an approach 'targeted to the issues raising substantial barriers to trade for business and/or deterring consumers from buying cross-border'.[94]

What followed was the Commission's *Green Paper on policy options for progress towards a European Contract Law for consumers and businesses* issued in 2010.[95] The *Green Paper* reemphasised certain barriers in the completion of the internal market, some of which had been mentioned in the 2001 Communication as well. It proposed seven options as guidance for choosing the best instrument for European contract law: (i) publishing the results of the Expert Group set up by the Commission in 2010 in charge of studying the feasibility of a user-friendly instrument of European contract law;[96] (ii) creating an official 'toolbox' for national; (iii) adopting a Commission Recommendation on European Contract law; (iv) adopting an optional instrument as a regulation; (v) adopting a directive on European contract law; (vi) adopting a regulation on European contract law; and (vii) adopting a regulation on a European civil code.[97] The Green Paper made reference to 'full' harmonisation, although once again, it did not define it.[98]

Full harmonisation was deemed to be a 'balanced way forward' by Viviane Reding,[99] and could also be found in Andreas Schwab's working paper on the proposal for the Consumer Rights Directive, referenced by Reding in the same speech.[100] Although not explicitly mentioned, this approach aimed to strike a balance between those areas of consumer law where protection standards can be maximised and applied uniformly, and some other areas that would continue to be covered by minimum standards. In Schwab's words, it was '[...] a comprehensive solution, harmonizing consumer rights at a European level as much as possible, but always with a view to what is realistic and achievable'.[101]

94 Commission Staff Working Paper, 'Report on the Outcome of the Public Consultation on the Green Paper on the Review of the Consumer *Acquis*', p. 3; 'full harmonisation' and 'targeted full harmonisation' became central to the preparatory work on the Consumer Rights Directive and the report submitted by the Committee on the Internal Market and Consumer Protection and the draft opinion of the Legal Committee.

95 European Commission, 'Green Paper on policy options for progress towards a European Contract Law for consumers and businesses', COM(2010) 348 final (not published in the Official Journal); see also Expert Group, 'A European contract law for consumers and businesses: Publication of the results of the feasibility study carried out by the Expert Group on European contract law for stakeholders' and legal practitioners' feedback'.

96 Commission Decision of 26 April 2010 setting up the Expert Group on a Common Frame of Reference in the area of European Contract Law, *OJ* L105 of 27 April 2010.

97 For a more extensive discussion over the Green Paper see for instance Halson & Campbell 2013, p. 104; Gutman 2014, p. 260; Zachariasiewicz 2011, p. 471; Beale 2011, p. 119; Gutman 2011, p. 151; Cristas 2011, p. 314; Mak 2011d, p. 257; Augenhofer 2011, p. 195; Reich 2012, p. 1.

98 COM(2010) 348 final, p. 10.

99 Reding 2010, available at: <http://europa.eu/>, last accessed on 27 July 2016.

100 *Ibid.*

101 Schwab 2010, available at: <www.eppgroup.eu/press>, last accessed on 27 July 2016.

Commissioner Reding and her Directorate-General for Justice drafted a proposal for a Common European Sales Law in late 2011.[102] This legislative proposal took the form of a Regulation, therefore leaving no leeway for Member States to diverge from it in the transposition process.[103] However, the proposal was eventually withdrawn by the Commission for reasons of further modification in order to fully benefit from the potential of e-commerce under the Digital Single Market.[104] On a similar note, the *Digital Single Market Strategy for Europe* adopted by the Commission in May 2015 focuses on the strong potential of the internet as an environment for the cross-border provision of goods and services. Both minimum and full harmonisation are mentioned, but not much detail about the harmonisation policy is provided within the scope of the strategy, which rather calls for simplified and modern rules for online purchases instead.[105]

In December 2015, the Commission issued two new proposals on the topic of contract law: on consumer online and distance sales (complementing the Consumer Sales Directive), and on digital content.[106] Both proposals mention targeted full harmonisation as the policy alternative chosen by the Commission in the light of the withdrawal of the Common European Sales Law.

102 European Commission, 'Proposal for a Regulation of the European Parliament and of the Council on a Common European Sales Law', COM(2011) 635 final, *OJ* C37 of 10 February 2012.

103 For a general overview of the features of the Common European Sales Law see for example, Twigg-Flesner 2015, p. 231; Smits 2012b, p. 904.

104 Clive 2015, available at: <www.epln.law.ed.ac.uk/2015/01/07/proposal-for-a-common-european-sales-law-withdrawn/>, last accessed on 27 July 2016..

105 European Commission, 'Communication from the Commission to the European Parliament, the Council, the European Economic and Social Committee and the Committee of the Regions – A Digital Single Market Strategy for Europe', COM(2015) 192 final (not yet published), p. 4; see also the earlier communications on the Digital Single Market, European Commission, 'Communication from the Commission to the European Parliament, the Council, the European Economic and Social Committee and the Committee of the Regions – A Digital Agenda for Europe', COM(2010) 245, *OJ* C121 of 19 April 2011; European Commission, 'Communication from the Commission to the European Parliament, the Council, the European Economic and Social Committee and the Committee of the Regions – A coherent framework for building trust in the Digital Single Market for e-commerce and online services', COM(2011) 942 final, *OJ* C102 of 5 April 2012.

106 Proposal for a Directive of the European Parliament and of the Council on certain aspects concerning contracts for the online and other distance sales of goods, 9 December 2015, COM(2015) 635 final ; Proposal for a Directive of the European Parliament and of the Council on certain aspects concerning contracts for the supply of digital content, 9 December 2015, COM(2015) 634 final; as for the policy reasons behind these developments, on page 2, the first Proposal reads: '[b]y eliminating the key contract law-related barriers hindering cross-border trade, the rules put forward in the proposals will reduce the uncertainty faced by businesses and consumers due to the complexity of the legal framework and the costs incurred by businesses resulting from differences in contract law.'

2.3.3. Types

Despite harmonisation being an operative tool included in EU law terminology, the European legislator has left its meaning to be determined by the context in which it is used. The TFEU often refers to harmonisation within the syntagm 'excluding any harmonisation of the laws and regulations of the Member States'[107] and Directives mention harmonisation in their preamble to emphasise the goal of rule implementation.[108] As seen in the chronological overview, little attention is paid to defining or clarifying what harmonisation really is and what shapes it can take. At best, such answers lie hidden in policy documents that lack any binding force. However, different types of harmonisation can be individualised in the light of the overview above:

i) *Minimum harmonisation*: the legislative form of EU intervention in the field of private law has to this point highlighted a process of identifying a high standard of consumer protection and turning it into the level playing field for all Member States. Should any of the Member States want to impose an even higher level of consumer protection, they could make use of this possibility. In a nutshell, this is what minimum harmonisation entails. However, in the light of how fragmented minimum harmonisation directives have been, this has inevitably led to a 'piecemeal approach' to the harmonisation of European private law.[109] In the 1999 *Travel Vac* case the Court of Justice illustrated the potential incoherence and confusion arising from the *acquis*:[110] if a salesman sells timeshare away from business premises, the consumer simultaneously has a *cancellation/renunciation* right under the Doorstep Selling Directive[111] and a right of *withdrawal* under the Timeshare Directive.[112]

ii) *Full harmonisation (maximum harmonisation)*: this standard was developed to achieve a high level of convergence in consumer protection.[113] All in all, it entails that Member States cannot go beyond the scope of European rules in their transposition, which is considered to lead to a more compact and unitary system of consumer protection. In itself, this action can deter trade as well, since it is claimed that a certain amount of regulatory diversity can lead to enhanced competition on the internal market as far as the price is concerned.[114]

107 Articles 19, 79(4), 84, 166(4), 167(5), 196(2) TFEU.

108 Directive 1999/44/EC.

109 European Commission, 'Communication from the Commission to the Council and the European Parliament on European Contract Law, COM(2001) 398 final.

110 Case C-423/97, *Travel Vac SL v Manuel José Antelm Sanchis* [1999], ECR I-02195.

111 Council Directive 85/577/EEC.

112 Council Directive 94/47/EC of 26 October 1994 on the protection of purchasers in respect of certain aspects of contracts relating to the purchase of the right to use immovable properties on a timeshare basis, *OJ* L280 of 29 October 1994; see also López-Rodríguez 2003-2004, p. 1198.

113 Smits 2010b, p. 5-10; Faure 2008, p. 440; Mak 2009, p. 55-73; Whittaker 2009, p. 223.

114 Collins 1994, p. 229, 232.

(iii) *Targeted full harmonisation:* the Commission Staff Working Paper on the review of the consumer *acquis* does not draw a clear line between full and targeted full harmonisation, thus implying that the latter is a subcategory of the first. As reflected in the two most recent proposals issued at the end of 2015, this seems to be the favoured policy option of the Commission.[115] One distinction, however, can be observed in instruments like the Unfair Commercial Practices Directive. Here some parts of the Directive (e.g. the black listed practices) are full harmonisation rules, while others are only minimum harmonisation. For this reason, it can be said that targeted full harmonisation is only partial full harmonisation.

To sum up, what the reader needs to take away from this trichotomy is that with time, European approximation policies have seen a development from a less intrusive top-down intervention (minimum harmonisation) to a stricter interference in national rules. Since the main criticism brought to minimum harmonisation is that it still nurtured divergent national rules and created a rather unfortunate and puzzling 'piecemeal' approach,[116] imposing more rigid standards that national legislators cannot deviate from was seen as the solution for this problem. However, as it is mentioned in the next Section, maximum harmonisation raises various doubts over whether the EU has the constitutional prerogative to justify such measures in the field of private law. To clarify these matters, the discussion now shifts to the competence of the European legislator to harmonise private law matters in general.

2.3.4. Competence

Not only does the notion of private law harmonisation lack an official definition, but it also does not have an explicit legal basis embedded in the TFEU. This is, to a certain extent, understandable since EU competences are determined according to a more functionalist approach, in which distinctions such as private/public law do not hold much sway.[117] For this reason, the EU does not have as such a general

115 In the Staff Working Paper the syntagm 'full (targeted) harmonisation' is used; see Commission Staff Working Paper, 'Report on the Outcome of the Public Consultation on the Green Paper on the Review of the Consumer Acquis', p. 4. Even though the distinction is not clear in policy papers, authors like Howells and Schulze support this view by drawing a comparison between targeted full harmonisation and complete full harmonisation when discussing the Proposal for the Consumer Rights Directive; see Howells & Schulze 2009, p. 8. Micklitz also acknowledges the lack of clarity as to what 'targeted full harmonisation' means, but is of the opinion that the European legislator must justify why, for instance, in the Proposal on the Consumer Rights Directive certain articles would be aimed to fully harmonise specific practices; see Micklitz 2009b, p. 53. See also COM(2015) 635 final and COM(2015) 634 final.

116 See Twigg-Flesner 2012c, p. 1370.

117 Mańko 2015, p. 3; see also Semmelmann 2012; Reich 2010, p. 56-89; Michaels & Jansen 2006, p. 843; Schmid 2005, p. 211.

competence to regulate private law. The discussion below relates to the main legal provision justifying whatever competence the EU does have.

According to Article 4 TFEU, the EU may regulate specific areas such as the internal market (paragraph a) and consumer protection (paragraph f). Since this competence is not exclusive, it must be considered in the light of the principle of subsidiarity. According to Article 5 TEU, this principle entails that the EU may only act if Member States cannot sufficiently achieve objectives that can better be achieved at EU level.[118]

This being said, the most common basis for the harmonisation of contract law has been Article 114 TFEU, operating under the ordinary legislative procedure.[119] Under this provision, contract law - and more specifically consumer contract law - is seen as an area that can help strengthen the internal market.[120] Given this inferred competence, not few are the voices arguing that the European legislator is stretching the TFEU in terms of the measures it is constitutionally allowed to take in matters of private law.[121] A prominent example of a measure that fell outside the ambit of Article 114 TFEU was Directive 98/43, which was central to the judgment rendered by the Court of Justice in *Tobacco Advertising I*.[122] This directive imposed a ban on tobacco advertising and sponsorship in all media channels apart from television, including posters displayed in cafes and ads featured in magazines.

To defend this measure, the Parliament and the Council stated that competition was distorted because of the differences in legislation covering tobacco advertising, which allowed unequal revenue for companies that had the competitive advantage given by the states that did not prohibit such advertising.[123] However, apart from there not being a link between the internal market arguments and the amount of trade the Directive touched upon, the Court held that the Directive was just a hidden health protection measure that did not fulfil the requirements of Article 114 and annulled the Directive.[124]

Shortly after, the *British American Tobacco (BAT)* case built on *Tobacco Advertising I* and in upholding Directive 2001/37 the Court assessed a genuine link

118 See also Cauffman 2015, p. 71; Poto 2007, p. 837; Wimmer 2014, p. 337; Chalmers *et al.* 2010, p. 368. The applicability of the proportionality principle to contract law was confirmed by the Court of Justice in Case T-154/01, *Distilleria F. Palma SpA v Commission of the European Communities* [2004] ECR II-01493.

119 Mańko 2015, p. 3; Riesenhuber 2005, p. 304; Low 2011, p. 48; Conway 2010, p. 968; Twigg-Flesner 2012a, p. 8; Twigg-Flesner 2008a, p. 19.

120 Two other articles are always mentioned in the literature on the topic: (i) Article 169, regarding consumer protection, that makes reference to 114 in subparagraph 2(a) and which is thus not used by itself; and (ii) Article 115, which operates under the special legislative procedure and was used for early consumer directives; see Low 2011, p. 49; Mańko 2015, p. 9.

121 Weatherill 2004, p. 646; Goode 2003, p. 13; Wilhelmsson 2004, p. 317; Collins 2013, p. 910.

122 Case C-376/98, *Germany v Parliament & Council (Tobacco Advertising I)* [2000] ECR I-8419; see also Weatherill 2011a, p. 827; Beck 2013, p. 421-422.

123 Chalmers *et al.* 2010, p. 687.

124 *Tobacco Advertising I*, para. 83.

between the Directive and the objectives of improving the functioning of the internal market inherent to Article 114:[125]

> 'it follows from that case-law that while recourse to [Article 114] as a legal basis is possible if the aim is to prevent the emergence of future obstacles to trade resulting from multifarious development of national laws, the emergence of such obstacles must be likely and the measure in question must be designed to prevent them'.[126]

This remark allows further interpretation according to which Article 114 does not only become applicable when barriers to trade already exist, but also when they consist of 'future obstacles' (preventive approximation).[127] In the same vein, the Court found in subsequent cases that when 'smooth operation of the internal market by preventing or eliminating differences between the legislation and practice of the various Member States' cannot be achieved through the exclusive legislation of a Member State, then Article 114 could indeed be used as the legal basis.[128]

In *Vodafone et al v Secretary of State* Article 114 was revisited.[129] At the core of proceedings layed Regulation 717/2007 that capped roaming charges on public mobile networks for voice calls and aimed at curing the uncompetitive operation of the market by harmonising the prices imposed by private service providers. This time, however, the Court upheld the legislative choice and clarified that the measure was preventively adopted to avoid divergent national price control measures.

Given the available case law on Article 114, Weatherill suggests that a circular relationship has been created between the EU legislator and the Court of Justice – legislative institutions use case law as a 'drafting guide' and fall back on this argument if brought before the Court. The effect of this circularity, Weatherill infers,

125 Liu 2009; Slater 2003, p. 137.

126 Case C-491/01, *Queen v Sec'y of State for Health, ex parte British Am. Tobacco (Inv.) Ltd. & Imperial Tobacco Ltd.* [2002] ECR I-11453, para. 61. In 2006, a case was brought against Directive 2003/33 replacing Directive 98/43/EC considered in *Tobacco Advertising I* and the Court upheld the Directive: 'While a mere finding of disparities between national rules is not sufficient to justify having recourse to Article 95 EC, it is otherwise where there are differences between the laws, regulations or administrative provisions of the Member States which are such as to obstruct the fundamental freedoms and thus have a direct effect on the functioning of the internal market', Case C-380/03, *Germany v Parliament and Council (Tobacco Advertising II)* [2006] ECR I-11573, para. 37.

127 Low 2011, p. 51.

128 Case C-377/98, *Netherlands v Parliament and Council* [2001] ECR I-7079, para. 32; see also Case C-210/03, *R v Secretary of State for Health, ex p Swedish Match* [2004] ECR I-11893; Case C-66/04, *United Kingdom v Parliament and Council (Smoke flavourings)* [2005] ECR I-10553, para. 45; Case C-380/03, *Germany v Parliament and Council* [2006] ECR I-11573; Case C-301/06, *Ireland v. Parliament and Council* [2009] ECR I-593.

129 Case C-58/08, *Vodafone Ltd, Telefónica O2 Europe plc, T-Mobile International AG, Orange Personal Communications Ser- vices Ltd v Secretary of State for Business, Enterprise and Regulatory Reform* [2010], ECR I-04999; see also Maletic 2011, p. 199; Brenncke 2010, p. 1793; Weatherill 2011, p. 827; Ackermann 2010, p. 426; Alemanno & Garde 2013, p. 1761.

is that a successful claim challenging the proportionality of measures adopted under Article 114 seems to be the exception rather than the rule.[130]

Much more could be said about the future of EU competences especially in the light of the recent developments on the Common European Sales Law.[131] However, this discussion goes well beyond the aim of this Section, which was meant to familiarise the reader with the most common legal basis for the adoption of measures concerning consumer contract law. Nevertheless, what must be said in conclusion is that the EU legislator claims that Article 114 covers both minimum as well as full harmonisation,[132] although this point remains questionable.[133]

2.4. *Reasons for and against Harmonisation*

Having looked at what harmonisation is, how it evolved, what forms it can take and how it fits with the competence of the EU legislator, it is now essential to understand the motives for and against it.

As it has been explored earlier, trade pushes legal convergence, and this remark is also applicable to the harmonisation of laws in Europe. The strengthening of the internal market seems to be the umbrella argument against nationally-oriented legislation, as it 'provides the most powerful motivation, and driving force, for legal harmonisation and contract law [...] obviously particularly closely related to the internal market'.[134] The overall view according to which legal harmonisation strengthens the European economy is a core belief that helped build the internal market.[135] However, when speaking about harmonisation the present discussion does not focus on market forces as such, but it rather looks at the main arguments given by academic and policy literature to support and/or raise doubts about what triggers harmonisation.

On this note, there are many accounts of how/whether to justify harmonisation.[136] The starting point of the arguments presented below takes for granted the fact that harmonisation is already an ongoing process and the supposed benefits of this process are presented. To counterbalance these views, theories that deny the gains of harmonisation are then considered. For a better structure of the pros and cons, four main arguments have been chosen: a) transaction costs; b) legal certainty; c) consumer confidence; and d) European identity.

130 Weatherill 2011a, p. 843.

131 An example of another provision as a basis for a potential optional instrument on European contract law is the flexibility clause, namely Article 352 TFEU. This Article has already been used to create optional instruments in, for instance, IP law; see Mańko 2015, p. 12.

132 *Ibid.*, p. 6.

133 *Ibid.*

134 Zimmermann 2009, p. 484.

135 Stuyck 2009, p. 138.

136 See for instance some economic reasons supporting but also criticizing harmonisation: Van den Bergh & Visscher 2009, p. 146.

2.4.1. Transaction Costs

One of the most cited arguments supporting harmonisation is that differences between legal systems in Europe bring high transaction costs that deter businesses from engaging in transboundary activities.[137] To be able to trade with each other, companies within Member States stumble upon two categories of transaction costs: non-legal and legal.

Firstly, to find trading partners and reach agreements with them, businesses need to tackle the problems of different languages, commercial cultures and merchant practice.[138] This process of collecting information is vital, since information asymmetry can trigger an adverse selection problem, which is nothing else than an imbalance in negotiation power.[139] At the same time, companies are at risk because it might be more difficult to monitor business relationships across borders, or to make use of protective measures (e.g. warranties, letters of credit, etc.).

Secondly, business cultures in turn reflect the legal environment, although some might argue that behavioural and sociological aspects of contract law cannot be qualified as legal and can only be dealt with by other disciplines like psychology, anthropology or behavioural economics.[140] The costs of either specialising own legal advisers in a particular foreign law or hiring local offices to work with bureaucracy webs generally occur because of the lack of uniformity. More specifically for contract law, such costs entail costs of contracts (e.g. knowledge of foreign statutory law, procedural matters, doing research, etc.) or costs of legal disputes (much higher than national disputes).[141] Based on these considerations, it is theoretically accepted that legal harmonisation is endorsed to protect trade and lower transaction costs.[142]

However, even if this argument makes sense when talking about economies of scale and coordinating legal reform in a way that avoids the creation of externalities within Europe, businesses seem to be of a different opinion in practice. Empirical studies, such as the one conducted by the Oxford Institute of European and Comparative Law on 100 European businesses, found the existence of different legal systems to lead to a very interesting phenomenon of competition of laws: 23 per cent of the participants favoured English law while 14 per cent chose German law.[143] Moreover, when asked whether familiarity with other jurisdictions existed, 74 per cent of respondents answered in the affirmative,[144] which only shows how legal diversity is not only not a danger to trade, but it is also a tool businesses use

137 COM(2001) 398 final, p. 9; Lando 2000b, p. 343; Collins 2002, p. 270; Rott 2005, p. 386; De Vries 2012, p. 930; Oosterhuis 2013, p. 996; Estrella-Faria 2009, p. 16. See also COM(2015) 634 final and COM(2015) 635 final.

138 Van den Bergh 2010, p. 66.

139 Linarelli 2002, p. 339.

140 Smits 2007, p. 46.

141 See Wagner 2012, p. 541; see also Hondius 2004, p. 860.

142 Lando 2000a; Weatherill 2005, p. 162.

143 See the final results of the Vogenauer empirical analysis of civil justice systems in Europe: Vogenauer 2008; see also Cuniberti 2014, p. 455.

144 Vogenauer 2008.

when they want to exploit advantages offered by particular jurisdictions. There are others, such as Collins, who claim that law is seldom an impediment to trade, because it only affects very specific circumstances. For him, this is the case of insurance policy, namely the cross-border sale of which can be affected when laws diverge; or marketing techniques, whereby businesses that need to change their marketing approaches because of diverging rules are at risk.[145]

Another landmark study on this subject was done by Cuniberti in 2014.[146] Having scrutinised around 4,427 international contracts, Cuniberti found two particular categories of parties for which transaction costs would not raise issues: (i) sophisticated parties ready to incur necessary transaction costs - parties that are willing to apply a foreign law to their contracts because the benefits of doing so overweigh the costs; and (ii) sophisticated parties unwilling to incur necessary transaction costs - parties who are likely to apply national law anyhow.[147]

Regardless of what transaction costs actually entail, the main question mark arising out of this argument has to do with the level of transaction costs reduced by harmonisation. Is that level considerable, making harmonisation a necessary endeavour, or is it insignificant, thus turning transaction costs into a very unconvincing case? The latter option is well adhered to,[148] as it seems difficult to measure the proportion affecting transaction costs. In this circumstance, any change must be considered against another category of costs, namely harmonisation costs. In addition, the size of actors matters as well.[149] This view also plays a role in the discussion on the next argument for and against harmonisation, namely the need of legal certainty.

2.4.2. Legal Certainty

In spite of legal certainty being sometimes discussed under the heading of transaction costs,[150] the reason for selecting it as a self-standing argument is two-fold: firstly, there are numerous surveys undertaken in the past years reflecting the opinions of a wide range of legal practitioners, where legal certainty is of pivotal importance for businesses or their representing law firms; and secondly, legal certainty is crucially linked to the coverage of harmonisation. Legal certainty is stronger when promoted by maximum harmonisation as opposed to minimum harmonisation, for the simple reason that the former strives for the same standards,

145 Collins 2004, p. 15; Twigg-Flesner 2008a, p. 184.

146 Cuniberti 2014.

147 *Ibid.*, p. 509-512. Cuniberti identified two more categories, namely (i) sophisticated parties bounded rationally - parties who care about the applicable law but do not have enough information to make a fully rational decision, and (ii) unsophisticated parties - parties who do not really understand the implications of a choice of law clause.

148 Gómez & Ganuza 2011a, p. 32; see also Van Boom 2009, p. 446.

149 Kabacinska 2011, p. 7, available at: <http://en.zpc.wpia.uw.edu.pl/wp-content/uploads/-2011/01/European-Constitutionalism-paper-NKabacińska.pdf>, last accessed on 27 July 2016.

150 Estrella-Faria 2009, p. 16; Van den Bergh 2010, p. 86; Wagner 2005, p. 30.

while the latter only imposes the same minimum standard.[151] Since the discussion on the degree of harmonisation is dealt with quite extensively in the following Section, the present analysis focuses on the survey argument.

Such surveys are important because they add numbers to policy perspectives while showing the problems practice is concerned with. What these surveys have in common is the goal of exploring legal realities by using empirical tools in support of the theoretical debate.

In 2005, Clifford Chance did a survey of 175 European businesses[152] to find out that in average, variation in legal systems has one of the highest impacts on cross-border transactions.[153] In the 2008 Oxford study quoted above, outcome predictability was the fourth most important reason determining the choice of governing contract law.[154] Conversely, in a 2010 study undertaken by Law Society of England and Wales, legal certainty ranked first on the list of important factors. The Law Society study was divided in the Firms Omnibus covering a sample of 602 private practice firms in England and Wales and the Online Survey of private practitioners and in-house solicitors covering 63 private practitioners and 65 in-house solicitors.[155] It was found that 73 per cent of firm representatives and 68 per cent of private practitioners and in-house solicitors legal certainty was the most important factor influencing the choice of governing law for their clients' transactions.[156] This is to say that for actors with resources to deal with foreign law, legal certainty is indeed essential. However, can the same be inferred for consumers? Looking at the 2011 study conducted on behalf of Allen & Overy on a sample of 3,024 online shoppers in six different European countries, only a mere 26 per cent are concerned about the laws governing the terms and conditions of sale.[157] To summarise, what all these studies show is that legal certainty has different importance for different actors.

On the other hand, legal certainty is affected when actors involved in transactions are not sure about the legal effects of their actions.[158] However, the accurate coverage of legal certainty depends on many contextual factors: in the case of European contract law it is important to keep in mind, among others, which actors it affects and what interests it protects.[159] Trade involves both businesses and consumers, and it is already clear that legal preferences are different depending on whoever answers a question related to that.[160] Consumers are considered to be in a risky position, given the general presumption that they will have little resources to

151 Miller 2011, p. 138; De Vries 2012, p. 930; Mak 2011d, p. 265.

152 Clifford Chance Survey on European Contract law, April 2005.

153 *Ibid.*; 'Variation in legal systems' scored 5.35 out of 10, as the second most important factor after 'Tax', 5.64.

154 Vogenauer 2008.

155 Law Society of England and Wales, 'Firms Cross-Border Work' Survey, December 2010.

156 *Ibid.*, p. 13-14.

157 Ipsos Mori for Allen&Overy, Online Consumer Research, January 2011, p. 10.

158 Wagner 2007, p. 2; Mak 2011b, p. 339; Case 99/79, *Lancôme v Etos & Albert Heyn* [1980] ECR 2511, para. 16.

159 Mak 2011d, p. 262-266.

160 See for instance the overview made by O'Hara O'Connor 2011, p. 505.

understand and relate to foreign law. If this lack of understanding is considered to deter transactions governed by such law, then consumers will be reluctant to buy foreign products. In turn, businesses of different sizes tend to also diverge in their preferences as well. Small and medium sized enterprises do not benefit from the same strong bargaining power that is meant to aid them in gaining essential expertise in dealing with foreign jurisdictions.[161]

So far, legal certainty was discussed in the context of choice of law and more explicitly, in cases when economic actors need to differentiate between domestic law, foreign law and European law. Still, legal certainty can also be threatened when there is no alternative applicable law. A suitable example of uniform law is the Vienna Convention on the Sale of Goods (CISG). Disregarding the opt-out aspects, interpretation issues challenge its entire uniform character.[162] Open-ended concepts are illustrations of such challenges. Turning back to European contract law, even if it is assumed it could exclusively be shaped by universal mandatory standards, general clauses such as good faith or reasonableness and fairness pose a danger of clashing with legal certainty, thus rendering harmonisation superficial.[163] Even so, this is again a theoretical argument, since there is no empirical study to date that proves that blanket clause interpretation is consistently different within and between jurisdictions in such a manner that it affects harmonisation.

2.4.3. Consumer Confidence

Turning to the third argument for and against harmonisation, in the Commission's view, legal certainty as specified above is a precondition for building confidence between contracting parties,[164] as it only displays once again how inter-related harmonisation arguments are. It has been shown that consumers have been a centre of interest for the debate on contract law, since their modest involvement in the legal understanding of every day transactions turns them into protected actors.[165]

When talking about European legal harmonisation, policy documents such as those from the Directorate-General for Internal Policies place the allocation of basic rights to citizens participating actively in the internal market within one of the EU constitutional limits.[166] This tendency to activate the role of consumers can be noted in European legislation. Recital five of the Consumer Sales Directive reads:

> 'Whereas the creation of a common set of minimum rules of consumer law, valid no matter where goods are purchased within the Community, will strengthen consumer confidence and enable consumers to make the most of the internal market'.[167]

161 Smits 2005a, p. 168.
162 Cuniberti 2006, p. 1517.
163 De Vries 2011, p. 8, available at: <http://ssrn.com/abstract=1703078>, last accessed on 27 July 2016.
164 COM(2010) 348 final, p. 2.
165 See also Hesselink 2008, p. 10; Meli 2006, p. 159; Rott 2005, at 386.
166 Howells & Reich 2010, p. 8.
167 Directive 99/44/EC.

However, there are voices warning against consumer confidence being used as a flagship for the promotion of more aggressive harmonisation.[168] With Directives on Distant Marketing of Financial Services,[169] Unfair Commercial Practices and Consumer Credit[170] justifying maximum harmonisation, consumer confidence is quoted as the main driving force behind this shift.[171] Consumer confidence seems to be a powerful argument when consulting what consumers actually have to say about cross-border transactions. The Eurobarometer Special Report 252, a study conducted on behalf of the Commission, seems to indicate that consumers generally feel less confident when purchasing online goods from a different Member State than their own.[172]

Having said that, two points of criticism can be made. Firstly, market research shows that consumers are interested in aspects other than law when they purchase a product or a service. Product familiarity (which in turn raises a competitive marketing practices issue), payment methods, the ability to compare products, peer-reviews, etc. are examples of factors that might influence consumers in their spending habits,[173] and most of the time, these factors underline a general need for trust. In a 2014 survey over the global share community, consumer research company Nielsen found that 69 per cent of its respondents use the internet to voice concerns or offer praise over customer service.[174] This way, peer feedback strengthens trust and influences consumer decision-making. Another example of consumer confidence-boosters is the use of trustmarks. Trustmarks are electronic labels or logos that can be used either online on websites or offline on material products. These logos are supposed to guarantee towards consumers that certain standards are respected in the production process.[175] A wellknown such trustmark is Fairtrade®.[176] Supermarkets are currently abundant in products that display the

168 See Wilhelmsson 2004.

169 Directive 2002/65/EC.

170 Directive 2008/48/EC.

171 Stuyck 2009, p. 138.

172 Eurobarometer Special Report 252, 'Consumer Protection in the Internal Market', p. 44; EOS Gallup Europe, 'Consumers survey', January 2002.

173 It is questionable if empirical evidence can accurately account for *all* the factors that drive consumer decision-making, as Oren Bar-Gil puts it: 'We consumers are imperfectly rational, our decisions and choices influenced by bias and misperception. Moreover, the mistakes we make are systematic and predictable. Sellers respond to those mistakes. They design products, contracts, and pricing schemes to maximize not the true (net) benefit from their product, but the (net) benefit as perceived by the imperfectly rational consumer. Consumers are lured, by contract design, to purchase products and services that appear more attractive than they really are', in Bar-Gill 2012, p. 2. In the same vein, Ariely claims that individuals look for things around them in relation to others, and this entails that not only consumers themselves have a good handle on their own preferences; see Ariely 2009, p. 45.

174 The Nielsen Company, 'Is Sharing the New Buying – Reputation and Trust Are Emerging as New Currencies', May 2014, p. 10.

175 ECC-Net, 'Trustmark Report 2013 – Should I trust the Trustmark?', October 2013, p. 6.

176 Fairtrade® is a Fairdtrade International trustmark: 'Products bearing these Marks meet the internationally-agreed social, environmental and economic Fairtrade Standards', definition available at: <www.fairtrade.net>, last accessed on 27 July 2016.

Fairtrade® mark, ranging from chocolate and coffee to flowers and wine, favoured by consumers who want to get engaged in more conscious shopping habits.[177] For the average consumer, shopping in a supermarket does not entail a background check on what law is applicable to their transaction, and what repercussions this might have. If consumers respond to visual identities with marketing affiliations, then perhaps public relations campaigns over laws themselves might enhance consumer confidence better than harmonised rules.

Secondly, other studies show that consumers even choose not to care about the legal matters surrounding their contracts.[178] The most prominent example in this respect is the clicking of the 'I agree' button without actually reading terms and conditions. Even at the risk of becoming bound by dubious boilerplate clauses, consumers do not invest their time in reading contractual clauses, which once again, could be, in some cases, linked back to the trust issue as discussed above.

2.4.4. European Identity

Another argument brought up to endorse the idea of European contract law harmonisation, this time of a cultural nature, is the argument that Europe needs to feel European. In other words, contract law must commit to the development of a supranational European identity.[179] To answer the question of whether strengthening a European political identity is imminent or to the contrary, even probable,[180] one must take a step back and try to understand what role national identity plays in multi-layered governance: does the future coexistence of economies, cultures and values lie in unity, or in diversity?

Some views acknowledge that law can be the means by which further integration between European jurisdictions might be possible.[181] In the same way that national civil codes are representative of national legal cultures, a potential European civil code might lead to the creation of a supra-national legal culture.[182] Moreover, it has been said that embracing a European identity does not necessarily conflict with national identities. The first is 'complex and intangible' and it is derived from a special relationship between the citizens and the European Union that does not entail any direct filiation, whereas the latter stems from a direct vertical relationship between the citizens and the state.[183]

177 For more insights as well as the empirics of consumer response to fairtrade products, psychology or marketing studies can be of further assistance; see for instance De Pelsmacker *et al.* 2005, p. 50; Stratton & Werner 2013, p. 363; Gielissen 2011, p. 21; Thøgersen *et al.* 2010, p. 1787; Martinez Gandara 2013, p. 128-131.

178 Bakos *et al.* 2014, p. 1; Ben-Shahar & Schneider 2010; Verkerke 2015, p. 899; Korobkin 2003, p. 1217.

179 Smits 2006, p. 55-107.

180 Study Group on Social Justice in European Contract Law 2004, p. 653.

181 Friedman & Teubner 1986, p. 370; Pintens 2003, p. 29; Wilhelmsson 2014, p. 200.

182 For a more in-depth discussion over the implications and future of a European Civil Code see for instance Collins 2008a; Hartkamp *et al.* 2010; Smits 2005b; Hesselink 2006; Niglia 2015; Schmidt-Kessel 2012; Schulze & Stuyck 2011.

183 Sefton-Green 2006, p. 282-283; see also Hesselink 2008a, p. 77.

Counterarguments however submit that the necessary political consensus for a European identity milestone such as a European civil code is difficult if not impossible to reach anytime soon.[184] Furthermore, political opposition to this idea also stems from concerns over the preservation of national legal cultures.[185] In the same vein, the 2008 financial crisis, the 2015 developments of the Greek debt situation, and the 2016 Brexit referendum have left Europe fragmented, and in the face of turmoil, Member States might prefer to tend to domestic issues rather than support even further European integration.[186]

3. Aims of this Study and Methodology

3.1. *Harmonisation: The Two Perspectives of this Study*

So far convergence and harmonisation were discussed to clarify their meaning and understand how they relate to one another. It was established that in the context of European consumer contract law harmonisation is the policy means employed by the European legislator and convergence is the subsequent effect of legal rules becoming similar. These clarifications lay at the foundation of this study.

One of the striking aspects of the harmonisation discussion is the lack of a yardstick to determine whether harmonisation has in fact a converging effect on law. Moreover, in spite of the wide use of harmonisation as a European policy, there is a clear lack of knowledge regarding what its effect actually is. This study aims to contribute to the understanding of convergence that follows from the harmonisation of consumer sales law. It does so by offering a substantive comparison and a numerical analysis.

3.1.1. The Substantive Comparison

Firstly, this study intends to make a substantive comparison between five directives from the consumer *acquis* and their transposition into the national legislation of seven Member States.[187] The comparative analysis is structured on the basis of a number of different criteria:

(i) the goals of harmonisation according to the European legislator;
(ii) the role of the Court of Justice as a creator of European consumer law; and

184 Loos 2007b, p. 522.
185 Legrand 1997, p. 44; Legrand 2002, p. 61.
186 Sachs 2015, available at: <www.project-syndicate.org/commentary/greece-endgame-eurozone-default-by-jeffrey-d-sachs-2015-06>, last accessed on 27 July 2016; Krugman 2015, available at: <http://goo.gl/xZBjRp>, last accessed on 27 July 2016. Moreover, the 2014 European Parliament elections saw the rise of Euroscepticism, see BBC News 2014, available at: <www.bbc.com/news/world-europe-27575869>, last accessed on 27 July 2016.
187 The concept of 'consumer *acquis*' refers to the body of European legal rules adopted in the field of consumer law. Although consumer law as such is much broader, in this book, this concept will only reflect consumer contract law rules that have European origin.

(iii) the similarities and differences between the different transpositions of European consumer rules in national legal systems.

The criteria chosen for the comparative analysis take the shape of questions then applied to each of the five directives:

(i) what the rationale and scope of the directive are;
(ii) what the standard of harmonisation set by the European legislator is;
(iii) what the reception of the standard of harmonisation by Member States is like; and
(iv) what comparative notes on the transposition can be made.

In addressing these issues, both the European as well as the national level of governance are considered. On the one hand, understanding what exactly the goal of the European legislator was when adopting consumer protection rules, and looking into why the rules are shaped the way they are, is the starting point of this analysis. On the other hand, *transposition* plays a very important role in the process of harmonisation, because it reflects choices made by the national legislator.[188] To frame this research, two questions have been chosen as the general research questions of the substantive comparison:

1. What are the standards of convergence behind the rules on consumer sales developed by the European legislator and how has the Court of Justice interpreted these standards?
2. How did national legislators transpose these rules, and what issues arose from this process?

From a methodological point of view, the comparative analysis is carried out through an extensive literature review of policy developments both at European as well as national level. The case law of the Court of Justice serves as guidance for the further interpretation of European consumer contract law, and its role vis-à-vis national legislation is also explored. Moreover, national case law is also used selectively, to showcase potential issues national courts have to deal with in the

188 Once again the issue of potential terminological confusion arises. Literature often refers to the process of transposition to mean the same as the process of implementation. However, a distinction must be drawn between the two. While transposition envisages the adoption of national rules to mirror the results of the protection standard determined by a directive, implementation has a wider meaning, including activities that might go well beyond the rules themselves. Implementation can thus refer to administrative rules that are adopted to ensure the effectiveness of the protection standard, but also to the interpretation and application of the protection standard by national courts. The TFEU does not tackle 'transposition' or 'implementation' in Article 288 regarding the legal acts of the European Union; see also Tomkin 2004, p. 130; OECD, 'Better Regulation in Europe: An OECD Assessment of Regulatory Capacity in the 15 Original Member States of the EU (Project Glossary)', p. 6-13, available at: <www.oecd.org/gov/regulatory-policy/44952782.pdf>, last accessed on 27 July 2016; Mullerat 2010, p. 6.

transposition process. The selection of directives and Member States included in the research is extensively addressed in Section 4 (Limitations).

3.1.2. The Numerical Analysis

To complement the comparative overview of European rules on consumer contract law and their transposition, the second contribution this research aims to bring consists of a numerical analysis of harmonisation. For this purpose, a statistically inspired Convergence Index is developed. It must be stressed that apart from the consumer-oriented indicators given by EuroStat (e.g. 'Consumer prices', 'Consumer electronic and household appliances', etc.), legal harmonisation is not, as of yet, reflected in any statistical study attempting to measure it. This being the case, due attention must of course be paid to the reasons behind the lack of such information. Is the lack of harmonisation indicators perhaps a sign that they would bring no contribution to the harmonisation debate? The very attempt to answer this question is by no means an easy endeavour. Whether turning harmonisation into numbers can add any value to the debate on legal convergence depends to a great extent on how exactly this is done. In making a point about the importance of one of his methods, namely numerical comparative law, Siems quotes Lord Kelvin, according to whom 'when you can measure what you are speaking about and express it in numbers, you know something about it; but when you cannot measure it, when you cannot express it in numbers, your knowledge is of the meagre and unsatisfactory kind'.[189] The Convergence Index aims to build on the increasingly used numerical comparative law methodology[190] and provide a solution to the question above.

On the basis of data visualisation, the resulting Convergence Index aims to offer new ways of looking at the harmonisation of consumer protection. Studying the law normally entails discussing it in a way that has not changed much from the times of Aristotle, who said about rhetoric:

> 'Of the modes of persuasion furnished by the spoken word there are three kinds. The first kind depends on the personal character of the speaker; the second on putting the audience into a certain frame of mind; the third on the proof, or apparent proof, provided by the words of the speech itself'.[191]

Writing about the law largely reflects the act of persuading an audience by bringing proof (arguments) to criticise the law that is (*lege lata*) and/or support the law that should be (*lege ferenda*). The vast majority of these arguments are reflective, analytical and/or evaluative to such an extent that legal thinking becomes a self-standing category of logical reasoning, or as Smits calls it, legal doctrine.[192] For some, it might be counterintuitive to consider that the law can stand arguments based on numbers. However, as it is shown later in this study, there is great

189 Siems 2014a, p. 146.
190 *Ibid.*
191 Aristotle, Rhetoric, 1356a.
192 Smits 2016.

potential in exploring this perspective. In a world faced with a volume of information exponentially increasing, data visualisation has some strong benefits: (i) simultaneously showing multiple dimensions of a specific issue; (ii) revealing stories from the gathered information and adding new light on pattern identification;[193] (iii) reconsidering how to communicate information with the surrounding world;[194] (iv) gaining the 'big picture',[195] or in other words understanding the complexity and scope of a certain phenomenon. Applying the potential of data visualisation to European consumer law and more specifically the process of legal convergence in this field can bring a novel perspective and contribute to the further understanding of contractual harmonisation. In the light of this complementary perspective, it must be again emphasised that extracting data from consumer protection directives and representing them in various shapes does not replace the need to continue investigating developments in consumer law in a qualitative fashion. The numerical analysis attempts to answer two main research questions:

3. What has harmonisation achieved and how can the resulting convergence process be measured?
4. Which policy recommendations follow from this for the European and national legislators, as well as other institutions?

Methodologically speaking, the numerical analysis builds, as mentioned before, on numerical comparative law as coined by Siems, taken together with the OECD Manual on Composite Indicators. The end result is the construction of the Convergence Index, a composite indicator reflecting quantified factors that influence the harmonisation process. The name 'Convergence Index' has been favoured to 'Harmonisation Index' especially because of the distinction drawn on several occasions already. While harmonisation is a policy method, convergence is the result achieved with this method. Furthermore, it is necessary to once again underline that the purpose of working with an index is to offer an innovative perspective to a longstanding discussion over legal convergence in European consumer contract law.

The full extent of the methodology used in developing the numerical analysis is discussed at length in Chapter 3.

3.2. *Selected Directives*

To avoid setting an unreachable goal by referring to harmonisation and convergence in too broad of a sense, certain filters had to be considered. The first such filter deals with the field of law chosen for the analysis, namely consumer sales law. Five directives have been selected in this respect:

193 Kirk 2012, p. 12.
194 On this topic, see Chapter 1 ('Why Visualize: From Information to Wisdom) from Cairo 2013.
195 Fry 2005, p. 1.

- the Doorstep Selling Directive (1985);[196]
- the Unfair Contract Terms Directive (1993);[197]
- the Distance Selling Directive (1997);[198]
- the Consumer Sales Directive (1999);[199] and
- the Unfair Commercial Practices Directive (2005).[200]

It has already been pointed out that European contract law as it currently exists is far from being a comprehensive and unitary collection of rules, but is more similar to a consumer law puzzle.[201] To be able to assess convergence in the context of the present study, it is first necessary to explain the decision to select the instruments mentioned above.

One of the filters used to narrow down the research question was the substantive scope of the analysis. Choosing to focus on a specific part of consumer law made it easier to navigate through the consumer *acquis*. As this is a study regarding sales law, any selection must revolve around one fundamental aspect: the definition of the contract of sale. Inspiration is now drawn from various legislative and theoretical definitions of the contract of sale.

Turning to the national contract law of the UK, the classical definition of the contract of sale can be found in Section 2(1) of the Sale of Goods Act 1979:

> 'A contract of sale of goods is a contract by which the seller transfers or agrees to transfer the property in goods to the buyer for a money consideration, called the price. [...]'[202]

In addition, the notion of 'consumer contract' was inserted[203] through an amended version of the Sale and Supply of Goods Act 1994,[204] making reference to Section 25(1) of the Unfair Contract Terms Act 1977:

> [...]
>
> ''Consumer contract' means a contract in which –
>
> (a) one party to the contract deals, and the other party to the contract ('the consumer') does not deal or hold himself out as dealing, in the course of a business, and
>
> (b) in the case of a contract such as is mentioned in section 15(2)(a) of this Act, the goods are of a type ordinarily supplied for private use or consumption;[...]'.

196 Directive 85/577/EEC.
197 Directive 93/13/EEC.
198 Directive 97/7/EC.
199 Directive 99/44/EC.
200 Directive 2005/29/EC.
201 COM(2001) 398 final.
202 Section 2, Sale of Goods Act 1979.
203 Section 61(1), Sale of Goods Act 1979.
204 Schedule 2, para. 5(9)(a)(i), Sale and Supply of Goods Act 1994.

In German law, the elements defining the contract of sale can be found in § 433 of the *Bürgerliches Gesetzbuch* (BGB):

> (1) By a purchase agreement, the seller of a thing is obliged to deliver the thing to the buyer and to procure ownership of the thing for the buyer. The seller must procure the thing for the buyer free from material and legal defects.
>
> (2) The buyer is obliged to pay the seller the agreed purchase price and to accept delivery of the thing purchased.

French law clarifies the nature of a contract of sale in Article 1582 *Code Civil* (CC):

> 'Sale is a convention by which one party promises to deliver a thing, and the other promises to pay the price.
>
> It may be done by authenticated act or under private signature'.

The *Code de la Consommation* completes the dispositions of the Civil Code on the contract of sale by distinguishing between two different types of parties: the professional and the consumer,[205] but failing to provide for a clear consumer sale definition. The legal systems discussed above are just illustrations of how most Member States identify elements inherent to the contract of sale, such as the principle of reciprocity,[206] through definitions that are either explicit or implicit.[207]

Zooming out of national legal systems and moving to the European perspective, three sources of inspiration for unified definitions applicable to the contract of sale come to mind: the Principles on European Contract Law (PECL),[208] the Principles of European Law of Sales (PEL S),[209] and the Draft Common Frame of Reference (DCFR). While the PECL tends to be highly abstract so that it can be applicable to any contract regardless of its type,[210] meaning that it does not directly address the contract of sale, but is directly applicable to it, the PEL S address definitional issues for both the contract of sale and consumer sale in Articles 1:101 (2) and respectively 1:202:

> 'A contract for the sale of goods is a contract under which one party, the seller, undertakes to another party, the buyer, to transfer the ownership of goods to the buyer, or a third person, either immediately on conclusion of the contract or at some future time, and the buyer undertakes to pay the price'.

205 E.g. Articles L113 (1)-(5) of the Code de la Consommation on price and conditions of sale.

206 Fauvarque-Cosson & Mazeaud 2008, p. 8.

207 Austria CC Article 1053; Belgium CC Article 1582(1); Czech Republic CC Article 588; Estonia Law of Obligations Act Article 208(1); Greece CC Article 513; Hungary CC Article 365(1); Latvia CC Article 2002; Lithuania CC Article 6:305; Netherlands CC Article 7:1; Portugal CC Article 874; Spain CC Article 1445; Nordic countries leave the definition to legal literature.

208 Lando *et al.* 2000; Lando *et al.* 2003.

209 See for instance Hondius 2004.

210 Article 1:101 PECL.

> [...]
>
> 'For the purpose of these Principles, a consumer sale is a contract under which a natural or legal person who is acting to any extent for purposes related to that person's trade, business or profession (the professional) sells goods to a natural person who is acting primarily for purposes which are not related to that person's trade, business or profession (the consumer)'.

As the PEL S were the basis for the sales section of the DCFR, it is not surprising that the definition of a sales contract has been taken over in Article 1:202. However, the distinction is reflected in Article 1:204, where a consumer sale is defined in terms of the contracting parties rather than the relative consequences of their capacities:

> [...]
>
> 'For the purpose of this Part of Book IV, a consumer contract for sale is a contract for sale in which the seller is a business and the buyer is a consumer'.

Looking at these definitions, it becomes clear that differences between national frameworks and the theoretical structure of the two sets of Principles and the DCFR can be noticed in terms of clarity and consistency: first of all, not all Member States have a clear definition of the contract of sale; second of all, not all Member States have a clear definition of the contract of consumer sale. For this consideration, the present study draws inspiration from a supranational characterisation of sales in its consumer dimension. Thus, a consumer contract of sale is to be understood as a contract under which one party, the seller (business), undertakes to another party, the buyer (consumer), to transfer the ownership of goods to the buyer, or a third person, either immediately upon the conclusion of the contract or at some future time, and the buyer (consumer) undertakes to pay the price.

3.3. *Member States Included in the Research*

Another filter used to narrow down the ambit of the study deals with the selection of Member States. This study includes seven Member States: Belgium; France; Germany; Ireland; the Netherlands; Romania; and the United Kingdom. Two main considerations led to selecting these Member States.

Firstly, it was important to make sure that both the common law as well as the civil law legal families were represented. This does not only concern comparative law design in general, but it is equally important from a substantive perspective. For instance, one of the Directives in this study is the Consumer Sales Directive creating a new hierarchy of remedies for consumers who deal with products not in conformity with the contract. The first set of remedies in this hierarchy is repair and replacement.[211] Considered to be specific performance remedies, it is interesting to

[211] See Section 2.4.

look into how they have been accommodated by a Member State such as the United Kingdom or Ireland, whose primary remedy in case of non-performance has historically been the granting of damages. The same can be said about the Unfair Contract Terms Directive that focuses on a general clause making reference to good faith. Looking at the reception of the standards envisaged by the Directive would be incomplete without taking into consideration the rules in the United Kingdom or Ireland. These are jurisdictions where good faith is known not to have played the same role as on the continent. Substantive aspects of the issues dealt with can also be mentioned in the case of unfair commercial practices. Since German law was the model according to which the Unfair Commercial Practices Directive was drafted, looking into the German transposition cannot be set aside when taking about unfair practices.

Secondly, legal developments in new Member States must be integrated alongside older Member States. On the one hand, newer Member States such as Romania, Bulgaria or Croatia must catch up in terms of comprehensive evaluations of the body of European rules applicable within their legal systems. Not only is literature in English on new Member States scarce, but it can be beneficial to a wide variety of market actors who are interested in studying the rules available otherwise exclusively in the national language. On the other hand, the very results of such an academic undertaking can help draw comprehensive conclusions that can answer the question: how are newer Member States coping with the transposition of European law?

4. Novelty

Much literature exists on the substantive aspects of harmonisation of European consumer law. However, the same cannot be said about the *effect* of harmonisation, namely how it can be measured, and what policy consequences could follow from this measurement. These are questions the present thesis is aiming to answer. What is novel about this approach is that in so far as the effect of harmonisation is concerned, no literature exists.[212]

It has been indicated in the very beginning of the first Chapter that this thesis aims to identify and fill this gap and analyse harmonisation by focusing on its converging effect. In doing so, the thesis aims to develop a methodology to measure legal convergence, and it subsequently applies this methodology to the field of European consumer sales law.

Bearing these considerations in mind, the novelty of this study lies in three things.

Firstly, this study combines a substantive comparison with a numerical analysis. In doing so, not only are the refined details of transposition dealt with, but the conclusions drawn on the basis of the substantive comparison are also tested against the findings of the numerical analysis.

[212] Existing studies that include elements of quantifying the law are examined in Section 3.2; however, none of them deal with European consumer contract law.

Secondly, it creates and applies a new methodology by developing a so-called composite index in the area of consumer sales law. The Convergence Index does not only aim to be a tool in the numerical analysis of European consumer law, but it can also contribute in answering questions about convergence in other fields. For this reason, the Convergence Index may be considered the beta version of a method that can be built upon, reinterpreted and reapplied to other areas of (private) law as well. In addition, the Convergence Index makes use of the OECD Composite Indicators handbook,[213] which has not been done before in the field of consumer sales law before.

Thirdly, it combines a diverse mix of directives and Member States. Four of the directives chosen for the study are minimum harmonisation instruments, and one is a maximum harmonisation instrument. Moreover, both old and new, Western European and Eastern European Member States are included in the research. The diversity of both directives and Member States can be used to explain (i) the advantages and/or disadvantages of how the EU legislator dealt with specific aspects of consumer contract law; and (ii) the advantages and/or disadvantages of how national legislators have responded to European law.

5. Limitations

While Section 3 of this Chapter referred to what *is* included in this research, it is equally necessary to address what is *not* included. To detail the choices made, some clarifications are in order. To start with, it can be argued that the consumer *acquis* includes other directives that could easily fit the definition of consumer sale covered in Section 3.3. The decision not to include any directives other than the five mentioned above was based on the reasons below:

(i) The non-selected directives cover transaction logistics rather than substantive obligations. Two examples that can be mentioned in this sense are the Payment Services Directive and the E-commerce Directive.[214] Besides covering payment service providers and authorisation schemes, the Payment Services Directive focuses more on the facilitation of operations rather than the actual content of sales law. Similarly, the Ecommerce Directive deals – albeit to a lesser extent – with authorisation issues for information society service providers, but also with technical requirements dealing with online contracts, hosting, caching and other features of working with online platforms. While these aspects are more than relevant to concluding online contracts for instance, the mere fact that their focus lies with practical matters and not with the content of substantive rights and obligations was central to the decision of not including them in the study.

213 OECD & European Commission 2008.

214 Directive 2007/64/EC of the European Parliament and of the Council of 13 November 2007 on payment services in the internal market amending Directives 97/7/EC, 2002/65/EC, 2005/60/EC and 2006/48/EC and repealing Directive 97/5/EC, *OJ* L319/1 of 5 December 2007; Directive 2000/31/EC.

(ii) The non-selected directives apply a higher level of consumer protection. This is the case with directives covering financial instruments. On the one hand, directives such as the Consumer Credit Directive lay at the heart of the consumer acquis.[215] On the other hand, getting a EUR 300,000 mortgage to buy a house is different than shopping for a pair of EUR 50 shoes on asos.com. Indeed, the reverse is possible as well - a EUR 1,000 loan for personal use/limit on a credit card is different than buying a EUR 10,000 couture gown on net-a-porter.com. However, shopping for fashion and undertaking restrictive financial obligations are two different sides of consumer protection: while the first might be considered rather mundane, and regardless of the price, the transaction does not raise major comprehension issues for the consumer, the same cannot be said about credit contracts. This distinction mandates financial transactions to be handled with more care towards the consumer. In the light of these considerations, financially-oriented directives have been left out of this study.

(iii) The non-selected directives have recently come into force. This is the case for only one instrument, namely the Consumer Rights Directive.[216] Even though it has repealed two of the directives included in the study (Distance Selling and Doorstep Selling), given its recent entry into force in June 2014, it could not be an appropriate replacement for the CJEU and national case law considered in both the substantive comparison and the numerical analysis. For this reason, while reference is made to the Consumer Rights Directive to highlight the most recent developments regarding distance and doorstep selling, this Directive is not as such included in the instruments analysed by this study. Moreover, while the Consumer Rights Directive changed the scope of the rules applicable to doorstep and distance selling,[217] it simply builds on the previous two directives: consumer protection is still based on information duties and withdrawal rights. For this reason, any discussions relating to the repealed directives is still relevant under the regime governed by the Consumer Rights Directive.

6. Structure

Chapter 1 was dedicated to providing a background for the entire research. It looked at convergence as a global phenomenon, and it acknowledged harmonisation as a policy tool that is supposed to achieve convergence. Harmonisation was then examined from a chronological point of view, and its types, as well as the competence of the European legislator to pursue this policy were addressed.

215 Directive 2008/48/EC.

216 Directive 2011/83/EU.

217 The Consumer Rights Directive is an example of targeted full harmonisation, unlike the Doorstep Selling and the Distance Selling Directives. Moreover, the period applicable to withdrawal rights was changed from a minimum of seven days to a one-size-for-all 14 days.

In what follows, Chapter 2 focuses on the substantive comparative overview as indicated in Section 3.1.1 of this Chapter. The five selected directives - Doorstep Selling, Unfair Contract Terms, Distance Selling, Consumer Sales Law and Unfair Commercial Practices - are discussed by addressing each of the four criteria mentioned earlier: (i) the rationale scope of the directive; (ii) the standard of harmonisation set by the European legislator; (iii) the reception of the standard of harmonisation by Member States; and (iv) comparative notes on the transposition of the Directives. After analysing the policy behind the directives at the EU level of governance, national transpositions are then discussed for the selected jurisdictions: Belgium, France, Germany, Ireland, the Netherlands, Romania and the UK. The transposition discussions leads, for each of the directives, to a comparative overview highlighting similarities and differences. The chapter ends with a short discussion regarding overlaps between the rules of the various instruments.

Chapter 3 is dedicated to the numerical analysis. This analysis builds on an existing theory of numerical comparative law, according to which law and its inherent characteristics can be turned into numbers to add new perspectives in order to help understand the complexity of a vast topic such as legal convergence. In doing so, the information gathered in Chapter 2 serves as inspiration for the modelling of a measurement tool, called the Convergence Index. Chapter 3 elaborates on the factors included in the creation of the Convergence Index, and explains how the latter was methodologically constructed. Subsequently, on the basis of the identified factors, information is retrieved from the selected directives and the selected national transpositions, once again mirroring the comparative substantive analysis in the previous Chapter. This information is later on coded according to very specific methodological considerations, finally creating comparative Convergence Index values for each of the five directives and seven Member States under scrutiny.

Furthermore, the data collected in Chapter 3 is visualised using various chart formats, in order to facilitate the development of new perspectives over the legal convergence debate in consumer contract law. Findings resulting from this enhanced visualisation are also comprehensively discussed. Chapter 3 also includes an interactive virtual tool that can unfortunately not be supported by text format: this virtual tool is a Google Motion Chart, created on the basis of the data gathered in this Chapter. This Motion Chart is currently hosted on https://iconsume.eu and can be consulted online.

Lastly, Chapter 4 is dedicated to drawing concluding remarks on the study as a whole, but also various individual aspects, such as the novel methodology used for the analysis. This Chapter aims to bring symmetry to the present study, and makes an overview of the findings in the light of the proposed research questions. What is more, Chapter 4 also drafts policy recommendations and explores creative ways in which the present study can contribute to the design of more hands-on solutions for policy-makers.

Chapter 2

THE SUBSTANTIVE COMPARISON

1. Introduction and Aim of the Chapter

As mentioned above in the methodological discussion, harmonisation in European consumer sales law is firstly addressed using a substantive comparison. In doing so, the five selected directives are discussed in the light of four questions. To remind the reader, these questions touched upon:

(i) the rationale and scope of the directive;
(ii) the standard of harmonisation set by the European legislator;
(iii) the reception of the standard of harmonisation; and
(iv) comparative notes on the transposition.

The reason why these criteria were chosen is three-fold. Firstly, discussing what the directives were designed to achieve, and more importantly how (criteria i and ii), is useful in recreating the policy developments envisioned by the European legislator. Secondly, by understanding how Member States have transposed European rules, the success and/or shortcomings of national alignment to these policy developments can be evaluated (criterion iii). Lastly, the comparative notes on the transposition (criterion iv) help determine which policy objectives were achieved and which weaknesses were identified in the process.

This Chapter aims to familiarise the reader with the rules applicable to distance selling, doorstep selling, unfair contract terms, consumer sales and unfair commercial practices, both on a European level and a national one, in the light of the overall convergence theme. The five directives are discussed in chronological order, and the four criteria above are then applied to each individual directive. The Chapter thus focuses on comparing national laws - and it does so under the comparative notes - but finally the directives are also compared in a discussion relating to an eventual overlap between their provisions. What is more, the substantive comparison is not only a self-standing methodological perspective, as mentioned in Chapter 1, but it also constitutes the basis of the numerical analysis in Chapter 3 as is seen later.

Two main points need to be taken into account when looking at the structure of this Chapter. Firstly, instead of discussing directives as a whole, the Chapter focuses on selected provisions from each of the five directives. This is because while the rationale and scope of the directives can be easily addressed altogether, not the same can be said about the said directives' transposition. Works such as the Consumer Law Compendium database have successfully focused on outlining, article-by-article, the performance of national legislation in accommodating consumer contract directives. This approach, however, is not one followed by the present study. Leaving aside the differences between the scope and goals of the five chosen directives, it is acknowledged that in its complexity, each directive addresses consumer law-related topics in different layers (e.g. definitional matters, rights/systems set in place, enforcement issues, etc.). In an attempt to narrow down the present analysis, not all articles are looked at, but rather several provisions are selected from each directive, as they are considered a reflection of the most important rules in the directive that help it attain its identified goal. In a nutshell, as far as the national transposition part is concerned, the discussion surrounding it has been designed to reflect the selected European rules.

In doing so, the main challenge has been to identify *which* transposing legislation to consider, as some Member States (e.g. Belgium) have modified transposing legislation more than others (e.g. Ireland). Moreover, because of the scope of national legal reforms, which at times have been quite considerable and changed the design of law itself (e.g. the German *Schuldrechtsreform*, the French *Code de la Consommation*, the Belgian *Code de Droit Economique*, the Dutch *Burgerlijk Wetboek*, etc.), several choices had to be made to ensure methodological cohesion.

For this purpose, as a general rule, the transposition discussion focuses on the *initial* transposing legislation. However, a set of strict exceptions has been applied to French and German law as follows.

(i) French Law

The earliest directive included in this study is the Doorstep Selling Directive adopted in 1985 and entering into force in late 1987. French law initially transposed this Directive through a 1989 amendment of the already-existing Law no. 72-1137 on canvassing and door-to-door sales. With the introduction of the Consumer Code in 1993, France reformed its consumer legislation. A specific choice has been made to discuss the content of the Consumer Code, and not that of the pre-existing law, for two reasons. Firstly, the French legislator transposed the Doorstep Selling Directive long after the transposition deadline, and thus the intermediary rules were in force for a mere four years. The Consumer Code adopted through Law no. 93-949 from 26 July 1993 was the codification of an earlier piece of legislation, namely Law no. 78-22 from 10 January 1978. At the same time, the project for the creation of a Consumer Code did not occur spontaneously in 1993, but it had been in the contemplation of policy-makers as early as the 1985 Calais-Auloy bill.[1] Secondly, the

1 Jean-Jacques M. Robert, 'Rapport fait au nom de la commission des Affaires économiques et du Plan (1) sur le projet de loi relatif au code de la consommation (partie législative)' (Report →

very existence of the Consumer Code is a fundamental feature of the French legal system when it comes to consumer law. Focusing on the transposition of the Doorstep Selling Directive in the Consumer Code can thus preempt concerns regarding the fact that the resulting analysis would otherwise not truly reflect the characteristics of this jurisdiction.

(ii) German Law

The methodological problem surrounding the transposing German laws occurred in two of the selected directives: the Unfair Contract Terms Directive and the Distance Selling Directive. The overarching problem deals with the fact that the German law of obligations went through a wide-reaching reform in 2002, and the question has been whether to focus on separate transposing laws in existence before this reform, or to consider the rules as they were embedded in the German Civil Code. The latter solution has been opted for and the arguments for this choice are outlined below.

As far as the Unfair Contract Terms Directive is concerned, even though the initial transposition occurred in a different decade than the reform, Civil Code rules are of the essence because unfair terms are a pivotal topic in consumer protection. Focusing on the ambit of the old rules to the detriment of those in the Civil Code would thus create an impression of German law that general literature might not equally reflect.

In the case of the Distance Selling Directive, just as with the French example given above, the initial transposing law entered into force in mid 2000, and the new rules in the Civil Code would be applicable as of the beginning of 2002, leading to a one and a half year expiry date on the intermediary rules.

These exceptions are not considered lightly. However, it is submitted that using these exceptions to strengthen the aforementioned methodological vision does not cause a detriment to the analysis, since the particular features of the legislation in question have been considered.

Lastly, this Chapter includes visual support in the form of timeline graphs, showing the legislative process of the adoption of each directive, taken over from Eur-Lex. By adding the graphs, the reader is given additional support in understanding the historical evolution of consumer law-related matters.

made in the name of the commission of economic affairs and of the plan (1) on the bill relating to the consumer code (legislative part)), French Senate, 2nd ordinary session 1992–1993, p. 15.

2. The Doorstep Selling Directive (1985)

2.1. *What are the Rationale and Scope of the Directive?*

Figure 3: Doorstep Selling Directive Adoption Timeline (source: Eur-Lex)

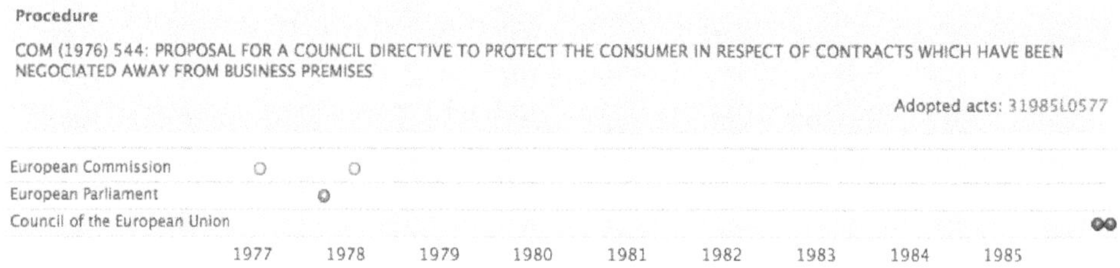

Based on Article 115 TFEU (ex Article 94 TEC),[2] the Doorstep Selling Directive is the oldest instrument of its kind and it was established with the purpose of protecting consumers' interests in contracts of sale concluded under the commercial practices in existence at the time of its drafting.[3] This very drafting had started as of 1977,[4] and involved three different Directorates: DG Environment as the leading service, DG III Industry and DG XV Internal Market and Financial Services.[5] Doorstep selling involves much more pressure than buying on the trader's premises, and it also does not allow consumers to compare prices.[6] Other consumers try to stay away from these types of contracts because of lack of trust in the salespersons, or due to already established retail preferences.[7] Fundamentally, what the Directive became most known for was its coverage of a right called the right of cancellation/renunciation, which was in other words a right to withdraw from the contract.[8] This right was also linked to the trader's duty to inform the consumer

2 Twigg-Flesner 2007, p. 367.

3 Directive on the protection of consumers in respect of contracts negotiated away from business premises 85/577/EEC; Discussion Paper on the Review of Directive 85/577/EEC to protect the consumer in respect of contracts negotiated away from business premises (Doorstep Selling Directive), p. 4; see also Wilhelmsson 1993, p. 26.

4 Proposal For a Council Directive to Protect the Consumer in Respect of Contracts Which Have Been Negociated Away From Business Premises, COM(76) 544 final, 12 January 1977; see also Council Opinion on the proposal for a Council Directive to protect the consumer in respect of contracts which have been negotiated away from business premises, 77/C 180/11; Amendment to the Proposal for a Council Directive to Protect the Consumer in Respect of Contracts Which Have Been Negotiated Away From Business Premises, COM(78) 2 final.

5 See <www.eurlex.eu>, last accessed on 27 July 2016.

6 Office of Fair Trading, 'Doorstep selling: A report on the market study', May 2004, p. 2, available at: <www.oft.gov.uk/shared_oft/reports/consumer_protection/oft716.pdf>, last accessed on 27 July 2016.

7 *Ibid.*

8 It is important to keep in mind this terminological distinction, as the Doorstep Selling Directive mentions a right to cancel the contract, whereas the Distance Selling Directive speaks about a right to withdraw from the contract. Both notions reflect the same content, namely the cooling off period in which the consumer can change his mind about the concluded contract for whatever reason.

about his possibility to cancel the contract within seven days from receipt,[9] and for this reason it can be stated that the Directive affected the rules on contract formation.[10] This term was to be calculated from the time the consumer was given notice of his right to withdraw from the contract, or as the Directive called it, the right of cancellation.[11] In other words, in a more rational decision-making sense, consumers were given the opportunity to make a comparative cost-benefit analysis with other competing offers in order to determine whether they really wanted to conclude the contract.[12] The Directive interpreted contracts negotiated away from business premises to cover contracts concluded: when the trader organised an excursion outside his business premises; or when the trader visited the consumer's home or place of work without having been invited by the consumer to do so.[13] The situation in which the consumer did request to be visited by the trader but then the latter offered to supply goods or services that the consumer did not know or could not reasonably have known were part of the trader's commercial activity was also covered.[14]

2.2. *What Standard of Harmonisation is Set by the European Legislator?*

The Doorstep Selling Directive was a minimum harmonisation instrument in the consumer *acquis*. It was also one of the eight minimum harmonisation consumer directives reviewed at the initiative of the Commission's Green Paper,[15] and in 2014 it was repealed by the entry into force of the Consumer Rights Directive.[16] The Doorstep Selling Directive aimed at protecting consumers by giving them the possibility to reconsider their transactions and exercise a right of withdrawal, available not only in their home country, but in any other Member State. Thus one of the goals of the European legislator was to harmonise national rules in this respect, as the Court of Justice pointed out in the 1994 *Recreb Srl* case:

> '[...] the directive is intended to improve consumer protection and eliminate discrepancies between national laws providing such protection.'[17]

However, the Directive left much discretion to national legislators, as can be seen for instance in Article 7, where it was made clear that matters such as the legal effects of the right of renunciation were not dealt with by the Directive, but by

9 Article 4, Directive 85/577/EEC, *OJ* L372 of 31 December 1985.
10 Wilhelmsson 1993, p. 26.
11 See Case C-481/99, *Georg Heininger and Helga Heininger v Bayerische Hypo- und Vereinsbank AG* [2001] ECR I-9945; Case C-227/08, *Eva Martín Martín v EDP Editores SL* [2009] ECR I-11939.
12 Eidenmueller *et al.* 2011, p. 1085.
13 Article 1(1), Directive 85/577/EEC, *OJ* L372 of 31 December 1985.
14 Article 1(2), Directive 85/577/EEC, *OJ* L372 of 31 December 1985.
15 European Commission, 'Green Paper on the Review of the Consumer Acquis', COM(2006) 744, Annex II.
16 Kawakami & Goanta 2015, p. 157.
17 Case C-91/92, *Paola Faccini Dori v Recreb Srl* [1994] ECR I-03325, para. 5.

national rules.[18] In practice, the right of cancellation was likely to lead to an obligation for each party, in case performance was already rendered: the trader must reimburse the consumer, who must then return the goods received. Since the Directive was silent on any potential effects,[19] the Court of Justice held that in spite of the Directive allowing Member States to deal with certain aspects arising from the right of cancellation, this did not affect the minimum protection offered by the Directive, namely the seven days cooling-off period.[20]

However, the Court made it clear that even the cooling-off period has its limitations. This was decided in *Hamilton*.[21] Annelore Hamilton had concluded an off-premise loan agreement with a bank whose rights were later acquired by Volksbank. Given that Mrs. Hamilton was given wrong information about her cancellation right, the seven days term would only start as of the moment when she became aware of its existence, which she did by reading the Court's decision in the *Heiniger* case.[22] Still, the German transposing legislation, namely the *Gesetz über den Widerruf von Haustürgeschäften und ähnlichen Geschäften* of 16 January 1986 stated that the cancellation right would lapse after one month from the moment when the contractual obligations were performed. The Court agreed with this limitation.[23]

2.3. *How was the Directive Transposed by Member States?*

Two characteristics of this Section must be acknowledged. Firstly, to better compare national transpositions, it does not address all articles in the Doorstep Selling Directive, but a selection thereof. This Directive has the least number of articles out of all the directives under scrutiny, and since Article 5 establishing the right of renouncing the effects of the contract (right of cancellation) lies at its centre, it is the only selected provision for the purposes of the comparisons made in this Section.

Secondly, as stated above, the Doorstep Selling Directive has been repealed by the Directive on Consumer Rights,[24] and is no longer applicable as of 2014. Since the current Chapter focuses on surveying legislation relating to the selected directives, the rules adopted in the light of this development are included in order to provide the reader with a comprehensive overview of the legislative modifications. What is more, where this information is necessary, the rules existing before the transposition of the directives are accounted for. However, neither of the two categories form part of the analysis as such. The goal of this Chapter is to follow national legislation as it existed after the initial transposition.

18 Terryn 2008, p. 157; von Bar & Drobnig 2004, p. 257.

19 Loos 2009, p. 266.

20 Case C-91/92, *Paola Faccini Dori v Recreb Srl* [1994] ECR I-03325, para. 17.

21 Case C-412/06, *Annelore Hamilton v Volksbank Filder eG* [2008] ECR I-02383, para. 40.

22 Mak 2012a, p. 330; see also Calliess 2002.

23 *Annelore Hamilton v Volksbank Filder eG*, para. 40; this period has been subsequently changed, since in the proposal for a Consumer Rights Directive it was raised to three months, see Twigg-Flesner & Metcalfe 2009, p. 382.

24 See Section 1.6, p. 36.

The transposition of Article 5 in the national laws of Member States is thus analysed in what follows.

2.3.1. Belgium

Provisions on doorstep selling used to be covered in Belgian law by the Trade Practices Law of 1971 and the Royal Decree 82 of 28 November 1939 on itinerant trade activities, later replaced by Law of 13 August 1986 regarding the exercise of itinerant activities.[25] With a transposition deadline on 23 December 1987,[26] the Doorstep Selling Directive was only transposed in Belgian law with the adoption of the Act of 14 July 1991 on trade practices and consumer information and protection (Articles 86-92),[27] entering into force on 29 February 1992, after a delay of 50 months.[28] Articles 88 and 89 specifically deal with the right to renounce the contract, which could be exercised by the consumer for seven days starting as of the day after the conclusion of the contract, by means of sending the seller a registered letter and notifying him about the renunciation. It was deemed sufficient if the notification was sent before the expiry of the seven-day term. Interestingly, the Belgian legislator had specified in Article 88 that consumer sales outside of business premises would only come into being if eventually concluded in writing, before or at the latest at the time of the delivery of the product or performance of the service.[29]

These rules were subsequently modified with the entry into force of the Act of 6 April 2010 on market practices and consumer protection. According to this Act, the requirements of Article 5 of the Directive were spread throughout Articles 60-62 as follows: the right to renounce the effects of the contract within a period of not less than seven working days,[30] together with the effects of renunciation were mirrored

25 *Loi du 13/08/1986 relative à l'exercice des activités ambulantes (Wet van 13/08/1986 betreffende de uitoefening van de ambulante activiteiten)*, Moniteur belge of 24 September 1986, p. 12941; see also Stuyck 1978, p. 133-151.

26 The Consumer Law Compendium establishes 31 December 1987 as the transposition deadline; however Article 9 of the Directive mentions in para. 1 that 'Member States shall take the measures necessary to comply with this Directive within 24 months of its notification', which occurred on 23 December 1987.

27 *Loi du 14/07/1991 sur les pratiques du commerce et sur l'information et la protection du consommateur (Wet van 14/07/1991 betreffende de handelspraktijken en de voorlichting en bescherming van de consument)*, Moniteur belge of 29 August 1991, p. 18712.

28 Schulte-Nölke *et al.*, *Consumer Law Compendium*, p. 50, available at: <www.eu-consumer-law.org/consumerstudy_full_en.pdf>, last accessed on 27 July 2016. This body of work has also been published in book format: Schulte-Nölke *et al.* 2008. However, this book version does not include information about Romanian and Bulgarian law, given that its publication overlapped the accession of the two already-mentioned Member States. For this reason, and for the fact that the Consumer Law Compendium database has been created to serve as an online tool, the research refers to the study published on the website, the link to which is provided above.

29 Article 88 of the 1991 Law used to read: '*[…] les ventes au consommateur visées par la présente section doivent, sous peine de nullité, avant ou au plus tard lors de la livraison du produit ou de la prestation du service, faire l'objet d'un contrat écrit, rédigé en autant d'exemplaires qu'il y a de partie contractantes ayant un intérêt distinct.*'

30 Schulte-Nölke *et al.* 2008, p. 195.

in Article 61 (first and second sentence) and Article 62, while compliance with the time limit by dispatching notice was covered by Article 60 (second sentence).

As of December 2013, these rules have been incorporated in the Code of Economic Law.

2.3.2. France

Before the Doorstep Selling Directive, door-to-door sales were generally prohibited in France by virtue of Law no. 72-1137 on canvassing and door-to-door sales, which is said to have influenced the drawing up of the Directive.[31] France transposed the doorstep selling rules in a special law that pre-dated the introduction of the Consumer Code in 1993. This initial law, namely Law no 89-421 of 23 June 1989 served as an intermediary transposition, modifying Law no. 72-1137 until the latter was repealed by the Consumer Code. Setting aside the complicated legislative developments at the time, one aspect is certain - the transposition deadline was not respected.[32] Since the in-between law was a short-term solution for the transposition, and the Consumer Code is a distinguishable feature of French consumer protection, the Consumer Code transposition is of the essence.

The right to renounce the effects of the transaction within a period of no less than seven calendar days was covered by Article L. 121-25 and the suggested forms to be used by traders for withdrawal were mentioned in Articles R. 121-3 to 6. Compliance with the time limit by dispatching notice was also tackled by Article L. 121-25, while French law stayed silent on the effect of renunciation. What French law did add, however, was a prohibition on providing services during the period of withdrawal. According to Article L. 121-26, 'no person or entity shall demand or obtain from the client, whether directly or indirectly, on any grounds, any remuneration or any undertaking nor provide any service of any kind.'[33] As of 17 March 2014, these rules have been changed to fit the transposition duties under the Consumer Rights Directive, and at the moment can be found in Article 121-21, up to 121-21-8 of the Consumer Code.

2.3.3. Germany

The initial transposition of doorstep selling rules into German law took place well before the transposition deadline, through the Doorstep Selling Cancellation Act, entering into force on 1 May 1986.[34] As the Consumer Law Compendium emphasises, this Act was adopted almost at the same time as the Directive itself,[35]

31 *Ibid.*, p. 175.

32 *Ibid.*, p. 76; *Loi Numéro 89-421 du 23/06/1989 relative à l'information et à la protection des consommateurs ainsi qu'à diverses pratiques commerciales*, Journal Officiel du 29.06.1989, p. 8047.

33 Micklitz *et al.* 2010, p. 263.

34 *Gesetz über den Widerruf von Haustürgeschäften und ähnlichen Geschäften vom 16/01/1986*, Bundesgesetzblatt Teil I vom 22.01.1986, p. 122; see also Magoulas & Schwartze 1986, p. 225; Rott 2006, p. 1110.

35 Schulte-Nölke *et al.* 2008, p. 82.

and the legislative technique chosen for this transposition has been deemed as a 'first phase' of German legislative techniques of transposition. Early on in the development of European private law, and more specifically consumer contract law the German legislator transposed European directives by modifying existing laws.[36]

Initially, § 1 reflected the content of Article 5 of the Doorstep Selling Directive, thus creating a right of withdrawal (*Recht auf Widerruf*). This entailed a written revocation of the consumer's declaration of intent within a period of one week. As of 1 January 2002, with the reform of the law of obligations, these rules were taken over by the Civil Code (e.g. §§ 13, 14, 312, 312a, 312f, 355- 359 BGB). Furthermore, as of that point in time, the right to renounce the effects of the contract within a period of not less than seven days was to be found in § 312(1) and § 355 BGB.[37] The latter also covered compliance with the time limit by dispatching notice. As for the effects of renunciation, a series of provisions stemming from the general regime were equally applicable: §§ 346-348, § 355(1) and § 357 BGB.[38]

As of 13 June 2014, different rules apply, as the German Federal Parliament passed the Act on the Implementation of the EU Consumer Rights Directive and on the Amendment of the Law on Housing (*Gesetz zur Umsetzung der Verbraucherrechterichtlinie und zur Änderung des Gesetzes zur Regelung der Wohnungsvermittlung*).

2.3.4. Ireland

The European Communities (Cancellation of Contracts Negotiated away from Business Premises) Regulations 1989 were the rules transposing the Doorstep Selling Directive into Irish law on 1 November 1989, meaning that the transposition was not timely.

Until the transposition of the Directive, general contract law used to apply to contracts concluded outside of business premises (e.g. Sale of Goods Act 1893; Sale of Goods and Supply of Services Act 1980; etc.). It has been pointed out that even though the Act of 1980 allowed the Minister responsible to issue orders on consumer withdrawal, this option was not used.[39]

Regulations 5 and 6 reflect Article 5 of the Directive, as follows: Regulation 5(1) covered the withdrawal right of seven days (according to which the consumer can withdraw from a contract by handing in or sending a cancellation form) as well as the compliance with the time limit by dispatching the notice and Regulations 5(3) and 6(1) dealt with the effects of withdrawal (the contract was void and any sums paid had to be returned to the consumer).

Statutory Instrument No. 484 of 2013 European Union (Consumer Information, Cancellation and Other Rights) Regulations 2013 changed this regime by further transposing the Consumer Rights Directive into Irish law.

36 *Ibid.*, p. 83.
37 BGH (2005) DB 1516; BGH (2002) I ZR 55/00.
38 See also Rott 2008, p. 7-33.
39 Schulte-Nölke *et al.* 2008, p. 100.

2.3.5. The Netherlands

Dutch law already addressed doorstep selling in the Doorstep Selling Law of 7 September 1973.[40] The right of withdrawal was covered by Article 25, paragraphs (1)-(2) and (4). Article 25(1) established the right of withdrawal, while paragraph (2) specified that the notification of withdrawal must be made no later than on the eight day calculated as of the day following the day when the contract was concluded.

Paragraph (4) mentioned the effects of withdrawal, but the wording of the paragraph reveals some complications. It made reference to '*ontbinding*', which is the term used for contractual termination.[41] The Doorstep Selling Law applied until the transposition of the Consumer Rights Directive that came into force on 13 June 2014,[42] and entailed the modification of (among others), Book 6 of the Dutch Civil Code.

2.3.6. Romania

1999 marked the transposition of the Doorstep Selling Directive into Romanian law. As Romania was not a Member State at the moment of the adoption of the Directive, it fulfilled its duty to adopt community legislation prior to joining the European Union. Thus it can be stated that the transposition was timely. Rules on doorstep selling were covered by Government Ordinance regarding consumers contracts negotiated away from business premises no. 106/30.08.1999 as approved and amended by Law no. 60 of 16 January 2002.[43] Before the adoption of this instrument, Romanian law did not have any specific rules on doorstep selling, although it had established a basis for consumer protection in general under the regime of Government Ordinance 21/1992, which continues to apply even to date.

According to the Ordinance, Article 9(1) and (2) covered the seven-day term that began when the contract was concluded or alternatively, when the product was delivered. Moreover, the Romanian rule in Article 9(2) provided that the parties may stipulate a longer term. Paragraph (3) specified that notification must be done via mail, in writing, and the date of dispatch must fall within the term stipulated in the contract. Article 14 covered the effects of renunciation, which released the parties from any obligation.

As of 13 June 2014, these rules were modified by the entry into force of Emergency Ordinance 34/2014 transposing the Consumer Rights Directive.[44]

40 *Colportagewet wijziging van 03/07/1989*, Staatsblad nummer 1989-301 van 25.07.1989.

41 Hijma & Valk 2004, p. 30.

42 For an analysis of the new rules see Luzak & Mak 2014b.

43 *Ordonanta Guvernului nr. 106/1999 privind contractele încheiate în afara spatiilor comerciale*, Monitorul Oficial nr. 431 din 31.08.1999.

44 *Ordonanța de Urgentă nr. 34/2014 privind drepturile consumatorilor în cadrul contractelor încheiate cu profesioniștii, precum și pentru modificarea și completarea unor acte normative*, Monitorul Oficial nr. 427 din 11.06.2014.

2.3.7. The United Kingdom

Before the adoption of the Directive, there were no specific doorstep selling rules in the UK with the exception of inertia selling.[45]

The Consumer Protection (Cancellation of Contracts concluded away from business premises) Regulations 1987 entered into force on 1 July 1988. Article 5 was mirrored by Regulation 8, which stated that a consumer must send the cancellation notice within the cancellation period and the dispatch theory is used for this purpose (paragraphs 1 and 5); if cancelled, the contract was considered as never having been entered into (paragraph 2); Schedule 4 Part II included a cancellation form, but it was not mandatory for the consumer to use it as long as the notification indicated the intention to cancel de contract (paragraph 3); and as a later addition, the possibility of cancelling a doorstep contract by sending an e-mail was also taken into account (paragraph 6).

As of 13 June 2014, doorstep selling rules can be found in the Consumer Contracts Regulations (Information, Cancellation and Additional Charges) Regulations 2013.

2.4. *Comparative Notes on the Transposition*

It has been pointed out that the Doorstep Selling Directive is a minimum harmonisation directive, and that there has been quite some leeway for Member States to transpose it. Moreover, being the earliest consumer contract law directive, its scope has been rather narrow, restricted to information duties and the right to cancel the contract. In what follows, the national transposing rules are discussed in the light of three selected points relevant from the perspective of convergence.

Perhaps even before looking at these issues it must be emphasised that the Doorstep Selling Directive is one of the earliest directives in the consumer *acquis* overall. Some of its features include conciseness (it is the least lengthy directive out of all the five analysed in this study), but also the narrow scope – apart from very brief information duties and the cancellation right, the Doorstep Selling Directive does not stand out from a harmonisation perspective. It is somehow understandable that without a clearly shaped vision of the consumer *acquis*, the European legislator developed rules on distance selling on a micro level, that is to say without having in mind how this Directive can lay the grounds for consumer harmonisation well beyond its substantive ambit.

Going back to the three points, firstly, there is the issue of terminology. Member States understood to transpose the main right given by the Directive in diverging ways. A lot of confusion ensued not only from national provisions, but also from the different language versions of the Directive. The English version of the Directive used the term of 'right of cancellation', or as Article 5 stated, 'right of renouncing the effects of the contract'. The German and Dutch versions spoke about a 'right of cancellation' ('*Widerrufsrecht*' and '*het recht om de overeenkomst op te*

45 Schulte-Nölke *et al.* 2008, p. 164.

zeggen'), while the French and Romanian versions referenced a right to terminate the contract ('*droit de résilier le contrat*'; '*dreptul de a rezilia contractul*'). Interestingly enough, the Belgian and French transposing terminologies moved away from the aforementioned language versions, and developed the concepts '*le droit de se rétracter de son achat*', and namely '*faculté de renonciation*', signalling a departure from the traditional remedies in civil law available on national level. Romanian law moved in the opposite direction by transposing the cancellation right through the concept of unilateral termination ('*dreptul de a denunța unilateral contractul*'). A similar situation existed in Dutch law, where Article 25(4) of the Dutch Doorstep Selling Law used the term '*ontbinden*', which is normally used for termination. German law faced a similar issue, given that the '*Widerrufsrecht*' had been used with a different connotation, namely to indicate the possibility of withdrawing an offer – a particularity of the BGB.[46] The main inconvenience with terminology in this case is that if a legal system embeds a European concept by removing its identity and fully transforms it into a national remedy, this no longer showcases the European origin of the right. It is shown later that this could be detrimental to attaining convergence.

The terminological issues discussed above are linked to the second point of this comparison: the legal nature of the right of withdrawal. The Netherlands and Romania connected withdrawal to termination, while the UK and Ireland provided detailed rules regarding the special effect of withdrawal. Moreover, there is also the aspect of when the contract is actually concluded. While some authors suggest that the conclusion of the contract only occurs after the expiry of the withdrawal period, other opinions suggest that the contract is concluded before the withdrawal period starts, however, 'withdrawing from the contract unwinds the contract retroactively'.[47] As the Distance Selling Directive provided no guidance as to the exact legal nature of the cancellation right (the right of withdrawal) and its effects, the Consumer Rights Directive added new provisions in this respect. However, the new provisions fall short of solving this issue. Article 12 of the Consumer Rights Directive mentions that 'the exercise of the right of withdrawal shall *terminate* the obligations of the parties [emphasis added]'. While it is true that the formulation used by the English version of the Directive is not shared by the French version,[48] the legal nature of the right of withdrawal is still not clarified. Moreover, Article 12 of the Consumer Rights Directive also mentions in sub-paragraph (b) that where 'an offer was made by the consumer, the right of withdrawal terminates the obligations of the parties to conclude a contract'. The wording of this sub-paragraph is dubious at best. It refers to a situation where a contract was never concluded, in which case withdrawal can be easily mistaken with the withdrawal of the offer that was already mentioned in German law.

Thirdly, some Member States (e.g. France, United Kingdom) standardised the cancellation procedure by supplying traders with a cancellation form they could

46 Rott 2006, p. 1112.

47 Micklitz *et al.* 2010, p. 263.

48 The French version reads: 'L'exercice du droit de rétractation a pour effet d'éteindre l'obligation des parties […]'.

then use and make available to consumers. While this might seem a rather technical or administrative endeavour, businesses tend to relate their compliance to law to transaction costs. If rules might be costly to comply with (e.g. having an external lawyer draft a model cancellation form; or alternatively bearing the risk of not entirely following cancellation right requirements), businesses could, in theory, choose not to comply with them in the way a lawmaker would expect.[49] For this reason, providing standard forms in order to help traders fulfil their obligations could be considered to lead to a more uniform national practice, and therefore to a higher level of convergence. It is thus surprising that this has not been a measure supported by the Directive itself, and it was up to a few Member States to come up with it.

To sum up, before moving to the discussion relating to the Unfair Contract Terms Directive, this Section tried to select three perspectives from which to compare the national transposition rules discussed so far.

3. The Unfair Contract Terms Directive (1993)

3.1. *What are the Rationale and Scope of the Directive?*

Figure 4: Unfair Contract Terms Directive Adoption Timeline (source: Eur-Lex)

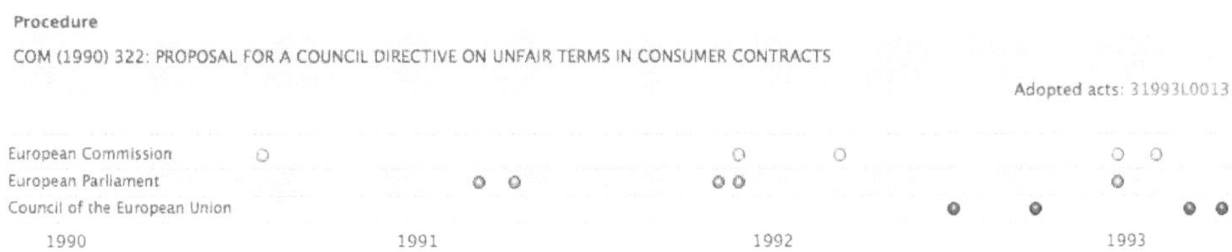

The Unfair Contract Terms Directive, based on Article 114 TFEU (ex Article 95 TEC)[50] is seen as a cornerstone in European consumer policy and its main purpose is to control standard contract terms.[51] Although the leading directorate involved in the procedure was DG Health and Consumers, up to 11 associated agencies were overall involved in the drafting of the Unfair Contract Terms Directive.[52] In the

49 See for instance Ben-Shahar & Posner 2011; see also Levmore 2013.

50 Dean 1993, p. 582.

51 Grundmann *et al.* 2001, p. 29; see also Bright 2000, p. 331; Wilhelmsson 2004, p. 317; Lawson 2011, p. 311; Schulte-Nölke *et al.* 2008, p. 341; Bernitz 2000, p. 13; Report from the Commission on the Implementation of Council Directive 93/13/EEC of 5 April 1993 on Unfair Terms in Consumer Contracts, COM(2000) 248 final, p. 5.

52 According to EurLex, the following associated services were involved in the adoption process: DG VII - Transport; DG III - Industry; DG XXIII - Enterprise Policy, Distributive Trades, Tourism and Cooperatives; Eurostat; DG Research and Innovation; Secretariat-General; DG XV - Internal Market and Financial Services; DG Competition; DG Employment, Social Affairs and Inclusion; DG Agriculture and Rural Development; DG II - Economic and Financial Affairs; and DG Information Society and Media.

making for around 19 years,[53] the Unfair Contract Terms Directive has a twofold rationale, just like the Doorstep Selling Directive: (i) strengthening the internal market by (ii) harmonising consumer law. It has been highlighted that directives adopted under Article 114 (ex Article 95) 'harmonise national laws as a means to improve the functioning of the market'.[54]

The Unfair Contract Terms Directive was driven by two major consumer concerns: the lack of transparency of consumer contract terms, and the lack of a bargaining process essentially limiting freedom of contract.[55] In Ben-Shahar's words, 'real people don't read standard form contracts', because they are consumers, and what matters to them is the product or service they purchase, rather than the means, methods and conditions or even the legal effects of that purchase.[56] In more detail, in *Commission v Kingdom of Sweden*, a case revolving around Sweden's transposition of the Directive's Annex, the Commission claimed that the Unfair Contract Terms Directive aims at approximating rules in Member States relating to unfair terms in consumer contracts and at improving existing consumer information on what rules are applicable in such contracts.[57] This is also laid in Article 1 and the second recital to its preamble.

The main way in which the Unfair Contract Terms Directive seeks to realise these aims is to provide courts with an unfairness test applicable to standard contract terms, but also to list an indicative and non-exhaustive selection of terms that may be considered unfair.[58] This policy reflects a Community strategy on the protection of consumers that has been on the European agenda ever since the adoption of the Preliminary Programme for a Consumer Protection dating back to 1975.[59]

The Directive indirectly addresses the different bargaining positions of the seller, as a business, and the buyer, as a consumer. This is embedded in Article 3(1), according to which a contract term shall be deemed unfair if, contrary to the requirement of good faith, it causes a significant imbalance in the parties' rights and obligations arising under the contract, to the detriment of the consumer. As the Court held in *Océano Grupo*:

53 Woodroffe & Lowe 2010, p. 162.

54 Weatherill 2011b, p. 190; see also Recital 5 of the Unfair Commercial Practices Directive: 'Whereas, generally speaking, consumers do not know the rules of law which, in Member States other than their own, govern contracts for the sale of goods or services whereas this lack of awareness may deter them from direct transactions for the purchase of goods or services in another Member State'; see also Loos 2003, p. 702.

55 Willett 1997, p. 223; see also Preamble of the Unfair Contract Terms Directive.

56 Ben-Shahar 2009, p. 2; Ben-Shahar & Schneider 2010, p. 42; see also White 2000, p. 1693; Faure & Luth 2011, p. 348; *Suisse Atlantique Société d'Armement Maritime SA v Rotterdamsche Kolen Centrale NV*, [1967] HL AC 361, para. 406.

57 Case C-478/99, *Commission of the European Communities v Kingdom of Sweden* [2002] ECR I-04147, para. 10.

58 Article 3(3) Directive 93/13; see also the Annex of this Directive.

59 Council Resolution of 14 April 1975, *OJ* C92/1 of 24 April 1975; see also European Commission, 'Communication of the Commission to the Council on unfair terms in consumer contracts', COM(84) 55 final; Posch 1997, p. 135.

'[...] it should be noted that the system of protection introduced by the Directive is based on the idea that the consumer is in a weak position vis-à-vis the seller or supplier, as regards both his bargaining power and his level of knowledge. This leads to the consumer agreeing to terms drawn up in advance by the seller or supplier [...]'.[60]

Even though there have been discussions on possibly extending the application of the Directive to commercial contracts as well,[61] it is clear the Directive is a harmonisation effort limited to the sphere of consumer law.[62] For this reason it only applies to consumer transactions as identified by the definitions provided in Article 2:

'[...](b) 'consumer' means any natural person who, in contracts covered by this Directive, is acting for purposes which are outside his trade, business or profession;

(c) 'seller or supplier' means any natural or legal person who, in contracts covered by this Directive, is acting for purposes relating to his trade, business or profession, whether publicly owned or privately owned.'

As for the types of contracts covered by the Directive, after Germany's interference in the drafting procedure, the draft was changed from including any unfair contract term, to terms that have not been individually negotiated.[63] This category is described in Article 3(2) which views a term not individually negotiated as a standard term drafted in advance without any involvement from the consumer as to its substance. While the Recitals explicitly leave out contracts relating to employment, succession rights, rights under family law and the incorporation and organisation of companies or partnership agreements, insurance contracts are included in the scope.[64] A group of transactions concerns contracts for the sale of immovables. Is the Unfair Contract Terms Directive applicable to real estate/land contracts as well? The answer remains disputed even in light of the drafting history. It is said that this directive had been initially formulated in French and should normally cover land contracts as well.[65] Lastly, from a formal perspective it must also be noted that the Directive does not only cover written terms, but also oral terms.[66]

There are two dimensions of the discussion relating to how the unfairness test in Article 3 and its inherent blanket clauses affect harmonisation. To start with, very

60 Joined cases C-240/98 to C-244/98, *Océano Grupo Editorial SA v Roció Murciano Quintero; Salvat Editores SA v José M. Sánchez Alcón Prades; José Luis Copano Badillo; Mohammed Berroane; and Emilio Viñas Feliú* [2000] ECR I-04941, para. 24.

61 Hondius 1994, p. 36.

62 See also Laws LJ's interpretation of the Directive's scope of application in *The London Borough of Newham v kathu, Zeb nd Iqbal, and the Office of Fair Trading (Interested Party)* [2004] EWCA Civ 55 (22.2.2004); Lete 1997, p. 205; Davo 1997, p. 157; Reich 1997, p. 165; Collins 2008b, p. 1-18.

63 Hondius 1994, p. 37; Micklitz & Radeideh 2005, p. 326-327.

64 Weatherill 2005, p. 117.

65 Bright & Bright 1995, p. 655; Hartley 1996, p. 265.

66 Lawson 2011, p. 311.

similarly to the Doorstep Selling Directive, it seems that the text of the Directive itself may lead to confusion. Luckily, the *travaux preparatoires* were very insightfully accounted for in literature. Deciding on the scope of the Directive's protection (e.g. coverage of any contractual term as opposed to non-individually negotiated terms), as well as deciding on the content of the general test was no easy task.[67] If early in the drafting process, good faith was considered a self-standing test, it was changed during the many amendments taking place between 1990-1992, and it was confined to a supplementary test:

> 'A contractual term which has not been individually negotiated shall be regarded as unfair if, contrary to the requirement of good faith, it causes a significant imbalance in the parties' rights and obligations arising under the contract, to the detriment of the consumer.'[68]

Following a literal interpretation of Article 3, it can be once again stated that the four conditions (non-individually negotiated term; contrary to good faith; causing significant imbalance; and bring a detriment to the consumer) are cumulative. It has been claimed that by adding the good faith standard as a supplementary condition, this conflicts with one of the other criteria used, that of 'significant imbalance', whereby no term causing a significant imbalance can be in line with good faith.[69] In other words, good faith encompasses any significant imbalance. This finding is specifically important when analyzing the way in which Member States have transposed the test and its specific open-ended concepts, which is the second level of the harmonisation discussion. If the general unfairness test was designed to have a vague yet targetted form, it becomes essential that Member States preserve this meaning, and transpose the very same elements making up this test, without being skeptical about their content:

> '[o]nce the good faith principle has become a European principle, all national judges should apply it in a similar way. This means that national judges shall indirectly take into account existing case-law and doctrine and principles being developed in other Member States'.[70]

67 Tenreiro 1995, p. 275.

68 Article 3, Unfair Contract Terms Directive. For comparison, Article 2 of the proposal submitted on 3 September 1990 (COM(90) 322 final) reads: 'A contractual term is unfair if, of itself or in combination with another term or terms of the same contract, or of another contract upon which, to the knowledge of the person or persons who conclude the first-mentioned contract with the consumer, it is dependent:
- it causes to the detriment of the consumer a significant imbalance in the parties' rights and obligations arising under the contract; or
- it causes the performance of the contract to be unduly detrimental to the consumer; or
- it causes the performance of the contract to be significantly different from what the consumer could legitimately expect; or
- it is incompatible with the requirements of good faith.'

69 Tenreiro 1995, p. 279.

70 *Ibid.*

These are the words of one of the witnesses to the creation of the Unfair Contract Terms Directive, and the hopes he had expressed in his 1995-written article were by no means modest. However, this perspective clarifies perhaps the reason why no definition of 'good faith', 'significant imbalance' or 'detriment' were ever provided for in the Directive. To a certain extent there was an unspoken expectation that Member States would acknowledge and pursue harmonisation via their national courts.

3.2. *What Standard of Harmonisation is Set by the European Legislator?*

Just like the Doorstep Selling Directive, the Unfair Contract Terms Directive adopts a minimum harmonisation standard.[71] The Directive is said to have triggered a real harmonisation process for sales law,[72] notwithstanding the fact it had only established minimum protection standards. The Court of Justice confirmed in *Caja de Ahorros* that Article 8 allows Member States to impose more stringent provisions in the field of consumer law with the condition that these measures 'are designed to afford consumers a higher level of protection'.[73]

Even so, the consumer playing field was levelled by the introduction of possibly the most important aspect of the Directive, namely its fairness test, briefly addressed just above. In *Freiburger Kommunalbauten*, the Court was asked to rule on the fairness of a contract term requiring the consumer to pay the price before the seller or supplier had performed his obligations. The Court did not answer fairness questions directly, but it held it is up to national courts to apply the fairness test of Article 3(1) with due regard to Article 4, which puts forward objective criteria for the determination of fairness. These criteria include the nature of goods or services and the circumstances under which the contract was concluded, which the Court went on and mentioned were to be found in national law.[74]

But how does this finding, seen in the light of the fact that the Unfair Contract Terms Directive operates with two important open-ended concepts, namely fairness and good faith, relate to the overarching harmonisation objective? In other terms, why is the Court so eager to ask national courts to anchor their fairness test in national law, when the Preamble of the Unfair Contract Terms Directive clearly acknowledges the need for further harmonisation?

One answer to this question might lie in the fact that open-ended concepts have always proved to be difficult when incorporated in legislation, because of their dual nature. On the one hand, these are norms lacking a concise and determined content, but which can contribute to the development of legal thought as their

71 Micklitz, 'The Proposal on Consumer Rights and the Opportunity for a Reform of European Unfair Terms Legislation in Consumer Contracts', EUI Working Papers LAW 2010/2, p.1; Ebers 2010a, p. 34.

72 Grundmann 2002, p. 22.

73 Case C-484/08, *Caja de Ahorros y Monte de Piedad de Madrid* [2010] ECR I-04785, para. 40.

74 Case C-237/02, *Freiburger Kommunalbauten GmbH Baugesellschaft & Co. KG* [2004] ECR I-03403, para. 21; see also Case C-478/99, *Commission of the European Communities v Kingdom of Sweden* [2002] ECR I-4147, para. 17.

interpretation varies on a case-by-case basis – a feature reflecting the flexibility law ought to have. On the other hand, interpreting a vague concept can lead to opposing results, an outcome possibly against the aim of harmonisation, and surely leading to less convergence.

However, the interplay between what is too abstract and what is too detailed is affected by many factors.[75] Since Chapter 3 deals with open-ended concepts extensively, the discussion focuses here on only two of these factors. Firstly, the regulatory technique and its connection to judicial discretion must be taken into account. Where the former is very specific with respect to what path interpretation should follow, judicial discretion will not be so wide. Similarly, when legislation leaves room for discretion through the use of open norms, this will be reflected in the activity of a judge to supplement contractual intentions of the parties, to fill the gaps.[76] This should hold without a problem in civil law systems, while for common law it is not necessarily the case. Where judges already have the freedom to shape the law, open-ended concepts are not so much needed.[77]

The second aspect to take into account deals with the fact that interpretation can tilt the rights and obligations either in favour of the trader or in that of the consumer.[78] The background ethic of such interpretation can thus either take the form of a self-interest and self-reliance theory that reflects market confidence,[79] or the form of consumer protection, one of the expressions of social justice.[80]

This Directive has led to the highest number of preliminary questions out of all the studied instruments, and most certainly out of many consumer directives in general. As of March 2016, there were 45 relevant judgments and orders that have undoubtedly contributed to the understanding of the Directive's goal, and new judgments and orders are issued with unprecedented speed.[81] To address this case law in full would need a separate volume. For this reason, while a list of cases is included in Chapter 3,[82] in what follows, a brief overview is made of one particular case, interesting for the purposes of this analysis. *Verein für Konsumenteninformation* is a case about unfair contract terms and data protection, dealing with Amazon's general terms and conditions that were challenged in injunction procedures by the Austrian Consumer Association. While the issues posed by the terms, dealing with

75 Whittaker 2006, p. 57.

76 Hesselink 2005, p. 58.

77 Grundmann 2006a, p. 9.

78 In *DGFT v First National Bank* [2001] 3 W.L.R. 1297 at 1307 Lord Bingham discusses the existence of a significant imbalance as imposed by the transposing rules of the Unfair Contract Terms Directive Article 3(1) to mean that the unfair term disadvantages the consumer to the benefit of the trader.

79 Willett 2012, p. 413.

80 See Study Group on Social Justice in European Private Law 2004, p. 653; Collins 2011, p. 133-166; see also Hesselink 2008a.

81 See for instance Case C-7/16, *Banco Popular Español SA and PL Salvador, S.A.R.L. v Maria Rita Giraldez Villar and Modesto Martínez Baz* [2016] ECLI:EU:C:2016:523; Case C-191/15, *Verein für Konsumenteninformation v Amazon EU Sàrl* [2016] ECLI:EU:C:2016:612; another order was issued in Case C-537/15 as well, however the preliminary question was not admissible in the end, see Case C-537/15, *Euro Bank SA v Marek Łopaciński* [2016] ECLI:EU:C:2016:143.

82 See Chapter 3, Section 3, p. 191.

data protection as well as private international law, were analysed under different directives, the question addressed in the light of Article 3(1) of the Unfair Contract Terms Directive dealt with whether a standard term establishing choice of law for the law of a Member State in which the seller or supplier is established. The Court answered that in so far as such a term confuses the consumer that the chosen law exclusively applies to the contract, the term is unfair. What is interesting to notice is that the Court relied on Article 6(2) of Rome I in saying that the unfairness must be further determined through national interpretation. This case shows how interconnected the Unfair Contract Terms Directive is, and how many fields it can impact beyond the already classical consumer credit sector.

Whether open-ended concepts hinder harmonisation or not, it remains to be determined, and the empirical part of this study strives to contribute to this debate. For now, this analysis aims to assess whether the Commission's standard of harmonisation has indeed been achieved by the transposition of the Directive in the national laws of the Member States. In what follows, the legislation of Member States is briefly looked into.

3.3. *How was the Directive Transposed by Member States?*

The Unfair Contract Terms Directive is a highly complex piece of legislation. This is not only because of its very wide scope, but also because of its features, such as: the unfairness test, open-ended concepts and a general lack of rules on enforcement. Since it is not feasible to address the Directive in its entirety, a selection of provisions is made, for the reason that they are considered to be central to the analysis. The Articles this Section focuses on are:

- Article 3 – (unfairness test);
- Article 4 – (assessing unfairness);
- Article 5 – (clarity and *contra proferentem* rule);
- Article 6 – (effects of unfair contract terms);
- Article 7 – (control of unfair contract terms).

The transposition of these provisions into the several jurisdictions is now addressed.

3.3.1. Belgium

In anticipation of the Unfair Contract Terms Directive, the Belgian legislator had introduced the Law of 14 July 1991 on trade practices and consumer information and protection, including rules on unfair contract terms.[83] The date of transposition

[83] According to the Report issued by the Commission on the transposition of the Unfair Contract Terms Directive into Belgian law, the following laws were notified: *Loi sur les pratiques et sur l'information et la protection du consommateur (Chapitre X, Article 31-34); Loi du 12.06.1991 sur le crédit à la consommation, modifiée par la loi du 06.07.1992Loi du 25.06.1992 sur le contrat d'assurance terrestre; Loi du 04.08.1992 relative au crédit hypothécaire; Loi du 03.04.1997 relative aux clauses abusives dans les contrats conclus avec leurs clients par les titulaires de* →

(29 February 1992) thus predated the due transposition date (31 December 1994). This is said to reflect the way in which the Belgian legislator did not solely rely on horizontal contract law harmonisation, but nationally intervened in a vertical or sectoral approach.[84] Article 31 of this Law put forward a definition of an unfair term, by using the criterion of the expressed lack of balance (*déséquilibre manifeste*) between the obligations of the parties. Article 31 makes no reference to good faith.[85] In the application of this Article, judges could make use of their discretionary power of appreciation.[86] Article 32 of the same law drew a list of 21 clauses presumed to be unfair. Furthermore, according to Article 33(1), the judge has the discretion to annul clauses falling under Article 31, and according to Article 33(2), the clauses in Article 32 are considered by the Belgian legislation to be void and prohibited (*nulles et interdites*).[87] One important particularity to be observed in Belgian legislation dealt with the type of contracts covered by the Law of 14 July 1991. Initially, it did not apply to real property contracts, but this aspect was dealt with by the Law of 7 December 1998 modifying the Law of 14 July 1991, and real property contracts were explicitly integrated in a new Article 31(2)(1).[88] Moreover, in terms of which actors were covered by the 1991 law, Belgian legislation chose to exclude the services provided by liberal professions, and regulate these contracts in a separate law, the Law of 3 April 1997, replaced by the Law of 2 August 2002.[89] Article 7 of this law stated that unfair clauses in a contract concluded with a client by a holder of a liberal profession are prohibited and void.

These rules are now included in the Code of Economic Law.

3.3.2. France

The sources of rules governing the obligations of parties in consumer contracts in French law are manifold. The earliest attempt to regulate this sector has been put into practice as early as 10 January 1978, with Chapter IV of Law no. 78-23.[90] Under this law, the Commission for Unfair Clauses (*Commission de Clauses Abusives*) could submit advice to the government with respect to the limitation and regulation of unfair clauses used in consumer contracts.[91] In 1991, it was also established that

professions libérales; and Loi du 07.12.1998 sur les pratiques du commerce et sur l'information et la protection du consommateur; see Report from the Commission on the Implementation of Council Directive 93/13/EEC of 5 April 1993 on Unfair Terms in Consumer Contracts, COM(2000) 248 final, p. 37.

84 Bourgoignie 1999, available at: <http://ec.europa.eu/consumers/policy/developments/-unfa_cont_term/uct04_en.pdf>, last accessed on 27 July 2016.

85 Article 31 of the 1991 law reads: 'Pour l'application de la présente loi, il faut entendre par clause abusive, toute clause ou condition qui, à elle seule ou combinée avec une ou plusieurs autres clauses ou conditions, crée un déséquilibre manifeste entre les droits et les obligations des parties.'

86 Balate 1997, p. 143.

87 *Ibid.*

88 Schulte-Nölke *et al.* 2008, p. 206.

89 *Ibid.*

90 Schulte-Nölke *et al.* 2008, p. 210.

91 Youngs 1998, p. 417.

courts can evaluate whether contractual terms fulfil the standard set by this law, namely to render the terms invalid if they are detrimental to the consumer or are imposed on the consumer by an abuse of economic power.[92] As the French legislator notified the Commission, the transposition of the Directive was achieved through *Loi N° 95-96 du 1.02.1995 concernant les clauses abusives et la présentation des contrats régissant diverses activités d'ordre économique et commercial*, which brought changes to the already existing regime.[93]

The provisions of Law no. 78-23 were integrated in the *Code de la consommation* (Article L. 132-1 - Article L. 135-1), again slightly modified in 1995 for the transposition of Directive 93/13.[94] Particularities of the transposition process include:

(i) the French legislator provides, in Article L. 132-1 of the *Code de la Consommation*, that the annex containing the list of unfair terms is an indicative non-exhaustive list of unfair terms, meaning it is neither a black nor a grey list;[95]
(ii) Article L. 132-1 of the *Code de la Consommation* containing the definition of unfair terms does not make reference to good faith, similarly to Belgian law;[96]
(iii) the same Article L. 132-1 to 4 of the *Code de la Consommation* outlines the applicability of this set of rules to any contract regardless of its type or object, therefore offering a more generous standard of protection than the Directive;[97]
(iv) and finally, French law made this regime applicable to contracts concluded between professionals and non-professionals (incompetent party to a contract; professionals contracting outside their technical specialisation) or consumers, unlike the Directive that only mentions consumers.[98]

3.3.3. Germany

Statutory control of general conditions had been introduced in Germany starting with the 1976 Act Concerning the Regulation of the Law of Standard Business Terms (*Gesetz zur Regelung des Rechts der Allgemeinen Geschäftsbedingungen*).[99] To accommodate the requirements of the Unfair Contract Terms Directive, Germany adapted the 1976 Act by inserting two new provisions: § 12 and § 24a.[100] Further

92 Träger 2008, p. 70.
93 *Loi No. 78-23 du 10.01.1978* and *Loi No. 88-14 du 05.01.1988*.
94 Davo 1997, p. 157; Report from the Commission on the Implementation of Council Directive 93/13/EEC of 5 April 1993 on Unfair Terms in Consumer Contracts, COM(2000) 248 final, p. 37.
95 Davo 1997, p. 159.
96 Fauvarque-Cosson & Mazeaud 2008, p. 194.
97 Davo 1997, p. 162.
98 *Ibid.*, p. 163.
99 Schulte-Nölke *et al.* 2008, p. 361; see also Grundmann 2006b, p. 77; Schauer 2006, p. 83.
100 *Gesetz vom 19.07.1996 zur Änderung des AGB-Gesetzes und der Insolvenzordnung* (BGBl. I N° 36/1996); see Reich 1997, p. 167.

developments occurred once the German law of obligations was reformed in 2002. Book 2, Division 2 of the BGB (*Bürgerlichen Gesetzbuch*) now regulates the drafting of contractual obligations by means of standard business terms in § 305-§ 310.[101] § 305 defines standard terms by imposing the condition that in order to be considered as standard, they must be used in at least three contracts. The general clause for the evaluation of standard terms was incorporated in § 307(1) in a form close to that of the Directive's Article 3(1). § 307(2) goes on and establishes a familiar test for unfairness, namely the balance between statutory obligations of the parties and their agreement, but also the rights and obligations that are essential for the purpose of the contract. In addition to the general clause, there are two lists of terms which the German legislator has compiled: § 308 contains a list of clauses which are prohibited but can still be evaluated in court, while § 309 lists contract terms which are prohibited without any possibility of evaluation.[102] § 306 and § 307 deal with the legal effect of a term being unfair, namely rendering the term ineffective.

3.3.4. Ireland

The relevant sources of Irish law handling standard contract terms used to be the Sale of Goods Acts 1893 and 1980 and Sale of Goods and Supply of Services Act 1980.[103] The Unfair Contract Terms Directive was transposed into Irish law through the European Communities (Unfair Terms in Consumer Contracts) Regulations, 1995 (SI No. 27/1995) in a form close to the wording of the Directive.[104] Article 3(1) of the Directive was even kept in its initial wording.[105] Furthermore, in 2000 the Regulations were amended (SI No. 307/2000) and consumer organisations were introduced alongside consumers as beneficiaries of the protection conferred by Regulation 8 of the Principal Regulations, referring to the right to seek orders against the (continued) use of unfair terms.[106]

3.3.5. The Netherlands

Influenced by German legislation, the new Dutch Civil Code brought specific provisions for the regime of unfair contract terms (Articles 6:231-6:247 BW), which had not existed before.[107] Given the general nature of these provisions, they are not only applicable to B2C transactions, but also to B2B, with some exceptions set forth in Article 6:235. This Article lists terms which for the Dutch legislator are always unfair, while Article 6:237 compiles terms presumed to be unfair, where the burden of proof is on the business to prove they are not unfair. Article 6:233a provides a

101 Gordley & von Mehren 2006, p. 493.
102 Schulte-Nölke *et al.* 2008, p. 361.
103 *Ibid.*, p. 363.
104 Statutory Instrument 95, No. 27 of 1 February 1995: Unfair Terms in Consumer Contracts.
105 Cafaggi 2008b, p. 311.
106 Schulte-Nölke *et al.* 2008, p. 363.
107 Grundmann 2006b, p. 215; Hondius 2006, p. 70.

general test and renders a standard term voidable (*vernietigbaar*)[108] and additionally establishes the elements for the evaluation of unfair terms.[109] This regime was already amended twice: first, in 1999, for compliance with a Court of Justice Judgment asking for the explicit mention of the principle of transparency (now Article 6:231 and Article 6:238),[110] and second in 2004, when the regime on unfair terms also became applicable to contracts which were not written.[111] Article 6:238(2) second sentence also incorporates the *contra proferentem rule* as of 1999,[112] which had equally not been integrated into Dutch law at the moment of the initial transposition into the Dutch Civil Code.[113]

The Dutch transposition raised some concerns reflecting the way in which the Dutch legislator chose to accommodate the provisions of the Directive. For instance, while Article 6:233 might address the same terms as Article 3 of the Directive, it does not as such fully transpose it because, among other differences, it does not make reference to good faith. As Hondius states, '[t]he Dutch government apparently is of the opinion, that the existence of a general good faith paragraph (Article 248 Book 6), together with the requirement to interpret legislation in conformity with the Directive, should suffice.'[114] To support that claim, in the case filed by the Commission against the Netherlands, no reference was made to any faulty implementation of Article 3 of the Directive.[115]

3.3.6. Romania

In Romania, the first attempt to regulate unfair clauses was initiated by Law No. 193/2000 regarding unfair terms (*clause abuzive*) in contracts concluded between businesses and consumers. Prior to the entry into force of this law, general contract law governed the management of contract terms. Law No. 193/2000 was subsequently modified (Law. No. 65/2002; Law No. 363/2007; Law No. 161/2010) in order to reaffirm the transposition of community law, but also to adapt the list of terms considered to be unfair. Article 4(1) of this Law establishes the general clause transposing Article 3(1) of the Unfair Contract Terms Directive, maintaining the European standard of only being applicable to standard terms, and not to the outcome of individual negotiation, but also by making express reference to good

108 Terms included in either the grey or black list have the same legal effect.

109 See also Verschraegen 2006, p. 113.

110 Case C-144/99, *Commission v Kingdom of the Netherlands* [2001] ECR I-03541; see also Smits 2001, p. 853; Van Boom & Kottenhagen 2006, p. 139; Pavillon 2006, p. 26.

111 Schulte-Nölke *et al.* 2008, p. 368.

112 Wissink 2002, p. 151. The *contra proferentem* rule had not been explicitly transposed into Dutch law prior to 1999, see Schulte-Nölke *et al.* 2008, p. 368: 'After the ECJ (C-144/99) criticised that Dutch Law does not contain explicit provisions on the principle of transparency, the legislator amended CC Article 6:231 and 6:238 and clarified moreover, that in case of doubt about the meaning of a term, the interpretation most favourable to the consumer shall prevail.'

113 Hondius 1997, p. 194.

114 *Ibid.*, p. 194.

115 Case C-144/99, *Commission v Kingdom of the Netherlands* [2001] ECR I-03541.

faith.[116] The Annex contains 20 terms reflecting examples of contractual terms presumed to be unfair according to Article 4(4). Article 4(5) and (6) indicate the circumstances which are to be taken into account for the determination of additional unfair terms. As Article 1(3) prohibits the use of unfair terms by businesses, the Romanian legislator chose to apply two types of sanctions for the violation of this provision: (i) contraventions with determined administrative fines if the act does not meet the requirements of special criminal law; and (ii) criminal offences if the act falls under the competence of criminal jurisdiction (Article 16). Civil courts are empowered to evaluate the fairness of terms (Articles 8-15).[117] In addition to these provisions, the Law governing the Consumer Code (Law No. 296/2004, republished in 2008) entered into force in 2007. Apart from literally reiterating some concepts from earlier legislation (e.g. the definition of 'unfair clause'; the *contra proferentem* principle, principle of transparency, etc.), the Consumption Code extended consumer protection to consumer organisations as well (Articles 29-34), and also established the National Consumption Institute, to coordinate with the National Authority for the Protection of Consumers.

3.3.7. The United Kingdom

In the United Kingdom, prior to the adoption of specific rules on unfair terms, case law was the tool used by courts to review contracts.[118] As early as 1977 though, legislation on the matter was introduced, with the enactment of the Unfair Contract Terms Act applying well beyond consumer transactions.[119]

The Unfair Contract Terms Directive was transposed by means of the Unfair Terms in Consumer Contracts Regulations in 1994, revised in 1999, and replaced in 2015 by the Consumer Rights Act.[120] The Regulations used to have a very high degree of resemblance to the Directive: as a general clause, Regulation 5-(1)A was a restatement of Article 3(1) of the Directive, applying to standard terms; the Regulations did not associate legal persons with consumers, as it was stated in Regulation 3-(1); Schedule 2 listed terms which may be regarded as unfair; and finally Regulation 8 specified that no legal effect were to be given to unfair terms. At the same time, the Unfair Contract Terms Act continued to be applicable, with a different scope, leaving consumer protection in the United Kingdom to 'run in two streams'.[121] While in practice, the two pieces of legislation led to major divergences given the English law influence on the draft Directive,[122] differences can easily be

116 See Ruen 2011, p. 66.

117 See World Bank 2009, p. 9, available at: <http://siteresources.worldbank.org/-INTECAREGTOPPRVSECDEV/Resources/RO_-_CPFL_Vol_I.pdf>, last accessed on 27 July 2016; Alternative means of dispute resolution are however encouraged by practitioners; see Sîrbu & Gorghiu 2007, p. 136.

118 Howells & Weatherill 2005, p. 263.

119 Schulte-Nölke *et al.* 2008, p. 374-375; Beale 1978, p. 115; see also Coote 1978, p. 312; Burgess 1986, p. 255.

120 Bright 2000, p. 332.

121 Howells & Weatherill 2005, p. 269.

122 *Ibid.*, p. 282; Dean 1993, p. 585.

observed.[123] Perhaps one of the most noticeable differences lays in the fact that the Act imposes an unreasonableness test, while the Regulations dealt with an unfairness test that introduced the statutory concept of good faith in English law.[124] The fear of English law and more precisely English courts having to deal with a completely foreign concept was however alleviated by the issuing of guidelines for the assessment of unfair terms.[125]

3.4. *Comparative Notes on the Transposition*

The Unfair Contract Terms Directive has imposed a standard of legislative approximation based on minimum harmonisation, a feature very often acknowledged by the Court of Justice.[126] This entails that Member States are allowed to impose more stringent rules, as long as they provide consumers with an enhanced protection regime. As a very complex instrument, the Directive on Unfair Terms poses many issues. Two such issues have been selected for a brief comparative overview: (i) the explicit requirement of 'good faith'; and (ii) the legal consequences of unfair terms.

(i) The Explicit Requirement of 'Good Faith'

The 'good faith' discussion started earlier is now briefly revisited. Article 3(1) imposes an unfairness test the clarity of which made a difference in the reception of the Directive's standards.[127] While three states (Ireland, Romania and the United Kingdom) refer directly to good faith in the same manner as in the Directive, others do not explicitly mention it (e.g. Belgium and France). It is presumed the latter category, not integrating the requirement of good faith, lowers the burden of proof for the consumer. However, the majority of countries do take into account the balance between the contracting parties, imposing the 'significant imbalance' threshold.[128] What is more, it is important to determine to what degree the inconsistent transposition of the requirement of good faith has affected legal convergence. This question is further addressed in Chapter 3.

123 The Law Commission and the Scottish Law Commission, 'Unfair Terms In Contracts: A Joint Consultation Paper', July 2002, p. 12, available at: <http://lawcommission.-justice.gov.uk/docs/cp166_Unfair_Terms_In_Contracts_Consultation.pdf>, last accessed on 27 July 2016.

124 Teubner 1998, p. 11-12; see also Twigg-Flesner 2006, p. 235-261; Willett 2007, p. 193; Macdonald 2002, p. 768; Willett 1997, p. 232.

125 Office of Fair Trading, 'Unfair Contract Terms Guidance - Guidance for the Unfair Terms in Consumer Contracts Regulations 1999', September 2008, available at: <www.oft.gov.uk/-shared_oft/reports/unfair_contract_terms/oft311.pdf>, last accessed on 27 July 2016. Interestingly though, the 2015 Consumer Rights Act maintains the good faith test almost verbatim, although no definition is provided for the open-ended term.

126 Case C-484/08, *Caja de Ahorros y Monte de Piedad de Madrid* [2010] ECR I-4785, paras. 28-29; Case C-453/10, *Jana Pereničová and Vladislav Perenič v SOS financ spol. s r. o.* [2012], para. 34; Case C-618/10, *Banco Español de Crédito SA v Joaquín Calderón Camino* [2012], para. 70.

127 Hondius 1995, p. 246.

128 See also Schulte-Nölke *et al.* 2008, p. 393.

(ii) The Legal Consequences of Unfair Terms

Perhaps one of the most difficult provisions to assess the transposition of is Article 6(1) Unfair Contract Terms Directive:

> 'Member States shall lay down that unfair terms used in a contract concluded with a consumer by a seller or supplier shall, as provided for under their national law, not be binding on the consumer and that the contract shall continue to bind the parties upon those terms if it is capable of continuing in existence without the unfair terms.'

Unfortunately, the Directive does not shed any light on how exactly Member States need to apply this provision in practice; the decision on the type of measure to achieve the goal of Article 6(1) has been left to the discretion of Member States.

These distinctions are important in order to determine what legal consequences Member States chose to give to unfair terms. In *Cofidis*, the Court of Justice tried to bring clarity on the protection standards imposed by the Unfair Contract Terms Directive in ruling on the question whether a French court could annul unfair terms on its own motion even after the prescription period of two years for the application against such terms had passed:

> 'It is therefore apparent that, in proceedings aimed at the enforcement of unfair terms brought by sellers or suppliers against consumers, the fixing of a time-limit on the court's power to set aside such terms, of its own motion or following a plea raised by the consumer, is liable to affect the effectiveness of the protection intended by Articles 6 and 7 of the Directive. To deprive consumers of the benefit of that protection, sellers or suppliers would merely have to wait until the expiry of the time-limit fixed by the national legislature before seeking enforcement of the unfair terms they would continue to use in contracts.'[129]

In the Court's assessment, the two year prescription term limiting the consumer's right to have an unfair term annulled is not in conformity with the purpose of the Directive. It is however unclear whether the Court tried to imply that relative nullity as such is not a suitable transposition of the legal consequences envisaged by the Directive, or whether it simply stated that a two year term is insufficient for the exercise of this right. Still, what is sure is that the Court underlined the necessity to closely look at any procedural provision affecting the application of Community law, and consider it in the light of the procedural setting as a whole.[130]

In a more recent judgment, the Court even went as far as to interpret Article 6(1) as prohibiting national courts from revising the term and thus modifying the contract, since courts have to disregard the particular term and keep the remainder of the contract intact.[131]

129 Case C-473/00, *Cofidis SA v Jean-Louis Fredout* [2002] ECR I-10875, para. 35; see also Case C-120/78, *Rewe-Zentral AG v Bundesmonopolverwaltung für Branntwein* [1979] ECR 00649; Case C-261/95, *Rosalba Palmisani v Istituto nazionale della previdenza sociale (INPS)* [1997] ECR I-04025.

130 *Cofidis SA v Jean-Louis Fredout*, para. 37; Case C-137/08, *VB Pénzügyi Lízing v Ferenc Schneider* [2010] ECR I-10847, para. 47.

131 *Banco Español de Crédito SA v Joaquín Calderón Camino*, para. 65.

4. The Distance Selling Directive (1997)

4.1. *What are the Rationale and Scope of the Directive?*

Figure 5: Distance Selling Directive Adoption Timeline (source: Eur-Lex)

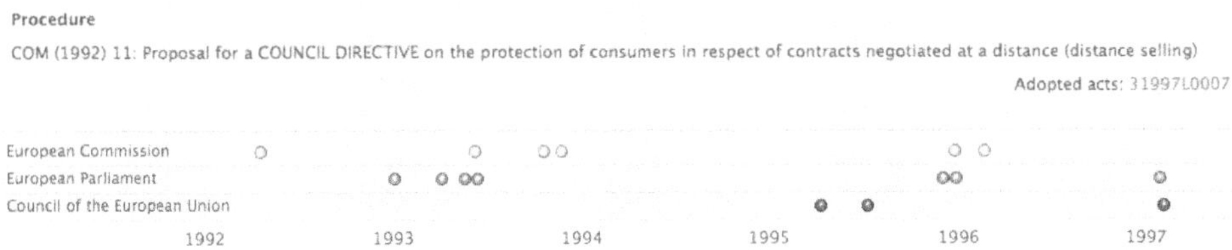

The policy behind the Distance Selling Directive focused on strengthening consumer protection and confidence. Similarly to the Doorstep Selling Directive, this Directive was modelled to apply to situations when contracts would not be classically concluded on business premises. In this case, mainly contracts concluded over the phone and/or online. The intention of the legislature in passing rules on distance contracts had two dimensions. Firstly, there was the balance between the interests of the contracting parties. When consumers cannot directly assess the quality and condition of the goods they are interested in, they purchase them 'in the dark'.[132] This circumstance is said to weaken their position, making them more prone to abuse; not only in cases when the goods do not correspond to the legitimate expectations of the buyer, but also because the seller's reputation might be unknown or even worse, unreliable.[133] More than that, thinking about the features of online commerce and how consumers very rarely read the standard terms of contracts they click into,[134] it is justifiable to say they need additional protection. In the light of these conditions, the main goal of the Directive is undoubtedly reflected in the enhancement of consumer protection in distance contracts. However, as was emphasised by the Court of Justice in *easyCar* where it had to defend the existence of stipulated exceptions to this protection,[135] the interests of suppliers of certain services also fall within the Directive's scope. The exception touched upon one of the essential features of the Distance Selling Directive, namely the establishment of a right of withdrawal. Tackling whether the right of withdrawal was justified in the situation of services booked via the internet, the *easyCar* case made it clear that the suppliers of such services must be exempted from complying with the right of withdrawal. This was done in order for them not to suffer 'disproportionate consequences arising from the cancellation at no expense and with no explanation of services which have given rise to a booking'.[136]

132 Dickie 1998, p. 217; Borges & Irlenbusch 2007, p. 85; Rothchild 1998, p. 295; see also Cafaggi & Nicita 2012, p. 265.

133 Henderson & Poulter 2002, p. 289; Mik 2012, p. 397; Rekaiti & Van den Bergh 2000, p. 373.

134 Ben-Shahar 2009, p. 2; Winn & Bix 2006, p. 178.

135 Case C-336/03, *easyCar (UK) Ltd v Office of Fair Trading* [2005] ECR I-01947.

136 *Ibid.*, para. 28; see also McDonald 2005, p. 192.

Secondly, there was once again the internal market argument, namely the internal market can profit from the expansion of distance sale. Over time, distance selling started revealing the potential of trading online on the European wide web. While this might not have been an initial aim of the Directive, it had grown into a very strong policy argument.[137] The Internet is providing opportunities for increasing types of goods to be sold in cross-border transactions.[138] Still, in spite of booming technological innovations, such as the increasing use of smartphones[139] with, amongst others, apps for online banking and QR code scanning that allows them to instantaneously buy products advertised in train stations, the single market is underdeveloped when it comes to the digital economy. Only 2-4 per cent of all European trade is conducted online, as digital markets are still profoundly national and consumers lack the confidence necessary to purchase goods on unfamiliar websites.[140] The Distance Selling Directive identified the potential of this sector, although it did not directly mention any internet-based technologies.[141] In the third recital, the Directive specifies that 'cross-border distance selling could be one of the main tangible results of the completion of the internal market'. It can therefore be said that developing a trade sector able to take economic integration even further is a subsidiary goal of the consumer protection regime envisaged by the Distance Selling Directive.[142]

While the Distance Selling Directive focused on the vulnerability of consumers as they cannot see what they purchase, the nature of this transaction does bring some other types of benefits:

- the comfort of not having to travel for purchasing goods or services;
- the opportunity to compare prices more easily (e.g. by using Google Product Search, etc.) and to look into peer reviews;
- lower overall prices (less transaction costs as no stores are necessary);
- the possibility to choose from a larger pool of suppliers, or to shop from suppliers who are not physically present in the consumer's geographical proximity;
- the option to pre-order an item and not to have to queue up for it;

137 European Commission, 'Communication from the Commission to the European Parliament, the Council, the European Economic and Social Committee and the Committee of the Regions - A Digital Agenda for Europe', COM(2010) 245 f/2, p. 7.

138 *Ibid.*

139 Arthur & Garside, 'Smartphones take the lead in European phone market', 8 September 2011, available at: <www.guardian.co.uk/technology/2011/sep/08/smartphones-take-lead-in-mobile-phone-market>, last accessed on 27 July 2016.

140 European Commission 'Towards a Single Market Act', COM(2010) 608 final, p. 10; European Commission, 'Communication from the Commission to the European Parliament, the Council, the European Economic and Social Committee and the Committee of the Regions – A Digital Agenda for Europe', COM(2010) 245, p. 5; DG Internal Policies, 'A Pan-European Trustmark for E-Commerce: Possibilities and Opportunities', p. 11, available at: <www.europarl.europa.eu>, last accessed on 27 July 2016.

141 Bradgate 1997.

142 Mak 2011c, p. 31; see also Loos 2009, p. 245.

- the lack of time constraints (the internet is open 24/7);
- the possibility of creating customer preference profiles, or to personalise searches, which again reduces the time spent shopping.[143]

Online consumer behaviour classically profiles consumers into two types: passive and active.[144] When a consumer is passive, he does not put a lot of effort into accumulating information about the transaction, be it by not reading the terms he agrees to, or simply by not spending time to research these products. Ben-Shahar argues many consumers in this position are rational enough to simply choose *not to care* about what is in the contract.[145] However, it is hard to tell whether the 'passive consumer' category can stand in the contemporary world wide web, when content reaches people through an explosion of channels. Take for instance an unhappy customer who shares his experience on Facebook, leading the information to appear in the newsfeed of his Facebook friends. Not having actively pursued the gathering of information about a specific product, individuals are still reached by information, and even if that is not the case, it is still easy to conclude contracts. Online contracts have developed in such a way that by simply ticking a box and clicking a button (clickwrap), or by merely browsing through a supplier's page or using some of its services or products on the site (browsewrap), a contract is concluded.[146] As for the second category, active consumers do invest time in informing themselves over the transactions they enter into and they are the ones likely to return products if not fully satisfied with them.

The question to ask here is whether it makes any sense to differentiate between the aforementioned categories when drafting consumer protection legislation. I would tend to believe it does not. When shopping online, users are indeed aware of some risks, but their preferences might be so different, that a more efficient alternative to a one-size-fits-all rule that would take into account some degree of differentiation, would not be representative. Shopping for clothing from a brand one is familiar with and might have even tried in a store, simply to benefit from lower prices, is very different than purchasing a record player the consumer has no experience with. In the same vein, there are too few products which are exclusively available online. It must also be kept in mind that consumers will be willing to bear these risks depending on the value of the contract. Consider the difference between purchasing EUR 20 worth of music and buying a EUR 5,000 car on eBay. Nevertheless, the lower the price of the contract, the less likely it is to think the consumer will take the effort to return a good; the higher the prices are, the more likely it is to claim consumers might need to either protect themselves, or be protected by the law.

143 Schafer *et al.*, 'E-Commerce Recommendation Applications', Grouplens Paper, p. 2, available at: <www.grouplens.org/papers/pdf/ECRA.pdf>, last accessed on 27 July 2016.
144 Meier & Stormer 2009, p. 79.
145 Ben-Shahar 2009, p. 15.
146 Conklin 2007-2008, p. 327; see also Tracy 2005, p. 164; Streeter 2002, p. 1363; Kunz *et al.* 2003-2004, p. 279; Founds 1999-2000, p. 99; Davis 2007, p. 577.

To sum up, consumers are aware of the risks they take when shopping online. They cope with these risks differently, depending on whether they are passive or active and also depending on the price of the contract. However, the fact that consumers acknowledge and internalise these risks might prove to be a more intense deterrent for the effective exercise of withdrawal, than the requirement set by the Distance Selling Directive according to which sellers need to make sure withdrawal rights are free of charge for the consumer (Article 6(2)).

Having established what policies the Directive stands for, the next step is to determine what their exact range is. In order to do so, attention must be first given to the types of contracts covered by this instrument.

According to Article 2, distance contracts are defined as:

> '[...] any contract concerning goods or services concluded between a supplier and a consumer under an organised distance sales or service-provision scheme run by the supplier, who, for the purpose of the contract, makes exclusive use of one or more means of distance communication up to and including the moment at which the contract is concluded;'

There is no mention of new electronic technologies in the Distance Selling Directive, as the definition above strived to form a generic category able to support unforeseen technological innovations.[147] The same is valid for novel situations arising from the complicated components of the modern chain of distribution. For example, when websites provide discount offers, such as socialdeal.nl, a question arises as to which company has what obligations towards the consumers.[148] Another difficulty is to determine liability when an intelligent agent, or 'virtual butler', assists the supplier.[149] However, in drafting a general definition, terminology becomes heavily conceptual and this can raise clarity problems. As reflected in the responses to the consultation initiated by the Commission on the subject of distance selling, some stakeholders supported an eventual clarification of the term 'organised distance sales or service provision scheme',[150] which only stands to show there was a lot of space for improvement as far as clarity was concerned.

Going further, Article 3(1) excludes the following contracts from the application of the Directive: contracts dealing with financial services; concluded at vending machines or automated commercial premises; concluded with telecommunications operators using public payphones; related to immovable

147 Annex 1 to the Distance Selling Directive contains however an indicative list of the means covered by the Directive; see also Twigg-Flesner & Metcalfe 2009, p. 370-371; Poulter *et al.* 2003, p. 329, available at: <www.iadis.net/dl/final_uploads/200301L042.pdf>, last accessed on 27 July 2016.

148 Platforms such as <socialdeal.nl> often distribute offers made by other companies.

149 Lodder & Voulon 2002, p. 278.

150 Working Document of the Commission, 'Responses to the Consultation on Distance Selling Directive 97/7/EC contained in Communication 2006/514/EC', retrieved from <http://ec.europa.eu/consumers/cons_int/safe_shop/dist_sell/sum_responses_consultations_en.pdf>, last accessed on 27 July 2016; see also Dickie 1998, p. 219.

property rights except for rental; and contracts concluded by auction.[151] Among these exceptions, contracts concluded by auctions seem to make up the most problematic category, since a lot of the online trade occurs on websites such as eBay, Amazon and other platforms with online auction services.[152] The Directive itself does not distinguish between real life and online auctions, so the debate concerning the extent to which the exception applies is still highly relevant.[153] National policies on the matter are thoroughly discussed later in this Section. Moreover, according to Article 3(2), the rules enshrined in the Directive only partially apply to contracts over foodstuffs, beverages or similar goods. These rules also apply to contracts for the provision of accommodation, transport, catering or leisure services with a specified performance date or period, which are exactly the cases referred to earlier, where the seller of a good or the supplier of a service also need protection from the disadvantages of cancelling reservations for fixed periods of time.[154]

The discussion so far focused on what contracts used to be covered by the Directive; but what exactly were the rights and obligations imposed within these contractual relationships? Even if the Distance Selling Directive formulated numerous detailed rules designed to increase the level of consumer protection, some of them stood out as essential: (i) the provision of prior information (Article 4); (ii) the seven day withdrawal period (Article 6); and (iii) the 30 day performance period (Article 7).

(i) The Provision of Prior Information (Article 4)

As it has already been mentioned, since the consumer is unable to inspect the desired goods, certain information must be handed to him before the conclusion of the contract, to ensure the predictability of the transaction. Similarly, since digital identity can be easily manipulated, it is important for the consumer to know whom he contracts with. With these dangers in mind, it becomes clear why Article 4 asks suppliers to provide the following information before the contract was concluded: his identity and address (in the case when advance payment is required); the main characteristics of the goods/services; the price (with taxes); eventual delivery costs; payment, delivery or performance arrangements; the existence of a right of withdrawal; the validity of the offer; and finally for permanent or recurrent contracts, the minimum duration.

Although the Article outlined the information consumers should be aware of, paragraph (2) introduced the supplementary obligation of providing the information in conformity with the principle of good faith in commercial

151 See Hedley 2006.

152 Poulter *et al.* 2003, p. 330.

153 See Spindler 2005, p. 725; Riefa 2009a, p. 178; Gu 2007, available at: <www.bileta.ac.uk/>, last accessed on 27 July 2016.

154 These contracts are excluded from the application of Articles 4, 5, 6 and 7(1) and in exceptional circumstances for service contracts, Article 7(2); see Bech Serrat 2010, p. 77.

transactions.[155] A similar open-ended standard was also used to determine time limits: information must be given to the consumer in 'good time'.[156]

The interpretation of Article 4(1) was visited by the Court of Justice in the *Content Services* case.[157] There, the Court noted the differences in linguistic formulation between Article 4(1) and Article 5(1), whereby the former only required relevant information to be 'provided', whereas the latter entailed more effort on behalf of businesses to make sure consumers 'receive'/are 'given' prior information. The Court thus decided that since information was neither 'given' by the undertaking nor 'received' by the consumer because it was found that the business simply sent an e-mail to the consumer with a link that the consumer had to himself access. Moreover, the Court also decided that a website like the one *Content Services* used cannot be regarded as a 'durable medium', since the company could at all times change the information that was available to consumers upon visiting the linked website address:

> Article 5(1) of Directive 97/7/EC of the European Parliament and of the Council of 20 May 1997 on the protection of consumers in respect of distance contracts must be interpreted as meaning that a business practice consisting of making the information referred to in that provision accessible to the consumer only via a hyperlink on a website of the undertaking concerned does not meet the requirements of that provision, since that information is neither 'given' by that undertaking nor 'received' by the consumer, within the meaning of that provision, and a website such as that at issue in the main proceedings cannot be regarded as a 'durable medium' within the meaning of Article 5(1).[158]

(ii) The Seven Day Withdrawal Period (Article 6)

The traditional reason justifying the introduction of withdrawal rights is to support the consumer's bargaining position, by allowing him to change his mind and undo the contract, no questions asked.[159] Recourse to this right can be made when the buyer receives the goods purchased and they are below his expectations. Parallel redress might exist in rules concerning performance or defects, but making a cooling off period available is considered to be a more efficient scenario for the consumer. The downside of the cooling off period as a statutory rule is that it comes with asymmetric effects and costs, and its overall economic efficiency is controversial, however, these are debates lying beyond the ambit of the present Chapter.[160]

The withdrawal right set forth by Article 6 gave the consumer a seven working days period to change his mind about buying a good or contracting a service. This

155 See Twigg-Flesner 2008b, p. 101; Silkenat *et al.* 2009, p. 304; Coteanu 2005, p. 118; Twigg-Flesner 2012b, p. 487; Twigg-Flesner 2008a, p. 69.

156 Kierkegaard 2007, p. 6; Donnelly & White 2005, p. 216.

157 Case C- 49/11, *Content Services Ltd v Bundesarbeitskamer* [2012].

158 *Content Services Ltd v Bundesarbeitskamer*, para. 52; see also Goanta 2013, p. 643.

159 Ben-Shahar & Posner 2011, p. 118; Rekaiti & Van den Bergh 2000, p. 373; Rott 2007, p. 51; Loos 2009, p. 238.

160 For arguments in this sense see Andrews 2004-2005, p. 90; Rothchild 1998, p. 294; Smits 2011, p. 679; Wagner 2010, p. 58.

period was calculated from the moment when the contract was concluded, and could extend up to three months if the seller did not comply with the obligations in Article 5 (written confirmation requirement).[161] Paragraph (3) excluded the existence of the right to withdraw in the following cases: contracts of services when performance has begun; contracts the price of which depends on financial fluctuations; contract for personalised or rapidly deteriorating objects; contracts for audio/video or software products which were subsequently unsealed; contracts over newspapers, periodicals and magazines; and contracts for gaming and lotteries. These exceptions were supposed to limit the situations in which the right of withdrawal could be abused. A typical example consists of the case when a consumer buys computer software, installs it and then decides to get out of the contract by invoking his withdrawal right.[162] However, other items such as books were not on the exception list. The resulting situation has been tackled at national level; for instance, Germany imposed a so-called usage fee (§ 357(3) BGB).[163] This measure was brought to the attention of the Court of Justice in the *Messner* case.[164] In December 2005, Pia Messner bought a second-hand computer in an online transaction and decided to withdraw from the contract in November 2006, due to a screen defect. Since German law kept withdrawal valid for an undetermined period of time when no notice of the withdrawal right was sent, she was still able to use this right after almost one year. Stefan Krüger, the seller, claimed he was entitled to compensation since Mrs. Messner had used the laptop since the purchase. The Court was thus asked to decide on whether a national measure giving rise to a right to compensation derived from the use of a good purchased in a distance contract would be precluded by Article 6 of the Distance Selling Directive. In rendering its judgment, the Court took notice of how Article 6(1) explicitly mentioned that the only charge to be imposed on the consumer with respect to the withdrawal right is that arising from returning the goods, as 'the consumer could be dissuaded from exercising that right if it involved adverse financial consequences'.[165] Based on this argument, the Court specified that in general, compensation would not be in line with the objectives of the Distance Selling Directive and in particular of the right of withdrawal. However, the Court's decision is far from straight-forward, because it goes on to say that in principle, Articles 6(1) and (2) do not preclude national law from allowing fair compensation for the seller when the buyer has used the good in a manner against the principles of civil law, such as good faith and unjustified enrichment.[166] This decision has been subjected to intense scrutiny, since some commentators consider the Court had a civil law bias in reinstating the importance

161 Andrews 2004-2005, p. 86; Hörnle *et al.* 2002, p. 18.
162 Henderson & Poulter 2002, p. 295.
163 Borges & Irlenbusch 2007, p. 86.
164 Case C-489/07, *Pia Messner v Firma Stefan Krüger* [2009] ECR I-07315.
165 *Ibid.*, para. 19.
166 *Ibid.*, para. 26.

of the principle of good faith, while others consider it is a clear statement of the Court leaving remedial autonomy to Member States.[167]

(iii) The 30 Day Oerformance Period (Article 7)

Article 7 aimed to set a deadline on the performance of the contract, and it must be read in the light of Recital 15 in the Preamble, where it was stated that a time limit for the performance of the contract was necessary.[168] If the parties did not agree on a specific date when performance should take place, the Directive laid down the rule that performance must occur within a 30 day period calculated from the day following that when the consumer forwarded the order (Article 7(1)).

If performance did not occur because the goods or services were not available, paragraph (2) stated that the consumer was entitled to obtain a refund of all sums paid. However, according to paragraph (3), there was another option available to the supplier, namely to provide goods of equivalent quality and price, if this option was provided for before the contract was concluded, or was included therein.

As with the other directives, the rights consumers have in distance selling are part of a binding statutory framework for businesses.[169] Article 12 Distance Selling Directive mentioned that rights obtained under the transposition of the Distance Selling Directive are non-waivable.[170] It is interesting to notice that unlike the Doorstep Selling Directive (Article 6), the choice of wording in Article 12 did not relate to rights conferred on the consumer by the *Directive*, but by the transposition of the Directive into *national law*.[171] However, as it is clear from the case law of the Court of Justice on provisions of the Distance Selling Directive, the objectives of the Directives are pivotal in discerning whether national legislation respects the level of consumer protection set forth by the Directive.

Moreover, Article 12(2) also referred to situations arising from choice-of-law clauses of non-Member States. It has been suggested that using such clauses could trigger cases where consumers in Member States would be deprived of their protection if sellers intentionally used a legal system with lower protection standards. The Directive did not fully cover this situation, as it contained a condition of a 'close connection with the territory of one or more Member States'. If this condition was fulfilled, the consumer did not lose his protection. If it was not, then the consumer was subjected to the non-EU state regime, according to what used to be the 'close connection' principle in Article 7 of the Rome Convention.[172]

167 See Hesselink 2011b, p. 61; Mak 2012a, p. 333; Mak 2011c, p. 32; Purnhagen 2012, p. 854; Rott 2010, p. 187; Trstenjak & Beysen 2011, p. 115.

168 Donnelly & White 2005, p. 220.

169 Wagner 2010, p. 48.

170 Hörnle *et al.* 2002, p. 30.

171 Dickie 1998, p. 227.

172 Reich & Halfmeier 2001-2002, p. 130; Rowe 1998, p. 234; see also Kramer 2002, p. 227; Swire 1998, p. 991.

4.2. *What Standard of Harmonisation is Set by the European Legislator?*

Similarly to the Doorstep Selling and the Unfair Contract Terms Directive, the Distance Selling Directive was a minimum harmonisation Directive that was applicable prior to the entry into force of the Consumer Rights Directive, shifting the protection to a maximum harmonisation standard. This was stated in Article 14 allowing Member States to introduce measures ensuring a higher level of protection.[173] The European legislator specifically chose not to interfere with national legal systems in such a way to entirely overarch contract law rules exclusively applicable to all the phases of distance contracts. Rather, it chose to promote a standard of consumer protection resting on essential rights conferred to the consumer, such as the withdrawal right. This way, the European legislator remained neutral towards each of the Member State's classical theory of contract,[174] which was at best amended to ensure access to these rights.

As far as trade organisations are concerned, Recital 18 of the Distance Selling Directive made reference to Commission Recommendation 92/295/EEC. Issued at the same time as the adoption of the Distance Selling Directive proposal by the Commission, on 7 April 1992, the recommendation offered guidance to trade associations of suppliers in the sense of suggesting the adoption of codes of conduct reflecting the rules enshrined in the Distance Selling Directive.[175] This encouragement to inform consumers about self-regulation, also referred to in Article 16, consisted in the idea that suppliers can make their own codes of conduct, which would not be legally binding but have a transparency effect to boost consumer confidence.[176] It is noted however, that this approach seemed to be flawed from two main perspectives: firstly, by the time the Directive was published in 1997, the Commission had ended its initiatives of supporting codes of conduct by providing a presumption of conformity of the codes with legislation; and secondly, the effectiveness of consistent and uniform self-regulation was questioned.[177] On the one hand, even if it is perhaps inherent for self-regulation to be asymmetric, the past decade has seen codes of conduct flourish in Europe. On the other hand, the Commission has been recently revisiting its support for such codes, and even taking one step further by looking into the feasibility of an eventual EU trustmark.[178]

Furthermore, as it has already been discussed, since the Court of Justice has the legitimate role of interpreting European legislation, its case law serves as an

173 Mak 2008, p. 431; Reich & Halfmeier 2001-2002, p. 114; Rott 2006, p. 1135.

174 Riefa 2009b, p. 9.

175 92/295/EEC: Commission Recommendation of 7 April 1992 on codes of practice for the protection of consumers in respect of contracts negotiated at a distance (distance selling), *OJ* L156, 10 June 1992.

176 Girot 2001, p. 69.

177 Howells *et al*. 2006, p. 200.

178 DG Internal Policies, 'A Pan-European Trustmark for E-Commerce: Possibilities and Opportunities', p. 70. This is only one of the five policy options it is currently looking into; the other four include: (a) no intervention; (b) encouraging self-regulation; (c) co-regulation; and (d) establishing an EU trustmark accreditation scheme.

important guide for the application of consumer law by national courts.[179] Six cases were brought before the Court of Justice in relation to the Distance Selling Directive. Out of these cases, only four are relevant for the discussion of consumer law interpretation. The remaining two consist of a non-implementation matter,[180] and a dismissal by the Court after the *Bundesgerichtshof* deemed its own reference for a preliminary ruling as subsequently stripped of object.[181] In what follows, the remaining four cases are looked at chronologically, in order to determine how the Court's views helped interpret the Distance Selling Directive.

The 2005 *easyCar* case[182] was the first time in the European Court's proceedings when a problem arose in connection to the Distance Selling Directive. In brief, easyCar was a self-drive car hire company operating exclusively via the Internet. To enter into a contract with easyCar, customers were supposed to agree to the condition that in case they cancelled the contract for other reasons than the ones specified as exceptions, they could obtain no refund. These exceptions made reference to 'unusual and unforeseeable events beyond [his] control including... serious illness of the driver which results in the driver being unfit to drive; natural disaster; acts or restraints of governments or public authorities; and war, riot, civil commotion or acts of terrorism' or 'at the discretion of our Customer Service Manager in other extreme circumstances'.[183] The Office of Fair Trade, representing numerous consumers who had complained about easyCar contracts, took the position that such practice was against the purpose of the protection granted by the Directive, according to which full reimbursement must be given to the consumer in case of withdrawal from the contract. As previously stated, the Distance Selling Directive also deals with exceptions from the protection which the OFT correctly highlighted as the purpose of the Directive. These exceptions were laid down in Article 3(2) and made direct reference to contracts for the provision of transport services, with the condition that these contracts specified a date or period for performance. With this factual background in mind, the Court of Justice had to determine whether contracts concluded for car hire services fell under the ambit of Article 3(2). In order to answer this question, the Court looked at the *travaux préparatoires* of the Distance Selling Directive and determined that the legislator had intentionally not used the wording 'carriage of persons or goods' since it would narrow down the applicability of the exception to situations where passengers would be carried by the service provider. However, the final version of the Distance Selling Directive referred to a more general category of the transport services sector,[184] which could indeed cover the types of contracts concluded with easyCar. The Court went on to argue the nature of the exception. Since arrangements had to be made for the provision of services on specifically arranged dates, whenever these

179 Van Gerven 1997, p. 295.

180 Case C-414/01, *Commission of the European Communities v Kingdom of Spain* [2002] ECR I-11121.

181 Case C-146/09, *Prof. Dr. Claus Scholl v Stadtwerke Aachen AG* [2009].

182 Case C-336/03, *easyCar (UK) Ltd v Office of Fair Trading* [2005] ECR I-01947; see also Whittaker 2007, p. 340.

183 *easyCar (UK) Ltd v Office of Fair Trading*, para. 10.

184 *Ibid.*, para. 23.

services were cancelled by virtue of the right to withdraw, the provider of the service suffered losses which destroyed the balance between the interests of the parties.[185] This is how the Court justified bringing car hire contracts under the ambit of Article 3(2) Distance Selling Directive.

In 2009, the *Messner* case was decided.[186] As the reader is already familiar with the facts of the case from earlier, it can be said that the resulting ruling fell very much in line with *easyCar*. The Court once again looked at the balance between the interests of the parties to the contract concluded over the sale of the laptop. The Court was ambivalent in ruling over the appropriateness of compensation in the light of the Distance Selling Directive, which forbade any additional charges to be imposed on the consumer. Restating the purpose of the Distance Selling Directive, the Court determined that in general, compensation did not meet this purpose. However, it also stated that as a matter of principle, compensation can be envisaged by national laws, because if a buyer used a good and then wanted to return to the *status quo ante*, by making legitimate use of his right of withdrawal, then this use would be unfair to the seller.

The *easyCar* and *Messner* decisions can be interpreted in the light of two aspects. First, it can be argued that in building the case argumentation, the Court acknowledged the limits of the consumer protection regime instituted by the Distance Selling Directive. It analysed one of the exemptions referred to in Article 3(2) and it looked at compensation as a legitimate influence over the effective exercise of the right of withdrawal. Second, it can also be said that the Court paid due regard to the interests of the parties concluding the contract, without overlooking the purpose and objective of the Distance Selling Directive.

Then, in 2010 the Court delivered yet another judgment, namely *Handelsgesellschaft Heinrich Heine*.[187] The company in this case was operating by mail order and imposed a flat-rate delivery cost of EUR 4.95, non-returnable in the case of the consumer's withdrawal from the contract. This company was sued by Verbraucherzentrale Nordrhein-Westfalen, a German consumer association that applied for an injunction on the imposition of the non-refundable charge. Article 6(1) of the Directive established that the only charge that might be imposed on the consumer because of the exercise of his right of withdrawal is that of returning the goods. The same rule is reinstated in paragraph (2), which furthermore tells that all sums paid by the consumer must be reimbursed, except for the return costs. Thus the Court had to interpret whether the construct 'sums paid by the consumer' is wide enough to include delivery costs, and similarly, whether the condition expressed by the wording 'because of the exercise of his right of withdrawal' implies that delivery costs should be regarded as 'subsequent to the implementation of that right',[188] as argued by the German government. The Court determined that

185 *Ibid.*, para. 29.

186 See also Piedelièvre 2010, p. 21; Jacquemin 2009, p. 273; Eickelmann 2009, p. 398; Paisant 2009, p. 25; Avena-Robardet 2009, p. 2161.

187 Case C-511/08, *Handelsgesellschaft Heinrich Heine GmbH v Verbraucherzentrale Nordrhein-Westfalen e*V [2010] ECR I-03047 [2010].

188 *Ibid.*, para. 35.

'sums paid' include delivery costs. The main argument reflected the fact that the Distance Selling Directive distinguished between different types of payable sums (e.g. price of goods, delivery costs, etc.) in Article 4 but the distinction was not applied to Article 6, which was then to be regarded as covering all the sums that a consumer paid by entering into the contract. Moreover, the Court also looked at the official translations to determine whether the words 'because of the exercise of his right of withdrawal' then 'relate not to all of the costs to be charged to the consumer, but only to those connected with the exercise of the right of withdrawal'.[189] Here it was decided that an interpretation favouring a wide coverage of Article 6 to refer, as indicated above, to all costs incurred by all phases of the contract, is in line with the purpose of the Directive.[190]

The *Handelsgesellschaft Heinrich Heine* decision focused on one main consideration: imposing a charge on the consumer in the case of withdrawal is an exception, and interpreting the words 'the only charge' must be strict. However, as we have already explored in the *Messner* case the Court did find another charge than that of returning the goods (compensation) *could* be legitimately imposed. What then made the Court come to such a different conclusion in *Handelsgesellschaft Heinrich Heine*? One answer could be that the Court raised its own interpretation standard. Simply put, the Court was pro-consumer, a claim that is in no way new about the CJEU.[191] Otherwise, in the light of existing case law it could have very well restated that as a matter of principle, other charges are not against the purpose of the Distance Selling Directive as long as they are fundamental to the balance between the interests of the parties. As Loos puts it, the costs of consumer protection must also be borne by the consumer himself, and the payment of delivery fees are a clear example of this in practice.[192] In the light of the same argument, as it was put forward by the German government, in contracts concluded on business premises, the consumer is the one making the trip to the business location and bearing all costs thereof.[193]

Another element to keep in mind is that the Distance Selling Directive did not distinguish between different types of delivery fees. A consumer could have insisted to have a good shipped with urgency, and pay this high cost of delivery. However, if withdrawn from the contract, based on the rationale of the *Heinrich Heine* case, the supplier had to reimburse the contract price, as well as this high cost. The Consumer Rights Directive addresses this issue by introducing new rules for distance contracts. For example, in Article 13(2), the Directive imposes the reimbursement of delivery fees only to the extent covered by the least expensive delivery offered by the trader.

Going back to the argumentation of the CJEU, a more recent case on the Distance Selling Directive is reviewed below.

189 *Ibid.*, para. 48.
190 *Ibid.*, para. 52.
191 Reich 2006, p. 43.
192 Loos 2007a, p. 16.
193 *Handelsgesellschaft Heinrich Heine GmbH v Verbraucherzentrale Nordrhein-Westfalen eV*, para. 26.

Content Services is a case dating from 2012.[194] Registered under English law, Content Services was a company operating in Germany, its services also being accessible in Austria. It offered trial or paid versions of different types of software. To access these products, consumers were supposed to fill in a registration form, which they could only complete by ticking a box to agree with the general terms and conditions. Among others, the standard terms included a withdrawal rights waiver. After this, the user received an e-mail displaying a link to the website where the consumer could log in, and the user name and password destined for the login. The e-mail made no mention of a right of withdrawal. Another e-mail attaching an invoice for EUR 96 then notified the consumer about having been granted access to the website for 12 months, and about the waived right to cancel the subscription. The *Bundesarbeitkammer* brought an action against this practice. The question before the Court was whether it conformed to Article 5(1) of the Directive, which requires the receipt by the consumer of written confirmation of the relevant information, or confirmation on another durable medium available. Since the e-mails did not contain such information, one of the main issues was to determine whether information offered by clicking a link was to be considered as fulfilling the durable medium requirement. The Court determined that placing information on a server entails that the information was neither 'given' to nor 'received' by the consumer, which was the wording utilised in Article 5(1). These requirements, the Court added, must be seen in the light of recital 11 of the preamble, striving 'to avoid a situation where the use of means of distance communication leads to a reduction in the information provided to the consumer.'[195] Building onto this, the durable medium question was answered in the negative. A link to a website was considered not to fulfil the same functions as paper form because the information could be altered and did not ensure permanent accessibility,[196] which eventually meant that Content Services was infringing the requirements of Article 5(1). However, this begs the question: should a website and its characteristics actually fulfil the same functions as paper, or can there simply be an equivalent between the two, regarded from the perspective of the potential of technological innovations? The Court left this outside the discussion, and did not address the possible technical solutions that Content Services could have employed in order to fulfil this requirement.

Perhaps the most challenging case available on the Distance Selling Directive, *Content Services* raised questions related to how the Distance Selling Directive was supposed to be applied to the intricacies of e-commerce. It was also challenging because it stood as a reflection of widespread practices in German-speaking countries, where online companies tried to commit consumers to their services by leaving consumers with no exit possibilities. Moreover, as Advocate General Mengozzi briefly observed, another important legal issue - unfortunately not included in the subject-matter of the reference to the preliminary ruling - was the lawfulness of waiving the right to withdrawal in the first place. Still, from the facts

194 *Content Services Ltd v Bundesarbeitskammer.*

195 *Ibid.*, para. 36.

196 *Ibid.*, para. 43; see also Case E-4/09, *Inconsult Anstalt v Finanzmarktaufsicht* [2010] EFTA Court Report.

of the case it seems difficult to understand how Content Services treated this waiver.[197] Even so, the same facts portrayed an intransparent and unfair commercial practice, which in itself justified the application of the Distance Selling Directive purpose. Nevertheless, what the Court failed to achieve was to clarify when exactly a website would be a durable medium, taking into account the numerous web-hosting services provided nowadays, as well as the practices of online traders.

An example of such an analysis can be seen in the case law of the Court of the European Free Trade Association in the *Inconsult Anstalt* case. There, the EFTA Court looked at what conditions must be met in order for a website to be a durable medium:

> 'The Internet site in question must constitute an instrument which (a) enables the customer to store information addressed personally to him, (b) enables him to store such information in a way accessible for future reference for a period of time adequate to the purposes of the information, and (c) allows for the unchanged reproduction of the information stored.'[198]

In the same vein, the European Securities Market Expert group (ESME), to which the EFTA court refers to, distinguishes between so-called 'ordinary' and 'sophisticated' websites, specifying that the latter category can very well be assimilated to the notion of 'durable medium' because they can:

> '- allow users personally to address e-mails to themselves attaching .pdf files of, for example, terms and conditions which are sent to and immediately stored on the user's computer [...] or
> - permit (or even require before access to a service is granted) users to print off the information in question, at which point, the information has clearly been provided in a durable medium.'[199]

It can be claimed that the Court of Justice did not go into depth with the analysis of what a durable medium means, for the mere reason that the Content Services website only had ordinary features and it failed to provide the information as required by Article 5(1). By thoroughly analysing the question, the Court could have explicitly taken the application of the Distance Selling Directive from its earlier envisaged use, namely to cover contracts concluded by post, to a more contemporary context, surrounding internet users who only have online contact with their suppliers. Given that the requirement of a durable medium is also set forth in Article 7 of the new Consumer Rights Directive (CRD) which reforms the rules applicable to distance contracts, the interpretation could have also been important for the implementation of the CRD. What the Court chose to do instead

197 Opinion of Advocate General Mengozzi, Case C-49/11, *Content Services Ltd v Bundesarbeitskammer*, para. 15.

198 *Inconsult Anstalt v Finanzmarktaufsicht*, para. 32.

199 European Securities Market Expert group (ESME), 'Report on Durable Medium – Distance Marketing Directive and Markets in Financial Instruments Directive', available at: <http://ec.europa.eu/internal_market/securities/docs/esme/durable_medium_en.pdf>, last accessed on 27 July 2016.

was to focus on the facts and apply the protection regime as set forth in Article 5(1) to ensure the consumer was safeguarded in the face of dubious commercial practices.

It was mentioned earlier that in the *easyCar* and *Messner* cases, the Court took into account a certain limitation of consumer protection and it assessed the balance between the interests of contractual parties. However, in *Heinrich Heine* and most recently in *Content Services*, these elements are not present. On the one hand, the Court did not go beyond the interpretation of the wording 'all sums' to determine whether the reimbursement of the delivery fee is fair in the light of the Distance Selling Directive. On the other hand, it also did not analyse the conditions for a 'durable medium' as a matter of principle, to shed light on the standard that must be met by the business practices of online suppliers.

4.3. *How was the Directive Transposed by Member States?*

Having seen how the Court of Justice has interpreted the Distance Selling Directive in its case law, in what follows, the legislation of selected Member States is now addressed, with an emphasis on the three essential provisions: (i) the provision of prior information (Article 4); (ii) the seven day withdrawal period (Article 6); and (iii) the 30 day performance period (Article 7).

4.3.1. Belgium

Belgium had implemented the Distance Selling Directive in due time, by revising the Law of 14 July 1991 on trade practices and consumer information and protection (Trade Practices Law) through the Law of 25 May 1999 (Articles 77-81).[200] Further updates to the rules reflecting the content of the Distance Selling Directive took place in 2010, when the Law of 6 April on market practices and consumer protection entered into force and in 2014, when the Code of Economic Law was introduced in the aftermath of the adoption of the Consumer Rights Directive.

Going back to the initial transposition, with regards the content of these rules, the information duties imposed by Article 4(1) of the Distance Selling Directive can be read in Article 45 of the Trade Practices Law. These duties closely reflected the Directive's wording, except for the mention of good faith in commercial transactions, which was left out. The right of withdrawal (Article 6 Distance Selling

200 Mougenot 2002, p. 313; Biquet-Mathieu 2007, p. 2, available at: <www.henricapitant.be/documents/jcolombiennes_rapport.pdf>, last accessed on 27 July 2016; Patrick Van Eecke & Maarten Truyens, 'Benchmarking of Existing National Legal E-Business Practices. Country Report - Belgium', DG/ENTR/04/68, p. 5; see also Anne Salaun, 'Transposition de la directive contrats à distance en droit belge, commentaire de l'article 20 de la loi du 25 mai 1999', Droit des nouvelles technologies, available at: <www.droit-technologie.org>, last accessed on 27 July 2016; Vanessa Veriter, 'De elektronische handel: een nieuwe muze voor wetgevers', Beroep Instituut van Erkende Boekhouders en Fiscalisten, 15 July 2001, available at: <www.bibf.be/page.aspx?pageid=1364&menuid=1090>, last accessed on 27 July 2016.

Directive) was governed by Article 47 of the Trade Practices Law, granting the consumer a cooling off period of 14 calendar days and underlining that the only charge to be imposed on the consumer because of the exercise of his right of withdrawal (*en raison de l'exercise de son droit de rétractation*) was the direct cost of returning the goods. Apart from making reference to a longer cooling off period, paragraph 1 of Article 6 was transposed entirely and had three important features. Firstly and most significantly, according to Article 47 § 1er, rules for notification were provided. Here, withdrawal was considered to have occurred with the twin condition that it was made in writing or on a durable medium which the supplier has access to and that it was made before the expiration of the 14 calendar days. The reader must not forget that the Distance Selling Directive was silent on the provision of any rules on notification. Secondly, § 2 of the Trade Practices Law dealt with the situation in which the supplier failed to provide the consumer with the written confirmation (Article 5 Distance Selling Directive, Article 46 Trade Practices Act) but did so within the period of three months to which the right of withdrawal was extended, similar to Article 6(1) of the Directive. The particularity of this section consisted of the fact that the Belgian legislator added the situation of contracts concluded for the successive delivery of goods, when it determined that the right of withdrawal started with the day following that of the first delivery. Lastly, Belgian law applied a slightly different wording for the calculation of the moment when the cooling off period started. While the Directive established that the seven day period started from the moment (day) when the goods were delivered or when the service contract was concluded, Article 47 calculated these terms starting with the day following that of the delivery or of the conclusion of the contract (with the exception of the terms when the supplier did not fulfil the confirmation duties, calculated just as in the Distance Selling Directive). Paragraphs 2 and 3 of Article 6 Distance Selling Directive are also covered by Article 47.

Article 48 of the Trade Practices Act implemented the performance obligations envisaged in Article 7 Distance Selling Directive, establishing the same 30-day period for the supplier to honour the contract, and the subsequent 30 days to reimburse any paid sums. Moreover, it established that if the period for performance was not respected, the consumer was given a right over the resolution of the contract, which he could exercise by way of notification and without making recourse to proceedings before the court. As for the binding nature of the consumer rights in distance contracts, Article 56 § 2 clearly stated that all clauses whereby the consumer renounced the rights given to him were rendered void.

4.3.2. France

In France, the Distance Selling Directive was transposed in 2001 in the *Code de la Consommation* starting with Article L. 121-16 (and until Article L. 121-20-7). This regime was subsequently modified in 2005, 2006, 2008 and 2010.[201] The general

[201] Ordinance no. 2005-648 of 6 June 2005; Law no. 2005-841 of 26 July 2005; Law no. 2006-387 of 31 March 2006; Law no. 2008-3 of 3 January 2008; Law no. 2010-853 of 23 July 2010.

particularity of French law was the lack of an explicit definition of consumer in statutory provisions, which was then developed by case law.[202] Article L. 121-16 defined the ambit of application for subsequent rules, by mentioning distance contracts in a different wording than the Distance Selling Directive, but with the same effect. Article L. 121-17 took over the exceptions based on Article 3 Distance Selling Directive, with the distinction that French law mentioned 'public auctions', while the Directive only specifies 'auctions'. Article L. 121-18 went on to enumerate the information which needed to be offered to the consumer in the offer: a) the name of the seller or supplier, telephone number, registered office (for moral persons) and the address of the offeror (if different); b) delivery costs, where appropriate; c) the arrangements for payment, delivery or performance; d) the existence of a right of withdrawal and its eventual limits or, in the case when that right is not applicable, reference to the lack of this right; e) the period for which the offer or the price remains valid; f) the cost of using the means of distance communication, where it is calculated other than at the basic rate; and finally g) where appropriate, the minimum duration of the contract in the case of contracts for the supply of products or services to be performed permanently or recurrently. There were two additional requirements in the Directive, namely the indication of the essential characteristics of the good or service, and the indication of the price of the good or service with all taxes included. However, French law dealt with these issues under the more general part over the formation of consumer contracts, in Article L. 111-1 (*les caractéristiques essentielles du bien*) and respectively Article L. 113-3 (*les prix, les limitations éventuelles de la responsabilité contractuelle et les conditions particulières de la vente*). Article L. 121-18 also contained a second indent implementing Article 4(2) of the Distance Selling Directive, with the particularity that no mention of the principle of good faith in commercial transactions was made. Article 4(3) Distance Selling Directive was transposed almost literally, requesting the seller or supplier to specify his identity and commercial purpose at the beginning of any telephonic conversation with the customer.

Article L. 121-20 established the right of withdrawal (*droit de rétractation*). The main deviation of French law from the Distance Selling Directive came from the duration of this right. While the Distance Selling Directive imposed seven working days (*jours ouvrables*), French law operated with normal 24-hour days (*jours francs*), which included weekends and holidays if they fell within the duration of the term, but are extended to the next day if the right expired on either weekend days or holidays. Article L. 121-20-1 mentioned that in case of withdrawal the consumer had 30 days to be reimbursed. Additionally, French law specified that after the passing of the 30 days, reimbursable sums were productive of legal interest. Reimbursable sums could be returned through any means of payment, and it was further specified that at the proposal of the seller or supplier, another mode of reimbursement could be selected. Article L. 121-20-2 imposed the same limitations on the right of withdrawal as Article 6(3) Distance Selling Directive.

202 Cass. 1re civ. 21 January 1995; Cass. 1re civ., 15 March 2005, n°02-13.285; Civ.1ère 5 March 2002 n°00-18202.

Performance of the contract was dealt with in Article L. 121-20-3. French law first tackled the case when a contract had a fixed date. Failure to perform the contract would, according to Article L. 114-1, grant the consumer the right to obtain the resolution of the contract and be reimbursed for sums paid. Then, if failure to perform arose out of the unavailability of the good, the Distance Selling Directive model was followed, and the consumer may be provided with a good or service of equivalent quality and price. Moreover, French law allowed the seller or supplier to be released of responsibility if they could prove that the failure to perform, or the defective performance was due to an insurmountable event (e.g. *force majeure*), or was imputable to the consumer.

As far as the mandatory character of the provisions is concerned, there was no explicit transposition in this regard. However, Article L. 121-20-16 did specify that the entire section had a public order character.

After the transposition of the Consumer Rights Directive, these rules have been changed through Law no. 2014-344 of 17 March 2014.

4.3.3. Germany

Germany had initially implemented the Distance Selling Directive in 2000, with the Distance Selling Act. However, subsequent to the German reform of the law of obligations, consumer rules on distance contracts had been inserted into the BGB, in §§ 13, 14, 241a, 312b-312d, 312f, 355-359 and 676h. Additionally, Articles 2 and 14 of the Regulation on duties to supply information in civil law were also applicable.[203]

§§ 13 and 14 BGB determined the definitions of consumers and suppliers, in an almost identical manner to the Directive, while distance contracts were defined in § 312b I.[204] The interesting particularity of German law was that it explicitly recognised electronic business dealings (e-commerce contracts) in § 312g.

Although Article 4 of the Distance Selling Directive was reflected in § 312c, the list of information itself was not available in the BGB, but were, however, found in Article 246 sections (1) and (2) of the Introductory Act to the German Civil Code (*Einführungsgesetz zum Bürgerlichen Gesetzbuch*),[205] which accurately implemented all the requirements of the Directive. However, no specific mention of good faith in commercial transactions was made.

The right to withdraw from distance contracts was codified in § 312 d BGB, where two types of rights were differentiated: the right of revocation, and the right of return. In distance contracts, the German legislator made available for the consumer a general right of revocation (§ 355 BGB), and whenever the contract dealt with the sale of goods, the consumer could make recourse to the right of return (§ 356 BGB). According to § 355, the consumer was not required to give any reason for wishing to revoke the contract, which he can do within 14 days. This period was extended by law to one month if the supplier did not meet his confirmation

203 Schulte-Nölke *et al.* 2008, p. 539.

204 Wiesemann & Falletti 2006, p. 3.

205 *Ibid.*

obligation set forth by Article246 sections (1) and (2) of the Introductory Act to the German Civil Code, but could not be any longer than six months (§ 355 (4) BGB). German law also clearly regulated the legal consequences of revocation and return in § 357 BGB, departing from the main consideration of the Directive in this case, namely that no other charge than the return fee can be imposed on the consumer. According to German law, it was generally the responsibility of the seller or supplier to bear the costs and risks of the return parcel. However, when these costs were less than EUR 40, they could be charged to the consumer. The same could be applied if the consumer had not yet rendered consideration or given a part payment, with the exception of goods supplied that do not correspond to the order. The exceptions for contracts where no right of withdrawal was applicable were embodied in § 312d(4)(1). Apart from taking over the requirements in the Directive, the German legislator chose to specifically refer to auctions as well.

When it comes to performance, the rules were rather dispersed amongst general law of obligations provisions. To start with, § 271 BGB made a distinction between the case when the parties agreed on a specific date of performance and the case when no such date was determined, where German law saw the good to be delivered or the service to be supplied as eligible to be demanded immediately. Still, no explicit term of maximum 30 working days as envisaged by the Directive for the performance of the contract had been transposed. For this reason, § 271 BGB must be read together with § 308 BGB prohibiting contractual clauses that are either unreasonably long or insufficiently specific. Furthermore, based on §§ 323 and 346 BGB, if performance was not rendered, or it was not rendered according to the contract, the consumer could revoke the contract and any eventual performance received or any emolument taken was to be returned. § 275 established the situations in which a seller or supplier is excused from performance if he is in the impossibility of fulfilling his contractual obligations, while § 346 stated that in the situation of impossibility, the obligee (in our case the consumer) can revoke the contract.

Just like with the rules on the Doorstep Selling Directive, the provisions on distance selling have been changed by the transposition of the Consumer Rights Directive through the Act on the Implementation of the EU Consumer Rights Directive and on the Amendment of the Law on Housing (*Gesetz zur Umsetzung der Verbraucherrechterichtlinie und zur Änderung des Gesetzes zur Regelung der Wohnungsvermittlung*).

4.3.4. Ireland

The Distance Selling Directive was transposed into Irish Law by the EC (Protection of Consumers in respect of contracts made by means of distance communication) Regulations 2001.[206] Regulation 2(1) defined the notion of 'consumer' just as it lies in the Distance Selling Directive. Regulation 3 reflected the meaning of 'distance

206 Statutory Instrument 207 of 2001.

contract', once again borrowing the Directive's text, with the addition of the Article 3 Distance Selling Directive exemptions.

The obligation to provide information was included in Regulation 4(1)a that made reference to the annexed Schedule 3. This Schedule layed out exactly the same requirements as the Directive. Moreover, Regulation 4(1)c explicitly referred to the principle of good faith in commercial transactions.

Regulation 6 dealt with the right of withdrawal, which under Irish law is called the right of cancellation, and was referred to as an implied condition. According to this regulation, the consumer was given the minimum period prescribed by the Distance Selling Directive, namely seven working days, to return the goods, without having any other charges or penalties imposed onto him except for the direct cost of returning the goods. The Irish legislator thus implemented the Distance Selling Directive in a very literal manner. When the confirmation of the provision of information was not received by the consumer, the right of cancellation was extended to a maximum of three months, starting: for goods, when they are received by the consumer; for services, upon the conclusion of the contract. Just like many other regulations in the present statutory frame, Regulation 6 specified that if its provisions are not respected, the person in violation was guilty of an offence. This entails the possibility of having the offences prosecuted and enabling liability on summary conviction to a fine not exceeding EUR 3,000.

Regulation 9 articulated exactly the same obligations as expressed in Article 7 Distance Selling Directive: the period for performance was maximum 30 days, the consumer could receive replacement goods or services, and the unavailability of goods attracted a period of 30 days of reimbursement.

Regulation 18 specified that a consumer could not waive his rights under the protection of the Regulations (Article 12 Distance Selling Directive).

The Consumer Rights Directive changed the aforementioned rules through Statutory Instrument No. 484 of 2013 European Union (Consumer Information, Cancellation and Other Rights) Regulations 2013 to fit the new maximum harmonisation policy.

4.3.5. The Netherlands

Book 7 of the Dutch Civil Code used to be the main source of rights and duties of parties involved in transactions concluded at a distance.

Article 7:46c BW transposed the duty to provide information. Although the information Dutch law required was simply similar to the Directive, two comments must be made. Firstly, this part of the Civil Code dealt with special contracts, namely sale contracts. For this reason, the wording of Article 7:46c(1)(b) only refers to physical objects (*zaken*) and not to services. However, by virtue of the express reference in Article 7:46i(1), the same rules apply *mutatis mutandis* to services other than financial services. A second clarification that needs to be made is that the Dutch legislator did not make express reference to the principle of good faith, even though in the Dutch translation of the Directive, it is presented as the principle of honesty in commercial transactions (*beginselen van eerlijkheid bij commerciële transacties*).[207] Nevertheless, it can be argued that Dutch law had already imposed a general obligation of conducting contractual relations in good faith (*redelijkheid en billijkheid*) in Articles 6:2 BW and 6:248 BW, wide enough to apply to distance contracts as well.

The right of withdrawal could be found in Article 7:46d BW and it was transposed by complying with the minimum period prescribed by the Distance Selling Directive, namely seven working days. Even if the Directive used the term '*herroepingsrecht*', which is the equivalent of the English 'right of withdrawal', the Dutch Civil Code only referred to the dissolution of the contract ('*ontbinding*'). Again, similarly to the provisions of the Distance Selling Directive, the possibility to dissolve the contract was extended to a minimum of three months in case the confirmation of information, as integrated by the Dutch legislator in Article 7:46c(2). Also, the right of the consumer to not be charged fees other than those affiliated with the return of the product had been implemented in Article 7:46d(2), while the next paragraph gave the seller or supplier a maximum of 30 days to reimburse all sums paid by the buyer, without any additional fees. As far as the exceptions were concerned, all the requirements of the Distance Selling Directive were met, by having been codified either in Article 7:46d(4) or 7:46i(5) BW.

Performance of the contract, as envisaged in Article 7:46f, did not raise any compatibility problems, as the Civil Code literally spells out the same requirements as the Distance Selling Directive. The same can be said about the mandatory nature of consumer rights in distance selling and according to Article 7:46j(1), these rights cannot be waived by agreement. The content of these rules was changed by the transposition of the Consumer Rights Directive, which entailed the modification of Book 7, where the initial rules had been transposed and the addition of part 2B in Book 6 Title 5 of the Civil Code.

4.3.6. Romania

Romania had firstly implemented legislation referring to distance selling in 2000, quite a long time before joining the European Union, through Ordinance no. 130 from 21 August 2000 on consumers' protection regarding the conclusion and performance of distance selling contracts. However, this law was incomplete, as it was notified by letter from the European Commission.[208] Thus the Romanian legislator modified the distance-selling regime in November 2008 through Emergency Ordinance 174/2008, amending the 2000 law.[209]

207 Hesselink 2011c, p. 476; see for comparison the new rules implementing the Consumer Rights Directive: Luzak & Mak 2014a, p. 127; see also *Memorie van implementatie van de Richtlijn consumentenrechten*, Kamerstukken II 2012/2013, 33520, nr 3, 6 *et seq*.

208 Letter from the European Commission to the Romanian Government, SANCO/B2/ADG/ew D(2008)220354 of 19 September 2008.

209 *Ordonanța nr. 130/2000 privind regimul juridic al contractelor la distanță, Monitorul Oficial* nr. 431 din 09.02.2000.

Article 3 offered the information needed to be given to the consumer by the seller or supplier and it almost literally transposed Article 4 Distance Selling Directive, with two additions. Firstly, in case of advance payment, Article 3(1)(a) of the Ordinance not only required the identity and address of the trader, but also asked for the phone number, e-mail address and the trader's commercial registration code. Secondly, Article 3(1)(j) obliged the trader to inform the consumer on the maximum performance period. Romanian law did not, however, make specific reference to the principle of good faith, as it chose to refer to good commercial practices in transactions (*principiile de bunã practicã comercialã*).

One of the specificities of this law is reflected by the fact that the Romanian legislator expressly stated in Article 5 of the Ordinance that the moment when the distance contract was considered to have been concluded was the moment when the consumer received the confirmation of his order, unless parties had otherwise agreed.

The right of withdrawal was governed by Articles 7 and 8 and it consisted of a period of 10 working days. The obligations enshrined in the Directive were almost fully met, with the sole exception that in the case of the extension of the right of withdrawal, instead of three months, Romanian law only spoke about 90 days, which was very close but did not meet the minimum standard imposed by the Distance Selling Directive. Also, even if the Romanian language version of the Directive referred to a specific right of withdrawal (*drept de retractare*), the Ordinance did not take over the terminology and only referred to a right of the consumer to unilaterally terminate the contract (*drept de denunțare unilateralã*).

Performance could be found in Article 11 and once again very closely followed the obligations imposed by the Distance Selling Directive. One important distinction was that Romanian legislation did not take over the obligation of the supplier to reimburse the consumer as soon as possible, but only referred to the maximum period in which this reimbursement could take place, which was just like in the Directive, 30 days. However, sellers or suppliers who did not respect this provision were subject to fines, according to Article 17 of the Ordinance.

Lastly, Article 26 stated that the rights conferred to the consumer under the regime of the Ordinance could not be waived.

As of 13 June 2014, Emergency Ordinance 34/2014 transposing the Consumer Rights Directive changed the content of the rules applicable to distance selling.

4.3.7. The United Kingdom

The UK is one of the Member States that chose to implement the Distance Selling Directive in an overall almost literal manner. The Consumer Protection (Distance Selling) Regulations 2000 were the implementing statutory instrument.

Regulation 7 referred to the obligation to provide information prior to the conclusion of the contract. This Regulation also drew from other obligations enshrined in the Distance Selling Directive and referred to the duty of the seller or supplier to inform the consumer about the possibility to receive substitute goods, as indicated in Regulation 7(1)(b), but also that returning substitute goods would be paid for by the trader, in Regulation 7(1)(c). UK law mirrored the Distance Selling Directive when it comes to implementing the requirement of providing information in accordance to the principle of good faith in commercial transactions, even if it had been acknowledged that English law was not familiar with such concept and what is more, the very notion of good faith might differ from consumer contracts to commercial ones.[210]

The UK legislator had found a national equivalent for the right of withdrawal in the so-called right to cancel, featured in Regulation 10. Regulations 11 and 12 distinguished between the nature of the contractual object and established separate rules for goods and services. Still, the same terms applied: seven working days for the right to cancel, and if the confirmation of information was not respected, the right could be extended to a maximum of three months. Regulation 14 established that when the right to cancel was exercised, any sum paid by the consumer must be returned as soon as possible and after no longer than 30 days.

Performance was covered mainly by Regulation 19 and it respected the 30 days limit imposed by the Directive, in the case when parties did not convene on a specific term for performance. Additionally, in conjunction with Regulation 7, the supplier could provide substitute goods, if this information was offered and if this possibility was stated in the contract.

Progressing to an eventual waiver of consumer rights, Regulation 25(1) deemed void any term inconsistent with the protection envisaged by the 2000 Regulations. As of 13 June 2014, the Consumer Contracts Regulations (Information, Cancellation and Additional Charges) Regulations 2013 transposing the Consumer Rights Directive replaced these rules.

4.4. *Comparative Notes on the Transposition*

The analysis of the Distance Selling Directive and its subsequent implementation had the goal of firstly identifying several essential obligations established under the Directive's ambit and then analysing their subsequent transposition into the laws of the Member States. By doing so, problems dealing with the consistency and divergence in national transposition could be brought to light. In what follows, a brief comparative overview is provided in order to highlight some of the issues arising from national transposition standards.

It can be agreed that no significant differences have been identified in the above featured country reports. However, this does not entail that differences lack completely. Three aspects of legislation can be looked at when dealing with divergences between national transpositions: (i) open-ended norms; (ii) specific rules v general rules; and (iii) duration of terms. Minimum harmonisation is discussed in each of these categories.

(i) Open-ended Norms

The reason why it is important to be aware of the fact that Article 4 employs two open-ended concepts is mainly because in theory 'good time' and 'the principle of good faith in commercial transactions' can be said to have the same root: a general

210 Bradgate 1997; see also Bain & Subirana 2003, p. 282.

sense of fairness which in this case must dominate commercial transactions. This being said, there are several problems that arise from their use in the text of the Directive.

Firstly, when considering the notion of 'good time', its context must be mentioned. The seller or provider of services must offer the consumer information on the goods or services at stake, to allow the consumer to have a clear view over the transaction he is about to enter into. Article 4(1) of the Directive imposed that this information is offered in good time prior to the conclusion of the contract. However, there are two issues with this 'good time' standard. On the one hand, depending on the specific means of distance communication, the standard can be stretched or shrunk. Imagine the situation in which a person on the Shetland Islands who does not have an Internet connection is interested in buying a product that he saw advertised in a magazine. The only options he would have to purchase such a good are either to communicate via phone or regular mail. This begs the question: what is good time when a consumer is involved in a phone conversation, and what is good time when the information must physically travel in order to reach him? It is difficult to imagine one clear answer to this question, and to a certain extent this is a positive aspect of open-ended concepts - they can be tailored to very specific situations. However, the problem is that a high degree of specificity will automatically attract diversity. Moreover, this process might be too focused on local preferences, to the detriment of the creation of a unified time standard. On the other hand, using the Internet as a means of communication implies a different set of questions. Looking at the kind of information a seller is supposed to share with a consumer, Article 4(1) listed items such as the identity and contact details of the seller (address and phone number, etc.), the main characteristics of the goods or services, the price including all taxes, delivery costs, arrangements for payment, etc.

Many of these items had an educational nature - among others, sellers and suppliers were mandated by law to indicate the final price of a good or service, rather than being allowed to lure consumers with incomplete prices; they needed to reveal their commercial identity so that consumers can hold them liable in case the contract goes wrong; they also needed to specify that consumers were entitled to make use of their right of withdrawal and send the good back without any specific reason, etc. However, many of these items also happen to reflect rather common sense questions that consumers ask themselves when shopping online: how much a product costs (probably the best feature of internet-shopping is the ability to compare prices easily); how long it takes to have the product delivered, and how much it costs; whether they can pay by credit card or not; etc. Without clarifications like those, online shoppers would most likely be reluctant to engage in any transaction. From this narrow perspective, the requirement of providing the information in good time becomes redundant, because it can be seen as a prerequisite for engaging consumer interest to start with. All in all, if the good time requirement is bound, as it inherently should be, to particularities such as preferences and usage of a specific type of means of communication, this can have major drawbacks on the harmonisation of the obligations Article 4 imposes.

Secondly, when dealing with good faith, it is important to remind the readers that the Directive does not speak about just any obligation related to fairness, but it emphasises the *principle* of good faith in commercial transactions. This specific reference to a principle of law rekindles the debate surrounding the value and applicability of good faith throughout the laws of the Member States. While for some jurisdictions it is indeed a fundamental principle of law that leads to rules of direct application,[211] some others have seen it as a legal irritant and only implemented it in the light of transposition obligations, but did not give it the standing of a principle of law.[212] Still, it must be acknowledged that even within the national laws where this is the case, other principles and rules have served a similar purpose. From this viewpoint, it seems that in practice there should be no difference between whether a jurisdiction embraces good faith as a principle or applies a reasonable person standard instead. This being said, the burden finally lies with the courts before which the application of these different standards comes into play, as they should be fully aware of such a mirror-effect and try to link the concepts to one another.

With the exception of France, all other Member States had made it clear that information must be given and confirmed to the consumer in 'good time'. The main deficiency, as noted by Schülte-Nolke in the Consumer Law Compendium, was a lack of clarity as to what precisely 'good time' should entail.[213]

'Good faith in commercial transactions' does not enjoy the same treatment however. Only three out of the seven Member States have transposed this requirement: one (Romania) has done so without referencing the already-existing civil law concept of good faith (*bună credință*); the other two Member States that borrow the wording of the Directive are Ireland and the United Kingdom. These are common law systems that do not share the civil law tradition and history of the principle of good faith.

Open-ended norms have often been the subject of controversy.[214] The main critique is that by allowing the use of standards that cannot be consistently determined and are too interpretable, legal certainty is endangered. However, the focus in this debate rarely falls on the overall effect created by a certain resistance of national law to embrace the open-ended concepts in directives. Good faith is the best example when it comes to the Distance Selling Directive and there are two ways in which this standard has not been taken over by four of the member states.

Firstly, Member States might claim that the purpose of implementing a provision like Article 4(2) is met if information 'shall be provided in a clear and comprehensible manner in any way appropriate to the means of distance communication used'. In other words, good faith only comes to supplement a requirement that already makes it clear that the seller or supplier must inform the consumer in such a manner that the consumer understands the information. Still, one issue is overlooked: the fact that the Distance Selling Directive governs technology, and technology is constantly evolving. For this reason, we might ask ourselves: what exactly is appropriate when using a specific means of distance

211 DCFR, Introduction, para. 72.

212 Teubner 1998, p. 11.

213 Schulte-Nölke *et al.* 2008, p. 503.

214 Smits 2010a, p. 99.

communication? Can that be objectively determined when assessing a specific means of communication? And even more, what happens when various means of communication overlap? In my view, the mere presence of adjectives such as 'clear', 'comprehensible' and 'appropriate' might be of some help in understanding these questions, but in no circumstance does it offer an answer for them. This is because in order to make legislation receptive to technological developments, good faith as a flexible standard of consumer protection seems to be a very suitable solution.

Secondly, Member States might equally claim that there is no need to implement the good faith standard, because their national legislation already uses a similar norm. Take for instance German law: the famous *Treu und Glauben* provision (§ 242 BGB) might explicitly mention that it covers performance of the contract alone, but case law and subsequent academic literature have long recognised the fact that it gives rise to supplementary obligations, *inter alia*, the duty to inform.[215] It can then be argued that since good faith already extends over information duties, there is no need for the German legislator to carry on with a separate implementation of the good faith standard. However, while this choice could be said to solve some issues occurring in the transposition process, other problems arise. German law has pursued the concretisation of § 242 by the creation of case groups (*Fallgruppen*). It follows from this that while it might be possible for the § 242 framework to give effect to the good faith standard in the Distance Selling Directive, connecting the two might not be so achievable in practice.

As previously mentioned, the Distance Selling Directive makes reference to the principle of good faith in commercial transactions in Article 4(2). After looking at eight Member States it becomes clear that tackling the implementation of this principle indeed creates legislative divergence.

A first category of Member States does not make any reference to good faith, such as Germany, the Netherlands and France. Would this incomplete implementation affect in any way the obligation according to which the information due to the consumer must be given in a way that is fair towards him and takes his own interests into account? Perhaps not, because both French and German law have a long standing of operating with general principles of either objective or subjective good faith. However, the debate does not end here, as good faith can be applicable to different stages of the contract (pre-contractual duties, formation and performance) but also to contractual interpretation.[216]

215 Whittaker & Zimmermann 2000, p. 24; Palandt/Heinrichs (n. 67) § 242, nn. 23 ff.

216 Emily M. Weitzenböck, 'Good Faith and Fair Dealing in the Context of Contract Formation by Electronic Agents', Proceedings of the AISB 2002 Symposium on Intelligent Agents in Virtual Markets, 2-5 April 2002, available at: <http://folk.uio.no/emilyw/documents/-Good%20Faith%20-%20Contract%20Formation%20%26%20source.pdf>, last accessed on 27 July 2016; Peter Schlechtriem, 'Good Faith in German Law and in International Uniform Laws', Saggi, Conferenze e Seminari 24, Roma (February 1997), available at: <http://cisgw3.law.pace.edu/cisg/biblio/schlechtriem16.html>, last accessed on 27 July 2016; Nedzel 1997, p. 97; see also Article 1134 of the French Civil Code and § 242 BGB; Omer Tene, 'Good Faith in Precontractual Negotiations: A Franco-German-American Perspective', 8 November 2006, p. 10, available at: <http://ssrn.com/abstract=943383>, last accessed on 27 July 2016.

The second category would consist of Member States who implemented the good faith requirement, but give it a different name, such as Romania. Romania only refers to good commercial practices, which again say nothing with respect to the eventual discrepancies between commercial good faith and consumer good faith, adding to the confusion. Insofar as the application of good faith to distance contracts is hindered by these two types of implementation, the minimum harmonisation standard would not be met.

A third category is represented by Ireland and the UK that chose to transpose the obligation literally. Issues arise however from the fact that normally these systems do not acknowledge a clear principle of good faith, and its applicability has been questioned.

(ii) Civil Codes v Satellite Laws

Another point of divergence between the legal systems consists in either the fragmentation or combination of rules under a specific regime. While France, Romania, and Belgium have separate special laws which they apply to distance selling, Germany and the Netherlands have incorporated these rules into their civil codes. This does not pose any problems in itself, but the incorporation also then took into account already existing rules (e.g. performance in Germany), leading to a rather dispersed body of rules applicable to distance contracts. Still, this should not necessarily lead to legal divergence, but it is an observation that deals with the method of implementation.

(iii) Duration of Terms

Making sure that national implementation respects the terms established by the Directive is one of the instances where minimum harmonisation becomes of utmost importance. As France only imposes a seven-day (*jours francs*) withdrawal period, it is clear this does not meet the standard imposed by the Directive. In the same vein, Romania extends this right to a maximum of 90 days in the case the seller fails to inform the consumer about the right to withdraw, which is under the three months term within the Distance Selling Directive. This is perhaps the most problematic point, since terms are expressed in numbers and it is clear when minimum numbers are not met. Still, Member States like Germany even go beyond the scope of the Directive by offering an extension of six months to the withdrawal right, or by extending the withdrawal right itself, again like Germany, to a maximum of 14 days.

Minimum harmonisation gives, in this case, the opportunity of Member States to enhance the regime for consumer protection if they so wish. However, as it has been shown in this section, this leads to great differences, and whatever convergence takes place can only be related to in terms of the minimum standards which have been achieved. Nevertheless, sometimes not even these standards are met, and the question which still needs to be answered is whether the resulting differences, though slight, affect the object and purpose of the Directive.

5. Consumer Sales (1999)

5.1. *What are the Rationale and Scope of the Directive?*

Figure 6: Consumer Sales Directive Adoption Timeline (source: Eur-Lex)

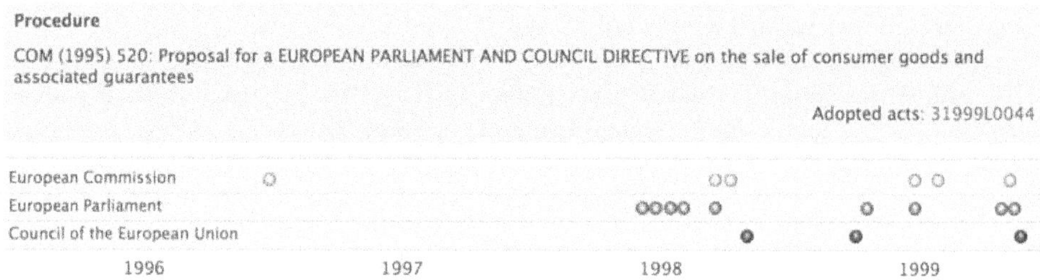

The Consumer Sales Directive[217] was adopted in order to ensure 'a uniform minimum set of fair rules governing the sale of consumer goods'.[218] The intervention of the European legislator aimed to fill a gap in national private law regimes at the time of the Directive's adoption in 1999: there were no common rules on contractual conformity in the case of sale of goods.[219]

A European action plan on consumer guarantees and after-sales services had already been in existence as early as 1993,[220] leading to the publication of the Commission's Green Paper on the same topic later that year.[221] Acknowledging the progress made by the adoption of the Unfair Contract Terms Directive by imposing the prohibition of unfair terms in standard contracts, the Green Paper also discusses the need to implement a positive measure in the form of conferring consumers certain rights in sales contracts.[222] This specific need for positive harmonisation became clear after a study was conducted on existing national legislation on legal warranties.[223] The findings of the Commission were that not only is the consumer deterred from making major purchases in foreign countries, but vendors and manufacturers are also threatened by distortions in competition.[224] This is when the idea of a directive on consumer guarantees was born.[225] The Consumer Sales

217 Directive 1999/44/EC.
218 Recital 2 of the Preamble to the Directive
219 Parisi 2004, p. 404; Zollers *et al.* 1999, p. 107.
220 Commission Action Plan, 'Placing the Single Market at the Service of European Consumers', COM(93) 378 final, 28 July 1993; see also Jeloschek 2006, p. 15.
221 European Commission, 'Green Paper of 15 November 1993 on guarantees for consumer goods and after-sales services', COM(93) 509 final, *OJ* C338 of 15 December 1993.
222 *Ibid.*, p. 12.
223 *Ibid.*, p. 17.
224 *Ibid.*, p. 71; see also Eurobarometer No. 35 of July 1991.
225 European Commission, 'Green Paper of 15 November 1993 on guarantees for consumer goods and after-sales services', COM(93) 509 final, p. 101.

Directive is another example of the minimum harmonisation policy,[226] and this can be seen in Article 8(2) that leaves leeway for Member States to adopt more stringent rules to the benefit of consumers.

The Directive has been very often compared to the CISG, on the grounds that it strives to achieve the same goal, namely uniformity in sales law.[227] Arguments related to the resemblance of the two instruments are well founded, if one keeps in mind how the Directive's proposal was drafted in the lines of the CISG. This is noticeable in the legislative history not only in terms of the wording of certain articles, but also in their scope.[228] The full extent of this comparison falls outside the ambit of the present study, but it is however noteworthy to mention there is one strong distinction between the Directive and the CISG: while the first applies to consumer sales, the latter only applies to B2B transactions.[229]

The purpose of tailoring sales rules for consumers in the context of the internal market made it possible for the Directive to be adopted on the basis of Article 114 TFEU (ex Article 95 TEC). This is reflected in the Preamble, either directly in recital one, or by describing the reasons to be considered in the harmonisation of sales law such as: disparate rules do not encourage consumers to enter transboundary transactions, which leads to their role in the completion of the internal market to be undermined;[230] or the markets for consumer goods should not differ and be compartmented at national level.[231] The Preamble thus gives a description of pro-harmonisation arguments very similar to those found in other Directives discussed so far in this book, operating alongside 'a double line of reasoning',[232] with which the reader might have become quite familiar. Firstly, the Directive is a tool that enhances consumer protection by setting a standard of rights throughout the Union. Secondly, higher protection leads to more confident consumers who will increase their purchases in cross-border transactions, thereby consolidating the European market.[233]

226 Scotton 2001, p. 298; Twigg-Flesner 2011, p. 239.
227 Kruisinga 2001, p. 178; Grundmann 2003, p. 237; Kingisepp 2008, p. 219.
228 See Article 2(b) of the Consumer Sales Directive, which is the literal reflection of Articles 2(c) and (f) of the CISG; see also Proposal for a European Parliament and Council Directive on the sale of consumer goods and associated guarantees, COM(95) 520 final, *OJ* C307/8 of 16 October 1996; Common Position (EC) no 51/98 adopted by the Council on 24 September 1998 with a view to adopting Eurpean Parliament and Council Directive 98/EC, on certain aspects of the sale of consumer goods and associated guarantees, *OJ* C333/46 of 30 October 1998; Communication from the Commission to the EP on the Common Position of the Council on the proposal for a Directive on the sale of consumer goods and associated guarantees of 25 September 1998, SEC(1998) 1553 final; European Commission Opinion of 19 January 1999, COM(1999) 16 final.
229 Except from when the seller does not know the buyer is a consumer. Moreover, the Consumer Sales Directive applies to EU Member States, while the CISG applies internationally.
230 Recital four of the Preamble to the Consumer Sales Directive.
231 Recital three of the Preamble to the Consumer Sales Directive.
232 Staudenmayer 2000, p. 548.
233 *Ibid.*; see also Van Zelst 2008, p. 13; Deards 1998, p. 100.

In determining the ambit of the Consumer Sales Directive, the nature of contracts covered as well as the contracting parties must be taken into account. Starting with the first point, it becomes clear from Article 1(1) that the Consumer Sales Directive is not a general sales regime, but it only covers sales contracts in aspects related to consumer guarantees. Moreover, as it is stated in Article 1(2)(4), service contracts can also fall within the protective ambit of the Directive, as long as they are 'contracts for the supply of consumer goods to be manufactured or produced'. However, this has been deemed as an incomplete regime.[234] On the one hand, including services under sale of goods might prevent national laws from recognizing such contracts in separate categories (e.g. the work and materials contract in English law could be seen as a sales contract under the Consumer Sales Directive).[235] On the other hand, only a narrow category of services is considered under the Consumer Sales Directive, which leaves the remaining types of services on the European market either unregulated or fragmented.[236] Article 1(2)(b) defines consumer goods as tangible movable items, but exceptionally leaves out several types of goods: those sold by way of execution or otherwise by authority of law; water and gas (if not offered in a limited volume or set quantity); and electricity. As for the second point, contracting parties are defined in Article 1(2)(a) and (c) establishing the parties to the transaction: the seller, or 'any natural or legal person who, under a contract, sells consumer goods in the course of his trade, business or profession', and the consumer, 'any natural person who, in the contracts covered by this Directive, is acting for purposes which are not related to his trade, business or profession'.[237]

Having understood to what contracts and between which parties the Directive applies, it is now time to consider its essential provisions in order to determine the content of the minimum standard of protection: (i) conformity with the contract (Article 2); (ii) rights of the consumer (Article 3); (iii) time limits (Article 5); and (iv) guarantees (Article 6).

(i) Conformity with the Contract (Article 2)

The importance of Article 2 flows from two aspects. Firstly, it establishes the obligation of the seller to deliver the good in conformity with the agreement between himself and the consumer, and second, it ascertains the presumption of conformity in four situations:

> '(a) comply with the description given by the seller and possess the qualities of the goods which the seller has held out to the consumer as a sample or model;
>
> (b) are fit for any particular purpose for which the consumer requires them and which he made known to the seller at the time of conclusion of the contract and which the seller has accepted;

234 European Consumer Law Group 1998, p. 92.

235 Howells & Weatherill 2005, p. 154.

236 See Marco Loos, 'Service contracts', January 2010, p. 1, available at: <http://papers.ssrn.com/sol3/papers.cfm?abstract_id=1542506>, last accessed on 27 July 2016.

237 See also Twigg-Flesner 2003b, p. 8; Atiyah *et al.* 2005, p. 299.

(c) are fit for the purposes for which goods of the same type are normally used;

(d) show the quality and performance which are normal in goods of the same type and which the consumer can reasonably expect, given the nature of the goods and taking into account any public statements on the specific characteristics of the goods made about them by the seller, the producer or his representative, particularly in advertising or on labelling.'[238]

Although it is a highly theoretical remark, it must be noted that the four situations enumerated above do not represent conditions of contractual conformity, but are rather presumptions of such conformity.[239] Their role is to support the seller's position before a court, as the burden of proof rests with the consumer who must, in some cases, prove non-conformity and thus rebut the presumption.[240]

Another feature worth mentioning is that Article 2 operates with the standard of reasonableness, mostly visible in paragraphs (3) and (4). The liability of the seller for non-conformity will undoubtedly depend on whether the consumer was aware or could have been aware as any reasonable person of the non-conformity at the moment of the conclusion of the contract. Hondius and Schelhaas mention that this refers to the situation when anyone can see the defect.[241] Paragraph (4) shields the seller from being bound by public statements in the cases when he was not aware of such statements on specific characteristics of the goods in advertising or on labelling.

Lastly, Article 2 is significant because it integrates a so-called IKEA clause in paragraph (5).[242] The Article establishes lack of conformity in cases when the consumer incorrectly installs goods using installation instructions provided by the seller.

(ii) Rights of the Consumer (Article 3)

Perhaps the most important provision in the Directive, Article 3 deals with the remedies available to the consumer for lack of conformity with the contract. While paragraph (1) establishes the liability of the seller as starting from the moment of delivery, the remaining provisions (paragraphs (2)-(6)) lay out a two-stage approach of solving non-conformity.

Looking at the seller's liability, it is striking that the European legislator chose to hold the seller liable in spite of situations where non-conformity stems from the production process. Read together with the right of redress enshrined in Article 4, this provision seems to be rather detrimental to the interests of sellers who are part of a complex supply chain. To make matters even more complicated, the actions available to the seller to bring a claim against the producer are further left to the discretion of national law. However, the right of the seller to a remedy under Article

238 Article 2(2) of the Consumer Sales Directive.

239 Staudenmayer 2000, p. 551. Not all Member States have transposed this as such, for instance Belgium made the requirements under Article 2 of the Directive conditions for conformity.

240 Recital 8 of the Preamble to the Consumer Sales Directive.

241 Hondius & t Schelhaas 2001, p. 333.

242 Staudenmayer 2000, p. 553; Twigg-Flesner 2001, p. 122.

4 may be interpreted as being absolute,[243] as the seller would only be able to renounce this right if he takes an active step in this respect, since adding an exclusion clause in his general terms might not suffice.[244]

Turning to the remedies consumers have access to, it must be pointed out that two categories of remedies are given: primary (repair and replacement) and secondary (price reduction and rescission). According to Article 3(3), the consumer must first give the seller another chance to perform by asking the goods to be remedied free of charge by either repair or replacement,[245] unless this is impossible or disproportionate.[246] A remedy shall be deemed disproportionate if it imposes unreasonable costs in comparison with 'the alternative remedy'. The wording of Article 3(3) second sentence thus shows that this test will only be applied between the two primary remedies in relation to one another.[247] Secondly, the consumer can either have the price reduced or the contract rescinded in the cases mentioned in Article 5(3), namely if '[...] the consumer is entitled to neither repair nor replacement, or if the seller has not completed the remedy within a reasonable time, or if the seller has not completed the remedy without significant inconvenience to the consumer.' The Directive does not specify what is meant with the first situation, namely the cases in which the consumer may not be entitled to repair or

243 Bradgate & Twigg-Flesner 2002, p. 359.

244 Micklitz 1999, p. 487.

245 Luzak 2015, p. 691.

246 Twigg-Flesner 2003a, p. 13; see also Recital 10 of the Preamble to the Consumer Sales Directive.

247 Recital 11 establishes disproportionality in an objective fashion. Moreover, even if only one remedy is possible, and thus the proportionality test cannot apply as such, the seller cannot deny this possible remedy, as stated in *Weber*: '[a]lthough the second subparagraph of Article 3(3) of the Directive consequently precludes national legislation from granting the seller the right to refuse the only possible remedy because of its absolute lack of proportionality, that article nevertheless allows effective protection of the legitimate financial interests of the seller, which is additional, as stated in paragraph 58 of the present judgment, to the protection provided for in Articles 4 and 5 of the Directive; *Gebr. Weber GmbH v Jürgen Wittmer* C-87/09 *Ingrid Putz v Medianess Electronics GmbH*, para. 73. However, if replacement is the only possible remedy, and it involves disproportionate costs - where disproportion is calculated objectively - then the buyer might have to support a part of these costs. In this situation, if paying the costs of replacement in part leads to an inconvenience to the consumer, then he can ask the seller for one of the second tier remedies: termination or price reduction: 'It must be observed in that regard that, concerning in particular the specific situation referred to by the referring court, in which replacement of the defective goods, as the only possible remedy, involves disproportionate costs because of the need to remove the goods not in conformity from where they were installed and to install the replacement goods, Article 3(3) of the Directive does not preclude the consumer's right to reimbursement of the cost of removing the defective goods and installing the replacement goods from being limited, where necessary, to an amount proportionate to the value the goods would have if there were no lack of conformity and the significance of the lack of conformity. Such limitation leaves intact the consumer's right to seek replacement of goods not in conformity', *Gebr. Weber GmbH v Jürgen Wittmer* C-87/09 *Ingrid Putz v Medianess Electronics GmbH*, para. 74.

replacement.[248] The seller may choose to offer price reduction or termination in place of or together with repair or replacement, but because of the two-step remedy system he cannot impose the offered secondary remedies before the legal requirements therefore are satisfied.

It must be born in mind that a common element is mentioned in both paragraph (2) and (3) - the goods must be brought into conformity by way of repair or replacement, free of charge. As it was pointed out in *Quelle*, not charging the consumer for available remedies is 'an essential element of the protection afforded to consumers by the Directive',[249] since in the absence of such protection consumers might be deterred from exercising their rights. *Quelle* is one of the cases where the CJEU had the possibility to interpret the remedies set forth in Article 3 (compensation for the replaced good), and this discussion was continued in joined cases *Gebr. Weber GmbH* and *Ingrid Putz* (refusal of replacement and replacement costs).[250] Each of these cases is discussed in what follows.

In *Quelle*, the Court had to decide whether Article 3 of the Directive can be interpreted as allowing national legislation to impose compensation on the buyer for using a faulty good until the seller would replace that good. In August 2002, Ms Brüning ordered a 'stove set' from Quelle, and only noticed the appliance's lack of conformity in early 2004. Quelle subsequently replaced the appliance, as repair was not possible, but also charged Ms Brüning EUR 69.97 representing the enrichment the buyer had gained from using the initial product.[251] To rule on this issue, the CJEU looked at Article 3 as a whole and acknowledging the seller's liability for non-conformity, clarified the rights to which the consumer is entitled:

> 'Article 3(2) of the Directive lists the rights which the consumer may rely on against the seller in cases where the goods delivered are not in conformity. Initially, the consumer has the right to require the goods to be brought into conformity. If that is not possible, he may subsequently require a reduction in the price or rescission of the contract.'[252]

Moreover, the Court established that on the grounds of the *travaux préparatoires*, it was the intention of the European legislature to make repair or replacement available to the consumer without any significant inconvenience. It is for this reason the Court came to the conclusion that the availability of such remedies 'free of charge' is an essential element of the Directive's protection regime. In spite of the very intuitive rationale used by the CJEU in the *Quelle* judgment, it has been argued in academic literature that the Court is in pursuit of a so-called effectiveness trend.[253] This is to say that consumer directives are interpreted by the CJEU in a way

248 The situation when repair or replacement is impossible certainly falls under this category in any case, but it is for the Court of Justice to determine in future cases whether the scope of this sub-paragraph extends beyond impossibility.

249 Case C-404/06, *Quelle AG v Bundesverband der Verbraucherzentralen und Verbraucherverbände* [2008] ECR I-2685, para. 33; see also Rott 2009, p. 172; Heiderhoff 2011, p. 112.

250 *Gebr. Weber GmbH v Jürgen Wittmer.*

251 *Quelle AG v Bundesverband der Verbraucherzentralen und Verbraucherverbände*, paras. 12-14.

252 *Ibid.*, para. 27.

253 Mak 2011c, p. 33.

which gradually eliminates all costs for consumers in the light of one overarching argument: consumers would be dissuaded from enforcing their rights if there is an effort attached to this enforcement.

The same can be noticed in *Gebr. Weber GmbH*, a case focusing on a contract of sale concluded between Mr. Wittmer and Mr. Weber for polished tiles priced at EUR 1,382.87. In the course of installing the tiles, Mr. Wittmer noticed a visible fault in the products, namely a shading of the tiles. After having unsuccessfully complained to Mr. Weber, the buyer appointed an expert who determined the shading was a result of micro-brush-marks that could not be removed. For Mr. Wittmer, this meant the only remedy available was the replacement of the tiles, valued by the expert at EUR 5,830.57. After the *Landgericht Kassel* (Regional Court, Kassel) granted a reduction in price consisting of EUR 273.10, on appeal Mr. Wittmer was granted by the *Oberlandesgericht Frankfurt* (Higher Regional Court, Frankfurt) the delivery of a new set of tiles free of defects and the payment of EUR 2,122.37 as costs deriving from the replacement.

In *Ingrid Putz*, an Internet sales contract over a dishwasher was considered. Ms. Putz had ordered a new dishwasher from Medianess Electronics, in the value of EUR 367 to which EUR 9.52 were added as payment-on-delivery costs. Shortly after the dishwasher was installed, Ms. Putz noticed a defect, which could not have arisen out of the installation of the device. After the seller agreed to replace the dishwasher, Ms. Putz also demanded the removal of the defective machine and the installation of a new one. Since Medianess Electronics refused to cover the two additional costs, Ms. Putz rescinded the contract.[254] Proceedings were brought before the *Amtsgericht Schorndorf* (Local Court, Schorndorf) for reimbursement of the price paid.[255] The Local Court stayed proceedings and asked the CJEU to answer the question whether under Article 3 of the Directive it is the seller who must bear the costs corresponding to the replacement of goods.

Given the close connection of the two cases (*Gebr. Weber GmbH* and *Putz*), the Court of Justice decided in favour of their joinder, in order to tackle the issue of whether it is the obligation of the seller to pay any costs affiliated not only with the removal of goods not in conformity with the contract, but also with the subsequent instalment of replacement goods. To answer this question, the CJEU noted that: 'In the first place, the consumer has the right to require the goods to be brought into conformity. If that is not possible, he may subsequently seek a reduction in the price or rescission of the contract.'[256] As Advocate General Mazák highlighted, performance-oriented remedies are preferred, because the '*synallagma*' is in this way restored and the consumer can derive the benefit of his original intention under the contract, namely to enjoy its performance.[257]

254 *Gebr. Weber GmbH v Jürgen Wittmer*, paras. 24-28.

255 It must be noted at this point that German law requires the buyer to grant the seller an effective period of time for subsequent performance, therefore conditioning the validity of rescission; see §§ 433-439 BGB.

256 *Gebr. Weber GmbH v Jürgen Wittmer*, para. 44.

257 Opinion of Advocate General Mazák, Case C-65/09, *Gebr. Weber GmbH v Jürgen Wittmer*, para. 47.

In addition, the Court noted that repair and replacement are two methods of bringing goods in conformity that strive for the same level of consumer protection.[258] As a reference, the analysis was centered on comparing a legal transaction characterised by the non-conformity of the delivered good, with a situation where the consumer actually receives what he has contracted for. Had the seller delivered a good free of defects, the consumer would only have to bear the cost of installation once. However, if the good is not in conformity with the contract, other costs arise, namely for the removal of the defective good, and for a second installation.[259] The Court thus argued that if it were for the buyer to support any incidental costs, it would be contrary to Article 3(2) and (3). Moreover, it also stated that free of charge is to be associated with costs of postage, labour and materials. The Court also noted in *Quelle* that this list is rather illustrative rather than exhaustive, which is to say it could also include costs arising out of the removal of defective goods and the installation of new ones. Therefore, in connection to the *Ingrid Putz* referral question, the CJEU made it clear these costs are to be borne by the seller, as long as the buyer had installed the machine in good faith.[260]

Turning back to *Gebr. Weber GmbH,* the main issue is trying to determine whether Article 3 deals with absolute or relative proportionality between the costs of replacement and the other available remedies. Looking at the wording of the Article, but also at recital 11, the Court said that the European legislator had intended to allow the seller to turn down repair or replacement in the cases when there remedies would be relatively disproportionate.[261] However, if replacement is the only remedy available to bring the goods in conformity, then even in the case of absolute disproportionality the seller must meet the buyer's request for replacement.[262] Still, the Court held in parallel that in the latter case, Article 3(3) must not be interpreted as precluding national legislation from limiting the consumer's right to reimbursement of prices paid for the removal and reinstallation of goods.[263] The resulting argumentation was based on a fair balance of the interests of the parties. On the one hand, the consumer must be put in a position he would be in if the contract had been concluded, but on the other hand, the seller must not be charged with an excessive amount for removal and reinstallation of new goods.

After *Quelle* and *Gebr. Weber GmbH* and *Ingrid Putz,* there is one mention that must still be made referring to the remaining remedy of rescinding the contract. Rescission is also addressed in Article 3(5) as an alternative to price reduction, in three situations: (a) if the consumer is not entitled to repair or replacement; (b) if the seller had a reasonable time and still did not complete the remedy; and (c) if repair

258 *Gebr. Weber GmbH v Jürgen Wittmer,* para. 51.

259 *Ibid.,* para. 47.

260 *Ibid.,* para. 60.

261 *Ibid.,* para. 71.

262 Except for the situation when this would constitute a significant inconvenience for the consumer, which opens for him the possibility to inkove a secondary remedy.

263 *Gebr. Weber GmbH v Jürgen Wittmer,* para. 74. It must also be noted that when the consumer needs to bear part of the installation costs, this constitutes significant inconvenience to the consumer, who might instead chose to claim termination or price reduction.

or replacement bring about a degree of significant inconvenience to the consumer. Moreover, according to Article 3(6), the consumer cannot rescind the contract if the lack of conformity is minor.[264] The Directive is silent on what can be considered as a minor lack of conformity, but this is generally interpreted to represent 'a lack of conformity of slight importance'.[265] Indeed, inspiration can be drawn from the criteria embedded in Article 2(2), which clearly explains that conformity is to be regarded in terms of fitness for purpose, and compliance with the description and qualities of the good.[266]

It has been argued that the rights of the consumer under this Article, reflected in the set of remedies offered to him in the two-tier system, are rather limited. The main remedy left out from the ambit of Article 3 is the granting of damages. In this situation, it is said that for the coverage of consequential loss, the consumer must nevertheless turn towards national sales law or tort law.[267] What is more, the Directive is silent on whether goods may be rejected, and what connection this would have to the two-tier remedies.[268]

(iii) Time Limits (Article 5)

Article 5 of the Directive establishes that the seller is liable for the lack of conformity that becomes visible within two years calculated from the moment of the delivery of the goods. The time of delivery is also the moment when a mandatory limitation period commences. This two-year limitation is designed to align national legislation that might otherwise impose different prescriptions for the remedies offered to the consumer in the light of this Directive.

Article 5(2) establishes that Member States may choose whether to impose a requirement according to which the consumer must make a notification about the lack of conformity to the seller within two months since the lack of conformity was detected. This approach has been characterised as 'cautious' in the light of the Directive's controversial drafting history. While the initial proposal included a cut-off rule, the final text transformed the notification obligation into an option Member States could individually choose to implement.[269]

What is more, paragraph 3 operates with a presumption regarding the lack of conformity: any such lack that becomes visible within six months from the moment of delivery is presumed to have existed at the time of delivery. Two exceptions to this presumption are further envisaged: firstly, no lack of conformity will be presumed if the nature of the goods rejects such a presumption; and secondly, the very lack of conformity might be of a nature that it cannot be presumed to have existed at the moment of delivery. This presumption, literally taken over in Article

264 To compare, the CISG uses the notion of fundamental breach, see Article 49(1) CISG.
265 Bianca & Grundmann 2002, p. 202.
266 These requirements are similar to the DCFR, see Article IV. A. - 2:301-302 DCFR.
267 Bianca & Grundmann 2002.
268 *Ibid.*, p. 177; Twigg-Flesner 2009, p. 169.
269 Jeloschek 2006, p. 157-160.

IV.A.-2:308 DCFR,[270] is said to place the burden of proof on the seller, who needs to prove lack of conformity not only by 'casting doubt as to whether the non-conformity existed at the moment when risk passed, but is required to positively prove that such non-conformity did not exist at that time.'[271] This is a relevant reversal of the burden of proof which national legislation normally sets on the shoulders of the buyer.[272]

(iv) Guarantees (Article 6).

Article 1(2)(e) defines the concept of guarantees as meaning:

> '[...] any undertaking by a seller or producer to the consumer, given without extra charge, to reimburse the price paid or to replace, repair or handle consumer goods in any way if they do not meet the specifications set out in the guarantee statement or in the relevant advertising [...]'.

Even though the Directive uses both legal and commercial guarantees, the reference in Article 1(2)(e) only refers to the latter category. The Directive does not as such use the terms 'legal' and 'commercial' guarantees, which may make this distinction prone to confusion. In the Green Paper, commercial guarantees were referred to as 'contractual guarantees';[273] however the Directive did not integrate this wording. Interestingly enough, some authors indicate that the reason why the Directive does not explicitly mention commercial guarantees is because calling a guarantee 'commercial' would have been confusing in some jurisdictions.[274]

Legal guarantees stem from the rights conferred upon the consumer in Article 3, and they are to be implemented and interpreted in accordance with the goals envisaged by the Directive itself.[275] Commercial guarantees reflect the independent will of the seller to promise certain characteristics in advertising statements or during the sale, but also the creation of rights, should these characteristics lack.[276] In other words, the seller consents to be bound by the advertising of certain characteristics of the good sold.[277] This means commercial guarantees will often exceed legal guarantees, for reasons including competitiveness stimulation or marketing strategies.[278] Moreover, the guarantee reflects the level of confidence the guarantor has in the products he offers.[279]

270 Beale/Herre/Huet/Schlechtriem/Storme/Swann/Varul/Veneziano/Zoll, Notes under II, no. 7 to Article IV.A.-2:308 DCFR, p. 1314.
271 Marco Loos, Sales Law in the DCFR, Centre for the Study of European Contract Law, Working Paper Series No. 2010/04, p. 18.
272 Janssen 2005, p. 13.
273 COM(93) 509 final, p. 105.
274 Bianca & Grundmann 2002.
275 Van Zelst 2008, p. 186.
276 Janssen 2005; see also PEL/Hondius/Heutger/Jeloschek/Sivesand/Wiewiorowska, *Sales*, Chapter 6, p. 358.
277 PEL/Hondius/Heutger/Jeloschek/Sivesand/Wiewiorowska, *Sales*, Chapter 6, p. 362.
278 Bianca & Grundmann 2002, p. 221-222.
279 Wiewiórowska-Domagalska 2013, p. 6.

In practice, such guarantees will not necessarily be fully included in the general terms and conditions applicable to the transaction, but are handed over to the consumer in separate documents, or printed on the back of the invoice. When the seller makes use of various leaflets and other advertising materials, he will be legally bound by the specifications therein, which will be regarded as complementary to the guarantee statement.[280] It must be borne in mind that the types of commercial guarantees referred to in Article 6 are guarantees offered free of charge. Apart from this category, there can also be insurance-like guarantees that consumers are charged extra for. However, if paid guarantees restrict the rights offered to consumers under the Directive, this becomes problematic. The Apple Care debate is a good example of this problem.[281]After Viviane Reding's efforts to raise awareness amongst Member States over Apple's one-year warranty (another term for guarantee) advertisements in Europe[282] and a EUR 900,000 fine from the Italian Competition Authority for unfair commercial practices,[283]Apple amended its policy and started offering three different warranties: first, there is the statutory warranty, associated with EU consumer law, provided at no additional cost, with a claim period of two years from the date of delivery; second, the Apple warranty, or the so-called commercial warranty, again provided at no additional cost, with a claim period of one year from the date of purchase; third, the AppleCare Protection Plan, an additional commercial warranty offered as a product for additional costs, with a claim period ranging from two to three years.[284]

Problems start to arise when considering electronic commerce. Article 6(3) states that the consumer can request the guarantee to be 'made available in writing or feature in another durable medium available and accessible to him'. The durable medium condition discussed earlier is of particular interest.[285] The reason why it is worth looking into this issue is two-fold: firstly, once again no definition of durable medium is provided by the text of the Directive, leaving its interpretation open to inspiration directed from other sectors of consumer law with more stringent levels of protection;[286] secondly, this condition could be fulfilled by placing the guarantee statement at the disposal of the consumer on an electronic environment (e.g. a website). According to Article 6, the guarantee is made available at the request of

280 Bianca & Grundmann 2002, p. 224.

281 It should be noted that common law gives a double meaning to the term 'warranty': first, it can indicate a guarantee of the like included in the Consumer Sales Directive; second, it can indicate a contractual term the breach of which will entitle the innocent party to claim damages but that will not lead to the termination of the contract.

282 Aoife White, 'Apple Warranty Ads Should Be Examined in EU, Reding Says', 1 October 2012, available at: <www.bloomberg.com/news/2012-10-01/apple-warranty-ads-should-be-examined-by-eu-states-reding-says.html>, last accessed on 27 July 2016.

283 Italian Competition Authority, '*Garanzia di conformitàdelvenditore: antitrust sanzionailgruppo Apple per complessivi 900 mila Euro*', press release, 27 December 2011, available at: <www.agcm.it/stampa/news/5829-sanzioni-per-complessivi-900mila-euro-al-gruppo-apple-per-pratiche-commerciali-scorrette.html>, last accessed on 27 July 2016.

284 More details regarding the Apple statutory guarantee available on the Apple website: <www.apple.com/uk/legal/statutory-warranty/>, last accessed on 27 July 2016.

285 See Chapter 2, p. 79.

286 *Ibid.*

the consumer. If the consumer does not request this document, he is later put in the position of having to find proof of his guarantee in advertising materials.[287]

An additional point must be addressed when discussing commercial guarantees. While in the case of conformity the Directive identifies the seller to be liable, when it comes to guarantees, the language used refers to 'offerors' and Article 1(2) includes both producers and sellers in this category. A guarantee can thus be either offered by the producer, by any other actor in the distribution chain, or by both. This can be viewed to have both positive and negative aspects. On the negative side, it creates confusion. Commercial guarantees become an exceptional circumstance in which the Directive, otherwise solely targeting seller liability, touches upon an eventual liability of producers. Subsequently, this may lead to confusion amongst consumers, who will most likely not make a difference between conformity and liability, sellers and producers. Still, on the positive side, the availability of options might not be so detrimental to consumers after all. As consumers will seldom focus on liability, they will try to uphold their rights under the guarantee.[288] All in all, as complex as it might be, the interaction and potential overlap between the legal and commercial guarantees remains a theoretical debate. As reflected in the EU Consumer Law Compendium, national courts very rarely deal with issues relating to the interpretation of national legislation transposing Article 6.[289] To date, the Court of Justice has not given any decision relating to this article.

5.2. *What Standard of Harmonisation is Set by the European Legislator?*

Together with Article 1 dealing with the scope of the Directive, this provision very clearly reflects that the Consumer Sales Directive is an instrument promoting minimum harmonisation, adopted on the basis of Article 114 TFEU (ex Article 95 TEC).[290] On a policy note, recital five of the preamble mentions that a common set of minimum rules available throughout Members State legislation will enhance consumer confidence and thus lead to the increase in cross-border trade.

The scope of harmonisation was briefly touched upon in *Quelle*, where the Court acknowledged that even though the protection provided by the Directive is minimal and Member States may adopt more stringent national measures, 'they may not undermine the guarantees laid down by the Community legislature'.[291] This rationale was once again used by the Court in *Gebr. Weber GmbH*.[292] At the time when the Green Paper was drafted in 1993, minimum harmonisation was seen by the Commission as a solution to the main issue behind the need for new rules on

287 Bianca & Grundmann 2002, p. 225.

288 Wiewiórowska-Domagalska 2013, p. 17.

289 *Oberlandesgericht Hamm (DE)*, 12 May 2009, 28 U 42/09; *Oberlandesgericht Naumburg (DE)*, 07 December 2005, 6 U 24/05; *Rb. Eupen (BE)*, 21 June 2010; *Curtea Constituţională (RO)*, 12 July 2011, 2858D/2010.

290 Consumer Sales Directive preamble, recital 1; see also Article 8(2) of the Directive.

291 *Quelle AG v Bundesverband der VerbraucherzentralenundVerbraucherverbände*, para. 36.

292 *Gebr. Weber GmbH v Jürgen Wittmer*, para. 60.

consumer sales and associated guarantees - diversity and imprecision. On a practical level, consumers used to have great difficulties in exchanging or repairing products purchased abroad.[293] On a policy level, even though Member States shared some of the legal rationales, conditions and rules shaping national regimes of liability for defective goods, considerable differences still remained.[294] It is in this framework that the Commission identified a broader goal, namely securing the 'free movement' of consumers as purchasers of goods.[295]

Going back to the manner in which the Commission deemed it fit to approach this issue, two paths were suggested: the private international law solution and the harmonisation solution. Using private international law to overcome problems arising out of the sale of defective products might better the position of individual consumers on a case by case basis, but legal divergence would still linger and eventually create disproportionate results amongst buyers. Harmonisation, as the preferred solution, was supposed to overcome any discriminatory treatment; and since general harmonisation was counted out at the offset because of the cumbersome efforts it would entail, the only possibility left was sector-specific harmonisation, which the Commission deemed to be sufficient for the objectives pursued, without clashing with the principle of subsidiarity.[296]

The line of argumentation offered by the Commission in the Green Paper is rather well-built - there was a real issue arising out of the difficulties consumers encountered when shopping abroad. Minimum harmonisation was chosen to fast-track the adoption of measures promoting the interests of these consumers, as it sets 'the floor below which national legislation cannot fall'.[297] While the standard of minimum harmonisation established by the European legislator for the Consumer Sales Directive is very clear, what remains to be resolved is whether in the light of various trends in European private law moving towards maximum harmonisation, the Directive is interpreted beyond its characteristics. For this purpose, several cases that were mentioned earlier are revisited in what follows. A total of ten cases touching upon the Consumer Sales Directive have been registered with the Court of Justice according to the database of the Court. Out of those, three are proceedings concerning failures by Member States (Belgium, France and Luxembourg) to implement the Directive,[298] while two other judgments ruled out the application of specific Consumer Sales Directive provisions.[299] Thus the remaining five cases constitute landmark judgments for the interpretation of rules on consumer sales and associated guarantees: *Quelle*, the joint cases *Gebr. Weber GmbH* and *Ingrid Putz,*

293 Eurobarometer No. 35, July 1991.
294 COM(93) 509 final, p. 16.
295 *Ibid.*, p. 9.
296 *Ibid.*, p. 83.
297 Barnard 2007, p. 600.
298 Case C-310/03, *Commission of the European Communities v Grand Duchy of Luxemburg* [2004] ECR I-01969; Case C-312/03, *Commission of the European Communities v Kingdom of Belgium* [2004] ECR I-01975; Case C-311/03, *Commission of the European Communities v France.*
299 Case C-318/08, *Filomena Califano v Wind SpA* [2010] ECR I-02213; Case C-320/08, *Multiservice Srl v Telecom Italia SpA* [2010] ECR I-02213.

Soledad Duarte Hueros, and the most recent judgment, *Froukje Faber*.[300] Each of these cases are now be discussed in an attempt to understand the impact of each judicial outcome on the Directive's overall standard of harmonisation.

As noted above, *Quelle* underlined a tendency of the Court to interpret the wording of the Directive in such a manner that excludes any potential risk burdening the consumer. Once again, the key issue revolved around whether sellers are entitled to demand compensation-for-use from consumers when replacing sold goods. The Court specifically excluded the interpretation of the German government that claimed Recital 15 of the preamble allows national law to legislate compensation for use.[301] The Court put emphasis on the second sentence of the recital, which seems to imply that the compensation referred to only covers situations arising out of contractual termination.[302] Advocate General Trstenjak's analysis followed the same line of argumentation.[303]

To start with, one thing is very clear - the Directive is completely silent on the effects of replacement. While Article 3(3) empowers the consumer to ask for repair or replacement 'free of charge', the actual wording of the Directive does not go any further to indicate a clear perspective on what exact costs qualify under this rule. Indeed, Article 3(4) mentions some examples in that respect. As indicated by AG Trstenjak and the Court itself, the examples given by the Directive do not make up an exhaustive list,[304] and 'free of charge' should cover any costs burdening the consumer to an extent where he would not have effective access to his rights under the Directive. However, the main argument used to exclude replacement from the meaning of recital 15 is its teleological interpretation. According to a very circular argumentation made by both the AG and the Court, recital 15 cannot cover replacement, since Article 3(3) is supposed 'to provide effective protection to consumers'. In her written opinion, the AG developed this line of reasoning to show that there might be cases where sellers could make replacement conditional on the payment of compensation, to the detriment of consumers effectively enjoying their rights. The AG indicates this to be 'practice', but fails to bring any proof in this respect and does not elaborate on whatever ambit or trend such practice might have in specific trade sectors. Assuming *arguendo* this is indeed a deterrent for consumers *vis-à-vis* their right to replacement, it can always be claimed that consumers can deem such replacement to cause inconvenience in the meaning of Article 3(5) and proceed to terminate the contract according to the same provision.

Going back to recital 15, in spite of not having binding nature, it serves to help establish the purpose and object of the Directive. Two important terms have been, however, overlooked in the Court's analysis. The first sentence of the recital

300 Case C-32/12, *Soledad Duarte Hueros v Autociba SA, Automóviles Citroën España SA* [2013]; see also Jansen 2014, p. 975; Case C-497/13, *Froukje Faber v Autobedrijf Hazet Ochten BV* [2015].

301 *Quelle AG v Bundesverband der VerbraucherzentralenundVerbraucherverbände*, para. 25.

302 *Ibid.*, paras. 38-39.

303 Opinion of Advocate General Trstenjak, Case C-404/06, *Quelle AG v Bundesverband der VerbraucherzentralenundVerbraucherverbände*.

304 *Ibid.*, para. 46; *Quelle AG v Bundesverband der VerbraucherzentralenundVerbraucherverbände*, para. 31.

mentions that '*any* reimbursement' can be subject to reduction. It is very clear from the formulation of the sentence that no limitation to rescission is placed on the reimbursement referred to therein. For this reason, the first sentence can be interpreted to touch upon any remedy made available by the Consumer Sales Directive that involves reimbursements. Repairing goods is thus excluded, because of the very nature of the actions it involves. Nevertheless, replacement and price reduction can imply repayment: in the first situation, the Directive does not provide a definition for replacement, so that it is feasible to argue that replacement could also cover the re-delivery of goods which might not be identical or have an identical price. In the second case, price reduction refers to the situation where repayment is due to the consumer, to compensate for a lower value of the good. It is true that it would be difficult to argue compensation for use could apply to price reduction. Nevertheless, as the remedies conferred by the Directive recognise multiple situations in which reimbursement could take place, it cannot be claimed that recital 15 exclusively refers to termination. Rather, it can be said that recital 15 second sentence is the procedural step with regards to reimbursement occurring as an effect of termination. By virtue of the different approaches taken by European jurisdictions on the matter of termination, it can, among others, be seen that termination is not always given retroactive effect.[305] What is more, common law differs considerably from continental traditions on this point. For instance, English law makes use of non-contractual rules (e.g. the law of restitution) to re-establish the initial positions of the parties.[306]

It can be claimed it is the intricate nature of termination that is acknowledged in recital 15 and for which 'detailed arrangements', as the second sentence reads, are necessary. Looking at the outcome of *Quelle*, it can be concluded that it strengthened the role of the Directive, by enhancing the high level of consumer protection against any other economic consideration arising out of the contractual relationship.[307]

Two other judgments having to do with the replacement of goods were joint cases *Gebr. Weber GmbH* and *Putz*. Here, as noted previously,[308] the main question was whether under the provisions of the Consumer Sales Directive, the seller is obliged to replace goods which are not in conformity with the contract by removing the faulty ones and installing new, defect-free goods. To illustrate what such actions would entail, the *Weber* case can serve as an example, where alongside the price of new tiles under the initial contract, worth EUR 1,382.27 for approximately 45 m^2, additional costs of EUR 5,830.57 for the removal of the defective tiles and a new subsequent installation would be added. As Johnston and Unberath have very well pointed out, this represents an increase of 522 per cent in the value of the initial contract.[309] In spite of the excessive difference, the Court answered this question in

305 Articles 1183, 1184 French Civil Code and Belgian Civil Code recognise the retroactive nature of termination; Article 6:271 Dutch Civil Code, § 346 German Civil Code do not recognise termination to be retroactive but do acknowledge an inherent obligation of restitution.

306 Dannemann 2009, p. 60.

307 *Quelle AG v Bundesverband der VerbraucherzentralenundVerbraucherverbände*, para. 36.

308 See Chapter 2, p. 100.

309 Johnston & Unberath 2012, p. 796.

the affirmative and stated that such obligation exists under consumer law regardless of whether the seller was the one who had to perform the installation under the sales contract or not. In claiming so, the Court relied on several key arguments: first, the consumer must not be held to pay the price of installation twice as this standard would not meet the level of consumer protection imposed by the Directive;[310] second, the seller's interests are protected by the structure of remedies conferred in Article 3, but also by his right to redress affirmed in Article 4.[311]

However, this line of argumentation was not fully supported by AG Mazák, who very neatly illustrated how the Directive must deliver its consumer protection goals with due regard to the legitimate interests of the other party to the contract: '[…] the scheme of remedies under the directive may not simply favour either the consumer or the seller, but must instead seek to strike a fair balance between their respective interests.'[312] The AG also disagreed with the exclusive use of the literal method of interpretation in determining whether the verb 'to replace' would actually refer to an obligation to take any measure necessary for the substitution of the goods. In his view, such interpretation would be neither conclusive nor sufficient. For this reason, AG Mazák turned to a contextual reading of Article 3. His main finding, considerably divergent from the Court's key arguments, is that seller's liability must be envisaged under the original contract. In this vein, the only way in which a seller who did not bare the initial obligation of installing the goods could be held liable to remove the defective goods and reinstall defect-free goods, would be by means of damages; and since damages are not conferred by the Directive as a remedy to the consumer, this liability exceeds the Directive's protection.[313]

Unfortunately, the Court did not find inspiration in AG Mazák's view, but rather followed its own rationale in *Quelle* to achieve the same result: a more generous interpretation of consumer rights, to the detriment of the seller.. The Court ultimately relied on the insufficient literal interpretation of the term 'replacement' to surprisingly include not only the removal of the defective goods, but also the subsequent reinstallation of conforming goods in the meaning of the term. Moreover, the judgment was also criticised for the Court's tendency to formulate so-called 'self-evident' arguments:[314] '[…] in a situation where neither party to the contract is at fault, it is justified to make the seller bear the cost of removing the goods not in conformity and installing the replacement goods, since those additional costs, first, would have been avoided if the seller had at the outset correctly performed his contractual obligations and, second, are now necessary to bring the goods into conformity'.[315]

Moving to *Duarte Hueros*, the case facts follow the misfortune of Ms. Duarte Hueros, a Spanish national who purchased a car with a sliding roof from Autociba

310 *Gebr. Weber GmbH v Jürgen Wittmer*, para. 47.
311 *Ibid.*, para. 58.
312 Opinion of Advocate General Mazák, *Gebr. Weber GMBH v Jürgen Wittmer*, para. 30.
313 *Ibid.*, paras. 58-60.
314 Johnston & Unberath 2012, p. 799.
315 *Gebr. Weber GMBH v Jürgen Wittmer*, para. 57.

in July 2004. Soon after, the buyer returned the vehicle because the roof was not properly isolated and thus it rained inside the car. Several repair attempts were done, but to no avail, so Ms. Duarte Hueros asked for the replacement of the car. Autociba did not want to grant this to their buyer, so they were taken before the *Juzgado de Primera Instancia no 2 of Badajoz* (Court of First Instance, Section No 2, Badajoz). On the basis of Spanish procedural law Ms. Duarte Hueros could not change her claim, and the national judge ascertained that the contract would most probably not be rescinded, as the defect was minor. However, having concerns that Ms. Duarte Hueros would still be entitled to ask for price reduction, the Court of First Instance decided to turn to the Court of Justice. It thus asked the CJEU whether a national court could invoke price reduction out of its own motion, even though the consumer only asked for the rescission of the contract. The Court established that the Directive precludes national legislation which does not allow a national court to invoke an alternative remedy, in this case price reduction *ex officio*.

At the heart of this case, very similarly to many Unfair Contract Terms Directive cases, lie procedural provisions that are supposed to support the effective application of EU law, and in this situation, of the consumer rights granted by Article 3 of the Directive. Since Spanish rules in the Code of Civil Procedure could have hindered this effectiveness, the Court stated that national courts must set those provisions aside. In other words, while the AG mentioned that Article 3 does not include any explicit provisions regarding national courts, if procedural rules do not allow a consumer to change the claim during the proceedings or ask for price reduction in a subsequent claim, because of the effect of *res judicata*, then the national judge needs to take this into account.

Lastly, Article 5 of the Consumer Sales Directive was thoroughly discussed by the Court in *Froukje Faber*. Mrs. Faber had purchased a second hand car from the Autobedrijf Hazet garage on 27 May 2008, and almost three months later, the vehicle caught fire and was completely destroyed. Mrs. Faber only formally complained about the total loss in May 2009, which raised an issue of whether her claim was made in a timely fashion. Moreover, since she had not indicated at the moment of the conclusion of the contract what purpose the vehicle was going to have, there were also doubts as to whether Mrs. Faber was acting in her capacity as consumer. Seven very complex questions were forwarded on the basis of these facts to the Court of Justice, dealing with: (1) whether the national court should investigate *ex officio* whether a party to a dispute is a consumer; (2) especially since not enough information to determine this status is available; (3) and this matter was expressly left open in appeal; (4) whether Article 5(3) of the Consumer Sales Directive relating to the six-month presumption of non-conformity should be seen as equivalent to a rule of public policy; (5) whether Dutch law could specify that the consumer has to present facts and adduce evidence relating to the duty of notifying the seller (in due time) of the lack of conformity; (6) what exactly the consumer must prove in terms of lack of conformity; and (7) whether it matters if the consumer was assisted by a lawyer.

Among others, the Court determined that indeed, the national court must establish whether a party is a consumer or not (and if the Directive is applicable) even if that party had not relied on the consumer status. This was determined also in the light of the answer to the fourth question, as the CJEU did give Article 5(3) of the Directive a standing equivalent to Dutch national public policy rules. Moreover, the Court took notice of the option taken by the Netherlands to require a notification of the lack of conformity in good time, the lack of which would deprive the consumer of its reliance on the lack of conformity. However, the Court stated that in order for the consumer to be able to exercise his rights, the notification in question would only refer to the existence of the lack of conformity, and that it would further be for the seller to prove that the lack of conformity only occurred after delivery.

5.3. *How was the Directive Transposed by Member States?*

5.3.1. Belgium

The Belgian legislator chose to implement the Consumer Sales Directive by amending the Civil Code.[316] Articles 1649bis-1649octies were introduced as almost literal reflections of the rules embodied in the Directive. It is acknowledged that the Belgian legislator wanted to make use of the Directive's minimum harmonisation orientation, and not deprive the consumer of other more protective remedies.[317]

While Article 1649terties takes over the same criteria used in the Directive to install the European notion of conformity with the contract, Article 1649quinquies mirrors the Directive's hierarchy of remedies.[318]Article 1649quater § 1er reflects the time limits imposed by Article 5 of the Consumer Sales Directive and acknowledges the seller's liability for defects that exist at the moment of delivery and become apparent within two years from that specific moment. What is more, according to the third sentence of § 1, for second hand goods, parties are open to shorten the two-year legal guarantee period, but without going below one year. When the lack of conformity does not become apparent at the end of the two year period, general sales law revives the remedies for hidden defects.[319]

In § 3, the Belgian legislator establishes a prescription period of one year for consumer actions, to start on the day when the consumer has taken notice of the lack of conformity,[320] but which cannot expire before the end of the two-year term in § 1. However, the paragraph goes on to mention that the prescription period shall not expire before the passing of the two-year time limit discussed above. Moreover, according to § 2 of the same article, the seller and the buyer may agree on setting a time during which the consumer must inform the seller about the existence of a lack

316 See comments in the Belgian Senate over the Project-law of 1 September 2004 transposing the Consumer Sales Directive into Belgian law. See also Van Oevelen 2005, p. 29.

317 Stuyck 2010, p. 37.

318 Rutten *et al.* 2009, p. 198.

319 *Ibid.*

320 Article 1649quater reads in § 3: '*L'action du consommateur se prescrit dans un délai d'un an à compter du jour où il a constaté le défaut de conformité, sans que ce délai puisse expirer avant la fin du délai de deux ans, prévu au § 1er.*'

of conformity, which cannot be any shorter than two months, calculated from the day when the consumer discovered the lack of conformity. The Belgian legislator did not impose a notification duty, but left it up to the parties to determine whether they want to agree on the use of such a notification period.

Finally, Article 1649septies § 1 transposes the conditions embedded in Article 6 of the Directive almost word by word. However, one distinction needs to be emphasised: Article 1649bis § 1 did not take over the mention 'given without extra charge' in the definition of 'guarantee'. In doing so, Belgian legislation did not embrace the Directive's distinction between commercial guarantees and after-sale services based on the payment of a price, but rather left it to the actual content of the agreements themselves to determine whether a promise made by the guarantor would fall in the category of guarantees or not.[321]

5.3.2. France

In order to accommodate the requirements of the Consumer Sales Directive, French law adapted its Consumer Code based on Ordinance no 2005-136 from 17 February 2005.[322] The transposition of the Directive has given rise to an extended national debate concerning the legislative choice - amending the Consumer Code or triggering a more in-depth reform of the Civil Code.[323]

Articles L. 211-4, L. 211-5, L. 211-6 and L. 211-8 reflect the obligations enshrined in the Directive's Article 2, namely the establishment of conformity. Just as in Belgian law, conformity as such was dealt with in France through a two-tier approach consisting in the seller's obligation to deliver a good on the one hand, and his obligation to stand liable for hidden defects on the other.[324] By establishing the conformity principle, the Directive is said to impose a so-called 'monist' view on the legal obligations of the seller.[325] However, as it has been observed by the National Consumer Institute, the transposition of the Directive has been made *a minima*, and as such does not exclude from application the action in the guarantee of hidden defects (*l'action en garantie des vices cachés*), reflected in the French Civil Code Articles 1641 and following.[326] The similarities between Directive-based conformity and general French law can be particularly noticed when taking a look at Article 1641. In the light of this provision, the two criteria chosen to delineate hidden defects focus on functionality: (1) the fitness for use and (2) diminution of use.[327]

321 Rutten *et al.* 2009, p. 204.

322 *Ordonnance n° 2005-136 du 17 février 2005 relative à la garantie de la conformité du bien au contrat due par le vendeur au consommateur*, JORF n°41 du 18 février 2005.

323 Patricia Foucher & Françoise Hébert-Wimart, '*La garantie de la conformité du bien au contrat*', Institut National de la Consommation Hebdo no. 1367, 5-11 December 2005.

324 Article 1604 French Civil Code.

325 Valériane König, 'La transposition de la directive européenne du 25 mai 1999 surcertains aspects de la vente et des garanties des biens de consommation en droit français', presentation held at the Franco-German seminar on sales law, University of Panthéon-Assas (Paris II) and Humboldt University Berlin, p. 9.

326 Foucher & Hébert-Wimart 2005, p. I.

327 Cass. Civ. I, 16.6.1993, Bull. civ. I no. 224.

One major criticism brought to the notion of conformity vis-à-vis French law has focused on the fact that since it only deals with qualitative standards of delivered goods, conformity does not cover non-delivered or late delivered goods, and neither does it cover goods delivered in too little of a quantity. For these situations, French law continues to apply general contract law.[328]

The rights of the consumer are governed by Articles L. 211-8, L. 211-9, L. 211-10 and L. 211-11, and reflect Directive Article 3 very closely.

Regarding time limits, Article L. 211-12 mentions that the action resulting from defects of conformity is prescribed after two years from the date of delivery. However, general contract law can protect the consumer even further than this period, as it provides for an action (*l'action résultant des vices rédhibitoires*) to be brought by the buyer within two years after the discovery of the defects.[329] Moreover, French law chose not to transpose the optional notification requirement, on the basis of which the consumer should inform the seller about the defects within two months from its discovery.

Articles L. 211-15 and L. 211-16 deal with commercial guarantees. Disregarding the definitions in Article 1 of the Directive, the French transposition emphasises the elements of commercial guarantees rather than their targeted meaning. For this purpose, it is considered that the commercial guarantee shall meet the requirement of being drafted in writing and presented to the buyer. The written guarantee must detail the content of the guarantee, as well as other aspects such as its territorial application and contact details of the guarantor. Moreover, Article L. 211-15 makes clear reference to Articles 1641-1649 Civil Code in mentioning that the seller remains liable for hidden defects as determined by general sales law.

5.3.3. Germany

Division 8 Title 1 of the German Civil Code served to transpose the Consumer Sales Directive in the German law of obligations. The transposition reflected in part the impetus of the German legislator to reform not only sales law, but also the entire law of obligations.[330] In this light, it was decided that the provisions inserted by § 433ff BGB would not only apply to consumer sales, but also to commercial transactions.[331]

With respect to conformity, Article 2 of the Directive is translated into the BGB by § 434(1) and (2) and § 442. While § 433 establishes the contractual duties of the parties to the contract of sales, § 434(1) sets out the rule according to which a thing is free of material defects if the thing has the agreed quality at the moment of the passing of the risk. The sections go on to mention that if the quality has not been agreed upon, there are two criteria to look at for the determination of eventual defects: '(1) if it is suitable for the use intended under the contract, or (2) if it is suitable for the customary use and its quality is usual in things of the same kind and

328 Foucher & Hébert-Wimart 2005, p. IV.

329 Article 1648 French Civil Code.

330 Rott 2004, p. 240.

331 Rott & Twigg-Flesner 2007, p. 128; Jeloschek 2006, p. 22.

the buyer may expect this quality in view of the type of the thing.' Quality is further defined as to include characteristics drawn from public statements made either by the seller, the producer or any affiliated assistants, with the exception of the cases when the seller was neither aware of such statements nor had a duty to be aware of them. Other exceptions from public statements related to characteristics include the situation when such statements did not affect the buyer's decision of purchasing the thing. The Commission saw these criteria as hierarchical rather than cumulative, as the Directive had intended to make them.[332]

Interestingly, German law specifies in § 434(3) BGB that supplying a different thing, or a lesser amount of the thing is considered a material defect.

Another particular feature of German law is that conformity as such is not the governing concept having to deal with defective performance. In this regard, German law adopted an original approach: As it has been already discussed, § 434 establishes material defects, whereas § 435 talks about legal defects. Legal defects are seen as eventual rights third parties can oppose against the buyer. A clear example is given for the sale of immovables, where a right that does not exist but has been registered in the Land Registry is assimilated to a legal defect. However, the sale of immovables is outside the ambit of the Directive, and so are legal defects. Moreover, § 442 develops the exception in the Directive's Article 2(3), whereby a consumer who is aware of the defects of the things purchased will not be able to avail himself of any lack of conformity. § 442 states that in such cases the buyer will be deprived of his rights, and the buyer is not aware of defects due to gross negligence, it is only if the seller fraudulently hid the defect from the buyer, or gave a guarantee, that the buyer can assert his rights.

One of the most relevant particularities of German law in the transposition of the Consumer Sales Directive can be seen in the hierarchy of remedies available to the consumer. In this case, the main provision dealing with the rights of the consumer found in Directive Article 3 is § 437 BGB; however, a plethora of other provisions comes to complement this rule. Under § 437(1) BGB a consumer can demand cure (repair or replacement as part of the second chance to perform) according to § 439 BGB taken together with § 275 BGB governing impossibility to perform. If the consumer chooses to exercise this right, the seller must then bear all costs associated with the second performance, 'in particular transport, workmen's travel, work and materials costs'.[333]

Subsequently, § 437(2) BGB specifies that the contract can be terminated according to §§ 440, 323 and 326(5) BGB, or the price can be reduced as mentioned in § 441 BGB. Reimbursement of futile expenditure is also included, by virtue of § 284 BGB.

332 European Commission, 'Communication from the Commission to the Council and the European Parliament on the implementation of Directive 1999/44/EC of the European Parliament and of the Council of 25 May 1999 on certain aspects of the sale of consumer goods and associated guarantees including analysis of the case for introducing direct producers' liability', COM(2007) 210 final, p. 5.

333 § 439(2) BGB. The initial transposition allowed the seller to withhold compensation for use; see Rott & Twigg-Flesner 2007, p. 121, 141.

Even though § 437 BGB does not explicitly lay down a hierarchy between the remedies offered to the consumer, and what is more, the third remedy consisting in damages can always be cumulated with either specific performance (repair and replacement) or termination, the rule is interpreted in a restrictive manner. It is thus acknowledged that consumers must set out a period of time for the seller to comply with his contractual obligations before asking for termination. This is what made some academics reflecting on the topic to actually support the view that even if not explicitly, the system of remedies available in German law is nothing more than a reflection of the hierarchy embedded in the Directive.[334]

Still, there have been voices arguing that German rules on consumer remedies for non-conformity do depart from the Directive's format. One opinion mentions that while the Directive allows for termination if a reasonable period of time has been set for repair and replacement, German law allows the consumer to set this very period of time, and when the consumer is not aware of this right, it is questionable whether termination is still possible.[335]

Such view must be rejected based on two arguments: first, § 323 BGB does not make specific reference to a reasonable period of time, but the principle of giving the seller a second chance to perform is also reflected in other provisions, such as § 281 BGB, where it is expressly stated that for damages in lieu of performance to be accessible, the creditor must first set a reasonable period of time. Reasonableness is reiterated in § 430 BGB dealing with the termination of sale, according to which 'Except in the cases set out in section 281 (2) and section 323 (2), it is also not necessary to specify a period of time if the seller has refused to carry out both kinds of cure under section 439 (3) or if the kind of cure that the buyer is entitled to receive has failed or cannot *reasonably* be expected of him (emphasis added).' In the light of these provisions it can be stated that German law mirrors the provisions of the Directive. Secondly, even if *assuming arguendo*, German law does not reflect the Directive in its entirety when it comes to the rights of the consumer and more specifically the hierarchy of remedies, German courts have already acknowledged the need to interpret national rules in the light of their European origin,[336] which should pose no issue for the interpretation of § 323 BGB.

Furthermore, according to § 475(2) BGB, parties cannot agree to lower the two year period calculated from the statutory beginning of limitation (or one year for second-hand movable goods). The general rule on ineffectiveness of termination (§ 218 BGB) applies concomitantly.

Guarantees are covered by §§ 443, 477 and 126b. The only distinction from the wording of the Directive is the fact that German law did not implement paragraph 4 of Article 6, allowing Member States to draft the guarantee in one of more Community languages.[337]

334 Rott 2004, p. 248.
335 Sivesand 2007, p. 147.
336 BGH (DE), 26 November 2008, VIII ZR 200/05.
337 Rott 2004, p. 253.

5.3.4. Ireland

In Ireland, the Consumer Sales Directive has been transposed by means of the Consumer Sales Regulations 2003,[338] coming to supplement the regime already in force governed by the Sale of Goods and Supply of Services Acts 1893 and 1980. Overall, it can be said that Ireland followed the Directive almost literally, which is to say it did not make use of the minimum harmonisation nature of the Directive, but rather addressed the modification of consumer rules in a narrow manner.[339] Also, White draws attention to the chosen form of transposition, as an independent piece of legislation rather than a reform brought to existing law, and motivates this choice on the structure of the Irish private law system with very strong English influences.[340]

Conformity is dealt with in Regulations 5 & 6, and the rights of the consumer are covered by Regulation 7. Even if the latter provision uses exactly the same terminology as the Directive, the remedies available to the consumer are restructured. Whereas repair or replacement are brought together under the ambit of Regulation 7(2)(a) as means of bringing the goods into conformity, there is a subsequent division made by paragraphs 2(b), dealing with price reduction, and 2(c), dealing with rescission. To illustrate how general contract rules overlap the 2003 Regulations, reference can be made to paragraph 8 of Regulation 7, excluding rescission for the cases where defects are minor. According to Sale of Goods Act 1980, the consumer still has access to rescission in these cases. The co-existence of two consumer law regimes creates complications when determining the priority of rules applicable to consumers. Moreover, in the light of harmonisation efforts it can also be noted that such implementation choices ensure compliance with the obligation to transpose European legislation, but in practice the question remains whether the effectiveness of such legislation can be guaranteed.

With respect to time limits, Ireland only transposed paragraph 3 of Directive Article 5 in accordance with the criteria set forth by the European legislator.[341] The prior two paragraphs do not have an express transposition, since on the one hand, Ireland chose to apply the general limitation period for actions concerning breach of contract, and on the other hand it did not embark on the option given by the Directive in relation to imposing notification obligations on the consumer.

Commercial guarantees, covered by Regulation 9, are another example of the dual regime feature of Irish contract law. In spite of its *mot à mot* transposition of Article 6 of the Directive, general sales law will complement commercial guarantees.[342] The Irish legislator did not choose to make use of the legislative embedded in Article 6 dealing with language specifications.

338 S.I. No. 11/2003 – European Communities (Certain Aspects of the Sale of Consumer Goods and Associated Guarantees) Regulations 2003.

339 Schulte-Nölke *et al.* 2008, p. 656.

340 White 2009, p. 372.

341 Regulation 8 of the Consumer Sales Regulation 2003.

342 For example, see Section 12 of the Sale of Goods Act 1980 on aftersale services.

5.3.5. The Netherlands

After the general private law reform in 1992 when large parts of the new Civil Code were enacted, the Dutch legislator had generally updated the consumer regime to reflect European standards.[343] However, several inadequacies led to further changes in the BW. An example is the initial lack of a clear price reduction remedy, which was eventually rectified by its specific introduction in Article 7:22b BW.[344] Another aspect worth mentioning is that rules on sale distinguish between consumers and non-consumers, giving rise to two separate legal regimes. For instance, the consumer's possibility to opt for termination and damages is more limited than the rights available under the general regime.[345] Moreover, the proportionality test is not limited to the primary remedies, which is in clear contradiction to the hierarchy of remedies as established by the Directive.[346]

As far as conformity with the contract is concerned, it has been integrated in Articles 7:17 and 7:18 BW. Furthermore, Article 7:17(3) specifying that non-conformity is deemed to occur whenever an object of a different type, quality, size or weight is delivered.

Consumer rights (Article 3 of the Directive) are reflected in the specific rules on sale in Articles 7:21, 7:22 and 7:24 BW, but also link back to general termination rules in Article 6:265 BW. Once again, certain provisions go beyond the protection conferred by the Directive. In paragraph 1, Article 7:21 BW fills the gap left by the Directive in terms of incomplete delivery, and puts forward a right of the consumer to have the missing goods delivered. Moreover, paragraph 6 of the same article elaborates on the repair remedy, granting the consumer the option to have the repair carried out by a third party and to recover the costs made in this respect from the seller. This is yet again a situation where Dutch law fills the grey areas of the Directive, as we have seen previously, repair can raise issues relating to practical or absolute impossibility. The solution chosen by the Dutch legislator makes it easier for the consumer to rely on repair.

The rules in Directive Article 5 can be found in Articles 7:18(2) and 7:23 BW. Here, Dutch law departs from the lines of the Directive: first, paragraph 1 of Article 7:23 BW does not make reference to the two year time period within which conformity must become evident, but it actually refers to a reasonable period; second, the limitation period is calculated as of the moment of notification, and not that of delivery. Concerning the consumer notification requirement, the Dutch legislator chose to make use of this option, and decided that notifications must take place within a due period of time after the defect is discovered, and that a notification made within a period of two months after the discovery of the defect is considered to be made in time (Article 7:23(1) BW).

343 Smits 2000b, p. 1825; Hondius & Schelhaas 2001, p. 328.
344 Hijma 2009, p. 94.
345 Sivesand 2007, p. 138.
346 Article 7:21(5) BW.

Consumer guarantees are embedded in Articles 7:6a and 7:36 BW. No specific legislative transposition has been put in place for language provisions regarding the drafting of guarantees.

5.3.6. Romania

Law no. 449 from 2003 regarding the sale of products and associated guarantees is the instrument through which the Consumer Sales Directive was transposed in Romanian law. In spite of the Romanian Civil Code having been entirely reformed in 2011, the Romanian legislator chose to keep earlier instruments governing consumer contracts in force, as *lex specialis*.[347] It could be argued that having satellite laws gravitating around a main codification of the law of obligation can reach the same result as in Ireland, namely the co-existence of rules with different content. However, in the case of Romanian legislation, two observations are necessary: in light of the recent reform, the content of the Civil Code has been restructured and updated; and the principle of *lex specalis derogat generalibus* is a principle closely followed not only in Romanian legal theory but also by the Supreme Court.[348]

As for the actual content of Law 449/2003, Articles 5-8 govern conformity, in an almost literal transposition. The rights of the consumer are covered by Articles 9-14, and are once again very faithful to the wording of the Directive, with one specific addition: while the Directive is silent on defining impossibility, Romanian law provides for a definition. Article 11(3) of Law 449/2003 indicates that a reparatory measure (replacement) will be deemed impossible if the seller cannot provide an identical good for replacement purposes. Although additional definitions may be considered positive legislative developments especially for the purpose of aiding courts in the interpretation of contract rules, the definition of impossibility as currently existing under Law 449/2003 is somewhat misleading.[349] The impossibility/disproportionality test envisaged by Directive Article 3(3) refers to both repair and replacement. Romanian law, however, mentions in Article 11(3) of Law 449/2003 that in the case of replacement, impossibility entails the lack of identical goods, a distinction which is not made by the Directive.

On a different note, the transposed time limits have the same ambit, as can be seen in Articles 16-18 of Law 449/2003. The Romanian legislator chose to even implement the optional obligation of the consumer to notify the seller within a lime limit of two months.

347 Article 1177 Romanian Civil Code.

348 *Înalta Curte de Casaţie şi Justiţie, Secţia Civilă şi de Proprietate Intelectuală*, Decizia nr. 399, Dosar nr. 2572/35/2006, 24 ianuarie 2008.

349 Article 11(3) of Law 449/2003: 'O măsură reparatorie va fi considerată ca imposibilă dacă vânzătorul nu poate asigura produse identice pentru înlocuire sau piese de schimb pentru reparare, inclusiv ca urmare a lipsei utilajelor sau a tehnologiei aferente.' (A reparatory measure shall be deemed impossible if the seller cannot ensure identical products for replacement of spare parts for repair, including the situation of the lack of machinery or affiliated technology).

Guarantees are governed by Articles 19-21 of Law 449/2003. Apart from the conditions specified in the Directive, Romanian law elaborates on certain matters. An example is Article 20(2) that specifies certain information to be included in the guarantee (e.g. the modalities of exercising the guarantee, such as maintenance, repair, replacement, etc.).

5.3.7. The United Kingdom

The United Kingdom has often chosen to transpose European law almost literally, which made some commentators tag the approach as 'copy-paste'.[350] However, in the case of the Consumer Sales Directive, several Acts were amended to accommodate the new consumer regime. It was thus through the Sale and Supply of Goods to Consumers Regulations 2002 (SI 2002/3045) that the Sale of Goods Act 1979, Supply of Goods and Services Act 1982 and Supply of Goods (Implied Terms) Act 1973, together with the Unfair Contract Terms Act 1977 were modified.[351]

Although there was no general definition of conformity, a functional equivalent of Article 2 of the Directive was reflected by the specification in Section 48 F of the SoGA that 'goods do not conform to a contract of sale if there is, in relation to the goods, a breach of an express term of the contract or a term implied by section 13, 14 or 15 above'. A similar reference existed in Section 11S of the SGSA, completed by the specific mention of installation issues. No Ikea clause existed in the SoGa.

Article 3 also had its own particular transposition issues. Above all, the consumer law provisions particularly in the SoGA represented a fundamental departure from the system of remedies at common law by integrating specific performance as a right, rather than an equitable remedy.[352] This posed serious questions not only with respect to the hierarchy of remedies, with damages most often leading the list,[353] but also to the transformation of certain remedies, as specific performance, into institutions of law characterised by a certain duality.

What is more, Sections 48B (3) and (4) SoGA and Sections 11M (3) and (4) SGSA determined the proportionality test in Article 3. However, a remedy was deemed to be disproportionate not only by comparing the first tier remedies - repair and replacement - but also termination and price reduction, as it could be seen in Section 48B3(c) SoGA. This does not correspond with the test envisaged by the Directive. Moreover, paragraph 6 of Article 3 had not been transposed at all, shedding unclarity over rescission in cases of minor lack of conformity. One step further, it seems English law had expressly regulated termination to acknowledge the use of the good in Section 48C (3) SoGA.

The same problem with the lack of transposition could be seen in the case of Article 5(1) and (2). Firstly, there was no reference to the two-year expiry period, as the general limitation period for legal action on breach of contract was taken into

350 Schulte-Nölke *et al.* 2008, p. 164.
351 Howells 2007, p. 129.
352 Twigg-Flesner & Bradgate 2000.
353 Watterson 2001, p. 209.

account; and second, there was no notification obligation on the consumer's guarantees, as Article 6(1) alone had been implemented in Regulation 15(1) of the Sale Regulations.

This regime has been changed with the introduction of the Consumer Rights Act 2015, which entered into force in October 2015.

5.4. *Comparative Notes on the Transposition*

It has been pointed out earlier that the Consumer Sales Directive is a legislative act adopted under the strategy of minimum harmonisation. Several legal systems have been examined with respect to the national transposition of four different Consumer Sales Directive articles. While so far national experiences with the transposition process have been put forward in a descriptive fashion, in what follows a brief comparative overview of some of the issues arising out of the transposition is discussed.

For this purpose, some of the differences that resulted from the transposition of the Directive have been selected: (i) compensation for use; (ii) the proportionality test; (iii) the consumer's obligation to notify; (iv) the amendment of organic private law vis-à-vis the adoption of a separate instrument; (v) the similarity of national texts with the Consumer Sales Directive texts; and (vi) the separation between B2B and B2C regimes. Compensation for use and the notification obligation are presented in the light of the choices made by Member States with respect to the possibility of taking consumer protection further than the *de minimis* rules enshrined in the Directive.

(i) Compensation for Use

Compensation for use covers the situations in which a consumer requesting a remedy for non-conforming goods has made use of that good to the extent that whatever remedies he receives will be diminished with the value of the use. The question once again arising is: are all four remedies covered by compensation for use?

Since compensation for use can only occur as long as the seller receives a good back, repair is not included in this list. What is more, as we have seen from the *Quelle* case, replacement was held by the Court of Justice to be offered free of charge, so that no costs could be placed on the consumer; in its interpretation of recital 15 of the Preamble, the Court thus determined that reimbursement to the consumer may only be reduced in the case of rescission and price reduction. In this case, the Law Commissions in England and Scotland held in a study on consumer remedies that even in the case of rescission, deduction for use must be removed. Amongst the motives cited, the following were included: consumers would feel aggrieved if they would be charged for use after they would repeatedly try to have the good repaired or replaced; since it is a second tier remedy, consumers would have already suffered delays and inconveniences; such compensation can be tricky to calculate; or consumers do not have the equivalent right of asking for compensation for costs associated with the second tier remedy such as time off work, telephone calls or general inconvenience. The overall perspective was thus that whatever inconvenience consumers suffer is going to set off whatever use has been made of the good.[354]

Compelling evidence of a general negative perception consumers have on compensation for price reduction has been assembled by the same Law Commissions.[355] However, an additional question must be posed: should there not be a distinct category of potential cases where compensation *may* be used, so that a balance between the interests of both parties is reached?

To answer this question it must be stated that cases might occur when price reduction is the only remedy pursued by the parties. In this instance, inconveniences caused might not amount to unreasonable delays and aggrieved consumers. Also, in cases where the lack of conformity is signalled after the passing of more than one year, there might be certain goods the value of which can drop significantly (e.g. technology products). In these cases, since the consumer has been enjoying the use of such goods, it is difficult to come up with practical reasons explaining why the consumer would not have to account for their very use. In certain cases, even if a product lacks conformity, it may still be used. If one buys a computer that turns out to have a defective wireless card but still uses the computer for gaming, the keyboard may, with time, start showing signs of usage. After all, the nature of price reduction itself adds to this argument - price reduction does not entail that the consumer changes the defective good, or that he returns it; but it actually means the consumer is sufficiently motivated to keep using the good. In no way does this view exclude the possibility of asking for a price reduction, but equally, if the consumer is satisfied to continue using the good, this has to be reflected by the remedies at hand.

Generally, compensation for use, whether stemming from rescission (where it is given as an option by the Directive) or price reduction (where the option is not explicit, but neither is the prohibition), is a tool the design of which can help balance the interests of both seller and consumer, in spite of its lack of popularity in the interpretation of the Directive.

(ii) Proportionality Test

Belgium, France and Ireland have transposed the proportionality test in Article 3 quite closely to the Directive. Germany and the Netherlands transposed the Directive in the Civil Code, and in consequence had to incorporate it in provisions that in part also address non-consumer transactions. For this reason, German law operates with the concept of 'material defects' that leads to a departure from the

354 The Law Commission and the Scottish Law Commission, 'Consumer Remedies for Faulty Goods', November 2009, paras. 6.40 - 6.50; see also Department for Business Innovation & Skills, Enhancing consumer confidence by clarifying consumer law - Consultation on the supply of goods, services and digital content', July 2012, available at: <https://www.gov.uk/government/uploads/system/uploads/attachment_data/file/31350/12-937-enhancing-consumer-consultation-supply-of-goods-services-digital.pdf>, last accessed on 27 July 2016, p. 69.

355 Appendix A to the Consultation Paper on Consumer Remedies for Faulty Goods (Law Com CP 188; Scot Law Com DP 139).

original proportionality test established by the Directive's hierarchy of remedies. In § 439(3) BGB, the German legislator mentions that the seller may refuse the cure chosen by the buyer, if that cure entails disproportionate expenses. Also departing from the wording of the Directive is Dutch law, that transposed the proportionality test in a way that does not only take into account the first tier remedies, but that applied to any remedy.

Similarly to Dutch law, the UK did not only include the first tier remedies to determine impossibility, but actually included price reduction and rescission in this comparison as well.

Moreover, Romania actually defined impossibility, unlike the wording of the Directive. The definition deems repair or replacement impossible if an identical product is not available, or if the seller does not have the spare parts necessary to repair the product.

(iii) The Consumer's Obligation to Notify

Article 5(2) of the Directive establishes the notification obligation which Member States may adopt. This notification obligation is considered to be one of the weaknesses of the Directive, since its present form represents a compromise between several proposals either making it mandatory or removing it entirely.[356]

Belgium, the Netherlands and Romania made use of the choice, with the following comments: Belgium has left it to the contracting parties to decide whether to include a notification duty in their contract (Article 1649quater § 2 Civil Code) and the Netherlands mentions a reasonable period of time and deems a notification taking place within two months from the discovery of the defect to be timely (Article 7:23(1) BW). France, Germany, Ireland and the UK did not make use of this choice.

(iv) The Amendment of Organic Private Law vis-à-vis the Adoption of a Separate Instrument

Belgium, Germany and the Netherlands have chosen to integrate consumer sales rules in their Civil Codes by amending them. Ireland, Romania and the United Kingdom have accommodated these rules by means of satellite legislation, namely laws (Romania), regulations (Ireland) and existing sales law (United Kingdom). As an intermediate category, France implemented the Consumer Sales Directive by making amendments to its Consumer Code. Having Consumer Codes govern consumer transactions establishes a clear body of *lex specialis*. The problem occurs when legislation updates are not included in the Consumer Code. This is the case of Romania, where a Consumer Code has been put in place as of 2004.[357] However, instead of amending it to accommodate the Consumer Sales Directive, the Romanian legislator chose to adopt a separate law (Law no. 449/2003). In consequence, consumer protection becomes over-fragmented, as is the case with

356 Staudenmayer 2000, p. 558; see also Twigg-Flesner 2009, p. 29.

357 Law no. 296 of 28 June 2004 regarding the Consumer Code, Romanian Official Gazette no. 224 of 24 March 2008.

satellite laws, which can lead to legal confusion.[358] Still, choosing to amend Civil Codes comes with drawbacks as well. Incorporating European rules into a rooted private law framework might just as well lead to an inherent lack of clarity; distinguishing which provisions have European origin and which are national can become difficult.[359]

(v) The Similarity of National Texts with the Consumer Sales Directive Texts

Belgium, Ireland, Romania and the UK have adopted rules that resemble the content of the Directive almost literally. The Netherlands and Germany preferred to change the operating concepts. For instance, the Dutch version of the Directive speaks of conformity with the contract as *'overeenstemming met de overeenkomst'*, while Article 7:17(1) BW refers to conformity in different terms, namely *'de overeenkomst beantwoorden'*. This is not to say the two Dutch versions lead to fundamentally different results, but it does show a tendency of the Dutch legislator to really integrate the European rules into national legislation and align them to existing law. Similarly, § 433(1) and § 434(1) BGB refer to an object being free of physical defects, rather than explicitly referring to conformity. France cannot be said to have transposed the Directive literally, but neither does it make use of individualised concepts, like Germany.

To exemplify the similarities between the text of the Directive and the French rules, Article L. 211-5 Consumer Code can be mentioned. As the reflection of the Directive's Article 2, it refers to criteria which establish the presumption of conformity. Directive Article 2(2) paragraphs (a) - (d) have been integrated in an order that does not coincide with the original text and has changed the wording. Still, in Article L. 211-4(1) Consumer Code the term *'défauts de conformité'* is used, seemingly closer to the Directive's conformity concept. This aspect can be underlined especially in relation to German law, where as it has been mentioned above, some concepts reflected the spirit of the Civil Code more than that of the Directive. Interestingly, France could have used its own Civil Code inspired concepts of *'défauts cachés'* or *'vices apparents'*.

(vi) The Separation between B2B and B2C Regimes

Germany is the only Member State that has chosen to unify the sales regimes applicable to B2B and B2C transactions by means of reforming its law of obligations. Belgium, France, Ireland, the Netherlands, Romania, and the UK follow a clear division between consumer law and commercial law. Consumer sales law, whether derived from Civil Codes, Consumer Codes or special laws, must be complemented by general contract law. On the one hand, the main positive aspect about

358 In spite of the clear mention in Aricle 1 that the law governs '[...] aspects regarding the sale of products [...] and associated guarantees in view of prividing consumer protection [...]', Law no. 449/2003 has been invoked by commercial parties to be applicable to commercial contracts, see *Curtea de Apel Bucureşti - Secţia a V-a Comercială, Decizia comercială nr. 255 din 25.05.2009; Curtea de Apel Galaţi, Secţia Comercială, Maritimă şi Fluvială, Decizia comercială nr. 21 din 19 Martie 2008.*

359 Smits 2012a, p. 163.

Germany's legislative choice is the efficient application of laws. Sales law applies concomitantly with general contract law; however, no distinction must be made between consumers or non-consumers, which can in principle be said to lead to the simplification of applicable law. This strategy could be of help not only to courts but also to contracting parties, to the extent that debates regarding the consumer status of commercial representatives would not be of relevance; what is more, businesses engaged in consumer sales could have lower transaction costs when dealing themselves with other businesses. Still, one main aspect must be kept in mind - the BGB only unifies the B2B and B2C regimes in respect to sales law, which is not to say that the entire law of obligations applies to consumers and non-consumers in the same manner.[360] On the other hand, separate regimes for B2B and B2C transactions allow for different standards to be applicable. Based on some classical arguments favouring consumer protection, such as the weak negotiating position or information asymmetry, consumers should be given certain rights which can level the contract playing field,[361] thus derogating from general contract law regimes. However, in order to understand why such separation might not be optimal, there are two aspects which deserve further attention.

First, B2B transactions cannot be all placed under the same category, as not all businesses have the same market position. The now-retracted proposal on the CESL is the first European contract law instrument to recognise new actors in between consumers and businesses, namely SMEs.[362] This development shows that businesses with limited resources might have market-related difficulties placing them in an inferior position in relation to some of their business partners.

Second, B2C regimes are incomplete, and often apply together with certain provisions governed by general contract law, that also applies to B2C sales. It has already been seen that for instance in Ireland, the consumer is not entitled to have rescission under the Regulations implementing the Consumer Sales Directive, but he does have this right under general contract law.[363] The result is the overlap of the two regimes (B2B and B2C), which defeats the purpose of separating them in the first place.

The essential point which needs to be made in relation to the Court's role in the harmonisation process is reflected by the fact that the increasing bias towards consumers currently identified in the interpretation of Consumer Sales rules can be said to lead to a second wave of harmonisation. Through case law, the Court of Justice addresses aspects of the Consumer Sales Directive that may not have been explicitly laid down in the provisions of the directive. Since what the Court does is interpret provisions which may sometimes be considered grey areas, it follows that it has a margin of appreciation in determining how they must be applied. It seems, however, that within this margin of appreciation, the Court of Justice is increasingly

360 See for instance the consumer right of withdrawal, § 356 BGB.

361 Coteanu 2005, p. 5.

362 See Proposal for a Regulation of the European Parliament and of the Council on a Common European Sales Law, COM(2011) 635 final; see also European Commission Recommendation 2003/361[13] of 6 May 2003 on the definition of SMEs.

363 See p. 106.

supporting more consumer-friendly interpretations. Member States that have already implemented the Directive upon its adoption are now faced with the problem of having to adapt national legislation to the new limits imposed by the current reading of the Directive. Germany and England are two relevant examples in this case. On the one hand, Germany, after having amended the Civil Code by adding a new section to § 474(2), still needs to determine the most promising legislative manoeuvre to address the modifications needed by § 439, as *Weber* and *Putz* shed doubt on how the *Bundesgerichtshof* interpreted the latter paragraph.[364] At the same time, after having to accommodate multiple judgments with the general contract law framework chosen by the German legislator for consumer rules, issues regarding the success of this implementation method seem to pop up.[365] On the other hand, taking a look at the consumer law framework in England, in order for national courts to achieve the same result, authors such as Johnston and Unberath call for reform - either in the method of interpretation used by courts for the newly established obligations imposed on the seller, or in the very amendment of legal texts.[366]

6. Unfair Commercial Practices (2005)

6.1. *What are the Rationale and Scope of the Directive?*

Figure 7: Unfair Commercial Practices Adoption Timeline (source: Eur-Lex)

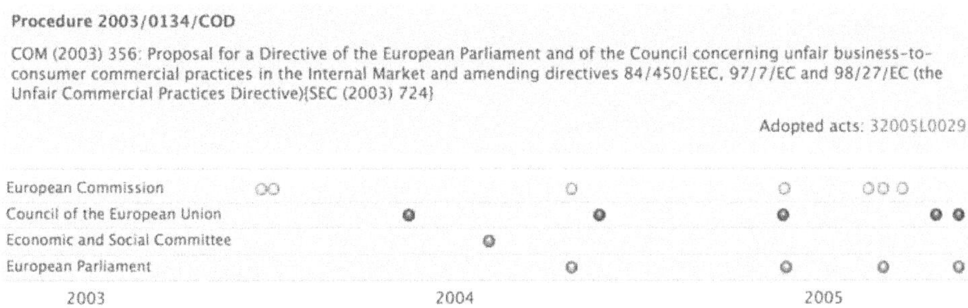

364 *Gebr. Weber GMBH v Jürgen Wittmer*, para. 21 reads: 'The Bundesgerichtshof notes that it would however not be necessary to answer that question if Weber were entitled to refuse to reimburse the cost of removing the tiles which were not in conformity because the cost is disproportionate. That court states that, under Paragraph 439(3) of the BGB, the seller may refuse the type of subsequent performance chosen by the buyer not only where that type of performance would result in disproportionate cost in comparison to the alternative type of performance ('relative lack of proportionality'), but also where the cost of the method chosen by the buyer, even if it is the only method possible, is inherently disproportionate ('absolute lack of proportionality')'.

365 Johnston & Unberath 2012, p. 806.

366 *Ibid.*, p. 805.

Unlike the other Directives included in this study, the Unfair Commercial Practices Directive does not *per se* fall in the category of directives dealing with consumer sales; rather, it covers sales indirectly, as it relates to advertising and promotion aspects arising outside contractual relationships.[367] The Directive was included in this research by virtue of its role in the wider fair trading debate, which had also led in 1993 to the adoption of the Unfair Contract Terms Directive.[368] It is not only fair trading that brings these two Directives together - they even resemble one another in content, as both make use of a general clause in order to define unfair commercial practices and respectively unfair contract terms.

The Unfair Commercial Practices Directive is another highly debated legislative measure taken in the field of consumer protection.[369] Pushed into public consultations as early as 2001 by the European Commission's Green Paper on consumer protection,[370] it was adopted four years later, in 2005, as a shift towards a novel maximum harmonisation approach.[371] According to a Report issued by the Commission in March 2013, the Directive aims to protect consumers from misleading advertising and aggressive marketing and make sure that consumers have truthful and accurate information that can help them make an informed choice in their transactions.[372]

Before looking at the subject matter in more detail, it is first necessary to understand what drove the European legislator to take further action in the regulation of commercial practices. Not only was there a framework of other Directives governing unfair trade, but an underlying system of national private laws also existed, under which remedies could be provided to consumers by means of general (or even consumer) contract law. To this end, it is necessary to mention the two-fold rationale behind the Directive.[373]

367 Stuyck 2011, p. 118; see also Recital 13 of the Preamble to the Unfair Commercial Practices Directive.

368 For comparative research on fair trading, see *Institut für Europaisches Wirtschafts und Verbraucherrecht*, 'Study on the Feasibility of a General Legislative Framework on Fair Trading', November 2000, available at: <http://ec.europa.eu/dgs/health_consumer/-library/surveys/sur21_vol2_en.pdf>, last accessed on 27 July 2016.

369 See Meyer 2007, p. 169.

370 Green Paper on European Union Consumer Protection, COM(2001) 531 final, 2 October 2001, electronically available at: <http://ec.europa.eu/consumers/cons_int/safe_shop/fair_bus_pract/green_pap_comm/fair_comm_greenpap_en.pdf>, last accessed on 27 July 2016; see also Howells 2006, p. 19.

371 Miller 2011, p. 85.

372 See also Report from the Commission to the European Parliament, the Council and the European Economic and Social Committee, 'First Report on the application of Directive 2005/29/EC of the European Parliament and of the Council of 11 May 2005 concerning unfair business-to-consumer commercial practices in the internal market and amending Council Directive 84/450/EEC, Directives 97/7/EC, 98/27/EC and 2002/65/EC of the European Parliament and of the Council and Regulation (EC) No 2006/2004 of the European Parliament and of the Council ('Unfair Commercial Practices Directive')', COM(2013) 139 final, March 2013, p. 2.

373 See also Willett 2010, p. 247-248.

First, it strives to promote a higher and uniform level of consumer protection across the jurisdictions of the Member States, by introducing maximum harmonisation. Unlike the minimum harmonisation initiatives discussed earlier in this study, the new standard leaves no room for Member States to operate individually. The question arising is thus how exactly maximum harmonisation can be described. A starting point in this regard is reflected in the agenda set out by the European Commission in its 2004 Communication on contract law: '[t]he [...] key goals remain to enhance consumer and business confidence in the internal market through a high common level of consumer protection [...]'.[374] This goal must be viewed in the light of serious alleged shortcomings of minimum harmonisation, such as legal fragmentation.[375] This was regarded by the Commission in the same document as unable to considerably remove differences between national legislation arising out of the implementation of various consumer directives. In brief, maximum harmonisation - or more specifically, full harmonisation as it is called in the Directive itself[376] - entails the setting aside of any national provision overlapping the material scope of the Unfair Commercial Practices Directive that in any way goes below or above the Directive's established level of protection.

The main point to be made about maximum harmonisation in relation to the scope of the Directive deals with its function of introducing two types of obligations on Member States: the positive obligation of implementing consumer protection matching the Directive; and the negative obligation of refraining from offering consumers any other level of protection than the one prescribed therein.[377]

The second goal pursued by the Unfair Commercial Practices Directive is the well-functioning of the internal market perceived from an end-to-end perspective: on the one hand, businesses can benefit from more legal certainty derived from further harmonisation efforts, while on the other, consumers can be empowered to engage in cross-border trade under the protection of their strengthened rights.[378]

In brief, the Directive is rather clear in structuring the two arguments - the proper functioning of the internal market is promoted by a high-reaching and uniform consumer protection policy.[379] This double-purpose approach is reiterated in Article 1.[380]

Another relevant aspect touching upon the discussion of the Directive's scope is its material application. Although it is not the first measure taken to limit the impact of unfair commercial practices,[381] it is, for good reasons, considered to have

374 Communication from the Commission to the European Parliament and the Council, 'European Contract Law and the revision of the acquis: the way forward', COM(2004) 651 final.

375 Weatherill 2005, p. 155.

376 Recital 14 Preamble Unfair Commercial Practices Directive.

377 See generally, Collins 2005, p. 417; Abbamonte 2006, p. 695; Stuyck *et al.* 2006, p. 107; Shears 2007, p. 781.

378 De Vries 2012, p. 914.

379 See for instance Recital five of the Preamble.

380 COM(2013) 139 final, p. 3.

381 Directive 2006/114/EC of the European Parliament and of the Council of 12 December 2006 concerning misleading and comparative advertising, *OJ* L376/21; Council Directive →

the widest ambit because of its extensive applicability to seemingly all B2C commercial practices.[382] The Directive is however a first in tackling aggressive practices, as can be seen in recital 11 of the Preamble.

Article 1 also refers to the Directive's material ambit as generally consisting of 'unfair commercial practices harming consumers' economic interests'. However, to flesh out what this actually covers, Article 3 must be further consulted. According to paragraph 1, the Directive applies to (i) B2C; (ii) unfair commercial practices occurring at any point surrounding a commercial transaction (iii) in relation to a product. Each of the three conditions are discussed separately.

(i) B2C

Before the adoption of the Unfair Commercial Practices Directive, it was the 1984 Misleading Advertising Directive that governed whatever European rules existed for consumers against false advertising.[383] One year after the adoption of the Unfair Commercial Practices Directive, in 2006, the Misleading and Comparative Advertising Directive entered into force. This Directive, based on minimum harmonisation,[384] came to replace the 1984 Directive and its design sought to protect traders against the unfair consequences of misleading advertising.[385] In more recent years, more specifically in the Communication on misleading marketing practices from 2012, the Commission defended its choice of focusing on the impact of advertising on trade in terms of the need to promote truthful and professional diligence.[386]

Businesses are depicted in the Directive by the use of the term 'traders', defined in Article 2(b) as 'any natural or legal person who, in commercial practices covered by this Directive, is acting for purposes relating to his trade, business, craft or profession and anyone acting in the name of or on behalf of a trader'. The definition poses no problem in identifying traders as the very suppliers of goods and/or services, although with the thriving of internet-specific services, the delineation is not so clear anymore. An example in this sense can be represented by professional comparison shopping engines (CSEs), which simply feed consumers information on a diverse array of prices for specific products, as well as consumer reviews.[387] CSEs are said to fall under the trader category, and when they promote biased information, as was the case with the grocery comparison website

84/450/EEC of 10 September 1984 relating to the approximation of the laws, regulations and administrative provisions of the Member States concerning misleading advertising, *OJ* L250.

382 Stuyck *et al.* 2006, p. 107; Anagnostaras 2007, p. 147.

383 See Leistner 2005, p. 153.

384 Article 7, Misleading and Comparative Advertising Directive.

385 Article 1, Misleading and Comparative Advertising Directive.

386 European Commission, 'Protecting businesses against misleading marketing practices and ensuring effective enforcement', COM(2012) 702 final.

387 See for instance <www.ciao-shopping.nl>, last accessed on 27 July 2016.

quiestlemoinscher.com powered by Carrefour, website owners can be held to respect unfair commercial practices rules.[388]

(ii) Unfair Commercial Practices Occurring at Any Point Surrounding a Commercial Transaction

Article 5 uses a principle-based approach to define unfair commercial practices, which are deemed to be either contrary to professional diligence (Article 5(2)(a)) or likely to distort the economic behaviour of the average consumer (Article 5(2)(b)). Paragraph 4 of the same Article specifies two types of unfair commercial practices: misleading (Articles 6 and 7) and aggressive (Articles 8 and 9).

Given the general nature of these principles and the lack of designated sectors of application, paragraphs 2-4 impose certain limitations. To the extent that more specific legislation is available, such as contract law rules on validity, formation and effect (paragraph 2), special rules will prevail, should there be a conflict of law (paragraph 4). It must also be noted that there is no restriction relating to the moment in the consumer transaction when these practices must occur - Article 3 covers all possible moments - before, during or after a commercial transaction.

(iii) In Relation to a Product

According to the definitions in Article 2, the term product is not limited to goods, but rather refers to both goods and services and it includes immovable property, as well rights and obligations. The recent 2013 Commission Report emphasises that products must not only be regarded as part of offline transactions, but should also reflect the online dimension.[389]

As wide as this definition might appear, certain limitations apply here as well. The most straightforward limitation in this respect is reflected in Article 5(10), according to which the Unfair Commercial Practices Directive excludes from its ambit any impact over the application of laws, regulations and administrative provisions taken by Member States in the field of standards of fineness of articles of precious metal.

A more complicated exception is contained in paragraph 9 of the same Article, which derogates from the maximum harmonisation regime and entails that in the case of financial services and immovable property, more 'restrictive or prescriptive' requirements can be adopted by Member States. This is to say that in these restricted fields, Member States are not compelled to keep the unified standard imposed by the Unfair Commercial Practices Directive, but can go above it,[390] as the standard applicable to these cases is that of minimum harmonisation.

For the purpose of determining how harmonisation played out in the nine Member States under scrutiny, the following analysis is anchored in three aspects

388 Commission Staff Working Document, 'Guidance on the Implementation/Application of Directive 2005/29/EC on Unfair Commercial Practices', 3 December 2009, SEC(2009) 1666, p. 8, discussing French case law, *Tribunal de commerce de Paris – 29 mars 2007 – Carrefour c/Galaec (la coopérative groupement d'achat des centres Leclerc)*.

389 COM(2013) 139 final, p. 2.

390 Howells *et al.* 2006, p. 80.

covered by the Directive, which could be counted to have an indirect impact on sales law: a) Articles 5-9 dealing with and detailing the general prohibition of unfair commercial practices as well as the division of misleading and aggressive practices; b) Article 10 covering voluntary harmonisation in the form of codes of conduct; and c) Article 11 dealing with the enforcement of claims based on unfair commercial practices. The selection of the three categories of Articles has been made in such a way to portray the multi-faceted features of the Unfair Commercial Practices Directive; both Articles 10 and 11 are exceptions to the maximum harmonisation standard set up by Articles 5-9. The three categories are now examined one by one.

a) Articles 5-9: the general prohibition of unfair commercial practices and its division in misleading and aggressive practices

Articles 5-9 represent the core of the Directive. Brought together under Chapter 2, called 'unfair commercial practices', these rules start off with the general clause laid down in Article 5 (general prohibition), and subsequently elaborate on two specific categories of unfair commercial practices: misleading practices (Articles 6 and 7) and aggressive practices (Articles 8 and 9).

Going back to Article 5, the general clause consists of a two-tier cumulative test. According to paragraph 2, for a commercial practice to be unfair, it must: (i) be contrary to the requirements of professional diligence; and it must (ii) materially distort (or be likely to materially distort) the economic behaviour of the average consumer or of the average member of a group of consumers.[391] To aid the general nature of this clause, paragraph 5 makes reference to Annex 1, which lists commercial practices deemed unfair under any circumstance. The Annex contains 23 misleading practices and eight aggressive practices, which are blacklisted to the extent that they do not need any further examination by national courts but are considered unfair as a matter of principle.[392]

This Article poses certain issues on three different levels: by inserting the requirement of professional diligence; by introducing the statutory average consumer standard; and by imposing a closed list to which Member States cannot add.

First, one of the conditions against which unfair commercial practices are tested is that of professional diligence. Article 2(h) defines it as '[...] the standard of special skill and care which a trader may reasonably be expected to exercise towards consumers, commensurate with honest market practice and/or the general principle of good faith in the trader's field of activity [...]'. It follows that in order for commercial practices to be fair, traders must display behaviour which upon objective evaluation must show special skill and care, reflective of honest market practice and/or good faith. Viable questions regarding the application of such new concepts to consumer law, like professional diligence and honest market practice, have already been posed. Reporting to the Department of Trade and Industry on the application of the Directive, Twigg-Flesner and his research team have emphasised

391 See also Case C-540/08, *Mediaprint Zeitungs-und Zeitschriftenverlag GmbH & Co. KG v 'Österreich'-Zeitungsverlag GmbH*, para. 31.

392 See also Recital 17, Unfair Commercial Practices Directive Preamble.

that a standard focusing on 'special' skill and care will not add much to the general duty of skill and care, and traders will not be bound to follow the highest standards in their field of activity. According to the Explanatory Memorandum accompanying the Unfair Commercial Practices Directive proposal, 'generally recognised standards of business practice' need to be looked at.[393] However, the difficulty arises in the situation when generally recognised standards are actually poor business standards; still, it seems that if traders comply with poor standards for the mere reason that they are the average norm in a specific sector, the Directive's requirement will be considered as not having been fulfilled.[394] It is also noteworthy that the requirement of professional diligence in Article 5 may be derogated from if Articles 6-9 apply, given the general presumption that misleading and aggressive practices always imply the lack of professional diligence.[395] This rationale stemmed out of the Explanatory Memorandum,[396] but more recently has been detailed by AG Wahl's interpretation in *Tour Services*.[397] The case surrounds two Austrian travel operators, CHS and Team4 Travel, and overlapping reservations they had made with the same accommodation provider. Since CHS was also able to make accommodation bookings, it brought Team4 Travel to court to stop them from advertising the listed accommodations in their brochures as 'exclusive'. After both *Landesgericht Innsbruck* (Regional Court Innsbruck) and *Oberlandesgericht Innsbruck* (High Regional Court Innsbruck) passed the same decisions refusing CHS an injunction against Team4Travel's use of advertising materials, it was the *Oberster Gerichtshof* that referred the interpretation of Article 5 to the CJEU. AG Wahl disagreed with the opinion that misleading or aggressive practices, as detailed in Annex 1 pursuant to Article 5(5) or as laid down in Articles 6-9, would be mere examples of unfair practices, with the effect that the general clause would still be applicable. He thus builds on the view expressed in the Explanatory Memorandum and concludes that when a commercial practice falls under the black list referred to by Article 5(4), traders can be held liable for unfair practices regardless of whether they have acted with professional diligence or not.[398] However detailed his analysis has been in terms of the interaction between the different paragraphs of Article 5, the Advocate General did not go into one of the more stringent issues - the interpretation of the definition of professional diligence. For this reason, it is still

393 European Commission, Proposal for a Directive of the European Parliament and of the Council concerning unfair business-to-consumer commercial practices in the Internal Market and amending Directives 84/450/EEC, 97/7/EC and 98/27/EC (the Unfair Commercial Practices Directive), COM(2003) 356 final, para. 53.

394 Christian Twigg-Flesner *et al.*, 'An Analysis of the Application and Scope of the Unfair Commercial Practices Directive', Report for the UK Department of Trade and Industry, p. 4-5.

395 *Ibid.*, p. 5.

396 European Commission, Proposal for a Directive of the European Parliament and of the Council concerning unfair business-to-consumer commercial practices in the Internal Market and amending Directives 84/450/EEC, 97/7/EC and 98/27/EC (the Unfair Commercial Practices Directive), COM(2003) 356 final, para. 56.

397 Opinion of Advocate General Wahl, Case C-435/11, *CHS Tour Services GmbH v Team4 Travel GmbH*.

398 *Ibid.*, para. 31.

unclear whether this standard, by virtue of its reference to honest market practices is descriptive, meaning that national courts may use own concepts to fulfil it, or whether it is normative, and thus Member States would have to integrate it as a novel concept stemming from European law.

Secondly, the average consumer standard must be addressed. While it might not be a new concept for CJEU case law, statutory reference to the average consumer for the goal of profiling the segment of protected interests is an elaborate development.[399] In this sense, Article 5 distinguishes between two categories of average consumers: the ones mentioned in the general clause (paragraph 2), and others who are 'particularly' vulnerable (paragraph 3). The main shortcoming of this development is the general lack of a clear definition, which was removed by the Council in its Common Position.[400] This is not to say that there are no indications whatsoever to the more precise content of these concepts.

When speaking about the first category, it must be stated that recital 18 explains the choice of the European legislator to introduce the notion of an average consumer. To describe this consumer, the recital in question refers to '[...] the average consumer, who is reasonably well-informed and reasonably observant and circumspect, taking into account social, cultural and linguistic factors, as interpreted by the Court of Justice [...]'. This can be held to represent a codification of the analysis already made by the Court of Justice in its case law.[401] To a certain degree, the use of this benchmark has been rather consistent in the fields from where it emerged: free movement of goods, misleading advertising, labelling, and trademark infringements;[402] and since it has now been made part of the Unfair Commercial Practices Directive, the Court will be bound by it narrowly. Still, uniformity remains the primary challenge. If the CJEU must apply the average consumer test in unfair commercial practices, it could do so in other fields related to consumer contracts. Unfair practices are not bound to a given medium or a given moment within the conclusion of consumer contracts, and thus their relevance is quite wide. This is to say that unfair practices could easily occur in or around Internet contracts, which could subsequently enable the Court of Justice to draw inspiration from this benchmark in its own interpretations over distance selling. However, the Court showed exactly the opposite in *Content Services*,[403] where it profiled the consumer as not having to undertake any effort, not even clicking a mouse button, to access the

399 Willett 2010, p. 269; Barron 2008, p. 298.

400 Wilhelmsson 2006, p. 131.

401 European Commission, Proposal for a Directive of the European Parliament and of the Council concerning unfair business-to-consumer commercial practices in the Internal Market and amending Directives 84/450/EEC, 97/7/EC and 98/27/EC (the Unfair Commercial Practices Directive), COM(2003) 356 final, para. 35; Case C-315/92, *Verband Sozialer Wettbewerb eV v Clinique Labatories SNC and Estée Lauder Cosmetics GmbH* [1994] ECR I-317; Case C-210/96, *Gut Springheide GmbH v Oberkreisdirektor des Kreises Steinfurt* [1998] ECR I-4657; Case C-299/12, *Green – Swan Pharmaceuticals CR, a.s. v Státní zemědělská a potravinářská inspekce, ústřední inspektorát* [2013]; Case C-122/10, *Konsumentombudsmannen v Ving Sverige AB* [2011] ECR I-03903; see also Mak & Braspenning 2012, p. 312.

402 Poncibò & Incardona 2007, p. 22.

403 *Content Services Ltd v Bundesarbeitskammer.*

information confirmed by the trader via a durable medium.[404] This conflict stems from the relation between the average consumer profile and the confident consumer goal, which has been shaping consumer law in areas like sales or unfair terms.[405] As of yet, it is unclear where this interplay will lead. What is more, it must be asked whether having a one-fits-all average consumer standard is desirable at all. As it has been shown in sector-specific case law such as that of OHIM, profiling consumers in one area does not automatically imply the same can be done for the entire sector: 'The clothing sector (...) comprises goods which vary widely in quality and price. Whilst it is possible that the [average] consumer is more attentive to the choice of mark where he or she buys a particular item or clothing, such an approach on the part of the consumer cannot be presumed without evidence with regard to all goods in that sector.'[406]

In its turn, Article 5(3) talks about certain objective criteria used to determine the pool of average vulnerable consumers: the existence of mental of physical infirmity; age; and credulity. It is furthermore important that not only are these factors present, but the trader must be expected to reasonably foresee them. As useful as they might appear, the criteria are much too vague. While it can be argued that mental or physical infirmity enjoy a certain degree of clarity since it might prove easier to determine a pool of vulnerable consumers with such features, the same cannot be said about age and credulity. On the one hand, the age argument can go either way, and it can be claimed that it is not only seniors who can be the victims of unfair practices, but youngsters below legal age limits might be facing the same problem.[407] Age itself does not entail that a certain age group is necessarily challenged. Moreover, as technology advances and its use becomes more widespread, the age segments of those who can benefit from it are constantly increasing. To take an example, in 2005, over 80 per cent of individuals between 65 and 74 claimed to never have used the Internet. In 2011, this percentage dropped to 65 per cent.[408] On the other hand, credulity has the same problem - it must be determined who the individuals described by this feature are, and how this criterion is to be put in practice.

Thirdly, as it has already been discussed to a certain extent, Article 5(5) blacklists practices which are in any circumstances unfair, meaning that fulfilling the general requirements in Article 5 or the more specific conditions in Articles 6-9 is not required.[409] Since the Directive intends to fully harmonise the law relating to unfair commercial practices,[410] a very high number of cases before the CJEU

404 See Goanta 2013.

405 Wilhelmsson 2004, p. 321.

406 Joint cases T-117/03 to T-119/03 and T-171/03, *New Look Ltd v Office for Harmonisation in the Internal Market (Trade Marks and Designs)*, para. 43.

407 It must be however mentioned that this age category will have limited capacity to conclude contracts.

408 Digital Agenda Scoreboard 2012, 'Life Online', p. 4.

409 Wilhelmsson 2006, p. 158; see also Poncibò & Incardona 2005, p. 321; Micklitz 2009a, p. 110.

410 Joint cases C-261/07, *VTB-VAB NV v Total Belgium NV* and C-299/07, *Galatea BVBA v Sanoma Magazines Belgium NV* [2009] I-02949; Case C-304/08, *Zentrale zur Bekämpfung unlauteren Wettbewerbs eV v Plus Warenhandelsgesellschaft mbH* [2010] ECR I-00217.

surrounded the possibility of national courts prohibiting practices from the offset, similarly to those in the black list, without interpreting such practices in the light of the particular details of the case. One of the cases dealing with this matter is *Citroën Belux*.[411] In 2010, car manufacturer Citroën initiated a campaign offering interested purchasers of a new car six months' worth of free comprehensive car insurance. The Federation for Insurance and Financial Intermediaries (FvF) considered such offer to constitute a prohibited combined offer in the understanding of Belgian legislation; Article 72 of the Law of 6 April on market practices and consumer protection (*Wet van 6 april 2010 betreffende marktpraktijken en consumentenbescherming/Loi du 6 avril 2010 relative aux pratiques du marché et à la protection du consommateur*) prohibited (with certain exceptions) any combined offer to the consumer which has at least one finance service component. The *Rechtbank van koophandel te Brussel* agreed with the Federation, and Citroën subsequently lodged an appeal with the *Hof van beroep te Brussel*. It was the latter Court that decided to submit a question to the CJEU for a preliminary ruling in relation to Article 3(9): Does Article 3(9) preclude national law from prohibiting combined offers where at least one component is a financial service?'

It was not the first time that the CJEU was analyzing combined offers. On several other occasions, including in 2009 in the *VTB-VAB NV* and *Galatea* joint cases, as well as in 2010 in *Zentrale zur Bekämpfung unlauteren Wettbewerbs eV*, the Court stated that the Unfair Commercial Practices Directive precludes national prohibitions of commercial offers whereby the availability of certain services is linked to the purchase of goods, since they were not listed in the Directive's black list. Nevertheless, it was the first time when combined offers involved financial services, which are as such outside the boundaries of the process of fully harmonising unfair commercial practices.

The fact remains that Article 3(9) clearly leaves financial services and immovable property out of the scope of the Directive's full harmonisation policy, since as it is stated in recital nine to the Preamble, these sectors come with inherent serious risks and great complexity and thus require detailed conditions. This is to say that, as the Court observed in paragraph 27 of the judgment, the EU legislator wanted to leave it to the Member States to impose conditions in respect of governing these sectors in ways that are either more restrictive or prescriptive.

b) Article 10: voluntary harmonisation and codes of conduct

It is clear from the Explanatory Memorandum that the European legislator saw the potential of codes of conduct to foster further harmonisation, by allowing Member states to encourage private actors to set soft law rules regarding their commercial activity.[412] To justify this support, the Commission quoted two surveys[413] showing

411 Case C-265/12, *Citroën Belux NV v Federatie voor Verzekerings-en Financiële Tussenpersonen (FvF)* [2013].

412 European Commission, Proposal for a Directive of the European Parliament and of the Council concerning unfair business-to-consumer commercial practices in the Internal Market and amending Directives 84/450/EEC, 97/7/EC and 98/27/EC (the Unfair Commercial Practices Directive), COM(2003) 356 final, para. 24.

that 65 per cent of the business respondents considered codes of conduct to be a very or fairly efficient in facilitating their cross-border sales and/or advertising within the European Union.[414] Two of the other options the participants could choose from, namely 'Better information on all regulations related to consumer protection' and 'Harmonised national regulations on consumer protection' both scored 68 per cent.[415]

Article 10 acknowledges the supplementing role of codes of conduct, in addition to available court or administrative enforcement procedures.[416] Article 2(g) indicates what the Unfair Commercial Practices Directive defines as a code of conduct:

> '[...] an agreement which defines the behaviour of the traders who undertake to be bound by the code in relation to one or more particular commercial practices or business sectors [...]'.

This being said, there are no indications whatsoever as to whether the codes referred to are European or national, nor are there any specifications regarding the content, form, or any other conditions for such codes to come into being.

Regardless of how well self-regulation might complement statutory law, their combination in the same instrument, save that different standards of harmonisation apply, is to a certain extent self-defeating. On the one hand, the Directive promotes the full harmonisation of unfair commercial practices by imposing a test accompanied by a list of practices which are always unfair. This is done to ensure a more uniform understanding of the rules supposed to combat these practices. On the other hand, the Unfair Commercial Practices Directive lays the foundations for Member States to take codes of conduct into their own hands and to choose firstly whether to engage in their promotion, and secondly what codes to stimulate. In other words, codes of conduct are double-voluntary in nature: it is voluntary for businesses to adhere to codes of conduct, and it is voluntary for Member States to support their actions. Some authors argue that codes of conduct did not really contribute to the Directive's harmonisation goal, for cultural and legal reasons,[417] yet arguments supporting the view that codes of conduct may lead to further convergence are presented in Chapter 3.

413 Flash Eurobarometer 128, 'Views on Business-to-Consumer Cross-border Trade', January 2015; Standard Eurobarometer 57.2, 'Health Issues, Cross-Border Purchases, and National Identities', February 2003.

414 The European Opinion Research Group EEIG and EOS Gallup Europe, 'Public Opinion in Europe: Views On Business-To-Consumer Crossborder Trade - Report B', November 2002, p. 52.

415 *Ibid.*

416 Pavillon 2012, p. 272.

417 *Ibid.*, p. 285.

c) Article 11: the enforcement of claims based on unfair commercial practices

Article 11 was at the heart of the *Köck* judgment.[418] In 2010, Mr. Köck, an Innsbruck-based trader, posted an announcement in a local newspaper that he would put his products on a 'total clearance' sale. He also displayed window banners and stickers indicating 'Everything must go' and 'Up to 90 per cent off'. The problem Mr. Köck faced when he was brought before the *Landesgericht Innsbruck* (Regional Court Innsbruck) by the Association for Protection against Unfair Competition (*Schutzverband gegen unlauteren Wettbewerb*) was that he had not applied for authorisation from the district administrative authority. As such, the authorisation requirement was rendered necessary by Paragraph 33b of the Law against unfair competition (*Gesetz gegen den unlauteren Wettbewerb*). In those circumstances, the CJEU was asked to rule on whether the Unfair Commercial Practices Directive must be interpreted '[...] as precluding a national court from ordering a commercial practice to cease on the sole ground that the practice has not been the subject of prior authorisation by the competent administrative authority, without itself carrying out an assessment of whether the practice is unfair'.[419]

The Directive was designed in such a way that left enforcement to the considerable discretion of Member States.[420] According to Article 11(1), the main obligation imposed at national level is that the means to combat unfair practices are adequate and effective. Some general principles are further laid down in Article 11. Firstly, Member States may choose whether they want courts to deal with legal action arising out of unfair commercial practices, whether they enable administrative authorities to be the relevant forum, or whether they want to make both options available to consumers. Such facilities will then be made available regardless of whether consumers affected are in the territory of the Member State where the trader is located. In addition, it is up to national law to determine whether prior to the lodging of the legal action/complaint, any additional procedures must be fulfilled.[421] Secondly, courts or administrative authorities enabled by national legislation have the power to issue injunctions and desist orders. Proof of actual loss or damage, or intention in the case of negligence (on the part of the trader) is not necessary. Moreover, Member States may confer upon courts or administrative authorities the power to determine whether the publication of such decisions is necessary.[422] Lastly, administrative authorities must be impartial, have adequate powers and give reasons for their decisions.[423]

These enforcement details were mentioned because as the Commission suggested, they did not reflect a new system, since other Directives had already mentioned these aspects.[424] Still, this is not to say it is a complete enforcement

418 C-206/11, *Georg Köck v Schutzverband gegen unlauteren Wettbewerb* [2013].

419 *Ibid.*, para. 24.

420 Weber 2012, p. 290; Budaite & Van Dam 2007, p. 108.

421 Article 11(1), Unfair Commercial Practices Directive.

422 Article 11(2), Unfair Commercial Practices Directive.

423 Article 11(3), Unfair Commercial Practices Directive.

424 Articles 4-6 of Directive 84/450/EEC; Article 11 of Directive 97/7/EC; see European Commission, Proposal for a Directive of the European Parliament and of the Council →

system, but one which is to be complemented by other rules, such as the ones embedded in the Injunctions Directive.[425] The Injunctions Directive itself acknowledges in recital three of the Preamble that '[c]urrent mechanisms available [...] both at national and at Community level, do not always allow infringements harmful to the collective interests of consumers to be terminated in good time'. In those circumstances, Article 3 of the Injunctions Directive enables both private and public bodies to safeguard the collective interests of the consumer. What this has led to is an eclectic enforcement of claims based on unfair commercial practices, from which three models of delegation can be distinguished: (i) private bodies have the right to file actions for injunctions but are not obliged to do so; (ii) private bodies that are not eligible to bring claims before courts assist public agencies; and (iii) both public and private bodies have rights to bring claims, but the extent to which they do is limited by national institutional patterns and culture.[426]

6.2. *What Standard of Harmonisation is Set by the European Legislator?*

As it has been emphasised before, the Unfair Commercial Practices Directive is a maximum harmonisation directive, which has been pointed out to be the second strongest feature of centralised rule-making after regulations.[427] Although not explicitly specified in the body of the Directive, maximum, or full harmonisation, entails that Member States may not impose more protective rules than those of the Unfair Commercial Practices Directive. The Court of Justice elaborated on this matter on a number of occasions. Between 2009 and 2013, the Court explicitly referred to full harmonisation on four occasions.[428] In the understanding of the Court, this principle stems directly out of Article 4. The shift towards maximum harmonisation is justified, as can be read in recital 5 of the Preamble, by the existence of disparities in national rules, leading to barriers affecting both businesses and consumers. For this reason, the Directive proposes to eliminate such barriers by 'establishing uniform rules at Community level which establish a high level of consumer protection and by clarifying certain legal concepts at Community level to the extent necessary for the proper functioning of the internal market and to meet the requirement of legal certainty'.[429] In those circumstances, the European

concerning unfair business-to-consumer commercial practices in the Internal Market and amending Directives 84/450/EEC, 97/7/EC and 98/27/EC (the Unfair Commercial Practices Directive), COM(2003) 356 final, para. 77.

425 Directive 2009/22/EC of the European Parliament and of the Council of 23 April 2009 on injunctions for the protection of consumers' interests (Codified version), *OJ* L110 of 1 April 2009.

426 Cafaggi & Micklitz 2008, p. 424-425.

427 Keirsbilck 2011, p. 182; see also Ramsay 2012, p. 161.

428 *VTB-VAB NV v Total Belgium NV and Galatea BVBA v Sanoma Magazines Belgium NV, para. 52; Zentrale zur Bekämpfung unlauteren Wettbewerbs eV v Plus Warenhandelsgesellschaft mbH*, para. 41; *Mediaprint Zeitungs- und Zeitschriftenverlag GmbH & Co. KG v 'Österreich'-Zeitungsverlag GmbH*, para. 30; *Citroën Belux NV v Federatie voor Verzekerings- en Financiële Tussenpersonen (FvF)*, para. 20.

429 Recital 5, Unfair Commercial Practices Directive Preamble.

legislator seems to have relied on two separate measures: (i) setting up uniform rules reflecting a high standard of consumer protection; and (ii) clarifying legal concepts to promote the functioning of the internal market and legal certainty.

It is not contested that these two measures are said to govern the entire body of rules in the Directive; however, the fact remains that the goal of full harmonisation is not reflected in all the articles in the Directive. This difference can be explained through the following factors: (i) minimum rather than maximum harmonisation applies to certain sectors by way of exception; (ii) the interpretation of certain provisions leads to diverging results in such a way that cannot support the goal of maximum harmonisation; and (iii) certain matters (such as enforcement or codes of conduct) are specifically left outside full harmonisation.

To exemplify the first case, namely where minimum rather than maximum harmonisation applies, reference can be made to Article 3(9). In relation to this article, the judgment in *Citroën Belux* is quite clear: financial services and immovable property are not subject to full harmonisation in the Unfair Commercial Practices Directive, and thus national legislation has a serious degree of discretion to deal with their regulation in relation to commercial practices.[430] As a result, Member States may impose measures which are more protective than those enshrined in the Directive. The Commission's Communication from March 2013 emphasised that unfair practices still linger in the fields of financial services and immovable transactions but that it is inappropriate to remove the minimum harmonisation character from these two sectors.[431] This policy draws on one of the conclusions that had been put forward by Civic Consulting in their Study on the application of Directive 2005/29/EC on Unfair Commercial Practices in the EU conducted for DG Justice in 2011.[432] Civic Consulting claims it is desirable to maintain the competence of Member States to impose more protective measures. Such measures may take the form of prohibitions imposed by national law, which would as such give Member States the possibility to add to the otherwise closed list in Annex 1 Unfair Commercial Practices Directive.[433] Civic Consulting emphasised that financial services and immovable property are sectors which entail higher risk and higher vulnerability for consumers, and that Member States should be able to draft their own prohibitions to better react to country-specific unfair practices.[434]

430 *Citroën Belux NV v Federatie voor Verzekerings-en Financiële Tussenpersonen (FvF).*

431 Communication from the Commission to the European Parliament, the Council and the European Economic and Social Committee on the application of the Unfair Commercial Practices Directive, 14 April 2013, COM(2013) 138 final, p. 6.

432 Civic Consulting, 'Study on the application of Directive 2005/29/EC on Unfair Commercial Practices in the EU', Part 1 – Synthesis Report, December 2011; Civic Consulting, 'Study on the application of Directive 2005/29/EC on Unfair Commercial Practices in the EU', Part 2 – Country Reports, December 2011.

433 *Ibid.*, p. 155.

434 *Ibid.*

It is clear from the 2013 Communication that the Commission fully embraced this view.[435] However, what the Commission did not do was provide answers to the following questions: why are financial services still governed by minimum harmonisation in the Unfair Commercial Practices Directive when they are already subject to full harmonisation as governed by other Directives?[436] And also, what makes unfair practices in financial services and immovable property more country-specific then other types of consumer matters?

It might be that it is perhaps the intention of the European legislator not to individualise a separate area for unfair practices with respect to financial services, albeit certain rules stemming out of financial services directives touch upon commercial practices that might pass the unfairness test.[437] As for the argument of specificity, it creates the impression that distinct consumer culture and preferences are better served by minimum harmonisation. This situation might reflect another directive that uses a general clause, namely the Unfair Contract Terms Directive. Still, this does not explain why the preference claim only fits financial services and immovable property. All in all, if the exemption in Article 3(9) remains a policy choice made by the Commission, it must be defended on different grounds.

The second factor under scrutiny is the fact that the interpretation of certain provisions leads to diverging results in such a way that cannot support the goal of maximum harmonisation. The Directive was said to have an 'inverted pyramid' structure (Figure 8), which would reveal one of its essential features: that the rules it refers to are 'future proof'.[438]

Figure 8: Classification of Unfair Practices (source: Giuseppe B. Abbamonte[439])

GENERAL CLAUSE		

MISLEADING PRACTICES		AGGRESSIVE PRACTICES
ACTIONS	OMISSIONS	

BLACK LIST

435 Communication from the Commission to the European Parliament, the Council and the European Economic and Social Committee on the application of the Unfair Commercial Practices Directive, 14 April 2013, COM(2013) 138 final, p. 6.

436 See Recital 9, Preamble, Directive 2008/48/EC of the European Parliament and of the Council of 23 April 2008 on credit agreements for consumers and repealing Council Directive 87/102/EEC, L 133/67; Recital 13, Preamble, Directive 2002/65/EC of the European Parliament and of the Council of 23 September 2002 concerning the distance marketing of consumer financial services and amending Council Directive 90/619/EEC and Directives 97/7/EC and 98/27/EC.

437 For instance, Articles 9 and 10 of Directive 2002/65/EC governing unsolicited services or communications.

438 Abbamonte 2007, p. 20-21.

439 *Ibid.*

Given that the Directive is based on a general clause, it is considered that whatever practice fails to be categorised as either misleading or aggressive can still be tested using Article 5. If that happens, two of the most important factors able to determine whether a practice is unfair or not, are the concepts already discussed: professional diligence and average consumer. In spite of the definition given in Article 2 for 'professional diligence', or the already-mentioned case law pinpointing at the characteristics of the average consumer, such concepts remain rather open to interpretation and are not appropriate for a one-fits-all application template. A template of this sort would be undesirable, if thinking of the entire consumer and business segments these concepts address; unlike other Directives in the consumer *acquis*, the Unfair Commercial Practices Directive does not preclude specific business sectors from applying its rules. Open-ended concepts such as professional diligence and average consumer are rather well placed and fit to deal with any developments shown by market trends and consumer behavior. The only issue with the general clause is its maximum harmonisation nature.

It has been claimed that prior to the adoption of the Directive, several Member States such as Germany, Denmark and Sweden, applied national standards of unfair competition going well beyond the protection proposed by the Directive.[440] In those circumstances, it is essential to determine how national courts eventually interpret the implementation of the Unfair Commercial Practices Directive in practice. It can be argued that the courts in question might echo a legal culture where the consumer is over-protected. In the analysis of national legal systems, Germany is one of the Member States of interest for this book, so this matter is looked at in greater detail under subsection 6.3.

Lastly, the third feature of interest is the fact that certain matters are specifically left outside the harmonisation goal of the Directive. It has been pointed out earlier that the Unfair Commercial Practices Directive does not apply harmonisation to matters such as enforcement and codes of conduct. In the case of enforcement, even though it was stated that it follows an already existing policy direction,[441] it is not clear what this policy wants to achieve. The enforcement system referred to in the Directive is in line with the earlier one stemming out of Articles 4-6 of Directive 84/450/EEC on misleading advertising, which was to a certain extent also used in Article 11 of the Distance Selling Directive.[442]

6.3. *How Was the Directive Transposed by Member States?*

As it is stated in Article 3(5) of the Directive, Member States had a transitional period of six years to continue applying their national laws as opposed to the

440 Bernitz 2007, p. 37.

441 See p. 16.

442 European Commission, Proposal for a Directive of the European Parliament and of the Council concerning unfair business-to-consumer commercial practices in the Internal Market and amending Directives 84/450/EEC, 97/7/EC and 98/27/EC (the Unfair Commercial Practices Directive), COM(2003) 356 final, para. 77.

Directive's unified regime. This period expired on 12 June 2013. In what follows, the transposition of the articles discussed above is now discussed.

6.3.1. Belgium

Initially, Belgian law accommodated unfair commercial practices in its Law on Commercial Practices and Consumer Information.[443] Even though it is a law that incorporates a vast number of provisions regarding consumer protection in general, it must be noted that in the light of the transposition choice, the Law of 14 July 1991 is a satellite law, as opposed to being part of the Civil Code. Before the entry into force of the Unfair Commercial Practices Directive, this law was modified to include the legislative changes.[444] However, in 2010 these rules were replaced with the Law on Market Practices and Consumer Protection.[445] For the purposes of this section, the 2010 law is analysed for one main reason. When it comes to unfair commercial practices, Belgian law had transposition issues which led to no less than three cases which gave the Court of Justice the possibility to evaluate the national implementation of several articles in both the 1991 as well as the 2010 laws.[446] Since the Belgian legislator was often faced with the problem of consolidating national rules to fall in line with their European inspiration, looking at the initial transposition would disregard these subsequent harmonisation efforts.

Chapter 4 of the Law on Market Practices dealt with prohibited practices (*pratiques commerciales déloyales*), and Articles 84-94 emphasised those practices occurring in relation to consumers. The general clause in Article 5 of the Directive and its components were transposed by the Law on Market Practices in an identical language, divided between three Articles: 84 (general clause), 85 (reference to the lists of misleading and aggressive practices) and 86 (general prohibition). The content of rules on misleading actions and omissions (Articles 6 and 7 Unfair Commercial Practices Directive) was taken over literally from the Directive, as can be shown in the wording of Articles 89 and 90, with Article 91 displaying the same list of misleading commercial practices as shown in Annex I to the Directive.[447]

The same can be said for the rules covering aggressive commercial practices: Articles 8 and 9 were taken over as such in Articles 92 and 93. Article 94 copied the

443 Budaite & Van Dam 2007, p. 115; Reiner Schulze & Hans Schulte-Nölke (eds.), 'Analysis of National Fairness Laws Aimed at Protecting Consumers in Relation to Commercial Practices', study commissioned by the Directorate-General Health and Consumer Protection of the European Commission (DG SANCO), 2003, p. 12.

444 *Wet van 5 juni 2007 tot wijziging van de wet van 14 juli 1991 betreffende de handelspraktijken en de voorlichting en bescherming van de consument*, B.S. 21.06.2007, 34272.

445 Cauffman 2012, p. 1328; see also Case C-657/11, *Belgian Electronic Sorting Technology NV v Peelaers and another* [2013], para. 13; *Citroën Belux NV v Federatie voor Verzekerings- en Financiële Tussenpersonen* (FvF), para. 6.

446 *VTB-VAB NV v Total Belgium NV and Galatea BVBA v Sanoma Magazines Belgium NV, para, 52; Belgian Electronic Sorting Technology NV v Peelaers and another*, para. 13; See also *Citroën Belux NV v Federatie voor Verzekerings- en Financiële Tussenpersonen* (FvF), para. 6.

447 See also Keirsbilck 2011, p. 161.

list in Annex I of the Directive regarding aggressive commercial practices considered as unfair in all circumstances.

Moving on to Article 10 of the Directive, it must be determined whether there were any explicit provisions in the Law on Market Practices on code owners controlling unfair commercial practices.[448] Scanning through the 2010 law, it seems there were no such provisions. While codes of conduct were indeed acknowledged by the Belgian legislator in the context of misleading commercial practices,[449] there was no specific provision endorsing the control of unfair commercial practices by owners of codes of conduct. However, it must be mentioned that several codes of conduct had been adopted by the Advertising Council (*Raad voor de Reclame*).[450]

As for enforcement, Chapter 6 (Articles 110-118) of the Law on Market Practices dealt with injunctions. In more detail, Belgian law allowed for injunctive relief not only against the advertiser, but also against publishers, printers, directors or distributors of the advertisement, when the advertiser did not reside nor had a designated responsible person in Belgium (Article 110 of the Law on Market Practices). Similarly, proceedings may have been brought not only by interested parties, but also by: the Minister or Director-General of the Directorate-General for Supervision and Mediation of the Federal Public Service Economy, SMEs, Self-Employed and Energy; trade or inter-trade organisations provided they have legal personality; and consumer organisations (Article 113 of the Law on Market Practices). Moreover, injunctions had a provisional effect (Article 118 of the Law on Market Practices), and could have only been published if they were likely to contribute to the cessation of the practice (Article 116 EMPC, second sentence).

As of 2014, these rules have been taken over by the Code of Economic Law.

6.3.2. France

Given that French law incorporates consumer protection in the Consumer Code, the Unfair Commercial Practices Directive was implemented by way of amending the Code, which took place on two different occasions during the same year (2008).[451] Commercial practices are as such covered by Title II.

The general clause (Article 5 Unfair Commercial Practices Directive) was integrated by the French legislator in Article L. 120-1. Starting with the general prohibition of unfair commercial practices (*pratiques commerciales déloyales*), the wording of the Article closely follows the Directive, with one relevant distinction: while the Unfair Commercial Practices Directive introduces the concept of 'average consumer', the standard used in Article L. 120-1 is that of the 'normally informed

[448] Article 2(31) explains what a code of conduct is according to the same definition as the Unfair Commercial Practices Directive in its Article 2(f).

[449] See for instance Article 91(3) of the Law on Market Practices.

[450] Keirsbilck 2011, p. 455.

[451] *Loi no 2008-776 du 4 août 2008 de modernisation de l'économie, Journal Officiel de la République Française (JORF)*, 05 August 2008; *Loi no 2008-3 du 3 janvier 2008 pour le développement de la concurrenceau service des consommateurs, Journal Officiel de la République Française (JORF)*, 04 January 2008; see also Keirsbilck 2011, p. 164; Ambroise-Castérot 2009, p. 22.

and reasonably observant and circumspect' (*normalement informé et raisonnablement attentive et avisé*). This is nothing else than the definition of the average consumer, as referred to in recital 18 of the Unfair Commercial Practices Directive, which shows the proximity of the French legislation to the Directive's goal. A slight departure from the wording of the Directive can be noticed in the second paragraph of Article L. 120-1, implementing Article 5(3) Unfair Commercial Practices Directive. There, the French legislator specifies that 'the unfair character of the commercial practice that targets a particular category of consumers or a group of consumers who are vulnerable due to mental or physical infirmity, age or credulity shall be assessed in relation to the average judgment capacity of the category or the group'.[452] The technical departure of the French text from the Directive's content touches upon three elements.

Firstly, the French article does not take over the Directive's condition that it is commercial practices 'which are likely to materially distort the economic behaviour only of a clearly identifiable group of consumers' that shall be subjected to an assessment using the 'average member of the group' test. The reason why this condition is important is because it sets forth an objective standard, represented by the material distortion of the economic behaviour, whereas the French legislator included a subjective standard bearing on judgment capacity (*capacité moyenne de discernement*). However, it is hard to determine whether the two standards lead to diverging results in practice. On the one hand, in order to determine what is average about a group of consumers, a judge might order a survey, which is only as clear as the questions composing it. On the other hand, to determine capacity, a judge normally orders a psychological examination;[453] still, it is difficult to tell how this procedure would contribute to revealing the average vulnerable consumer.

Secondly, it is interesting to notice that in the Unfair Commercial Practices Directive, the assessment of commercial practices is made 'from the perspective' of the average member of a group (*du point de vue du membre moyen de ce groupe*), while Article L. 120-1 second paragraph mentions that the evaluation of commercial practices will be made *in relation to* (emphasis added) the average judgment capacity (*au regard de la capacité moyenne de discernement de la catégorie ou du groupe*). It can be argued that the Directive's test requires the judge to put himself in the position of the average vulnerable consumer when identifying which practices may be detrimental to his interests. However, the French test would only require the judge to take into account the vulnerable consumer's position when balancing interests. However, once again, it must be mentioned that even though theoretical arguments can be made on the basis of this difference, it remains very difficult to prove that the two interpretations would diverge in practice.

Thirdly, French law does not take into account the condition according to which the vulnerability of the consumers is something that the trader could reasonably be expected to foresee.

452 Translation by author.

453 *CA Toulouse, CH. 02 SECT*, n° 07/0513901, 4 February 2009.

Going back to the transposition of Article 5(3), it must be added that Article L. 120-1 did not transpose the exception regarding the common and legitimate advertising practice of making exaggerated statements.

The last paragraph of Article L. 120-1 mentions that misleading commercial practices as defined by Articles L. 121-1 and L. 121-1-1, and aggressive commercial practices as defined by Articles 122-11 and L. 122-11-1 constitute unfair commercial practices.

Article L. 121-1 I transposes Article 6 of the Directive. Several further differences can be noticed: (i) French law does not specify the fundamental causal link between the practice and the transactional decision as indicated in Article 6(1) of the Directive;[454] (ii) French law departs from the terminology of the Directive, but it can be said that overall, the conditions in Article 6(1) are still fulfilled;[455] (iii) French law does not recognise separate categories for misleading actions and omissions;[456] (iv) Article 6(2) is only partially found in French law - no reference is made to commercial practices being regarded as misleading if they involve non-compliance by the trader with his undertaken commitments in his code of conduct.[457] Article L. 121-1-1 lists commercial practices regarded as unfair in any case. With the exception of one, all commercial practices mentioned in Annex I of the Directive are found in Article L. 121-1-1.[458]

Article L. 122-11 I covers aggressive commercial practices and has a different format than Article 8 Unfair Commercial Practices Directive. The differences can be catalogued on the basis of the aggressive means used to conclude the contract, or the causal test as follows: (i) the Directive refers to aggressive means used to conclude the contract, namely harassment and coercion, including the use of physical force, or undue influence; French law refers to repeated and persistent solicitations or the use of physical or psychological coercion; (ii) the Directive uses a causal test between the aggressive mean to conclude the contract and the consumer's decision to undertake the transaction; Article L. 122-11 does not specifically identify such a test, although it can be argued that paragraph 2° of the same Article makes reference to the vitiation of the consumer's consent, which in

454 Article 6(1), Unfair Commercial Practices Directive: '[...] causes or is likely to cause [the consumer] to take a transactional decision that he would not have taken otherwise [...]'.

455 E.g. see Article L. 121-1 (paragraph 1°a), *Code de la Consommation: '[...] l'existence, la disponibilité ou la nature du bien ou du service [...]'*; compare with Article 6(1)(a) Unfair Commercial Practices Directive: '[...] the existence or nature of the product'.

456 Article 7 Unfair Commercial Practices Directive is transposed in Article L. 121-1 II Consumer Code.

457 However, Article L. 121-1-1 (paragraph 3) does refer to codes of conduct in that it deems the claiming that a code of conduct has endorsement when it does not, as being a misleading commercial practice, just as in Annex I of the Unfair Commercial Practices Directive.

458 Paragraph 14 of Annex I Unfair Commercial Practices Directive was not transposed: 'Establishing, operating or promoting a pyramid promotional scheme where a consumer gives consideration for the opportunity to receive compensation that is derived primarily from the introduction of other consumers into the scheme rather than from the sale or consumption of products.'

turn could lead to the same causal test being applied;[459] (iii) Article 8 uses the standard of the average consumer; this standard is absent from Article L. 122-11.

Moving on, the content of Article 9 was incorporated literally in paragraph II of Article L. 122-11. The same can be said for the list of aggressive commercial practices in Article L. 122-11-1, taking over the content of Annex I: all but one aggressive practice in the Directive are listed in the Consumer Code.[460]

Although the Consumer Code operates with the concept of codes of conduct, it is neither defined nor elaborated upon. For this reason it can be stated that with respect to the possibility to encourage the control of unfair commercial practices by code owners (Article 10 of the Directive), the French legislator did not take any specific measures.

Articles L. 121-2 to L. 121-6 deal with enforcement matters. According to Article L. 121-2, it is possible for certain state agents to take note of unfair commercial practices and ask the responsible party to submit documentation in order to defend their practice.[461] The record of such practices (*procés-verbal*) observed by state agents are sent to the national prosecutor. Furthermore, Article L. 121-3 clearly specifies that the *juge d'instruction* may order injunction, either at the request of the public ministry or *ex officio*, as per Article 11(2) of the Directive.

6.3.3. Germany

Germany implemented the Unfair Commercial Practices Directive by amending its Act against Unfair Competition (*Gesetz gegen den unlauteren Wettbewerb*, hereinafter UWG) only at the end of 2008. In July 2008 the Commission had launched an infringement procedure for untimely transposition.[462] Unfortunately, that was not the only problem faced by the German implementation process. Many provisions can be held to contradict the rules of the Directive, for one general reason: they do not align to the Directive's standard of harmonisation.

§ 3 UWG transposes the general clause found in Article 5 of the Directive. Although not a literal transposition, the essence of the rules is maintained by the German legislator: there is a general prohibition of unfair commercial practices; professional diligence and the average consumers are used as standards, reference is made to vulnerable consumers and the reasonable foreseeability obligation placed on the shoulders of the trader. Still, no exception is made in the case of common and legitimate advertising practices of making exaggerate statements (Article 5(3)

459 See for instance Article 1116 French Civil Code.

460 Paragraph 29 of Annex I Unfair Commercial Practices Directive is currently not listed in French law (Paragraph 6 of Article 122-11-1 was repealed): 'Demanding immediate or deferred payment for or the return or safekeeping of products supplied by the trader, but not solicited by the consumer except where the product is a substitute supplied in conformity with Article 7(3) of Directive 97/7/EC (inertia selling).'

461 According to Article L. 121-2, these agents are: agents in the fields of competition, consumer matters, fraud repression, agents working at the general directorate for food matters (within the ministry for agriculture) and agents working at the metrology service (within the ministry for industry).

462 Case C-326/08, *Commission v Germany* [2009].

second sentence). Although the UWG contains an Annex listing commercial practices that are always deemed unfair, § 4 includes 11 examples of unfair commercial practices. One of these situations has been deemed by the Court of Justice to have been inconsistent with the maximum harmonisation goal of the Directive. For instance, in *Zentrale zur Bekämpfung unlauteren Wettbewerbs eV*,[463] the CJEU stated that the Directive precludes national legislation (§ 4(6) UWG) from imposing a general prohibition without taking account specific circumstances.

§ 5 mirrors Article 6 of the Directive. Once again, even though the wording and structure differ, German law can be said to make reference to the same standards, save for some alterations. Notable differences include: no specific reference to the causal test between the deceiving elements and the consumer's transactional decision; the list of such elements (leading to the consumer's deceit) does not refer to the existence or nature of the product (Article 6(1)(a)) separately, but it includes nature together with the characteristics of the product (§ 3(1)(1) UWG); the elements relating to the extent of the trader's commitments, the motives for the commercial practice and the nature of the sales process are left out of § 3(1) UWG.

Perhaps the most controversial transposition choice has been § 5(1)(6) UWG, stating that whenever a code owner undertakes to be bound by his code of conduct and does not comply with this obligation, the practice can be deemed misleading.[464] As such, this circumstance is just the same as that referred to in Article 2(b)(ii) of the Directive. The problem is that by using a different structure, the German legislator places this specific situation under a chapeau it does not belong to (§ 5(1)UWG). Consequently, having to interpret it together with the requirement that an unfair commercial practice shall be deemed misleading if it contains untruthful information,[465] the result is different: a commercial practice can be considered to be misleading if the trader *provides untruthful information* regarding his compliance with a code of conduct he has undertaken to be bound to.[466]

Moreover, § 5(4) UWG specifies that the advertising of a price reduction in the case when the price concerned is only offered for a short period of time is presumed to be misleading, and thus unfair. There is no doubt that should this paragraph end up under the scrutiny of the Court of Justice, the case would be deemed to have the same faith as *Zentrale zur Bekämpfung unlauteren Wettbewerbs eV*, since the Court clearly stated that the German legislator cannot go beyond the standard of harmonisation imposed by the Directive, and can thus not create a presumption of unfairness to situations other than the ones included in Annex I. This would be, in the light of the Court's rationale in *Zentrale zur Bekämpfung unlauteren Wettbewerbs*

463 *Zentrale zur Bekämpfung unlauteren Wettbewerbs eV v Plus Warenhandelsgesellschaft mbH*, para. 68.

464 See for instance Beckers 2014, p. 178.

465 This is actually the transposition of Article 6(1), Unfair Commercial Practices Directive.

466 For a more detailed analysis of codes of conduct under the UWG see Beckers 2014, p. 176.

eV, a stricter rule which would entail a higher level of consumer protection than what the Directive prescribes.[467]

Article 7 is reflected in the newly created § 5a UWG, titled 'Misleading by omission'. Although in this case it seems the German legislator kept the structure of the Directive, upon a closer look, one essential aspect is missing in the determination of what may represent a misleading commercial practice: the standard of the average consumer. Both paragraphs 1 and 2 of Article 7 use this standard to determine the influence of certain practices on transactional decision-making. § 5a UWG does not replicate this standard: subparagraph 1 tests concealment of facts against generally accepted standards (*Verkehrsauffassung*); and subparagraph 2 simply refers to consumer's ability of reaching a decision, without implementing the Unfair Commercial Practices Directive's view according to which it is the average consumer who must be taken into account in doing so.

Article 8 can be considered to have been transposed in § 4, although tracking back the legislative change of 2008, only mild amendments have been brought to the UWG 2004 in this sense, subparagraph 2 being the only one that suffered total change.[468] Moreover, Article 9 of the Directive consisting of the factors which may help to determine which commercial practices are aggressive has not been accommodated by German legislation. This being said, § 4 UWG does make reference to very detailed circumstances, some of which overlap the content of Article 8. For instance, § 4(1) UWG specifies refers to commercial practices that impair the freedom of decision by pressure and influence, and § 4(9) UWG speaks of deception and unreasonable exploitation.

The *Bundesgerichtshof* has analysed § 4 UWG on several occasions. In 2010, in one case regarding the awarding of vouchers for the purchase of fixed-price pharmaceuticals, the *Bundesgerichtshof* concluded that there was no conflict between § 4(11) UWG and the Unfair Commercial Practices Directive.[469] One year later (2011), the *Bundesgerichtshof* looked into a case regarding the transparency of participating in a raffle, and explicitly analysed § 4(5) UWG in conjunction with Article 7(1) and (2) of the Directive.[470]

Nevertheless, regardless of how § 4 UWG combines misleading and aggressive practices, or how it combines new paragraphs and initial rules, it still poses one significant problem - it looks more like a black list than a particular test. The Directive promotes maximum harmonisation by virtue of its own structure: Article 5 is the general test, Articles 6-9 are the particular tests (misleading and aggressive practices), and the Annex is the black list. In other words, no other commercial practices than those included in the Annex can be unfair as a matter of principle, without looking at the circumstances of the case. This is exactly what is missing from § 4 UWG; instead of mentioning that its 11 subparagraphs are factors

467 *Zentrale zur Bekämpfung unlauteren Wettbewerbs eV v Plus Warenhandelsgesellschaft mbH*, para. 41.

468 First Act Amending the Unfair Competition Act of 22 December 2008, Federal Gazette 2008, Part I no. 64, 29 December 2008.

469 BGH, *Unser Dankeschön für Sie*, I ZR 193/07.

470 BGH, *Einwilligungserklärung für Werbeanrufe*, I ZR 50/09, para. 15.

which can test unfairness, the chapeau reads that these 11 situations are considered to be particularly unfair (*'Unlauter handelt insbesondere, wer [...]'*).

Moving on to the content of the Annex of the Directive, it can be seen from the Amending Act that the German legislator added it to the UWG in 2008.[471] Although the transposition has a high degree of similarity to the Directive, several observations can be made. Firstly, the UWG Annex does not distinguish between misleading and aggressive practices. Secondly, paragraph 26 of the Directive's Annex (on persistent and unwanted solicitations) was not transposed in the UWG.

After browsing through the provisions of the UWG it becomes clear that Article 10 on codes of conduct, does not have an equivalent in the German act. This does not mean that no such codes of conduct exist in practice. For instance, the German Advertising Standards Council, a self-regulatory body for the advertising industry in Germany, uses codes of conduct for several areas of the advertising trade. Moreover, the Council claims to assess advertising practices from the perspective of the reasonably well-informed and rational consumer.[472]

Provisions on the enforcement of rules combating unfair commercial practices (Article 11 of the Directive) can be found in Chapter 2 of the UWG. These rules stem from the 2004 version of the UWG, and the 2008 amendment did not affect their substance.[473] The level of detail and legal conceptualisation of the enforcement rules confirms their national nature. For instance, German commentaries categorise injunctive relief as referred to in § 8 UWG to be a substantive pecuniary claim, and not a mere procedural remedy.[474] Recourse to injunctions entails the risk of recurrence of the unfair practices referred to in § 3 and § 7 UWG (§ 8(1) UWG).[475] According to § 8(3) UWG, the parties who can ask for injunctive relief are: competitors, business associations, consumer associations and the Chamber of Industry and Commerce. Before requesting the injunction, the interested party must send a notification to warn the infringer about legal proceedings and ask him to cease and desist (§ 12(1) UWG).[476] Injunctions are provisional and the court has discretion in deciding whether their publication is necessary (§ 12(2) and (3) UWG). What is specific about the enforcement procedure of the UWG is that it also creates conciliation boards.

471 First Act Amending the Unfair Competition Act of 22 December 2008, Federal Gazette 2008, Part I no. 64, 29 December 2008.

472 German Standards Advertising Council Rules on Advertising and its Appraisal (October 2007), available at: <www.werberat.de/sites/default/files/uploads/media/dw_general_principles_en.pdf>, last accessed on 27 July 2016.

473 UWG § 8 Beseitigung und Unterlassung, Bergmann/Goldmann/Harte-Bavendamm/-Henning-Bodewig, UWG, 3. Auflage 2013, Rn 63.

474 UWG § 8 Beseitigung und Unterlassung, Piper/Ohly/Sosnitza, Gesetz gegen den unlauteren Wettbewerb, 5. Auflage 2010, Rn 5.

475 *Ibid.*, Rn 7.

476 *Ibid.*, Rn 11.

6.3.4. Ireland

The Unfair Commercial Practices Directive was implemented in Ireland through The Consumer Protection Act 2007, a piece of legislation that also served the purpose of establishing The National Consumer Agency (hereinafter the NCA).[477] The creation of the NCA was part of a wider consumer policy strategy devised by the Consumer Strategy Group, set up by the Minister for Enterprise, Trade and Employment in 2004.[478]

The general prohibition against unfair commercial practices (Article 5) is enshrined in Section 41 and reflects the same elements as the Directive. The professional diligence and average consumer standards have been taken over from the Unfair Commercial Practices Directive. One specific feature is that vulnerable consumers and particular groups of consumers are not mentioned in Section 41 but are actually covered by the definitions in Section 2.

Article 6 of the Directive is reflected in Sections 44 and 45, which do not deviate from the Directive's content in other way than structure-wise. Similarly, Article 7 was transposed in Section 46.

Aggressive commercial practices as envisaged in Articles 8-9 of the Directive can be found in Sections 52-54, once again with unchanged content. Section 55 lists the commercial practices which are prohibited under any circumstance. Although once again the structure differs quite extensively,[479] the content of the black-listed practices remains the same the same when transposed in Irish law.

Moving on to Article 10, the Consumer Protection Act 2007 includes not only details regarding the authority of the NCA to review codes of practice (Section 8 subparagraph k), but also the approval procedure for such codes. According to Section 88, a person representing one or more traders may submit a code of practice to the NCA's review. The NCA then evaluates if the code is consistent with the provisions of the Consumer Protection Act 2007. In order to provide assistance to traders with respect to unfair commercial practices in general and codes of practice in particular, the NCA can issue guidelines (Section 90). Going one step further, Section 89 even puts forward a procedural rule relating to the fact that codes of conduct, whether approved by the NCA under Section 88 or not, are admissible in court as evidence.

Regarding enforcement, Irish law is particular in that it did not only include public enforcement provisions, but it also provided consumers with a private right to damages.[480] To start with, Section 71, governing civil proceedings, allows any

477 UK Department of Enterprise, Trade and Employment, 'Consumer Protection (National Consumer Agency) Bill 2006 – Screening Regulatory Impact Analysis', August 2006, p. 3.

478 *Ibid.*

479 The most evident difference can be seen when it comes to pyramid promotional schemes: instead of being listed in Section 55 together with the other black-listed practices, pyramid schemes are instead dealt with quite extensively in Sections 64-66.

480 The Law Commission (England and Wales), 'A private right of redress for unfair commercial practices? Preliminary Advice to the Department for Business, Enterprise and Regulatory Reform on the Issues Raised', November 2008, p. 3; see also Collins 2010, p. 113.

person (including the NCA and other public bodies) to apply for prohibition orders to prevent a trader or person from committing or engaging in prohibited acts or practices (Article 11(2)). In assessing such applications, the Irish Circuit Court of High Court must take public interest into account (among others), which is specifically prescribed for in Article 11(2) of the Directive.

According to Section 74, in the case of unfair commercial practices other than those specified in Sections 45 (misleading practices) and 65(1) (pyramid schemes), a consumer may avail itself of a right of action for relief by way of damages (including exemplary damages). Sections 76-84 govern criminal proceedings.

6.3.5. The Netherlands

The Netherlands has a history of assimilating consumer contract legislation in its Civil Code, and the Unfair Commercial Practices Directive is no exception. On 25 September 2008, an Act was passed by the Dutch Parliament to amend Books 3 and 6 of the Civil Code in order to accommodate the Unfair Commercial Practices Directive.

The general prohibition in Article 5 Unfair Commercial Practices Directive is reflected in Article 6:193b BW,[481] which takes over the concept of average consumer but does not make any reference to the material distortion of consumer behaviour. It can, of course, be argued that while the wording might not be there, the meaning behind it is actually embedded in the norm. Vulnerable consumers are said to be a variant of the average consumer standard, and are mentioned in the definitions encompassed by Article 6:193a(2) BW.

Article 6:193c BW reflects misleading practices (Article 6 of the Directive). Even though the criteria used to determine the misleading nature of practices in both subparagraphs are the same as in the Directive, two main differences can be pointed out. Firstly, Article 6:193c(1) BW leaves out the explicit mention in Article 6(1) that even if the information provided to the consumer is factually correct, a practice can still be misleading. However, it can be argued that the lack of this specification does not change the essence of the Dutch provision that continues to be in conformity with the Directive, given that it provides for the possibility that the consumer is misled as an alternative to the provision of factually incorrect information.[482] Secondly, the chapeau of Article 6:193c(2) BW is simplified to the extent that it does not specify being applicable on a case-by-case basis, given that the situations it refers to are not part of the black list, but must always be considered in the light of their context and circumstances.[483]

Articles 6:193d-e BW reflect misleading omissions without posing any transposition questions, and the same can be said for Articles 6:193h-i BW, which

481 Cherednychenko & Kuiper 2008, p. 2.

482 Article 6:193c(1) BW reads: 'Een handelspraktijk is misleidend indien informatie wordt verstrekt die feitelijk onjuist is of die de gemiddelde consument misleidt of kan misleiden, al dan niet door de algemene presentatie van de informatie, zoals ten aanzien van [...]'.

483 Article 6:193c(2) BW reads: 'Een handelspraktijk is eveneens misleidend indien [...]'.

are a copy-paste version of the Directive's Annex. Article 6:193h BW deals with aggressive practices in exactly the same manner as Articles 8-9 of the Directive.

When it comes to consumer codes, the Dutch legislator has been a keen supporter of self-regulation.[484] However, there are no specific provisions in the body of rules transposing this Directive that explicitly showcase this support.

As far as enforcement is concerned (Article 11), Article 3:305d BW prescribes that cessation orders may be applied for in light of Article 1.1k of the Consumer Protection (Enforcement) Act (*Wet handhaving consumentenbescherming*). The procedure may be initiated by consumers and public bodies alike.

6.3.6. Romania

In Romania, the Unfair Commercial Practices Directive was transposed by virtue of satellite law 363/2007 (hereinafter 'Law 363/2007') regarding the combating of unfair commercial practices in relation to consumers and the harmonisation of national provisions with European consumer protection law.[485] Just as in the case of other Directives, the Romanian legislator adopted a 'copy/paste' transposition technique.

On a terminological note, the translation used in the Romanian law for 'unfair practices', namely 'incorrect practices' (*practici incorecte*), is different than the Romanian version of the Directive.[486] This being said, no fundamental issues can be said to arise out of this particular terminology, since practice would not necessarily distinguish between unfair or incorrect.

Looking at transposition more closely, it can be seen that Article 5 of the Directive is reflected in Article 4 of Law 363/2007, keeping the vast majority of the initial content. The only main difference is that unlike in the Directive, Article 4 does not put forward a general prohibition of unfair commercial practices. However, this prohibition can be found in Article 15, which states that unfair commercial practices are seen as contraventions and are sanctioned according to administrative law with a fine ranging from RON 5.000 to 50.000.[487]

Misleading practices are embedded in Article 6 (actions) and Article 7 (omissions) of Law 363/2007 and follow the wording of the Directive. The same can be said for Articles 8 and 9 of Law 363/2007 (aggressive practices). The average consumer test, the elements which are listed to be taken into account when applying the specific unfairness tests in the cases of unfair actions/omissions and aggressive practices - all the pivotal concepts in the Directive can be found in more or less the

484 Pavillon 2012, p. 283; Van Mierlo 2007; Castermans 2011, p. 360.

485 Law no. 363 of 28 December 2007, Romanian Official Gazette no. 899 of 28 December 2007.

486 The Romanian version of the Directive uses the term 'disloyal practices' (*practici neloiale*).

487 Contraventions are defined in Article 1, Ordinance 2 of 12 July 2001 (Romanian Official Gazette no. 410 of 25 July 2001) as: '[...] acts established and sanctioned by law, ordinance, Government decision [...], committed with intention [...]'; the amount of the fine was increased in 2010 by Law no. 130 of 30 June 2010 (Romanian Official Gazette no. 453 of 2 July 2010), and was the only modification brought to Law 363/2007.

same form in Romanian legislation. Moreover, the Annex to Law 363/2007 is identical to the Directive's Annex.

Moving to Article 10 of the Directive, Law 363/2007 does not contain any explicit provision encouraging codes of conduct. However, Article 14 specifies that the owners of codes of conducts may establish a certain control over unfair commercial practices, given that this control does not limit the rights of consumers, consumer associations, or other interested parties to start procedures before the National Authority for Consumer Protection or the competent courts. One example of such a code owner is the Romanian Advertising Council, a non-governmental organisation which embraced self-regulation, employs such a code of conduct in practice (the Code of Advertising Practice).[488] The influences of the Unfair Commercial Practices Directive on this code can be noticed upon a closer reading of its rules,[489] and the code itself specifies in its Preamble that attention was paid to guidelines issued by the International Chamber of Commerce in this respect.

As for enforcement, Articles 10-16 of Law 363/2007 elaborate on how Romanian law sanctions unfair commercial practices. Two public institutions are involved in the policing of unfair commercial practices: the National Authority for Consumer Protection, which is granted authority to hear complaints from interested persons (Article 10), and the National Audiovisual Council of Romania, which can be asked by the National Authority for Consumer Protection, or by the competent courts to provide the identification details of the natural and/or legal persons involved in unfair commercial practices relating to advertising (Article 13(1)(c)).

According to Article 13, in urgent cases (and specifically in matters dealing with public interest), the competent courts or the National Authority for Consumer Protection may take certain measures even without proof of loss or effective prejudice, and also without proof of intention or negligence on behalf of the commercial party. These measures imply the triggering of the necessary legal procedures to cease and desist from unfair commercial practices (Article 13(1)(a) and (b)).

Once the court judgment prohibiting commercial practices as unfair or establishing cease and desist is issued, the court may request the partial or full publication of the judgment, as well as the publishing of corrective statements, at the expense of the commercial party (Article 13(2) and (3)).

6.3.7. The United Kingdom

The United Kingdom accommodated the European rules on unfair commercial practices by passing the Consumer Protection from Unfair Trading Regulations (CPRs) entering into force in May 2008 and replacing several regimes that had been

488 Romanian Advertising Council, The Code of Advertising Practice, available online at: <www.rac.ro/EN/cod>, last accessed on 27 July 2016.

489 For instance, the average consumer is defined as a 'consumer considered to be reasonably informed, careful and cautious, taking into account the social, cultural and linguistic factors'.

applicable to unfair trade to that date.[490] Before the CPRs, UK law left the control of unfair commercial practices to a variety of statutes, the application of which was facilitated by a sustained use of business codes.[491] The new regime thus marked a shift towards principle-based regulation,[492] which was supposed to overhaul the applicable law by simplifying its sources and harmonizing its content. Overall, the CPRs can be said to have three fundamental parts: the general prohibitions; offences; and enforcement. While the general prohibitions part is visibly influenced by the Directive, when it comes to offences and enforcement it can be noted that some traditional features of UK law have been taken over. In comparison to the other UK national transposition provisions addressed in this book, the CPRs can undoubtedly be considered as a change in the policy of the UK lawmaker, well-known for its copy-paste transposition techniques. Moving on to the rules themselves, Regulation 3 serves to implement Article 5(1)-(2) and (4)-(5) Unfair Commercial Practices Directive by using the same content. Although at first sight the vulnerable consumer standard in Article 5(3) Unfair Commercial Practices Directive seems to be missing, it was actually taken over and developed in Regulation 2(2)-(6) dealing with interpretation. The Office of Fair Trading accompanied the CPRs with a set of guidelines for the application of the new law.[493] According to these guidelines, unfair commercial practices can be seen as follows:

Figure 9 – UK Office of Fair Trading classification of unfair commercial practices (Source: UK Office of Fair Trading)

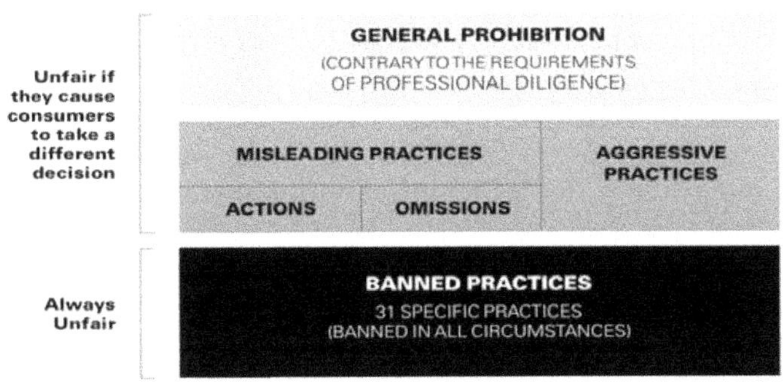

490 The CPRs repealed, amongst others, the following acts in full: Fraudulent Mediums Act 1951, Trading Representations (Disabled Persons) Act 1958, Mock Auctions Act 1961. Schedule 4 to the CPRs lists a total of 40 acts the provisions of which have been repealed in part or in full (including the ones mentioned above). See also Duivenvoorde 2015, p. 150.

491 Keirsbilck 2011, p. 144-146; Collins 2004, p. 26.

492 Williams & Hare 2010, p. 381.

493 Office of Fair Trading, Guidance on the UK Regulations (May 2008) implementing the Unfair Commercial Practices Directive, available at: <www.oft.gov.uk/shared_oft/-business_leaflets/cpregs/oft1008.pdf, last accessed on 27 July 2016.

Article 6 of the Directive regarding misleading actions has been fully and accurately transposed by Regulation 5, while Article 7 dealing with misleading omissions is completely reflected by Regulation 6. What the latter does add, however, is a definition for 'material information', which it takes to mean 'the information which the average consumer needs, according to the context, to take an informed transactional decision; and [...] any information requirement which applies in relation to a commercial communication as a result of a Community obligation'. Still, this brief definition integrated in Regulation 6 does not add any novel elements, but it simply links back to the Directive's concept of 'transactional decision'.

In turn, Articles 8 and of the Directive regarding aggressive commercial practices have been accommodated by Regulation 7 with exactly the same content. The only notable distinction is that Regulation 7 leaves out physical force when enumerating the means of aggressive commercial practices in paragraph 1, but that it solely because paragraph 3 later mentions that coercion includes the use of physical force. On the same interpretative note of Regulation 5(3) it is worth remarking that undue influence is also defined as 'exploiting a position of power in relation to the consumer so as to apply pressure, even without using or threatening to use physical force, in a way which significantly limits the consumer's ability to make an informed decision'.[494] Unlike other Member States, UK law is probably the closest to the concept of undue influence as employed by the Directive and still the CPRs spell out what is understood by undue influence.[495] This transposition choice can be interpreted to give national judges a tool of clarity and separation between already existing national concepts and European terminology. What is more, Schedule 1 of the CPRs has precisely the same content as the Unfair Commercial Practices Directive's black list.

Moving on to Article 10 of the Directive, as it has been already mentioned, codes of conduct have flourished in the UK and have seriously contributed to the setting of commercial standards.[496] The spread use of such codes can be attributed to an OFT policy dating from back in 2001, when it started encouraging the development of codes created on the basis of OFT core criteria. According to the consultations conducted by the OFT at that time, the response received from industry representatives was not only high, but also enthusiastic, which allowed the OFT to draw the conclusion that self-regulation was welcomed not only by

494 This definition stems from Article 2(j) Unfair Commercial Practices DirectiveUnfair Commercial Practices Directive.

495 See for instance other language versions of the Unfair Commercial Practices Directive Unfair Commercial Practices Directive: the French translation uses the term *influence injustifiée*, a concept not inherent to French contract law, which could have been replaced by the French doctrine of *violence*; the same can be said about the Romanian translation *influență nejustificată*, a concept unknown to Romanian contract law. For a general overview of the problems posed by ambiguity in translations see McAuliffe 2014, p. 65.

496 Pavillon 2012, p. 283.

businesses and business associations, but consumer associations as well.[497] For this reason, the OFT drafted core criteria for consumer codes and created a so-called Consumer Codes Approval Scheme: if code sponsors fulfil OFT criteria, their code is approved.

Taking this system to reflect principle-based regulation, it might be that in this case it combines the best of two worlds: on the one hand, industry representatives can have a say in rule management as they are allowed to draft their own rules, but on the other hand their discretion has a fixed ambit, as a government agency ensures a given level of consumer protection. The OFT seems to be equally supportive of self-regulation: '[t]he aim of the scheme is to put the 'self' back into self-regulation [...]'.[498]

Still, in spite of the proliferation of codes of conduct in the UK, the implementation of the Directive by virtue of the CPRs does not add much.[499] Apart from the few references in the Regulations simply mirroring the Unfair Commercial Practices Directive, only one additional Regulation tackles codes of conduct. According to Regulation 4, code owners may not promote unfair commercial practices in their codes.

In what concerns enforcement, Regulations 19-23 detail the applicable procedures. However, what these rules provide for only covers the powers vested in national authorities with respect to conducting inspections, making test purchases, etc. No specific reference to a possible injunction procedure can be found in the CPRs, most likely because as the OFT pointed out in its pre-implementation consultation response, '[t]he practices are sufficiently specific that a trader should not need to be told not to engage in the practice by an injunction - rather, strict sanctions should be available in order to act as a serious deterrent [...]'.[500] What is more, only enforcement authorities may take action for breaches of unfair commercial practices provisions.

This seems to be indeed the case if we take a look at Regulations 8-18, covering offences. If found guilty of the offences detailed therein, traders can be convicted to the payment of a fine and/or imprisoned for a term up to two years (Regulation 13).

The fact that consumers have been given no direct recourse in situations involving unfair commercial practices has had the academic community ask

497 Office of Fair Trade, Consumer Codes of Practice: The OFT's response to the Consultation, OFT344, July 2001, p. 1, available at: <www.oft.gov.uk/shared_oft/Approvedcodesof-practice/oft344.pdf>, last accessed on 27 July 2016.

498 Office of Fair Trading, 'Consumer Codes Approval Scheme; Core Criteria and Guidance', OFT390, March 2008, p. 5, available at: <www.oft.gov.uk/shared_oft/Approvedcodes-ofpractice/oft390.pdf>, last accessed on 27 July 2016.

499 Even though the OFT is as such acknowledged to play a role in the enforcement of rules against unfair commercial practices, as stated in Regulation 19 in conjunction with Regulation 2(1), the CPRs are silent on the OFT procedure and the link between it and the Directive's Article 10.

500 Office of Fair Trading, 'Implementing the EU Directive on Unfair Commercial Practices and Amending Existing Consumer Legislation', OFT839, March 2006, p. 28, available at: <www.oft.gov.uk/shared_oft/reports/oft_response_to_consultations/oft839.pdf>, last accessed on 27 July 2016.

whether a private right of redress should be included in the CPRs.[501] According to Consumer Focus, 40 per cent of consumers in a sample of 1,000 online interviews conducted with adults in England, Scotland and Wales considered themselves victims of unfair commercial practices within a time-span of 24 months.[502] Out of these, 57 per cent did not consider taking any legal action.

An impact assessment conducted by the Department for Business, Innovation and Skills suggested different policy option: introducing a limited right of redress; using voluntary codes of conduct; introducing a comprehensive right of redress.[503] The same Department then went on to draft an amendment to the CPRs, introducing two individual rights to redress: the right to unwind (get a refund) and the right to a discount.[504] The proposal is part of a wider programme to reform consumer law in the UK, in the light of the implementation schedule of the Consumer Rights Directive.

6.4. *Comparative Notes on the Transposition*

The Unfair Commercial Practices Directive is the only maximum harmonisation directive included in this research. What is more, it is also the only directive that considers the potential of self-regulation as a form of co-regulation. In what follows, a brief account of some of the issues faced in the transposition process by Member States is given in a comparative manner.

In March 2013 the Commission issued a Communication on the application of the Unfair Commercial Practices Directive,[505] highlighting the improvement it brought to the regulatory environment and the obstacles it removed in cross-border commerce. While some beneficial impacts might be revealed when looking at national case law, the Commission claims the Directive improved the percentage of consumers willing to engage in cross-border transactions as reflected in Flash

501 The Law Commission, 'A private right of redress for unfair commercial practices? Preliminary advice to the Department for Business, Enterprise and Regulatory Reform on the issues raised, November 2008, available at: <http://lawcommission.justice.gov.uk/docs/-rights_of_redress_advice1(2).pdf>, last accessed on 27 July 2016; Howells 2011, p. 135.

502 Kate Roberts, 'The Extent of Unfair Commercial Practices', March 2009, p. 1, available at: <www.consumerfocus.org.uk/assets/1/files/2009/11/UCPDresearch.pdf>, last accessed on 27 July 2016.

503 Department for Business, Innovation and Skills, 'Consumer Redress for Misleading and Commercial Practices. Impact Assessment: Final', August 2013, available at: <https://www.gov.uk/government/uploads/system/uploads/attachment_data/file/226641/bis-13-1110-consumer-redress-for-misleading-and-aggressive-commercial-practices-impact-assessment-final.pdf>, last accessed on 27 July 2016.

504 See Department for Business, Innovation and Skills, 'The Consumer Protection from Unfair Trading (Amendment) Regulations 2013', August 2013, available at: <https://www.gov.uk/government/uploads/system/uploads/attachment_data/file/226640/bis-13-1112-the-consumer-protection-from-unfair-trading-amendment-regulations-2013-draft-regulations.pdf>, last accessed on 27 July 2016.

505 COM(2013) 138 final.

Eurobarometer 332.[506] However, further evidence is necessary to determine whether the growth in trade volume was affected by the introduction of a European directive.

In general, it can be said that the national regimes under scrutiny can be divided into three main categories which are not mutually exclusive and which depend on whether the transposition by Member States (i) poses content issues (Germany, Belgium, France); (ii) poses terminology issues (using terminology that does not fully reflect the Directive's rules, but that does capture their essence: France, Ireland, the Netherlands and the United Kingdom); (iii) applies the copy-paste approach to a considerable extent (Belgium, Romania, the Netherlands).

What is more, in what concerns the transposition technique, five Member States have transposed the Unfair Commercial Practices Directive by virtue of a satellite law (Belgium, Germany, Ireland, Romania, the United Kingdom), one Member State made use of a consumer code (France) and one Member State made use of its civil code to implement the Unfair Commercial Practices Directive (the Netherlands).

7. Concluding Remarks over the Substantive Comparison

This Chapter was dedicated to the substantive analysis of five directives and their subsequent transposition into the national laws of seven Member States. This analysis focused on the harmonisation discussion, and tried to what standards the drafters of these directives aimed for when creating them. Then, a selection of provisions from these directives, chosen in the light of their content, were taken as markers to determine how national law accommodated European rules.

In total, 40 legal regimes were observed. From the perspective of their substance, the similarities and differences are too detailed to be encapsulated in a doctrinal discussion. This is one of the main arguments why Chapter 3 pursues a more numerical methodology. However, some concluding remarks regarding the substantive comparison are presented below.

One of the issues affecting the consumer *acquis* has to do with definitional issues surrounding the concepts of seller and consumer,[507] but this was not addressed in too much detail in Chapter 2 because of the growing redundancy of questions on this matter. In what concerns the Unfair Contract Terms Directive, Recital 10 of its Preamble indeed indicates which are the contracts covered by the Directive, namely 'all contracts concluded between sellers or suppliers and consumers'. This somehow suggests that the Directive is only applicable to contracts for sale and contracts for the supply of goods. This confusion arises

506 Flash Eurobarometer 332, 'Consumers' Attitudes Towards Cross-border Trade and Consumer Protection', May 2012.

507 See Mak 2009, p. 55; Loos 2008, p. 117; Kingisepp & Värv 2011, p. 44; Robert Bradgate *et al.*, 'Review of the Eight EU Consumer Acquis Minimum Harmonisation Directives and Their Implementation in the UK and Analysis of the Scope for Simplification', Independent Report prepared for the Department of Trade and Industry, September 2005, retrieved at <www.bis.gov.uk/files/file27200.pdf>, last accessed on 27 July 2016.

especially since the Doorstep Selling Directive utilises the precise term of 'trader', the use of which makes reference to a larger scope of transactions. However, it must be noted that it is not commonly accepted that the Unfair Contract Terms Directive does not only apply to the sale of goods but also to the supply of services.[508]

In what concerns the right to cancellation, in the light of the Doorstep Selling Directive the consumers' obligations arisen in the exercise of this right were governed by national laws, whereas the Distance Selling Directive allowed the seller to impose the cost of returning the goods on the consumer.[509] Very much in relation to the right to cancellation, it must also be mentioned that the time span in which the consumer could take the decision to cancel the contract (cooling-off period) is set differently in the directives included in the research than it is in other directives in the consumer *acquis*, for example in the Directive on Timeshare. While the first gives the consumer a cooling-off period of seven days,[510] the second allocates 14 days for the same purpose.[511] On a more general note, taking into account how the Doorstep Selling Directive and the Distance Selling Directive were interrelated, it has been suggested to unify the two in a set of rules applicable both to 'surprise' contracts but also contracts concluded via distance communication[512] which has indeed been achieved with the Consumer Sales Directive.

Moreover, the Distance Selling Directive and the Doorstep Selling Directive protected consumers using the same tool, namely the right to cancel the contract. While the Doorstep Selling Directive called this right a cancellation right, the Distance Selling Directive called it a withdrawal right. Moreover, as it has been explained when the Doorstep Selling Directive was analysed, the right of cancellation gave rise to a cooling off period of at least seven days, whereas the right of withdrawal entitled the consumer to a period of at least seven working days. This leads to two categories of problems: firstly, the different interpretations of 'days'; and secondly, the lack of a common European understanding of 'working day'.[513] Moreover, the notification of withdrawal was also a point of divergence. While the Doorstep Selling Directive covered some indications over dispatch in Article 5, it made reference to notification procedures governed by national law. In comparison, the Distance Selling Directive did not specify anything about notification. Similarly, when it comes to the legal effects of cancelling the contract, the cancellation right (Doorstep Selling) did not clarify what the effects were, making once again reference to national law for supplementary rules. However, the Distance Selling Directive tried to minimise the impact of making effective recourse

508 Report from the Commission on the implementation of Council Directive 93/13/EEC of 5 April 1993 on unfair terms in consumer contracts, COM(2000) 248 final, p. 31.

509 Article 6, Directive 97/7/EC.

510 Article 5, Directive 85/577/EEC.

511 Article 6, Directive 2008/122/EC.

512 Hans-W. Micklitz *et al.*, 'Door to Door Selling - Pyramid Selling - Multilevel Marketing, A study commissioned by the European Commission, Final Report, Volume II: Analysis', November 1999, p. 95.

513 *Ibid.*, p. 91; see also Twigg-Flesner & Schulze 2010, p. 146.

to the right of withdrawal on the consumer, by indicating in Article 6 that no other fee than the one paid to return the goods shall be imposed on the consumer.

As for codes of conduct, it has already been discussed that recital 18 of the Distance Selling Directive preamble mentioned that the minimum harmonisation rules would be supplemented 'by voluntary arrangements among the traders concerned', to the extent of disseminating information over consumer rights through codes of practice (Article 16). Similarly, codes of conducts are mentioned in the preamble of the Unfair Commercial Practices Directive, and fully elaborated upon in Article 10 of the same Directive.

Overall, it can be stated that Member States react to transposition obligations differently. Political implications aside, the analysis in Chapter 2 focused on trying to unveil the particularities of different transposition techniques. Looking at how these Member States have transposed European consumer law, two issues worthy of discussion come to mind.

Firstly, there is the matter of the impact of European law over the national legal system. In this respect, countries like Ireland, Romania and the United Kingdom (with the exception of the Consumer Sales Directive) opted for a copy-paste solution in transposing European rules. France and Belgium have made serious attempts to stay close to the wording of the Directives, while Germany and the Netherlands have filtered the wording used by the directives. It has not been within the ambit of this study to prove how or why these discrepancies occurred, or what exactly they reflect, but several speculative arguments have been addressed throughout Chapter 2: that sometimes Member States adopt European regimes only to tick a box, but national regimes remain applicable in parallel (e.g. the United Kingdom and the Consumer Sales Directive); that Member States deeply embed European rules in the national legal systems and in doing so lose the European nature of these rules (e.g. the Netherlands and Germany transposing rules in their respective Civil Codes); or that newer Member States are busy catching up with the European framework that they do not make express reform efforts to accommodate harmonisation as such (e.g. the example of Romanian law, which currently has many pieces of legislation dating from before the accession, which need to be reconciled with European rules).

Secondly, there is the question of equivalence. This matter is most important in the case of Member States that chose which parts of the directives to transpose expressly. A great example in this respect is the Netherlands. By leaving out of the transposition process, concepts such as 'good faith' or rights such as the *contra proferentem* interpretation - both examples stemming out of the Unfair Contract Terms Directive - the transposition seems to be incomplete. It can indeed be said that general contract rules can supplement consumer rules, so there might not be a need to restate some of the transposing provisions. However, it is difficult to draw a line and claim that not adding an article in Book 6 that uses a general test based on good faith (as the Directive on Unfair Terms prescribes) is equivalent to the application of the national concept of reasonableness and fairness.

Chapter 2 has detailed all the aforementioned issues, in an attempt to give the readers a systematic overview of both European and national regimes, and set the foundation for the following Chapter which now proceeds to use this information as a self-standing dataset for further analysis.

Chapter 3

THE NUMERICAL ANALYSIS

The previous Chapter focused on discussing specific transposition issues of the consumer *acquis* in the national laws of seven Member States: Belgium, France, Germany, Ireland, the Netherlands, Romania and the UK. The central purpose of this comparative analysis, in line with the vast majority of writings covering the topic, was to provide a starting point for the exploration of factors that influence convergence. This Chapter focuses on the following points: in Section 1, the aim of the Chapter is presented together with a brief overview of previous work that is of interest for this study. Next, Section 2 explains the methodology leading to the creation of the Convergence Index, the novel tool this study aims to contribute with in measuring the legal convergence resulting out of harmonisation policies. On the basis of this methodology, Section 3 focuses on gathering data from the five directives and their transposition in the laws of the Member States as described in the previous Chapter. Section 4 uses the aforementioned data to 'code' values for the Convergence Index, and finally, Section 5 presents some preliminary conclusions.

1. Aim of the Chapter and Background in Previous Work

As comprehensive as descriptive analyses on the harmonisation of consumer law are, one perspective of this discussion remains under-represented in literature - the need to empirically *measure* the said harmonisation process. Previous works such as the compilation of the Consumer Law Compendium,[1] or directive-oriented implementation studies[2] are of tremendous help in understanding how European law is integrated into national legal systems. Accordingly, these studies look at contract law directives in a targeted manner and address legal issues in detail. However, apart from executive summaries and comparative tables, no other tools

1 Schulte-Nölke *et al.* 2008.

2 See for instance Civic Consulting, Study on the application of Directive 2005/29/EC on Unfair Commercial Practices in the EU, Final Report for European Commission - DG Justice; see also Micklitz *et al.* 1999.

are used to highlight the overall findings of these comprehensive studies. The present research aims to fill this gap and contribute to the current framework with a comparative approach that looks at harmonisation in a cross-directive/cross-country manner and evaluates the process on the basis of pre-determined factors, in order to measure its converging effect.

The initial reaction to this idea might lead to the question why developing a method to measure law would be of any added value, especially when dealing with a process so complex as harmonisation. Recent trends in the study of law show a tendency to promote evidence-based approaches,[3] questioning the classical black-letter method,[4] or suggesting the creation of unitary legal methods.[5] What is advocated in this sense is that alternative methodologies might offer a fresh approach to comparative law aimed at reducing its complexity.[6]

This study is by no means the first attempt to measure the law. Different methods have been used before, mainly originating in economical (including law and economics) or social science literature. Several examples in this sense include: the economic theory analysis models used by Gomez and Ganuza, Philipsen, Faure and Ogus or Dari-Mattiacci;[7] the econometric testing done by Klick and Helland;[8] the logic-based fuzzy set Qualitative Comparative Analysis (fsQCA) done by Kaeding;[9] the Atlas.ti qualitative data analysis coded by Falkner, Hartlapp and Treib;[10] or the questionnaire method undertaken by Reimann and Halberstam[11] to name a few. The present methodology draws considerable inspiration from two other studies written by Siems and respectively Djankov *et al.*[12]

First of all, Siems' contribution to the 'Does Law Matter?' volume, and his theory of numerical comparative law embrace the view that legal science is currently accommodating novel methodologies that can add to a very classical framework of legal understanding. Secondly, the 'Courts' study by Djankov *et al.* was pivotal for the chosen design. The 'Courts' paper aggregated what it called a 'Formalism Index' as a measurement of substantive and procedural intervention

3 Rachlinski 2011, p. 910; Bar-Gill 2012, p. 2-3.

4 Van Gestel & Micklitz 2014, p. 293. See also the literary method proposed by Heinze 2014, p. 17; Husa 2014, p. 28.

5 Hesselink 2008b, p. 20; Neergaard & Nielsen 2012, p. 7.

6 Siems 2005, p. 534. See also Cabrelli & Siems 2015, p. 109; Siems 2014b, p. 119; Wagner-von Papp 2014, p. 137; Katelouzou 2014, p. 43.

7 Gómez-Pomar & Ganuza 2011b, p. 275; Faure *et al.* 2008, p. 361; Giuseppe Dari-Mattiacci, 'Soft Negligence and Cause In Fact: A Comment on Ganuza and Gomez', October 2004, George Mason University School of Law Working Papers Series, Working Paper 4; Gómez-Pomar & Gili-Saldaña 2014, p. 331.

8 Helland & Klick 2013.

9 Kaeding 2007.

10 Falkner *et al.* 2007, p. 395.

11 Halberstam & Reimann 2014, p. 3-67.

12 Djankov *et al.* 2003, p. 453-517; Siems 2011, p. 115. Siems has further developed additional methods to quantify information about, among others, legal systems as such, see Siems 2016, p. 1.

mandated by statutory law in court cases at lower-level civil trial.[13] In spite of the wave of critique brought to earlier studies conducted by Djankov et al. within the authors' participation in World Bank research projects,[14] the critical observations on this body of work do not have a direct impact on the measurement of harmonisation, for the simple reason that the main inspiration source was the very creation of the Formalism Index and not its subsequent econometric applications.[15]

What is more, the European Commission itself has been trying to develop metrics in various policy areas such as competitiveness and innovation, corruption and governance, education and learning, or the information society.[16] To this end, the Commission has even created a Composite Indicators Research Group.[17] This group also works on developing indicators for the internal market, but the only output in this field makes reference to the Internal Market Index, as well as to the Internal Market Scoreboard, which is an measurement of, among others, transposition deficiencies that names and shames Member States who lag behind in their transposition of internal market-related directives.[18] Another indicator compiled by the Institute for the Protection and Security of the Citizen was the Consumer Empowerment Index, a pilot exercise on consumer measurement of skills, awareness and empowerment that has led to a Special Eurobarometer on this topic.[19]

To summarise what has just been described, there are some studied promoting metrics in various fields of law and policy, whether academic in nature or issued by European institutions. However, neither of them addresses the effect of harmonisation. In the light of these reasons, the Convergence Index in its *beta* version adds value to existing literature from four perspectives: (i) it starts a discussion over the measurement of what has been achieved so far through harmonisation; (ii) it tries to explore what factors are important for convergence and how these factors perform; (iii) it offers proof of how maximum harmonisation does not necessarily lead to much more convergence; and (iv) it opens the door for future

13 The Formalism Index includes the following indiced: '(i) professionals versus laymen, (ii) written versus oral elements, (iii) legal justi cation, (iv) statutory regulation of evidence, (v) control of superior review, (vi) engagement formalities, and (vii) independent procedural actions. The index ranges from zero to seven where seven means a higher level of control or intervention in the judicial process.', see Djankov *et al.* 2003, p. 469.

14 Helland & Klick 2011, p. 99.

15 Djankov *et al.* 2003.

16 See for instance the Regional and European Innovation Scoreboards, available at: <http://ec.europa.eu/growth/node/1378_de>, last accessed on 21 July 2016.

17 European Commission, Composite Indicators Research Group website, available at: <https://composite-indicators.jrc.ec.europa.eu>, last accessed on 21 July 2016.

18 European Commission, Internal Market Scoreboard website, available at: <http://ec.europa.eu/internal_market/score/index_en.htm>, last accessed on 21 July 2016; see also Andrea Saltelli, 'Indicators for the Internal Market? An Unfinished Business', JRC Scientific and Policy Reports, 2014, p. 3.

19 Michela Nardo *et al.*, 'The Consumer Empowerment Index', JRC Scientific and Technical Reports, 2011, available at: <http://ec.europa.eu/consumers/consumer_empowerment/-docs/JRC_report_consumer_empowerment_en.pdf>, last accessed on 21 July 2016; Special Eurobarometer 342, April 2011.

possibilities of actually testing the claims of the European Commission that more harmonisation leads to the better functioning of the internal market.[20]

2. Methodology

By looking at available methods such as the ones indicated above, and thinking about what added value they would bring if applied to the field of European consumer sales law, the choice was made to measure harmonisation by putting together a composite indicator, namely the Convergence Index. The OECD Composite Indicators Handbook has been chosen as the starting point in terms of index design.[21] According to the OECD, an indicator is 'a quantitative or a qualitative measure derived from a series of observed facts that can reveal relative positions (e.g. of a country) in a given area',[22] whereas a composite indicator reflects 'individual indicators [...] compiled into a single index on the basis of an underlying model'.[23] I will use the terms 'composite indicator' and 'aggregate index' interchangeably, since I attach the same meaning to them.

As an aggregate measurement tool, the Convergence Index is the sum of multiple individual indicators. The strength of coding such an index stems from the fact that it has the power to contribute to the country comparison and to help illustrate a complex policy like harmonisation. The Convergence Index thus offers a model to measure the level of convergence.

In terms of the nature of this index, certain aspects must be clarified. The Convergence Index is based on both legal and statistical considerations, and for this reason it reflects a *hybrid legal methodology*, characterised by the following features:

20 The fact that the European regulatory framework in consumer law does not currently justify its policies with hard evidence has been one of the vulnerabilities of European consumer protection explored at a conference focusing on the Common European Sales Law at the University of Chicago in 2012; see for instance Richard Epstein's comments: 'But the Brussels Commissioners do not explain why or how this one single strategy works better than a decentralised approach that consciously puts multiple Member States in direct competition with each other.', in Richard Epstein, 'Harmonisation, Heterogeneity and Regulation: Why the Common European Sales Law Should Be Scrapped', p. 6, available at: <www.law.uchicago.edu/files/files/RAE%20paper.pdf>, last accessed on 21 July 2016.

21 OECD, European Commission, 'Handbook on Constructing Composite Indicators', 2008. Additional research has been consulted on this matter, but the OECD Handbook is preferred because of its completeness, as opposed to other more topic-based papers that address issues specific to various sectors or methodologies, see for instance European Commission, 'Exploratory Research Report: The Integration of Thematic Composite Indicators', Institute for the Protection and Security of the Citizen Research Paper, 2003, available at: <https://composite-indicators.jrc.ec.europa.eu/sites/default/files/EUR20682%20EN.pdf>, last accessed on 21 July 2016; moreover, the staff of Econometrics and Applied Statistics Unit of the Joint Research Center of the European Commission have been involved in the drafting of the OECD Handbook.

22 *Ibid.*, p. 13.

23 *Ibid.*

(i) the focus mainly lays with the *construction* of the Index, and it will not be subsequently used in econometrical analyses. This is an important point to make because the Index is purely illustrative, and does not aim at proving neither correlation nor causation between any of its factors and the resulting effect of convergence in general.
(ii) the creation of the Index is an attempt to establish a self-standing alternative method of comparative law – the index is not built as a purely statistical tool, but it borrows statistical considerations and uses them in combination with the legal discipline.[24]

These features reflect the aims of the Convergence Index: to comparatively discuss its factors, to have an overview of directive/country-based results, and in the light of those findings to make policy recommendations. In addition, by virtue of the alternative methodology, the Convergence Index contributes to the discussion on the importance of 'law and…' research on the one hand,[25] and the need to better understand contract law harmonisation through the creation of adequate novel tools on the other.

Chapter 2 has made an overview of the regulatory framework for the transposition of selected European rules in the national laws of seven Member States. This overview has been the starting point in creating the Index. The literature survey behind Chapter 2 focused both on the features of the five European directives, as well as the issues faced by Member States in accommodating these rules. This research was valuable in understanding how the Index should be built, and what features it should have, given that there are no indicators focusing on legal convergence already in existence. The resulting approach has been to try to make a list of the most important such characteristics of both European and national law, and turn these characteristics into factors which would subsequently be coded. In other words, during the time dedicated to compiling Chapter 2, I have been searching for so-called 'markers' of harmonisation, on the basis of a rather simple question: 'What affects the process of harmonisation at European as well as at national level?' My answer to this question – the set of factors – reflects multiple dimensions of the harmonisation process and thus several typologies can be set up:

(i) depending on the *level* where harmonisation takes place, the factors may have a European or a national scope;

24 The OECD Composite Indicators Handbook indicate a 10-step method of building an indicator: 1. Developing a theoretical framework; 2. Selecting variables; 3. Imputation of missing data; 4. Multivariate analysis; 5. Normalisation of data; 6. Weighting and aggregation; 7. Robustness and sensitivity; 8. Back to the details; 9. Links to other variables; 10. Presentation and dissemination). In addition, Siems suggests a set of numerical comparative law guidelines: 1. Necessity; 2. Methodical awareness; 3. Transparency; 4. Compatibility; 5. Functional equivalents; 6. Reflections.
25 Smits 2014, p. 75.

(ii) depending on the *stakeholder* in the harmonisation process, the factors may reflect the activity of the European legislator, the national legislator, the CJEU, national courts, or private actors;
(iii) depending on *data availability*, the factors may be either observational, namely reflecting objective features of legislative instruments or judicial decisions, or they may be interpretative, meaning that they reflect a pre-defined and well-detailed explanation of substantive law;

To add to these classifications, from a statistical perspective, depending on the *measurement unit*, the factors may be either binary, meaning that they can be expressed in terms of 'Yes' or 'No', or they may be non-binary, meaning they might be expressed in values beyond those corresponding to 'Yes' or 'No' alone. To a certain extent, this might be problematic for the composition of the Index, and for this reason the non-binary factors are normalised. More details on this procedure are provided in Sections 3 and 4 of this Chapter.

One major point that needs to be acknowledged about the list of factors is that the methodology used to determine them has not been externalised for more objectivity. One argument justifying this choice is simply that the practice of having the author of the study make design choices is rather accepted in empirical legal academia.[26] Moreover, as long as the findings of this study are interpreted in the light of the selected factors and are not generalised to encompass questions that have not been addressed in their selection, transparency can also help alleviate whatever methodological concerns might be raised in this sense. Lastly, the Convergence Index as described in this study is a *beta* tool, meaning that it could most certainly benefit from a lot of additional work and fine-tuning in further research. This being said, this initial version of the Convergence Index is by no means perfect; however, it is a measurement tool developed in a field that has not been measured so far, and that in itself contributes to the harmonisation debate.

Keeping in mind the considerations addressed above, as well as the fact that this analysis exclusively relates to the regulatory framework of European consumer law, the factors/individual indicators included in the Convergence Index are:

A. European level
a) Law v policy
b) Type of European instrument (Directive/Regulation)
c) Nature of policy (minimum/maximum harmonisation)
d) Reference to self-regulation
e) General clause
f) Black list
g) CJEU case law

B. National level
a) National transposition technique

26 See for instance the acclaimed empirical legal work of Marotta-Wurgler 2007, p. 679.

b) Reception of selected novel concepts
c) Reception of selected open-ended norms
d) Reference to European law in end legislation
e) Timely transposition (date of national legislation)
f) Infringement procedures (resulting in CJEU decisions - excluding timely transposition issues)

These factors have been selected in the light of three main limitations described below.

1. The Convergence Index does not include data from national courts
As pointed out above, in drafting the factors, attention was paid to a very important design issue, which has also been the main limitation, namely data availability. Law is not a dataset-friendly field of research, and the challenge was to construe information that could somehow be quantified from available sources. In doing so, the purpose was to isolate the relationships between the European legislator and the CJEU on the one hand, and the EU and the national legislator on the other. No quantifiable reference to national case law was included in the set for very practical reasons, such as information asymmetry. The publication of national case law in databases follows non-transparent patterns, making comparisons difficult and potentially too biased to make a significant contribution to the Convergence Index.[27] For this reason, the Index is only limited to the *legislative process* and does not express any enforcement application by national courts. The case law of the Court of Justice is however included in the Index for two reasons: (i) it is retrieved from the same transparent source (www.curia.eu) and (ii) given the interpretative powers of the CJEU, the case law based on the preliminary reference procedure enshrined in Article 267 TFEU is integrated in the obligations stemming from the directives themselves.

2. The Convergence Index does not include factors influencing harmonisation by proxy
The second limitation is related to the fact that harmonisation could be affected by factors going well beyond a legislative or judicial process. Examples in this sense include: national legal culture and history (the legal cultural background of a given legal system); consumer empowerment (consumers being aware of their rights); consumer preferences (whether consumers need more or less protection, for more or less expensive goods and services); the number of cases per judge (determining whether case overloads can lead to less awareness of the European nature of a rule, or if it is a sign of resilience to harmonisation by private actors not complying with European standards); judge training (judge awareness of European law developments and applicability in own court); the number of lawyers specialised in European law in relation to the total number of lawyers (practitioner awareness regarding European law developments which can be brought before judges in

27 See for instance <www.rechspraak.nl<; <www.beck.de<; <www.indaco.ro; www.dalloz.fr>, last accessed on 27 July 2016.

national disputes). As important as these factors might be, the Convergence Index is limited to the regulatory framework and for this reason it does not look into indicators that might have a social or administrative dimension.

3. The Convergence Index does not have predictive value

One aspect already emphasised above is that the Convergence Index is designed as a quantitative analysis tool that is used to further explain the legal harmonisation occurring in European consumer sales law. The aim of the Index is to test the extent to which a numerical comparative perspective makes a contribution to the understanding of this process. This entails that any conclusions this Index supports are to be interpreted exclusively in the light of its design and more than anything, its aim. For this reason, the methodology it is based on does not have an inherent statistical nature, but it is rather *inspired* from statistical methods of data analysis. This mention is necessary to understand that the audience envisioned for this research is not the econometric world, but that of legal academics. In the light of this perspective, the Convergence Index is there to show that legal scholarship can turn to a more numerical evidence-based methodology that can complement the generous amount of classical legal doctrine.

Having outlined the limitations of the Convergence Index, time has come to look at the actual content of its individual variables. Outlining these variables is essential for the coding of the Index, since for every factor there is an assumption and it is only in the light of these assumption that the entire analysis is to be taken into account. These assumptions operate as rules, or in other words they are the context of the Convergence Index. Outside this context, the conclusions the Index eventually leads to may be misleading.

A. European level

a) Law v policy

Assumption: mandatory law leads to a higher level of convergence than policy.

The role of this factor is to determine whether the European contract law instrument is either mandatory or voluntary. One of the features of this distinction is based on the architecture of desired convergence. On the one hand, if an instrument is mandatory, taking the example of a Directive, the national implementation efforts reflect *top-down* harmonisation. On the other hand, if Member States take it upon themselves to draw inspiration from soft law, such as the Draft Common Frame of Reference, or the Open Method of Coordination, the harmonisation process is inversed, and it becomes a *bottom-up* approach.

It might be stated that the Open Method of Coordination might lead to more convergence because it does not require political consensus in the Parliament and it does not have to undergo a long transition from policy to practice. The Open Method of Coordination was first defined by the European Council as 'the means of spreading best practice and achieving greater convergence towards the main EU goals.'[28] This method is meant 'to help Member States to progressively develop their own policies',[29] however, it is not designed to pursue harmonisation in the same manner indicated in Article 114 TFEU, the general legal basis of Directives on consumer contract law.[30] Moreover, Radaelli states that the results of the Open-Method of Coordination have been rather modest since they do not fulfil the purpose of the method, namely to achieve bottom-up learning:

> '[...] the poor results in terms of learning reflect the lack of bottom-up participation, the underestimation of the peculiarities of learning in a political context, and the limitations in the current use of benchmarking.'[31]

While the importance of this Method for legal convergence is acknowledged, it is not a policy applied to European private law.[32]

Similarly, it can be said that optional instruments may also fall under the 'policy' category, as they are not fully mandatory. The CESL can be cited as an example: if the regulation establishing this instrument had passed, it would have been applicable in all Member States, but that does not mean it would have covered all consumer transactions in a given jurisdiction given its voluntary nature.

b) Type of European instrument
Assumption: some EU instruments envisioned by Article 288 TFEU (Regulations and decisions) lead to a higher level of convergence than others (directives, recommendations and opinions).

This factor focuses on types of legislative acts. When dealing with consumer sales law, the main legislative acts are directives (e.g. Unfair Contract Terms, Unfair Commercial Practices, etc.), but attention must be paid to the fact that in recent years the CESL proposal has been shaping the potential future existence of a

28 European Council, Presidency Conclusions at the Lisbon meeting, 23-24 March 2000, para. 37; see also De Ruiter 2014, p. 63; Tholoniat 2010, p. 94.

29 Communication from the Commission to the Council and the European Parliament - 2003 Environment Policy Review - Consolidating the environmental pillar of sustainable development, COM(2003) 745 final, *OJ* C96 of 21 April 2004.

30 See for instance fields when the Open Method of Coordination has been used: European employment strategy (Articles 129-130 TFEU; Broad Economic Policy Guidelines (Article 99 TFEU); Pensions (Article 140 TFEU); or Taxation (no TFEU basis); for more research on the Coordination Method see Claudio M. Radaelli, 'The Open Method of Coordination: A new governance architecture for the European Union?', Swedish Institute for European Policy Studies, Report no. 1 March/2003, p. 33; for pitfalls of the Open Method of Coordination such as the 'lemming effect' (following wrong policy as good practice) or the 'lamp-post syndrome' (focusing on easy-to-measure fields as opposed to fields where indicators are scarce), see Souto-Otero *et al.* 2008, p. 245.

31 Radaelli 2003, p. 9.

32 Walter van Gerven uses the Open Method of Coordination to propose the creation of an Open Method of Convergence, see Van Gerven 2008, p. 34; another policy-based convergence suggestion was made by Colombi Ciacchi in terms of case-law convergence - however, even if points of confluence can be determined *prima facie* by comparing national case law, the process remains unchartered - see Colombi Ciacchi 2005, p. 296.

consumer contract law regulation. However, the CESL has been to date withdrawn by the Commission.

Out of the five different types of instruments, only regulations and directives are taken into account for two reasons: (i) recommendations and opinions have no binding force and would not fall within the ambit of this variable; and (ii) decisions are legal acts undertaken by the Commission or the Council in areas other than contract law, so of little relevance for the Convergence Index.

Going back to directives and regulations, regulations have a higher value for harmonisation for the reason that they achieve uniformity in the content of the obligations placed on Member States, as the text stays the same. Directives, however, require transposition through national legislation that must only follow the purpose of the instrument. As shown in the previous chapter, this process is sometimes detrimental to harmonisation.[33]

c) Nature of policy (minimum/maximum harmonisation)
Assumption: maximum harmonisation leads to more convergence than minimum harmonisation.

When it comes to consumer contract law, policy objectives set by the European legislator aim at a specific degree of harmonisation. While in the days of the Doorstep Selling Directive or even of the Unfair Contract Terms Directive this degree reflected a default standard, recent years have seen a shift towards maximum harmonisation.[34] This shift undoubtedly affects the way in which national jurisdictions accommodate European law. Moreover, this shift marks an assumption that by not being able to derogate from the common standards,[35] national regimes are more similar.

The Convergence Index surveys five directives. Out of those five, only one (the Unfair Commercial Practices Directive) is a maximum harmonisation directive, while the rest are minimum harmonisation instruments. The reason for this distribution reflects the nature of the topic chosen. The five selected directives are the most important instruments covering European consumer sales law. The only one directive left out of this study is the Consumer Rights Directive, replacing the Doorstep and Distance Selling Directives. The reasons why this Directive was not included deal with its much too recent entry into force, an argument elaborated on earlier in Chapter 1.[36]

d) Reference to self-regulation
Assumption: explicit reference to forms of self-regulation in the Directive (e.g. codes of conduct) leads to more harmonisation.

33 See also Twigg-Flesner 2011, p. 238.
34 De Vries 2012, p. 917.
35 Cauffman 2012, p. 1327; see also Rutgers & Sefton-Green 2008, p. 439; Mak 2012b, p. 214.
36 See Chapter 1, p. 38.

This factor is designed to verify any self-regulation references in a given European instrument and whether that instrument promotes it. Simply because the European legislator enacts rules on contract law, it does not necessarily mean that private actors will not create their own standards (e.g. trustmarks, codes of conduct, etc.).[37] Acknowledging the activity of the private sector may lead to the creation of public-private structures that can overview this activity and make sure it does not fall short of the European standards it is supposed to fulfil. This has been called the 'carrot approach', meant to grant public approval and endorsement to codes of conduct.[38] For instance, this could be observed in the Consumer Codes Approval Scheme (CCAS) that had been governed until April 2013 by the Office of Fair Trading in the United Kingdom.[39] Upon the closing of the Office of Fair Trading, this procedure was taken over by the Trading Standards Institute (TSI). This independent institution now manages the approval of consumer codes, which is in other words a neutral (former state-affiliated) business endorsement, designed to enhance consumer protection as well as business reputation. When looking at the criteria required for code approval, most of it taken over from the previous format, it becomes clear that the TSI actually uses standards that are common to the rules set up by different consumer directives. One example is Criterion 3l, according to which '[t]he code shall address the additional effort/help to be provided to vulnerable consumers as appropriate to the sector'. This requirement, as general as it may sound given that it must cover a wide ambit of business activities, still echoes the very specific category of consumers referred to in Article 5(3) of the Unfair Commercial Practices Directive, namely that of vulnerable consumers, who should benefit from even better protection. What this example shows is the existence of a possible 'European creep' in self-regulation. Whether it is the result of institutional design (e.g. the Office of Fair Trading was a state-affiliated institution that was itself held to respect the European rules), or the mere spontaneous standardisation of a higher consumer protection business target, such accreditation schemes prove that self-regulation is indeed affected by European law-making, and it can itself become a vessel of further harmonisation.

As beneficial as self-regulation might be for harmonisation, it also poses certain dangers, as too much self-regulation might lead to fragmentation rather than harmonisation. This is very much the case of trust-marks, whose rapid proliferation might leave users - consumer and businesses alike - confused.[40] However, the centralisation of such practices by means of a public-private partnership like the one elaborated on above shows that self-regulation can be influenced by European law and in turn, can positively affect convergence. This is exactly what Article 10 of the

37 Bull *et al.* 2015, p. 110.

38 Pavillon 2012, p. 272.

39 Trading Standards Institute, 'Consumer Codes Approval Scheme - New codes approval criteria - consultation paper', 24 October 2012, p. 4, available at: <https://www.recc.org.uk/-images/upload/news_62_TSI-Codes-Criteria-Consultation.pdf>, last accessed on 27 July 2016.

40 Commission Staff Working Document, 'Consumer Confidence in E-Commerce: lessons learned from the e-confidence initiative', SEC(2004) 1390, p. 7.

Unfair Commercial Practices Directive stands for – the recognition of private actors collaborating with state mechanisms designed to protect consumer interests.[41]

e) General clause
Assumption: instruments establishing general clauses lead to less convergence than those not using such clauses.

To understand what this factor refers to, the concept of 'general clauses' must first be defined. There are many references in legal literature to 'general clauses'.[42] A lot of these references are made in relation to the principle of good faith.[43] In the particular context of the Convergence Index, a general clause is to be understood as a provision in the text of the Directive that uses a general test in order to determine whether the professional has fulfilled a specific legal standard. The general test is set up to include several generic conditions that might make reference to open-ended norms. For the purposes of this study, open-ended norms are considered to be behavioural and moral standards that parties are held to respect in a given contractual situation, characterised by their content being circumstantial and determinable on a case-by-case basis.

In Ramsay's words, general clauses 'pose questions rather than provide answers'.[44] The main issue with general clauses is that they leave a lot of leeway for their interpretation, and thus the views of national courts may diverge when the general clause is applied. This can be seen in the case law of the Court of Justice when dealing with two of the most important directives in consumer law: the Unfair Contract Terms Directive and the Unfair Commercial Practices Directive. These two directives together have generated over 70 preliminary reference questions, as is detailed in Section 3 of this Chapter.[45]

f) Black list
Assumption: instruments that annex a black list of practices lead to more convergence.

This variable is determined by the fact that if the European legislator sets out examples of practices which national courts are required to follow, then it is more likely that legal systems converge more, since the list has a unifying role in relation to practice.[46] This is the example of the black list found in the Unfair Commercial Practices Directive. This factor can also include the case of directives that make use of practical examples to relate to some of their more abstract content. Apart from the Unfair Commercial Practices Directive and the Unfair Contract Terms Directive,

41 Article 10 makes reference to Article 11 in terms of acknowledging the intertwaining of enforcement mechanisms.
42 Beale 2006, p. 12; Klauer 2000, p. 187.
43 Lando 2007, p. 841.
44 Ramsay 2012, p. 164.
45 See Section 3 of Chapter 3, p. 171.
46 Ramsay 2012, p. 161.

there are no other directives in this study that have such exemplificatory lists. Another important distinction to be made is the difference between black and grey lists. While black lists have the unifying effect mentioned before, the same cannot be said for grey lists. Normally such lists will only include examples of practices that must still be tested against circumstantial facts.

g) CJEU case law
Assumption: the more questions are sent to the CJEU about the interpretation of a specific instrument, the less convergence that instrument leads to.

This factor emphasises that apart from discussing CJEU case law in case-specific details, it is equally necessary to understand the story behind the overall number of cases. All the existing preliminary reference cases on each of the five directives are looked at, in an attempt to determine what drives national courts to send questions to the Court of Justice. This factor is supposed to shed light on whether case law trends per directive show any similarities, or whether there are any outliers - for example directives that have a very high number of preliminary reference questions.

There are several ways in which the number of cases before the Court of Justice may be interpreted. Firstly, one could argue that the more judgments there are the more convergence this leads to, since national courts can subsequently rely on more guidance from the European court. This interpretation is plausible in so far as it be said that courts are under an obligation to take into account CJEU judgments and they acknowledge this obligation for all of the cases before them. However, the very existence of Article 99 of the Rules and Procedure of the Court of Justice places doubt on the reliability of this interpretation. According to this Article:

> '[w]here the answer to a question referred to the Court for a preliminary ruling may be clearly deduced from existing case-law or where the answer to the question referred for a preliminary ruling admits of no reasonable doubt, the Court may at any time, after hearing the Advocate General, give its decision by reasoned order'.[47]

In recent years, especially when dealing with the Unfair Contract Terms Directive, the Court started issuing orders instead of judgments.[48] These orders are procedurally justified using Article 99 above. The fact that the Court still issues reasoned opinions in spite of the high load of existing case law on a given directive, such as the case of the Unfair Contract Terms Directive, can be interpreted to mean that national courts simply do not understand how to apply transposing legislation. A number of seven such orders can be consulted below in Section 3.3 of this Chapter, dealing with the aforementioned Directive. Romanian, Spanish, Hungarian and Slovak courts behind these specific preliminary references have asked questions that the Court had addressed before. This stands to show that even in spite of the growing body of case law on the Unfair Contract Terms Directive,

47 See for instance Case C-342/13, *Katalin Sebestyén v Zsolt Csaba Kővári and others.*
48 See case law overview in Section 3.2, p. 190.

national courts continue to look at the Court of Justice for the interpretation of Article 3 its interaction with national law.

Alternative argumentations can be proposed (e.g. temporarily de-cluttering national courts, etc.), but the very complexity of instruments such as the Unfair Contract Terms Directive or the Unfair Commercial Practices Directive must be borne in mind. On the one hand, the Unfair Contract Terms Directive has been used in the aftermath of the economic crisis in 2008 to protect consumers who had taken loans from banks and ended up with the banks enforcing boilerplate clauses without taking recourse of normal court proceedings. On the other hand, but still in connection with the point just made, neither of the two instruments address their impact on national procedural law, or on general contract law in order to determine the effect of unfair terms or commercial practices. These two arguments come to support the foundations of the assumption that more case law reflects more confusion.

Another interpretation that can be ruled out is the claim that the more case law exists on a directive, the more prevalent it is in practice. The example of internet sales shows why this argument cannot stand. Since 1997 when the Distance Selling Directive was introduced and until 2013 when it was repealed, it has only led to a number of five cases. In other words, for 16 years the Court of Justice has barely ruled on matters dealing with online contracts, which might seem rather shocking. Still, the Court has ruled over as many as 19 cases on unfair commercial practices, and over 45 cases on unfair contract terms. By comparing these numbers, it seems feasible to consider that a higher number of cases might point to a specific directive, the transposition of which did not suffice to make national courts understand how to apply the European rules.

B. National level

a) National transposition technique

Assumption: the transposition of a directive through satellite laws or specialised codes leads to more convergence than its transposition through civil codes.

This variable entails that if a national legislator chooses to transpose European legislation by means of a specialised code or satellite law, the rules are likely to retain their European identity. On the contrary, if new consumer rules derived from the European level are taken over into the national web of the civil code, it is likely that they will have to fit the existing framework and thus the converging force weakens. One argument supporting this view is that when integrated into a civil code, rules on consumer protection must follow the terminological pattern already provided by the civil code. This danger is lessened in the case of specialised codes, given their focus on special law, such as that covering consumer protection.

In the case of satellite laws terminology is not necessarily an issue, since national legislators using satellite laws to transpose European law have a tendency to use a copy-paste approach to the content of the obligations. This factor has been inspired, among others, by the Consumer Law Compendium analysis, which thoroughly assessed how consumer directives were transposed by Member States in their national legislation and accounted for transposition techniques.

b) Reception of selected novel concepts
Assumption: accurately incorporating European legal concepts into national legislation leads to a higher level of convergence.

European terminology is an essential aspect of a unified European legal order. To start with, it can be held that any term used in a European context adds to this supranational terminology. The present factor focuses on a defined selection of so-called 'novel concepts'. Novel concepts are understood here to mean notions that give rise to European legal rights or obligations, independent from any similar rights or obligations existing at national level. The reason why this factor is part of the Convergence Index is because it can be easily coded on the basis of the theoretical analysis already covered in Chapter 2.

In the light of the articles indicated for every directive, a selection of novel concepts is made. Although this selection might seem rather subjective, it is by no means arbitrary and it reflects the essential features of each directive, equally discussed in Chapter 2.

c) Reception of selected open-ended norms
Assumption: accurately incorporating open-ended norms into national legislation leads to a higher level of convergence.

As indicated above, this study takes open-ended norms to mean behavioural and moral standards that parties are held to respect in a given contractual situation, with circumstantial content that is determined on a case-by-case basis. This factor is partially connected to terminology, just like the novel concepts variable. Similarly to the latter, a selection of open-ended norms is made on the basis of directive-based characteristics.

The contribution this factor makes from a convergence perspective lays in the fact that Member States transplanting European open-norms into their national legal framework indirectly 'download' the separate European terminology. What is also important to mention is that this terminology comes with a separate content, which should ideally be treated independently from whatever equivalents might exist in national law.

This is a flexible indicator, meaning that it goes beyond a terminological match, and it takes into account functional equivalents of the open-ended norms mentioned in the European instrument.[49]

d) Reference to European law in end legislation
Assumption: reference to the European instrument made in transposing legislation leads to more convergence.

49 Anne de Vries, 'Maximum Harmonisation and General Clauses - Two Conflicting Concepts?', January 2011, available at: <http://ssrn.com/abstract=1703078>, last accessed on 27 July 2016.

This factor focuses on European law awareness and it entails that explicit reference to the European instrument can signal the source of the rules. Being aware that specific consumer rules stem from the European legislator helps practitioners to interpret them in the light of European law, instead of mistaking this identity for a national framework. In the light of the assumption this factor entails, it is not necessary to focus on the official publication journals, but to select generally-accepted trustworthy online databases which practitioners normally use on a day-to-day basis.

e) Timely transposition (date of national legislation)
Assumption: transposing a directive within the time frame established by the European legislator leads to more convergence.

This variable has two dimensions: an objective one, reflecting the dates when Member States enacted transposing laws; but also a subjective one, reflecting one of two situations - the national legislator was either unable or unwilling to comply with the transposition obligations. Regardless of which situation a Member State may be in, untimely transposition can be considered to hinder harmonisation. As such it has been said that failure to transpose the Directive by a specified date entails that national courts need to interpret national law in the light of the purpose of the Directive, as mandated by direct effect.[50] However, sometimes it might prove difficult for national courts to do just that. In such a case, the consumer is only left with having to take recourse against the Member State, which might have a deterring effect. Although untimely transposition may also be the subject of infringement procedures, many applications started in this sense may be removed from the Registry of the Court because the Member States in question have, in the meantime, enacted implementing legislation. So in order to avoid the bias of overlooking these cases, only the dates of initial implementation will be taken into account instead. Similarly to the 'Transposition techniques' factor, choosing timely transposition as a variable was equally inspired by the analysis included in the Consumer Law Compendium, where timely transposition was also discussed for the directives under scrutiny. Moreover, the Internal Market Scoreboard also tracks timely transposition in one of the tools it offers.[51]

f) Infringement procedures
Assumption: transposing a directive correctly leads to more convergence.

Similarly to timely transposition, infringement procedures are one way of looking at Member State behaviour when assessing willingness to engage in harmonisation efforts. Infringement procedures may be taken against a Member State pursuant to Article 258 TFEU for the failure to fulfil an obligation under the Treaties, be it regarding the untimely adoption of transposing measures, or issues regarding the

50 Steiner *et al.* 2012, p. 357; Woodroffe & Lowe 2010, p. 163.
51 European Commission, Internal Market Scoreboard website, available at: <http://ec.europa.eu/internal_market/score/index_en.htm>, last accessed on 21 July 2016.

conformity and correct application of these measures. However, this last factor only takes into account resilience to harmonisation, manifested in the incorrect transposition of European law. To avoid any overlap with timely transposition, only those infringement procedures resulting in CJEU decisions on incorrect transposition are taken into account. I acknowledge there might be a bias in what concerns infringement procedures, since it is not always clear how the Commission chooses the Member States it wants to bring before the Court. However, infringement procedures are still relevant to the Convergence Index in spite of this issue. Regardless of how they are selected, infringement procedures for incorrect transposition can still be interpreted to show that the Member State in question has not complied with the desired harmonisation outcome. Moreover, the European Union itself included this aspect in the Internal Market Scoreboard.[52]

I have so far listed a total of 13 variable. Seven belong to the European level and six to the national one. The two levels are also the two main dimensions of the Convergence Index, designed to not only facilitate cross-Member State, but also cross-directive comparison. This means that once computed, the Convergence Index will have values compiled on the basis of each directive (five in total) and each Member State (seven in total). The Convergence Index has a minimal value of 0 (no convergence) and a maximal value of 13 (maximum convergence). The Index is coded in the next Chapter. However, until then it is important to investigate how individual variables perform when applied to concrete examples. What follows now is a descriptive application of the variables to the directives and Member States in question.

To sum up, this Section focused on making the reader familiar with the components of the Convergence Index. These components - or as they have been referred to above, factors - are features of the harmonisation process of European consumer contract law, taken into account at multiple levels of governance (European and national). In Section 3, these factors are used in order to gather data from the five directives and their respective transposition into the national laws of the Member States.

3. Gathering Data from the Five Directives

Having looked at the background of the present methodology and its components, this Section is dedicated to the gathering of data from the five directives, subsequently coded into the Convergence Index. The factors presented above are first applied to each of the Directives under scrutiny, and then to the national transposition in the laws of the Member States.

At times, legal arguments are discussed briefly, in the light of the particularities of a given factor. However, as such, the aim of this Section is to take each factor through every piece of European/national legislation, and retrieve relevant information. For this reason, this Section has a rather repetitive and concise style.

52 *Ibid.*

One additional mention must be made regarding the use of tables. Since a lot of the legal information available had to be standardised, or in other words be gathered in systematic overviews, this Section makes use of multiple types of tables. Since the substantive information comprised in the tables has already been mostly discussed in Chapter 2, this Section seeks to simply display it, and not analyse its merits.

3.1. *Doorstep Selling Directive*

In the present Section the focus is on the earliest Directive in this analysis, namely the Doorstep Selling Directive.

Given that this Directive is a very early effort to harmonise consumer legislation, it does not have too many substantive provisions dealing with consumer protection. For this reason, the main provision examined here is Article 5, giving consumers the possibility to make use of their 'right of cancellation'.

A. European level

a) Law v policy

As measures protecting consumers in contracts concluded away from business premises have been adopted under the auspices of Article 115 TFEU (ex-Article 100 EEC), they take the form of a Directive. According to Article 288 TFEU, Member States are obliged to apply the same standards, but are free to determine on their own the measures which they will use for this end result. Thus unlike with the case of regulations, where 'every 't' must be crossed and every 'i' must be dotted',[53] directives leave implementation discretion to Member States.[54]

b) Type of European instrument

As explained above, the instrument under analysis is a Directive. This stands to explain not only the differences between the ways in which Member States have chosen to transpose the Distance Selling Directive, but also the variation in the type of obligations that can arise out of it: while Member States are bound to implement the Directive, they can choose to add additional requirements in their national laws. This discretion plays an equally important role in the discussion regarding minimum/maximum harmonisation and it is addressed in the description of the next factor as well.

The fact that this legislative instrument is a Directive impacts legal convergence to the extent that it inherently promotes diversity in transposition. By giving national legislators the discretion to steer both the language and the content of the Directive as long as its result is achieved, it could be argued that more space for divergence is created: not only are Member States different legal systems and different legal languages, but they also have to apply rules that eventually look differently. Depending on the impact of these differences (whether it is simply a

53 Craig & De Búrca 2003, p. 106.
54 *Ibid.*

matter of innocent rephrasing or going so far as to changing the meaning and content of the Directive's rules), the consequences on harmonisation will either be greater, to the extent that legal systems are only randomly converging, or lesser, in that more convergence is possible.

c) Nature of policy

Like the majority of the Directives in this book (four out of five), the Doorstep Selling Directive applies a minimum harmonisation standard, which stems out of Article 8 of the Directive. Minimum harmonisation might look like a suitable political compromise, and if the goal of the European legislator is to *approximate* national laws, as it is stated in Article 115 TFEU, then it follows that as long as national laws become similar without necessarily being the same, this goal is fulfilled. However, the main challenge that minimum harmonisation poses is the problem of identifying what exactly similar is. It is not outside of the question to imagine how minimum harmonisation could promote considerable gaps between how some jurisdictions embrace higher consumer protection while others simply embrace the Directive standard.

d) Reference to self-regulation

No specific reference to self-regulation is made within the selected Article (Article 5).

e) General clause

The Doorstep Selling Directive does not make use of a general clause.

f) Black list

The Doorstep Selling Directive does not make use of a black list.

g) CJEU case law

A total number of eight cases have been decided by the Court of Justice on the Doorstep Selling Directive between 1985 and 2014, when the Directive was repealed (a total of 26 years). It is interesting to note that the preliminary questions only originate from two Member States: Germany (five) and Spain (three). An overview of these cases is available below, and the information displayed under the column 'Ruling' has been selected in such a way to very carefully reflect the operative part of the respective judgments.

Table 1: CJEU Case Law on the Doorstep Selling Directive

Overview				**Outcome**
Year	**Case number and name**	**Court**	**Member State**	**Citation of operative part of the judgment**
1999	Case C-423/97 *Travel-Vac, S.L. and Manuel José Antelm Sanchís*	*Juzgado de Primera Instancia de Valencia*	Spain	1. Council Directive 85/577/EEC of 20 December 1985 to protect the consumer in respect of contracts negotiated away from business premises applies to a contract relating to the acquisition of a right to use immoveable property on a time-share

				basis and to the provision of services whose value is higher than that of the right to use the immoveable property. 2. A contract concluded in a situation in which a trader has invited a consumer to go in person to a specified place at a certain distance from the place where the consumer lives and which is different from the premises where the trader usually carries on his business and is not clearly identified as premises for sales to the public, in order to present to him the products and services he is offering, must be considered to have been concluded during an excursion organised by the trader away from his business premises within the meaning of Directive 85/577. 3. The consumer can exercise his right of renunciation under Article 5(1) of Directive 85/577 where the contract has been concluded in circumstances such as those described in Article 1 of that directive, without there being any need to prove that the consumer was influenced or manipulated by the trader. 4. Directive 85/577 does not preclude a Member State from adopting rules providing that the notice of renunciation provided for by Article 5(1) of the directive is not subject to any condition as to form. 5. Directive 85/577 precludes the inclusion in a contract of a clause imposing payment by the consumer of a lump sum for damage caused to the trader for the sole reason that the consumer has exercised his right of renunciation.
2001	Case 481/99 *Georg Heininger and Helga Heininger v Bayerische Hypo- und Vereinsbank AG*	*Bundes-gerichtshof*	Germany	1. Council Directive 85/577/EEC of 20 December 1985 to protect the consumer in respect of contracts negotiated away from business premises is to be interpreted as applying to a secured-credit agreement such as that in point in the main proceedings, with the result that the right of cancellation provided for in Article 5 of that directive is available to a consumer who has entered into a contract of that type in one of the cases specified in Article 1. 2. Directive 85/577 precludes the

				national legislature from imposing a time-limit of one year from the conclusion of the contract within which the right of cancellation provided for in Article 5 of that directive may be exercised, where the consumer has not received the information specified in Article 4.
2004	Case C-229/04 *Crailsheimer Volksbank eG v Klaus Conrads and Others*	*Hanseatisches Oberlandes-gericht in Bremen*	Germany	1. Articles 1 and 2 of Council Directive 85/577/EEC of 20 December 1985 to protect the consumer in respect of contracts negotiated away from business premises must be interpreted as meaning that when a third party intervenes in the name of or on behalf of a trader in the negotiation or conclusion of a contract, the application of the Directive cannot be made subject to the condition that the trader was or should have been aware that the contract was concluded in a doorstep- selling situation as referred to in Article 1 of the Directive. 2. Directive 85/577, and Article 5(2) thereof in particular, does not preclude: - a requirement that a consumer who has exercised his right to cancel under the Directive must pay back the loan proceeds to the lender, even though according to the scheme drawn up for the investment the loan serves solely to finance the purchase of the immovable property and is paid directly to the vendor thereof; - a requirement that the amount of the loan must be paid back immediately; - national legislation which provides for an obligation on the consumer, in the event of cancellation of a secured credit agreement, not only to repay the amounts received under the agreement but also to pay to the lender interest at the market rate; However, in a situation where, if the Bank had complied with its obligation to inform the consumer of his right of cancellation, the consumer would have been able to avoid exposure to the risks inherent in investments such as those at issue in the main proceedings, Article 4 of the Directive requires Member States to ensure that their legislation protects consumers who have been unable to avoid

				exposure to such risks, by adopting suitable measures to allow them to avoid bearing the consequences of the materialisation of those risks.
2005	Case C-350/03 *Elisabeth Schulte and Wolfgang Schulte v Deutsche Bausparkasse Badenia AG*	*Landgericht Bochum*	Germany	1. Article 3(2)(a) of Council Directive 85/577/EEC of 20 December 1985 to protect the consumer in respect of contracts negotiated away from business premises must be interpreted as excluding from the scope of the Directive contracts for the sale of immovable property even where they are merely a component of an investment scheme financed by a loan for which the negotiations prior to the conclusion of the contract were held in a doorstep-selling situation, both as regards the contract for the purchase of the immovable property and the loan agreement serving solely to finance that purchase. 2. Directive 85/577 does not preclude national rules which limit the effect of cancellation of the loan agreement to the avoidance of that agreement, even in the case of investment schemes in which the loan would not have been granted at all without the acquisition of the immovable property. 3. Directive 85/577 does not preclude: - a requirement that a consumer who has exercised his right to cancel under the Directive must pay back the loan proceeds to the lender, even though according to the scheme drawn up for the investment the loan serves solely to finance the purchase of the immovable property and is paid directly to the vendor thereof; - a requirement that the amount of the loan must be paid back immediately; - national legislation which provides for an obligation on the consumer, in the event of cancellation of a secured credit agreement, not only to repay the amounts received under the agreement but also to pay to the lender interest at the market rate. However, in a situation where, if the Bank had complied with it obligation to inform the consumer of his right of cancellation, the consumer would have been able to avoid exposure to the risks inherent in investments such as those at issue in the main

				proceedings, Article 4 of Directive 85/577 requires Member States to ensure that their legislation protects consumers who have been unable to avoid exposure to such risks, by adopting suitable measures to allow them to avoid bearing the consequences of the materialisation of those risks.
2008	Case C-412/06 *Annelore Hamilton v Volksbank Filder eG*	*Oberlandes-gericht Stuttgart*	Germany	Council Directive 85/577/EEC of 20 December 1985 to protect the consumer in respect of contracts negotiated away from business premises must be interpreted as meaning that the national legislature is entitled to provide that the right of cancellation laid down in Article 5(1) of the directive may be exercised no later than one month from the time at which the contracting parties have performed in full their obligations under a contract for long-term credit, where the consumer has been given defective notice concerning the exercise of that right.
2009	Case C-227/08 *Eva Martín Martín v EDP Editores SL*	*Audiencia Provincial de Salamanca*	Spain	Article 4 of Council Directive 85/577/EEC of 20 December 1985 to protect the consumer in respect of contracts negotiated away from business premises does not preclude a national court from declaring, of its own motion, that a contract falling within the scope of that directive is void on the ground that the consumer was not informed of his right of cancellation, even though the consumer at no stage pleaded that the contract was void before the competent national courts.
2010	Case C-215/08 *E. Friz GmbH v Carsten von der Heyden*	*Bundes-gerichtshof*	Germany	Two questions were brought before the CJEU in this case, and the Court determined that: (i) the Doorstep-Selling Directive applies to contracts regarding real property funds established as partnerships, even when the purpose for joining is investment and not becoming a member; and (ii) Member States may impose legislation establishing that if a consumer withdraws from such a contract, he will have a claim against the partnership but may only retrieve less than the value of his initial contribution.

2012	Case C-166/11 *Ángel Lorenzo González Alonso v Nationale Nederlanden Vida Cía. de Seguros y Reaseguros, S.A.E.*[55]	*Audiencia Provincial de Oviedo*	Spain	A contract concluded away from business premises, under which life assurance is offered in return for payment of a monthly premium to be invested, in varying proportions, in fixed-rate investments, variable-rate investments and financial investment products of the company offering the contract falls outside the scope of Council Directive 85/577/EEC of 20 December 1985 to protect the consumer in respect of contracts negotiated away from business premises, in accordance with Article 3(2)(d) thereof.

B. National level

a) National transposition technique

The manner in which the national transposition technique is analysed focuses on dividing national instruments into two categories: (i) civil codes; and (ii) specialised codes and satellite laws. On the one hand, the category 'civil codes' is self-evident and only covers transpositions that are embedded in the existing civil codes. On the other hand, the category 'specialised codes and satellite laws' encompasses the wide range of codification projects undertaken at national level that are focused on consumer law: consumer codes, economic codes, special laws etc. This category refers to rules that exist outside of the main codification projects.

An overview of the various instruments used to transpose the Doorstep Selling Directive follows below. It must be borne in mind that many subsequent legislative changes have taken place in the majority of the Member States in the aftermath of the adoption and entry into force of the Consumer Rights Directive. The addition of the most recent legislative developments to the present section was not necessary, given that the focus here lies on trying to understand how the factors included in the numerical comparison look like when applied to initial legislation.[56] The same arguments have already been pointed out in Chapter 2, when the rules analysed here were discussed in greater detail.[57] To ensure methodological consistency, but also to bring clarity to the factors belonging to the Convergence Index, only the initial transposition provisions are considered. An overview of the transposition techniques can be consulted below in the Initial National Transposition Techniques table, followed by a graph aimed at the visual representation of this transposition.

55 See Weatherill 2012, p. 221.
56 See Chapter 1, p. 37.
57 See Chapter 2, p. 41-42.

Table 2: Initial national transposition techniques table (Doorstep Selling Directive)

Member State	Transposition technique
Belgium	*Loi du 14/07/1991 sur les pratiques du commerce et sur l'information et la protection du consommateur (Wet van 14/07/1991 betreffende de handelspraktijken en de voorlichting en bescherming van de consument)*
France	*Loi Numéro 72-1137 du 22/12/1972 relative à la protection des consommateurs en matière de démarchage et de vente à domicile; Loi Numéro 89-421 du 23/06/1989 relative à l'information et à la protection des consommateurs ainsi qu'à diverses pratiques commerciales*
Germany	*Gesetz über den Widerruf von Haustürgeschäften und ähnlichen Geschäften*
Ireland	European Communities (Cancellation of Contracts negotiated away from business premises) Regulations 1989
Netherlands	*Colportagewet*
Romania	*Ordonanța Guvernului nr. 106/1999 privind contractele încheiate în afara spațiilor comerciale; Lege nr. 60/2002 pentru aprobarea Ordonanței Guvernului nr. 106/1999 privind contractele încheiate în afara spațiilor comerciale*
United Kingdom	The Consumer Protection (Cancellation of Contracts Concluded away from Business Premises) Regulations 1987

Figure 10: Initial national transposition techniques map (Doorstep Selling Directive)

As can be seen in the graph above, this Directive shows that all national legislators provided consumers with protection in case of contracts negotiated away from business premises by means of imposing rules that are separate from their existing regimes on the law of obligations. One factor that might explain this tendency, especially when seen in comparison with the rest of the Directives analysed here (see next sub-chapters), might be the fact that the Doorstep Selling Directive is the first consumer directive with a contractual ambit. For this reason it can be stated that Member States did not have enough experience with the transposition of consumer protection rules in the field of contract law, which inherently touches upon already existing contractual regimes.

b) Reception of selected novel concepts

The most important concept that originated from the Doorstep Selling Directive was the right of cancellation: consumers are to 'renounce the effects of his undertaking by sending notice within a period of not less than seven days from receipt by the consumer of the notice referred to in Article 4, in accordance with the procedure laid down by national law'. Making use of the right of cancellation entailed that consumers were released from any of their obligations under the contract. From the point of legal convergence, the right of cancellation is one of the earliest European innovations in terms of consumer contract law - a right that is independent from other remedies existing under national law and that has an autonomous identity.

In the case of the Doorstep Selling Directive, there is one fundamental novel concept that has been identified, namely the right of cancellation. This right has a similar meaning and ambit as the right of withdrawal under the Distance Selling Directive, even though the European legislator has termed the two differently. In this circumstance, the right of cancellation/right of withdrawal points to an issue that can affect the convergence process: inconsistencies in legislation at European level. Should any such inconsistencies be determined, their presence is taken into account when measuring the harmonisation factors in the next Section. A transposition table is available below.

Table 3: Transposition of novel concepts (Doorstep Selling Directive)

Member State	Directive version in original language	Implementation
		Form
Belgium[58]	*droit de résilier le contrat/ het recht de overeenkomst op te zeggen*	*droit de renoncer/ het recht [om zonder kosten [...] zijn aankoop] af te zien*
France[59]	*droit de résilier le contrat*	*faculté de renonciation*
Germany[60]	*Widerrufsrecht*	*Recht auf Widerruf*
Ireland[61]	right of cancellation	cancellation
Netherlands[62]	*het recht de overeenkomst te opzeggen*	*de overeenkomst te ontbinden*
Romania[63]	*dreptul de a rezilia contractul*	*dreptul de a denunța unilateral contractul*
United Kingdom[64]	right of cancellation	right to cancel the contract

58 Article 88, Law of 14 July 1991.

59 Article R121-3, Consumer Code.

60 § 1(2) HWiG.

61 Regulation 4(1), European Communities (Cancellation of Contracts negotiated away from business premises) Regulations, 1989.

62 Article 24(1) of the Doorstep Selling Law.

63 Article 8(1) of Ordinance nr. 106/30.08.99 regarding consumers contracts negotiated away from business premises.

64 Regulation 7(2), The Cancellation of Contracts made in a Consumer's Home or Place of Work etc. Regulations 2008.

From the perspective of legal convergence, the Doorstep Selling Directive is a complicated instrument. Being an early attempt at regulating consumer contract law in a very narrow field of interest, it has a fundamental deficiency: it does not clarify what role European rules play vis-à-vis what Member States had already provided for in their default regimes. There are two ways in which this lack of clarity can be determined: by looking at the terminology used in the Directive itself, and by looking at how Member States understood to transpose it.

To address the first point, in Article 4 of the Directive, the English version speaks about the 'right of cancellation', and not the common law notion of rescission, which can be considered to create a new ground for consumer claims in the case of contracts concluded away from business premises. This becomes clear in the Preamble of the Doorstep Selling Directive, where not only was the cancellation right affirmed, but it was given a very specific content: 'the consumer should be given a right of cancellation over a period of at least seven days in order to enable him to assess the obligations arising under the contract'.[65] In other words, the European legislator identified a specific area where it considered action was necessary in order to protect consumers, and had set up a specific right to reflect this protection. However, other versions of the Directive do not use terminology that shows the equivalent of this novel right. For instance the French version of the Doorstep Selling Directive uses '*droit de résilier*'. In comparison, the French version of the Distance Selling Directive, which is analysed later in this chapter, and which builds on this right of cancellation (renaming it as a withdrawal right), speaks about '*droit de rétractation*'. The main difference is that while the latter reflected the individual identity of the European consumer right of withdrawal, the former was translated by using national concepts such as termination.[66] By overlapping termination with withdrawal from the contract, it became unclear what legal nature of the cancellation right has, and moreover, whether there was any hierarchy between default rules and consumer protection. The same issue was found in the Dutch and Romanian versions of the Directive.

Secondly, it can be seen in Table 3 that some Member States had not followed the specific language version terminology when transposing the cancellation right: the French as well as the Belgian legislators (both the French and Dutch versions of the Market Practices Law) had used concepts that have an individual identity and showcase the special nature of European consumer protection. The Netherlands and Romania, on the other hand, chose to stay close to the specific language versions of the Directive that posed the issues addressed under the first point of this discussion. Germany, Ireland and the United Kingdom followed the Directive closely as well.

Another aspect that has already been briefly hinted at is how this Directive interacted with the Distance Selling Directive. The two instruments were rather similar in that they created the same consumer right for specific situations. The common factor was thus not only the fact that both Directives set up a

[65] Recital 5 of the Preamble of the Doorstep Selling Directive.

[66] Withdrawal may lead to similar effects, the legal nature is different, especially since this Directive does not deal with termination at all, unlike Directive 1999/44/EC.

cancellation/withdrawal right, but also that the choice of contracts in which this right is offered was guided by the same rationale: the consumer was not in a normal purchasing environment on the premises of the trader, where he had informational advantages, but he was either home or away from business premises and was physically approached by the trader (doorstep selling), or he had not had any physical contact with the seller at all (distance selling). From the convergence perspective, problems start occurring as the European legislator did not take these similarities into account and did not take measures to clarify that it is indeed the same right. Luckily, the Consumer Rights Directive is proof of this awareness; it does not only bring national legislation to the same level by virtue of maximum harmonisation, but it also harmonises European terminology and brings full equivalence between the withdrawal right in the Distance Selling Directive and the cancellation right in Doorstep Selling.

c) Reception of selected open-ended norms

No open-ended norms have been identified in Article 5. This factor will thus have to be normalised when coding the Convergence Index. Simply put, normalisation is a statistical procedure that aims that the selected indicators of a composite index are not overrepresented, and that individual indicators are comparable. In this case, normalisation is done by adding an average value for all Member States, calculated on the bases of the minimum and maximum values this factor can have.

d) Timely transposition

According to Article 9, the transposition deadline was 24 months from the publication of the Directive, thus 31 December 1987. An overview of how Member States complied with this deadline is available below.

Table 4: Overview of transposition deadline (Doorstep Selling Directive)

Member State	National legislation	Transposition date	Timely transposition
Belgium	Law of 14 July 1991 on Commercial Practices and Information and Consumer Protection	14 July 1991	No
France	L. Article 121-21 *et seqq.* Consumer Code	29 June 1989	No
Germany	Doorstep Selling Cancellation Act	1 May 1986	Yes
Ireland	European Communities (Cancellation of Contracts Negotiated away from Business Premises) Regulations, 1989	1 November 1989	No

Netherlands	Law on Doorstep Selling	Modification of 26 July 1989[67]	No
Romania	Government Ordinance regarding consumers contracts negotiated away from business premises no. 106/1999	30 September 1999	Yes
United Kingdom	Consumer Protection (Cancellation of Contracts concluded away from business premises) Regulations 1987	1 July 1988	No

e) Infringement procedures
No infringement procedures were identified for this Directive.

f) Reference to European law in end legislation
The table below shows an overview of legislation as it appears in the indicated databases. The selection of the databases has not been made with a view to capturing the formal aspects of publishing legislation, but rather because of the practical reliance on online sources by legal practitioners.

Table 5: Overview of reference to European law (Doorstep Selling Directive)

Member State	National legislation	Reference to European law	Database
Belgium	*Loi du 14/07/1991 sur les pratiques du commerce et sur l'information et la protection du consommateur (Wet van 14/07/1991 betreffende de handelspraktijken en de voorlichting en bescherming van de consument)*	No	Ejustice
France	Article L. 121-21 *et seqq*. Consumer Code	No	Legifrance
Germany	Doorstep Selling Cancellation Act	No	Juris
Ireland	European Communities (Cancellation of Contracts Negotiated away from Business Premises) Regulations, 1989	Yes	Irish Statute Book (Office of the Attorney General)
Netherlands	Law on Doorstep Selling	No	Overheid
Romania	Government Ordinance regarding consumers contracts negotiated away from business premises no. 106/1999	Yes	Lege 5
United Kingdom	Consumer Protection (Cancellation of Contracts concluded away from business premises) Regulations 1987	No	The National Archives

67 MvT, *Kamerstukken* II 1987-1988, 20443, nr. 3 (*Wijziging van de Colportagewet*).

3.2. *Unfair Contract Terms Directive*

When the Unfair Contract Terms Directive was described in the prior chapter, the following articles were analysed:

- Article 3 - (unfairness test);
- Article 4 - (assessing unfairness);
- Article 5 - (clarity and *contra proferentem* rule);
- Article 6 - (effects of unfair contract terms);
- Article 7 - (control of unfair contract terms).

These articles are now be used for the application of the factors.

A. European level

a) Law v policy
Given that the measures protecting consumers against unfair terms in consumer contracts have been adopted on the basis of Article 114 TFEU, they take the form of a Directive. From this perspective, the Unfair Contract Terms Directive can be considered to represent binding law.

b) Type of European instrument
As explained above, the instrument under analysis is a Directive.

c) Nature of policy
As can be seen in Article 8 of the Unfair Contract Terms Directive, it is an instrument promoting minimum harmonisation.[68]

d) Reference to self-regulation
No provisions encouraging self-regulation were identified within the rules set forth in Articles 3-7.

e) General clause
Article 3 of the Unfair Contract Terms Directive can be qualified as a general clause.

f) Black list
Although the Unfair Contract Terms Directive does make use of an annex, it is not considered a 'black list'. The purpose of the 'black list' factor is to assume that the more indications are given with respect to the application of the rules in a particular directive, the more convergence this may lead to. In the case of the Unfair Contract Terms Directive, such a black list does not exist. The examples of unfair contract

68 See also M.W. Hesselink & M.B.M. Loos, 'Unfair contract terms in B2C contracts', Briefing Note for the European Parliament's Committee on Legal Affairs, p. 7; Hondius 1995, p. 242-243.

terms in the Annex are mere examples of terms that *may* be considered as unfair under the test in Article 3.

g) CJEU case law

By gathering all the cases generated by the transposition of a specific Directive which have reached the Court of Justice by means of the Article 267 TFEU procedure (preliminary reference), two aspects can be clarified. Firstly, case law taken together can be an indication of eventual problems national courts struggle with, reflecting the characteristics of Member State transposition. Secondly, analysing the case law of the Court of Justice allows for a step-by-step assessment of the Court's role as a creator of law, with focus on one Directive at a time. If one searches the Curia database for a list of all judgments referring to the Unfair Contract Terms Directive, a total of 102 cases are found (as of March 2016); however, not all these cases deal with the Directive, and out of those which do, not all resulted in judgments.

A table overviewing the judgments of the Court of Justice on the Unfair Contract Terms Directive is presented below.

Table 6: CJEU Case Law on the Unfair Contract Terms Directive

Overview				**Outcome**
Year	**Case number and name**	**Court**	**Member State**	**Citation of operative part of the judgment**
2000	Cases C-240/98 to C-244/98 *Océano Grupo Editorial SA v Rocío Murciano Quintero; Salvat Editores SA v José M. Sánchez Alcón Prades; José Luis Copano Badillo; Mohammed Berroane; Emilio Viñas Feliu*	*Juzgado de Primera Instancia No. 35 de Barcelona*	Spain	1. The protection provided for consumers by Council Directive 93/13/EEC of 5 April 1993 on unfair terms in consumer contracts entails the national court being able to determine of its own motion whether a term of a contract before it is unfair when making its preliminary assessment as to whether a claim should be allowed to proceed before the national courts. 2. The national court is obliged, when it applies national law provisions predating or postdating the said Directive, to interpret those provisions, so far as possible, in the light of the wording and purpose of the Directive. The requirement for an interpretation in conformity with the Directive requires the national court, in particular, to favour the interpretation that would allow it to decline of its own motion the jurisdiction conferred on it by virtue of an unfair term.
2001	Joined cases C-541/99 and C-542/99	*Giudice di Pace di Viadana*	Italy	The term 'consumer, as defined in Article 2(b) of Council Directive 93/13/EEC of 5 April 1993 on unfair

	Cape Snc v Idealservice Srl; Idealservice MN RE Sas v OMAI Srl			terms in consumer contracts, must be interpreted as referring solely to natural persons.
2002	Case C-437/00 *Cofidis SA v Jean-Louis Fredout*	*Tribunal d'instance de Vienne*	France	Council Directive 93/13/EEC of 5 April 1993 on unfair terms in consumer contracts precludes a national provision which, in proceedings brought by a seller or supplier against a consumer on the basis of a contract concluded between them, prohibits the national court, on expiry of a limitation period, from finding, of its own motion or following a plea raised by the consumer, that a term of the contract is unfair.
2004	Case C-237/02 *Freiburger Kommunalbauten GmbH & Co. KG v Ludger Hofstetter & Ulrike Hofstetter*	*Bundes-gerichtshof*	Germany	It is for the national court to decide whether a contractual term such as that at issue in the main proceedings satisfies the requirements for it to be regarded as unfair under Article 3(1) of Council Directive 93/13/EEC of 5 April 1993 on unfair terms in consumer contracts.
2006	Case C-168 *Elisa María Mostaza Claro v Centro Móvil Milenium SL*	*Audiencia Provincial de Madrid*	Spain	Council Directive 93/13/EEC of 5 April 1993 on unfair terms in consumer contracts must be interpreted as meaning that a national court seized of an action for annulment of an arbitration award must determine whether the arbitration agreement is void and annul that award where that agreement contains an unfair term, even though the consumer has not pleaded that invalidity in the course of the arbitration proceedings, but only in that of the action for annulment.
	Case C-302/04 *Ynos kft v János Varga*	*Szombathelyi Városi Bíróság*	Hungary	In circumstances such as those of the dispute in the main proceedings, the facts of which occurred prior to the accession of a State to the European Union, the Court of Justice does not have jurisdiction to answer the first and second questions.
2009	Case C-40/08 *Asturcom Telecomunicaciones SL v Cristina Rodríguez Nogueira*	*Juzgado de Primera Instancia No 4 de Bilbao*	Spain	Council Directive 93/13/EEC of 5 April 1993 on unfair terms in consumer contracts must be interpreted as meaning that a national court or tribunal hearing an action for enforcement of an arbitration award which has become

				final and was made in the absence of the consumer is required, where it has available to it the legal and factual elements necessary for that task, to assess of its own motion whether an arbitration clause in a contract concluded between a seller or supplier and a consumer is unfair, in so far as, under national rules of procedure, it can carry out such an assessment in similar actions of a domestic nature. If that is the case, it is for that court or tribunal to establish all the consequences thereby arising under national law, in order to ensure that the consumer is not bound by that clause.
	Case C-243/08 *Pannon GSM Zrt. V Erzsébet Sustikné Györfi*	*Budaörsi Városi Bíróság*	Hungary	1. Article 6(1) of Council Directive 93/13/EEC of 5 April 1993, on unfair terms in consumer contracts, must be interpreted as meaning that an unfair contract term is not binding on the consumer, and it is not necessary, in that regard, for that consumer to have successfully contested the validity of such a term beforehand. 2. The national court is required to examine, of its own motion, the unfairness of a contractual term where it has available to it the legal and factual elements necessary for that task. Where it considers such a term to be unfair, it must not apply it, except if the consumer opposes that non-application. That duty is also incumbent on the national court when it is ascertaining its own territorial jurisdiction. 3. It is for the national court to determine whether a contractual term, such as that which is the subject-matter of the dispute in the main proceedings, satisfies the criteria to be categorised as unfair within the meaning of Article 3(1) of Directive 93/13. In so doing, the national court must take account of the fact that a term, contained in a contract concluded between a consumer and a seller or supplier, which has been included without being individually negotiated and which confers exclusive jurisdiction on the court in the territorial

				jurisdiction of which the seller or supplier has his principal place of business may be considered to be unfair.
2010	C-137/08 *VB Pénzügy Lízing v Ferenc Schneider*	*Budapesti II. és III. kerületi bíróság*	Hungary	1. The first paragraph of Article 23 of the Statute of the Court of Justice does not preclude a provision of national law which provides that the court which initiates a preliminary reference procedure is at the same time to inform, of its own motion, the Minister with responsibility for Justice in the Member State concerned. 2. Article 267 TFEU must be interpreted as meaning that the jurisdiction of the Court of Justice of the European Union extends to the interpretation of the concept of 'unfair term' used in Article 3(1) of Council Directive 93/13/EEC of 5 April 1993 on unfair terms in consumer contracts and in the annex thereto, and to the criteria which the national court may or must apply when examining a contractual term in the light of the provisions of that Directive, bearing in mind that it is for that court to determine, in the light of those criteria, whether a particular contractual term is actually unfair in the circumstances of the case. 3. The national court must investigate of its own motion whether a term conferring exclusive territorial jurisdiction in a contract concluded between a seller or supplier and a consumer, which is the subject of a dispute before it, falls within the scope of Directive 93/13 and, if it does, assess of its own motion whether such a term is unfair.
	Case C-484/08 *Caja de Ahorros y Monte de Piedad de Madrid v Asociación de Usuarios de Servicios Bancarios (Ausbanc)*	*Tribunal Supremo*	Spain	1. Articles 4(2) and 8 of Council Directive 93/13/EEC of 5 April 1993 on unfair terms in consumer contracts must be interpreted as not precluding national legislation, such as that at issue in the main proceedings, which authorises a judicial review as to the unfairness of contractual terms which relate to the definition of the main subject- matter of the contract or to

				the adequacy of the price and remuneration, on the one hand, as against the services or goods to be supplied in exchange, on the other hand, even in the case where those terms are drafted in plain, intelligible language. 2. Articles 2 EC, 3(1)(g) EC and 4(1) EC do not preclude an interpretation of Articles 4(2) and 8 of Directive 93/13 according to which Member States may adopt national legislation which authorises a judicial review as to the unfairness of contractual terms which relate to the definition of the main subject- matter of the contract or to the adequacy of the price and remuneration, on the one hand, as against the services or goods to be supplied in exchange, on the other hand, even in the case where those terms are drafted in plain, intelligible language.
	Case C-76/10*Pohotovosť s. r. o. v Iveta Korčkovská*	*Krajský súd v Prešove*	Slovakia	1. Council Directive 93/13/EEC of 5 April 1993 on unfair terms in consumer contracts requires a national court, hearing an application for enforcement of a final arbitral award issued by default and without the participation of the consumer, of its own motion, where the necessary information on the legal and factual state of affairs is available to it for this purpose, to consider the fairness of the penalty contained in a credit agreement concluded by a creditor with a consumer, that penalty having been applied in that award, where, according to national procedural rules, such an assessment may be conducted in similar proceedings under national law. 2. It is for the national court concerned to determine whether a term in a credit agreement such as that at issue in the main proceedings providing, according to the findings of that court, for the consumer to pay a disproportionately high sum in compensation, must, in the light of all the circumstances attending the conclusion of the contract, be regarded as unfair within the

				meaning of Articles 3 and 4 of Directive 93/13. If that is the case, it is for that court to establish all the consequences thereby arising under national law, in order to ensure that the consumer is not bound by that term. 3. In circumstances such as those in the main proceedings, the failure to mention the annual percentage rate in a consumer credit contract, the mention of the annual percentage rate being essential information in the context of Directive 87/102/EEC of 22 December 1986 for the approximation of the laws, regulations and administrative provisions of the Member States concerning consumer credit, as amended by Directive 98/7/EC of the European Parliament and of the Council of 16 February 1998, may be a decisive factor in the assessment by a national court of whether a term of a consumer credit agreement concerning the cost of that credit in which no such mention is made is written in plain, intelligible language within the meaning of Article 4 of Directive 93/13. If that is not the case, that court has the power to assess, of its own motion, whether, in the light of all the circumstances attending the conclusion of that contract, the failure to mention the annual percentage rate in the term of that contract concerning the cost of that credit is likely to confer on that term an unfair nature within the meaning of Articles 3 and 4 of Directive 93/13. However, notwithstanding the power which is given to assess that contract in the light of Directive 93/13, Directive 87/102 is to be interpreted as allowing national courts to apply of their own motion the provisions transposing Article 4 of the latter directive into national law and as providing that the failure to mention the annual percentage rate in a consumer credit contract means that the credit granted is deemed to be interest-free and free of charge.

2012	C-618/10 *Banco Español de Crédito v Joaquín Calderón Camino*	*Audiencia Provincial de Barcelona*	Spain	1. Council Directive 93/13/EEC of 5 April 1993 on unfair terms in consumer contracts must be interpreted as precluding legislation of a Member State, such as that at issue in the main proceedings, which does not allow the court before which an application for an order for payment has been brought to assess of its own motion, in limine litis or at any other stage during the proceedings, even though it already has the legal and factual elements necessary for that task available to it, whether a term relating to interest on late payments contained in a contract concluded between a seller or supplier and a consumer is unfair, in the case where that consumer has not lodged an objection. 2. Article 6(1) of Directive 93/13 must be interpreted as precluding legislation of a Member State, such as Article 83 of Royal Legislative Decree 1/2007 approving the consolidated version of the General Law for the protection of consumers and users and other supplementary laws (Real Decreto Legislativo 1/2007 por el que se aprueba el texto refundido de la Ley General para la Defensa de los Consumidores y Usuarios y otras leyes complementarias) of 16 November 2007, which allows a national court, in the case where it finds that an unfair term in a contract concluded between a seller or supplier and a consumer is void, to modify that contract by revising the content of that term.
	Case C-472/10 *Nemzeti Fogyasztóvédelmi Hatóság v Invitel Távközlési Zrt*	*Pest Megyei Bíróság*	Hungary	1. It is for the national court, ruling on an action for an injunction, brought in the public interest and on behalf of consumers by a body appointed by national law, to assess, with regard to Article 3(1) and (3) of Council Directive 93/13/EEC of 5 April 1993 on unfair terms in consumer contracts, the unfair nature of a term included in the general business conditions of consumer contracts by which a seller or supplier provides for a unilateral amendment of fees connected with

				the service to be provided, without setting out clearly the method of fixing those fees or specifying a valid reason for that amendment. As part of this assessment, the national court must determine, inter alia, whether, in light of all the terms appearing in the general business conditions of consumer contracts which include the contested term, and in the light of the national legislation setting out rights and obligations which could supplement those provided by the general business conditions at issue, the reasons for, or the method of, the amendment of the fees connected with the service to be provided are set out in plain, intelligible language and, as the case may be, whether consumers have a right to terminate the contract. 2. Article 6(1) of Directive 93/13, read in conjunction with Article 7(1) and (2) thereof, must be interpreted as meaning that: - it does not preclude the declaration of invalidity of an unfair term included in the standard terms of consumer contracts in an action for an injunction, provided for in Article 7 of that directive, brought against a seller or supplier in the public interest, and on behalf of consumers, by a body appointed by national legislation from producing, in accordance with that legislation, effects with regard to all consumers who concluded with the seller or supplier concerned a contract to which the same general business conditions apply, including with regard to those consumers who were not party to the injunction proceedings; - where the unfair nature of a term in the general business conditions has been acknowledged in such proceedings, national courts are required, of their own motion, and also with regard to the future, to take such action thereon as is provided for by national law in order to ensure that consumers who have concluded a contract with the seller or supplier to which those

				general business conditions apply will not be bound by that term.
	Case 453/10 *Jana Pereničová, Vladislav Perenič v SOS financ spol. s r. o.*	*Okresný súd Prešov*	Slovakia	1. Article 6(1) of Council Directive 93/13/EEC of 5 April 1993 on unfair terms in consumer contracts must be interpreted as meaning that, when assessing whether a contract concluded with a consumer by a trader which contains one or more unfair terms can continue to exist without those terms, the court hearing the case cannot base its decision solely on a possible advantage for one of the parties, in this case the consumer, of the annulment of the contract in question as a whole. That directive does not, however, preclude a Member State from providing, in compliance with European Union law, that a contract concluded with a consumer by a trader which contains one or more unfair terms is to be void as a whole where that will ensure better protection of the consumer. 2. A commercial practice such as that at issue in the main proceedings which consists in indicating in a credit agreement an annual percentage rate of charge lower than the real rate must be regarded as 'misleading' within the meaning of Article 6(1) of Directive 2005/29/EC of the European Parliament and of the Council of 11 May 2005 concerning unfair business-to-consumer commercial practices in the internal market and amending Council Directive 84/450/EEC, Directives 97/7/EC, 98/27/EC and 2002/65/EC of the European Parliament and of the Council and Regulation (EC) No 2006/2004 of the European Parliament and of the Council ('Unfair Commercial Practices Directive') in so far as it causes or is likely to cause the average consumer to take a transactional decision that he would not have taken otherwise. It is for the national court to ascertain whether that is the case in the main proceedings. A finding that such a commercial practice is unfair is one

				element among others on which the competent court may, pursuant to Article 4(1) of Directive 93/13, base its assessment of the unfairness of the contractual terms relating to the cost of the loan granted to the consumer. Such a finding, however, has no direct effect on the assessment, from the point of view of Article 6(1) of Directive 93/13, of the validity of the credit agreement concluded.
2013	Case C-397/11 *Erika Jőrös v Aegon Magyarország Hitel Zrt.*	*Fővárosi Bíróság*	Hungary	1. Council Directive 93/13/EEC of 5 April 1993 on unfair terms in consumer contracts must be interpreted as meaning that where a national court, dealing with an appeal concerning the validity of terms in a contract concluded between a seller or supplier and a consumer on the basis of a form prepared in advance by that seller or supplier, has the power, under its internal procedural rules, to examine any grounds for invalidity clearly apparent from the elements submitted at first instance and, if necessary, to redefine, depending on the facts determined, the legal basis relied upon to establish that those terms are invalid, it must assess, of its own motion or by redefining the legal basis of the application, whether those terms are unfair in the light of the criteria in that directive. 2. Article 6(1) of Directive 93/13 must be interpreted as meaning that a national court which has established that a contractual term is unfair is required, first, without waiting for the consumer to make an application in that regard, to draw all the consequences which, under national law, result from that finding in order to satisfy itself that that consumer is not bound by that term and, secondly, to assess, in principle on the basis of objective criteria, whether the contract concerned can continue in existence without that term. 3. Directive 93/13 must be interpreted as meaning that a national court which has, of its own

				motion, established that a contractual term is unfair must, as far as possible, apply its internal procedural rules in such a way as to draw all the consequences which, under national law, result from a finding that the term at issue is unfair, in order to satisfy itself that the consumer is not bound by that term.
	Case C-92/11 *RWE Vertrieb AG v Verbraucher-zentrale Nordrhein-Westfalen e.V.*	*Bundes-gerichtshof*	Germany	1. Article 1(2) of Council Directive 93/13/EEC of 5 April 1993 on unfair terms in consumer contracts must be interpreted as meaning that that directive applies to provisions in general terms and conditions, incorporated into contracts concluded between a supplier and a consumer, which reproduce a rule of national law applicable to another category of contracts and are not subject to the national legislation concerned. 2. Articles 3 and 5 of Directive 93/13 in conjunction with Article 3(3) of Directive 2003/55/EC of the European Parliament and of the Council of 26 June 2003 concerning common rules for the internal market in natural gas and repealing Directive 98/30/EC must be interpreted as meaning that, in order to assess whether a standard contractual term by which a supply undertaking reserves the right to vary the charge for the supply of gas complies with the requirements of good faith, balance and transparency laid down by those directives, it is of fundamental importance: - whether the contract sets out in transparent fashion the reason for and method of the variation of those charges, so that the consumer can foresee, on the basis of clear, intelligible criteria, the alterations that may be made to those charges. The lack of information on the point before the contract is concluded cannot, in principle, be compensated for by the mere fact that consumers will, during the performance of the contract, be informed in good time of a variation of the charges and of their right to terminate the contract

				if they do not wish to accept the variation; and - whether the right of termination conferred on the consumer can actually be exercised in the specific circumstances. It is for the national court to carry out that assessment with regard to all the circumstances of the particular case, including all the general terms and conditions of the consumer contracts of which the term at issue forms part.
	Case C-415/11 *Mohamed Aziz v Caixa d'Estalvis de Catalunya, Tarragona i Manresa (Catalunyacaixa)*	*Juzgado de lo Mercantil No 3 de Barcelona*	Spain	1. Council Directive 93/13/EEC of 5 April 1993 on unfair terms in consumer contracts must be interpreted as precluding legislation of a Member State, such as that at issue in the main proceedings, which, while not providing in mortgage enforcement proceedings for grounds of objection based on the unfairness of a contractual term on which the right to seek enforcement is based, does not allow the court before which declaratory proceedings have been brought, which does have jurisdiction to assess whether such a term is unfair, to grant interim relief, including, in particular, the staying of those enforcement proceedings, where the grant of such relief is necessary to guarantee the full effectiveness of its final decision. 2. Article 3(1) of Directive 93/13 must be interpreted as meaning that: - the concept of 'significant imbalance' to the detriment of the consumer must be assessed in the light of an analysis of the rules of national law applicable in the absence of any agreement between the parties, in order to determine whether, and if so to what extent, the contract places the consumer in a less favourable legal situation than that provided for by the national law in force. To that end, an assessment of the legal situation of that consumer having regard to the means at his disposal, under national law, to prevent continued use of unfair terms, should also be carried out;

				- in order to assess whether the imbalance arises 'contrary to the requirement of good faith', it must be determined whether the seller or supplier, dealing fairly and equitably with the consumer, could reasonably assume that the consumer would have agreed to the term concerned in individual contract negotiations. Article 3(3) of Directive 93/13 must be interpreted as meaning that the annex to which that provision refers contains only an indicative and non-exhaustive list of terms which may be regarded as unfair.
	Case C-472/11 *Banif Plus Bank Ztr v Csaba Csipai, Viktória Csipai*	*Fővárosi Bíróság*	Hungary	1. Articles 6(1) and 7(1) of Council Directive 93/13/EEC of 5 April 1993 on unfair terms in consumer contracts must be interpreted as meaning that the national court which has found of its own motion that a contractual term is unfair is not obliged, in order to be able to draw the consequences arising from that finding, to wait for the consumer, who has been informed of his rights, to submit a statement requesting that that term be declared invalid. However, the principle of audi alteram partem, as a general rule, requires the national court which has found of its own motion that a contractual term is unfair to inform the parties to the dispute of that fact and to invite each of them to set out its views on that matter, with the opportunity to challenge the views of the other party, in accordance with the formal requirements laid down in that regard by the national rules of procedure. 2. The national court must, in order to determine whether the contractual term on which the claim brought before it is based may be unfair, take account of all of the other terms of the contract.
	Case C-488/11 *Dirk Frederik Asbeek Brusse, Katarina de Man Garabito v Jahani BV*	*Gerechtshof Amsterd*	Nether-lands	The Unfair Contract Terms Directive applies to residential tenancy agreements concluded between a professional landlord and a consumer, provided that they are not limited by national mandatory

				statutory or regulatory rules. Moreover, where a national court has the procedural powers to examine of its own motion whether contract terms are against rules on public policy, it must give the same treatment to the establishment of unfair terms, provided that they fall within the scope of the directive. Similarly, if the national court is given the power to determine and apply the sanctions applicable to terms contrary to public policy, it should give the same treatment to unfair terms, but only after having invited the parties to debate this issue. What is more, Article 6 must be interpreted to mean that if a court determines that a penalty clause is unfair, it may not reduce the amount of the penalty, even if this is provided for under national law, but must exclude the application of the clause entirely.
	Case C-413/12 *Asociación de Consumidores Independientes de Castilla y León v Anuntis Segundamano España SL*	*Audiencia Provincial de Salamanca*	Spain	Council Directive 93/13/EEC of 5 April 1993 on unfair terms in consumer contracts and the principles of equivalence and effectiveness must be interpreted as not precluding national procedural rules under which actions for an injunction brought by consumer protection associations must be brought before the courts where the defendant is established or has its address and whereby no appeal lies against a decision declining territorial jurisdiction handed down by a court of first instance.
	Joined cases C- 537/12 *Banco Popular Español SA v Maria Teodolinda Rivas Quichimbo, Wilmar Edgar Cun Pérez* C- 116/13 *Banco de Valencia SA v Joaquín Valldeperas Tortosa, María Ángeles Miret Jaume*	*Juzgado de Primera Instancia e Instrucción No. 1 de Catarroja*	Spain	1. Council Directive 93/13/EEC of 5 April 1993 on unfair terms in consumer contracts must be interpreted as precluding legislation of a Member State, such as that at issue in the main proceedings, which does not allow the court responsible for the enforcement, in mortgage enforcement proceedings, either to assess of its own motion or at the consumer's request, the unfairness of a term contained in the contract which gives rise to the debt claimed and which constitutes the basis of the right to enforcement, or to grant interim relief capable of

				staying or terminating the mortgage enforcement proceedings, where such relief is necessary to ensure the full effectiveness of the final decision of the court hearing the declaratory proceedings before which the consumer argues that that term is unfair. 2. Article 3(1) and (3) of Directive 93/13 and Points 1(e) and (g) and 2(a) of the annex thereto must be interpreted as meaning that, in order to assess the unfairness of a contractual term accelerating the repayment of a mortgage, such as that at issue in the main proceedings, the following are of decisive importance: - whether the right of the seller or supplier to cancel the contract unilaterally is conditional upon the non-compliance by the consumer with an obligation which is of essential importance in the context of the contractual relationship in question, - whether that right is provided for in cases in which such non-compliance is sufficiently serious in the light of the contractual term and amount of the loan, - whether that right derogates from the rules applicable in the absence of agreement between the parties, so as to make it more difficult for the consumer, given the procedural means at his disposal, to take legal action and exercise rights of the defence, and - whether national law provides for adequate and effective means enabling the consumer subject to such a contractual term to remedy the effects of the unilateral cancellation of the loan agreement. It is for the national court to make such an assessment on the basis of the specific circumstances of the case before it.
2014	Case C-226/12 *Constructora Principado SA v José Ignacio Menéndez Álvarez*	*Audiencia Provincial de Oviedo*	Spain	Article 3(1) of Council Directive 93/13/EEC of 5 April 1993 on unfair terms in consumer contracts must be interpreted as meaning that: - the existence of a 'significant imbalance' does not necessarily

				require that the costs charged to the consumer by a contractual term have, as regards that consumer, a significant economic impact having regard to the value of the transaction in question, but can result solely from a sufficiently serious impairment of the legal situation in which that consumer, as a party to the contract, is placed by reason of the relevant national provisions, whether this be in the form of a restriction of the rights which, in accordance with those provisions, he enjoys under that contract, or a constraint on the exercise of those rights, or the imposition on him of an additional obligation not envisaged by the national rules; - in assessing whether there is a significant imbalance, it is for the referring court to take into account the nature of the goods or services for which the contract was concluded by referring to all the circumstances attending the conclusion of that contract, as well as all the other terms of contract.
	Case C-34/13 *Monika Kušionová v SMART Capital a.s.*	*Krajský súd v Prešove*	Slovakia	The Court found the Directive not to preclude national legislation that allows debt recovery by means of extrajudicial enforcement of a charge on immovable property as long as the rights conferred to consumers by the Directive are somehow protected. Moreover, interpreting Article 1(2), the Court ruled that if contractual terms reflect mandatory statutory or regulatory provisions, they do not fall within the ambit of the Directive.
	C-470/12 *Pohotovosť s.r.o. v Miroslav Vašuta*	*Okresný súd Svidník*	Slovakia	Council Directive 93/13/EEC of 5 April 1993 on unfair terms in consumer contracts, in particular Articles 6(1), 7(1) and 8 of that directive, read in conjunction with Articles 38 and 47 of the Charter of Fundamental Rights of the European Union, must be interpreted as not precluding national legislation which does not allow a consumer protection association to intervene in support of a consumer in proceedings for enforcement, against the latter, of a final arbitration award.

	C-342/13 *Katalin Sebastyén v Zsolt Csaba Kővári, OTP Bank, OTP Faktoring Követeléskezelő ZRT, Raiffeisen Bank Zrt*	*Szombathelyi Törvényszék*	Hungary	Article 3(1) and (3) of Council Directive 93/13/EEC of 5 April 1993 on unfair terms in consumer contracts, and point 1(q) of the Annex to that directive, must be interpreted as meaning that it is for the national court concerned to determine whether a clause contained in a mortgage loan contract concluded between a bank and a consumer – vesting exclusive jurisdiction in a permanent arbitration tribunal, against whose decisions there is no judicial remedy under national law, to hear all disputes arising out of that contract – must, having regard to all of the circumstances surrounding the conclusion of that contract, be regarded as unfair under those provisions. In the context of its assessment, the national court must, in particular: - verify whether the clause at issue has the object or effect of excluding or hindering the consumer's right to take legal action or exercise any other legal remedy; and - take account of the fact that the communication to the consumer, before the conclusion of the contract at issue, of general information on the differences between the arbitration procedure and ordinary legal proceedings cannot alone rule out the unfairness of that clause. If the clause is held to be unfair, it is for that court to draw the appropriate conclusions under national law in order to ensure that the consumer is not bound by that clause.
	C-153/13 *Pohotovosť* s.r.o. *v Ján Soroka*	*Okresný súd Bardejov*	Slovakia	The Court of Justice of the European Union manifestly lacks jurisdiction to answer the questions referred by the *Okresný súd Bardejov* (Slovakia) by decision of 15 February 2013.
	C-26/13 *Árpád Kásler, Hajnalka Káslerné Rábai v OTP Jelzálogbank Zrt*	*Kúria*	Hungary	Article 4(2) of Directive 93/13/EEC of must be interpreted as meaning that: - the expression the 'main subject-matter of a contract' covers a term, incorporated in a loan agreement denominated in foreign currency concluded between a seller

				or supplier and a consumer and not individually negotiated, such as that at issue in the main proceedings, pursuant to which the selling rate of exchange of that currency is applied for the purpose of calculating the repayment instalments for the loan, only in so far as it is found, which it is for the national court to ascertain having regard to the nature, general scheme and stipulations of the contract and its legal and factual context, that that term lays down an essential obligation of that agreement which, as such characterises it; - such a term, in so far as it contains a pecuniary obligation for the consumer to pay, in repayment of instalments of the loan, the difference between the selling rate of exchange and the buying rate of exchange of the foreign currency, cannot be considered as 'remuneration' the adequacy of which as consideration for a service supplied by the lender cannot be the subject of an examination as regards unfairness under Article 4(2) of Directive 93/13. Article 4(2) of Directive 93/13 must be interpreted as meaning that, as regards a contractual term such as that at issue in the main proceedings, the requirement that a contractual term must be drafted in plain intelligible language is to be understood as requiring not only that the relevant term should be grammatically intelligible to the consumer, but also that the contract should set out transparently the specific functioning of the mechanism of conversion for the foreign currency to which the relevant term refers and the relationship between that mechanism and that provided for by other contractual terms relating to the advance of the loan, so that that consumer is in a position to evaluate, on the basis of clear, intelligible criteria, the economic consequences for him which derive from it. Article 6(1) of Directive 93/13 must

				be interpreted as meaning that, in a situation such as that at issue in the main proceedings, in which a contract concluded between a seller or supplier and a consumer cannot continue in existence after an unfair term has been deleted, that provision does not preclude a rule of national law enabling the national court to cure the invalidity of that term by substituting for it a supplementary provision of national law.
	Case C-280/13 *Barclays Bank SA v Sara Sánchez Garcia, Alejandro Chacón Barrera*	*Juzgado de Primera Instancia No4 de Palma de Mallorca*	Spain	Council Directive 93/13/EEC of 5 April 1993 on unfair terms in consumer contracts and the principles of EU law relating to consumer protection and a balance in the parties' rights and obligations must be interpreted as meaning that statutory and regulatory provisions of a Member State, such as those at issue in the main proceedings, are excluded from their scope, when there is no contractual term altering the effect or ambit of those provisions.
	Case C-92/14 *Liliana Tudoran, Florin Iulian Tudoran, Ilie Tudoran v SC Suport Colect SRL*	*Judecãtoria Câmpulung*	Romania	The Unfair Contract Terms Directive is not applicable to the case at hand because the facts took place prior to Romania's accession to the European Union.
	Case C-169/14 *Juan Carlos Sánchez Morcillo and María del Carmen Abril García v Banco Bilbao Vizcaya Argentaria SA*	*Audiencia Provincial de Castellón*	Spain	Article 7(1) of Council Directive 93/13/EEC of 5 April 1993 on unfair terms in consumer contracts, read in conjunction with Article 47 of the Charter of Fundamental Rights of the European Union must be interpreted as precluding a system of enforcement, such as that at issue in the main proceedings, which provides that mortgage enforcement proceedings may not be stayed by the court of first instance, which, in its final decision, may at most award compensation in respect of the damage suffered by the consumer, inasmuch as the latter, the debtor against whom mortgage enforcement proceedings are brought, may not appeal against a decision dismissing his objection to that enforcement, whereas the seller or supplier, the creditor seeking enforcement, may bring an appeal

				against a decision terminating the proceedings or ordering an unfair term to be disapplied.
2015	Case C-96/14 *Jean-Claude Van Hove v CNP Assurances SA*	*Tribunal de grande instance de Nîmes*	France	Article 4(2) of Council Directive 93/13/EEC of 5 April 1993 on unfair terms in consumer contracts, must be interpreted as meaning that a term of an insurance contract intended to ensure that loan repayments payable to the lender will be covered in the event of the borrower's total incapacity for work falls within the exception set out in that provision only where the referring court finds: first, that, having regard to the having regard to the nature, general scheme and the stipulations of the contractual framework of which it forms part, and to its legal and factual context, that term lays down an essential component of that contractual framework, and, as such, characterises it, and; secondly, that that term is drafted in plain, intelligible language, that is to say that it is not only grammatically intelligible to the consumer, but also that the contract sets out transparently the specific functioning of the arrangements to which the relevant term refers and the relationship between those arrangements and the arrangements laid down in respect of other contractual terms, so that that consumer is in a position to evaluate, on the basis of precise, intelligible criteria, the economic consequences for him which derive from it.
	Case C-110/14 *Horaţiu Ovidiu Costea v SC Volksbank România SA*	*Judecătoria Oradea*	Romania	Article 2(b) of Directive 93/13/EEC must be interpreted as meaning that a natural person who practises as a lawyer and concludes a credit agreement with a bank, in which the purpose of the credit is not specified, may be regarded as a 'consumer' within the meaning of that provision, where that agreement is not linked to that lawyer's profession. The fact that the debt arising out of the same contract is secured by a mortgage taken out by that person in his capacity as

				representative of his law firm and involving goods intended for the exercise of that person's profession, such as a building belonging to that firm, is not relevant in that regard.
	Case C-32/14 *ERSTE Bank Hungary Zrt. v Attila Sugár*	*Fővárosi Törvényszék*	Hungary	Articles 6(1) and 7(1) of Directive 93/13/EEC must be interpreted as meaning that they do not preclude national legislation, such as that at issue in the main proceedings, which allows a notary who drew up, in due form, an authentic instrument concerning a contract concluded between a seller or supplier and a consumer, to affix the enforcement clause to that instrument or to refuse to cancel it when no review of the unfairness of the contractual terms has been performed at any stage.
	Case C-8/14 *BBVA SA v Pedro Peñalva López and Others.*	*Juzgado de Primera Instancia nº 4 de Martorell*	Spain	Articles 6 and 7 of Council Directive 93/13/EEC of 5 April 1993 on unfair terms in consumer contracts must be interpreted as meaning that they preclude a national transitional provision, such as that at issue in the main proceedings, which, as regards mortgage enforcement procee-dings which were instituted before the date of entry into force of the law of which that provision forms part and which were not concluded at that date, imposes a time-limit on consumers calcula-ted from the day following the publication of that law, to object to enforcement on the basis of the alleged unfairness of contractual terms.
	Case C-602/13 *Banco Bilbao Vizcaya Argentaria SA v Fernando Quintano Ujeta and María-Isabel Sánchez García.*	*Juzgado de Primera Instancia nº 2 de Santander*	Spain	Translation by author: Articles 6(1) and 7(1) of Council Directive 93/13/EEC of 5 April 1993 on unfair terms in consumer contracts must be interpreted as not precluding national provisions relating to ce sens qu'ils ne s'opposent pas à des dispositions nationales providing for the moderation of default interest on a mortgage agreement, as long as the national provisions: do not prejudice the assessment by the national judge of the mortgage execution procedure of the contract with unfair character relating to the clause on default interest; do not create an obstable for the judge to depart from the said

				clause in case he finds the clause to be unfair in the meaning of Article 3(1) of this Directive. Directive 93/13 must be interpretes as meaning that since the national judge has found the unfair character in the sense of Article 3(1) of Directive 93/13 or a clause in a contract concluded between a consumer and a professional, the circumstance that the clause had not been executed, does not, in itself, preclude a national judge to consider all the consequences of the unfair character of that clause.
	Case C-567/13 *Nóra Baczó and János István Vizsnyiczai v Raiffeisen Bank Zrt*	*Fővárosi Törvényszék*	Hungary	Article 7(1) of Council Directive 93/13/EEC of 5 April 1993 on unfair terms in consumer contracts must be interpreted as meaning that it does not preclude a national procedural rule pursuant to which a local court which has jurisdiction to rule on an action brought by a consumer seeking a declaration of invalidity of a standard contract does not have jurisdiction to hear an application by the consumer for a declaration of unfairness of contract terms in the same contract, unless declining jurisdiction by the local court gives rise to procedural difficulties that would make the exercise of the rights conferred on consumers by the European Union legal order excessively difficult. It is for the national court to carry out the necessary verifications in that respect.
	Case C- 537/13 *Birutė Šiba v Arūnas Devėnas*	*Lietuvos Aukščiausiasis Teismas*	Lithuania	Council Directive 93/13/EEC of 5 April 1993 on unfair terms in consumer contracts must be interpreted as applying to standard form contracts for legal services, such as those at issue in the main proceedings, concluded by a lawyer with a natural person acting for purposes which are outside his trade, business or profession.
	Joined cases C-482/13 *Unicaja Banco SA v José Hidalgo Rueda and Others* C-484/13	*Juzgado de Primera Instancia e Instrucción de Marchena*	Spain	Article 6 of Council Directive 93/13/EEC of 5 April 1993 on unfair terms in consumer contracts must be interpreted as not precluding a national provision under which the national court hearing mortgage enforcement proceedings is required

	Caixabank SA v Manuel María Rueda Ledesma and Rosario Mesa Mesa C-485/13 *José Labella Crespo and Others* C-487/13 - *Alberto Galán Luna and Domingo Galán Luna*			to adjust the amounts due under a term in a mortgage-loan contract providing for default interest at a rate more than three times greater than the statutory rate in order that the amount of that interest may not exceed that threshold, provided that the application of that national provision: is without prejudice to the assessment by that national court of the unfairness of such a term and; does not prevent that court removing that term if it were to find the latter to be 'unfair', within the meaning of Article 3(1) of that directive.
	Case C-143/13 *Bogdan Matei and Ioana Ofelia Matei v SC Volksbank România SA.*	*Tribunalul Specializat Cluj*	Romania	Article 4(2) of Council Directive 93/13/EEC of 5 April 1993 on unfair terms in consumer contracts must be interpreted as meaning that 'main subject-matter of the contract' and 'adequacy of the price and remuneration, on the one hand, as against the services or goods supplies in exchange, on the other' do not, in principle, cover the types of terms in the credit agreements concluded between a professional and consumers such as those at issue in the main proceedings, which, on one hand, allow, under certain conditions, the lender unilaterally to alter the interest rate and, on the other hand, provide for a 'risk charge' applied by the lender. However, it is for the referring court to verify that classification of those contractual terms having regard to the nature, general scheme and stipulations of the agreements concerned and the legal and factual context of which they form part.
	Case C-312/14 *Banif Plus Bank Zrt. v Márton Lantos, Mártonné Lantos*	*Ráckevei járásbíróság*	Hungary	Article 4(1)(2) of Directive 2004/39/EC of the European Parliament and of the Council of 21 April 2004 on markets in financial instruments amending Council Directives 85/611/EEC and 93/6/EEC and Directive 2000/12/EC of the European Parliament and of the Council and repealing Council Directive 93/22/EEC must be interpreted as meaning that, subject to verification by the referring court, an investment

				service or activity within the meaning of that provision does not encompass certain foreign exchange transactions, effected by a credit institution under clauses of a foreign currency denominated loan agreement such as the one at issue in the main proceedings, consisting in fixing the amount of the loan on the basis of the purchase price of the currency applicable when the funds are advanced and in determining the amounts of the monthly instalments on the basis of the sale price of that currency applicable when each monthly instalment is calculated.
	Case C-348/14 *Maria Bucura v SC Bancpost SA.*	*Judecătoria Câmpulung*	Romania	Translation by author: 1. Article 2(b) of of Council Directive 93/13/EEC of 5 April 1993 on unfair terms in consumer contracts must be interpreted as including a natural person as 'consumer' for the purposes of the current provisions, where that person is considered a co-debtor for the purposes of a contract concluded with a professional, so long as the natural person acts for purposes outside his occupation or profession. 2. Article 6(1) of Directive 93/13 must be interpreted as to consider that it is up to the national court to appreciate ex officio the unfair character, in the light of these provision, of the clauses in a contract between a consumer and professional, as the court is aware of the facts and law necessary to this end. 3. Articles 3-5 of Directive 93/13 must be interpreted to mean that in dealing with the unfair charactermof unfair terms in consumer credit contracts as referred to in Article 3(1) and (3) of this Directive, the national court must take into account all circumstances surrounding the conclusion of this contract. In this sense, it is up to the national court to check that in the case at hand all elements that can affect the scope of the consumer's obligation and that allow him to assess, among others, the total cost of his load, were brought to the attention of the

				consumer. A decisive role in this appreciation is played by, on the one hand, the aspect of whether the clauses are drafted in a clear and inteligible manner so to allow an average consumer, namely a normally informed and sufficiently attentive and knowledgeable consumer, to evaluate such a cost, and on the other hand, the circumstances relating to not mentioning the considered information in the credit agreement, taking into account the nature of the goods or services as essential to the conclusion of the contract, especially those mentioned in Article 4 of Directive 87/102 after modification.
	Case C-539/14 *Juan Carlos Sánchez Morcillo and María del Carmen Abril García v Banco Bilbao Vizcaya Argentaria SA.*	*Audiencia Provincial de Castellón*	Spain	Article 7(1) of Council Directive 93/13/EEC of 5 April 1993 on unfair terms in consumer contracts, read in conjunction with Articles 47, 34(3) and 7 of the Charter of Fundamental Rights of the European Union, must be interpreted as not precluding a national provision of the kind at issue in the main proceedings, by which the consumer, as a mortgage debtor against whom enforcement proceedings are brought, may bring an appeal against the decision rejecting his objection to the enforcement only when the court of first instance has not upheld an objection based on the unfairness of the contractual term upon which the enforcement is based even though the sellers or suppliers may, by contrast, appeal against any decision terminating proceedings regardless of the ground of objection on which that decision is based.
	Case C- 74/15 *Dumitru Tarcău, Ileana Tarcău v Banca Comercială Intesa Sanpaolo România SA and others*	*Curtea de Apel Oradea*	Romania	Translation by author: Article 1(1) and Article 2(b) of Council Directive 93/13/EEC of 5 April 1993 on unfair terms in consumer contracts must be interpreted as this Directive is applicable to an immovable security contract (*contract de garanție imobiliară*) or of surety (*fideiusiune*) concluded between a natural person and a credit institution with a purpose of offering security for the obligations which a company

				contracted towards the respective institution when this natural person acted for purposes not included in its professional activity and which do not have any functional report with the respective company.
2016	Case C-49/14 *Finanmadrid EFC SA v Jesús Vicente Albán Zambrano, María Josefa García Zapata, Jorge Luis Albán Zambrano, Miriam Elisabeth Caicedo Merino*	*Juzgado de Primera Instancia No 5 de Cartagen*	Spain	Council Directive 93/13/EEC of 5 April 1993 on unfair terms in consumer contracts precludes national legislation, such as that at issue in the main proceedings, which does not permit the court ruling on the enforcement of an order for payment to assess of its own motion whether a term in a contract concluded between a seller or supplier and a consumer is unfair, when the authority hearing the application for an order for payment does not have the power to make such an assessment.
	Case C-613/15 *Ibercaja Banco SAU v José Cortés González*	*Juzgado de Primera Instancia n° 5 de Alcobendas*	Spain	Translation by author: Council Directive 93/13/EEC of 5 April 1993 on unfair terms in consumer contracts must be interpreted as: - its Articles 3, paragraph 1 and 4, paragraph 1, preclude the national law of a Member State from restricting the discretion of appreciation of a national court as to the finding of the unfairness of the terms of a mortgage contract between a consumer and a professional, and - its Article 6, parahraph 1, and 7, paragraph 1, require that national law does not impede the national court from setting aside such a clause, should it conclude that it has an unfair character, in the meaning of Article 3, paragraph 1 of the said directive.

The increased case load of the Court of Justice on unfair terms has raised many unclarities regarding the role of the Court as a developer of consumer law.[69] The yearly number of cases, as well as the referring Member States have been fluctuating since 1993. Out of the total 102 cases in the Curia database consulted as of March 2016:

69 Mak 2014, p. 823; Micklitz & Kas 2014, p. 48; Micklitz & Reich 2014, p. 772.

- 19 are cases that only briefly refer to the Unfair Contract Terms Directive as they are based on other legal acts, and the Court does not rule on the Unfair Contract Terms Directive claims in the operative part;
- 19 are orders to remove cases from the Court's registry, for various reasons including the withdrawal of the preliminary reference by the national court;
- 13 cases are featured in the database but no information is available whatsoever regarding their content;[70]
- 6 cases deal with infringement procedures;
- in 4 cases jurisdiction was declined or the Unfair Contract Terms Directive was not applicable;
- 34 cases have resulted in judgments regarding provisions in the Unfair Contract Terms Directive;
- 7 cases have resulted in orders regarding provisions in the Unfair Contract Terms Directive.

Out of all these cases, only the last three categories are considered for this factor, leading to a total of 45 cases. These are the only ones that can be taken into account in order to assess how and why national courts struggle to interpret the Unfair Contract Terms Directive.

B. National level

a) National transposition technique

The Unfair Contract Terms Directive is one of the most problematic consumer instruments in the *acquis* in view of the convergence discussion, if only for the fact that it transplanted a general clause with a very ambitious reach.[71] Analysing national law in great detail, especially by focusing on the nature of the transposition, can shed light on the case law listed above, and completes the understanding of how national systems cope with European rules. To better view how Member States transposed the Unfair Contract Terms Directive, an overview is first provided in table format, followed by a more visual graph.

Table 7: Initial national transposition techniques table (Unfair Contract Terms Directive)

Member State	Transposition technique
Belgium	Satellite law - Act of 14 July 1991 on trade practices and consumer information and protection
France	Consumer Code
Germany	Civil Code[72]

70 This lists includes C-267/98 (*Cardeñosa*); C-266/98 (*Caminati*); C-265/98 (*Compañ Calbuig*); C-82/96 (*Consumers Association*); C-268/98 (*Casas Minguelez*); C-269/98 (*Villar Castelao*); C-270/98 (*Lopez Aznar*); C-271/98 (*Serrano Garido*); C-272/98 (*Arencom Salazar*); C-21/00 (*Hamadeh*); C-129/01 (*Condominio Facchinei Orsini*); see also Case C-82/96, *R. and Secretary of Trade ex-parte Consumers Association*, in Howells & Weatherill 2005, p. 294.

71 See the reference to the *travaux preparatoires* made earlier in this chapter.

72 In 2002, the Civil Code took over the rules from the *Gesetz zur Regelung des Rechts der Allgemeinen Geschäftsbedingungen*.

Ireland	Satellite law - European Communities (Unfair Terms in Consumer Contracts) Regulations, 1995 and 2000
Netherlands	Civil Code
Romania	Satellite law - Law no. 193 of 6 November 2000 on unfair terms in contracts between sellers and consumers
United Kingdom	Satellite law - Unfair Terms in Consumer Contracts Regulations 1999

Figure 11: Initial national transposition techniques graph (Unfair Contract Terms Directive)

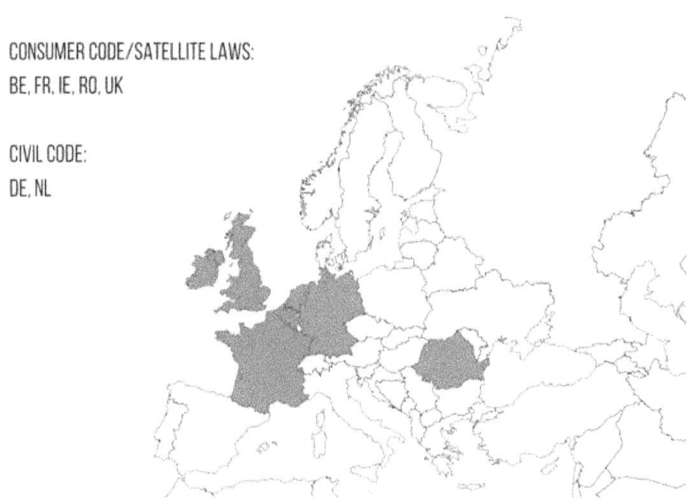

b) Reception of selected novel concepts

Before any discussion, it must be mentioned that the analysis of novel concepts is limited to Articles 3-7 of the Directive. Upon closer inspection of these articles, the main concept that can be said to have a *sui generis* European meaning is the broad notion of 'unfair terms'.

The Directive defines unfair terms through four aspects: firstly, the unfairness test (Article 3); secondly, the Annex containing an indicative and non-exhaustive list of terms which may be considered unfair (Article 3); thirdly, assessment factors (Article 4); and lastly, the lack of binding force (Article 6).

Preparatory works leading to the adoption of the Unfair Contract Terms Directive show that some Member States already had legislation dealing with unfair terms as early as the 1970s.[73] National legislation pre-dating the Directive was thus familiar with the majority of the four aspects now defining European unfair terms. For instance, in France, Article 35 of the Law no. 78-23 of 10 January 1978 prohibited certain clauses that 'seem[ed] to have been imposed on non-professionals or

73 European Commission, 'Unfair Terms in Contracts Concluded With Consumers', (based on COM(84) 55 final), p. 7.

consumers by abuse of the economic position of the other party, giving the latter an excessive advantage'.[74] The following sentence indicates that abusive clauses are considered void (*non écrites*).[75] Although not identical in wording, the French provisions show elements of the Directive's unfairness test as well as the lack of binding force. Although not included in this analysis as such, another example is Luxemburg's Law of 25 August 1983. Article 1 of this law mentioned that if contracts concluded between professional suppliers and consumers contain clauses that lead to an imbalance in the rights and obligations to the detriment of the consumer, such clauses will be considered null and void (*nulle et non écrite*).[76] This leads to a situation similar to French law - in 1983 Luxemburg law seemed to have already put into place an unfairness test, and it also specified the legal effect of terms deemed unfair. The law of the Federal Republic of Germany can be mentioned as an example as well. On 9 December 1976 it passed the Act concerning the Regulation of Standard Contract Terms.[77] Apart from specifying the legal consequences of exclusion and invalidity (§ 6), and establishing a general test that included the concept of good faith (§ 9), the Act also added two lists: a grey list with terms that may be void (§ 10) and a black list of terms that were always void (§ 11). These elements seem to be very familiar to the substance of European unfair terms.

The three examples from national laws as they existed in the 1970s and 1980s reveal that the European legislator did not reinvent the law when it passed the Unfair Contract Terms Directive. However, the degree of proximity between pre-existing legislation and the Directive is only limited. This is to say that before the drafting of the Directive, none of the Member States of the European Union treated unfair terms identically to the manner in which they are profiled by the Unfair

[74] Article 35, first sentence, *Loi no 78-23 du 10 Janvier 1978 sur la protection et l'information des consommateurs de produits et de services*; translation by author. The full text of the article reads: 'Dans les contrats conclus entre professionels et non-professionnels ou consommateurs, peuvent être interdites, limitées ou réglementées, par des décrets en Conseil d'Etat pris après avis de la commission instituée par l'article 36, en distinguant éventuellement selon la nature des biens et des services concernés, les clauses relatives au caractère déterminé ou déterminable du prix ainsi qu'à son versement, à la consistance de la chose ou à sa livraison, à la charge des risques, à l'étendue des responsabilités et garanties, aux conditions d'exécution, de résiliation, résolution ou reconduction des conventions, lorsque de telles clauses apparaissent imposées aux non-professionnels ou consommateurs par un abus de la puissance économique de l'autre partie et confèrent à cette dernière un avantage excessif.'

[75] Article 35, second sentence, *Loi no 78-23 du 10 Janvier 1978 sur la protection et l'information des consommateurs de produits et de services (France)*: 'De telles clauses abusives, stipulées en contradiction avec les dispositions qui précèdent, sont réputées non écrites.'

[76] Article 1, *Loi du 25 août 1983 relative à la protection juridique du consommateur (Luxemburg)*; translation by author. The full text of the article reads: 'Dans les contrats conclus entre un fournisseur professionnel de biens de consommation, durables ou non, ou de services et un consommateur final privé, toute clause ou toute combinaison de clauses qui entraîne dans le contrat un déséquilibre des droits et obligations au préjudice du consommateur est abusive et comme telle réputée nulle et non écrite.'

[77] *Gesetz zur Regelung des Rechts der Allgemeinen Geschaftsbedingungen (AGB-Gesetz - Germany)*; for a thorough analysis of this law see Sandrock & Moore Galston 1978, p. 551.

Contract Terms Directive.[78] It is for this reason that the European notion of 'unfair terms' can be seen to have an independent identity.

Some examples of the similarities between pre-existing national laws and the Directive have already been addressed. However, as similar as their laws may be, letting Member States regulate standard terms individually falls short of being a solution to the issue of legal divergence exposed by the Commission in the Explanatory Memorandum section of the Proposal for the Directive.[79] In the view of the Commission, 'differences between the laws of the Member States - even where they have adopted laws on unfair contract terms - have led and are likely to lead even more to unequal treatment of the Community's citizens.'[80]

This problem was supposed to be curbed by the introduction of a unitary regime governing unfair contract terms. Nevertheless, in the light of the chosen form of coordinating national policies on the matter (adopting a Directive), national laws remained divergent, even if in a different sense. For instance, the Commission's Report on the transposition of the Unfair Contract Terms Directive testifies to the fact that the notion of unfair terms was altered by the implementation effected by various Member States in that while some copy-pasted the provisions, others rephrased them.[81] What is more, Member States also had difficulties with the Annex, as some countries refused to transpose it, even though it was one of the defining factors of the European notion of 'unfair terms'.[82] The remaining disparities are analysed step by step under the factor 'Reception of selected novel concepts', to be addressed below.

Table 8: Transposition of novel concepts (Unfair Contract Terms Directive)

Member State	**Directive version in original language**	**Transposition**
		Form
Belgium[83]	*oneerlijk beding* *clause abusive*	*onrechtmatig beding* *clause abusive*
France[84]	*clause abusive*	*(clauses) abusives*

[78] For further comparison with other Member States see also Nordic Council of Ministers, 'Unfair Terms in Consumer Contracts in a European Perspective - Report from a Seminar in Copenhagen, 6 June 1990', *Nordiske Seminar- og Arbejdsrapporter*, p. 3; Hondius 1978, p. 525.

[79] European Commission, Proposal for a Council Directive on Unfair Contract Terms in Consumer Contracts, COM(90) 322 final, p. 2.

[80] *Ibid.*, p. 8.

[81] Report from the Commission on the Implementation of Council Directive 93/13/EEC of 5 April 1993 on Unfair Terms in Consumer Contracts, COM(2000) 248 final, p. 16.

[82] *Ibid.*

[83] Article 31 of Law of 14 July 1991.

[84] Article L. 132-1 para 1 Code de la Consommation.

Germany[85]	*mißbräuchliche Klauseln*	- (instead, the German legislator used the concept of 'ineffective provisions', meaning that the effect of the unfair rules is already indicated)[86]
Ireland[87]	unfair terms	unfair terms
Nether-lands[88]	*oneerlijke bedingen*	- (instead, the Dutch legislator uses the concept of 'voidable terms')[89]
Romania[90]	*(clauză) abuzivă*	*(clauză) abuzivă*
United Kingdom[91]	unfair terms	unfair terms

What can be noticed from the overview above is that while Belgium, France, Ireland, Romania and the United Kingdom have taken over the concept of 'unfair terms', the Netherlands and Germany do not make use of such concept. Instead, both national legislators decided to individualise unfair terms by directly referring to their effect, which is in both cases that of rendering the terms voidable. As such, this approach is not against the purpose of the Directive - Article 6 expressly mentions that Member States are required to guarantee consumers that unfair terms shall not be binding upon them. However, from a legislative technique perspective, this approach does not fully clarify the nature and the role of the Europeanised concept of 'unfair terms' in either German or Dutch law. For instance, in German law it seems that the transposing provision of Article 3(1) of the Directive sets up a wider general clause (*Generalklausel*) designed to test the invalidity of standard contract terms, without identifying an 'unfair terms' category.[92] Dutch law seems to pose a similar issue. However, it is stated that by not identifying the category of

85 § 307 BGB.

86 § 307(1) BGB reads: *'(1) Bestimmungen in Allgemeinen Geschäftsbedingungen sind unwirksam, wenn sie den Vertragspartner des Verwenders entgegen den Geboten von Treu und Glauben unangemessen benachteiligen. Eine unangemessene Benachteiligung kann sich auch daraus ergeben, dass die Bestimmung nicht klar und verständlich ist.'* (EN: 'Provisions in standard business terms are ineffective if, contrary to the requirement of good faith, they unreasonably disadvantage the other party to the contract with the user. An unreasonable disadvantage may also arise from the provision not being clear and comprehensible'; translation provided by the Langenscheidt Translation Service).

87 Regulation 3(2) European Communities (Unfair Terms in Consumer Contracts) Regulations.

88 Article 6:233 BW.

89 The article reads: *'Een beding in algemene voorwaarden is vernietigbaar: a. indien het, gelet op de aard en de overige inhoud van de overeenkomst, de wijze waarop de voorwaarden zijn tot stand gekomen, de wederzijds kenbare belangen van partijen en de overige omstandigheden van het geval, onredelijk bezwarend is voor de wederpartij; of b. indien de gebruiker aan de wederpartij niet een redelijke mogelijkheid heeft geboden om van de algemene voorwaarden kennis te nemen'.*

90 Article 4(1) *Lege nr. 193 din 6 noiembrie 2000 privind clauzele abuzive din contractele încheiate între comercianţi şi consumatori.*

91 Regulation 5(1) Unfair Terms in Consumer Contracts Regulations 1999.

92 Bruns/Münchener Kommentar zum VVG, BGB § 307 Inhaltskontrolle, Auflage 2010, Rn 56.

'unfair terms' as indicated in the Directive, Dutch law might not necessarily lead to a diverging outcome. Regardless of their content, transposing provisions are supposed to be interpreted in the light of the text of the Directive, but also the case law of the Court of Justice.[93] This argument applies universally to the implementation of any Directive. Still, if a national legislator strays away from the wording and meaning of Directive-based rules, for whatever reasons, proceedings on non-fulfillment might be brought against the Member State in question. This was the case when the Court of Justice was not convinced that (among others) Article 6:233 BW reflected an accurate transposition of the Directive on Unfair Terms, and declared in 2001 that the Netherlands had failed to fulfill its obligations under it.[94]

Another problem with the argument that directive-oriented interpretation might suffice is the question of awareness. In order to interpret national law in the light of European law, national judges must be aware of whether, in this case, the Unfair Contract Terms Directive would cover various nominate contracts. An example in this direction is the field of rental agreements, which have been, as of *Asbeek*,[95] explicitly placed by the Court of Justice under the ambit of the Directive. It has been a well known practice in various Member States for rental agencies to charge 'middle-man' fees to individuals looking for long-term accommodation, on the grounds of mediating their relation with landlords. Sometimes, agencies acts beyond their quality of accommodation-finders, but have the added role of contractually representing landlords in an eventual accord with their customers. This contractual triad implies that the agency (a company) representing an owner (an individual),[96] concludes a contract with a consumer. In spite of the complicated nature of this three-way relationship, it can very well be argued that if the agency uses general terms in its contract with the consumer, the Unfair Contract Terms Directive becomes applicable. However, at least in the Netherlands, recent case law seems not to make any reference to either the Directive or to Article 6:233 BW in such situations.[97] Although a clear conclusion is difficult to draw, it is not impossible to envisage how the piecemeal approach taken by the European legislator in terms of the harmonisation of contract law might leave national courts confused, and how an innacurate (even though not incorrect) transposition of European instruments does not really bring any clarity to the situation.

c) Reception of selected open-ended norms

The Unfair Contract Terms Directive is well known for the discussions it stirred around the use of the concept of good faith in its general clause. However, good

93 T&C BW/Valk, commentaar op Article 233 Boek 6 BW; see also T&C BW/Valk, commentaar op Article 234 Boek 6 BW; HR, 11-07-2008, nr C07/012HR.

94 Case C-144/99, *Commission of the European Communities v Kingdom of the Netherlands* [2001], ECR I-03541, paras. 14, 22.

95 See *Dirk Frederik Asbeek Brusse, Katarina de Man Garabito v Jahani BV*.

96 Although more research is necessary on this matter, it can be claimed that an individual renting out properties, depending on factors such as the number of rented properties, etc., might be considered a seller/supplier in the sense of Article 2(3) of the Unfair Contract Terms Directive.

97 Rechtbank Noord-Nederland, 2844681 CV EXPL 14-3775, 12 August 2014.

faith is not the only open-ended norm included in the Directive. Article 3 establishes a test that requires *unfair* terms in a non-individually negotiated contract to be contrary to *good faith* and cause a *significant* imbalance to create a *detriment* to the consumer (emphasis added). Assessing unfairness also implies that certain factors need to be taken into account, such as the rest of the terms in the contract or the circumstances in which the contract was concluded (Article 4), or the indication regarding the specific characteristics of drafting language (Article 5).

In the case of the aforementioned methodological limitation to Articles 3-7, the open-ended norms considered in this analysis are: 'unfair/unfairness'; 'good faith'; 'significant'; and 'detriment'.

Table 9: Transposition of open-ended norms (Unfair Contract Terms Directive)

Member State	Directive version in original language	Transposition
		Form
Belgium[98]	*(clause) abusive/ oneerlijk* *bonne foi/goede trouw* *significatif/aanzienlijk* *détriment/nadele*	*clause abusive/onrechtmatig beding* - *manifeste/ kennelijk* -
France[99]	*(clause) abusive* *bonne foi* *significatif* *detriment*	*abusives (les clauses)* - *significatif* *détriment*
Germany[100]	*mißbräuchlich* *Treu und Glauben* *erhebliches* *Nachteil*	- *Treu und Glauben* *unangemessen (benachteiligen)* -
Ireland[101]	unfair good faith significant detriment	unfair good faith significant detriment
Nether-lands[102]	*oneerlijk* *goede trouw* *aanzienlijk* *nadele*	- - *onredelijk* -
Romania[103]	*abuzivă* *bună credință* *semnificativ* *detrimentul*	*abuzivă* *bunei-credințe* *semnificativ* *detrimentul*

98 Article 31, Law of 14 July 1991.

99 Article L. 132-1(1) Code de la Consommation.

100 § 307 BGB.

101 Regulation 3(2) European Communities (Unfair Terms in Consumer Contracts) Regulations.

102 Article 6:233 BW.

103 Article 4(1) *Lege nr. 193 din 6 noiembrie 2000 privind clauzele abuzive din contractele încheiate între comercianti si consumatori.*

United Kingdom[104]	unfair good faith significant detriment	unfair good faith significant detriment

Once again it becomes evident that the two Member States that implemented the Directive in their Civil Codes are the ones who chose against taking over some of the open-ended concepts embedded in the Directive: the overall concept of 'unfair terms' (Germany and the Netherlands); the notion of 'detriment' (Germany and the Netherlands); and the concept of 'good faith' (Belgium, France, the Netherlands). While for the first two examples the same argumentation as above may hold true, the 'good faith' discussion has an additional dimension. All three jurisdictions that did not take over the requirement of good faith have a pre-existing principle of good faith applicable to contractual (and pre-contractual) obligations.

d) Timely transposition

According to Article 10, the transposition deadline was 31 December 1994.

Table 10: Overview of transposition deadline (Unfair Contract Terms Directive)

Member State	National legislation	Implementation date	Timely transposition
Belgium	Act of 14 July 1991 on trade practices and consumer information and protection	29 February 1992	Yes
France	Article L. 132-1 ff Consumer Code	28 February 1995	No
Germany	Act Concerning the Regulation of the Law of Standard Business Terms	25 July 1996	No
Ireland	European Communities (Unfair Terms in Consumer Contracts) Regulations, 1995	1 January 1995	Yes
Netherlands	Law of 28 October 1999 to the adaptation of Book 6 of the Civil Code to the Directive unfair terms in consumer contracts	17 November 1999	No
Romania	Law no. 193 of 6 November 2000 on unfair terms in contracts between sellers and consumers	10 December 2000	Yes
United Kingdom	Unfair Terms in Consumer Contracts Regulations 1994	1 July 1995	No

e) Infringement procedures

The following infringement procedure was retrieved from a search through the Curia database.[105]

[104] Regulation 5(1) Unfair Terms in Consumer Contracts Regulations 1999.

Table 11: Infringement Procedures (Unfair Contract Terms Directive)

Date of judgment	Case number and name	Member State	Proceedings	Ruling
10 May 2001	Case C-144/99 *Commission of the European Communities v Kingdom of the Netherlands*	Netherlands	Failure by a Member State to fulfil its obligations - Directive 93/13/EEC - Unfair terms in consumer contracts - Incomplete transposition of the directive into national law	The Netherlands failed to fulfil its obligations under the Directive by not adopting appropriate implementation measures.

Apart from the two cases mentioned above, there are five more infringement procedures the Commission brought against other Member States that are outside the ambit of this study: Italy,[106] Malta,[107] Spain[108] and Sweden.[109]

f) Reference to European law in end legislation
Table 12: Overview of reference to European law (Unfair Contract Terms Directive)

Member State	National legislation	Reference to European law	Database
Belgium	*Loi du 14/07/1991 sur les pratiques du commerce et sur l'information et la protection du consommateur (Wet van 14/07/1991 betreffende de handelspraktijken en de voorlichting en bescherming van de consument)*	No	Ejustice
France	Consumer Code	No	Legifrance
Germany	Civil Code	Yes	Juris
Ireland	European Communities (Unfair Terms in Consumer Contracts) Regulations, 1995 and 2000	Yes	Irish Statute Book (Office of the Attorney General)
Netherlands	Civil Code	No	Overheid

105 France was also brought before the Court; however, the case was removed from the registry before the judgment. See Case C-244/01, *Commission v France* [2001]; Brigitta Jud, 'Staatshaftung für judikatives Unrecht', *Ecolex*, 2003 p. 385-387.

106 Case C-372/99, *Commission v Italian Republic* [2002] ECR I-00819.

107 Case C-220/09, *Commission v Malta* [2009] (the Commission dropped the case after Malta addressed its implementation issues voluntarily).

108 Case C-318/97, *Commission v Kingdom of Spain* [1998] ECR I-05451; Case C-70/03, *Commission v Kingdom of Spain* [2004] ECR I-07999.

109 Case C-478/99, *Commission v Kingdom of Sweden* [2002] ECR I-04147.

Romania	Law no. 193 of 6 November 2000 on unfair terms in contracts between sellers and consumers	No	Lege 5
United Kingdom	Unfair Terms in Consumer Contracts Regulations 1999	Yes	The National Archives

3.3. *Distance Selling Directive*

To remind the reader which provisions of the Distance Selling Directive have been described earlier in Chapter 2, they are be briefly restated below:

- Article 4 (the provision of prior information);
- Article 6 (the seven day withdrawal period);
- Article 7 (the 30 day performance period);
- Article 12 (the mandatory nature of the consumer rights enshrined in the Directive).

Some of the factors which are dealt with shortly (e.g. the nature and type of European instrument, etc.) do not make direct reference to the articles above, as they can be assessed overall. However, some other factors (e.g. novel concepts, text similarity, etc.) exclusively reflect the analysed articles, and not the entire body of the directive.

A. European level

a) Law v policy
Given that the measures protecting consumers in distance contracts have been adopted under the auspices of Article 114 TFEU, they take the form of a Directive. Article 288 TFEU explicitly states that Directives are binding upon the Member States it is addressed to with respect to the result it needs to achieve, but the form of transposition is left to the national legislator. From a harmonisation perspective, Member States are obliged to apply the same standards, so we cannot assess to what extent national legislatures actually support their enactment. Some inferences can however be made by looking at whether Member States have transposed the Directive correctly and in a timely manner. Each of these aspects are dealt with in the following factors where applicable.

b) Type of European instrument
As explained above, the instrument under analysis is a Directive. This acts to explain not only the differences between the ways in which Member States have chosen to transpose the Distance Selling Directive, but also the variation in the type of obligations that can arise out of it: while Member States are bound to transpose the Directive, if it aims at minimum harmonisation, they can choose to add additional requirements in their national laws. This discretion plays an equally important role in the discussion regarding minimum/maximum harmonisation and it is discussed in the next factor as well.

c) Nature of policy

As stated in Article 14 of the Distance Selling Directive, it is a minimum harmonisation instrument. As explored before, this entails that the Directive levels the playing field with respect to certain rights given to the consumer and obligations imposed on sellers, but it does allow Member States to adopt legislation ensuring a higher level of consumer protection.

d) Reference to self-regulation
No specific reference to self-regulation is made within the Articles under analysis.[110]

e) General clause
The Distance Selling Directive does not make use of a general clause.

f) Black list
No annexes which can be deemed to be black lists are attached to the Distance Selling Directive.

g) CJEU case law
The CJEU is the supreme interpreter of European law. In this position, its findings become integral part of the consumer *acquis* and by virtue of clarifying different European provisions may set a new standard for Member States to abide by. While of the cases affecting the Directives in this study, several have already been touched upon and others have been discussed at length, the need to take CJEU case law and turn it into a harmonisation factor stems from two reasons: firstly, *an outcome-oriented representation* of available case law per directive is necessary to determine whatever consumer contract law trends are set by the Court; and secondly, a statistical overview of these cases can contribute to a wider understanding of how Member States transposed the five directives.

When it comes to the Distance Selling Directive, a total of five cases have been brought to the Court under the Article 265 TFEU preliminary reference procedure.[111]

Table 13: CJEU Case Law (Distance Selling Directive)

Overview				Outcome
Year	**Case number and name**	**Court**	**Member State**	**Citation of operative part of the judgment**
2005	Case C-336/03 *easyCar (UK) Ltd v Office of Fair Trading*	High Court of Justice (England & Wales), Chancery	United Kingdom	Article 3(2) of Directive 97/7/EC of the European Parliament and of the Council of 20 May 1997 on the protection of consumers in respect of distance contracts is to be

110 Overall, the Distance Selling Directive does not make reference to self-regulation, with the exception of Article 11(4) that states: '4. Member States may provide for voluntary supervision by self-regulatory bodies of compliance with the provisions of this Directive and recourse to such bodies for the settlement of disputes to be added to the means which Member States must provided to ensure compliance with the provisions of this Directive'.

111 Micklitz & Kas 2014, p. 48.

		Division		interpreted as meaning that 'contracts for the provision of transport services' includes contracts for the provision of car hire services.
2008	C-205/07 *Lodewijk Gysbrechts, Santurel Inter BVBA*	*Hof van Beroep*	Belgium	Article 29 EC does not preclude national rules which prohibit a supplier, in cross-border distance selling, from requiring an advance or any payment from a consumer before expiry of the withdrawal period, but Article 29 EC does preclude a prohibition, under those rules, on requesting, before expiry of that period, the number of the consumer's payment card.
2009	Case C-489/07 *Pia Messner v Firma Stefan Krüger*	*Amtsgericht Lahr*	Germany	The provisions of the second sentence of Article 6(1) and Article 6(2) of Directive 97/7/EC of the European Parliament and of the Council of 20 May 1997 on the protection of consumers in respect of distance contracts must be interpreted as precluding a provision of national law which provides in general that, in the case of withdrawal by a consumer within the withdrawal period, a seller may claim compensation for the value of the use of the consumer goods acquired under a distance contract. However, those provisions do not prevent the consumer from being required to pay compensation for the use of the goods in the case where he has made use of those goods in a manner incompatible with the principles of civil law, such as those of good faith or unjust enrichment, on condition that the purpose of that directive and, in particular, the efficiency and effectiveness of the right of withdrawal are not adversely affected, this being a matter for the national court to determine.
2010	Case C- 511/08 *Handelsgesellschaft Heinrich Heine GmbH v Verbraucherzentrale Nordrhein-Westfalen eV*	*Bundes-gerichtshof*	Germany	Article 6(1), first subparagraph, second sentence, and Article 6(2) of Directive 97/7/EC of the European Parliament and of the Council of 20 May 1997 on the protection of consumers in respect of distance contracts must be interpreted as precluding national legislation which allows the supplier under a distance contract to charge the costs

				of delivering the goods to the consumer where the latter exercises his right of withdrawal.
2012	Case C-49/11 *Content Services Ltd v Bundesarbeitskammer*	*Oberlandesgericht Wien*	Austria	Article 5(1) of Directive 97/7/EC of the European Parliament and of the Council of 20 May 1997 on the protection of consumers in respect of distance contracts must be interpreted as meaning that a business practice consisting of making the information referred to in that provision accessible to the consumer only via a hyperlink on a website of the undertaking concerned does not meet the requirements of that provision, since that information is neither 'given' by that undertaking nor 'received' by the consumer, within the meaning of that provision, and a website such as that at issue in the main proceedings cannot be regarded as a 'durable medium' within the meaning of Article 5(1).

B. National level

a) National transposition technique

This factor stands to show how Member States have transposed the Distance Selling Directive in their national legislation. The transposition practices of each of the seven Member States considered in this book are analysed, and the content of national provisions are displayed in a comparative table. Furthermore, graphs are also used in order to offer a more visual understanding of the observations. Three different transposition techniques have been identified with respect to how the seven Member States in question have approached the Distance Selling Directive: four of them (Belgium, Ireland, Romania, UK) chose to transpose the Directive by means of a satellite law, two of them transposed it in their national civil codes (Germany, the Netherlands) and one integrated it into the national consumer code (France). Doing in-depth research in order to build on this factor has shown that various problems affecting harmonisation might arise in the implementation process, depending on the technique used by national legislators.

In terms of using a satellite law to transpose European legislation, the main benefit is that transposition will often be very targeted and the content of the rules remains closely related to the text of the Directive (with the exception of Belgium, Ireland, Romania and the UK usually adopt a copy-paste approach.

To the opposite, choosing to amend the civil code in order to accommodate new consumer rules makes sure that these rules are integrated into the general contractual regime. However, the transposition fragments the articles of the Directive to the extent that they need to be spread out into different sections of the civil code. What is more, sometimes already-existing civil code rules are used to justify the transposition of Directive rules. While in theory it sounds like a highly integrated system, in practice there is one underlying danger – the impossibility of tracing down the European nature of these rules, and their consequent interpretation through an exclusive national meaning.

Table 14: Initial national transposition techniques table (Distance Selling Directive)

Member State	Transposition technique
Belgium	Satellite law – Law of 14 July 1991
France	Consumer Code – Loi n° 2000-719 du 1er août 2000
Germany	Civil Code
Ireland	Satellite law – European Communities (Protection of Consumers in Respect of Contracts made by Means of Distance Communication) Regulations, 2001
Netherlands	Civil Code
Romania	Satellite law – Ordinance nr. 130 of 31 August 2000 on consumers' protection regarding the conclusion and performance of distance selling contracts
United Kingdom	Satellite law – Consumer Protection (Distance Selling) Regulations 2000

Figure 12: Initial national transposition techniques graph (Distance Selling Directive)

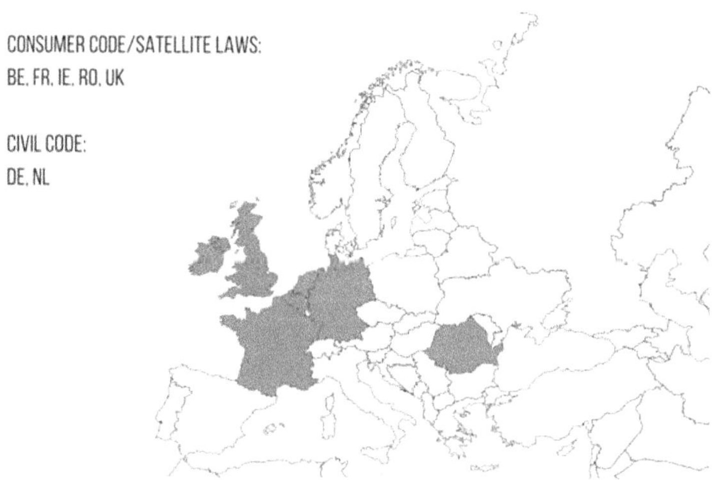

b) Reception of selected novel concepts

The most important concept that originated from the Distance Selling Directive and can also be reflected in the selected articles is the right of withdrawal. Regardless of its legal effects, the Directive did not call it 'termination', 'rescission' or 'cancellation'; it was simply a new concept. Not only was the right of withdrawal individualised as one of the tools consumers had to get out of a contract with a seller/supplier who is not in their physical proximity, but it is also given a very specific expiry date: the withdrawal right under the now-repealed Directive gives the consumer a total of at least seven working days to withdraw from the contract without any further conditions.

This factor strives to track down how Member States dealt with the introduction of concepts originating at European level. In the case of the Distance Selling Directive there is only one such concept that is analysed here: the right of withdrawal. A table of the official language versions of the Directive and the national transposition terminology is presented below:

Table 15: Transposition of novel concepts (Distance Selling Directive)

Member State	EU language version	National implementation
Belgium	*Droit de rétractation/ Herroepingsrecht*	*droit de renonciation/ verzakingsrecht*
France	*Droit de rétractation*	*Droit de rétractation*
Germany	*Widerrufsrecht*	*Widerrufsrecht*
Ireland	Right of withdrawal	Right of cancellation
Netherlands	*Herroepingsrecht*	*Recht de koop [...] te ontbinden*
Romania	*Dreptul de retractare*	*Dreptul de denuntare unilateralā a contractului*
United Kingdom	Right of withdrawal	Right to cancel

The right of withdrawal aims to support consumers in distance contracts by allowing them to get out of that contract without any reason whatsoever, and this context has been taken over by all seven Member States. With this in mind, the right of withdrawal still changes its nature when national law tries to embed it in an already existing framework, as opposed to working with the neologism offered by the official translation of the Directive in the respective language.

For example, Romanian law calls the right of withdrawal a right of unilateral termination (*drept de denuntare unilaterala*), which is a notion belonging to general civil law. To illustrate this statement, Article 1276 of the Romanian Civil Code can serve as an example. Article 1276(1) mentions that 'if the right to terminate the contract is given to one of the parties, this can only be exercised in so far as the performance of the contract has not yet begun'.[112] The general right of unilateral termination is thus very clearly described in the Civil Code. However, in contrast to this description, the withdrawal right, or as the Romanian version of the Directive calls it, *dreptul de retractare*, can be exercised by the consumer even after both parties have performed - the seller has delivered the good and the buyer has paid the price. Moreover, this right does not give rise to any possibility for the seller to negotiate whether to include it in the contract or not, given its mandatory nature. The result is the coexistence of two rights with the same name but with different characteristics, which can lead to confusion on two levels: (1) the confusion of courts as to the relation between the two rights (the special regime of consumer protection and the general regime of the Civil Code), and (2) the confusion of the consumer as to

112 Translation by author.

whether this is a pan-European right, or the protection it offers only covers contracts concluded with Romanian sellers.

d) Reception of selected open-ended norms

As described before, this factor will not reflect the Directive in its entirety, but only a selection of Articles, namely Articles 4, 6, 7 and 12. The content of each of these Articles has been checked for open-ended norms and the result is that two such concepts are used in Article 4: 'good time' and 'the principle of good faith in commercial transactions'. Both concepts are applied to the provision of prior information to a consumer. The first indicates the time frame in which information should be made available to the consumer prior to the conclusion of the contract. The second relates to how this information is communicated – a manner that is clear and comprehensible enough vis-à-vis the means of distance communication used. It is important to note that even though a brief reference is made to 'good time' in recital 13 of the Preamble,[113] the Directive contains no definitions or benchmarks for these concepts. In other words, while the European legislator recognised the need to create flexible standards in order to facilitate case-by-case application, the content of these concepts remains somewhat vague. An overview of how these norms have been transposed can be found below.

Table 16: Transposition of open-ended norms (Distance Selling Directive)

Member State	EU language version	National implementation
Belgium[114]	*temps utile/tijdig*	*temps utile/gelegener tijd*
	loyauté en matière de transactions commerciales/eerlijkheid bij commerciële transacties	-/-
France	*temps utile*	-
	loyauté en matière de transactions commerciales	-
Germany[115]	*rechtzeitig*	*rechtzeitig*
	der Lauterkeit bei Handelsgeschäften	-
Ireland	good time	good time
	good faith in commercial transactions	good faith in commercial transactions
Netherlands	*tijdig*	*tijdig*
	eerlijkheid bij commerciële transacties	-
Romania	*timp util*	*timp util*
	buna credinţă în materie de tranzacţii comerciale	*bună practică comercială in tranzacţii*

113 Recital 13 of the Preamble states: '(13) Whereas information disseminated by certain electronic technologies is often ephemeral in nature insofar as it is not received on a permanent medium; whereas the consumer must therefore receive written notice in good time of the information necessary for proper performance of the contract [...]'.

114 Article 83 ter, Law of 14 July 1991.

115 Article 246, § 1, *Einführungsgesetz zum Bürgerlichen Gesetzbuch.*

United Kingdom	good time	good time
	good faith in commercial transactions	good faith in commercial transactions

e) Timely transposition

According to Article 10, the transposition deadline was 4 June 2000.

Table 17: Overview of transposition deadline (Distance Selling Directive)

Member State	**National legislation**	**Implementation date**	**Timely transposition**
Belgium	Articles 76-83 of the Act of 14 July 1991 on trade practices and consumer information and protection	1 October 1999	Yes
France	Article L. 121-16 *et seqq*. Consumer Code	25 August 2001	No
Germany	Distance Selling Act	30 June 2000	No
Ireland	European Communities (Protection of Consumer in respect of Contracts made by means of Distance Communication) Regulations, 2001	15 May 2001	No
Netherlands	Law of 21 December 2000 to the adaptation of Book 7 of the Civil Code to Directive number 97/7/EC of the European Parliament and the Council of Europe of 20 May 1997 regarding the protection of consumers by distance selling	4 June 2000	Yes
Romania	Government Ordinance no. 130/2000 on consumers' protection regarding the conclusion and performance of distance selling contracts	2 October 2000	Yes
United Kingdom	Consumer Protection (Distance Selling) Regulations 2000 SI 2000/2334	31 October 2000	No

f) Infringement procedures

The infringement procedure factor is aimed at showing whether there has been any legal action taken by the Commission against Member States for transposition not in conformity with the Directive, or transposition that does not allow for the correct application of the Directive.[116] In the case of the Distance Selling Directive, there had only been one infringement procedure brought by the Commission against Spain; however this falls outside the scope of the selected jurisdictions.[117]

116 Article 258 TFEU.

117 Case C-414/01, *Commission of the European Communities v Kingdom of Spain* [2002] ECR I-11121.

Table 18: Infringement Procedures (Distance Selling Directive)

Date of judgment	Case number and name	Member State	Proceedings	Ruling
28 November 2002	Case C-414/01 *Commission of the European Communities v Kingdom of Spain*	Spain	Failure by a Member State to fulfil its obligations	The Kingdom of Spain has failed to fulfil its obligations under Article 15(1) of that directive.

g) Reference to European law in end legislation

If Member States incur severe delays in implementing European directives, or they do so in a faulty manner, the Member States in question might face a problem of resistance to harmonisation.

Table 19: Overview of reference to European law (Distance Selling Directive)

Member State	National legislation	Reference to European law	Database
Belgium	Act of 14 July 1991 on trade practices and consumer information and protection	No	Ejustice
France	Consumer Code	No	Legifrance
Germany	Civil Code	Yes	Juris
Ireland	European Communities (Protection of Consumer in respect of Contracts made by means of Distance Communication) Regulations, 2001	Yes	Irish Statute Book (Office of the Attorney General)
Netherlands	Civil Code	No	Overheid
Romania	Government Ordinance no. 130/2000 on consumers' protection regarding the conclusion and performance of distance selling contracts	No	Lege 5
United Kingdom	Consumer Protection (Distance Selling) Regulations 2000	Yes	The National Archives

3.4. *Consumer Sales Directive*

In what follows, legislative convergence in the specific area of contractual conformity is analysed from the perspective of the Consumer Sales Directive. In order to best apply the Convergence Index factors, it is important to remember the provisions that have been taken into account so far:

- Article 2 (conformity with the contract);
- Article 3 (rights of the consumer);

- Article 5 (time limits);
- Article 6 (guarantees).

A. European level

a) Law v policy
Introduced in the light of Article 114 TFEU, the Consumer Sales Directive translates into a body of rules that have become integral part of the consumer *acquis*, which is hard law - the set of norms that all Member States need to accommodate.

b) Type of European instrument
The rules on conformity with consumer contracts have been incorporated in a Directive.

c) Nature of policy
Like the majority of the Directives in this book (four out of five), the Consumer Sales Directive applies a minimum harmonisation standard. This policy choice is laid out in Article 8 of the Directive.

d) Reference to self-regulation
No specific reference to self-regulation is made within the Articles under analysis.[118]

e) General clause
The Consumer Sales Directive does not make use of an open clause.

f) Black list
The Consumer Sales Directive does not contain a black list.

g) CJEU case law
The general characteristics of this factor were described in the previous Section.[119] A total of four cases have been brought to the Court under the Article 265 TFEU preliminary reference procedure, with four resulting judgments.[120] This is the lowest number of preliminary references based on a directive out of the five directives this study focuses on.

Table 20: CJEU Case Law (Consumer Sales Directive)

Overview				Outcome
Year	**Case number and name**	**Court**	**Member State**	**Citation of operative part of the judgment**
2008	Case 404/06 *Quelle AG v Bundesverbandder*	*Bundes-gerichtshof*	Germany	Article 3 of Directive 1999/44/EC of the European Parliament and of the Council of 25 May 1999 on certain

118 Even beyond the selected articles, the Consumer Sales Directive does not make any reference to self-regulation.
119 See Chapter 3, Section 2, p. 173.
120 Micklitz & Kas 2014, p. 58.

	Verbraucherzentralen und Verbraucherverbände			aspects of the sale of consumer goods and associated guarantees is to be interpreted as precluding national legislation under which a seller who has sold consumer goods which are not in conformity may require the consumer to pay compensation for the use of those defective goods until their replacement with new goods.
2011	Joined cases C-65/09 and C-87/09 *Gebr. Weber GmbH v Jürgen Wittmer and Ingrid Putz v Medianess Electronics GmbH*	*Bundes-gerichtshof and Amtsgericht Schorndorf*	Germany	1. Article 3(2) and (3) of Directive 1999/44/EC of the European Parliament and of the Council of 25 May 1999 on certain aspects of the sale of consumer goods and associated guarantees must be interpreted as meaning that, where consumer goods not in conformity with the contract which were installed in good faith by the consumer in a manner consistent with their nature and purpose, before the defect became apparent, are restored to conformity by way of replacement, the seller is obliged either to remove the goods from where they were installed and to install the replacement goods there or else to bear the cost of that removal and installation of the replacement goods. That obligation on the seller exists regardless of whether he was obliged under the contract of sale to install the consumer goods originally purchased. 2. Article 3(3) of Directive 1999/44 must be interpreted as precluding national legislation from granting the seller the right to refuse to replace goods not in conformity, as the only remedy possible, on the ground that, because of the obligation to remove the goods from where they were installed and to install the replacement goods there, replacement imposes costs on him which are disproportionate with regard to the value that the goods would have if there were no lack of conformity and the significance of the lack of conformity. That provision does not, however, preclude the consumer's right to reimbursement of the cost of

				removing the defective goods and of installing the replacement goods from being limited, in such a case, to the payment by the seller of a proportionate amount.
2013	Case C-32/12 *Soledad Duarte Hueros v Autociba SA and Automóviles Citroën España SA*	*Juzgado de Primera Instancia nº 2 de Badajoz*	Spain	Directive 1999/44/EC of the European Parliament and of the Council of 25 May 1999 on certain aspects of the sale of consumer goods and associated guarantees must be interpreted as precluding legislation of a Member State, such as that at issue in the main proceedings, which does not allow the national court hearing the dispute to grant of its own motion an appropriate reduction in the price of goods which are the subject of a contract of sale in the case where a consumer who is entitled to such a reduction brings proceedings which are limited to seeking only rescission of that contract and such rescission cannot be granted because the lack of conformity in those goods is minor, even though that consumer is not entitled to refine his initial application or to bring a fresh action to that end.
2015	Case C-497/13 *Froukje Faber v Autobedrijf Hazet Ochten BV*	*Gerechtshof Arnhem-Leeuwarden*	Nether-lands	Directive 1999/44/EC must be interpreted as meaning that a national court before which an action relating to a contract which may be covered by that directive has been brought, is required to determine whether the purchaser may be classified as a consumer within the meaning of that directive, even if the purchaser has not relied on that status, as soon as that court has at its disposal the matters of law and of fact that are necessary for that purpose or may have them at its disposal simply by making a request for clarification. Article 5(3) of Directive 1999/44 must be interpreted as meaning that it must be regarded as a provision of equal standing to a national rule which ranks, within the domestic legal system, as a rule of public policy and that the national court must of its own motion apply any provision which transposes it into domestic law. Article 5(2) of Directive 1999/44

				must be interpreted as not precluding a national rule which provides that the consumer, in order to benefit from the rights which he derives from that directive, must inform the seller of the lack of conformity in good time, provided that that consumer has a period of not less than two months from the date on which he detected that lack of conformity to give that notification, that the notification to be given relates only to the existence of that lack of conformity and that it is not subject to rules of evidence which would make it impossible or excessively difficult for the consumer to exercise his rights. Article 5(3) of Directive 1999/44 must be interpreted as meaning that the rule that the lack of conformity is presumed to have existed at the time of delivery of the goods: - applies if the consumer furnishes evidence that the goods sold are not in conformity with the contract and that the lack of conformity in question became apparent, that is to say, became physically apparent, within six months of delivery of the goods. The consumer is not required to prove the cause of that lack of conformity or to establish that its origin is attributable to the seller; - may be discounted only if the seller proves to the requisite legal standard that the cause or origin of that lack of conformity lies in circumstances which arose after the delivery of the goods.

Looking at directives in terms of the latest interpretative case law or in terms of the quality of Court rationale independently may prove useful to understand harmonisation, but these views are definitely short of displaying the bigger picture. With the help of tables like the one above, made available for all directives deemed by this book to have contract law implications, the discussion on the harmonisation of consumer sales law is given a new dimension.

B. National level

a) National transposition technique

As far as the Consumer Sales Directive is concerned, three Member States have adopted transposing rules that have become part of the Civil Code (Belgium, Germany, Netherlands), one Member State has modified its Consumer Code to accommodate the Directive (France), and the remaining three have transposed the Directive through satellite legislation (Ireland, Romania, United Kingdom). It must be underlined that in terms of the areas covered by the Directive, contractual conformity was known to Member States in one form or another even before the adoption of the Directive in 1999.[121] Most Member States thus applied their default contractual regime together with the sales law regime to create a level of protection that was equally shared by consumers and businesses. For instance, Article L. 211-13 *Code de la Consommation* mentions that the special provisions of this Code do not deprive the consumer of the possibility to make use of his rights under Articles 1641-1649 *Code Civil*.[122] In this circumstance, the choice of transposition may be an indication of how unified Member States aimed for their national legislation to be in respect of the possibility that multiple regimes would be applicable.

To take yet another example, it can been seen when consulting the detailed transposition of the Consumer Sales Directive in Germany that available remedies are immediately linked back to the general regime of the BGB. However, Germany happens to be the only Member State under observation that is currently offering the same level of protection to both consumers and businesses. Still, there are issues with claiming that if the Directive is transposed in a codified version of private law then the regime applicable to the protection it conveys is more uniform.

A clear illustration of this issue is the case of the United Kingdom. To accommodate the Directive, the United Kingdom has passed Regulations amending several pivotal Acts, amongst which the Sale of Goods Act 1979 (SoGA 1979). Far from being a Civil Code, SoGA 1979 represents the default regime applicable to sales, and as of the transposition process it also contains express rules for consumers. Below, a table with the overview of transposition techniques, as well as a graph displaying these choices more visually can be found.

Table 21: Initial national transposition techniques table (Consumer Sales Directive)

Member State	**Transposition technique**
Belgium	Civil Code[123]
France	Consumer Code[124]

121 Schulte-Nölke *et al.* 2008, p. 652.

122 Article L. 211-13 *Code de la Consommation: 'Les dispositions de la présente section ne privent pas l'acheteur du droit d'exercer l'action résultant des vices rédhibitoires telle qu'elle résulte des articles 1641 à 1649 du code civil ou toute autre action de nature contractuelle ou extracontractuelle qui lui est reconnue par la loi'.*

123 Articles 1649bis-1649octies Belgian Civil Code.

124 Ordinance no 2005-136 from 17 February 2005.

Germany	Civil Code[125]
Ireland	Satellite law - Consumer Sales Regulations 2003
Netherlands	Civil Code[126]
Romania	Satellite law - Law no. 449 from 2003 regarding the sale of products and associated guarantees
United Kingdom	Satellite law - Sale and Supply of Goods to Consumers Regulations 2002 (SI 2002/3045) modifying the Sale of Goods Act 1979, Supply of Goods and Services Act 1982, Supply of Goods (Implied Terms) Act 1973, Unfair Contract Terms Act 1977

Figure 13: Initial national transposition techniques graph (Consumer Sales Directive)

c) Reception of selected novel concepts

Four different open-ended norms can be identified in the selected articles: reasonableness (e.g. reasonable expectations, awareness, etc.), appropriateness (in terms of the price reduction), disproportion (when determining the availability of a first tier remedy) and minority of defects (barring termination claims). The only open-ended norm that was defined in the Directive is the eventual disproportionate character of a remedy. Unlike the Unfair Contract Terms Directive, where good faith played a particularly important role because of its inclusion in the general clause, open-ended concepts in consumer sales seem to serve a different purpose. Overall, it could be argued that on the basis of how many times the aforementioned concepts are featured in the text (a total of eight times altogether), their main purpose is to fill any potential gaps in the interpretation of the detailed provisions. For example, it is very difficult, if not impossible, to map how a lack of conformity can affect the price of an object for the purposes of price reduction; it is thus more convenient to refer to price reduction as having to be 'appropriate'. As with any

125 § 433ff BGB.
126 Article 7:17 ff BW.

open-ended concept, it is indeed possible, at least in theory, for the application of the rules to be hindered by their divergent interpretation. However, it can be equally argued that should there be no such leeway, then law would be too rigid to deal with individual cases and particular facts.

In the case of the Consumer Sales Directive, there are several concepts that stood out in terms of their novelty: the notion of conformity, the two-tier remedy hierarchy and commercial guarantees (which although not specifically named 'commercial' are distinct from the so-called 'legal' guarantees, namely the mandatory legal effects of the lack of conformity).

Looking at the selected articles, three main concepts that characterise the Consumer Sales Directive can be derived: the notion of conformity with the contract, the hierarchy of remedies and the commercial guarantee. Although not always as compact as the withdrawal right that has been explored under distance selling, the three concepts are fundamental for the Directive because they reflect a set of rules that is inherently European.

Firstly, as far as conformity is concerned, Member States might have had legislation dealing with hidden and apparent defects,[127] or with the separate components of the conformity criterion (such as sale by description, etc.).[128] However, the introduction of an overarching notion of conformity can arguably be considered a novel concept. Even though the Directive provides no definition of conformity, a closer look at Article 2 demonstrates that this concept rests on four pillars: compliance with description and sample; specific fitness for purpose; general fitness for purpose; and general quality and performance features, either according to other goods of the same type or according to reasonable consumer expectations.

Secondly, dealing with the hierarchy of remedies, or as the heading of Article 3 mentions, 'Rights of the consumer', similar arguments are applicable. Remedies for general contract law (or even specific consumer remedies) have been present in national legislation even before the Consumer Sales Directive, whether directly stemming from national codes, or brought about by legislative reforms inspired by international commercial rules such as those of the CISG.[129] Nevertheless, the main reason why this hierarchy deserves to be labelled as novel is because of the fact that it provides for mandatory rules following a very specific remedy roadmap: if goods are not in conformity with the contract, consumers have a right to primarily be granted repair or replacement as a first tier remedy, as long as it is not impossible or disproportionate for the seller and it does not cause significant inconvenience to the consumer; the second tier remedies following from these exceptional circumstances are termination or price reduction.

Thirdly, the Consumer Sales Directive works with two types of guarantees: legal and commercial guarantees – Article 6 discusses the latter type.

127 For example § 433ff BGB; Article 1641ff French Civil Code.

128 Sections 12-15 Sale of Goods Act 1979; see also DCFR Commentary on Article IV.A.-2:302, p. 1311.

129 CISG Article 35.

Furthermore, two main arguments come to mind regarding the harmonisation importance of novel concepts in the Consumer Sales Directive: the fact that they reflect rules of a specific European nature, and that contractual conformity entails a very high degree of detail. Taken together, these arguments pinpoint at the vulnerabilities of choosing to transpose new, specific concepts via a directive.

The Directive was designed to level the playing field in terms of when a consumer would be entitled to protection from lack of contractual conformity and what that protection would entail. Multiple issues arose out of the transposition of this protection, and the most specific ones are visible in the table below. For instance, German law did not recreate the notion of conformity, but rather emphasised a rule according to which the object of the contract must be free from legal and physical defects (§ 434 BGB). Once again, by taking European concepts and integrating them into and existing legal framework, it can be stated that not only is the European nature of these rules lost, but it can also lead to application problems. If German law is to be applied in a way that does not infringe the Directive, it must be considered in the light of the rules therein; however, this is only the case in consumer contracts, and a different interpretation of the same rules may be allowed for B2B transactions.

Table 22: Transposition of novel concepts (Consumer Sales Directive)

Member State	Novel concept	EU language version	National implementation
			Form
Belgium[130]	conformity	*conformité/ overeenstemming*	*chose conforme au contrat/ overeenstemming*
	hierarchy	1st tier: *réparation ou remplacement/herstelling of vervanging* 2nd tier: *réduction adéquate du prix ou à la résolution/de prijs op passende wijze wordt verminderd of dat de koopovereenkomst [...] wordt ontbonden*	1st tier: *la réparation du bien ou son remplacement* 2nd tier: *réduction adéquate du prix ou la résolution du contrat/een passende prijsvermindering of de ontbinding van de koopovereenkomst te eisen*
	commercial guarantees	*garanties/garanties*	*garantie/garantie*
France[131]	conformity	*conformité*	*conformité*
	hierarchy	1st tier: *réparation ou remplacement* 2nd tier: *réduction adéquate du prix ou à la résolution*	1st tier: *choisir entre réparation et remplacement* 2nd tier: *rendre le bien et se faire restituer le prix ou garder le bien et se faire rendre une partie du prix*
	commercial guarantees	*garanties*	*garantie commerciale*

130 Articles 1649terties, 1649quinquies and 1649septies Belgian Civil Code.

131 Articles L. 211-4, L. 211-9,10 and L. 211-15 *Code de la Consommation.*

Germany [132]	conformity	*Vertragsmäßigkeit*	*Sache frei von Sach- und Rechtsmängeln*
	hierarchy	1st tier: *Nachbesserung oder Ersatzlieferung* 2nd tier: *angemessene Minderung des Kaufpreises oder auf Vertragsauflösung*	*1. Nacherfüllung verlangen* *2. dem Vertrag zurücktreten oder den Kaufpreis mindern* *3. Schadensersatz*
	commercial guarantees	*Garantien*	*Garantien*
Ireland[133]	conformity	conformity	conformity
	hierarchy	1st tier: repair or replacement 2nd tier: appropriate reduction made in the price or the contract rescinded	1st tier: repair or replacement 2nd tier: appropriate reduction made in the price or the contract rescinded
	commercial guarantees	guarantees	guarantees
Nether-lands[134]	conformity	overeenstemming	*aan de overeenkomst beantwoorden*
	hierarchy	1st tier: *herstelling of vervanging* 2nd tier: *de prijs op passende wijze wordt verminderd of dat de koopovereenkomst [...] wordt ontbonden*	1st tier: *herstel of vervanging van de afgeleverde zaak* 2nd tier: *de overeenkomst te ontbinden of de prijs te verminderen in evenredigheid met de mate van afwijking*
	commercial guarantees	*garanties*	*garantie*
Romania [135]	conformity	conformitate	conformitate
	hierarchy	1st tier: *reparare sau înlocuire* 2nd tier: *reducere de preţ corespunzătoare sau rezoluţiunea contractului*	1st tier: *reparare sau inlocuire* 2nd tier: *reducerea corespunzatoare a pretului ori de rezolutiunea contractului*
	Commercial guarantees	*garanţii*	*garanţii*

132 §§ 323, 326, 433, 437 and 443 BGB.

133 Regulations 5, 7 and 9, European Communities (Certain Aspects of the Sale of Consumer Goods and Associated Guarantees) Regulations 2003.

134 Articles 7:17(1), 7:21 and 7:22 BW.

135 Articles 5, 10 and 19, Law no. 449/2003.

United Kingdom[136]	conformity	conformity	conformity
	hierarchy	1st tier: repair or replacement 2nd tier: appropriate reduction made in the price or the contract rescinded	1st tier: repair or replacement 2nd tier: appropriate reduction made in the price or the contract rescinded
	commercial guarantees	guarantees	consumer guarantees

d) Reception of selected open-ended norms

One particularity of the Consumer Sales Directive is the fact that it does not operate with a general clause, and thus open-ended norms are not one of its fundamental characteristics. This being said, the Directive still employs a generous amount of blanket clauses. The ones this Section focuses on are reasonableness (e.g. reasonable expectations, awareness, etc.), appropriateness (in terms of the price reduction), disproportion (when determining the availability of a first tier remedy) and minority of defects (barring termination claims).

There are two aspects that are of interest at this point. Firstly, that keeping an open-ended norm in the same form as the Directive provides may underline once again the European nature of a rule. For instance, the disproportionality of a remedy forms an integral part of the remedy test that may take the consumer into either the direction of repair and replacement or in that of price reduction and termination. Secondly, as it can be consulted in the table below, some Member States such as Germany chose not to rely on the same wording as the Directive in order to suggest more precise standards of calculating for instance an appropriate price reduction. In this case the use of minimum harmonisation once again brings about the conclusion that the various transposition options may lead to divergent consumer results.

Table 23: Transposition of open-ended norms (Consumer Sales Directive)

Member State	Open-ended concept	EU language version	National implementation
Belgium[137]	reasonableness	*raisonnable*	*raisonnable*
	appropriateness	*adéquate*	*adéquate*
	disproportion	*disproportionné*	*disproportionné*
	minor lack of conformity	*le défaut de conformité est mineur*	*le défaut de conformité est mineur*

136 Regulation 15, Sale and Supply of Goods to Consumers Regulations 2002, Section 48B and F SoGA 1979.

137 Article 1649quinquies Belgian Code Civil.

France[138]	reasonableness	*raisonnable*	-
	appropriateness	*adéquate*	-
	disproportion	*disproportionné*	*disproportionné*
	minor lack of conformity	*le défaut de conformité est mineur*	*le défaut de conformité est mineur*
Germany[139]	reasonableness	*angemessen*	-
	appropriateness	*Angemessen/ vernünftigerweise*	*Bei der Minderung ist der Kaufpreis in dem Verhältnis herabzusetzen, in welchem zur Zeit des Vertragsschlusses der Wert der Sache in mangelfreiem Zustand zu dem wirklichen Wert gestanden haben würde.*
	disproportion	*unverhältnismäßig*	*unverhältnismäßigen*
	minority of defects	*geringfügigen Vertragswidrigkeit*	*Unerhebliches Pflichtverletzung*
Ireland[140]	reasonableness	reasonableness	reasonable
	appropriateness	appropriateness	appropriate
	disproportion	disproportion	disproportionate
	minor lack of conformity	minor lack of conformity	minor lack of conformity
Nether-lands[141]	reasonableness	*redelijke*	*redelijkerwijs*
	appropriateness	*passende*	*in evenredigheid met de mate van afwijking*
	disproportion	*buiten verhouding*	*niet gevergd kan worden*
	minor lack of conformity	*gering gebrek aan overeenstemming*	*geringe afwijking*
Romania[142]	reasonableness	*rezonabil*	*rezonabil*
	appropriateness	*corespunzător*	*corespunzător*
	disproportion	*disproporţionat*	*disproporţionat*
	minor lack of conformity	neconformitate minoră	*lipsă minoră a conformităţii*
United Kingdom[143]	reasonableness	reasonableness	reasonable
	appropriateness	appropriateness	appropriate
	disproportion	disproportion	disproportionate
	minor lack of conformity	minority of defects	-

138 Article L. 211-10 *Code de la Consommation*.

139 §§ 441(3), 439 and 323(5) BGB.

140 Regulation 7, European Communities (Certain Aspects of the Sale of Consumer Goods and Associated Guarantees) Regulations 2003.

141 Articles 7:21 and 7:22 BW.

142 Articles 5-7; 10-14, Law no. 449/2003.

143 Sections 14, 15 and 48B SoGA 1979.

e) Timely transposition

According to Article 10, the transposition deadline was 1 January 2002.

Table 24: Overview of transposition deadline (Consumer Sales Directive)

Member State	National legislation	Implementation date	Timely transposition
Belgium	Act of 1 September 2004 on the protection of consumers in respect of the sale of consumer goods	1 February 2005	No
France	Articles L. 211-1 et seq. C. Cons	17 February 2005	No
Germany	CC Articles 13, 14, 275, 323, 326, 346-354, 433-480, 651	1 January 2002	Yes
Ireland	European Communities (Certain Aspects of the Sale of Consumer Goods and Associated Guarantees) Regulations, 2003	22 January 2003	No
Netherlands	Civil Code	1 May 2003	No
Romania	Law no. 449/2003 regarding the sale of products and associated guarantees	1 January 2007	Yes
United Kingdom	Sale and Supply of Goods to Consumers Regulations 2002 (SI 2002/3045), amending Sale of Goods Act 1979, Supply of Goods and Services Act 1982 and Supply of Goods (Implied Terms) Act 1973; Unfair Contract Terms Act 1977	31 March 2003	No

f) Infringement procedures

Out of the Member States included in this analysis, Belgium and France have been brought before the Court of Justice by the Commission back in 2004 for its failure to fulfil its implementing obligations within the time prescribed by the Directive.[144]

Table 25: Infringement Procedures (Consumer Sales Directive)

Date of judgment	Case number and name	Member state	Proceedings	Ruling
19 February 2004	Case C-414/01 *Commission of the European Communities v the Kingdom of Belgium*	Belgium	Failure by a Member State to fulfil its obligations	The Kingdom of Belgium has failed to fulfil its obligations under that directive.

144 Case C-312/03, *Commission of the European Communities v Kingdom of Belgium*, ECLI:EU:C:2004:116; Case C-311/03, *Commission of the European Communities v France*, ECLI:EU:C:2004:405. Luxembourg was also brought by the Commission before the Court for non-implementation, see Case C-310/03, *Commission of the European Communities v Grand Duchy of Luxemburg*, ECLI:EU:C:2004:115.

1 July 2004	Case C-311/03 *Commission of the European Communities v France*	France	Failure of a Member State to fulfil obligations	France has failed to fulfil its obligations under that directive.

g) Reference to European law in end legislation

Table 26: Overview of reference to European law (Consumer Sales Directive)

Member state	National legislation	Reference to European law	Database
Belgium	Civil Code	No	Ejustice
France	Articles L. 211-1 *et seq*. Consumer Code	No	Legifrance
Germany	Civil Code	Yes	Juris
Ireland	European Communities (Certain Aspects of the Sale of Consumer Goods and Associated Guarantees) Regulations, 2003	Yes	Irish Statute Book (Office of the Attorney General)
Netherlands	Civil Code	No	Overheid
Romania	Law no. 449/2003 regarding the sale of products and associated guarantees	No	Lege 5
United Kingdom	Sale and Supply of Goods to Consumers Regulations 2002 (SI 2002/3045), amending Sale of Goods Act 1979, Supply of Goods and Services Act 1982 and Supply of Goods (Implied Terms) Act 1973; Unfair Contract Terms Act 1977	No	The National Archives

3.5. *Unfair Commercial Practices Directive*

The European and national factors are now applied to the same provisions analysed in the previous chapter:

- Articles 5-9 (the general prohibition of unfair commercial practices and its division in misleading and aggressive practices);
- Article 10 (voluntary harmonisation and codes of conduct);
- Article 11 (the enforcement of claims based on unfair commercial practices).

A. European level

a) Law v policy

The Unfair Commercial Practices Directive was adopted in the light of Article 114 TFEU, meaning that it leads to the creation of hard law that all Member States must follow.

b) Type of European instrument
As explained previously, harmonisation through directives leads to differences in transposition.

c) Nature of policy
The Unfair Commercial Practices Directive is the only Directive in this analysis that uses a maximum harmonisation standard. This is indirectly laid down in Article 3(5) of the Directive. Although this Directive is considered a landmark change in consumer protection policy, given that it strives to achieve a uniform standard rather than promote minimum harmonisation, there are still underlying issues. In spite of the Directive being advertised as a maximum harmonisation instrument,[145] not all its provisions operate to that effect.

d) Reference to self-regulation
The Unfair Commercial Practices Directive is the only instrument in this study that explicitly mentions codes of conduct. According to Article 10, no provision in the Directive impedes Member States in promoting codes of conduct in their national legislation.

The main reason why codes of conduct are important for convergence is because regardless of what legislative policy might be set by the European legislator or by Member States, the private sector may always take measures to standardise business practices. A brief example of this would be the Voluntary Code of Conduct on Pre-Contractual Information for Home Loans[146] (in the field of financial services), which was drafted by the European Associations of Consumers together with the European Credit Sector Associations. Adding specific codes-of-conduct provisions in national legislation has two major effects: first, it shows the voluntary nature of the harmonisation process (not through the content of the rules, but by the very adoption of the regulatory approach), and second, it strenghtens the value of mandatory harmonisation (by setting up registration schemes for codes of conduct, for instance, Member States can ensure the compatibility of these codes with European law).[147]

e) General clause
Article 5 is deemed to be the general clause of the Unfair Commercial Practices Directive.

145 Micklitz 2013, p. 39; see also Marco Loos, 'Full Harmonisation as a Regulatory Concept and its Consequences for the National Legal Orders: The Example of the Consumer Rights Directive', Centre for the Study of European Contract Law Working Paper Series No. 2010/03.

146 'European Agreement on a Voluntary Code of Conduct on Pre-Contractual Information for Home Loans', available at: <http://ec.europa.eu/internal_market/finservices-retail/-docs/home-loans/agreement_en.pdf>, last accessed on 27 Julu 2016.

147 Pavillon 2012.

f) Black list
The Unfair Commercial Practices Directive does indeed include an annex that has the role of a black list.

g) CJEU case law
According to the Curia database, a total of 19 cases have discussed the provisions of the Unfair Commercial Practices Directive. An overview of these cases is presented in what follows.

Table 27: CJEU Case Law (Unfair Commercial Practices Directive)

Overview				Outcome
Year	**Case number and name**	**Court**	**Member State**	**Citation of operative part of the judgment**
2009	Joined cases C-261/07 and C-299/07 *VTB-VAB NV v Total Belgium NV* and *Galatea BVBA v Sanoma Magazines Belgium NV*	*Rechtbank van Koophandel Antwerpen*	Belgium	Directive 2005/29/EC of the European Parliament and of the Council of 11 May 2005 concerning unfair business-to-consumer commercial practices in the internal market and amending Council Directive 84/450/EEC, Directives 97/7/EC, 98/27/EC and 2002/65/EC of the European Parliament and of the Council and Regulation (EC) No 2006/2004 of the European Parliament and of the Council ('Unfair Commercial Practices Directive') must be interpreted as precluding national legislation, such as that at issue in the disputes in the main proceedings, which, with certain exceptions, and without taking account of the specific circumstances, imposes a general prohibition of combined offers made by a vendor to a consumer.
2010	Case C-304/08 *Zentrale zur Bekämpfung unlauteren Wettbewerbs eV v Plus Warenhandelsgesellscaft mbH*	*Bundes-gerichtshof*	Germany	Directive 2005/29/EC of the European Parliament and of the Council of 11 May 2005 concerning unfair business-to-consumer commercial practices in the internal market and amending Council Directive 84/450/EEC, Directives 97/7/EC, 98/27/EC and 2002/65/EC of the European Parliament and of the Council and Regulation (EC) No 2006/2004 of the European Parliament and of the Council ('Unfair Commercial Practices Directive') must be interpreted as precluding national legislation, such as that at issue in the main proceedings, which

				provides for a prohibition in principle, without taking account of the specific circumstances of individual cases, of commercial practices under which the participation of consumers in a prize competition or lottery is made conditional on the purchase of goods or the use of services.
	Case C-540/08 *Mediaprint Zeitungs-und Zeitschriftenverslag GmbH & Co. KG v 'Österreich' – Zeitungsverslag GmbH*	*Oberster Gerichtshof*	Austria	1. Directive 2005/29/EC of the European Parliament and of the Council of 11 May 2005 concerning unfair business-to-consumer commercial practices in the internal market and amending Council Directive 84/450/EEC, Directives 97/7/EC, 98/27/EC and 2002/65/EC of the European Parliament and of the Council and Regulation (EC) No 2006/2004 of the European Parliament and of the Council ('the Unfair Commercial Practices Directive') must be interpreted as precluding a national provision, such as that at issue in the main proceedings, which lays down a general prohibition on sales with bonuses and is not only designed to protect consumers but also pursues other objectives; 2. The possibility of participating in a prize competition, linked to the purchase of a newspaper, does not constitute an unfair commercial practice within the meaning of Article 5(2) of Directive 2005/29, simply on the ground that, for at least some of the consumers concerned, that possibility of participating in a competition represents the factor which determines them to buy that newspaper.
2011	Case C-122/10 – *Konsumentombuds mannen v Ving Sverige AB*	*Mark-naomstolen* (Market Court)	Sweden	1. The words 'thereby enables the consumer to make a purchase' in Article 2(i) of Directive 2005/29/EC must be interpreted as meaning that an invitation to purchase exists as soon as the information on the product advertised and its price is sufficient for the consumer to be able to make a transactional decision, without it being necessary for the commercial communication also to offer an actual opportunity to

				purchase the product or for it to appear in proximity to and at the same time as such an opportunity. 2. Article 2(i) of Directive 2005/29 must be interpreted as meaning that the requirement relating to the indication of the price of the product may be met if the commercial communication contains an entry-level price, that is to say the lowest price for which the advertised product or category of products can be bought, while the advertised product or category of products are available in other versions or with other content at prices which are not indicated. It is for the national court to ascertain, on the basis of the nature and characteristics of the product and the commercial medium of communication used, whether the reference to an entry-level price enables the consumer to take a transactional decision. 3. Article 2(i) of Directive 2005/29 must be interpreted as meaning that a verbal or visual reference to the product makes it possible to meet the requirement relating to the indication of the product's characteristics, and that includes a situation where such a verbal or visual reference is used to designate a product which is offered in many versions. It is for the national court to ascertain, on a case-by-case basis, taking into account the nature and characteristics of the product and the medium of communication used, whether the consumer has sufficient information to identify and distinguish the product for the purpose of taking a transactional decision. 4. Article 7(4)(a) of Directive 2005/29 must be interpreted as meaning that it may be sufficient for only certain of a product's main characteristics to be given and for the trader to refer in addition to its website, on the condition that on that site there is essential information on the product's main characteristics, price and other terms in accordance with the requirements in Article 7 of that directive. It is for the national court

				to assess, on a case-by-case basis, taking into consideration the context of the invitation to purchase, the medium of communication used and the nature and characteristics of the product, whether a reference only to certain main characteristics of the product enables the consumer to take an informed transactional decision. 5. Article 7(4)(c) of Directive 2005/29 must be interpreted as meaning that a reference only to an entry-level price in an invitation to purchase cannot be regarded, in itself, as constituting a misleading omission. It is for the national court to ascertain whether a reference to an entry-level price is sufficient for the requirements concerning the reference to a price, such as those set out in that provision, to be considered to be met. That court will have to ascertain, inter alia, whether the omission of the detailed rules for calculating the final price prevents the consumer from taking an informed transactional decision and, consequently, leads him to take a transactional decision which he would not otherwise have taken. It is also for the national court to take into consideration the limitations forming an integral part of the medium of communication used; the nature and the characteristics of the product and the other measures that the trader has actually taken to make the information available to consumers.
	Case C-288/10 *Wamo BVBA v JBC NV and Modemakers Fashion NV*	*Rechtbank van koophandel te Dendermonde*	Belgium	Directive 2005/29/EC of the European Parliament and of the Council of 11 May 2005 concerning unfair business-to-consumer commercial practices in the internal market and amending Council Directive 84/450/EEC and Directives 97/7/EC, 98/27/EC and 2002/65/EC of the European Parliament and of the Council and Regulation (EC) No 2006/2004 of the European Parliament and of the Council ('Unfair Commercial Practices Directive') must be interpreted as precluding a national

				provision, such as that at issue in the main proceedings, which provides for a general prohibition of announcements of price reductions or announcements suggesting such reductions during the period preceding sales, in so far as the provision pursues objectives relating to consumer protection. It is for the national court to determine whether that is the situation in the case in the main proceedings.
	Case C-126/11 *INNO NV v Unie van Zelfstandige Ondernemers VZW (UNIZO) and Others*	*Hof van Cassatie*	Belgium	Translation by author: Directive 2005/29/EC must be interpreted as precluding a provision of national law, such as that at issue in the main proceedings, which lays down a general prohibition on announcements of price reductions and those suggestive of such reductions in the period preceding the period of sales, in so far as that provision pursues objectives related to consumer protection.
2012	Case C-559/11 *Pelckmans Turnhout NV v Walter Van Gastel Balen NV and others*	*Rechtbank van koophandel Antwerpen*	Belgium	Summary by author: The Directive does not apply to national legislation, such as the one in the case at hand, which does not focus on consumer protection.
	Case C-428/11 *Purely Creative Ltd and Others v Office of Fair Trading*	Court of Appeal (England & Wales Civil Division)	United Kingdom	Paragraph 31, second indent, of Annex I to Directive 2005/29/EC must be interpreted as prohibiting aggressive practices by which traders, such as those at issue in the main proceedings, give the false impression that the consumer has already won a prize, while the taking of any action in relation to claiming that prize, be it requesting information concerning the nature of that prize or taking possession of it, is subject to an obligation on the consumer to pay money or to incur any cost whatsoever; It is irrelevant that the cost imposed on the consumer, such as the cost of a stamp, is de minimis compared with the value of the prize or that it does not procure the trader any benefit; It is also irrelevant that the trader offers the consumer a number of methods by which he may claim the prize, at least one of which is free of

				charge, if, according to one or more of the proposed methods, the consumer would incur a cost in order to obtain information on the prize or how to acquire it; It is for the national courts to assess the information provided to consumers in the light of recitals 18 and 19 in the preamble to Directive 2005/29 and Article 5(2)(b) thereof, that is to say, by taking into account whether that information is clear and can be understood by the public targeted by the practice.
2013	Case C-206/11 *Georg Köck v Schutzverband gegen unlauteren Wettbewerb*	*Oberster Gerichtshof*	Austria	Directive 2005/29/EC of the European Parliament and of the Council of 11 May 2005 concerning unfair business-to-consumer commercial practices in the internal market and amending Council Directive 84/450/EEC, Directives 97/7/EC, 98/27/EC and 2002/65/EC of the European Parliament and of the Council and Regulation (EC) No 2006/2004 of the European Parliament and of the Council ('Unfair Commercial Practices Directive') must be interpreted as precluding a national court from ordering the cessation of a commercial practice not covered by Annex I to that directive on the sole ground that the practice has not been the subject of prior authorisation by the competent administrative authority, without itself carrying out an assessment of the unfairness of the practice in question against the criteria set out in Articles 5 to 9 of that directive.
	Case C-343/12 *Euronics Belgium CVBA v Kamera Express BV and Kamera Express Belgium BVBA*	*Rechtbank van koophandel te Gent*	Belgium	Directive 2005/29/EC of the European Parliament and of the Council of 11 May 2005 concerning unfair business-to-consumer commercial practices in the internal market and amending Council Directive 84/450/EEC and Directives 97/7/EC, 98/27/EC and 2002/65/EC of the European Parliament and of the Council and Regulation (EC) No 2006/2004 of the European Parliament and of the Council ('Unfair Commercial Practices Directive') must be interpreted as precluding a national

				provision, such as that at issue in the main proceedings, which provides for a general prohibition of offering for sale or selling at a loss in so far as that provision pursues objectives relating to consumer protection.
	Case C-265/12 *Citroën Belux NV v Federatie voor Verzekerings en FinanciëleTussen-personen (FvF)*	*Hof van beroep te Brussel*	Belgium	Article 3(9) of Directive 2005/29/EC of the European Parliament and of the Council of 11 May 2005 concerning unfair business-to-consumer commercial practices in the internal market and amending Council Directive 84/450/EEC, Directives 97/7/EC, 98/27/EC and 2002/65/EC of the European Parliament and of the Council and Regulation (EC) No 2006/2004 of the European Parliament and of the Council ('Unfair Commercial Practices Directive') must be interpreted, as must Article 56 TFEU, as not precluding a national provision, such as that at issue in the main proceedings, which lays down a general prohibition - save in the cases exhaustively listed by the national legislation - of combined offers made to consumers where at least one of the components of those offers is a financial service.
	Case C-435/11 *CHS Tour Services GmbH v Team4 Travel GmbH*	*Oberster Gerichtshof*	Austria	Directive 2005/29/EC of the European Parliament and of the Council of 11 May 2005 concerning unfair business-to-consumer commercial practices in the internal market and amending Council Directive 84/450/EEC, Directives 97/7/EC, 98/27/EC and 2002/65/EC of the European Parliament and of the Council and Regulation (EC) No 2006/2004 of the European Parliament and of the Council ('Unfair Commercial Practices Directive'), must be interpreted as meaning that, if a commercial practice satisfies all the criteria specified in Article 6(1) of that directive for being categorised as a misleading practice in relation to the consumer, it is not necessary to determine whether such a practice is also contrary to the requirements of professional diligence as referred to in Article 5(2)(a) of the directive in order for it legitimately to be

				regarded as unfair and, therefore, prohibited in accordance with Article 5(1) of the directive.
	Case C-59/12 *BKK Mobil Oil Körperschaft des öffentlichen Rechts v Zentrale zur Bekämpfung unlauteren Wettbewerbs eV.*	*Bundes-gerichtshof*	Germany	Directive 2005/29/EC of the European Parliament and of the Council of 11 May 2005 concerning unfair business-to-consumer commercial practices in the internal market and amending Council Directive 84/450/EEC, Directives 97/7/EC, 98/27/EC and 2002/65/EC of the European Parliament and of the Council and Regulation (EC) No 2006/2004 of the European Parliament and of the Council (the 'Unfair Commercial Practices Directive'), must be interpreted to the effect that a public law body charged with a task of public interest, such as the management of a statutory health insurance fund, falls within the persons covered by the directive.
	Case C-391/12 *RLvS Verlagsgesellschaft mbH v Stuttgarter Wochenblatt GmbH*	*Bundes-gerichtshof*	Germany	In circumstances such as those of the main proceedings, Directive 2005/29/EC of the European Parliament and of the Council of 11 May 2005 concerning unfair business-to-consumer commercial practices in the internal market and amending Council Directive 84/450/EEC, Directives 97/7/EC, 98/27/EC and 2002/65/EC of the European Parliament and of the Council and Regulation (EC) No 2006/2004 of the European Parliament and of the Council ('the Unfair Commercial Practices Directive') may not be relied on as against newspaper publishers, with the result that, in those circumstances, that directive must be interpreted as not precluding the application of a national provision under which those publishers are required to identify specifically, in this case through the use of the term 'advertisement' ('Anzeige'), any publication in their periodicals for which they receive remuneration, unless it is already evident from the arrangement and layout of the publication that it is an advertisement.

	Case C-281/12 *Trento Sviluppo srl und Centrale Adriatica Soc. Coop.arl v Authorità Garante della Concorrenza e del Mercato*	*Consiglio di Stato*	Italy	A commercial practice must be classified as 'misleading' for the purposes of Article 6(1) of Directive 2005/29/EC of the European Parliament and of the Council of 11 May 2005 concerning unfair business-to-consumer commercial practices in the internal market and amending Council Directive 84/450/EEC, Directives 97/7/EC, 98/27/EC and 2002/65/EC of the European Parliament and of the Council and Regulation (EC) No 2006/2004 of the European Parliament and of the Council ('Unfair Commercial Practices Directive') where that practice contains false information, or is likely to deceive the average consumer, and is likely to cause the consumer to take a transactional decision that he would not have taken otherwise. Article 2(k) of the directive must be interpreted as meaning that any decision directly related to the decision whether or not to purchase a product is covered by the concept of 'transactional decision'.
	Case C-515/12 *4Finance v State Consumer Rights Protection Authority and the Ministry of Finance*	*Lietuvos vyriausiasis administra-cinis tei*	Lithuania	Annex I, point 14, of Directive 2005/29/EC of the European Parliament and of the Council of 11 May 2005 concerning unfair business-to-consumer commercial practices in the internal market and amending Council Directive 84/450/EEC, Directives 97/7/EC, 98/27/EC and 2002/65/EC of the European Parliament and of the Council and Regulation (EC) No 2006/2004 of the European Parliament and of the Council ('Unfair Commercial Practices Directive'), must be interpreted as meaning that a pyramid promotional scheme constitutes an unfair commercial practice only where such a scheme requires the consumer to give financial consideration, regardless of its amount, for the opportunity to receive compensation that is derived primarily from the introduction of other consumers into the scheme

				rather than from the sale or consumption of products.
2015	Case C-13/15 *Cdiscount SA*	*Cour de cassation*	France	Directive 2005/29/EC of the European Parliament and of the Council of 11 May 2005 concerning unfair business-to-consumer commercial practices in the internal market and amending Council Directive 84/450/EEC, Directives 97/7/EC, 98/27/EC and 2002/65/EC of the European Parliament and of the Council and Regulation (EC) No 2006/2004 of the European Parliament and of the Council ('Unfair Commercial Practices Directive') must be interpreted as precluding national rules, such as those at issue in the main proceedings, and in so far as these pursue objectives relating to consumer protection, which impose a general prohibition on announcements of price reductions which do not show the reference price when the price is marked or displayed, when no case-by-case assessment has been undertaken to determine whether the announcements are unfair. It is for the referring court to determine whether that is so in the case in the main proceedings.
	Joined cases C-544/13 and C-545/13 *Abcur AB v Apoteket Farmaci AB (C-544/13), and Apoteket AB* and *Apoteket Farmaci AB (C-545/13)*	*Stockholms tingsrätt*	Sweden	1. [regards a different directive]. 2. Even where medicinal products for human use, such as those at issue in the main proceedings, fall within the scope of Directive 2001/83, as amended by Directive 2004/27, advertising practices relating to those medicinal products, such as those alleged in the main proceedings, can also fall within the scope of Directive 2005/29/EC of the European Parliament and of the Council of 11 May 2005 concerning unfair business-to-consumer commercial practices in the internal market and amending Council Directive 84/450/EEC, Directives 97/7/EC, 98/27/EC and 2002/65/EC of the European Parliament and of the Council, provided that the conditions for application of that directive are satisfied.

	Case C-388/13 *Nemzeti Fogyasztóvédelmi Hatóság v UPC Magyarország Kft.*	*Kúria*	Hungary	1. Directive 2005/29/EC of the European Parliament and of the Council of 11 May 2005 concerning unfair business-to-consumer commercial practices in the internal market and amending Council Directive 84/450/EEC, Directives 97/7/EC, 98/27/EC and 2002/65/EC of the European Parliament and of the Council and Regulation (EC) No 2006/2004 of the European Parliament and of the Council ('Unfair Commercial Practices Directive') must be interpreted as meaning that the communication, by a professional to a consumer, of erroneous information, such as that at issue in the main proceedings, must be classified as a 'misleading comer-cial practice', within the meaning of that directive, even though that information concer-ned only one single consumer. 2. Directive 2005/29 must be interpreted as meaning that, if a commercial practice meets all of the criteria specified in Article 6(1) of that directive for classification as a misleading practice in relation to the consumer, it is not necessary further to determine whether such a practice is also contrary to the requirements of professional diligence, as referred to in Article 5(2)(a) of that directive, in order for it legitimately to be regarded as unfair and, consequently, prohibited in accordance with Article 5(1) of that directive.

B. National level

a) National transposition technique

Just as with the other five directives, following pages include a table overviewing the initial transposition techniques. Then, the same information is shown in the form of a graph, aimed at visually comparing legislative choices.

Table 28: Initial national transposition techniques table (Unfair Commercial Practices Directive)

Member State	**Transposition technique**
Belgium	Satellite law - Law of 14 July 1991
France	Law n° 2008-3 of 3 January 2008 for the development of competition to the benefit of consumers (Consumer Code)
Germany	Satellite law - *Gesetz gegen den unlauteren Wettbewerb* (UWG)
Ireland	Satellite law - The Consumer Protection Act 2007
Netherlands	Civil Code
Romania	Satellite law - Law 363/2007 regarding the combating of unfair commercial practices in relation to consumers and the harmonisation of national provisions with European consumer protection law
United Kingdom	Satellite law - Consumer Protection from Unfair Trading Regulations 2008

Figure 14: Initial national transposition techniques graph (Unfair Commercial Practices Directive)

b) Reception of novel concepts

The Unfair Commercial Practices Directive is a complex instrument. Although very similar to the Unfair Contract Terms Directive in that it sets up a general clause and adds specific examples in an Annex, rules on commercial practices are much more detailed. The one main novel concept introduced by the Directive is the general category of 'unfair commercial practices'. These practices are further broken down into 'misleading commercial practices', 'misleading actions', 'misleading omissions' and 'aggressive commercial practices'. All of these concepts are considered novel for the purposes of this section. It must be mentioned here that many other terms used in Articles 5-11 could be labelled as novel. However, those not addressed here are discussed under the 'open-ended norms' section, because of the overlap between the two categories.

Regardless of whether any of the Member States had legislation covering unfair trade, the originality of the terms set forth by the Directive stems from their European nature, reflected in the definitions - all the above mentioned concepts are specifically defined.

Table 29: Transposition of novel concepts (Unfair Commercial Practices Selling Directive)

Member State	EU language version	Implementation
		Norms
Belgium	*pratiques commerciales déloyales* *pratiques commerciales trompeuses* *actions trompeuses* *omissions trompeuses* *pratiques commerciales agressives*	*pratiques commerciales déloyales*[148] *pratiques commerciales trompeuses*[149] -[150] *omissions trompeuses*[151] *pratiques commerciales agressives*[152]
France	*pratiques commerciales déloyales* *pratiques commerciales trompeuses* *actions trompeuses* *omissions trompeuses* *pratiques commerciales agressives*	*pratiques commerciales déloyales*[153] *pratiques commerciales trompeuses*[154] - - *pratiques commerciales agressives*[155]
Germany	*unlautere Geschäftspraktiken* *irreführende geschäftspraktiken* *irreführende Handlungen* *irreführende Unterlassungen* *aggressive Geschäftspraktiken*	*unlauterer geschäftlicher Handlungen* *irreführende geschäftliche Handlungen* - *Irreführung durch Unterlassen* -
Ireland	unfair commercial practices misleading commercial practices misleading actions misleading omissions aggressive commercial practices	unfair commercial practices[156] misleading commercial practices[157] -[158] -[159] aggressive commercial practices[160]

148 Article 84, Law on market practices.

149 Article 88, Law on market practices.

150 There is no specific transposition of the term '*action trompeuse*'. However, Article 88 of the Law on market practices has exactly the same wording as Article 6 of the Directive, which covers misleading actions.

151 Article 90, Law on market practices.

152 Article 92, Law on market practices.

153 Article L. 120-1, *Code de la consommation.*

154 *Ibid.*

155 *Ibid.*

156 Regulation 41, Consumer Protection Act 2007.

157 Regulation 42, Consumer Protection Act 2007.

158 There is no specific transposition of the term 'misleading action', however Regulation 43 of the Consumer Protection Act 2007 has exactly the same wording as Article 6 of the Directive, which covers misleading actions.

159 There is no specific transposition of the term 'misleading omission'. However, Regulation 46 of the Consumer Protection Act 2007 has exactly the same wording as Article 7 of the Directive, which covers misleading omissions.

160 Regulation 52, Consumer Protection Act 2007.

Nether-lands	*oneerlijke handelspraktijken* *misleidende handelspraktijken* *misleidende handelingen* *misleidende omissies* *agressieve handelspraktijken*	*oneerlijke handelspraktijken*[161] *misleidende handelspraktijken*[162] - *misleidende omissies*[163] *agressieve handelspraktijken*[164]
Romania	*practici comerciale neloiale* *practici comerciale înşelătoare* *acţiuni înşelătoare* *omisiuni înşelătoare* *practici comerciale agresive*	*practici comerciale incorecte*[165] *practici comerciale înşelătoare*[166] *acţiuni înşelătoare*[167] *omisiuni înşelătoare*[168] *practici comerciale agresive*[169]
United Kingdom	unfair commercial practices misleading commercial practices misleading actions misleading omissions aggressive commercial practices	unfair commercial practices[170] misleading commercial practices[171] misleading actions[172] misleading omissions[173] aggressive commercial practices[174]

d) Reception of selected open-ended norms

Open-ended terms may sometimes overlap the 'novel concept' factor above. That is because whenever directives specifically introduce new concepts, they underline the constant evolution of European terminology. Although some of these terms might have an open-ended nature it is not problematic for the current methodology of assessing harmonisation factors. There are four open-ended concepts identified in Articles 5-11: 'undue influence', 'professional diligence', 'average consumer' and 'vulnerable consumer'. Other terms in these articles might fit the 'open-ended' description, such as 'unclear', 'unintelligible', 'ambiguous' or 'untimely', however, a selection of concepts had to be made.

161 Article 6:139b BW.
162 Article 6:139c BW.
163 Article 6:139d BW.
164 Article 6:139b BW.
165 Article 4(1), Law 363/2007.
166 Article 4(3), Law 363/2007.
167 Article 5, Law 363/2007.
168 *Ibid.*
169 Article 4(3), Law 363/2007.
170 Regulation 3, Consumer Protection from Unfair Trading Regulations 2008.
171 Regulation 5, Consumer Protection from Unfair Trading Regulations 2008.
172 *Ibid.*
173 Regulation 6, Consumer Protection from Unfair Trading Regulations 2008.
174 Regulation 7, Consumer Protection from Unfair Trading Regulations 2008.

Table 30: Transposition of open-ended norms (Unfair Commercial Practices Selling Directive)

Member State	EU language version	Implementation
		Norms
Belgium	*influence injustifiée* *diligence professionnelle* *consommateur moyen* *consommateurs vulnérables*	*influence injustifiée*[175] *diligence professionnelle*[176] *consommateur moyen*[177] *consommateurs vulnérables*[178]
France	*influence injustifiée* *diligence professionnelle* *consommateur moyen* *consommateurs vulnérables*	*influence injustifiée*[179] *diligence professionnelle*[180] *consommateur normalement informé et raisonnablement attentif et avisé*[181] *consommateurs vulnérables*[182]
Germany	*unzulässige Beeinflussung* *berufliche Sorgfalt* *Durchschnittsverbraucher* *Schutzbedürftigverbrauchers*	*unzulässige Beeinflussung* *unternehmerische Sorgfalt* *durchschnittlichen Mitglieds* *Schutzbedürftigverbrauchers*
Ireland	undue influence professional dilligence average consumer vulnerable consumer	undue influence[183] professional diligence[184] average consumer[185] vulnerable consumer[186]
Nether-lands	*ongepaste beïnvloeding* *professionele toewijding* *gemiddelde consument* *vatbaar consumenten*	- *professionele toewijding* *gemiddelde consument*[187] -
Romania	*influență nejustificată* *diligență profesională* *consumatorul mediu* *consumator vulnerabil*	*influență nejustificată*[188] *diligență profesională*[189] *consumatorul mediu*[190] *consumator vulnerabil*[191]

175 Article 92, Law on market practices.
176 Article 84, Law on market practices.
177 *Ibid.*
178 *Ibid.*
179 Article L. 122-11, Code de la consommation.
180 Article L. 120-1, Code de la consommation.
181 *Ibid.*
182 *Ibid.*
183 Regulation 53(4), Consumer Protection Act 2007.
184 Regulation 41, Consumer Protection Act 2007.
185 Regulation 2, Consumer Protection Act 2007.
186 *Ibid.*
187 Article 6:193b BW.
188 Article 2(j), Law 363/2007.
189 Article 2(h), Law 363/2007.
190 Article 2(m), Law 363/2007.
191 Article 4(2), Law 363/2007.

United Kingdom	undue influence professional dilligence average consumer vulnerable consumer	undue influence[192] professional dilligence[193] average consumer[194] vulnerable consumer[195]

e) Reference to European law in end legislation

Table 31: Overview of reference to European law (Unfair Commercial Practices Directive)

Member State	**National legislation**	**Reference to European law**	**Database**
Belgium	Law of 14 July 1991	No	Ejustice
France	Law n° 2008-3 of 3 January 2008 for the development of competition to the benefit of consumers (Consumer Code)	No	Legifrance
Germany	*Gesetz gegen den unlauteren Wettbewerb*	Yes	Juris
Ireland	The Consumer Protection Act 2007	Yes	Irish Statute Book (Office of the Attorney General)
Nether-lands	Civil Code	No	Overheid
Romania	Law 363/2007 regarding the combating of unfair commercial practices in relation to consumers and the harmonisation of national provisions with European consumer protection law	No	Lege 5
United Kingdom	Consumer Protection from Unfair Trading Regulations 2008	Yes	The National Archives

f) Timely transposition

The deadline to transpose the Unfair Commercial Practices Directive was 12 June 2007.

Table 32: Overview of transposition deadline (Unfair Commercial Practices Directive)

Member State	**National legislation**	**Transposition date**	**Timely transposition**
Belgium	Law of 14 July 1991	01 December 2007	No
France	Law n° 2008-3 of 3 January 2008 for the development of competition to the benefit of consumers (Consumer Code)	05 January 2008	No

192 Regulation 7, Consumer Protection from Unfair Trading Regulations 2008; however, no definition of undue influence has been taken over from the Directive.

193 Regulation 2(1), Consumer Protection from Unfair Trading Regulations 2008.

194 *Ibid.*

195 Regulation 2(5), Consumer Protection from Unfair Trading Regulations 2008.

Germany	*Gesetz gegen den unlauteren Wettbewerb* (modification)	30 December 2008	No
Ireland	The Consumer Protection Act 2007	01 May 2007	Yes
Netherlands	Civil Code	15 October 2008	No
Romania	Law 363/2007 regarding the combating of unfair commercial practices in relation to consumers and the harmonisation of national provisions with European consumer protection law	31 December 2007	No
United Kingdom	Consumer Protection from Unfair Trading Regulations 2008	26 May 2008	No

g) Infringement procedures

Apart from the judgment issued in *Commission v Belgium*, as highlighted in the table below, there have been two other judgments[196] and four applications that resulted in the removal from the registry of the court.[197] Moreover, the Commission was also considering bringing an infringement procedure against France, but has yet not taken this step.[198]

Table 33: Infringement Procedures (Unfair Commercial Practices)

Date of judgment	**Case number and name**	**Member State**	**Proceedings**	**Ruling**
10 July 2014	Case C-421/12 *European Commission v Kingdom of Belgium*	Belgium	Failure of a Member State to fulfil obligations - Consumer protection - Unfair commercial practices - Directive 2005/29/EC - Complete harmonisation - Exclusion of the professions, dentists and physiotherapists - Restriction or prohibition of certain types of itinerant trading activities.	Kingdom of Belgium has failed to fulfil its obligations under Articles 2(b) and (d), 3 and 4 of Directive 2005/29.

196 Case C-321/08, *European Commission v Kingdom of Spain* [2009] ECR I-00063*; Case C-282/08, *European Commission v Grand Duchy of Luxembourg* [2009] ECR I-00013*.

197 Case C-326/08, *European Commission v Germany* [2009]; Case C-284/08, *European Commission v United Kingdom* [2009]; Case C-283/08, *European Commission v Netherlands* [2009]; Case C-270/08, *European Commission v Hungary* [2009].

198 Consumers: the European Commission asks Belgium and France to comply with EU rules on unfair practices, European Commission Press Release - IP/11/1096, 29/09/2011, available at: <http://europa.eu/rapid/press-release_IP-11-1096_en.htm?locale=en>, last accessed on 27 July 2016.

This part of Chapter 3 aimed to go through the factors on which the Convergence Index is based, in order to gather data from all the selected rules (both European and national). In doing so, a lot of the information has been clustered in comparative categories. On the basis of this data, Section 4 below creates the aggregate Convergence Index.

4. Factors Applied

4.1. *Aim of the Section*

This part of Chapter 4 translates the data gathered until now into statistical representations. The aim of this Section is to apply the methodology developed earlier in this Chapter. Before coding the values obtained in the previous Section, several remarks must be made.

Firstly, the actual coding of the Convergence Index is done by allotting values of either 0 or 1 to the data gathered so far. Exceptionally, the Index also integrates values between 0 and 1 when normalisation is necessary. As indicated above, normalisation is the process by which consistency is ensured between the separate indices putting together an aggregate index. The list of factors behind the Convergence Index and their affiliated assumptions are revisited below, and each of them are detailed in terms of the coding approach.

Secondly, this Section focuses on six comparative overviews: the Convergence Index as calculated solely for the European level of governance (with a maximum value of 7), which is subsequently added to the remaining five directive-based overviews (with a maximum value of 6). The latter overviews consist of a cumulation of both European and national factors, and the resulting Convergence Index has a maximum value of 13 (there are 6 national factors added to the 7 European ones). Graphs have been chosen to enhance the visualisation of the findings.

4.2. *Coding Method*

As noted above, the list of convergence factors are now revisited, to take the reader through the process of coding. The two levels of governance – European national – are the two so-called 'dimensions' of the Convergence Index.

Convergence Index: European level

a) *Law v policy*: law (1) leads to more convergence than policy (0).

b) *Type of European instrument*: Regulations (1) lead to more convergence than Directives (0).

c) *Nature of policy*: maximum harmonisation (1) leads to more convergence than minimum harmonisation (0).

d) *Reference to self-regulation*: if reference to self-regulation is made in an instrument (1), it leads to more convergence than if no such reference in made (0).

e) *General clause*: if an instrument does not contain a general clause (1), it leads to more convergence than if it does contain such a clause (0).

f) *Black list*: if an instrument contains a black list (1), it leads to more convergence than if it does not (0).

g) *CJEU case law*: the more preliminary references an instrument generates, the less convergence it leads to. This factor has been normalised by creating two categories of instruments – those with little case law (Doorstep Selling, Distance Selling, Consumer Sales = 1) and those with medium and high case law (Unfair Contract Terms, Unfair Commercial Practices = 0). For the first category, preliminary references range between four cases (Consumer Sales) and eight cases (Doorstep Selling). For the second category, the numbers are much higher, namely between 19 cases (Unfair Commercial Practices) to 45 cases (Unfair Contract Terms).

Convergence Index: National level

a) *National transposition technique*: transposing European law in a Consumer Code or a satellite law (1) leads to more convergence than transposing the rules in a Civil Code (0).

b) *Reception of selected novel concepts*: if the selected novel concepts have been transposed accurately (1 – this also includes functional equivalents), this leads to more convergence than if they have not (0). This factor sometimes requires normalisation, depending on the number of novel concepts selected. The normalisation is subsequently done by creating an average which then becomes the maximum value allotted to one individual such concept (e.g. if two concepts are identified, the maximum value given to each if the concept has been transposed correctly is 0.5).

c) *Reception of selected open-ended norms*: if the selected open-ended norms have been transposed accurately (1 – this also includes functional equivalents), this leads to more convergence than if they have not (0). The same normalisation approach as with the above factor is applied.

d) *Reference to European law in end legislation:* if there is a reference to the Directive in transposing legislation (1), it leads to more convergence than if there is none (0).

e) *Timely transposition (date of national legislation)*: if Member States transpose European law timely (1), it leads to more convergence than if they do not (0).

f) *Infringement procedures*: if a Member State has had no infringement procedures initiated against it (1), this entails more convergence than if infringement procedures have been brought against a State (0).

4.3. *The Convergence Index EU*

This Subsection displays the results of the coding process leading to the Convergence Index. For this reason, no substantive analysis accompanies the two main tools used for visualisation: the comparative table and the graph plotting the values in the table. As mentioned above, the first aggregation of the Convergence Index focuses on its European dimension, and it reflects the European factors as can be observed in the matrix below and in the subsequent chart.

Table 34: Convergence Index (European level)

Factor	Doorstep Selling	Unfair Contract Terms	Distance Selling	Consumer Sales	Unfair Commercial Practices
1. Law v policy	1	1	1	1	1
2. Type of European instrument	0	0	0	0	0
3. Nature of policy	0	0	0	0	1
4. Reference to self-regulation	0	0	0	0	1
5. General clause	1	0	1	1	0
6. Black list	0	0	0	0	1
7. CJEU case law	1	0	1	1	0
TOTAL VALUE (EU)	**3**	**1**	**3**	**3**	**4**

Figure 15: Convergence Index (European level)

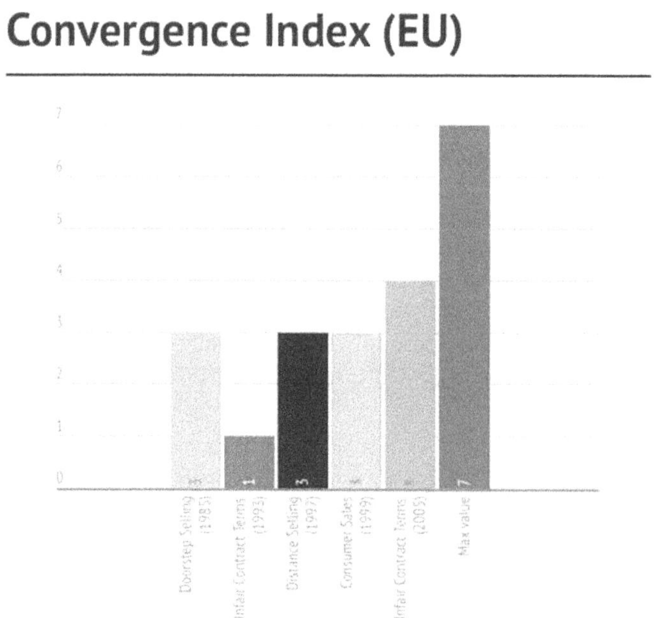

4.4. *Doorstep Selling Directive*

Next, the Convergence Index is calculated for each of the national transpositions, according to the selected directives. The national factors can be observed in the matrix below. The resulting values are added to the Convergence Index (EU) shown above and displayed once again in a graph.

As no open-ended norms have been coded for this particular Directive, this factor has been normalised by using the average value between 0 and 1, namely 0,5.

Table 35: Convergence Index (Doorstep Selling Directive)

Factor	BE	FR	DE	IR	NL	RO	UK
1. Transposition technique	1	1	1	1	1	1	1
2. Novel concepts	1	1	1	1	0	0	1
3. Open-ended norms	0,5	0,5	0,5	0,5	0,5	0,5	0,5
4. Timely implementation	0	0	1	0	0	1	0
5. Infringement procedures	1	1	1	1	1	1	1
6. Reference to EU law in end legislation	0	0	0	1	0	1	0
TOTAL VALUE (NAT) **AVG MS (NAT) = 3,78/6**	**3,5**	**3,5**	**4,5**	**4,5**	**2,5**	**4,5**	**3,5**

Figure 16: Convergence Index (Doorstep Selling Directive)

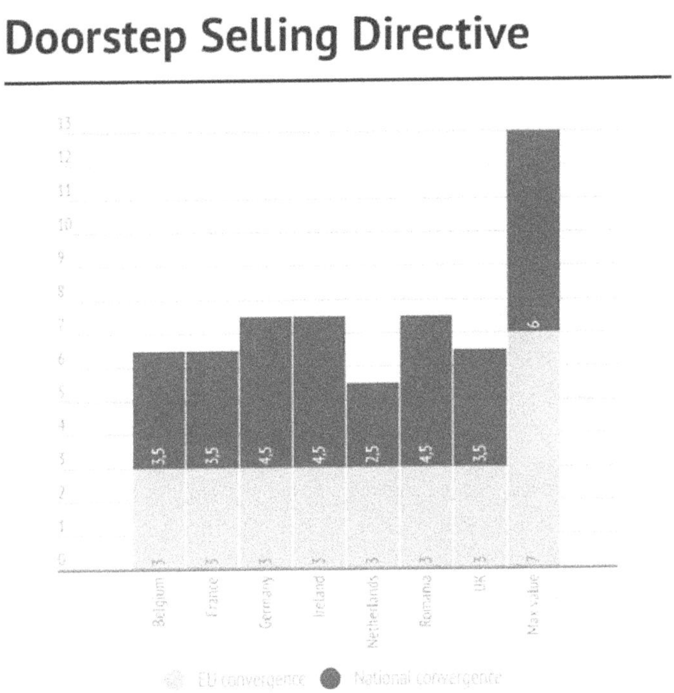

4.5. *Unfair Contract Terms Directive*

The same process as in Section 4.2. is followed.

Table 36: Convergence Index (Unfair Contract Terms Directive)

Factor	BE	FR	DE	IR	NL	RO	UK
1. Transposition technique	1	1	0	1	0	1	1
2. Novel concepts	1	1	0	1	0	1	1
3. Open-ended norms	0,5	0,75	0,5	1	0,25	1	1
4. Timely implementation	1	0	0	1	0	1	0
5. Infringement procedures	1	1	1	1	0	1	1
6. Reference to EU law in end legislation	0	0	1	1	0	0	1
TOTAL VALUE (NAT) **AVG MS (NAT) = 3,86/6**	**4,5**	**3,75**	**2,5**	**6**	**0,25**	**5**	**5**

Figure 17: Convergence Index (Unfair Contract Terms Directive)

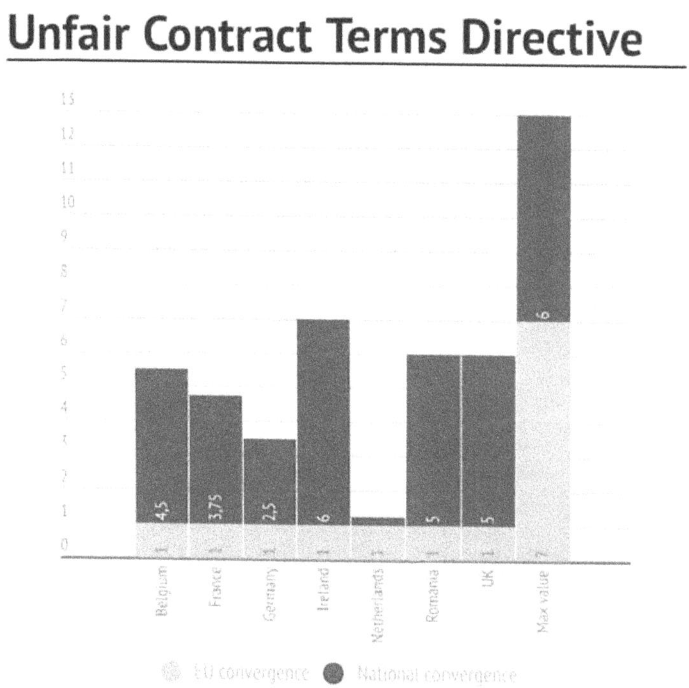

4.6. *Distance Selling Directive*

The same process as in Section 4.2 is followed.

Table 37: Convergence Index (Distance Selling Directive)

Factor	BE	FR	DE	IR	NL	RO	UK
1. Transposition technique	1	1	0	1	0	1	1
2. Novel concepts	1	1	1	1	0	0	1
3. Open-ended norms	0,5	0	0,5	1	0,5	0,5	1
4. Timely implementation	1	0	0	0	1	1	0
5. Infringement procedures	1	1	1	1	1	1	1
6. Reference to EU law in end legislation	0	0	1	1	0	0	1
TOTAL VALUE (NAT) **AVG MS (NAT) = 3,86/6**	**4,5**	**3**	**3,5**	**5**	**2,5**	**3,5**	**5**

Figure 18: Convergence Index (Distance Sellling Directive)

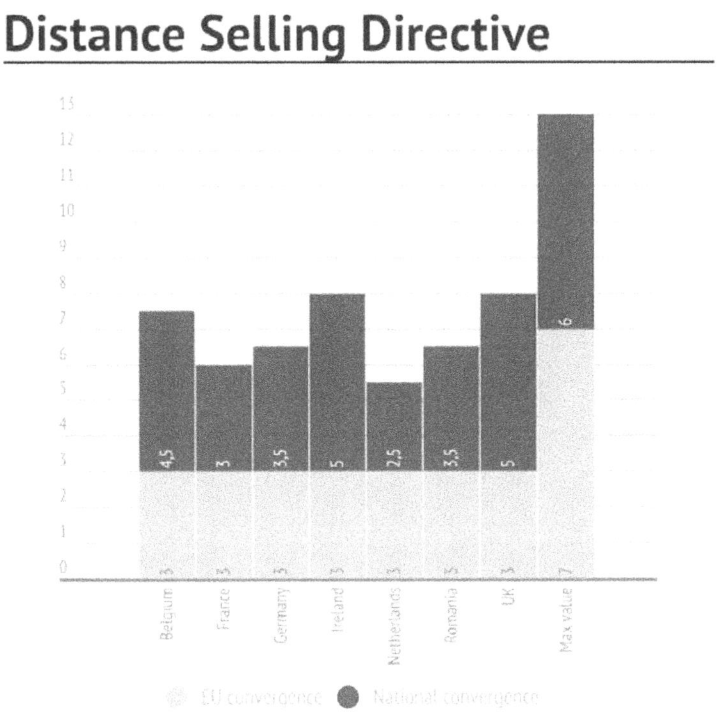

4.7. *Consumer Sales Directive*

The same process as in Section 4.2 is followed.

Table 38: Convergence Index (Consumer Sales Directive)

Factor	BE	FR	DE	IR	NL	RO	UK
1. Transposition technique	0	1	0	1	0	1	1
2. Novel concepts	1	0,83	0,33	1	0,66	1	1
3. Open-ended norms	1	0,5	0,5	1	0,25	1	0,75
4. Timely implementation	0	0	1	0	0	1	0
5. Infringement procedures	0	0	1	1	1	1	1
6. Reference to EU law in end legislation	0	0	1	1	0	0	0
TOTAL VALUE (NAT) **AVG MS (NAT) = 3,4/6**	**2**	**2,33**	**3,83**	**5**	**1,91**	**5**	**3,75**

Figure 19: Convergence Index (Consumer Sales Directive)

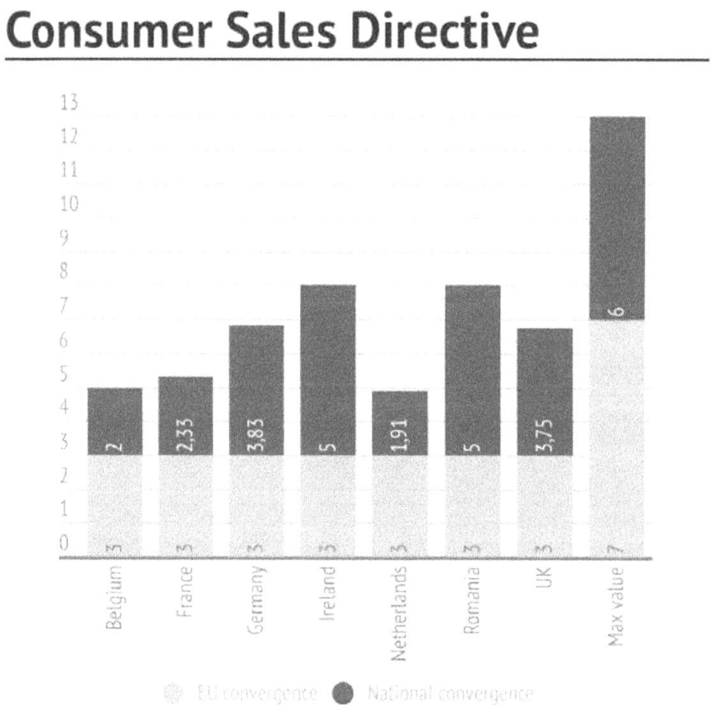

4.8. Unfair Commercial Practices Directive

The same process as in Section 4.2 is followed.

Table 39: Convergence Index (Unfair Commercial Practices Directive)

Factor	BE	FR	DE	IR	NL	RO	UK
1. Transposition technique	1	1	1	1	0	1	1
2. Novel concepts	0,8	0,6	0,6	0,6	0,8	0,8	1
3. Open-ended norms	1	1	0,75	1	0,5	1	1
4. Timely implementation	0	0	0	1	0	0	0
5. Infringement procedures	0	1	1	1	1	1	1
6. Reference to EU law in end legislation	0	0	1	1	0	0	1
TOTAL VALUE (NAT) **AVG MS (NAT) = 3,92/6**	**2,8**	**3,6**	**4,35**	**5,6**	**2,3**	**3,8**	**5**

Figure 20: Convergence Index (Unfair Commercial Practices Directive)

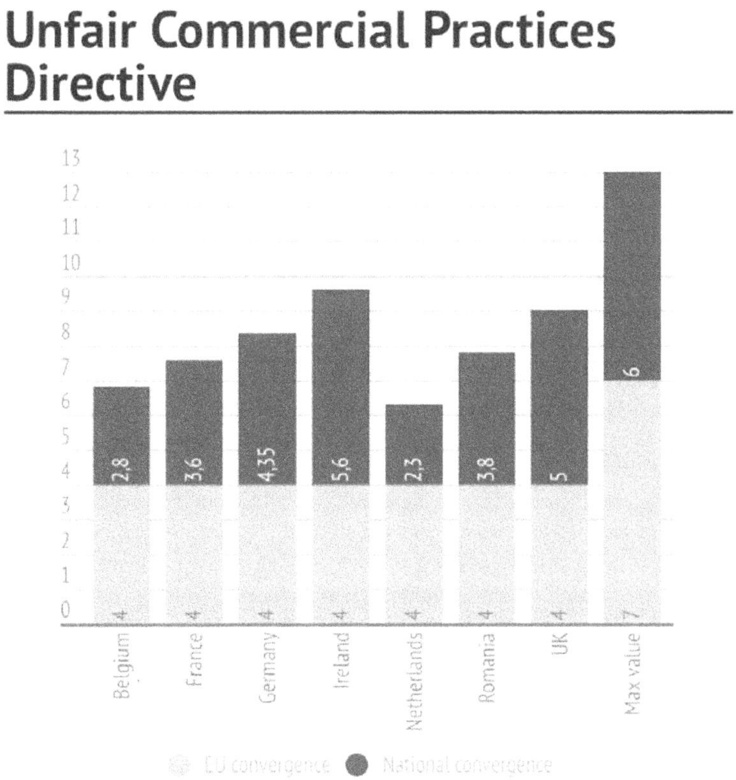

5. Using the Convergence Index to contribute to the Harmonisation Debate

5.1. *Introduction*

So far, the present Chapter had three particular goals. Firstly, it aimed to familiarise the reader with the methodology of numerical comparative law in general, and with the creation of the Convergence Index in particular. Secondly, it made an overview of the five directives and seven Member States on the basis of the factors behind the Convergence Index, in an attempt to gather data from the selected pieces of legislation. Lastly, this Chapter included the actual coding of the legal information available, and the subsequent conversion of the legal debate from textual arguments to numbers. Having pursued all these goals, now it is time to actually analyse the findings obtained with the help of the original methodology used by this study.

Before delving into some of the patterns and stories drawn from the data sets reflecting the five directives, several clarifications must be addressed.

In the first place, it is not the purpose of this research to claim that on the basis of Convergence Index conclusions can be drawn for either legal convergence or European legal harmonisation *in general*. The variances that continue to characterise European consumer law and policy make it difficult to assess all possible strong points and vulnerabilities. What this research aims to achieve is the isolation of several factors that influence harmonisation, and it is *solely in the light of these parameters* that any analyses are made.

Secondly, the selected convergence factors must also be interpreted in the light of the working assumptions developed earlier in this study at the beginning of this Chapter. According to the construction of the Index, these factors can only be valid if they are taken to have a very targeted meaning and role. Neither the Index, nor the factors can exist outside of the expressed assumptions.

The third point relates to the weight given to each of the factors. The starting point in this respect has been to consider all the factors mentioned above equally, and not allocate more than one point per factor. Justifying this decision is the fact that it would be difficult to state and prove that one factor is more important than another. Moreover, since they already cover rather diverse perspectives over harmonisation, it was important to make sure that all of these angles are represented. More specifically, the 13 factors reflect not only the actual transposition procedures (e.g. timely transposition; transposition technique; etc.), but they also reflect the very substance of the rules they stand for (e.g. novel concepts; open-ended norms; etc.). It is true that when it comes to the European dimension of the Convergence Index, several factors overlap (law v policy; type of European instrument; and nature of policy); however, in this particular case, it is submitted that the overlap simply strengthens the convergence effect by looking very closely at all the clues regarding what makes a European instrument be more convergence-friendly than others.

5.2. *Findings*

In the following pages, the data resulting from earlier in this Chapter are discussed. To start with, several classifications are made on the basis of a visualisation tool namely the Google Motion Graph. It is important to notice that while the x axis is expressed in time, this is nothing more than a graphic representation of the moments in time when the directives were adopted. For this reason, this graph is not a time series, as the observations are not dynamic and they only interact with one another from the perspective of the fact that they express legislative developments taken from isolated moments in time. Then, a general discussion is put together, focusing on different observations made on the basis of the Convergence Index data.

5.2.1. Classifications

Moving to some of the observations made on the basis of data visualisation, it can be observed that both the European as well as the national dimension of the Convergence Index can be clustered in different categories. These dimensions are nothing more than the different levels of governance which entail different features when it comes to legislation design.

A. The European dimension
On the basis of the European set of factors coded in the Convergence Index, each of the five directives can be labelled as either:

(i) *low convergence* – the Unfair Contract Terms Directive is the only instrument described in this category, given the fact that it promotes minimum harmonisation, does not make reference to self-regulation, has a general clause, does not include a black list and is the basis of the highest number of preliminary questions before the CJEU. The Unfair Contract Terms Directive has a CI(EU) score of 1/7.

(ii) *average convergence* – there are three directives in this category, namely the Doorstep Selling Directive, Distance Selling Directive and the Consumer Sales Directive. The characteristics of this group of directives focus on the fact the while they are minimum harmonisation, do not make reference to self-regulation, and neither do they include a black list: they also do not contain a general clause and have seldom been the basis of preliminary questions before the CJEU. The Doorstep Selling Directive, Distance Selling Directive and Consumer Sales Directive each have a CI(EU) score of 3/7.

(iii) *high convergence* – the Unfair Commercial Practices Directive is the only representative of this category, described through maximum harmonisation (it is the only maximum harmonisation instrument in the study) that includes a black list and reference to self-regulation, in spite of also containing a general clause and leading to a meaningful amount of cases before the CJEU. The Unfair Commercial Practices Directive has a CI(EU) score of 4/7.

B. The national dimension

Two subdivisions are possible here. Firstly, on the basis of the national set of factors shaping the Convergence Index, the distribution of observations reflecting the seven Member States on a timeline can be labelled as either:

(i) *J-shaped distribution* – this distribution can be observed for two Member States (Germany and the Netherlands). Although there might be differences in values between these observations (some Member States scored higher than others on the Convergence Index), their convergence pattern follows the same direction: between the Doorstep Selling Directive and the Unfair Contract Terms Directive, convergence values first decline before they start increasing. A slight variation is observed with respect to Germany, which sees its convergence values increase after the Consumer Sales Directive, whereas the value for the Netherlands, drops with the same Directive (see Figure 21 below).

Figure 21: J-shaped Distribution (Google Motion Graph)

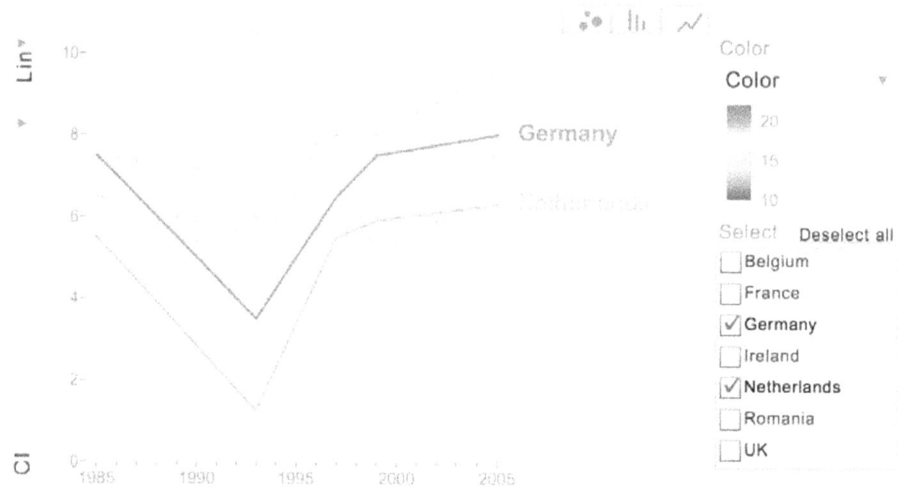

(ii) *W-shaped distribution* – this distribution is characteristic to three Member States, namely the UK, France and Belgium and it features the same starting value, a slight decrease marked by the Unfair Contract Terms Directive, a brief increase in convergence value for the Distance Selling Directive, followed by a sudden decrease prompted by the Consumer Sales Directive, afterwards redressed with an upward slope (see Figure 22 below).

Figure 22: W-shaped Distribution (Google Motion Graph)

(iii) *uniform distribution* – only one Member State can be described to have and almost uniform distribution, which in other words is the closest shape to an upward slope. It must be noted that even though the distribution of observations does not suffer any major negative impacts along the timeline (the only drop is of 0,5 on the Unfair Contract Terms Directive), it does display stagnation between the Doorstep Selling Directive and the Unfair Contract Terms Directive and between the Distance Selling Directive and the Consumer Sales Directive (see Figure 23). Ireland als has the overall highest values of convergence.

Figure 23: Uniform Distribution (Google Motion Graph)

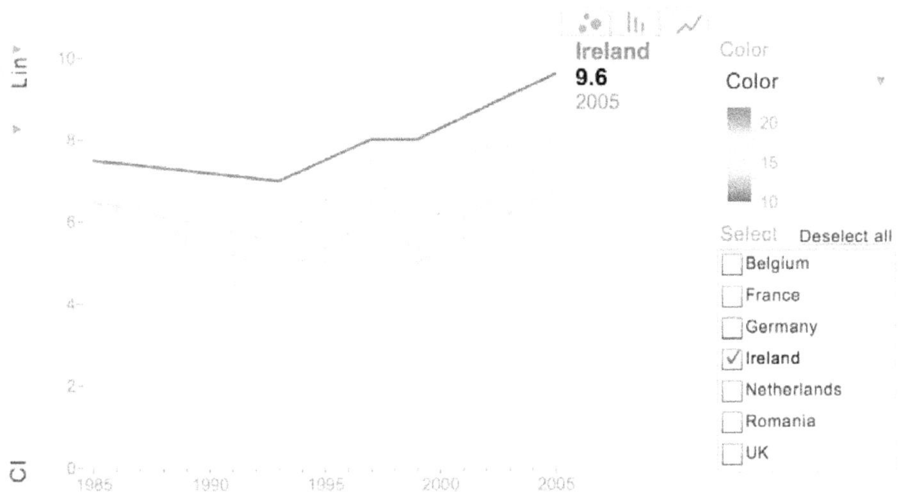

(iv) *overall decreasing value* - Romania is the only Member State that has a distribution characterised by a decrease in the score obtained on the most recent Directive under analysis.

Figure 24: Overall Decreasing Value

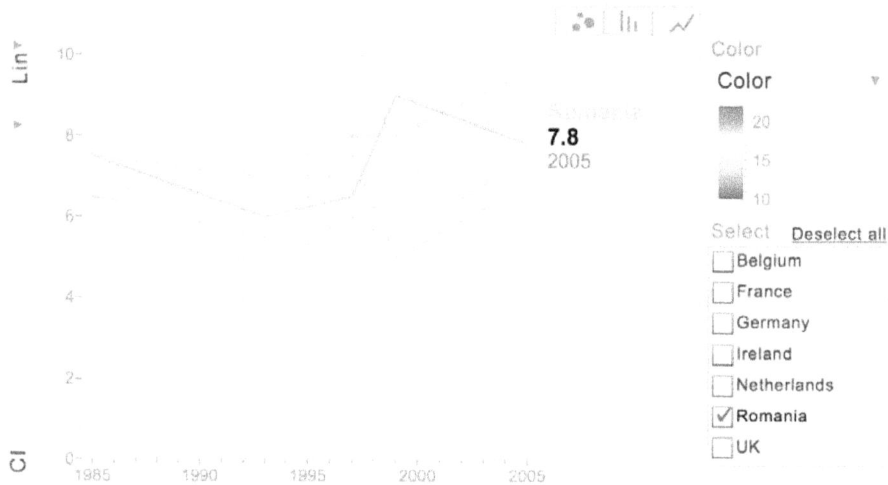

Secondly, on the basis of how steep the Index slope is towards the last set of observations (Unfair Commercial Practices Directive - maximum harmonisation), Member States can be divided into two groups:

(i) *convergence values increasing* - this group is formed out of Belgium, Ireland, France, Germany, the Netherlands and the UK, and entails a sudden spike in convergence values occasioned by the transposition of the Unfair Commercial Practices Directive;

(ii) *convergence values decreasing* - this is the situation of Romania, which peaked its convergence values with the occasion of the Consumer Sales Directive, and then suffered a drop on the value for the Unfair Commercial Practices Directive, in spite of the latter having the highest EU-value.

5.2.2. General Discussion

The graphs above (Figures 21-24) display convergence patterns that reflect the factors used in the Index. What follows now is a closer look at the most important of such patterns in order to determine how the Convergence Index can be used to better understand the harmonisation of European consumer law. A number of six patterns have been identified. Discussing these patterns has a dual purpose: firstly, to determine whether a new light can be shed on the harmonisation process using data visualisation; and secondly, to link back to Chapters 2 and 3 and reflect the more doctrinal part of this research, for the purpose of enhancing the accuracy of the newly discovered convergence patterns.

1. In general, and as defined by the factors shaping the Convergence Index, national consumer legislation is converging

Once again, it must be stated that the notion of convergence addressed in this chapter is inherently limited to the factors behind the Convergence Index, and does not reflect a wider concept. With this in mind and as can be seen in Figure 21 above, regardless of Convergence Index values, there is an upward trend in convergence for the majority of Member States. Looking at the graph, the Unfair Commercial Practices Directive is the point on the timeline when convergence values have the highest scores. The reason why Member States do so well with the transposition of the Unfair Commercial Practices Directive is two-fold. On the one hand, the European dimension of the Convergence Index was the highest of all Directives for the Unfair Commercial Practices Directive, given the positive scores on the following factors: maximum harmonisation, black listing and reference to self-regulation. The Unfair Commercial Practices Directive is the only directive in this study that combined all these features. On the other hand, the national dimension of the Convergence Index was very well represented: while there were some timely implementation issues (FR, DE, NL, UK), and some issues with the reception of open-ended concepts (FR, DE, NL), Member States ranked high on average.[199]

Going back to the upward trend, to a certain extent it confirms the Commission's perspective that full harmonisation might be better than minimum harmonisation.[200] However, the crucial question is: how much better exactly? The average Convergence Index for minimum harmonisation directives (6,47/13) is not very far away from the average score obtained by Member States on the Unfair Commercial Practices Directive (7,92/13), as seen below in Figure 25.

199 The average value of the national CI for the Unfair Commercial Practices Directive is 4,44/7, the highest of all directives.

200 There are more arguments used in the favour of maximum harmonisation, such as a high consumer protection level and the development of the internal market but as such only fragmentation is essentially linked to the debate surrounding convergence as a process; see Smits 2010b, p. 7.

Figure 25: Minimum Harmonisation v Maximum Harmonisation

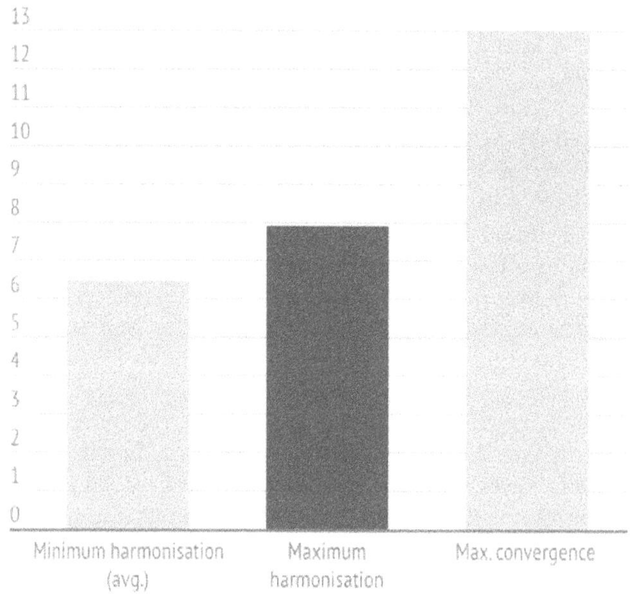

This perspective offers even more arguments to support the majority of views expressed in literature, criticizing maximum harmonisation.[201] However, we must remind ourselves what exactly makes researchers counter maximum harmonisation. In brief, the arguments presented against it relate to two distinct directions: that maximum harmonisation entails lowering consumer protection (the case of Member States that had to adopt rules less favourable to consumers than their prior national regimes) and that maximum harmonisation does not work in practice, because various features of the directives (open-ended norms, enforcement, etc.) would make it difficult for different national judges to reach the same outcomes in all cases.[202]

The Convergence Index is designed to reflect a maximum value (13) deemed as the ideal convergence standard in the light of the efforts of the European legislator. The fact that maximum harmonisation only mildly contributes to converging towards this standard is disappointing in the light of the promises maximum harmonisation was supposed to deliver. The Convergence Index makes it possible to assess the differences between these two policies in a clear and quantifiable manner.

201 Anne de Vries, 'Maximum Harmonisation and General Clauses - Two Conflicting Concepts?', January 2011, available at: <http://ssrn.com/abstract=1703078>, last accessed on 27 July 2016, p. 917; Hondius 2011, p. 164.

202 Schulte-Nölke even questions the uniformity of solutions given by national courts to B2B disputes in case of standard contract terms. See Schulte-Nölke 2015, p. 215.

2. The transposition of the Unfair Contract Terms Directive marks a decline in convergence values

For Member States with the J-shaped distribution,[203] the Unfair Contract Terms Directive brought about a downward trend. To reiterate, convergence values first decline between the Doorstep Selling Directive and the Unfair Contract Terms Directive, before they increase. All in all, the crash in values observed for the Unfair Contract Terms Directive raises two relevant points:

(i) the reasons why the Unfair Contract Terms Directive has a low convergence score;
(ii) the question of how Member States performed in transposing this Directive.

Firstly, the main driving factor behind the downward trend is the very low convergence score of the Unfair Contract Terms Directive (1 out of 7), impacting an otherwise consistent performance of the Member States in terms of national factors.[204] The Unfair Contract Terms Directive has been criticised on many occasions as having an unfitting form for the goal it is supposed to reach – harmonising the law of unfair standard terms.[205] Some of the critique points are mirrored in the Unfair Contract Terms Directive's performance vis-à-vis the Convergence Index. At this point it is useful to mention the assumptions made earlier in this Chapter – minimum harmonisation, no reference to self-regulation, the use of general clauses, the absence of a black list as well as a very heavy load of case law from the CJEU are all signs that harmonisation can only occur to a limited degree.

As it has already been discussed in Chapter 2, one of the features of the Unfair Contract Terms Directive that stems from CJEU case law is that the interpretation and application of key Unfair Contract Terms Directive provisions such as the fairness test will depend, to a great extent, on national law.[206] An example in this respect are all the Slovak and Spanish cases regarding national proceedings dealing with mortgage enforcement.[207] Although Slovakia and Spain are not included in the study, the preliminary references forwarded by their national courts to the CJEU seem to point in the same direction – a direction equally important in the discussion of harmonisation standards. Reviewing the unfairness of standard terms can reflect certain national procedures on enforcement, whether dealing with pre-set

203 See Figure 21, p. 265.
204 The MS average for Doorstep Selling Directive is 3.14 and the MS average for Unfair Contract Terms Directive is 3.96.
205 Anne de Vries, 'Maximum Harmonisation and General Clauses – Two Conflicting Concepts?', January 2011, available at: <http://ssrn.com/abstract=1703078>, last accessed on 27 July 2016.
206 Case C-237/02, *Freiburger Kommunalbauten GmbH Baugesellschaft & Co. KG v Ludger Hofstetter and Ulrike Hofstetter* [2004] ECR I-03403.
207 For a thorough exposé of case law on the Unfair Contract Terms Directive, see Micklitz & Reich 2014, p. 771.

arbitration clauses,[208] or with specific mortgage claims that appear to be common to countries like Spain, severely hit by the financial crisis.[209] But what exactly do these references stand for? Crossing the realm of substantive law and moving into procedural law makes the application of the Unfair Contract Terms Directive fully dependent on a review of these procedures which must nevertheless be made exclusively by the national court.

Another example in this respect is how the Unfair Contract Terms Directive lacks a unitary approach to the effect given to terms deemed to be unfair. By leaving this aspect to the appreciation of Member States, the Directive's converging effect is diminished. To illustrate this point, the 2014 developments of the Romanian law implementing the Unfair Contract Terms Directive have led to a very strict control of the effect of unfair terms: according to Article 13 of Law nr. 193/2000, should a court find a term to be unfair, then not only is it regarded as null and void, but the trader will be under the subsequent obligation of removing the term in question from any of its ongoing contracts.[210] These repercussions will have a powerful market impact, as banks have to change thousands and thousands of contracts in the aftermath of unsuccessful litigation. In Romania, these fears have been at the centre of debates that led to the postponement of the amendments brought to Law nr. 193/2000 twice.[211]

It can be argued that a regime like the one adopted by Romanian legislation is harmonisation-friendly, and it increases the practical level of consumer protection – a clause deemed unfair is a clause which the trader must automatically stop using. Other consumers affected by that clause in ongoing or future contracts can thus benefit from this protection. However, by leaving it up to Member States whether to provide for such implications or not, the Unfair Contract Terms Directive uncovers how weak of an effect it has in the uniform policing of unfair contract terms.

Still, in the light of the Convergence Index, the Unfair Contract Terms Directive seems to have scored poorly because of the features given to it by the European legislator, and not to so much because of transposition performances.

Secondly, and relating to what was just mentioned, from a national perspective Member States ranked overall better on the Unfair Contract Terms Directive than the Doorstep Selling Directive. While there have been problems with the transposition of open-ended norms (BE, FR, DE, NL) or with timely transposition (BE), it appears that Member States have more or less followed the

208 See for example Case C-168/05, *E.M. Mostaza Claro v Centro Movil Milenium* [2006] ECR I-10421; Liebscher 2008, p. 545; Case C-40/08, *Asturcom Telecommunicaciones SL v Cristina Rodríguez Nogueira* [2009] ECRI-9579, paras. 54–55; Ebers 2010b, p. 823.

209 See for instance Case C-169/14, *Juan Carlos Sánchez Morcillo and María del Carmen Abril García v Banco Bilbao Vizcaya Argentaria SA*; Case C-92/14, *Liliana Tudoran, Florin Iulian Tudoran, Ilie Tudoran v SC Suport Colect SRL*; Case C-280/13, *Barclays Bank SA v Sara Sánchez Garcia, Alejandro Chacón Barrera*; Case C-96/14, *Jean-Claude Van Hove v CNP Assurances SA*; Case C-110/14, *Horaţiu Ovidiu Costea v SC Volksbank România SA*; Case C-143/13, *Bogdan Matei and Ioana Ofelia Matei v SC Volksbank România SA*.

210 Comșa 2014, p. 108.

211 The amendments were first postponed until 1 July 2013 and subsequently until 1 October 2013; see also Dumitru 2012, p. 103.

policy direction of the Unfair Contract Terms Directive. This seems to contradict - at least from a legislative technique perspective - the literature available on the critiques brought to national transposition. For instance one of the most speculated upon divergences surrounding the implementation of the Unfair Contract Terms Directive - the UK and its good faith 'resistance'.[212]

Going back to doctrinal arguments, in a seminal decision delivered by Justice Mann in *Foxtons*, good faith does not seem to pose any problems. To the contrary, it is analysed not only in the light of the Unfair Terms in Consumer Contracts Regulations 1999, but also in the light of the Preamble of the Directive, in a way that individualises the European nature of the rules in the Regulations:

> 'That recital brings in the concept of good faith. This is an autonomous Community expression and has been elaborated in English authority as will in due course appear'.[213]

While the *Hoge Raad* as well as the *Bundesgerichtshof* might apply similar interpretational tools, it is important to notice that *Foxtons* is not a UK Supreme Court case, and yet Justice Mann delivers an impeccable interpretation of European consumer law. Simply put, Foxtons was brought to court in its quality of estate and letting agent by the Office of Fair Trading due to some of its standard terms relating to letting fees. In order to assess the fairness of these terms, good faith is discussed, and Justice Mann follows the line of argumentation developed by Lord Bingham in 2001 in *First National Bank*:

> 'The requirement of good faith in this context is one of fair and open dealing. Openness requires that the terms should be expressed fully, clearly, and legibly, containing no concealed pitfalls or traps. Appropriate prominence should be given to terms which might operate disadvantageously to the customer. Fair dealing requires that a supplier should not, whether deliberately or consciously, take advantage of the consumer's necessity, indigence, lack of experience, unfamiliarity with the subject matter of the contract, weak bargaining position or any other factor listed in or analogous to those listed in Schedule 2 to the Regulations. Good faith in this context is not an artificial or technical concept; nor, since Lord Mansfield was its champion, is it a concept wholly unfamiliar to British Lawyers. It looks to good standards of commercial morality and practice.'[214]

Discussing the role of good faith in English law goes beyond cases dealing with consumer contracts, as can be seen in the 2013 case of *Yam Seng Pte v International Trade Corporation Ltd*. In the words of Justice Leggatt:

212 Teubner 1998.

213 *The Office of Fair Trading v Foxtons Limited* [2009] EWHC 1681 (Ch), para. 18.

214 *Director-General of Fair Trading v First National Bank plc* [2002] 1 AC 481, para. 17; for a separate account given by Lord Bingham on matters dealing with good faith in English contract law, see also *Interfoto Picture Library Ltd v Stiletto Visual Programmes Ltd* [1989] 1 QB 433.

> 'In refusing, however, if indeed it does refuse, to recognise any such general obligation of good faith, this jurisdiction would appear to be swimming against the tide.'[215]

In summary, the UK was said to face problems with the implementation of a Directive asking its practitioners to use a seemingly foreign concept; and yet the UK adopted the Regulations 1999 and copy-pasted (among others) good faith into its statutory law. The subsequent development of consumer-specific case law such as *First National Bank* and *Foxtons* seems to indicate that regardless of the content of European consumer law, the UK legislator as well as UK courts take their harmonising role seriously. This perspective reflects the UK Convergence Index score for the Unfair Contract Terms Directive (6 out of 7).

However, the movements of the Convergence Index values points to a different problem when it comes to the UK and Ireland. Even with a very low directive score (Unfair Commercial Practices Directive), the overall values of the Convergence Index for the UK and Ireland are consistent, and in the case of the UK this value actually increased.[216] While the UK does not seem to be negatively impacted by the Unfair Commercial Practices Directive, this Member State has its own particularities. One of these particularities - and quite a pivotal one - deals with a different directive: the difficult accommodation of the Consumer Sales Directive to the system of already existing national remedies. Upon the transposition of the latter Directive by means of the Sale and Supply of Goods to Consumers Regulations 2002 by the UK legislator, concern was expressed in terms of the availability of remedies under the general rules for sale.[217] Keeping in mind the value attached to damages as a primary remedy in common law jurisdictions, the mere availability of a parallel regime might pose questions regarding the real ambit of the harmonisation process at national level. According to the Law Commission:

> 'Generally speaking, the Consumer Sales Directive remedies were inserted into SoGA as an additional layer of consumer protection, and there is little indication as to how the remedies are to interact'.[218]

215 *Yam Seng Pte v International Trade Corporation Ltd* [2013] EWHC 111 (QB), para. 124; Justice Leggatt acknowledges one of the classical cases quoted to prove the absence of a principle of good faith in English law, but addresses it with a caveat reflecting its factual circumstances: 'Another case sometimes cited for the proposition that English contract law does not recognise a duty of good faith is *Walford v Miles* [1992] 2 AC 128, where the House of Lords considered that a duty to negotiate in good faith is 'inherently repugnant to the adversarial position of the parties when involved in negotiations' and 'unworkable in practice' (per Lord Ackner at p. 138). That case was concerned, however, with the position of negotiating parties and not with the duties of parties who have entered into a contract and thereby undertaken obligations to each other', para. 122.

216 For the remaining Member States, even if national scores are high, the overall developments indicate a decrease in the Convergence Index values.

217 Watterson 2001, p. 219-220.

218 The Law Commission, 'Consumer Remedies For Faulty Goods', Cm 7725, SG/2009/Page 218, November 2009, para. 2.36; also, see the interpretation of the two-year period given in an →

How the existence of a parallel regime affects harmonisation cannot as such be reflected by the Convergence Index. However, there are several factors in the Convergence Index that can be further explained using views from literature. For instance, the UK did not transpose the Consumer Sales Directive in a timely manner. It can be argued this delay stems from an initial rejection of the Directive's consumer protection standard, which is said to be lower than the one provided for under UK law.[219] Although there were no timely implementation problems with respect to Ireland, similar issues with a parallel regime arise in this jurisdiction as well.[220]

3. Directives that make use of general clauses do not necessarily have a low convergence value

Some consumer directives tackle very specific areas of the law, in order to prevent a possible 'spill-over' effect and reduce the national legislator's legitimacy in governing contract law.[221] Examples in this respect are the Doorstep Selling Directive and the Distance Selling Directive.[222] However, several reforms in the process of Europeanising private law have led to rules of a much wider ambit, such as the Unfair Contract Terms Directive and Unfair Commercial Practices Directive. The general clauses reflected by these instruments set up tests for national courts to follow, and these tests come with benefits but also with complications. Firstly, the conditions included in these tests - for instance the unfairness tests in both the Unfair Contract Terms Directive and Unfair Commercial Practices Directive - depend on the circumstances of each individual case. Such an approach allows for a tailored application of the law - a penalty clause in a tenancy agreement will have inherent features and a specific context, making that clause different from an exclusive arbitration term in a credit agreement. A general clause will account for these features by way of flexibility. Secondly, it is precisely this flexibility that puts convergence into question.[223] Without further guidance, what is to say that Dutch fairness will be the same as Romanian or German fairness, even if the same conditions apply? The beauty of general clauses is however exactly what makes them unreliable in predicting the outcome of a case; such tests will always, to a certain extent, reflect the cultural, historical, social, economic or political roots of

information note prepared for the House of Commons: 'this requirement is not a two-year legal guarantee (although, rather confusingly, the Directive's title describes it as such); this is because goods are not legally required to last for those two years [...]', in 'The Sale and Supply of Goods to Consumers Regulations 2002 - is there a two years guarantee?', Standard Note, SN/HA/5235, December 2009.

219 Twigg-Flesner & Bradgate 2000.

220 Bird 2001, p. 279.

221 Klauer 2000, p. 190; also called 'spin-off effect' in Roth 2002, p. 770.

222 The same can be said for the Consumer Rights Directive, that brings together rules on distance and doorstep selling.

223 Danglehant 1995, p. 127.

law.[224] In Reich and Micklitz's words vis-à-vis the Unfair Contract Terms Directive, such a directive is a deliberate 'clear unclarity' or an 'unclear clarity'.[225]

This being said, general clauses have been coded in the Convergence Index to reflect a value of 0 when they are present in a directive (Article 3 Unfair Contract Terms Directive, Article 5 Unfair Commercial Practices Directive), and a value of 1 when they are absent. The underlying assumption is that general clauses are less likely to lead to convergence than rules with a more specific architecture. And yet, the scores obtained by the Unfair Contract Terms Directive and Unfair Commercial Practices Directive as the two directives making use of general clauses could not be more different. On the one hand, the Unfair Contract Terms Directive scored a mere 1 out of 7 for the European dimension of the Convergence Index, while the Unfair Commercial Practices Directive scored the most out of all directives, namely 4 out of 7. This difference seems to be explained by the additional pro-convergence features of the Unfair Commercial Practices Directive: it makes reference to self-regulation, it imposes a black list and it of course contains an 'internal market' clause establishing maximum harmonisation. These features are further discussed individually.

To start with, the reference to self-regulation as mentioned in Chapter 4 is presumed to be indicative of convergence for the mere fact that it 'nudges' Member States to take into account a potentially-coordinated bottom-up approach to harmonisation. Cases of codes of conduct governing commercial practices have been previously addressed.[226] Moreover, it must be acknowledged that there is a fine line between the qualification of commercial behaviour as a matter of unfair terms or a matter of unfair commercial practices.[227] It thus comes as no surprise that national bodies or agencies coordinating such codes for commercial practices may also have the legitimacy to tackle unfair contract terms. As such, self-regulation in the field of unfair contract terms has immense potential, because of what Cafaggi calls a 'standard-setting function':

> 'In relation to *standard setting*, [self-regulation] can often be an *agent of harmonisation* operating (1) outside of legislation in the realm of freedom of contract, or (2) as a complement of European legislation contributing to producing soft law instruments or (3) as a means of implementing European harmonising legislation in place of national legislation when there is formal delegation to private organisations.'[228]

Yet, even though Member States such as the UK have been using codes of conduct in the area of unfair contract terms ever since the 70's,[229] no reference to self-regulation is made in the Unfair Contract Terms Directive.

224 This perspective on law in context is what makes Legrand argue that European legal systems should value their distinctiveness rather than aim to converge their laws; see Legrand 2002, p. 63.

225 Micklitz & Reich 2014, p. 808.

226 See Chapter 3.

227 See Keirsbilck 2013a, p. 247.

228 Cafaggi 2007.

229 Hondius 1978, p. 532.

Second, the Unfair Commercial Practices Directive has a black list, whereas the Unfair Contract Terms Directive does not. The nature of the Unfair Contract Terms Directive list has been highly debated, since some authors call it a 'grey list',[230] while others disagree:

> '[...] an originally proposed 'black' and 'grey list' of incriminated terms was reduced to an 'indicative list' in the Annex, whose legal relevance remained deliberately unclear despite its rather detailed provisions (Article 3(3) and Annexes 1 and 2).'[231]

The lack of a clearly determined nature of the Unfair Contract Terms Directive list endangers the reaction national courts might have in applying the examples therein. In a Dutch case from 2012 dealing with an arbitration clause in a consumer contract, the *Hoge Raad* quashed a decision of the Leeuwarden Court of Appeals, on the ground that the latter had not considered the circumstances of the case and deemed the arbitration clause in question to be automatically unfair according to Article 6:236 BW.[232] This article reflects the choice of the Dutch legislator to actually transpose a black list in its legislation, together with a list of terms presumed to be unfair (Article 6:237 BW), which complicates matters even further. In the light of reasons such as the ones just expressed, calls for the transformation of the Unfair Contract Terms Directive Annex into more of an Unfair Commercial Practices Directive-like black list have been repeatedly made.[233]

Finally, the Unfair Contract Terms Directive is a minimum harmonisation directive, whereas the Unfair Commercial Practices Directive is maximum harmonisation. Ever since its adoption, the Unfair Contract Terms Directive was expected to disappoint business interests as well as consumer groups because of its minimum harmonisation character: '*Plus d'un seront déçus par la teneur de la directive*', Huet predicted as early as 1994.[234] In an attempt to describe the Unfair Contract Terms Directive more graphically, and in the light of its poor enforcement mechanisms, Micklitz and Reich call the Unfair Contract Terms Directive a 'toothless tiger'.[235] But how toothless is this tiger when it comes to legal convergence? As already seen, some Unfair Contract Terms Directive features (the grey/black list discussion for example) are interrelated with its minimum

230 Braucher 2013, p. 362.

231 Micklitz & Reich 2014, p. 773; Schulte-Nölke *et al.* 2008, p. 395. The Court of Justice held that '[t]he list thus offers the courts and other competent bodies, affected groups and individual consumers, sellers and suppliers - including those from another member state - a criterion for interpreting the expression unfair terms. Thus by giving concrete form to the open provision contained in Article3(1), that is to say, the first criterion for determining whether a contractual term is unfair, their certainty is reinforced', Case C-478/99, *Commission of the European Communities v Kingdom of Sweden* [2002] ECR I-04147, para. 29.

232 '[...] Het bestreden oordeel van het hof steunt niet op een waardering van de concrete omstandigheden van het geval maar plaatst als het ware het arbitrale beding op de zwarte lijst van Article 6:236 BW, en geeft derhalve blijk van een onjuiste rechtsopvatting [...]', HR 11/04598, 21 September 2012, para. 3.4.

233 Schulte-Nölke *et al.* 2008, p. 350.

234 Huet 1994, para. 1.309.

235 Micklitz & Reich 2014, p. 775.

harmonisation standard, and what results is an instrument with weak convergence power. The added perspective of the Convergence Index in this respect focuses on identifying these features (called factors in Chapter 4) and measuring them against one another in order to ask questions such as: what are the characteristics of a pro-convergence instrument? Since the answer to this question can be considered the corollary of the Convergence Index, it is dealt with in Chapter 4 (Conclusions and Recommendations).

Going back to the use of general clauses in directives, with some caveats, it can thus be claimed that using the general tests might not negatively affect the level of convergence as long as the instrument they belong to tries to balance the danger of legal uncertainty with other features.

4. Minimum harmonisation directives do not have a low convergence value

Three out of the four minimum harmonisation directives have been ranked as average convergence: these are the Doorstep Selling Directive, Distance Selling Directive and Consumer Sales Directive. They have all scored a 3 out of 7 on the European dimension of the Convergence Index. The pro-convergence features they share are the binding nature (law v policy), the fact that they do not make use general clauses and they have led to a very reduced volume of case law before the Court of Justice. On the negative side, they do not make use of black lists, neither do they include any reference to self-regulation and operate with minimum as opposed to maximum harmonisation. That the Unfair Contract Terms Directive has the lowest Convergence Index score has been established above and mainly reflects a rather unfortunate combination of factors impacting harmonisation: apart from its binding nature as a legal act of the EU, the Unfair Contract Terms Directive has nothing else to account for when it comes to coding the Index. However, the remaining three minimum harmonisation directives do not share the same outcome, which begs the question: how exactly are they different? To tackle this question, two arguments are explored in what follows: rule specificity versus general clauses, and the number of preliminary references before the CJEU.

To begin with, the Doorstep Selling Directive and the Distance Selling Directive are very similar in that they create well-determined rights and obligations: the withdrawal right and notification duties. Moreover, not only are these rules unambiguous, but their content can equally be expressed in numbers, as the Doorstep Selling Directive and the Distance Selling Directive both include a withdrawal right of seven working days. One could say that the instruction manual for how to transpose and apply these rules is considerably shorter than for the Unfair Contract Terms Directive. While some Member States had problems transposing even these very straight-forward rules (e.g. France used the notion of *'jours francs'*, which did not meet the minimum requirement), or other Member States chose to go beyond the minimum standard and thus varying the length of the rights (e.g. Germany had adopted a 14 day withdrawal right), specificity is a feature that facilitated harmonisation. Specific rights applicable to targeted fields (e.g. distance contracts) are easier to harmonise. It can be argued that as far as the Consumer Sales Directive is concerned, it does not necessarily have the same ambit as distance contracts, being applicable to a very wide variety of sales contracts and aiming at the change of national systems of remedies. However, even if one acknowledges the added complexity of the Consumer Sales Directive vis-à-vis the Doorstep Selling Directive or the Distance Selling Directive, this complexity is still rather specific: (i) the hierarchy of remedies is prescribed by the European legislator, and national implementations must reflect this choice; and (ii) while all remedies were recognised by national law even before the adoption of the Consumer Sales Directive (repair, replacement, termination and price reduction), the directive gives them a European dimension which goes beyond mere terminological connotations: just like the withdrawal right, reparation and replacement become European specific performance remedies. To illustrate the European nature of some substantive private law provisions, Schulze calls their implementations 'islands in a broad sea of Member States law'.[236] For these reasons, the Consumer Sales Directive is grouped together with the Doorstep Selling Directive and the Distance Selling Directive.

The exact opposite of rule specificity is the use of general clauses. This distinction is one of the lines drawn between the different Convergence scores of the Doorstep Selling Directive, Distance Selling Directive and Consumer Sales Directive, on the one hand, and the Unfair Contract Terms Directive on the other. As previously discussed under point 3 above, interpreting general clauses is prone to give rise to considerations that exist beyond the rules themselves.[237] Generel clauses have been accounted for in the Convergence Index.

The other example that makes a distinction between the various directives is the *number* of cases each has accumulated before the Court of Justice. Whereas the preliminary references that have as a ground either of the Doorstep Selling Directive, Distance Selling Directive or Consumer Sales Directive range from 4-8, the amount of cases based on the Unfair Contract Terms Directive is a staggering 45 and counting. The reasons why the Unfair Contract Terms Directive caseload has reached such a number are not mapped by literature yet. Some speculation has been put forward and deal mostly with the economical conditions in some Member States during or post-financial crisis.[238] The content of all these cases, as well as the role of the CJEU as a maker of private law have been thoroughly discussed by academics;[239] however more empirical research is necessary to understand the driving forces behind case load and harmonisation.

To summarise, what the Convergence Index adds to understanding convergence as promoted by minimum harmonisation directives is that rule specificity can make such directives achieve more convergence, even if it does not remove all the differences between the various Member States.

5. Member States with J-shaped distribution have similar transposition techniques

The Convergence Index is not designed to look beyond legislative transposition, due to the nature of its limitations. For this reason, the Index does not show the

236 Schulze 2005, p. 4.

237 See Chapter 3, p. 285.

238 Micklitz & Reich 2014, p. 806.

239 See for example Horsley 2013, p. 931; Keirsbilck 2013b, p. 1467; Micklitz & Reich 2014; Micklitz & Kas 2014.

wide picture of the Unfair Contract Terms Directive transposition in all Member States. However, among the objective observations that can be drawn, the following can be included: all Member States with the so-called 'J-shaped distribution' have similar transposition techniques. For these Member States, one common feature can be observed: the Unfair Contract Terms Directive is a convergence low. Moreover, with the exception of three situations (the Netherlands for Doorstep Selling, and Germany for Doorstep Selling and Unfair Commercial Practices), Germany and the Netherlands are the only Member States that have consistently transposed European consumer legislation into their national civil law provisions. This meant that other factors were affected as well, such as 'Novel concepts' and 'Open-ended concepts', the two substantive variables in this study. As national legislators tried to embed European law into national frameworks, a synchronisation process took place - European law became embedded in national law to the extent that it was absorbed by it. In the light of this process, national judges can thus not make distinctions between which rights are European in nature and which rights are national developments.

6. The Netherlands has the lowest scores out of all Member States

The Netherlands is the Member State with the lowest overall score for the Convergence Index. It scored the lowest for the Unfair Contract Terms Directive, and the Directive score itself was a 1.

Taking into account the reference to EU law in transposing laws, the Netherlands never managed to score anything but 0 on this factor. The main reason behind this is the fact that apart from the Doorstep Selling Directive, the Netherlands has only transposed European consumer rules into its own national Civil Code. In doing so, a national legislator limits the amount of information on the source of these rules which might be necessary to whoever consults the transposing provisions, whether a judge, a lawyer or a consumer.

Moreover, when it comes to late transposition, the Doorstep Selling, Unfair Commercial Practices and Distance Selling Directives were not transposed within the deadline; however only one infringement procedure was brought against the Netherlands by the Commission. When considering the substantive factors, the Netherlands did not do well with transposing novel concepts and open-ended terms (never maximum value). This could once again be put on the account of using the Civil Code as a source of consumer rights. Having to incorporate directives into an already existing and incredibly comprehensive private law context has proven to be detrimental to the goals of consumer law harmonisation. One example in this regard is the *Asbeek* judgment: while in the United Kingdom the Office of Fair Trading had elaborated guidelines for the application of the Unfair Contract Terms Directive in tenancy agreements, a Dutch court actually sent this question to the CJEU since it did not have sufficient information from the provisions in the Civil Code to answer this question.[240]

240 Case C-488/11, *Dirk Frederik Asbeek Brusse, Katarina de Man Garabito v Jahani BV* [2013], para. 22.

The very low values given to the Dutch versions of the Convergence Index are by no means indicative of the fact that the Netherlands is lagging behind in terms of consumer protection or that it has not done a good job keeping up with European standards of protection; what they do showcase however is that the seven factors inspired from the transposition process are vulnerable points for harmonisation as seen through the Dutch example.

6. Concluding Remarks over the Numerical Analysis

To sum up, this Chapter has been exclusively dedicated to the creation of the Convergence Index as an expression of numerical research in the field of European consumer law. The aim of the Chapter has been to complement the comparative analysis undertaken earlier in the study, and to that extent an overview of previous relevant quantitative work was made in Section 1. Building on Chapter 2, the numerical part of the research focused on designing and applying a method that would show to what extent convergence in consumer sales law exists. To meet this challenge, the Chapter first elaborated on the setup of the Convergence Index (Section 2), identifying its components: factors playing a role in the process of convergence. These factors were divided in two categories - European and national. In a nutshell, these factors are simply characteristics of the legislative transposition process as described in Chapter 2. In other words, the comparative analysis undertaken in Chapter 2 supported the opportunity of understanding what affects legal convergence: on the one hand, the nature of the instruments used for the adoption of European consumer rules or the design of such instruments could be mentioned, while on the other side, features such as the national transposition technique or the wording used in the transposition process are considered to play an important role. On the basis of the level of governance they occur at, a total of 13 factors were taken into account.

The factors were then coded into the Convergence Index as follows. The selected factors were given a value of either 0 or 1, with the exception of three factors (CJEU case law, reception of selected open norms, and reception of selected novel concepts) that received values between 0 and 1 and required normalisation, or in other words they needed to be made comparable to the other variables. The OECD Manual of Composite Indicators was the main source of inspiration for the design of the Index.

The Chapter then continued by gathering data from the five directives, by showing step by step how the selected transposing provisions from the seven Member States were analysed with a view to coding (Section 3). The results were then shown in the form of tables with values given to each factor, as well as graphs displaying both the European as well as the national levels of the Convergence Index (Section 4). Moreover, Section 5 elaborated on what new perspectives over convergence can be discovered by using the Index, and to this end screenshots of a Google Motion Chart were further added. The findings discussed in the same section touched upon the clustering of Directives and/or Member States according to the respective Convergence Index values.

Given that the selected Directives range between 1985 and 2005, the Convergence Index values occurring with the occasion of the entry into force of these instruments lead to an ascending trend on the basis of which it can be mentioned that convergence in European consumer law - as defined and interpreted by this study - is somewhat on the rise. However, one of the most important findings - a point that has not been proved in this manner before - is that the increase is actually not that significant.

It has also been observed that the five Directives in this research can be clustered in three categories: low, average or high convergence. While the Unfair Contract Terms Directive has the lowest convergence value, the Distance Selling and Doorstep Selling Directives as well as the Consumer Sales Directive have the same middle values. What is more, the Unfair Commercial Practices Directive scored the highest on the selected factors. The novelty of this classification stems from the fact that until now the content of these Directives had solely been discussed by describing certain characteristics (e.g. minimum/maximum harmonisation; the hierarchy of remedies; etc.), while comparing their convergence values shows a more complete picture. This is especially the case as the convergence values can be interpreted in the light of the European dimension of the Index: what makes Directives convergence-friendly? In a nutshell, a Directive with a high convergence value should be a maximum harmonisation instrument that makes reference to self-regulation, does not use general clauses, and creates uniform practices by using the so-called black lists.

Moving to Member States, the Convergence Index once again created a visual classification of how the selected Member States scored on the factors making up the Index: Ireland and the UK have the highest values, closely followed by Germany and Romania, in turn followed by France and Belgium. The Netherlands lagged behind and scored the lowest value out of all the Member States included in the research.

Member State performance reflects two important aspects: on the one hand, the formal choices of the national legislator in transposing the Directive (e.g. transposition deadlines and techniques or reference to EU law in end legislation), as well as substantive choices dealing with the actual content of the rules (e.g. the reception of novel concepts or the reception of open-ended norms). Keeping these two aspects in mind when analysing the resulting values of the Convergence Index can lead to conclusions that are not exclusively related to the political process of adopting implementing measures; the substantive transposition of the rules ends up being reflected in the Index as well, albeit to a lesser extent.

In addressing individual Member State findings, one clarification must be made. The Netherlands might be a low-score outlier, but all in all, the convergence values of the remaining six Member States do not lead to greatly different outcomes. This might be explained by the fact that with certain exceptions, Member States accommodate European legislation rather similarly. However, it might equally be the case that the current factors forming the Convergence Index are not enough to explain the particularities of each jurisdiction as they do not take into account the actual implementation (e.g. case law, national market practices, etc.).

Whether or not it may be said that common law systems have reacted more positively to harmonisation, is a question that the Convergence Index cannot fully answer. Some intuitive explanations might include the following ideas: (i) only civil law countries were brought before the Court of Justice in infringement procedures; (ii) with the exception of Romania, a well-known copy-paste Member State, none of the other civil law Member States managed to get the full score for the open-ended norms factor. Then again, there might be more value to the copy-paste transposition than substantive literature gives credit for. All Member States who adopted this approach for the Unfair Contract Terms Directive (Ireland, Romania, United Kingdom) scored high on the Convergence Index overall.

As far as the United Kingdom is concerned, its rather high score on the Unfair Contract Terms Directive might be coincidental. As it has been extensively shown by the Law Commission and the Scottish Law Commission, the adoption of Regulations that transposed the Unfair Contract Terms Directive in parallel with the already existing regime of the Unfair Contract Terms Act 1977 created a lot of confusion in UK law. Although the legal system was as such very familiar with the policing of unfair terms by courts, not only in B2C contracts but also in some B2B circumstances, the different terminology and sometimes conflicting rules did not make it easy for the accommodation of European consumer law.[241] However, apart from the limited practical considerations presented in the consultation paper, the Law Commissions fail to make a clear overview of the implications the overlap might have. Moreover, the Bill proposed in the light of this study goes well beyond discussing the overlapping regimes, as it is concerned with reforming consumer unfair terms in a broader (and substantive) sense that goes well beyond what the Directive envisaged.

The values of the six selected factors for the national dimension of the Index, show that certain Member States can indeed be grouped or they manage to set themselves apart from the rest of the countries. Examples in this respect are the UK and Ireland, who managed to obtain the maximum Convergence Index values. It so happens that both jurisdictions also preferred transposing the copy-pasted version of the Directives, which comes with the risk of not really accommodating the European rules into national practice, but rather ticking the transposition box in a way that might lead to the creation of parallel national regimes (EU law rights separate from common law rights). Interestingly, Romania happens to favour copy-paste transposition as well. In the light of this fact, one could say that the Index does not really reflect the reality of how law functions nationally, but it is only a measure of superficial and biased indicators. However, even if Member States transpose Directives in a literal manner to simply comply with their obligations under EU law, the effect of such technique must not be undermined. When English law opened itself to the inclusion of the requirement of good faith in the light of the Unfair Contract Terms Directive, it took over this concept into its national system. In doing

241 The Law Commission and the Scottish Law Commission, 'Unfair Terms in Contracts – Report on a reference under section 3(1)(e) of the Law Commissions Act 1965' (LAW COM No 292/SCOT LAW COM No 199).

so, any judge faced with an unfair contract terms claim on the basis of the transposing regulations would have to analyse and apply the general test using good faith. All in all, even what can be considered as effortless transposition - as copy-pasting a Directive would not necessarily entail a lengthy bill-drafting process - can be said to have a significant impact over the legal system as a whole.

As for the very low convergence value scored by the Netherlands, the observations showed that the reasons for this are mixed. Firstly, the Dutch legislator has taken a rather consistent approach (with the exception of the Doorstep Selling Directive) of transposing its consumer laws in the Civil Code. While this might be considered as a sign of integrating European law into national law as opposed to creating parallel regimes, this approach entails leaving out many of the rules that need to be transposed. An example in this respect can be the *contra proferentem* rule eventually added to book 6. The Dutch Civil Code and the case law based on it already developed rules on the interpretation of contracts that could be considered the equivalent of the *contra proferentem* rule in consumer law. However, not explicitly transposing such a rule has led to a situation where the Dutch legislator becomes selective with transposing the rules it is obliged to integrate in the national legal system. In one form or another, all national jurisdictions recognise interpretation rules that the consumer might make use of even outside the ambit of the specific rules reflecting the transposition of the Unfair Contract Terms Directive. Nevertheless, giving Member States the discretion of not transposing such rules just because they can be completed with Civil Code provisions renders the adoption of directives useless. And transposing rules in the Civil Code seems to raise these issues much more than if the same rules are transposed in separate legislation.

Secondly, linked to the first argument, the Netherlands has made specific substantive choices when transposing the provisions of the selected directives. One example in this respect is the general test of unfair terms. Not only does it lack the requirement of good faith from the same reason as mentioned above - namely because the Civil Code actually covers the principle of reasonableness and fairness separately - but the test itself lacks the criteria as they are mentioned in the Unfair Contract Terms Directive. Moreover, complications arose also when looking at the transposition of the hierarchy of remedies under the Consumer Sales Directive, as well as for the notion of right of return (also known as a withdrawal right) as entailed by the Doorstep Selling Directive.

In summary, the findings presented in Section 5 aimed at using data visualisation in order to discover new points of view that would further the understanding of how convergence works in the field of European consumer sales law. To this end, it can be stated that Chapter 3 is a 'data' image of Chapter 2. While the analysis in this Section focused on the use of the Google Motion Graph, given the impossibility to integrate multimedia features in a book, further resources are made available. The video format of the Google Motion Graph is currently hosted on iconsume.eu.

In what follows, Chapter 4 draws the overall conclusions relating to this study, and sets forth recommendations for the European and national legislator as well as for other stakeholders.

Chapter 4

CONCLUSIONS AND RECOMMENDATIONS

1. General Conclusions

This study aimed to bring a fresh contribution to the already-existing debate surrounding European consumer contract law. It did so by directing the discussion on two different paths - a comparative substantive overview and a mirroring numerical analysis. Three methodological conclusions can be mentioned in the light of this effort, and they are presented in what follows.

(i) Identifying a gap in the present discussion about the harmonisation of European consumer law

Firstly, as highlighted in Chapter 1, the harmonisation discussion is by no means novel. An ever-growing body of literature proves an increased interest in the field of European contract law, or more specifically, European consumer law. Recent developments such as the adoption of the Consumer Rights Directive or the withdrawal of the CESL announce thought-provoking times for contract lawyers. However, the nature of consumer contract law in itself, as well as the ever-growing body of knowledge that disseminates it, create a highly complex field that becomes more and more difficult to grasp in its entirety.

Moreover, while many authors venture into analysing specific Directives or national legal regimes, the attention paid to comprehensively studying the legal convergence arising from European consumer developments is not directly proportionate. Little attention is paid to the *extent* to which harmonisation, as a specific policy pursued by the European Commission leads to legal convergence as the effect of this policy. What is more, it is safe to say that to date, with the exception of the Convergence Index included in this study, no measurement tool has been developed to quantitatively assess this extent. For this reason, a gap has been identified in the harmonisation debate as it currently stands.

(ii) Filling the gap by developing a self-standing method

Secondly, the present study aims to fill the aforementioned gap. By developing a methodology that helps establish whether and to what extent there is convergence of laws in the field of European consumer contract law, this study wishes to further the academic and policy debates on the effects of European legislative design.

This novel method stands between two disciplines - law and statistics - and it is composed of two mirroring parts, the substantive comparison and the numerical analysis. The first is a classical expression of legal academic work: an overview of rules, their ambit and rationale and more importantly their interpretation. The second part is a numerical analysis leading to a composite indicator created according to an OECD manual. Taken together, these two parts give rise to a *sui-generis* method of assessing legal convergence as it results from the process of harmonisation. Furthermore, the structure and content of each of these two parts have been designed in the light of the overarching convergence theme, which adds another novel dimension to the analysis.

All in all, this method aims to trigger more interest for the quantification of legal convergence, by proving that, even with some inherent limitations, legal convergence *can* be measured.

(iii) Applying this method to a part of the consumer acquis

Lastly, another conclusion that can be drawn with respect to this study deals with what this methodology may lead to when applied. Beyond the very development of this method of measuring legal convergence, applying it as such can prove its potential. For instance, being able to visualise how Member States perform on a scale that entails the same criteria leads to a wider understanding of legal convergence in general and of consumer law in particular. What is more, the application of this method allowed for a clear distinction between European and national levels of convergence. Especially if looking at the Convergence Index values calculated for directives, the way in which the methodology was drafted allows for a demarcation between the features of the European legislative process and the subsequent transposition in national law. In other words, the Convergence Index can show the performance of the European instrument, the performance of the national legal system, but also the resulting overall level of convergence.

I called the three points examined above 'methodological conclusions' because they mostly focus on how the comparative and numerical analyses have fulfilled the aim of complementing existing research in the field of European consumer law. At the same time, more concrete conclusions can be drawn on the basis of the research questions asked in Chapter 1, presented below once more.

1. What are the standards of convergence behind the rules on consumer sales developed by the European legislator and how has the Court of Justice interpreted these standards?

Five directives (Doorstep Selling, Unfair Terms, Distance Selling, Consumer Sales and Unfair Practices) were selected for this study on the basis of their scope that reflected consumer sales law. While two of these instruments (Doorstep Selling and Distance Selling) have been repealed by the Consumer Rights Directive, they were included in the study because of the decades of influence already exercised over national regimes seeking to accommodate the concept of a cooling off period in consumer sales. Four of the instruments in this study promoted minimum harmonisation, while the most recent one (the Unfair Practices Directive) focused on targeted full harmonisation.

To begin with, it can be noted that the Doorstep Selling, Distance Selling and Consumer Sales Directive bear certain resemblances, not only if considered in the light of the literature review, but also on the basis of the findings in the numerical part of the analysis. All three Directives are rather brief, impose quite clear standards and while they might have specific grey areas (e.g. the nature of the right of withdrawal is not specified; the proportionality test in first-tier remedies may lead to complicated practical applications, etc.), the case law of the Court of Justice does not seem to indicate very complex concerns regarding the intricacies of these rules.

Not the same can be stated when looking at the remaining two Directives: Unfair Terms and Unfair Practices. The recent increase in preliminary references based on the Unfair Contract Terms Directive is definitely a cause for concern. In this study, it was assumed that the more case law exists on a given topic, the less likely it is that the instrument on which it is based would lead to convergence. Whether the reader agrees with this assumption or not, facts speak for themselves. A Directive dating from 1993 and leading to over 45 cases (and increasing) within the 20 years[1] it has been in force for is clearly somehow not understood by the national judges who continue to send preliminary questions to the Court of Justice. Literature echoes this concern.[2] As the Directive that includes a good faith test, the Unfair Contract Terms Directive has been under the constant attack of not being able to offer legal certainty. While legal certainty was indeed not part of this study as such, it was interesting to look at this Directive as well as the other four and envisage them as a sum of the factors behind the Convergence Index. Deconstructing each Directive and understanding its forming characteristics was very valuable for the development of the methodology. For instance, while the Unfair Commercial Practices Directive was praised (and feared) for its maximum harmonisation orientation, the Convergence Index factors emphasise that its unifying potential might come from other sources as well, such as the existence of a black list, or the reference to self-regulation.

Often different in scope and wording, the five directives do have a major concern in common: the problem that not even one of them sets rules comprehensive enough to be applied independently from national legal rules. In other words, the political compromise reached by the European legislator at the point of adoption left many gaps to be filled through interpretation. For doorstep and distance selling the nature and effect of the right to withdraw (or the cancellation right, as it is called in the Doorstep Selling Directive) are not explicitly mentioned, while for the Unfair Contract Terms open-ended norms like reasonableness or good faith receive no definition. These are just some examples of how the piecemeal approach to harmonisation consumer law works.[3]

The arguments tackled above shape the answer to the question on what standards of convergence were set by the European legislator. In brief, on the basis

1 This leads to an average of 2,25 cases per year.
2 Micklitz & Reich 2014.
3 COM(2001) 398 final.

of what has been examined in this study, these standards are often incomplete, due to the lack of a comprehensive framework of consumer law,[4] and they heavily rely on interpretation by the Court of Justice. However, it must be stated that the policy trend which can be noticed already with the adoption of the Unfair Commercial Practices Directive, and continued for instance with the Consumer Rights Directive, is to develop a more targeted harmonisation approach. This approach has two characteristics: it imposes a high standard of consumer protection when it comes to specific topics, and it constrains Member States to adopt it in a uniform manner.

2. *How did national legislators transpose these rules, and what issues arose from their transposition?*
Overall, this question has been dealt with in the comparative analysis, where the national legislation of the seven Member States in question (Belgium, France, Germany, Ireland, the Netherlands, Romania, and the United Kingdom) was closely scrutinised in order to understand how European rules have been accommodated. This effort took the shape of small-scale country reports. The small-scale characteristic stems from the fact that for each of the five directives, several provisions were selected:

- Doorstep Selling: Article 5;
- Unfair Contract Terms: Articles 3-7;
- Distance Selling: Articles 4, 6 and 7;
- Consumer Sales: Articles 2-3 and 5-6;
- Unfair Commercial Practices: Articles 5-9 and 10-11.

This approach was preferred to the overall discussion of the directives as it targets, in my view, what the five directives aim to achieve. As was said above, each of these instruments has gaps making their overall discussion a challenging endeavour. Moreover, as the substantive comparison in Chapter 2 looked not only at European rules, but also at their transposition in the selected national legal systems, working with selected provisions as opposed to entire directives made this effort possible; having full country reports on each of the five directives for each of the seven Member States would have made this study overly ambitious.

Member States accommodated European consumer rules in satellite legislation, consumer codes and civil codes. Since Directives do not need to be

[4] To clarify this claim it is necessary to refer to the new Proposal on on certain aspects concerning contracts for the online and other distance sales of goods (COM(2015) 635 final). While the Consumer Sales Directive is the current source of rules governing lack of conformity arising out of consumer transactions that are concluded at a distance, the said proposal wishes to distinguish two regimes: the regular face-to-face transactions would still be governed by the 1999 Directive, while the online/distance transactions would be taken over by the proposed directive. Not only are there substantive differences between the directive in force and the proposed instrument, but the first is a minimum harmonisation directive, while the latter endorses maximum harmonisation. What this would lead to in practice is even more confusion regarding the applicable rules, as Europe's top retailers operate online platforms besides the regular business premise model.

transposed *ad literam*, Member States (e.g. Germany and the Netherlands) often altered the wording of the transposing rules, to the extent that some European content was filtered out. This seldom led to infringement procedures (e.g. Belgium and the Netherlands), given the highly political nature of this action. However, the lack of infringement procedures does not entail that a given national transposition process is directive-proof (e.g. the initial failure to integrate a definition of 'consumer' in French law). Another aspect that Member States have taken with a great deal of discretion has been the timely transposition issue. For example, Ireland was the only Member State that transposed the Unfair Commercial Practice Directive within the June 2007 deadline set by the European legislator.

These choices shape how national lawmakers relate to harmonisation. Whether it is political resistance aimed at preserving the particularities of a national legal system (e.g. in those jurisdictions where comprehensive legal reforms took place, such as Germany or the Netherlands), or lack of experience with managing what has already been called the piecemeal harmonisation approach (e.g. Romania), the comparative analysis showed how some Member States use whatever discretion they can to influence the transposition process. However, the analysis also showed that many Member States often try to balance European and national interests in adhering to common standards.

3. How can the resulting convergence process be measured?

With regard to the third question, by analysing the Directives this study explored what factors lead to convergence, and showed that the overall performance of a Directive reflects not just one feature, but the interaction of multiple characteristics it may have as a legal instrument.

The 13 selected factors that influence harmonisation, or as they have been called before 'convergence markers', can be found at European level as well as national level:

- *European level*: (a) Law v policy; (b) Type of European instrument (Directive/-Regulation); (c) Nature of policy (minimum/maximum harmonisation); (d) Reference to self-regulation; (e) General clause; (f) Black list; (g) CJEU case law;
- *National level*: (a) National transposition technique; (b) Reception of selected novel concepts; (c) Reception of selected open-ended norms; (d) Reference to European law in end legislation; (e) Timely transposition (date of national legislation); (f) Infringement procedures.

These factors were first explained and defined within a very clear ambit. This ambit has been the context the Convergence Index needs for accuracy purposes. For this reason, any claims or suggestions made disregarding this context or outside of this context, are detrimental to the overall value that the Convergence Index has for the harmonisation debate.

Many observations were made on the basis of the visualisation resulting out of the charts and Google Graphs. An example of the type of conclusions drawn in this respect refers to transposition technique. Countries like Germany and the Netherlands, which consistently opted for the transposition of European consumer law in their national Civil Codes, have a poor overall Convergence Index performance. It is the way in which the convergence factors interact that leads to the final value. This being said, it has been speculated already that by using such legislative preferences, some Member States fail to fully transpose European rules. To give flesh to this argument, the good faith example can be recalled. If Germany or the Netherlands do not integrate a good faith test in the transposition of Article 3 of the Unfair Contract Terms Directive in their Civil Codes, commentators may say that no fowl has been done, as both Civil Codes already contain provisions dealing exclusively with *Treu und Glauben* or *redelijkheid en billijkheid*. However, this can be said for all other continental Member States (and to a certain extend about a functional equivalent at common law), regardless of where they choose to transpose European rules - certain general contractual principles and provisions will always complement consumer law. Still, this in itself is not a reason why Member States should make transposing legislation even more difficult to combine; certain European legislative acts are complicated in themselves, even when taken *ad literam* - complicating transposing legislation as well can undoubtedly well affect the desired harmonisation policy.

Overall, the observations arising out of visualizing the performances of the Convergence Index were classified under several headings as indicated below.

1. In general, and as defined by the factors shaping the Convergence Index, national consumer legislation is converging.
2. The transposition of the Unfair Contract Terms Directive marks a decline in convergence values.
3. Directives that make use of general clauses do not necessarily have a low convergence value.
4. Minimum harmonisation directives do not have a low convergence value.
5. Member States with J-shaped distribution have similar transposition techniques.
6. The Netherlands has the lowest scores out of all Member States.

These headings were addressed one by one, and the specific values of the Convergence Index were used to explain these findings.

So far, an attempt was made to outline the goals of this study and how they have been fulfilled. This was done so by first identifying an overall methodological outcome, and then subsequently providing an answer to three research questions posed in Chapter 1. Section 2 of this Chapter aims to offer an answer to the remaining research question: *Which policy recommendations follow from this for the European and national legislators, as well as other institutions?*

2. Policy Recommendations

2.1. *General Remarks*

So far, Section 1 of this Chapter addressed the overall conclusions drawn on the basis of this study. This Section builds on these conclusions outside of the context of the present research, with the aim of developing recommendations for the European lawmaker (Section 1.1), national lawmakers (Section 1.2) and other stakeholders (Section 1.3).

Before delving into the first of the aforementioned categories, a word on the desirability of convergence. All in all, Chapter 2 (the comparative analysis) looked at 35 national transposition measures of five directives into seven Member States, and Chapter 3 (the numerical analysis) explained the construction of the Convergence Index. These core parts of the research focused on identifying and applying factors deemed to be relevant for the process of convergence in European consumer sales law. As already mentioned in Chapter 1, the European Union has been promoting harmonisation as a policy and legislative technique as early as 1985. For this reason, any recommendation addressed to the European legislator must focus on identifying ways in which convergence can be enhanced. The same can be said about the national legislator, as Member States are under a Treaty obligation to transpose directives. Still, this is not to say that the following recommendations reflect the author's choice on whether convergence is desirable, but they highlight the factors that may lead to convergence, should this be a policy goal either at European or national level.

2.2. *Recommendations for the European Institutions*

Recommendation 1: The creation of a composite index by the EU (similar with or developed on the basis of the Convergence Index) to measure the extent of convergence in consumer sales law or any other field relating to consumer law.

As highlighted just above, the interest of the European legislator (and more directly of the European Commission) is to promote harmonisation, namely to make national laws of Member States become more similar. It has been emphasised throughout this study that the converging effect of harmonisation is influenced by various factors.[5] In Chapter 2, for methodological purposes, a distinction was even made between the 13 factors taken into consideration for the numerical analysis, and other factors that could still affect the impact of harmonising policies, albeit indirectly. This distinction is revisited in what follows.

To start with the first category, it must be acknowledged that the development of a composite index measuring the convergence effect of harmonisation has entailed a process of identifying the characteristics (or factors, as they have been called in this research) of the directive-based harmonisation policy created by the

5 See Chapter 3, p. 164.

European legislator. To do so, Chapter 2 has served as a concise description of how this policy was enacted in seven Member States with respect to five consumer law directives. This endeavour has implied a reflection on how the said characteristics of harmonisation could potentially lead to a higher degree of convergence. The assessment of what leads to more convergence has relied on a series of assumption, which the numerical analysis is dependent on.

When it comes to the European dimension of the factors affecting convergence, one important point must be acknowledged. The five European instruments included in this study are all directives. This is not to say, however, that the factors do not apply to regulations as well.[6] A regulation would have default maximum scores on most of the factors accounted for by the Convergence Index,[7] with the exception of: 'Reference to self-regulation'; 'General clause'; 'Black list'; 'CJEU case law'. To illustrative this, one could try to imagine the converging effect of the Unfair Contract Terms Directive had it been a regulation. Even with no transposition issues, national judges would still find it difficult to apply a test which might be considered as vague, namely to evaluate the very unfairness of a term. The lack of confidence in national interpretation could then be reflected, just as it is currently seen with this Directive, in a high number of cases before the Court of Justice. Confusion can be partially avoided by giving more guidance, in the form of examples when unfair terms are to always be considered unfair, in other words a black list. Moreover, a regulation that makes reference to, for instance, codes of conduct, could have a more consistent harmonizing impact.[8] A regulation including all the above characteristics would lead to maximum Convergence Index values (13 out of 13).

To this end, the European Union could very well replace directive-based harmonisation with the adoption of regulations.[9] However, as it may be speculated after the withdrawal of the Common European Sales Law, the political consensus

6 The factor called 'Type of European instrument' has been put forward under the assumption that a regulation leads to more convergence than a directive. There might be concerns that while this is technically accurate (e.g. regulations need not be transposed; it is clearer that they are directly applicable together with national law; Member States have no discretion in filtering the content of regulations; etc.), directives do bring about *some* convergence. This is indeed true, and in my opinion this occurs because directives are, after all, binding on Member States. The bindingness of directives is exactly what is considered under the factor 'Law v policy'.

7 A regulation would be conducive to convergence by default (a maximum value of 1 per each factor) when it comes to the following factors: 'Law v policy'; 'Type of European instrument (Directive/Regulation)'; 'Nature of policy (minimum/maximum harmonisation'; 'National transposition technique'; 'Reception of selected novel concepts'; 'Reception of selected open-ended norms'; 'Reference to European law in end legislation'; 'Timely transposition (date of national legislation)'; 'Correct transposition (infringement procedures resulting in CJEU decisions - excluding timely transposition issues)'.

8 Take for instance the example of a delegated act promoting main principles in the field of European structural and investment funds, Commision Delegated Regulation (EU) No 240/2014 of 7 January 2014 on the European code of conduct on partnership in the framework of the European Structural and Investment Funds, *OJ* L74/1 of 14 March 2014.

9 This idea had been endorsed before by academics, see Twigg-Flesner 2011.

that would be necessary for the promotion of such an instrument in the field of consumer law makes it an unfeasible option for the time being.[10]

In this context, how can a Directive lead to a similarly high score in terms of the Convergence Index?[11] In other words, if convergence is indeed the desired effect, how should a directive look like, and how should it be transposed?

The considerations mentioned above for regulations stand true for directives as well, as the four factors ('Reference to self-regulation'; 'General clause'; 'Black list'; 'CJEU case law') underline the content of the instrument rather than its form. In addition to that, the specific nature of policy, namely minimum or maximum harmonisation can have a different impact on the resulting convergence effect. The Unfair Contract Terms and the Unfair Commercial Practices Directives showcase this point rather well. In the case of the first, the Annex contains terms the unfairness of which still needs to be tested by courts; whereas for the second, the Annex blacklists terms that are unfair in any circumstance. Under minimum harmonisation, the transposition of the annex belonging to the Unfair Contract Terms Directive led to diverging approaches.[12] In the case of the Unfair Commercial Practices Directive, maximum harmonisation led to the obligation of blacklisting the terms in the annex by all Member States, a policy development meant to contribute to legal certainty.[13]

Moving on to how Member States choose to transpose a Directive, two points can be distinguished. First, when it comes to formal considerations, such as how and when transposing legislation is adopted, Member States must consider that they have a Treaty obligation of adopting legislation in a timely manner, as well as of adopting legislation that matches the provisions of a given directive (factors 'Timely transposition' and 'Infringement procedures').[14] Moreover, this legislation needs to preserve the European identity and goals of the provisions in a directive. To this end, transposing European rules in a civil code jeopardises the process; not

10 For a thorough analysis of the CESL and its future, see Rafał Mańko, 'Contract law and the Digital Single Market: Towards a New Online Consumer Sales Law?', European Parliamentary Research Service, September 2015.

11 It must be noted that in the light of the brief remarks in footnote 944, a Member State can only achieve a maximum of 12 out of 13 when the Convergence Index measures the transposition of a directive.

12 Rafał Mańko mentions that some Member States have a list of terms always considered unfair (Austria), some others have a so-called 'grey' list with terms presumed to be unfair, but the presumption may be rebutted (Poland), some have both a 'grey' and a 'black' list (Germany, the Netherlands), and some other Member States use the annex as an indicative list without establishing any presumptions (France); see Rafał Mańko, 'Unfair contract terms in EU law', European Parliamentary Library Briefing, September 2013, p. 3.

13 Namysłowska 2016, p. 67.

14 In 2015, in a case regarding Directives 93/104/EC and 2003/88/EC, the Dutch Supreme Court ruled for the first time on the matter of the State being liable for issuing national statutes that are not in line with European law. The Court established that introducing such rules could constitute a tort under national law. See HR 14/00189, 18 September 2015. This constitutes a departure from earlier situations in which the Dutch Supreme Court refused to apply the European rules and instead upheld the conflicting national provisions. See Conant 2002, p. 57.

only will these rules be independent from their source for the interpreters of the law ('Reference to European law in end legislation)', but they will also be synchronised with the existing web of rules in a given national legal system. While it could be argued that as such, this does not affect convergence, a mere reading of the Dutch civil code, or of the German civil code proves the opposite – terminology is one of the markers of this synchronisation. Second, two factors ('Reception of selected novel concepts' and 'Reception of selected open-ended norms') accounted for the substantive converging effect. In the case of novel concepts, or in other words concepts that have their self-standing European meaning (e.g. the withdrawal rights imposed by the Distance Selling Directive), discrepancies in terminology might cast doubts in terms of how these concepts may be applied. The same can be said for open-ended norms, which are already rather difficult to grasp. As there is no one-size-fits-all 'European good faith', references to 'good faith' in consumer sales law are bound to be interpreted in the light of the very specific instruments they are embedded in. Using a civil code's notion of 'good faith' fails to take this consideration into account.

With all of the above in mind, Recommendation 1 deals with creating a composite index similar to or based on the Convergence Index, as it could serve multiple goals including:

a) Research orientation – to determine the strengths and weaknesses of certain consumer instruments and their transpositions in order to further improve existing and future legislative initiatives;
b) Policy orientation – to provide further empirical evidence of the effect of legislative measures in various consumer fields during regulatory impact assessment processes;
c) Practice orientation – to rank the performances of Member States in order to communicate the effects of legislative developments more transparently to businesses and consumers.

While it might be hard to argue with the feasibility of the first two points, criticism may arise out of the idea that a EU-driven Convergence Index should aim at evaluating/scoring Member States, thereby potentially creating a situation of external pressure. To answer this concern it must be stated that the European Union would not be the first international organisation to engage in such an approach. The well-known 'Doing Business' report series issued every year by the World Bank focuses on comparing how different jurisdictions perform when assessed on the basis of given indicators.[15] Thus alternatively to Recommendation 1, Recommendation 3 proposes the development of a composite index by private actors.

The discussion above has so far focused on the factors that were included in the Convergence Index. As indicated earlier in this study, these are only a handful

15 See the yearly reports of the World Bank on the website of the Doing Business project: <www.doingbusiness.org/reports>, last accessed on 27 July 2016.

of characteristics of the harmonisation process that focus specifically on the transposition However, beyond transposition lies application, namely the actual implementation of European law, and it is here that other factors influencing the convergence process can be identified. A potential European Convergence Index could in principle cover a much broader array of factors. A brief list was made in this respect in Chapter 3: national legal culture and history (the legal cultural background of a given legal system); consumer empowerment (consumers being aware of their rights); consumer preferences (whether consumers support more or less protection, for more or less expensive goods and services); the number of cases per judge (determining whether case overloads can lead to less awareness of the European nature of a rule, or if it is a sign of resilience to harmonisation by private actors not complying with European standards); judge trainings (judge awareness of European law developments and applicability in own court); the number of lawyers specialised in European law in relation to the total number of lawyers (practitioner awareness regarding European law developments which can be brought before judges in national disputes). Including indices that would reflect such matters can further consolidate a legal measurement tool such as the Convergence Index.

Lastly under the heading of 'Recommendations for the European institutions', the role of the Court of Justice must be acknowledged. The Court has been called on many occasions a creator of European private law,[16] and the specific case law discussions covered in Chapter 2 stand to show that the Court has a lot of discretion in the interpretation of European law. It can thus be safely said that the CJEU impacts, one way or another, the process of legal convergence. For the purposes of this study, the focus was on trends that had been already highlighted in academic literature, such as the increase in preliminary references based on the Unfair Contract Terms Directive,[17] assuming that the more case law a directive generates, the less clear its application is, which in turn can affect legal convergence.

Generally, literature reviews of CJEU case law focus on the detailed interpretation of individual court rulings; this is a necessary step in the direction of understanding how the Court constantly develops European private law. However, looking at all the cases ruled on the basis of a specific directive, there is much more to observe, namely:

- Which are the Members States with courts that ask most questions?
- What is the total number of preliminary reference requests per directive?
- Are these numbers consistent across all consumer law directives, or do they fluctuate?
- Can the outcomes of the cases be measured in any way in order to outline eventual trends in the Court's interpretation?

16 See for instance Rafał Mańko, 'Methods for unifying private law in the EU', European Parliamentary Research Service, January 2014, p. 5.

17 Micklitz & Reich 2014.

Answering the questions above can bring a solid contribution to the understanding of harmonisation and the role the Court plays in this respect. For instance, if the total number of cases fluctuates in certain directives, it might be a sign that the directives in question have posed serious interpretation issues before national courts, deterring them from acting as EU courts. In the same vein, if compared to some of the other factors, as well as with the qualitative part of this research, looking at which Member States send the most preliminary questions might be a sign of how national courts add to the harmonisation of a system resisting EU influences. This being said, further research is necessary to understand *how* exactly the Court of Justice affects convergence and upholds harmonisation.[18]

2.3. *Recommendations for National Institutions*

Recommendation 2: The creation by national legislators of a National Transposition Guideline focused on the converging effect of European legislation. The National Transposition Guideline would be destined not only to national lawmakers themselves, but also to practitioners as well as to other stakeholders.

To increase the efficiency of legislative transposition, Member States already work with various transposition guides or tables that offer, in the best case, comprehensive information regarding the obligation of the Member State with respect to transposition, and the specific national legal measures to be taken in this respect.[19] While it is true that the starting point of such a guide is the national interest of the Member State, the standardisation of transposition procedures does not leave too much room for reflection on what could be perceived as more academic features of transposition. For instance, when deciding on transposition technique, the national legislator makes a choice in the light of existing national practice, and not in the light of existing comparative or European law.

However, a balance can definitely be struck between the consideration of national interests, on the one hand, and the contribution to a more cohesive national incorporation of European law on the other. One of the ways in which this can be achieved is through Option 2.

A National Transposition Guideline would be an inherently national instrument, created by a determined national authority, and using whatever

18 For instance, further research can focus on looking at what national courts do with the judgments of the Court of Justice after the preliminary reference procedure is complete – do they always follow the Court in applying national law subsequently, or are there Member States and/or national courts that still retain discretion on how to apply the Court's rulings? Answering questions like these can shed light on the eventual converging role of the Court's assessments.

19 See for example, Her Majesty's Government, 'Transposition Guidance: How to implement European Directives effectively', available at: <https://www.gov.uk/government/-uploads/system/uploads/attachment_data/file/229763/bis-13-775-transposition-guidance-how-to-implement-european-directives-effectively-revised.pdf>, last accessed on 27 July 2016; see also Dutch parliamentary proceedings working with a transposition table (*transponeringstabel richtlijn*).

national format may already exist after having been used for the overviewing of past transpositions. Moreover, this Guideline would not be a general transposition manual, but a Directive-specific set of instructions for the users of the transposing laws. The novelty regarding the suggested Guideline is two-fold.

Firstly, the Guideline would incorporate a convergence matrix, based on or similar to the national convergence factors identified in Chapter 3. The matrix would then be the basis of reporting information on, among others:

- the national transposition technique used out of the potential such techniques a Member State may use;
- whether novel concepts (concepts deemed earlier in this research to have a specific European identity) exist, and if so, whether and how they were transposed;
- whether open-ended norms (concepts deemed earlier in this research to have a meaning open for interpretation and which might also have a specific European identity) exist, and if so, whether and how they were transposed;
- whether the end transposing legislation makes reference to the European directive it transposes;
- transposition date.

Secondly, the Guideline would not be an executive set of instructions destined solely to the participants in the legislative process and dealing with the adoption of legislation, but it would be a guideline on the actual application of a transposing law, to be used by practitioners (judges, lawyers, etc.) and any other relevant stakeholders. In creating such a directive-based transposition report, practitioners would be able to better link the transposing legislation back to the original directive rules, while understanding national legislative choices in the process.

In a nutshell, the aim of the National Transposition Guideline would be to bring more structure to the transposition process, link the European perspective to the national transposition laws and familiarise practitioners with the European nature of the national piece of legislation.

As mentioned above, National Transposition Guidelines could not only be used by national lawmakers, but also by other stakeholders, such as national courts. In the current governance landscape, national courts are under an obligation to interpret national law in the light of European legislation, which must be transposed in due time, otherwise the Member State could be considered to commit a tort against some of its individuals.[20] Under Recommendation 1 the role of the Court of Justice in attaining legal convergence was explored. In turn, national courts can also be said to affect the harmonisation process.[21] As it has been seen in Chapter 2, discrepancies may arise between a directive and its transposing national legislation in a particular Member State. If this occurs, the national court must not

20 HR 14/00189, 18 September 2015.

21 Kadner Graziano speaks about soft harmonisation of the law within the context of regional integration: Kadner Graziano 2015, p. 38.

limit itself to applying national law, but it must do so while considering the European source - an eventual directive.[22] However, going beyond this point in understanding how national courts affect convergence is a complex undertaking, as was shown by Nowak *et al.* in their study dedicated exclusively to how national judges perceive and apply European law.[23]

2.4. *Recommendations for other Stakeholders*

Recommendation 3: Alternatively to Recommendation 1, the creation of a composite index by private actors (similar with or developed on the basis of the Convergence Index) to measure the extent of convergence in consumer sales law or any other field relating to consumer law.

Recommendation 1 focused on the creation of a composite indicator by the European legislator, as one of the core proposals of this study. Other international organisations developed indicators aimed at various stakeholders such as countries, businesses or individuals,[24] with the purpose of giving these stakeholders a wider perspective over highly complex topics (e.g. the standard of life or business conditions in a given country, etc.). From this perspective, a centralised indicator governed by the research power affiliated with a supra-state organisation such as the European Union would be a great development for European consumer law, as it could build on an already-existing preference of the European legislator for making evidence-based law.[25] Still, making use of an indicator means that Member States can be ranked, leading to some countries performing worse than others. That might be considered as a political *faux-pas*, especially in a European Union threatened first by Grexit and more recently by Brexit.[26]

As an alternative to Recommendation 1, private actors such as business or consumer associations, or academic institutions can design a composite index similar to the Convergence Index in order to create comparative information about convergence levels in all Member States. It may be stated that as authors of such a tool, different stakeholders have different interests: the Doing Business survey may be useful for businesses, but not so much for individuals (or more specifically consumers); similarly, the OECD Better Life Index can be a useful comparative

22 In assessing claims based on transposing consumer legislation, Supreme Courts will generally mention both national and European law. See for instance *Înalta Curte de Casaţie şi Justiţie (RO), Secţia a II-a civilă, Decizia nr. 860/2015 Dosar nr. 39074/3/2012, 18 martie 2015.*

23 Nowak *et al.* 2012.

24 See for example the OECD Better Life Index, or the World Bank Doing Business Reports.

25 See for instance law and economics as an example of the discussion regarding the practice of law for lawmaking and adjudication, Hacker 2015, p. 301-302.

26 'Grexit' refers to the 2012 political discussion regarding Greece's exit from the Eurozone: see Cinzia Alcidi *et al.*, "'Grexit': Who Would Pay for It?', CEPS Policy Brief No. 272, 2012. 'Brexit' refers to developments taking place in the United Kingdom around 2013, dealing with the country's potential withdrawal from the European Union: see G.I.P Ottaviano *et al.*, 'Brexit or Fixit? The trade and welfare effects of leaving the European union', CEP Policy Analysis, CEPPA016, 2014.

visualisation tool for individuals (including consumers), but it might only have marginal importance for businesses. However, when it comes to the assessment of legal convergence, this would not be an issue, as businesses and consumers are both impacted by the same consumer rules, and thus the information used to code the index would not be any different. In the same vein, different interests could lead to a different *use* of the resulting convergence values: if a given instrument has a high level of protection, consumers may choose to buy products from countries that have higher convergence values, whereas if businesses are not fond of the desired European level of protection, they can opt to start doing business in a jurisdiction with a low convergence value.

In the light of such usage, the availability of an online convergence tool might lead to enhanced consumer confidence. Online shops normally ask consumers what country they are based in (as a feature of using the website with a specific delivery policy or in a language of choice), and they display the applicable law to their contracts in the general terms and conditions. If, for instance, a consumer organisation develops an online convergence index, it may be able to display a map showing selected values comparatively (country of residence v country of purchase) that may empower the consumer in making a choice as to what other European jurisdictions to buy products from.

Academics can also further develop tools on the basis of the Convergence Index. One such option would entail enlarging the scope of the Convergence Index, which would then include, apart from elements of legislative transposition, the way in which this legislation is applied in practice. Such an option would potentially entail the creation of a convergence map, highlighting jurisdictions in accordance with their convergence values.[27]

Recommendation 4: The consolidation of multi-language databases on European consumer law such as the Consumer Law Compendium.

Beyond the possible applications of the Convergence Index, a lot remains to be said about doing more comparative analyses on consumer law. One of these endeavours has been the creation of the Consumer Law Compendium, which was extensively used for the purposes of this study. However, while its usefulness is beyond doubt, the Compendium has not been updated as of July 2012. The addition of more directives in the Compendium (e.g. Unfair Commercial Practices; Consumer Rights, etc.) would not only facilitate a more comprehensive perspective over the consumer *acquis*, but it would also gather information that could be the starting point of more numerical comparative law research in the field. Using visualisation software such as IBM's *Watson* or the freely available *Tableau*, the data generated by the Compendium could be analysed from new perspectives.

A link can be made once again to national courts. Retrieving information in a user-friendly manner is vital for case management, if one considers the heavy

27 This option was suggested to me by Omri Ben-Shahar in the context of the 'Consumers without Borders' conference held in Maastricht on 25 September 2015.

workloads courts all around Europe need to cope with. The phenomenon of global interaction between supreme or constitutional courts is already documented by academic literature, in works such as Lollini's foreign law patters.[28] Making databases available in a way that can facilitate judicial influence could possibly lead to spontaneous convergence, and national courts learning from one another how to interpret European law.[29]

One of the most problematic points of such a recommendation lays in language diversity,[30] as the European Union has no less than 24 official languages.[31] The many languages can be a pitfall in terms of the terminology itself, the translation of which could be confusing, but also from the perspective of generating sufficient translations. To solve the first issue, the Consumer Law Compendium could be enhanced with a 'Terminology' page, explaining European concepts comparatively, and emphasizing the European nature of what this study has called earlier 'novel concepts', namely concepts that are typical to European legislation and should be interpreted as such. As for the second issue, translation and interpretation algorithms either already exist, as in the case of the (in)famous Google Translate, or are currently being developed - an example in this sense is Skype Translate, a live interpretation service.[32] While some of this software might be in its infancy, one of its best features is that it learns from its users and is thus continuously fine-tuning output quality. Embedding a service such as Google Translate into the Consumer Law Compendium can allow the managers and users of the database to search and generate translations, instead of having to go through the excruciating and overly expensive process of translating every single posted document.

Recommendation 5: A call to more numerical academic representations of convergence in consumer sales law.

In the light of Option 4, not only is there an ongoing need for the comparative evaluation of the consumer *acquis*, but the nature of this evaluation should also take into account the fact that sheer volume of information currently amassed in this field has great potential for the development of quantitative research. If databases such as the Consumer Law Compendium are redesigned and updated, they can be

28 Lollini 2012, p. 56.

29 See for example another high profile database in the field of nationality law (Eudocitizenship), Vink & Chun Luk 2015, p. 157.

30 For a comprehensive overview regarding the issues posed by legal translations and comparative law see De Groot 2012, p. 538-549.

31 These languages are: Bulgarian, Croatian, Czech, Danish, Dutch, English, Estonian, Finnish, French, German, Greek, Hungarian, Irish, Italian, Latvian, Lithuanian, Maltese, Polish, Portuguese, Romanian, Slovak, Slovenian, Spanish, Swedish. See the overview made by DG Translation, available at: <http://ec.europa.eu/dgs/translation/translating/official-languages/index_en.htm>, last accessed on 27 July 2016.

32 Per Liljas, 'Skype Translator Will Be Able to Interpret Calls in Real Time', Time Magazine, 28 May 2014, available at: <http://time.com/121983/skype-translator-microsoft/>, last accessed on 27 July 2016.

used in numerical studies as such (e.g. how many provisions did German and Dutch law use to transpose the Consumer Sales Directive, etc.). Moreover, in such a context, not only established methodologies can be applied (e.g. law and economics), but new methods of comparative law can be created.

3. The Future Challenges for Legal Convergence in European Consumer Sales Law

2015 marked the withdrawal of probably the most ambitious proposal for the harmonisation of European consumer sales law (the Common European Sales Law). Much anticipated, whether with enthusiasm or criticism, the withdrawal of the proposal left an open question: how will the European legislator continue to pursue harmonisation? This has a direct bearing on what has been the main focus of this study, namely legal convergence. While the adoption of a consumer regulation would probably have increased the level of legal convergence in consumer sales, the European Union and its Member States might have much to wait for such a paradigm shift to take place.

In the meantime, the Consumer Rights Directive entered into force on 13 July 2014, and determining whether national transpositions manage to meet the high standards of consumer protection imposed by the Directive is very much a different research project.

Similarly, a lot can be said about the recent boom in preliminary reference procedures dealing with questions on the Unfair Contract Terms and Unfair Commercial Practices Directives. The growing number of judgments on the interpretation of these directives raises many challenges: what exactly drives so many different national courts to ask questions about unfair contractual clauses or unfair commercial practices? While it may be true that in the aftermath of the 2008 financial crisis a lot of consumer credit issues arose, this still does not explain why national courts tend to make use of the CJEU's interpretative authority even for matters that the Court had already dealt with, or matters which - at first sight - do not seem to need much interpretation. And what is more, what do all these cases actually say about legal convergence? For instance, if national judges encounter problems regarding the lack of special enforcement rules in transposing legislation, does that threaten whatever substantive convergence the Directive aimed to achieve?

These questions were intentionally left outside the ambit of this thesis, because of the fact that each of them may very well be the topic of a self-standing book. Nonetheless, one thing is clear: all these uncertainties can be further explored through research, in an attempt to bring more clarity to the complex yet fascinating phenomenon that is legal convergence.

SUMMARY

This is an empirical study about the converging effects of harmonisation policies used by the European lawmaker in consumer sales law. It aims to fill a gap in existing literature, by looking into what European consumer sales law harmonisation has achieved, and trying to develop a methodology to measure the convergence it has led to. The study encompasses both a substantive comparison as well as a numerical approach. While in the former, five directives and their subsequent transposition in the national laws of Member States are analysed, the latter focuses on the creation of the Convergence Index as a measurement tool for the effects of the harmonisation process. This research is dedicated to both academics as well as policy makers, as it aims to trigger more debate regarding benchmarking in European consumer law. Such a debate can play a role in further academic research aimed at determining whether harmonisation does indeed strengthen the internal market.

The study consists of four chapters.

Chapter 1 addresses the background to globalisation and legal convergence. Legal convergence, as a result of globalisation, is firstly defined, and subsequently explained by making an inventory of the driving forces behind it. This is essential for the clarification of a concept ('convergence') that has until now been used in many different ways and contexts. The chapter then places further emphasis on one specific policy behind convergence: the harmonisation of laws as practiced by the European Union. This opens the way for defining the aims and methodology of this study. Moreover, the Chapter also includes a discussion on the novelty of the study as well as its limitations. In laying the background for the rest of the study, Chapter 1 includes a brief historical scrutiny of European harmonisation as a policy tool that is supposed to achieve convergence. Harmonisation is then examined from a chronological point of view, and its types, as well as the competence of the European legislator to pursue this policy are addressed.

Chapter 2 focuses on the substantive comparative overview. It follows five selected directives (the Doorstep Selling Directive, the Unfair Contract Terms Directive, the Distance Selling Directive, the Consumer Sales Law Directive and the Unfair Commercial Practices Directive) which are discussed in the light of four criteria:

1. the rationale scope of the directive;
2. the standard of harmonisation set by the European legislator;
3. the reception of the standard of harmonisation by Member States; and
4. comparative notes on the transposition of the Directives.

After analysing the policy behind the directives at the EU level of governance, national transpositions are then discussed for the selected seven jurisdictions: Belgium, France, Germany, Ireland, the Netherlands, Romania and the United Kingdom. The transposition discussion leads, for each of the directives, to a comparative overview highlighting similarities and differences. The chapter ends with a short discussion regarding overlaps between the rules of the various instruments.

To summarise the discussions explored in Chapter 2, attention must be paid to the converging techniques used by the European lawmaker. Both minimum and maximum harmonisation directives are analysed, in an attempt to understand their defining characteristics, whether those are black lists, general clauses, or references to self-regulation. Two of the directives included in the study (the Doorstep Selling Directive and the Distance Selling Directive) are no longer applicable, having been repealed and replaced by the Consumer Rights Directive. However, understanding how the initial directives worked and what exactly they have achieved is crucial in determining whether this particular field (sales law) has undergone any meaningful changes after the change in policy.

Chapter 3 is dedicated to the numerical analysis. This analysis builds on an existing theory of numerical comparative law, according to which law and its inherent characteristics can be turned into numbers to add new perspectives in order to help understand the complexity of a vast topic such as legal convergence. In doing so, the information gathered in Chapter 2 serves as inspiration for the modelling of a measurement tool called the Convergence Index. The same Chapter elaborates on the factors included in the creation of the Convergence Index, and explains how the latter was methodologically constructed. Subsequently, on the basis of the identified factors, information is retrieved from the selected directives and the subsequent national transpositions, once again mirroring the comparative substantive analysis in the previous Chapter. This information is later coded according to very specific methodological considerations, finally creating comparative Convergence Index values for each of the five directives and seven Member States under scrutiny. Furthermore, the data collected in Chapter 3 is visualised using various chart formats, in order to facilitate the development of new perspectives over the legal convergence debate in consumer sales law. The Chapter includes an interactive virtual tool that can unfortunately not be supported by text format: this virtual tool is a Google Motion Chart, created on the basis of the data gathered in this Chapter. This Motion Chart is currently hosted on https://iconsume.eu and can be consulted online.

On the basis of the level of governance they occur at, a total of 13 factors were taken into account. The factors are coded as follows. The selected factors are given a value of either 0 or 1, with the exception of three factors (CJEU case law, reception of selected open norms, and reception of selected novel concepts) that receive values between 0 and 1 and required normalisation, or in other words they need to be made comparable to the other variables. The OECD Manual of Composite Indicators is the main source of inspiration for the design of the Index.

The Chapter then continues by gathering data from the five directives, and thus by showing step by step how the selected transposing provisions were analysed and subsequently coded. The results are shown in the form of tables with values given to each factor, as well as graphs displaying both the European as well as the national levels of the Convergence Index (Section 4). Moreover, Chapter 3 also elaborates on what new perspectives over convergence can be discovered by using the Index, and to this end screenshots of a Google motion chart were further added. Findings resulting from this enhanced visualisation are also comprehensively discussed in Chapter 3, and they relate to the following points:

1. *In general, and as defined by the factors shaping the Convergence Index, national consumer legislation is converging;*
2. *The transposition of the Unfair Contract Terms Directive marks a decline in convergence values;*
3. *Directives that make use of general clauses do not necessarily have a low convergence value;*
4. *Minimum harmonisation directives do not have a low convergence value;*
5. *Member States with J-shaped distribution have similar transposition techniques;*
6. *With the exception of the Consumer Sales Directive, the Netherlands has the lowest scores out of all Member States.*

The six patterns identified in these graphs have a dual purpose: firstly, to determine whether a new light can be shed on the harmonisation process using data visualisation; and secondly, to link back to Chapters 1 and 2 and reflect the more doctrinal analysis of this research, for the purpose of testing the accuracy of the convergence patterns.

Given that the selected Directives have been adopted between 1985 and 2005, the Convergence Index values occurring within this time lead to an ascending trend on the basis of which it can be mentioned that convergence in European consumer law - as defined and interpreted by this study - is actually on the rise. However, whether this rise is significant enough given the dramatic differences between minimum and maximum harmonisation as European policies, is another story.

The five Directives in this research can be clustered in three categories: low, average or high convergence. While the Unfair Contract Terms Directive has the lowest convergence value, the Distance Selling and Doorstep Selling Directives as well as the Consumer Sales Directive have the same middle values. What is more, the Unfair Commercial Practices Directive scores the highest on the selected factors. The novelty of this classification stems from the fact that until now the content of these Directives had solely been discussed by describing certain characteristics (e.g. minimum/maximum harmonisation; the hierarchy of remedies; etc.), while comparing their convergence values shows a more complete picture. This is especially the case as the convergence values can be interpreted in the light of the European dimension of the Index: what makes Directives convergence-friendly? In a nutshell, a Directive with a high convergence value should be a maximum harmonisation instrument that makes reference to self-regulation, does not use general clauses, and creates uniform practices by using the so-called black lists.

Moving to Member States, the Convergence Index once again creates a visual classification of how the selected Member States score on the factors making up the Index: Romania and Ireland have the highest values, closely followed by Belgium and the United Kingdom, in turn followed by Germany and then France. The Netherlands lags behind and scores the lowest value out of all the Member States included in the research.

Member State performance reflects two important aspects: on the one hand, the formal choices of the national legislator in transposing the Directive (e.g. transposition deadlines and techniques or reference to EU law in end legislation), as well as substantive choices dealing with the actual content of the rules (e.g. the reception of novel concepts or the reception of open-ended norms). Keeping these two aspects in mind when analysing the resulting values of the Convergence Index can lead to conclusions that are not exclusively related to the political process of adopting legislation; the substantive transposition of the rules ends up being reflected in the Index as well, albeit to a lesser extent.

In summary, the findings presented in Chapter 3 aimed at using data visualisation in order to discover new points of view that would further the understanding of how convergence works in the field of European consumer sales law. To this end, it can be stated that Chapter 3 is a 'data' image of Chapter 2.

Lastly, Chapter 4 is dedicated to drawing concluding remarks on the study as a whole, but also on various individual aspects, such as the novel methodology used for the analysis. Chapter 4 aims to bring symmetry to this research, and makes an overview of the findings in the light of the proposed research questions:

1. What are the standards of convergence behind the rules on consumer sales developed by the European legislator and how has the Court of Justice interpreted these standards?
Five directives (Doorstep Selling, Unfair Terms, Distance Selling, Consumer Sales and Unfair Practices) are selected for this study on the basis of their scope that comprises consumer sales law. While two of these instruments (Doorstep Selling and Distance Selling) have been repealed by the Consumer Rights Directive, they were included in the study because of the decades of influence already exercised over national regimes seeking to accommodate the concept of a cooling off period in consumer sales. Four of the instruments in this study promote minimum harmonisation, while the most recent one (the Unfair Practices Directive) focused on targeted full harmonisation.

To begin with, it can be noted that the Doorstep Selling, Distance Selling and Consumer Sales Directive bear certain resemblances, not only if considered in the light of the literature review, but also on the basis of the findings in the numerical part of the analysis. All three Directives are rather brief, impose quite clear standards and while they might have specific grey areas (e.g. the nature of the right of withdrawal is not specified; the proportionality test in first-tier remedies may lead to complicated practical applications, etc.), the case law of the Court of Justice does not seem to indicate very complex concerns regarding the intricacies of these rules.

Not the same can be stated when looking at the remaining two Directives: Unfair Terms and Unfair Practices. The recent increase in preliminary references based on the Unfair Contract Terms Directive is definitely a cause for concern. In this study, it was assumed that the more case law exists on a given topic, the less likely it is that the instrument on which it is based would lead to convergence. Whether the reader agrees with this assumption or not, facts speak for themselves. A Directive dating from 1993 and leading to over 45 cases (and increasing) within the 20 years it has been in force for is clearly somehow not understood by the national judges who continue to send preliminary questions to the Court of Justice. Literature echoes this concern. As the Directive that includes a good faith test, the Unfair Contract Terms Directive has been under the constant attack of not being able to offer legal certainty. While legal certainty was indeed not part of this study as such, it was interesting to look at this Directive as well as the other four and envisage them as a sum of the factors behind the Convergence Index. Deconstructing each Directive and understanding its forming characteristics was very valuable for the development of the methodology. For instance, while the Unfair Commercial Practices Directive was praised (and feared) for its maximum harmonisation orientation, the Convergence Index factors emphasise that its unifying potential might come from other sources as well, such as the existence of a black list, or the reference to self-regulation.

Often different in scope and wording, the five directives do have a major concern in common: the problem that not even one of them sets rules comprehensive enough to be applied independently from national legal rules. In other words, the political compromise reached by the European legislator at the point of adoption left many gaps to be filled through interpretation. For doorstep and distance selling the nature and effect of the right to withdraw (or the cancellation right, as it is called in the Doorstep Selling Directive) are not explicitly mentioned, while for the Unfair Contract Terms open-ended norms like reasonableness or good faith receive no definition. These are just some examples of how the piecemeal approach to harmonisation consumer law works.

These arguments shape the answer to the question on what standards of convergence were set by the European legislator. In brief, on the basis of what has been examined in this study, these standards are often incomplete, due to the lack of a comprehensive framework of consumer law, and they heavily rely on interpretation by the Court of Justice. However, it must be stated that the policy trend which can be noticed already with the adoption of the Unfair Commercial Practices Directive, and continued for instance with the Consumer Rights Directive, is to develop a more targeted harmonisation approach. This approach has two characteristics: it imposes a high standard of consumer protection when it comes to specific topics, and it constrains Member States to adopt it in a uniform manner.

2. How did national legislators transpose these rules, and what issues arise from their transposition?

Overall, this question has been dealt with in the comparative analysis, where the national legislation of the seven Member States in question (Belgium, France, Germany, Ireland, the Netherlands, Romania, and the United Kingdom) was closely scrutinised in order to understand how European rules have been accommodated.

This effort took the shape of small-scale country reports. The small-scale characteristic stems from the fact that for each of the five directives, several provisions are selected:

- Doorstep Selling: Article 5;
- Unfair Contract Terms: Articles 3-7;
- Distance Selling: Articles 4, 6 and 7;
- Consumer Sales: Articles 2-3 and 5-6;
- Unfair Commercial Practices: Articles 5-9 and 10-11.

This approach was preferred to the overall discussion of the directives as it targets, in my view, what the five directives aim to achieve. As was said above, each of these instruments has gaps making their overall discussion a challenging endeavour. Moreover, as the substantive comparison in Chapter 2 looked not only at European rules, but also at their transposition in the selected national legal systems, working with selected provisions as opposed to entire directives made this effort possible; having full country reports on each of the five directives for each of the seven Member States would have made this study overly ambitious.

These choices shape how national lawmakers relate to harmonisation. Whether it is political resistance aimed at preserving the particularities of a national legal system (e.g. in those jurisdictions where comprehensive legal reforms took place, such as Germany or the Netherlands), or lack of experience with managing what has already been called the piecemeal harmonisation approach (e.g. Romania), the comparative analysis showed how some Member States will use whatever discretion they can to influence the transposition process. However, the analysis also showed that many Member States will often try to balance European and national interests in adhering to common standards.

3. How can the resulting convergence process be measured?

With regard to the third question, by analysing the Directives this study explored what factors lead to convergence, and showed that the overall performance of a Directive reflects not just one feature, but the interaction of multiple characteristics it may have as a legal instrument.

The 13 selected factors that influence harmonisation, or as they have been called before 'convergence markers', can be found at European level as well as national level. To briefly remind the reader what these factors were, they are once more enumerated below:

- *European level*: (a) Law v policy; (b) Type of European instrument (Directive/-Regulation); (c) Nature of policy (minimum/maximum harmonisation); (d) Reference to self-regulation; (e) General clause; (f) Black list; (g) CJEU case law;
- *National level*: (a) National transposition technique; (b) Reception of selected novel concepts; (c) Reception of selected open-ended norms; (d) Reference to European law in end legislation; (e) Timely transposition (date of national legislation); (f) Infringement procedures.

These factors were first explained and defined within a very clear ambit. This ambit has been the context the Convergence Index needs for accuracy purposes. For this reason, any claims or suggestions made disregarding this context or outside of this context, are detrimental to the overall value that the Convergence Index has for the harmonisation debate.

What is more, Chapter 4 also drafts policy recommendations and explores creative ways in which the present study can contribute to the design of more hands-on solutions for policy-makers.

Recommendation for the European Institutions
Recommendation 1: The creation of a composite index by the EU (similar with or developed on the basis of the Convergence Index) to measure the extent of convergence in consumer sales law or any other field relating to consumer law.

Recommendation for National Institutions
Recommendation 2: The creation by national legislators of a National Transposition Guideline focused on the converging effect of European legislation. The National Transposition Guideline would be destined not only to national lawmakers themselves, but also to practitioners as well as to other stakeholders.

Recommendations for other Stakeholders
Recommendation 3: Alternatively to Recommendation 1, the creation of a composite index by private actors (similar with or developed on the basis of the Convergence Index) to measure the extent of convergence in consumer sales law or any other field relating to consumer law.

Recommendation 4: The consolidation of multi-language databases on European consumer law such as the Consumer Law Compendium.

Recommendation 5: A call to more numerical academic representations of convergence in consumer sales law.

VALORISATION ADDENDUM

1. What is the societal relevance?

The question of whether and how the European Union should contribute to the approximation of laws at Member State level is pivotal for 2016. This year will be remembered by history as the year when the United Kingdom held a referendum on the question of staying in the European Union, and its people answered in the negative. A lot can be said about the reasons leading to this monumental decision, and the extent to which private law harmonisation played a role is rather speculative at this point. However, what private law harmonisation and Brexit - as the unfortunate fall-out was named - have in common is the discussion of sovereignty. Where can one draw a line between EU interference and national legitimacy in decision-making? As it has been seen in this study, the European Commission has been pushing consumer protection trends that are purely normative, such as the maximum harmonisation standard. The data that European institutions use to justify these measures are scarce at best, and they fail to show any form of policy assessment. What has been achieved with minimum and maximum harmonisation? The Commission might have held consultations with a limited number of stakeholders, but do the preferences explained therein, which do not fully support maximum harmonisation, reflect better standards when applied to the internal market?

To a certain extent, these questions can and have been answered by means of doctrinary research. Nevertheless, the picture illustrated by doctrinary research is incomplete without an empirical assessment of minimum and maximum harmonisation. This is exactly what the present research results aimed to contribute to. The goal of creating the Convergence Index has been to open the floor to a wider debate on this matter. As indicated in the manuscript, the Index, as compiled here, is only a *beta* version, as it can and will be improved through subsequent research, to better reflect the factors it wishes to measure.

2. To whom are your research results of interest?

The findings in this manuscript are addressed to a wide array of stakeholders, from academics to policy-makers. One the one hand, as mentioned just above, the debate as to how to better measure the converging effects of harmonisation can be continued in the academic community, in an attempt to fine-tune a tool such as the Convergence Index, or create spin-offs.

On the other hand, the European Union already uses various benchmarking techniques (e.g. the Internal Market Scoreboard), but the authors of these tools themselves acknowledge that the indicators relating to the internal market are completely underdeveloped. With such a Convergence Index, the European institutions could keep track of Member State harmonisation activity, and could use the Index even further to actually test whether convergence is correlated with (or ideally causes) economic growth. What is more, private actors may become involved in the development of Index spin-offs as well, to perhaps justify whether the need for harmonisation has been actually overstated.

All in all, the very idea that more legal indicators can be developed for statistical purposes is encouraging, given the sheer lack of data in this respect. Where existent, European legal databases remain qualitative in nature, and make it difficult for measurement tools to be developed. As the Convergence Index is a composite indicator, it focuses on gathering data from the transposition process, in order to give a more visual overview as to how Member States embed the various consumer directives into their national legal systems.

3. Into which concrete products, services, processes, activities or commercial activities will your results be translated and shaped?

The Convergence Index has the potential of becoming either an academic, policy or consultancy tool, depending on the stakeholders engaged in its development. The academic dimension would envisage the further development of the Index by academic literature, both empirical as well as doctrinary. The policy dimension relates to the European legislator employing the tool to either determine Member State performance, or to further build on existing research in an attempt to empirically and economically make the case for more harmonisation. Finally, the consultancy dimension takes into account recent interest for benchmarking, reflected in similar tools that exist in other areas, such as nationality law. The Quality of Nationality Index by Henley & Partners and Dimitry Kochenov from the University of Groningen is an example in this respect.

The research results can be translated into an online tool that enables the visualisation of the factors composing the Convergence Index, as well as country performances. Moreover, given that the current research has been limited to a number of five directives and seven Member States, additional research could be done in the future to add more countries and more directives, in order to gain an even finer understanding of how harmonisation works and whether there is any major difference between the convergence effected by minimum harmonisation and the convergence that maximum harmonisation leads to.

4. To what degree can yur results be called innovative in respect to the existing range of products, services, processes, activities and commercial activities?

The Convergence Index is innovative on three different levels:

(i) Measuring the law in general

Generally speaking, as mentioned above, the indicators and overall data that exists on legal matters are very hard to find. A lot of indicators accounted for by EurStat are either economic or social, however none of them really deal with legal performance. It might be argued that it is difficult, if not impossible, to measure the law. However, at international level the UN and the OECD are currently measuring human development and quality of life, so if it is possible to put numbers next to these concepts, measuring the law might not be that much more difficult. Nevertheless, this field remains underdeveloped.

(ii) Measuring harmonisation

Also underdeveloped is the data showing the performance of selected policies such as minimum or maximum harmonisation. The few Eurobarometers that are often cited in policy papers make the case that harmonisation (either minimum or maximum) should be the desired policy aim, as it is favoured by some consumers and some businesses, due to the promised increase in consumer confidence levels, as well as the lowering of transaction costs. However, there is no study to date that proves whether this policy actually delivers on its economic promises; and even more, there is no study showing that maximum harmonisation is actually much different than minimum harmonisation. The need for a public debate in this respect is absolutel necessary, and the arguments (either for or against) can be strengthened through the use of empirical tools such as the Convergence Index.

(iii) Measuring consumer law

The Consumer Law Compendium is, to date, the largest academic study on the transposition of consumer law directives in the laws of the Member States. While this massive study is enlightnening in a quantitative comparative manner, it has not been designed to produce raw legal data that could further be used in an empirical way. The Convergence Index aims to fill this gap by making use of exactly such qualitative observations and turning them into an original dataset that can be used independently in quantitative research.

RELEVANT DOCUMENTS

1. European Legislation

Council Directive 84/450/EEC of 10 September 1984 relating to the approximation of the laws, regulations and administrative provisions of the Member States concerning misleading advertising, *OJ* L250 of 10 September 1984.

Council Directive 85/374/EEC of 25 July 1985 on the approximation of the laws, regulations and administrative provisions of the Member States concerning liability for defective products, *OJ* L210 of 7 August 1985.

Directive on the protection of consumers in respect of contracts negotiated away from business premises 85/577/EEC, *OJ* L372 of 31 December 1985.

Council Directive 86/653/EEC of 18 December 1986 on the coordination of the laws of the Member States relating to self-employed commercial agents, *OJ* L382 of 31 December 1986.

Council Directive 90/314/EEC of 13 June 1990 on package travel, package holidays and package tours, *OJ* L158 of 23 June 1990.

Council Directive 93/13/EEC of 5 April 1993 on unfair terms in consumer contracts, *OJ* L95 of 21 April 1993.

Directive 94/47/EC of the European Parliament and the Council of 26 October 1994 on the protection of purchasers in respect of certain aspects of contracts relating to the purchase of the right to use immovable properties on a timeshare basis, *OJ* L280 of 29 October 1994.

Directive 97/7/EC of the European Parliament and of the Council of 20 May 1997 on the protection of consumers in respect of distance contracts, *OJ* L144 of 4 June 1997.

Directive 98/26/EC of the European Parliament and of the Council of 19 May 1998 on settlement finality in payment and securities settlement systems, *OJ* L166 of 11 June 1998.

Directive 98/27/EC of the European Parliament and of the Council of 19 May 1998 on injunctions for the protection of consumers' interests, *OJ* L166 of 11 June 1998.

Directive 1999/44/EC of the European Parliament and of the Council of 25 May 1999 on certain aspects of the sale of consumer goods and associated guarantees, *OJ* L171 of 07 July 1999.

Directive 1999/93/EC of the European Parliament and of the Council of 13 December 1999 on a Community framework for electronic signatures, *OJ* L013 of 19 January 2000.

Directive 2000/31/EC of the European Parliament and the Council of 8 June 2000 on certain legal aspects of information society services, in particular electronic commerce, *OJ* L178 of 17 July 2000.

Directive 2001/95/EC of the European Parliament and of the Council of 3 December 2001 on general product safety, *OJ* L11/4 of 15 January 2002.

Directive 2002/47/EC of the European Parliament and of the Council of 6 June 2002 on financial collateral arrangements, *OJ* L168 of 27 June 2002.

Directive 2002/65/EC of the European Parliament and of the Council of 23 September 2002 concerning the distance marketing of consumer financial services, *OJ* L271 of 9 October 2002.

Directive 2005/29/EC of the European Parliament and of the Council of 11 May 2005 concerning unfair business-to-consumer commercial practices in the internal market and amending Council Directive 84/450/EEC, Directives 97/7/EC, 98/27/EC and 2002/65/EC of the European Parliament and of the Council and Regulation (EC) No 2006/2004 of the European Parliament and of the Council, *OJ* L149/22 of 11 June 2005.

Directive 2006/114/EC of the European Parliament and of the Council of 12 December 2006 concerning misleading and comparative advertising, *OJ* L376/21 of 27 December 2006.

Directive 2007/64/EC of the European Parliament and of the Council of 13 November 2007 on payment services in the internal market amending Directives 97/7/EC, 2002/65/EC, 2005/60/EC and 2006/48/EC and repealing Directive 97/5/EC, *OJ* L319/1 of 5 December 2007.

Directive 2008/48/EC on credit agreements for consumers, *OJ* L133/66 of 22 May 2008.

Directive 2009/22/EC of the European Parliament and of the Council of 23 April 2009 on injunctions for the protection of consumers' interests, *OJ* L110 of 1 April 2009.

Directive 2011/7/EU of the European Parliament and of the Council of 16 February 2011 on combating late payment in commercial transactions (recast), *OJ* L48/1 of 23 February 2011.

Directive 2011/83/EU of the European Parliament and of the Council of 25 October 2011 on consumer rights, amending Council Directive 93/13/EEC and Directive 1999/44/EC of the European Parliament and of the Council and repealing Council Directive 85/577/EEC and Directive 97/7/EC of the European Parliament and of the Council, *OJ* L304/64 of 22 November 2011.

2. Legislative Proposals

European Commission, Proposal For a Council Directive to Protect the Consumer in Respect of Contracts Which Have Been Negotiated Away From Business Premises, COM/76/544 final.

European Commission, Proposal for a Council Directive on Unfair Contract Terms in Consumer Contracts, COM(90) 322 final.

European Commission, Proposal for a European Parliament and Council Directive on the sale of consumer goods and associated guarantees, COM(95) 520 final.

European Commission, Proposal for a Directive of the European Parliament and of the Council concerning unfair business-to-consumer commercial practices in the Internal Market and amending Directives 84/450/EEC, 97/7/EC and 98/27/EC (the Unfair Commercial Practices Directive), COM(2003) 356 final.

European Commission, Proposal for a Regulation of the European Parliament and of the Council on a Common European Sales Law, COM(2011) 635 final.

European Commission, Proposal for a Directive of the European Parliament and of the Council on certain aspects concerning contracts for the supply of digital content, COM(2015) 634 final.

European Commission, Proposal for a Directive of the European Parliament and of the Council on certain aspects concerning contracts for the online and other distance sales of goods, COM(2015) 635 final.

European Commission, Composite Indicators Research Group website, available at: <https://composite-indicators.jrc.ec.europa.eu>, last accessed on 21 July 2016.

European Commission, Internal Market Scoreboard website, available at: <http://ec.europa.eu/internal_market/score/index_en.htm>, last accessed on 21 July 2016.

European Commission, 'Exploratory Research Report: The Integration of Thematic Composite Indicators', Institute for the Protection and Security of the Citizen Research Paper, 2003, available at: <https://composite-indicators.jrc.ec.europa.eu/sites/default/files/EUR20682%20EN.pdf>, last accessed on 21 July 2016.

European Commission, Internal Market Scoreboard website, available at: <http://ec.europa.eu/internal_market/score/index_en.htm>, last accessed on 21 July 2016.

Civic Consulting, Study on the application of Directive 2005/29/EC on Unfair Commercial Practices in the EU, Final Report for European Commission - DG Justice 2011

3. Decisions, Opinions, Recommendations and Resolutions

European Council, Resolution of 14 April 1975 on a preliminary programme of the European Economic Community for a consumer protection and information policy, *OJ* 75/C92/01.

European Council, Opinion on the proposal for a Council Directive to protect the consumer in respect of contracts which have been negotiated away from business premises, *OJ* 77/C180/11.

European Parliament, Resolution on action to bring into line the private law of the Member States, *OJ* 89/C158/05.

European Commission, Recommendation 92/295/EEC of 7 April 1992 on codes of practice for the protection of consumers in respect of contracts negotiated at a distance (distance selling), *OJ* L156.

European Parliament, Resolution on the harmonisation of certain sectors of the private law of the Member States, *OJ* 94/C205/05.

European Commission, Opinion of the Commission pursuant to Article 189 b(2)(d) of the EC Treaty, on the European Parliament's amendments to the Council's common position regarding the proposal for a European Parliament and Council Directive on the sale of consumer goods and associated guarantees, COM(99) 16 final.

European Parliament resolution on the approximation of the civil and commercial law of the Member States, COM(2001) 398, *OJ* C140 E.

European Commission Recommendation of 6 May 2003 concerning the definition of micro, small and medium-sized enterprises (notified under document number C(2003) 1422), *OJ* L124 of 20 May 2003.

European Parliament Resolution on the Communication from the Commission to the European Parliament and the Council, 'A more coherent European contract law', *OJ* 2004/C 076E/2.

Position of the European Parliament adopted at first reading on 23 March 2006 establishing a programme of Community action in the field of consumer protection (2007-2013).

European Commission Decision of 26 April 2010 setting up the Expert Group on a Common Frame of Reference in the area of European Contract Law, *OJ* L105/109.

European Commission Delegated Regulation (EU) No 240/2014 of 7 January 2014 on the European code of conduct on partnership in the framework of the European Structural and Investment Funds, *OJ* L74/1.

4. European Union Policy Documents

Executive Secretariat of the Commission, 'Approximation of legislation. Work undertaken between 1 June 1958 and 31 March 1965', Supplement to Bulletin of the European Economic Community No. 8/1966.

Executive Secretariat of the Commission, 'Community measures for the approximation of laws (1972-1974)', Bulletin of the European Communities Supplement 3/75.

Amendment to the Proposal for a Council Directive to Protect the Consumer in Respect of Contracts Which Have Been Negotiated Away From Business Premises, COM/78/2 Final.

European Commission, 'Communication of the Commission to the Council on unfair terms in consumer contracts', COM(84) 55 final.

European Commission, 'White Paper on Completing the Internal Market', COM(85) 310.

Commission Action Plan, 'Placing the Single Market at the Service of European Consumers', COM(93) 378 final.

Commission Green Paper of 15 November 1993 on guarantees for consumer goods and after-sales services, COM(93) 509 final.

European Commission, 'Communication from the Commission to the EP on the Common Position of the Council on the proposal for a Directive on the sale of consumer goods and associated guarantees', SEC(1998) 1553 final.

Common Position (EC) no. 51/98 adopted by the European Council on 24 September 1998 with a view to adopting European Parliament and Council Directive 98/EC, on certain aspects of the sale of consumer goods and associated guarantees.

European Commission, 'Communication from the Commission to the Council and the European Parliament on European contract law', COM/2001/0398 final, *OJ* C255 of 13 September 2001.

European Commission, 'Green Paper on European Union Consumer Protection', COM(2001) 531 final, *OJ* C125 of 25 May 2002.

European Commission, 'Communication from the Commission to the European Parliament, the Council, the Economic and Social Committee and the Committee of the Regions - Consumer Policy Strategy 2002-2006', COM/2002/0208 final, *OJ* C137 of 8 June 2002.

European Commission, 'Communication from the Commission to the European Parliament and the Council - A More Coherent European Contract Law - An Action Plan', COM(2003) 68 final, *OJ* C63 of 13 March 2003.

European Commission, 'Communication from the Commission to the Council and the European Parliament - 2003 Environment Policy Review - Consolidating the environmental pillar of sustainable development', COM/2003/0745 final, *OJ* C96 of 21 April 2004.

European Commission, 'Communication on European Contract Law and the revision of the *acquis*: the way forward', COM(2004) 651 final, *OJ* C14 of 20 January 2005.

European Commission Staff Working Document, 'Consumer Confidence in E-Commerce: lessons learned from the e-confidence initiative', SEC(2004) 1390.

European Commission, 'Green Paper on the Review of the Consumer *Acquis*', COM(2006) 744 final.

Working Document of the Commission, 'Responses to the Consultation on Distance Selling Directive 97/7/EC contained in Communication 2006/514/EC'.

European Commission, 'EU Consumer Policy Strategy (2007-2013) - Empowering consumers, enhancing their welfare, effectively protecting them', COM(2007) 99 final, *OJ* C181 of 3 August 2007.

Discussion Paper on the Review of Directive 85/577/EEC to protect the consumer in respect of contracts negotiated away from business premises (Doorstep Selling Directive), 2007.

European Commission, Communication from the Commission to the Council and the European Parliament on the implementation of Directive 1999/44/EC of the European Parliament and of the Council of 25 May 1999 on certain aspects of the sale of consumer goods and associated guarantees including analysis of the case for introducing direct producers' liability, COM(2007) 210 final.

European Commission, 'A Single Market for 21st Century Europe', Communication from the Commission to the European Parliament, the Council, the European Economic and Social Committee and the Committee of the Regions, Brussels, COM(2007) 724 final.

Letter from the European Commission to the Romanian Government, SANCO/B2/ADG/ew D(2008)220354 of 19 September 2008.

Commission Staff Working Paper, 'Report on the Outcome of the Public Consultation on the Green Paper on the Review of the Consumer *Acquis*', SEC(2008) 2544.

Commission Staff Working Document, 'Guidance on the Implementation/-Application of Directive 2005/29/EC on Unfair Commercial Practices', SEC(2009) 1666.

European Commission, 'A Digital Agenda for Europe', COM(2010) 245, *OJ* C121 of 19 April 2011.

European Commission, 'Green Paper on policy options for progress towards a European Contract Law for consumers and businesses', COM(2010) 348 final.

European Commission, Communication from the Commission to the European Parliament, the Council, the European Economic and Social Committee and the Committee of Regions, 'Towards a Single Market Act', COM(2010) 608 final.

European Commission, 'Communication from the Commission to the European Parliament, the Council, the European Economic and Social Committee and the Committee of the Regions – A coherent framework for building trust in the Digital Single Market for e-commerce and online services', COM/2011/0942 final, *OJ* C102 of 5 April 2012.

European Commission, 'Proposal for a Regulation of the European Parliament and of the Council on a Common European Sales Law', COM(2011) 635 final, *OJ* C37 of 10 February 2012

DG Internal Policies, 'A Pan-European Trustmark for E-Commerce: Possibilities and Opportunities', July 2012.

European Commission, 'Protecting businesses against misleading marketing practices and ensuring effective enforcement', COM(2012) 702 final.

European Commission, 'Communication from the Commission to the European Parliament, the Council and the European Economic and Social Committee on the application of the Unfair Commercial Practices Directive', COM(2013) 138 final.

European Commission, 'First Report on the application of Directive 2005/29/EC of the European Parliament and of the Council of 11 May 2005 concerning unfair business-to-consumer commercial practices in the internal market and amending Council Directive 84/450/EEC, Directives 97/7/EC, 98/27/EC and 2002/65/EC of the European Parliament and of the Council and Regulation (EC) No 2006/2004 of the European Parliament and of the Council ('Unfair Commercial Practices Directive')', COM(2013) 139 final.

European Commission, 'Communication from the Commission to the European Parliament, the Council, the European Economic and Social Committee and the Committee of the Regions - A Digital Single Market Strategy for Europe', COM(2015) 192 final.

5. Case Law

5.1. *Court of Justice of the European Union*

Case 120/78, *Rewe-Zentral AG v Bundesmonopolverwaltung für Branntwein* [1979] ECR 00649.

Case 99/79, *Lancôme v Etos & Albert Heyn* [1980] ECR 2511.

Case C-91/92, *Paola Faccini Dori v Recreb Srl* [1994] ECR I-03325.

Case C-315/92, *Verband Sozialer Wettbewerb eV v Clinique Labatories SNC and Estée Lauder Cosmetics GmbH* [1994] ECR I-317.

Case C-82/96 (*Consumers Association*) - case closed.

Case C-261/95, *Rosalba Palmisani v Istituto nazionale della previdenza sociale (INPS)* [1997] ECR I-04025.

Case C-82/96, *R. and Secretary of Trade ex-parte Consumers Association* - case withdrawn.

Case C-210/96, *Gut Springheide GmbH v Oberkreisdirektor des Kreises Steinfurt* [1998] ECR I-4657.

Case C-318/97, *Commission v Kingdom of Spain* [1998] ECR I-05451.

Case C-267/98 (*Cardeñosa*) - case closed.

Case C-266/98 (*Caminati*) - case closed.

Case C-265/98 (*Compañ Calbuig*) - case closed.

Case C-268/98 (*Casas Minguelez*) - case closed.

Case C-269/98 (*Villar Castelao*) - case closed.

Case C-270/98 (*Lopez Aznar*) - case closed.0

Case C-271/98 (*Serrano Garido*) - case closed.

Case C-272/98 (*Arencom Salazar*) - case closed.

Case C-423/97, *Travel Vac SL v Manuel José Antelm Sanchis* [1999] ECR I-02195.

Case C-376/98, *Germany v Parliament & Council (Tobacco Advertising I)* [2000] ECR I-8419.

Joined cases C-240/98 to C-244/98, *Océano Grupo Editorial SA v Roció Murciano Quintero; Salvat Editores SA v José M. Sánchez Alcón Prades; José Luis Copano Badillo; Mohammed Berroane; and Emilio Viñas Feliú* [2000] ECR I-04941.

Case C-21/00 (*Hamadeh*) - case closed.

Case C-377/98, *Netherlands v Parliament and Council* [2001] ECR I-7079.

Case C-481/99, *Georg Heininger and Helga Heininger v Bayerische Hypo- und Vereinsbank AG* [2001] ECR I-9945.

Case C-129/01 (*Condominio Facchinei Orsini*) - case closed.

Case C-244/01 (*Commission v France*) - case closed.

Case C-144/99, *Commission v Kingdom of the Netherlands* [2001] ECR I-03541.

Case C-144/99, *Commission of the European Communities v Kingdom of the Netherlands* [2001] ECR I-03541.

Case C-478/99, *Commission of the European Communities v Kingdom of Sweden* [2002] ECR I-04147.

Case C-491/01, *Queen v Sec'y of State for Health, ex parte British Am. Tobacco (Inv.) Ltd. & Imperial Tobacco Ltd.* [2002] ECR I-11453.

Case C-473/00, *Cofidis SA v Jean-Louis Fredout* [2002] ECR I-10875.

Case C-414/01, *Commission of the European Communities v Kingdom of Spain* [2002] ECR I-11121.

Case C-372/99, *Commission v Italian Republic* [2002] ECR I-00819.

Case C-478/99, *Commission v Kingdom of Sweden* [2002] ECR I-04147.

Case C-478/99, *Commission of the European Communities v Kingdom of Sweden* [2002] ECR I-04147.

Case C-237/02, *Freiburger Kommunalbauten GmbH Baugesellschaft & Co. KG* [2004] ECR I-03403.

Case C–210/03, *R v Secretary of State for Health, ex p Swedish Match* [2004] ECR I–11893.

Case T-154/01, *Distilleria F. Palma SpA v Commission of the European Communities* [2004] ECR II-01493.

Case C-310/03, *Commission of the European Communities v Grand Duchy of Luxemburg* [2004] ECR I-01969.

Case C-312/03, *Commission of the European Communities v Kingdom of Belgium* [2004] ECR I-01975.

Case C-311/03, *Commission of the European Communities v France* [2004].

Case C-70/03, *Commission v Kingdom of Spain* [2004] ECR I-07999.

Case C-237/02, *Freiburger Kommunalbauten GmbH Baugesellschaft & Co. KG v Ludger Hofstetter and Ulrike Hofstetter* [2004] ECR I-03403.

Case C-66/04, *United Kingdom v Parliament and Council (Smoke flavourings)* [2005] ECR I-10553.

Case C-336/03, *easyCar (UK) Ltd v Office of Fair Trading* [2005] ECR I-01947.

Case C-380/03, *Germany v Parliament and Council (Tobacco Advertising II)* [2006] ECR I-11573.

Case C-168/05, *E.M. Mostaza Claro v Centro Movil Milenium* [2006] ECR I-10421.

Case C-380/03, *Germany v Parliament and Council* [2006] ECR I-11573.

Case C-412/06, *Annelore Hamilton v Volksbank Filder eG* [2008] ECR I-02383.

Case C-404/06, *Quelle AG v Bundesverband der Verbraucherzentralen und Verbraucherverbände* [2008] ECR I-2685.

Case C-301/06, *Ireland v Parliament and Council* [2009] ECR I-593.

Case C-227/08, *Eva Martín Martín v EDP Editores SL* [2009] ECR I-11939.

Case C-489/07, *Pia Messner v Firma Stefan Krüger* [2009] I-07315.

Case C-146/09, *Prof. Dr. Claus Scholl v Stadtwerke Aachen AG* [2009].

Joint cases C-261/07, *VTB-VAB NV v Total Belgium NV* and C-299/07, *Galatea BVBA v Sanoma Magazines Belgium NV* [2009] I-02949.

Case C-326/08, *Commission v Germany* [2009].

Case C-220/09, *Commission v Malta* [2009] - case withdrawn.

Case C-321/08, *Commission v Kingdom of Spain* [2009] ECR I-00063*.

Case C-282/08, *Commission v Grand Duchy of Luxembourg* [2009] ECR I-00013*.

Case C-326/08, *Commission v Germany* [2009].

Case C-284/08, *Commission v United Kingdom* [2009].

Case C-283/08, *Commission v Netherlands* [2009].

Case C-270/08, *Commission v Hungary* [2009].

Case C-40/08, *Asturcom Telecommunicaciones SL v Cristina Rodríguez Nogueira* [2009] ECRI-9579.

Case C-58/08, *Vodafone Ltd, Telefónica O2 Europe plc, T-Mobile International AG, Orange Personal Communications Ser- vices Ltd v Secretary of State for Business, Enterprise and Regulatory Reform* [2010] ECR I-04999.

Case C-484/08, *Caja de Ahorros y Monte de Piedad de Madrid* [2010] ECR I-04785.

Case C-137/08, *VB Pénzügyi Lízing v Ferenc Schneider* [2010] ECR I-10847.

Case C-511/08, *Handelsgesellschaft Heinrich Heine GmbH v Verbraucherzentrale Nordrhein-Westfalen eV* [2010] ECR I-03047 [2010].

Case C-318/08, *Filomena Califano v Wind SpA* [2010] ECR I-02213.

Case C-320/08, *Multiservice Srl v Telecom Italia SpA* [2010] ECR I-02213.

Case C-540/08, *Mediaprint Zeitungs-und Zeitschriftenverlag GmbH & Co. KG v 'Österreich'-Zeitungsverlag GmbH* [2010] ECR I-10909.

Case C-304/08, *Zentrale zur Bekämpfung unlauteren Wettbewerbs eV v Plus Warenhandelsgesellschaft mbH* [2010] I-00217.

Case C-122/10, *Konsumentombudsmannen v Ving Sverige AB* [2011] ECR I-03903.

Case C-453/10, *Jana Pereničová and Vladislav Perenič v SOS financ spol. s r. o.* [2012].

Case C-618/10, *Banco Español de Crédito SA v Joaquín Calderón Camino* [2012].

Case C- 49/11, *Content Services Ltd v Bundesarbeitskamer* [2012].

Case C-32/12, *Soledad Duarte Hueros v Autociba SA, Automóviles Citroën España SA* [2013].

Case C-265/12, *Citroën Belux NV v Federatie voor Verzekerings-en Financiële Tussenpersonen (FvF)* [2013].

Case C-299/12, *Green – Swan Pharmaceuticals CR, a.s. v Státní zemědělská a potravinářská inspekce, ústřední inspektorát* [2013].

Case C-206/11, *Georg Köck v Schutzverband gegen unlauteren Wettbewerb* [2013].

Case C-657/11, *Belgian Electronic Sorting Technology NV v Peelaers and another* [2013].

Case C-488/11, *Dirk Frederik Asbeek Brusse, Katarina de Man Garabito v Jahani BV* [2013].

Case C342/13, *Katalin Sebestyén v Zsolt Csaba Kővári and others* [2014].

Case C-74/15, *Dumitru Tarcău, Ileana Tarcău v Banca Comercială Intesa Sanpaolo România SA and others* [2015] ECLI:EU:C:2015:772.

Case C-539/14, *Juan Carlos Sánchez Morcillo and María del Carmen Abril García v Banco Bilbao Vizcaya Argentaria SA* [2015] ECLI:EU:C:2015:508

Case C-348/14, *Maria Bucura v SC Bancpost SA* [2015] ECLI:EU:C:2015:447.

Case C-312/14, *Banif Plus Bank Zrt. v Márton Lantos, Mártonné Lantos* [2015] ECLI:EU:C:2015:794.

Case C-49/14, *Finanmadrid EFC SA v Jesús Vicente Albán Zambrano, María Josefa García Zapata, Jorge Luis Albán Zambrano, Miriam Elisabeth Caicedo Merino* [2016] ECLI:EU:C:2016:98.

Case C-7/16, *Banco Popular Español SA and PL Salvador, S.A.R.L. v Maria Rita Giraldez Villar and Modesto Martínez Baz* [2016] ECLI:EU:C:2016:523.

Case C-191/15, *Verein für Konsumenteninformation v Amazon EU Sàrl* [2016] ECLI:EU:C:2016:612.

Case C-537/15, *Euro Bank SA v Marek Łopaciński* [2016] ECLI:EU:C:2016:143.

Case C-613/15, *Ibercaja Banco SAU v José Cortés González* [2016] ECLI:EU:C:2016:195.

5.2. *Opinions of Advocates General (Court of Justice of the European Union)*

Opinion of Advocate General Trstenjak, *Case C-404/06, Quelle AG v Bundesverband der VerbraucherzentralenundVerbraucherverbände.*

Opinion of Advocate General Mazák, Case C-65/09, *Gebr. Weber GmbH v Jürgen Wittmer*, para. 47.

Opinion of Advocate General Mengozzi, Case C-49/11, *Content Services Ltd v Bundesarbeitskammer.*

Opinion of Advocate General Wahl, Case C-435/11, *CHS Tour Services GmbH v Team4 Travel GmbH.*

5.3. *Court of Justice of the European Free Trade Association States*

Case E-4/09, *Inconsult Anstalt v Finanzmarktaufsicht* [2010].

Joint cases T-117/03 to T-119/03 and T-171/03, *New Look Ltd v Office for Harmonisation in the Internal Market (Trade Marks and Designs).*

5.4. *National Case Law*

5.4.1. Belgium

Rb. Eupen (BE) 21 June 2010.

5.4.2. Germany

BGH (2005) DB 1516.

BGH (2002) I ZR 55/00.

BGH (DE) 26. Nov. 2008 VIII ZR 200/05.

BGH, *Unser Dankeschön für Sie,* I ZR 193/07.

BGH, *Einwilligungserklärung für Werbeanrufe,* I ZR 50/09.

Oberlandesgericht Hamm (DE) 12 May 2009 28 U 42/09.

Oberlandesgericht Naumburg (DE) 7 December 2005 6 U 24/05.

5.4.3. France

Cass. 1re civ. 21 Janvier 1995.

Cass. 1re civ., 15 Mars 2005, n°02-13.285.

Civ. 1ère 5 Mars 2002 n°00-18202.

Cass. Civ. I, 16.6.1993, Bull. civ. I no. 224.

Tribunal de commerce de Paris – 29 mars 2007 – Carrefour c/Galaec (la coopérative groupement d'achat des centres Leclerc).

CA Toulouse, CH. 02 SECT, n° 07/0513901, 4 February 2009.

5.4.4. Romania

Curtea Constituțională, 2858D/2010, 12 iulie 2011.

Înalta Curte de Casație și Justiție, Secția Civilă și de Proprietate Intelectuală, Decizia nr. 399, Dosar nr. 2572/35/2006, 24 ianuarie 2008.

Înalta Curte de Casație și Justiție (RO), Secţia a II-a civilă, Decizia nr. 860/2015 Dosar nr. 39074/3/2012, 18 martie 2015.

Curtea de Apel București – Secția a V-a Comercială, Decizia comercială nr. 255 din 25 aprilie 2009.

Curtea de Apel Galați, Secția Comercială, Maritimă și Fluvială, Decizia comercială nr. 21 din 19 Martie 2008.

5.4.5. The Netherlands

HR, C07/012HR, 11 July 2008.

HR, 11/04598, 21 September 2012.

HR, 14/00189, 18 September 2015.

Rechtbank Noord-Nederland, 2844681 CV EXPL 14-3775, 12 August 2014.

5.4.6. The United Kingdom

Suisse Atlantique Société d'Armement Maritime SA v Rotterdamsche Kolen Centrale NV [1967] HL AC 361.

The London Borough of Newham v kathu, Zeb nd Iqbal, and the Office of Fair Trading (Interested Party) [2004] EWCA Civ 55.

DGFT v First National Bank [2001] 3 W.L.R. 1297.

The Office of Fair Trading v Foxtons Limited [2009] EWHC 1681 (Ch).

Director-General of Fair Trading v First National Bank plc [2002] 1 AC 481.

Interfoto Picture Library Ltd v Stiletto Visual Programmes Ltd [1989] 1 QB 433.

Yam Seng Pte v International Trade Corporation Ltd [2013] EWHC 111 (QB).

5.4.7. The United States of America

Citizens United v Federal Election Commission, 558 U.S. 08-205 (2010).

6. Eurobarometers

Eurobarometer 35, 'Public Opinion in the European Community', June 1991.

Eurobarometer Special Report 252, 'Consumer Protection in the Internal Market', September 2006.

Flash Eurobarometer 332, 'Consumers' Attitudes Towards Cross-border Trade and Consumer Protection', May 2012.

Flash Eurobarometer 128, 'Views on Business-to-Consumer Cross-border Trade', January 2015.

Standard Eurobarometer 57.2, 'Health Issues, Cross-Border Purchases, and National Identities', February 2003.

Special Eurobarometer 342, April 2011.

BIBLIOGRAPHY

Abbamonte 2006
Abbamonte, G.B., 'The Unfair Commercial Practices Directive: An Example of the New European Consumer Protection Approach', *Columbia Journal of European Law*, 2006, Vol. 12, p. 695-712.

Abbamonte 2007
Abbamonte, G.B., 'The Unfair Commercial Practices Directive and its General Prohibition', in Weatherill, S. & Bernitz, U. (eds.), *The Regulation of Unfair Commercial Practices under EC Directive 2005/29*, Oxford: Hart Publishing, 2007, p. 11-32.

Abbott 2000
Abbott, S., *Understanding Analysis*, New York: Springer, 2000.

Ackermann 2010
Ackermann, Th., 'Vodafone: Price Regulation as a Substitute for Intervention under Article 102 TFEU', *Journal of European Competition Law & Practice*, 2010, Vol. 1(5), p. 426-428.

Alemanno & Garde 2013
Alemanno, A. & Garde, A., 'The Emergence of an EU Lifestyle Policy: The Case Of Alcohol, Tobacco and Unhealthy Diets', *Common Market Law Review*, 2013, Vol. 50, p. 1745-1786.

Ambroise-Castérot 2009
Ambroise-Castérot, C., 'Les nouvelles pratiques commerciales déloyales après la loi LME du 4 août 2008', *AJ Pénal*, 2009.22.

Anagnostaras 2007
Anagnostaras, G., 'The Unfair Commercial Practices Directive in Context: From Legal Disparity to Legal Complexity?', *Common Market Law Review*, 2007, Vol. 47, p. 147-171.

Anderson 2011
Anderson, L., 'Demystifying the Arab Spring', *Foreign Affairs,* 2011, Vol. 90(3), p. 2-7.

Andrews 2004-2005
Andrews, R., 'Electronic Commerce: Lessons Learned From the European Legal Model', *Intellectual Property Law Bulletin,* 2004-2005, Vol. 9, p. 81-94.

Ariely 2009
Ariely, D., *Predictably Irrational - The Hidden Forces that Shape Our Decisions,* New York: Harper Collins, 2009.

Atiyah *et al.* 2005
Atiyah, P.S. *et al., The Sale of Goods,* Essex: Pearson, 2005.

Augenhofer 2011
Augenhofer, S., 'A European Civil Law - for Whom and What Should it Include? Reflections on the Scope of Application of a Future European Legal Instrument', *European Review of Contract Law,* 2011, Vol. 7(2), p. 195-218.

Avena-Robardet 2009
Avena-Robardet, V., 'Faculté de rétractation dans les ventes à distance: entre illusion et réalité', *Recueil Le Dalloz,* 2009, p. 2161-2162.

Baffi & Santella 2011
Baffi, E. & Santella, P., 'The Economics of Legal Harmonisation', available at: <http://papers.ssrn.com/sol3/papers.cfm?abstract_id=1690967>, last accessed on 27 July 2016.

Bain & Subirana 2003
Bain, M. & Subirana, B., 'E-commerce Oriented Software Agents: Some Legal Challenges of Advertising and Semi-autonomous Contracting Agents', *Computer Law & Security Review,* 2003, Vol. 19(4), p. 282-288.

Balate 1997
Balate, E., 'La mise en oeuvre de la directive 93/13 ce concernant les clauses abusives dans les contrats conclus avec les consommateurs en droit belge', *European Review of Private Law,* 1997, Vol. 5(2), p. 143-150.

Bakos *et al.* 2014
Bakos, Y. *et al.*, 'Does Anyone Read the Fine Print? Consumer Attention to Standard Form Contracts', *Journal of Legal Studies,* 2014, Vol. 43(2), p. 1-35.

Bar-Gill 2012
Bar-Gill, O., *Seduction by Contract: Law, Economics, and Psychology in Consumer Markets,* Oxford: Oxford University Press, 2012.

Barnard 2007
Barnard, C., *The Substantive Law of the EU: The Four Freedoms,* Oxford: Oxford University Press, 2007.

Barron 2008
Barron, A., 'The Unfair Commercial Practices Directive - Alternatives in UK Law', in Parry, D. *et al.* (eds.), *The Yearbook of Consumer Law 2009,* Surrey: Ashgate Publishing, 2008, p. 289-305.

Beale 1978
Beale, H., 'Unfair Contract Terms Act 1977', *British Journal of Law and Society,* 1978, Vol. 5(1), p. 114-121.

Beale 2005
Beale, H., 'The Development of European Private Law and the European Commission's Action Plan on Contract Law', *Juridica International,* 2005, Vol. 10, p. 4-11.

Beale 2006
Beale, H., 'General Clauses and specific rules in the Principles of European Contract Law: the good faith clause', in Grundmann, S. & Mazeaud, D. (eds.), *General Clauses and Standards in European Contract Laws - Comparative Law EC Law and Codification Chapter,* The Hague: Kluwer Law International, 2006, p. 205-220.

Beale 2011
Beale, H., 'The Draft Academic Common Frame of Reference and the 'toolbox'', in Andenas, D. & Baasch Andersen, C. (eds.), *Theory and Practice of Harmonisation,* Cheltenham: Edward Elgar Publishing, 2011, p. 115-128.

Bech Serrat 2010
Bech Serrat, J.M., 'Why is there a Separation between Distance Selling in EU Law and the Tourism Industry?', *Journal of Consumer Policy,* 2010, Vol. 33, p. 75-89.

Beck 2013
Beck, G., *The Legal Reasoning of the Court of Justice of the EU,* Oxford: Hart Publishing, 2013.

Beckers 2014
Beckers, A., *Taking Corporate Codes Seriously,* PhD dissertation, Maastricht, 2014.

Ben-Shahar 2009
Ben-Shahar, O., 'The Myth of 'Opportunity to Read' in Contract Law', *European Review of Contract Law,* 2009, Vol. 5(1), p. 1-28.

Ben-Shahar & Posner 2011
Ben-Shahar, O. & Posner, E.A., 'The Right to Withdraw in Contract Law', *Journal of Legal Studies,* 2011, Vol. 40(1), p. 115-148.

Ben-Shahar & Schneider 2014
Ben-Shahar, O. & Schneider, C.E., *More Than You Wanted to Know: The Failure of Mandated Disclosure,* Princeton: Princeton University Press, 2014.

Bernitz 2000
Bernitz, U., 'Swedish Standard Contract Law and the EC Directive on Contract Terms', *Scandinavian Studies in Law,* 2000, Vol. 39, p. 13-27.

Bernitz 2007
Bernitz, U., 'Scope, Ambitions and Relation to Unfair Competition Law', in Weatherill, S. & Bernitz, U. (eds.), *The Regulation of Unfair Commercial Practices under EC Directive 2005/29,* Oxford: Hart Publishing, 2007, p. 33-46.

Bianca & Grundmann 2002
Bianca, M.C. & Grundmann, S. (eds.), *EU Sales Directive: Commentary,* Antwerp: Intersentia, 2002.

Bird 2001
Bird, T.C. 'Directive 99/44/EC on certain aspects of the sale of consumer goods and associated guarantees: its impact on existing Irish sale of goods law', *European Review of Private Law,* 2001, Vol. 9(2/3), p. 279-295.

Blair & Brent 2004
Blair, W. & Brent, R., 'A Single European Law of Contract?', *European Business Law Review,* 2004, Vol. 15(1), p. 5-21.

Boodman 1991
Boodman, M., 'The Myth of Harmonisation of Laws', *American Journal of Comparative Law,* 1991, Vol. 39(4), p. 699-724.

Borges & Irlenbusch 2007
Borges, G. & Irlenbusch, B., 'Fairness Crowded Out by Law: An Experimental Study on Withdrawal Rights', *Journal of Institutional and Theoretical Economics,* 2007, Vol. 163, p. 84-101.

Bourgoignie 1999
Bourgoignie, Th., '*La transposition de la directive 93/13/CEE dans le droit belge: un processus (très) évolutif et (trop) confidentiel*', available at: <http://ec.europa.eu/consumers/policy/developments/unfa_cont_term/uct04_en.pdf>, prepared with the occasion of the Brussels Conferende 'The 'Unfair Terms' Directive, Five Years On, Evaluation and Future Perspectives', last accessed on 27 July 2016.

Bradgate 1997
Bradgate, R., 'The EU Directive on Distance Selling', *Web Journal of Current Legal Issues,* 1997, Vol. 4.

Bradgate & Twigg-Flesner 2002
Bradgate, R. & Twigg-Flesner, C., 'Expanding the Boundaries of Liability for Quality Defects', *Journal of Consumer Policy*, 2002, Vol. 25(3), p. 345-377.

Brand 1996
Brand, R.L., 'Semantic Distinctions in an Age of Legal Convergence', *University of Pennsylvania Journal of International Economic Law*, 1996, Vol. 17, p. 3-5.

Braucher 2013
Braucher, J., 'Unfair Terms in Comparative Perspective: Software Contracts', in DiMatteo, L. & Zhou, Q. (eds.), *Commercial Contract Law – Transatlantic Perspectives*, New York: Cambridge University Press, 2013, p. 339-365.

Brenncke 2010
Brenncke, M., 'Case C-58/08, Vodafone Ltd and Others v. Secretary of State for Business, Enterprise and Regulatory Reform, Judgment of the Court of Justice (Grand Chamber) of 8 June 2010', *Common Market Law Review*, 2010, Vol. 47(6). p. 1793-1814.

Bright 2000
Bright, S., 'Winning the Battle against Unfair Contract Terms', *Legal Studies*, 2000, Vol. 20(3), p. 331-352.

Bright & Bright 1995
Bright, C. & Bright, S., 'Unfair Terms in Land Contracts: Copy Out or Cop Out?', *Law Quarterly Review*, 1995, Vol. 111, p. 655-673.

Buckland 2007
Buckland, W.W., *A Text-Book of Roman Law from Augustus to Justinian*, Cambridge: Cambridge University Press, 2007.

Budaite & Van Dam 2007
Budaite, E. & Van Dam, C., 'The Statutory Frameworks and General Rules on Unfair Commercial Practices in the 25 EU Member States on the Eve of Harmonisation', in Twigg-Flesner, C. *et al.* (eds.), *The Yearbook of Consumer Law 2008*, Surrey: Ashgate, 2007, p. 107-139.

Bull *et al.* 2015
Bull, W. *et al.*, 'Who Does What in Consumer Law? A Search for Criteria for Centralised Lawmaking', in Akkermans, B. *et al.* (eds.), *Who Does What?: On the Allocation of Regulatory Competences in European Private Law*, Antwerp: Intersentia, 2015, p. 97-124.

Burgess 1986
Burgess, A., 'Consumer Adhesion Contracts and Unfair Terms: A Critique of Current Theory and a Suggestion', *Anglo-American Law Review*, 1986, Vol. 15, p. 255-280.

Cabrelli & Siems 2015
Cabrelli, D. & Siems, M., 'Convergence, Legal Origins, and Transplants in Comparative Corporate Law: A Case-Based and Quantitative Analysis', *American Journal of Comparative Law,* 2015, Vol. 63, p. 109-153.

Cafaggi 2007
Cafaggi, F., 'Self-Regulation in European Contract Law', *European Journal of Legal Studies,* 2007, Vol. 1(1), p. 163-218.

Cafaggi 2008
Cafaggi, F., 'The Making of European Private Law: Governance Design', in Cafaggi, F. & Muir-Watt, H. (eds.), *Making European Private Law: Governance Design,* Cheltenham: Edward Elgar Publishing, 2008, p. 289-352.

Cafaggi & Micklitz 2008
Cafaggi, F. & Micklitz, H.-W., 'Collective Enforcement of Consumer Law: A Framework for Comparative Assessment', *European Review of Private Law,* 2008, Vol. 16(3), p. 391-425

Cafaggi & Nicita 2012
Cafaggi, F. & Nicita, A., 'The Evolution of Consumer Protection in the EU', in Eger, Th. & Schäfer, H.-B. (eds.), *Research Handbook on the Economics of European Union Law,* Cheltenahm: Edward Elgar Publishing, 2012, p. 263-278.

Cairo 2013
Cairo, A., *The Functional Art: An Introduction to Information Graphics and Visualisation,* Berkeley: New Riders, 2013.

Calliess 2002
Calliess, G.-P., 'The Limits of Eclecticism in Consumer Law: National Struggles and the Hope for a coherent European Contract Law. A Comment on the ECJ's and the FCJ's 'Heininger'- decisions', *German Law Journal,* 2002, Vol. 3(8), available at: <www.germanlawjournal.com>, last visted on 27 July 2016.

Calliess 2003
Calliess, G.-P., 'Coherence and Consistency in European Consumer Contract Law: a Progress Report The European Commission's Action Plan COM(2003) 68 final and the Green Paper on the Modernisation of the 1980 Rome Convention COM(2002) 654 final - PART I/II', *German Law Journal,* 2003, Vol. 4, available at: <www.germanlawjournal.com>, last visted on 27 July 2016.

Castermans 2011
Castermans,A.G., 'Towards a European Contract Law through Social Dialogue', *European Review of Contract Law,* 2011, Vol. 7(2), p. 360-367.

Cauffman 2012
Cauffman, C., 'The Impact of EU Law on Belgian Consumer Law Terminology', *European Review of Private Law,* 2012, Vol. 20(5/6), p. 1325-1352.

Cauffman 2015
Cauffman, C., 'The Principle of Proportionality and European Contract Law', in Rutgers, J. & Sirena, P. (eds.), *Rules And Principles In European Contract Law,* Cambridge: Intersentia, 2015, p. 69-98.

Chalmers *et al.* 2010
Chalmers, D. *et al., European Union Law,* Cambridge: Cambridge University Press, 2010.

Chalmers *et al.* 2011
Chalmers, D. *et al., European Union Law, Cases and Materials,* Cambridge: Cambridge University Press, 2011.

Cherednychenko & Kuiper 2008
Cherednychenko, O. & Kuiper, S.H., 'De Wet oneerlijke handelspraktijken en financiële dienstverlening', *Nederlands Tijdschrift voor Burgerlijk Recht,* 2008, Vol. 44, p. 1-18.

Chirico & Larouche 2013
Chirico, F. & Larouche, P., 'Conceptual Divergence, Functionalism and the Economics of Convergence - Contribution for Binding Unity/Diverging', in Larouche P. & Cserne, P. (eds.), *National Legal Systems and Globalisation,* The Hague: Asser Press, 2013, p. 9-34.

Chiu 2008
Chiu, I.H.-Y., *Regulatory Convergence in EU Securities Regulation,* Alphen aan den Rijn: Kluwer Law International, 2008.

Chomsky 2010
Chomsky, N., *Hopes and Prospects,* Chicago: Haymarket Books, 2010.

Collins 1994
Collins, H., 'Good Faith in European Contract Law', *Oxford Journal of Legal Studies* 1994, Vol. 14, p. 229-254.

Collins 2002
Collins, H., 'Transaction Costs and Subsidiarity in European Contract Law', in Grundmann, S. & Stuyck, J. (eds.), *An Academic Green Paper on European Contract Law,* The Hague: Kluwer Law International, 2002, p. 269-281.

Collins 2004
Collins, H., 'EC Regulation of Unfair Commercial Practices', in Collins, H. (ed.), *The Forthcoming EC Directive on Unfair Commercial Practices,* The Hague: Kluwer Law International, 2004, p. 1-42.

Collins 2005
Collins, H., 'The Unfair Commercial Practices Directive', *European Review of Private Law,* 2005, Vol. 1, p. 417-441.

Collins 2008a
Collins, H., *The European Civil Code – The Way Forward,* Cambridge: Cambridge University Press, 2008.

Collins 2008b
Collins, H., 'The Directive on Unfair Contract Terms: Implementation, Effectiveness and Harmonisation', in Collins, H. (ed.), *Standard Contract Terms in Europe: A Basis for and a Challenge to European Contract Law,* The Hague: Kluwer Law International, 2008, p. 1-18.

Collins 2010
Collins, H., 'Harmonisation by Example: European Laws against Unfair Commercial Practices', *Modern Law Review,* 2010, Vol. 73(1), p. 89-118.

Collins 2011
Collins, H., 'The Constitutionalisation of European Private Law as a Path to Social Justice?', in Micklitz, H.-W. (ed.), *The Many Concepts of Social Justice in European Private Law,* Cheltenham: Edward Elgar, 2011, p. 133-165.

Collins 2013
Collins, H., 'Why Europe Needs a Civil Code', *European Review of Private Law,* 2013, Vol. 4, p. 907-922.

Colombi Ciacchi 2005
Colombi Ciacchi, A., 'Non-Legislative Harmonisation of Private Law under the European Constitution: The Case of Unfair Suretyships', *European Review of Private Law,* 2005, Vol. 13(3), p. 285-308.

Comșa 2014
Comsa, P., 'A Fresh Approach to Unfair Terms in Commercial Contracts: Are the Latest Law Amendments Beneficial to Consumers?', *Challenges of the Knowledge Society. Private Law,* 2014, Vol. 4, p. 96-115.

Conant 2002
Conant, L., *Justice Contained – Law and Politics in the European Union,* New York: Cornell University Press, 2002.

Conklin 2007-2008
Conklin, R.S., 'Be Careful What You Click For: An Analysis of Online Contracting', *Loyola Consumer Law Review*, 2007-2008, Vol. 20, p. 325-347.

Conway 2010
Conway, G., 'Conflicts of Competence Norms in EU Law and the Legal Reasoning of the ECJ', *German Law Journal*, 2010, Vol. 11, p. 966-1005.

Coote 1978
Coote, B., 'Unfair Contract Terms Act 1977', *The Modern Law Review*, 1978, Vol. 41(3), p. 312-324.

Coteanu 2005
Coteanu, C., *Cyber Consumer Law and Unfair Trading Practices*, Hampshire/-Burlington: Ashgate Publishing, 2005.

Craig & De Burca 2003
Craig, P. & De Búrca, G., *EU Law. Texts, Cases and Materials*, Oxford: Oxford University Press, 2003.

Cristas 2011
Cristas, A., 'Green Paper on Policy Options for Progress Towards a European Contract Law for Consumers and Businesses What do we want?', *European Review of Contract Law*, 2011, Vol. 7(2), p. 314-334.

Cuniberti 2006
Cuniberti, G., 'Is the CISG Benefiting Anybody?', *Vanderbilt Journal of Transnational Law*, 2006, Vol. 39, p. 1511-1550.

Cuniberti 2014
Cuniberti, G., 'The International Market for Contracts: The Most Attractive Contract Laws', *Northwestern Journal of International Law & Business*, 2014, Vol. 34(3), p. 455-517.

Danglehant 1995
Danglehant, C., 'Commentaire de la loi n° 95-96 du 1er février 1995 concernant les clauses abusives et la présentation des contrats', *Recueil Dalloz*, 1995, p. 127-134.

Dannemann 2009
Dannemann, G., *The German Law of Unjustified Enrichment and Restitution: A Comparative Introduction*, Oxford: Oxford University Press, 2009.

Davis 2007
Davis, N.J., 'Presumed Assent: The Judicial Acceptance of Clickwrap', *Berkeley Technology Law Journal*, 2007, Vol. 22, p. 577-598.

Davo 1997
Davo, H., 'Clauses abusives: loi du février 1995 transposant la directive 93/13/CEE en droit français', *European Review of Private Law,* 1997, Vol. 5(2), p. 157-164.

Dean 1993
Dean, M., 'Unfair Contract Terms: The European Approach', *The Modern Law Review,* 1993, Vol. 56(4), p. 581-590.

Deards 1998
Deards, E., 'The Proposed Guarantees Directive: Is It Fit for the Purpose?', *Journal of Consumer Policy,* 1998, Vol. 21, p. 99-119.

De Groot 2012
De Groot, G.-R., 'Legal Translation', in Smits, J. (ed.), *Elgar Encyclopedia of Comparative Law,* Cheltenham: Edward Elgar, 2012, p. 538-549.

De Ruiter 2014
De Ruiter, R., 'Public Parliamentary Activities and Open Methods of Coordination', *The Journal of Legislative Studies,* 2014, Vol. 20(1), p. 62-77.

De Vries 2006
De Vries, S.A., *Tensions within the Internal Market,* Groningen: Europa Law Publishing, 2006.

De Vries 2012
De Vries, A., 'The Aim for Complete Uniformity in EU Private Law: An Obstacle to Further Harmonisation', *European Review of Private Law,* 2012, Vol. 20(4), p. 913-932.

Dickie 1998
Dickie, J., 'Consumer Confidence and the EC Directive on Distance Contracts', *Journal of Consumer Policy,* 1998, Vol. 21, p. 217-229.

Djankov *et al.* 2002
Djankov, S. *et al.*, 'Courts: the Lex Mundi project', National Bureau of Economic Research Working Paper 8890, 2002.

Donnelly & White 2005
Donnelly, M. & White, F., 'The Distance Selling Directives - A Time for Review', *Northern Ireland Legal Quarterly,* 2005, Vol. 56, p. 200-235.

Drucker & Gumpert 2010
Drucker, S.J. & Gumpert, G., 'Introduction: Regulating Convergence', in Drucker, S.J. & Gumpert, G., *Regulating Convergence,* New York: Peter Lang Publishing, 2010, p. 1-20.

Duivenvoorde 2015
Duivenvoorde, B.B., *The Consumer Benchmarks in the Unfair Commercial Practices Directive,* Cham: Springer, 2015.

Dumitru 2012
Dumitru, M., 'Considerations on the Modification of the Law Number 193/2000 Regarding the Abusive Clauses Included in the Contracts Entered into between Professionals and Consumers', *Jurnalul de Studii Juridice,* 2012, Vol. 3/4 p. 103-108.

Ebers 2010a
Ebers, M., 'From Minimum to Full Harmonisation - The Proposal for a Directive on Consumer Rights', *InDret,* 2010, Vol. 2, p. 1-47.

Ebers 2010b
Ebers, M., 'ECJ (First Chamber) 6 October 2009, Case C-40/08, *Asturcom Telecomunicaciones SL v Cristina Rodríguez Nogueira* - From Océano to Asturcom: Mandatory Consumer Law, Ex Officio Application of European Union Law and Res Judicata', *European Review of Private Law,* 2010, Vol. 18(4), p. 823-846.

Editorial Comments 2005
Editorial Comments, 'European Contract Law: Quo Vadis?', *Common Market Law Review,* 2005, Vol. 42, p. 1-7.

Eickelmann 2009
Eickelmann, S., 'No General Requirement to Pay Compensation for the Use of Goods after Withdrawal from a Distance Contract', *European Law Reporter,* 2009, p. 398-403.

Eichengreen & Boltho 2010
Eichengreen, B. & Boltho, A., 'The Economic Impact of European Integration', in Broadberry, S. & O'Rourke, K. (eds.), *The Cambridge Economic History of Modern Europe: Volume 2, 1870 to the Present,* Cambridge: Cambridge University Press, 2010, p. 267-295.

Eidenmueller *et al.* 2011
Eidenmueller, H. *et al.*, 'Towards a Revision of the Consumer Acquis', *Common Market Law Review,* 2011, Vol. 48, p. 1077-1123.

Epstein 2012
Epstein, R., 'Harmonisation, Heterogeneity and Regulation: Why the Common European Sales Law Should Be Scrapped', 2012, available at: <www.law.uchicago.edu/files/files/RAE%20paper.pdf>, last accessed on 21 July 2016.

Estrella-Faria 2009
Estrella-Faria, J.A., 'Future Directions of Legal Harmonisation and Law Reform: Stormy Seas or Prosperous Voyage?', *Uniform Law Review,* 2009, Vol. 14(1-2), p. 5-34.

European Consumer Law Group 1998
European Consumer Law Group, 'Opinion on the Proposal for a Directive on the Sale of Consumer Goods and Associated Guarantees', *Journal of Consumer Policy,* 1998, Vol. 21, p. 91-97.

Falkner *et al.* 2007
Falkner, G. *et al.*, 'Worlds of compliance: Why leading approaches to European Union implementation are only 'sometimes-true theories'', *European Journal of Political Research,* 2007, Vol. 46(3), p. 395-416.

Faure 2008
Faure, M., 'Towards a Maximum Harmonisation of Consumer Contract Law?', *Maastricht Journal of European & Comparative Law,* 2008, Vol. 15(4), p. 433-446.

Faure & Luth 2011
Faure, M.G. & Luth, H.A., 'Behavioural Economics in Unfair Contract Terms: Cautions and Considerations', *Journal of Consumer Policy* 2011, Vol. 34, p. 337-358.

Faure &Van der Walt 2010
Faure, M. & Van der Walt, A, (eds.), *Globalisation and Private Law, The Way Forward,* Cheltenham: Edward Elgar Publishing, 2010.

Faure *et al.* 2008
Faure, M. *et al.*, 'Enforcement Practices for Breaches of Consumer Protection Legislation', *Loyola Consumer Law Review,* 2008, Vol. 20, p. 361-401.

Fauvarque-Cosson & Mazeaud 2008
Fauvarque-Cosson, B. & Mazeaud, D. (eds.), *European Contract Law: Materials for a Common Frame of Reference: Terminology, Guiding Principles, Model Rules,* Munich: Sellier, 2008.

Fazio 2007
Fazio, S., *The Harmonisation of International Commercial Law,* Alphen aan den Rijn: Kluwer Law International, 2007.

Founds 1999-2000
Founds, G.L., 'Shrinkwrap and Clickwrap Agreements: 2B or Not 2B?', *Federal Communications Law Journal,* 1999-2000, Vol. 52, p. 99-124.

Friedberg 1990-1991
Friedberg, J.J., 'The Convergence of Law in an Era of Political Integration: The Wood Pulp Case and the Alcoa Effects Doctrine', *University of Pittsburgh Law Review,* 1990-1991, Vol. 52, p. 289-326.

Friedman & Teubner 1986
Friedman, L. & Teubner, G., 'Legal Education and Legal Integration', in Cappelletti, M. *et al.* (eds.), *Integration through Law - Europe and the Federal Experience,* Berlin: Wolter de Gruyter, 1986, p. 345-380.

Frier 1985
Frier, B.W., *The Rise of the Roman Jurists: Studies in Cicero's Pro Caecina,* Princeton: Princeton University Press, 1985.

Fry 2005
Fry, B., *Visualizing Data,* Sebastopol: O'Reilly, 2005.

Fukuyama 2011
Fukuyama, F., *New Ideas of Development after the Financial Crisis,* Baltimore: John Hopkins University Press, 2011.

Gambaro 2003
Gambaro, A., 'The *Plan d'Action* of the European Commission - A Comment', *European Review of Private Law,* 2003, Vol. 11(6), p. 768-781.

Ghemawat 2011
Ghemawat, P., *World 3.0 - Global Prosperity and How to Achieve It,* Boston: Harvard Business Review Press, 2011.

Gielissen 2011
Gielissen, R.B., 'Why Do Consumers Buy Socially Responsible Products?', *International Journal of Business and Social Science,* 2011, Vol. 2(3), p. 21-35.

Girot 2001
Girot, C., *User Protection in It Contracts: A Comparative Study of the Protection of the User Against Defective Performance in Information Technology,* The Hague: Kluwer Law International, 2001.

Glaeser & Schleifer 2002
Glaeser, E.L. & Schleifer, A., 'Legal Origins', *Quarterly Journal of Economics,* 2002, p. 1193-1229.

Goanta 2013
Goanta, C., 'Information Duties in the Internet Era: Case Note on *Content Services Ltd v Bundesarbeitskammer*', *European Review of Private Law,* 2013, Vol. 21(2), p. 643-659.

Gómez-Pomar 2011
Gómez-Pomar, F., 'Some Law and Economics of Harmonizing European Private Law', in Von Bar, C. & Hartkamp, A.S. (eds.), *Towards a European Civil Code,* Alphen aan den Rijn: Kluwer Law International, 2011, p. 401-426.

Gómez-Pomar & Ganuza 2011a
Gómez-Pomar, F. & Ganuza, J.J., 'Economic Underpinnings of European Private Law Harmonisation', in Schulze, R. & Schulte-Nölke, H. (eds.), *European Private Law - Current Status and Perspectives,* München: Sellier, 2011, p. 27-56.

Gómez-Pomar & Ganuza 2011b
Gómez-Pomar, F. & Ganuza, J.J., 'An Economic Analysis of Harmonisation Regimes: Full Harmonisation, Minimum Harmonisation or Optional Instrument?', *European Review of Contract Law,* 2011, Vol. 7(2), p. 275-294.

Gómez & Gili-Saldaña 2014
Gómez, F. & Gili-Saldaña, M., 'Termination as a Remedy in the Common European Sales Law: A Law and Economics Approach', *European Review of Contract Law,* 2014, Vol. 10(3), p. 331-364.

Goode 2003
Goode, R., 'Contract and Commercial Law: The Logic and Limits of Harmonisation', *Electronic Journal of Comparative Law,* 2003, Vol. 7(4).

Gordley & Von Mehren 2006
Gordley, J. & Von Mehren, A.T., *An Introduction to the Comparative Study of Private Law: Readings, Cases, Materials,* Cambridge: Cambridge University Press, 2006.

Gormley 2006
Gormley, L.W., 'The Internal Market : History and Evolution', in Nic Shuibhne, N. (ed.), *Regulating the Internal Market,* Cheltenham: Edward Elgar Publishing, 2006, p. 14-28.

Grundmann 2002
Grundmann, S., 'Introduction', in Bianca, M.C. & Grundmann, S. (eds.), *EU Sales Directive: Commentary,* Antwerp: Intersentia, 2002, p. 13-90.

Grundmann 2003
Grundmann, S., 'Consumer Law, Commercial Law, Private Law: How Can the Sales Directive and the Sales Convention Be So Similar?', *European Business Law Review,* 2003, Vol. 14(3), p. 237-257.

Grundmann 2006a
Grundmann, S., 'General Standards and Principles, *Clauses Générales* and *Generalklauseln* in European Contract Law', in Grundmann, S. & Mazeaud, D., *General Clauses and Standards in European Contract Law,* The Hague: Kluwer Law International, 2006, p. 1-20.

Grundmann 2006b
Grundmann, S., 'Structural Elements in the Contract Law Parts of the German Civil Code', in Grundmann, S. & Schauer, M., *The Architecture of European Codes and Contract Law,* The Hague: Kluwer Law International, 2006, p. 57-82.

Grundmann *et al.* 2001
Grundmann, S. *et al.*, 'Party Autonomy and the Role of Information in the Internal Market - an Overview', in Grundmann, S. *et al.* (eds.), *Party Autonomy and the Role of Information in the Internal Market,* Berlin: Walter de Gruyter, 2001, p. 3-38.

Gutman 2011
Gutman, K., 'The Commission's 2010 Green Paper on European Contract Law: Reflections on Union Competence in Light of the Proposed Options', *European Review of Contract Law,* 2011, Vol. 7(2), p. 151-172.

Gutman 2014
Gutman, K., *The Constitutional Foundations of European Contract Law: A Comparative Analysis,* Oxford: Oxford University Press, 2014.

Hacker 2015
Hacker, Ph., 'The Behavioral Divide - A Critique of the Differential Implementation of Behavioral Law and Economics in the US and the EU', *European Review of Contract Law,* 2015, Vol. 11(4), p. 299-345.

Halson & Campbell 2013
Halson, R. & Campbell, D., 'Harmonisation and Its Discontents: A Transaction Costs Critique of a European Contract Law' in Devenney, J. & Kenny, M. (eds.), *The Transformation of European Private Law - Harmonisation, Consolidation, Codification or Chaos?,* Cambridge: Cambridge University Press, 2013, p. 100-130.

Hartkamp *et al.* 2010
Hartkamp, A. *et al.* (eds.), *Towards a European Civil Code,* The Hague: Wolters Kluwer, 2010.

Hartley 1996
Hartley, T.C., 'Five Forms of Uncertainty in European Community Law', *Cambridge Law Review,* 1996, Vol. 55(2), p. 265-288.

Hedley 2006
Hedley, S., *The Law of Electronic Commerce and the Internet in the UK and Ireland,* London: Routledge, 2006.

Heiderhoff 2011
Heiderhoff, B., 'Constitutional Interpretation and European Interpretation in Private Law in Germany', in Zmij, G. & Heiderhoff, B. (eds.), *Interpretation in Polish, German and European Private Law,* Munchen: Sellier, 2011, p. 101-120.

Heinze 2014
Heinze, E., 'The Literary Model in Comparative Law: Shakespeare, Corneille, Racine', *Journal of Comparative Law,* 2014, Vol. 9(2), p. 17-27.

Heirbaut & Storme 2010
Heirbaut, D. & Storme, M.E., 'The Historical Evolution of European Private Law', in Twigg-Flesner, C. (ed.), *European Union Private Law,* Cambridge: Cambridge University Press, 2010, p. 20-32.

Helland & Klick 2011
Helland, E. & Klick, J., 'Legal Origins and Empirical Credibility', in Faure, M. & Smits, J. (eds.), *Does Law Matter – On Law and Economic Growth,* Antwerp: Intersentia, 2011, p. 99-114.

Helland & Klick 2013
Helland, E. & Klick, J., 'Regulation and Litigation: Complements or Substitutes?', in Buckley, F.H. (ed.), *The American Illness: Essays on the Rule of Law,* New Haven: Yale University Press, 2013, p. 118-136.

Henderson & Poulter 2002
Henderson, K. & Poulter, A., 'The Distance Selling Directive: Points for Future Revision', *International Review of Law Computers & Technology,* 2002, Vol. 16(3), p. 289-300.

Hermida 2004
Hermida, J., 'Convergence of Civil Law and Common Law Contracts in the Space Field', *Hong Kong Law Journal,* 2004, Vol. 34(2), p. 339-376.

Hesselink 2004
Hesselink, M.W., 'The European Commission's Action Plan: Towards a More Coherent European Contract Law?', *European Review of Private Law,* 2004, Vol. 12(4), p. 397-419.

Hesselink 2005
Hesselink, M., 'Non-Mandatory Rules in European Contract Law', *European Review of Contract Law,* 2005, Vol. 1(1), p. 44-86.

Hesselink 2006
Hesselink, M. (ed.), *The Politics of a European Civil Code,* The Hague: Kluwer Law International, 2006.

Hesselink 2008a
Hesselink, M., *CFR & Social Justice,* Munich: Sellier, 2008.

Hesselink 2008b
Hesselink, M., 'A European Legal Method? On European Private Law and Scientific Method', *European Law Journal,* 2008, Vol. 15, p. 20-45.

Hesselink 2011a
Hesselink, M.W., 'A Spontaneous Order for Europe? Why Hayek's Libertarianism is Not the Right Way Forward for European Private Law', in Micklitz, H.-W. & Cafaggi, F. (eds.), *European Private Law after the Common Frame of Reference,* Cheltenham: Edward Elgar Publishing, 2011, p. 123-146.

Hesselink 2011b
Hesselink, M., ''If You Don't Like our Principles We Have Others'; On Core Values and Underlying Principles in European Private Law: A Critical Discussion of the New 'Principles' Section in the Draft CFR', in Brownsword, R. *et al.* (eds.), *The Foundations of European Private Law,* Oxford: Hart Publishing, 2011, p. 59-72.

Hesselink 2011c
Hesselink, M., 'The Concept of Good Faith', in Hartkamp, A. *et al.* (eds.), *Towards a European Civil Code,* The Hague: Kluwer Law International, 2011, p. 619-650.

Hijma 2009
Hijma, J., 'Sale of Consumer Goods: The Adaptation of (Dutch) National Law to Transnational Demands', in Snijders, H.J. & Vogenauer, S. (eds.), *Content and Meaning of National Law in Transnational Context,* Munich: Sellier, 2009, p. 89-100.

Hijma & Valk 2004
Hijma, J. & Valk, W.L., *Wettelijke bedenktijd,* The Hague: Kluwer Law International, 2004.

Hondius 1978
Hondius, E., 'Unfair Contract Terms: New Control Systems', *American Journal of Comparative Law,* 1978, Vol. 26, p. 525-549.

Hondius 1994
Hondius, E., 'EC Directive on Unfair Terms in Consumer Contracts', *Journal of Contract Law,* 1994, Vol. 7, p. 34-52.

Hondius 1995
Hondius, E., 'The Reception of the Directive on Unfair Terms in Consumer Contracts by Member States', *European Review of Private Law,* 1995, Vol. 3, p. 241-255.

Hondius 1997
Hondius, E., 'Non-implementation of the Directive on Unfair Contract Terms - The Dutch Case', *European Review of Private Law,* 1997, Vol. 5(2), p. 193-196.

Hondius 2004
Hondius, E., 'European Private Law - Survey 2002-2004', *European Review of Private Law,* 2004, Vol. 12(6), p. 855-899.

Hondius 2006
Hondius, E., 'Clasifications', in Chorus, J. *et al.* (eds.), *Introduction to Dutch Law,* The Hague: Kluwer Law International, 2006, p. 69-74.

Hondius 2011
Hondius, E., 'The Proposal for a Directive on Consumer Rights: The Emperor's New Clothes?', *European Review of Private Law,* 2011, Vol. 19(2), p. 163-166.

Hondius & Schelhaas 2001
Hondius, E. & t Schelhaas, H., 'In conformity with the Consumer Sales Directive? Some remarks on transposition into Dutch law', *European Review of Private Law,* 2001, Vol. 9(2-3), p. 327-336.

Hörnle *et al.* 2002
Hörnle, J. *et al.*, 'Directive 97/7/EC on the Protection of Consumers in Respect of Distance Contracts', in Lodder, A.R. & Kaspersen, H. (eds.), *eDirectives: Guide to European Union Law on E-Commerce,* The Hague: Kluwer Law International, 2002, p. 11-31.

Horsley 2013
Horsley, Th., 'Reflections on the Role of the Court of Justice as the 'Motor' of European Integration: *Legal* Limits to Judicial Lawmaking', *Common Market Law Review,* 2013, Vol. 50, p. 931-964.

Howells 2002
Howells, G., 'Secola Conference Report', *European Review of Private Law,* 2002, Vol. 10(3), p. 475-477.

Howells 2006
Howells, G., 'Introduction', in Howells, G. *et al., European Fair Trading Law: The Unfair Commercial Practices Directive,* Hampshire: Ashgate Publishing Limited, 2006, p. 1-26.

Howells 2007
Howells, G., 'Consumer Concepts for a European Code?', in Schulze, R. (ed.), *New Features in Contract Law,* Munich: Sellier, 2007, p. 119-138.

Howells 2011
Howells, G., 'Unfair Commercial Practices - Future Directions', in Schulze, R. & Schulte-Nölke, H. (eds.), *European Private Law - Current Status and Perspectives,* Munich: Sellier, 2011, p. 133-144.

Howells & Schulze 2009
Howells, G. & Schulze, R., 'Overview of the Proposed Consumer Rights Directive', in Howells, G. & Schulze, R. (eds.), *Modernising and Harmonising Consumer Contract Law,* München: Sellier, 2009, p. 3-25.

Howells & Weatherill 2005
Howells, G. & Weatherill, S., *Consumer Protection Law,* Aldershot: Ashgate Publishing, 2005.

Howells *et al.* 2006
Howells, G.G. *et al.*, *European Fair Trading Law: The Unfair Commercial Practices Directive,* London: Ashgate Publishing, 2006.

Huet 1994
Huet, J., 'Propos amers sur la directive du 5 avril 1993 relative aux clauses abusives', *La semaine juridique,* 1994, Vol. 1.309.

Husa 2014
Husa, J., 'Interdisciplinary Comparative Law - Between Scylla and Charybdis', *Journal of Comparative Law,* 2014, Vol. 9(2), p. 28-42.

Jacquemin 2009
Jacquemin, H., 'Arrêt 'Messner': L'indemnité compensatrice parfois réclamée au consommateur en cas de rétractation dans un contrat à distance', *Journal de droit européen,* 2009, Vol. 163, p. 273-277.

Jansen 2014
Jansen, S., 'Price Reduction as a Consumer Sales Remedy and the Powers of National Courts: Duarte Hueros - Case C-32/12, *Soledad Duarte Hueros v Autociba SA, Automóviles Citroën España SA,* Judgment of the Court of Justice (First Chamber) of 3 October 2013', *Common Market Law Review,* 2014, Vol. 51(3), p. 975-991.

Janssen 2005
Janssen, A., 'The Dutch law after incorporation of the Consumer Sales Directive - Much ado about nothing?', in Ajani, G. & Ebers, M. (eds.), *Uniform Terminology for European Contract Law,* Baden-Baden: Nomos, 2005, p. 343-358.

Jeloschek 2006
Jeloschek, C., *Examination and Notification Duties in Consumer Sales Law,* Munich: Sellier, 2006.

Johnston & Unberath 2012
Johnston, A. & Unberath, H., 'Joined Cases C-65/09 & C-87/09, *Gebr. Weber GMBH v Jürgen Wittmer and Ingrid Putz v Medianess Electronics GMBH,* Judgment of the Court of Justice (First Chamber) of 16 June 2011 - Case Note', *Common Market Law Review,* 2012, Vol. 49(2), p. 793-807.

Kadner Graziano 2015
Kadner Graziano, Th., 'Is it Legitimate and Beneficial for Judges to Compare', in Andenas, M. & Fairgrieve, D. (eds.), *Courts and Comparative Law,* Oxford: Oxford University Press, 2015, p. 25-53.

Kaeding 2007
Kaeding, M., *Better Regulation in the European Union – Lost in Translation or Full Steam Ahead? The Transposition of EU Transport Directives across Member States*, Leiden: Leiden University Press, 2007.

Katelouzou 2014
Katelouzou, D., 'A Leximetric Approach to Comparative Corporate Governance: The Case of Hedge Fund Activism', *Journal of Comparative Law*, 2014, Vol. 9(2), p. 43-64.

Kawakami & Goanta 2015
Kawakami, M. & Goanta, C., 'Even Lawyers are Consumers: Perceiving Business Attitudes in Online Contracts', in Loos, M. & Samoy, I., *Information and Notification Duties*, Antwerp: Intersentia, 2015, p. 155-181.

Keirsbilck 2011
Keirsbilck, B., *The New European Law of Unfair Commercial Practices and Competition Law*, Oxford: Hart Publishing, 2011.

Keirsbilck 2013a
Keirsbilck, B., 'The interaction between consumer protection rules on unfair contract terms and unfair commercial practices: Pereničová and Perenič, Case C-453/10, *Jana Pereničová, Vladislav Perenič v SOS financ spol. s.r.o.*, Judgment of the Court of Justice (First Chamber) of 15 March 2012', *Common Market Law Review*, 2013, Vol. 50, p. 247-264.

Keirsbilck 2013b
Keirsbilck, B., 'The *erga omnes* Effect of the Finding of an Unfair Contract Term: *Nemzeti*, Case C-472/10, *Nemzeti v Invitel*, Judgment of the Court of Justice (First Chamber) of 26 April 2012', *Common Market Law Review*, 2013, Vol. 50, p. 1467-1478.

Keirse 2011
Keirse, A.L.M., 'European Impact on Contract Law: A Perspective on the Interlinked Contributions of Legal Scholars, Legislators and Courts to the Europeanisation of Contract Law', *Utrecht Law Review*, 2011, Vol. 7(1), p. 34-51.

Kierkegaard 2007
Kierkegaard, S.M., 'E-Contract Formation: U.S. and EU Perspectives', *Shidler Journal of Law, Computers & Technology*, 2007, Vol. 3, p. 1-22.

Kingisepp 2008
Kingisepp, M., 'European Consumer Sales Directive – the Impact on Estonian Law', *Juridica International*, 2008, Vol. 14, p. 219-227.

Kingisepp & Värv 2011
Kingisepp, M. & Värv, A., 'The Notion of Consumer in EU Consumer *Acquis* and the Consumer Rights Directive - A Significant Change of Paradigm?', *Juridica International,* 2011, Vol. 18, p. 44-53.

Kirk 2012
Kirk, A., *Data Visualisation: A Successful Design Process,* Birmingham: Packt Publishing, 2012.

Klauer 2000
Klauer, I., 'General Clauses in European Private Law and 'Stricter' National Standards: The Unfair Terms Directive', *European Review of Private Law,* 2000, Vol. 8(1), p. 187-210.

Korobkin 2003
Korobkin, R.B., 'Bounded Rationality, Standard Form Contracts, and Unconscionability', *University of Chicago Law Review,* 2003, Vol. 70, p. 1203-1295.

Kramer 2002
Kramer, J.J., 'Waive Goodbye: Choice Clauses, the Internet, Consumer Protection, and Other Issues Concerning the Unwary Investor', *Emory International Law Review,* 2002, Vol. 16, p. 227-262.

Kruisinga 2001
Kruisinga, S., 'What Do Consumer and Commercial Sales Law Have in Common? A Comparison of the EC Directive on Consumer Sales Law and the UN Convention on Contracts for the International Sale of Goods', *European Review of Private Law,* 2001, Vol. 9(2-3), p. 177-188.

Kunz *et al.* 2003-2004
Kunz, C.L. *et al.*, 'Browse-Wrap Agreements: Validity of Implied Assent in Electronic Form Agreements', *The Business Lawyer,* 2003-2004, Vol. 59, p. 279-312.

Lando 1993
Lando, O., 'Is Codification Needed in Europe? Principles of European Contract Law and the Relationship to Dutch Law', *European Review of Private Law,* 1993, Vol. 1, p. 157-170.

Lando 2000a
Lando, O., 'Optional or Mandatory Europeanisation of Contract Law', *European Review of Private Law,* 2000, Vol. 8(1), p. 59-69.

Lando 2000b
Lando, O., 'Some Features of the Law of Contract in the Third Millenium', *Scandinavian Studies in Law,* 2000, Vol. 40, p. 343-402.

Lando 2007
Lando, O., 'Is Good Faith an Over-Arching General Clause in the Principles of European Contract Law?', *European Review of Private Law* 2007, Vol. 15(6), p. 841-853.

Lando *et al.* 2000
Lando, O. *et al.* (eds.), *Principles of European Contract Law, Part I and II,* The Hague: Kluwer Law International, 2000.

Lando *et al.* 2003
Lando, O. *et al.*, *Principles of European Contract Law, Part III,* The Hague: Kluwer Law International, 2003.

Lawson 2011
Lawson, R., *Exclusion Clauses and Unfair Contract Terms,* London: Sweet & Maxwell, 2011.

Legrand 1996
Legrand, P., 'European Legal Systems are not Converging', *International and Comparative Law Quarterly,* 1996, Vol. 45, p. 52-81.

Legrand 1997
Legrand, P., 'Against a European Civil Code', *Modern Law Review,* 1997, Vol. 60(1), p. 44-64.

Legrand 2002
Legrand, P., 'On the Unbearable Localness of the Law: Academic Fallacies and Unseasonable Observations', *European Review of Private Law,* 2002, Vol. 10(1), p. 61-76.

Leistner 2005
Leistner, M., 'Unfair Competition or Consumer Protection', in Bell, J. & Dashwood, A. (eds.), *The Cambridge Yearbook of European Legal Studies,* Portland: Hart Publishing, 2005, p. 141-176.

Lete 1997
Lete, J., 'The Non Implementation of the EC Directive on Unfair Contract Terms in Spain', *European Review of Private Law,* 1997, Vol. 5(2), p. 205-212.

Levmore 2013
Levmore, S., 'Harmonisation, Preferences, and the Calculus of Consent in Commercial and Other Law', *Common Market Law Review,* 2013, Vol. 50, p. 243-260.

Liebscher 2008
Liebscher, C., 'Case C-168/05, *Elisa María Mostaza Claro v Centro Móvil Milenium SL*', *Common Market Law Review,* 2008, Vol. 45, p. 545-557.

Linarelli 2002
Linarelli, J., 'The Economics of Private Law Harmonisation', *American Society of International Law Proceedings,* 2002, Vol. 96, p. 339-342.

Liu 2009
Liu, H.-W., 'Harmonizing the Internal Market, or Public Health? - Revisiting Case C-491/01 (*British American Tobacco*) and Case C-380/03 (*Tobacco Advertising II*)', *Columbia Journal of European Law Online,* 2009, Vol. 15.

Lodder & Voulon 2002
Lodder, A. & Voulon, M., 'Intelligent Agents and the Information Requirements of the Directives on Distance Selling and E-commerce', *International Review of Law, Computers & Technology,* 2002, Vol. 16(3), p. 277-287.

Lohse 2011
Lohse, E.J., 'The Meaning of Harmonisation in the Context of European Union Law - A Process in Need of Definition', in Andenas, M. & Baasch Andersen, C. (eds.), *Theory and Practice of Harmonisation,* Cheltenham: Edward Elgar Publishing, 2011, p. 282-313.

Lollini 2012
Lollini, A., 'The South African Constitutional Court Experience: Reasoning Patterns Based on Foreign Law', *Utrecht Law Review,* 2012, Vol. 8(2), p. 55-87.

Loos 2003
Loos, M., 'ECJ, 24 January 2002, Case C-372/99, *Commission v Italian Republic* - Collective Action under the Unfair Contract Terms Directive', *European Review of Private Law,* 2003, Vol. 11(5), p. 701-707.

Loos 2007a
Loos, M., 'The Case for a Uniformed and Efficient Right of Withdrawal from Consumer Contracts in European Contract Law', *Zeitschrift für Europäisches Privatrecht,* 2007, Vol. 1, p. 5-36.

Loos 2007b
Loos, M., 'The Influence of European Consumer Law on General Contract Law and the Need for Spontaneous Harmonisation', *European Review of Private Law,* 2007, Vol. 4, p. 515-531.

Loos 2008
Loos, M., 'Review of the European Consumer Acquis', *Zeitschrift für Gemeinschaftsprivatrecht,* 2008, Vol. 3, p. 117-122.

Loos 2009
Loos, M., 'Rights of Withdrawal', in Howells, G. & Schulze, R. (eds.), *Modernising and Harmonising Consumer Contract Law,* Munich: Sellier, 2009, p. 237-278.

López-Rodríguez 2003-2004
López-Rodríguez, A.M., 'Towards a European Civil Code without a Common European Legal Culture? The Link between Law, Language and Culture', *Brooklyn Journal of International Law*, 2003-2004, Vol. 29, p. 1195-1120.

López-Rodríguez 2004
López-Rodríguez, A.M., 'The Rome Convention of 1980 and its Revision at the Crossroads of the *European Contract Law Project*', *European Review of Private Law*, 2004, Vol. 12(2), p. 167-191.

Low 2011
Low, G.W.L., *European Contract Law between the Single Market and the Law Market, A Behavioural Perspective*, Nijmegen: Wolf Legal Publishers, 2011.

Luzak 2015
Luzak, J., 'A Storm in a Teacup? On Consumers' Remedies for Non-conforming Goods after Weber and Putz', *European Review of Private Law*, 2015, Vol. 23(4), p. 689-704.

Luzak & Mak 2014a
Luzak, J. & Mak, V., 'Implementation of the Consumer Rights Directive - The Netherlands', *Journal of European Consumer and Market Law*, 2014, Vol. 2, p. 127-129.

Luzak & Mak 2014b
Luzak, J. & Mak, V., 'The Consumer Rights Directive', in Hartkamp, A. *et al.* (eds.), *De Invloed van het Europese Recht op het Nederlandse Privaatrecht*, The Hague: Kluwer Law International, 2014, p. 67-92.

Macdonald 2002
Macdonald, E., 'Scope and Fairness of the Unfair Terms in Consumer Contracts Regulations: Director General of *Fair Trading v First National Bank*', *The Modern Law Review*, 2002, Vol. 65(5), p. 763-773.

Magoulas & Schwartze 1986
Magoulas, G. & Schwartze, A., 'Das Gesetz über den Widerruf von Haustürgeschäften und ähnlichen Geschäften: Eine rechtliche und ökonomische Analyse', *Jüristische Arbeitsblätter*, 1986, Vol. 18(5), p. 225-235.

Mahbubani 2013
Mahbubani, K., *The Great Convergence - Asia, the West, and the Logic of One World*, New York: Public Affairs, 2013.

Mak 2008
Mak, C., 'Fundamental Rights and the European Regulation of iConsumer Contracts', *Journal of Consumer Policy*, 2008, Vol. 31, p. 425-439.

Mak 2009
Mak, V., 'Review of the Consumer Acquis - Towards Maximum Harmonisation?', *European Review of Private Law,* 2009, Vol. 17(1), p. 55-73.

Mak 2011a
Mak, C., 'Instrumentalisme, Legitimiteit en de Onderstroom Van Het Europees Contractenrecht', in Hesselink, M.W. *et al.* (eds.), *Groenboek Europees Contractenrecht: naar een optioneel instrument?,* The Hague: Boom Juridische uitgevers, 2011, p. 41-52.

Mak 2011b
Mak, C., 'Constitutional Aspects of a European Civil Code', in Von Bar, C. (ed.), *Towards a European Civil Code,* The Hague: Kluwer Law International, 2011, p. 333-352.

Mak 2011c
Mak, V., 'Standards of Protection: In Search of the 'Average Consumer' of EU Law in the Proposal for a Consumer Rights Directive', *European Review of Private Law,* 2011, Vol. 19(1), p. 25-42.

Mak 2011d
Mak, V., 'Policy Choices in European Consumer law: Regulation through 'Targeted Differentiation'', *European Review of Contract Law,* 2011, Vol. 7(2), p. 257-274.

Mak 2012a
Mak, C., 'Hedgehogs in Luxembourg? A Dworkinian Reading of the CJEU's Case Law on Principles of Private Law and Some Doubts of the Fox', *European Review of Private Law,* 2012, Vol. 20(2), p. 323-346.

Mak 2012b
Mak, V., 'Full Harmonisation in European Private Law: A Two-Track Concept', *European Review of Private Law,* 2012, Vol. 20(1), p. 213-236.

Mak 2014
Mak, C., 'On Beauty and Being Fair: The Interaction of National and Supranational Judiciaries in the Development of a European Law on Remedies', in Purnhagen, K. & Rott, P. (eds.), *Varieties of European Economic Law and Regulation. Liber Amicorum for Hans Micklitz,* Cham: Springer, 2014, p. 823-834.

Mak & Braspenning 2012
Mak, V. & Braspenning, J., '*Errare humanum est*: Financial Literacy in European Consumer Credit Law', *Journal of Consumer Policy,* 2012, Vol. 35, p. 307-332.

Maletic 2011
Maletic, I., 'The Story of the EU and the Happily Roaming Consumers - Case No. C58/08, *Vodafone Ltd, et al. v Secretary of State for Business, Enterprise and Regulatory Reform*', *Legal Issues of Economic Integration,* 2011, Vol. 38(2), p. 199-205.

Marotta-Wurgler 2007
Marotta-Wurgler, F., 'What's in a Standard Form Contract? An Empirical Analysis of Software License Agreements', *Journal of Empirical Legal Studies* 2007, Vol. 4(4), p. 677-713.

Martinez Gandara 2013
Martinez Gandara, A., *The Law and Economics of Eco-Labels*, Rotterdam: Erasmus University, 2013.

Mattei & Pes 2008
Mattei, U. & Pes, L.G., 'Civil Law and Common Law: Toward Convergence?', in Whittington, K.E. *et al.* (eds.), *The Oxford Handbook of Law and Politics*, Oxford: Oxford University Press, 2008, p. 267-280.

McAuliffe 2014
McAuliffe, K., 'Translating Ambiguity', *Journal of Comparative Law*, 2014, Vol. 9(2), p. 65-87.

McDonald 2005
McDonald, M., 'Distance Contracts Directive and Tourist Bookings: *easyCar v OFT*', *International Travel Law Journal*, 2005, Vol. 4, p. 192-202.

Meier & Stormer 2009
Meier, A. & Stormer, H., *eBusiness & eCommerce: Managing the Digital Value Chain*, Heidelberg: Springer, 2009.

Meli 2006
Meli, M., 'Social Justice, Constitutional Principles and Protection of the Weaker Contractual Party', *European Review of Contract Law*, 2006, Vol. 2(2), p. 159-166.

Merryman 1981
Merryman, J.H., 'On the Convergence (and Divergence) of the Civil Law and the Common Law', *Stanford Journal of International Law*, 1981, Vol. 17, p. 357-388.

Meyer 2007
Meyer, O., 'The Regulation of Unfair Commercial Practices under EC Directive 2005/29: New Rules and New Techniques - Results of the Conference which took place on 3 March 2006, at Oxford University', *European Review of Private Law*, 2007, Vol. 15(1), p. 169-171.

Michaels & Jansen 2006
Michaels, R. & Jansen, N., 'Private Law Beyond the State? Europeanisation, Globalisation, Privatisation', *The American Journal of Comparative Law*, 2006, Vol. 54(4), p. 843-890.

Micklitz 1999
Micklitz, H.-W., 'Die Verbrauchsgüterkaufs-Richtline', *Europäische Zeitschrift für Wirtschaftsrecht,* 1999, Vol. 10, p. 485-493.

Micklitz 2002
Micklitz, H.-W., 'An Expanded and Systematized Community Consumer Law as Alternative or Complement?', *European Business Law Review,* 2002, Vol. 13(6), p. 583-598.

Micklitz 2009a
Micklitz, H.-W., 'Unfair Commercial Practices and Misleading Advertising', in Micklitz, H.-W. *et al., Understanding EU Consumer Law,* Antwerp: Intersentia, 2009, p. 61-117.

Micklitz 2009b
Micklitz, H.-W., 'The Targeted Full Harmonisation Approach: Looking Behind the Curtain', in Howells, G. & Schulze, R., *Modernising and Harmonising Consumer Contract Law,* München: Sellier, 2009, p. 47-86.

Micklitz 2010
Micklitz, H.-W. *et al., Cases, Materials and Text on Consumer Law,* Oxford: Hart Publishing, 2010.

Micklitz 2013
Micklitz, H.-W., 'Minimum/Maximum Harmonisation and the Internal Market Clause', in Howells, G. *et al.* (eds.), *European Fair Trading Law: The Unfair Commercial Practices Directive,* London: Ashgate Publishing, 2013, p. 27-48.

Micklitz & Kas 2014
Micklitz, H.-W. & Kas, B., 'Overview of Cases before the CJEU on European Consumer Contract Law (2008–2013) – Part I', *European Review of Contract Law,* 2014, Vol. 10(1), p. 1-63.

Micklitz & Radeideh 2005
Micklitz, H.-W. & Radeideh, M., 'CLAB Europa – The European Database on Unfair Terms in Consumer Contracts', *Journal of Consumer Policy,* 2005, Vol. 28, p. 325-360.

Micklitz & Reich 2014
Micklitz, H.-W. & Reich, N., 'The Court and Sleeping Beauty: The Revival of the Unfair Contract Terms Directive', *Common Market Law Review,* 2014, Vol. 51, p. 771-808.

Micklitz *et al.* 1999
Micklitz, H.-W. *et al.*, 'Door To Door Selling – Pyramid Selling – Multilevel Marketing', 1999.

Van Mierlo 2007
Van Mierlo, T, 'Consumer Protection on the Single Market: Self-Regulation for Dating Services', in Boele-Woelki, K. & Grosheide, W.F. (eds.), *The Future of European Contract Law, Liber Amicorum E.H. Hondius,* The Hague: Kluwer Law International, 2007, p. 411-424.

Mik 2012
Mik, E., 'Mistaken Identity, Identity Theft and Problems of Remote Authentication in E-Commerce', *Computer Law & Security Review,* 2012, Vol. 28(4), p. 396-402.

Miller 2011
Miller, L., *The Emergence of Contract Law – Exploring Europeanisation,* Oxford: Oxford University Press, 2011.

Mougenot 2002
Mougenot, D., *Droit des Obligations. La Preuve,* Bruxelles: Larcier, 2002.

Namysłowska 2016
Namysłowska, M., 'The Blacklist of Unfair Commercial Practies: The Black Sheep, Red Herring or White Elephant of the Unfair Commercial Practices Directive?', in Van Boom, W. *et. al.* (eds.), *The European Unfair Commercial Practices Directive: Impact, Enforcement Strategies and National Legal Systems,* Oxon: Routledge, 2016, p. 65-89.

Nardo *et al.* 2011
Nardo M., *et al.*, 'The Consumer Empowerment Index', JRC Scientific and Technical Reports, 2011.

Nedzel 1997
Nedzel, N.E., 'A Comparative Study of Good Faith, Fair Dealing, and Precontractual Liability', *Tulane European and Civil Law Forum,* 1997, Vol. 12, p. 97-158.

Neergaard & Nielsen 2012
Neergaard, U. & Nielsen, R., 'Introduction', in Neergaard, U. & Nielsen, R. (eds.), *European Legal Method – In a Multi-Level EU Legal Order,* Copenhagen: DJØF Publishing, 2012, p. 7-24.

Niglia 2015
Niglia, L., *The Struggle for European Private Law: A Critique of Codification,* Oxford: Hart Publishing, 2015.

Nowak *et al.* 2012
Nowak, T. *et al.*, *National Judges as European Union Judges – Knowledge, Experience and Attitudes of Lower Court Judges in Germany and the Netherlands,* The Hague: Eleven, 2012.

Van Oevelen 2005
Van Oevelen, A., 'Het nieuwe begrip 'conformiteit'', in Stijns, S. & Stuyck, J. (eds.), *Het nieuwe kooprecht,* Antwerp: Intersentia, 2005, p. 29-53.

O'Hara O'Connor 2011
O'Hara O'Connor, E., 'The limits of Contract Law Harmonisation', *European Journal of Law and Economics,* 2011, Vol. 33(3), p. 505-519.

Oosterhuis 2013
Oosterhuis, J., 'Convergence and Unification of Nineteenth Century European Commercial Sales Law - Why the CESL Might Just Be an Intermezzo in the Game of Unifying European Commercial Sales Law', *European Review of Private Law,* 2013, Vol. 21(4), p. 991-1008.

Paisant 2009
Paisant, G., 'Le vendeur à distance ne peut, en principe, réclamer aucune indemnité pour utilisation du bien livré en cas de rétractation du consommateur dans les délais', *La Semaine Juridique,* 2009, Vol. 47, p. 25-29.

Parisi 2004
Parisi, F., 'The Harmonisation of Legal Warranties in European Law: An Economic Analysis', *American Journal of Comparative Law,* 2004, Vol. 52, p. 403-432.

Parisi 2008
Parisi, F., 'Harmonisation of European Private Law: An Economic Analysis', in Bussani, M. & Werro, F., *European Private Law: A Handbook,* Bern: Stämpfli Publications Ltd., 2008, p. 363-379.

Pavillon 2006
Pavillon, C., 'De wisselende betekenis van de Richtlijn oneerlijke bedingen in de Nederlandse rechtspraak: een drieluik', *Vermogensrechtelijke Annotaties,* 2006, Vol. 2, p. 25-70.

Pavillon 2012
Pavillon, C., 'The Interplay Between the Unfair Commercial Practices Directive and Codes of Conduct', *Erasmus Law Review,* 2012, Vol. 5(4), p. 267-288.

De Pelsmacker *et al.* 2005
De Pelsmacker, P. *et al.*, 'Consumer values and fair-trade beliefs, attitudes and buying behavior', *International Review on Public and Non Profit Marketing,* 2005, Vol. 2(2), p. 50-69.

Piedelièvre 2010
Piedelièvre, S., 'Chronique de jurisprudence de droit de la consommation', *Gazette du Palais,* 2010, Vol. 153-154, p. 21-24.

Pintens 2003
Pintens, W., 'Europeanisation of Family Law', in Boele-Woelki, K. (ed.), *Perspectives for the Unification and Harmonisation of Family Law in Europe,* Antwerp: Intersentia, 2003, p. 1-34.

Poncibò & Incardona 2005
Poncibò, C. & Incardona, R., 'The EU Commercial Practices Directive: A Faltering First Step', *London Law Review,* 2005, Vol. 1(2), p. 317-337.

Poncibò & Incardona 2007
Poncibò, C. & Incardona, R., 'The Average Consumer, the Unfair Commercial Practices Directive, and the Cognitive Revolution', *Journal of Consumer Policy Issue,* 2007, Vol. 30(1), p. 21-38.

Posch 1997
Posch, W., 'The Implementation of the EC Directive on Unfair Contract Terms into Austrian Law', *European Review of Private Law,* 1997, Vol. 5(2), p. 135-142.

Poto 2007
Poto, M., 'The Principle of Proportionality in Comparative Perspective - Part I/II', *German Law Journal,* 2007, Vol. 8, p. 835-870.

Purnhagen 2012
Purnhagen, K.P., 'Principles of European Private Or Civil Law? A Reminder of The Symbiotic Relationship Between the ECJ and the CFR in a Pluralistic European Private Law', *European Law Journal,* 2012, Vol. 18, p. 844-867.

Rachlinski 2012
Rachlinski, J.J., 'Evidence-Based Law', *Cornell Law Review,* 2011, Vol. 96(4), p. 901-923.

Ramsay 2012
Ramsay, I., *Consumer Law and Policy,* Oxford: Hart Publishing, 2012.

Reich 1997
Reich, N., 'The Implementation of Directive 93/13 on Unfair Terms in Consumer Contracts in Germany', *European Review of Private Law,* 1997, Vol. 5(2), p. 165-172.

Reich 2006
Reich, N., 'Protection of Consumers' Economic Interests by EC Contract Law - Some Follow-up Remarks', *Sydney Law Review,* 2006, Vol. 28, p. 37-61.

Reich 2010
Reich, N., 'The Public/Private Divide in European Law', in Cafaggi, F. & Micklitz, H.-W. (eds.), *European Private Law after the Common Frame of Reference,* Cheltenham: Edward Elgar, 2010, p. 56-89.

Reich 2012
Reich, N., 'EU Strategies in Finding the Optimal Consumer Law Instrument', *European Review of Contract Law*, 2012, Vol. 8(1), p. 1-29.

Reich & Halfmeier 2001-2002
Reich, N. & Halfmeier, A., 'Consumer Protection in the Global Village: Recent Developments in German and European Union Law', *Dickinson Law Review*, 2001-2002, Vol. 106, p. 111-137.

Reimann & Halberstam 2014
Reimann, M.W. & Halberstam, D., 'Federalism and Legal Unification: Comparing Methods, Results, and Explanations Across 20 Systems', in Halberstam, D. & Reimann, M.V. (eds.), *Federalism and Legal Unification, A Comparative Empirical Investigation of Twenty Systems*, New York: Springer, 2014, p. 3-67.

Rekaiti & Van den Bergh 2000
Rekaiti, P. & Van den Bergh, R., 'Cooling-Off Periods in the Consumer Laws of the EC Member States - A Comparative Law and Economics Approach', *Journal of Consumer Policy*, 2000, Vol. 23, p. 371-407.

Riefa 2009a
Riefa, C., 'A Dangerous Erosion of Consumer Rights: The Absence of a Right to Withdraw from Online Auctions', in Howells, G. & Schulze, R. (eds.), *Modernising and Harmonising Consumer Contract Law*, Munich: Sellier, 2009, p. 177-188.

Riefa 2009b
Riefa, C., 'The Reform of Electronic Consumer Contracts in Europe: Towards an Effective Legal Framework?', *Lex Electronica*, 2009, Vol. 14, p. 1-44.

Riesenhuber 2005
Riesenhuber, K., 'System and Principles of EC Contract Law', *European Review of Contract Law*, 2005, Vol. 1(3), p. 297-322.

Rosenberg 1976
Rosenberg, N., *Perspectives on Technology*, Cambridge: Cambridge University Press, 1976.

Rosett 1992
Rosett, A., 'Unification, Harmonisation, Restatement, Codification, and Reform in International Commercial Law', *American Journal of Comparative Law*, 1992, Vol. 40, p. 683-697.

Roth 2002
Roth, W.-H., 'Transposing 'Pointillist' EC Guidelines into Systematic National Codes - Problems and Consequences', *European Review of Private Law*, 2002, Vol. 10(6), p. 761-776.

Rothchild 1998
Rothchild, J., 'Making the Market Work: Enhancing Consumer Sovereignty Through the Telemarketing Sales Rule and the Distance Selling Directive', *Journal of Consumer Policy,* 1998, Vol. 21, p. 279-313.

Rott 2004
Rott, P., 'German Sales Law Two Years after the Implementation of Directive 1999/44/EC', *German Law Journal,* 2004, Vol. 5, p. 237-256.

Rott 2005
Rott, P., 'Consumer Guarantees in the Future Consumer Credit Directive: Mandatory Ban on Consumer Protection?', *European Review of Private Law,* 2005, Vol. 13(3), p. 383-404.

Rott 2006
Rott, P., 'Harmonising Different Rights of Withdrawal: Can German Law Serve as an Example for EC Consumer Law?', *German Law Journal,* 2006, Vol. 7(12), p. 1109-1136.

Rott 2007
Rott, P., 'Consumers and Services of General Interest: Is EC Consumer Law the Future?', *Journal of Consumer Policy,* 2007, Vol. 30, p. 49-60.

Rott 2008
Rott, P., 'Le droit de rétractation en Allemagne', in Terryn, E. (ed.), *Le droit de rétractation,* Brussels: Larcier, 2008, p. 7-34.

Rott 2009
Rott, P., ''Technical Harmonisation' versus Substantive Differences: Termination and Withdrawal in the Draft Common Frame of Reference', in Somma, A. (ed.), *The Politics of the Draft Common Frame of Reference,* Alphen aan den Rijn: Kluwer Law International, 2009, p. 163-175.

Rott 2010
Rott, P., 'The Balance of Interests in Distance Selling Law - Case Note on *Pia Messner v Firma Stefan Krüger*', *European Review of Private Law,* 2010, Vol. 18(1), p. 185-194.

Rott & Twigg-Flesner 2007
Rott, P. & Twigg-Flesner, C., 'No Closer to Harmonisation? The Implementation of Directive 1999/44/EC into English and German Law Three Years On', in Howells, G. *et al.* (eds.), *The Yearbook of Consumer Law,* London: Ashgate Publishing, 2007, p. 121-152.

Rowe 1998
Rowe, H., 'Legal Implications of Consumer-Oriented Electronic Commerce', *Computer Law & Security Report,* 1998, Vol. 14(4), p. 232-242.

Ruen 2011
Ruen, A., 'Paradoxurile juridice ale bunei-credinţe în contractile de consum. Privire comparativă între sistemul continental şi sistemul american', *SUBB Jurisprudentia*, 2011, Vol. 3, p. 41-76.

Rutgers & Sefton-Green 2008
Rutgers, J.W. & Sefton-Green, R., 'Revising the Consumer Acquis: (Half) Opening the Doors of the Trojan Horse', *European Review of Private Law*, 2008, Vol. 16(3), p. 427-442.

Rutten *et al.* 2009
Rutten, S. *et al.*, 'Rights of Redress and Direct Producer's Liability in Consumer Sales in Belgium: a Critical Appraisal', in Ebers, M. *et al.* (eds.), *European Perspectives on Producers' Liability*, Munich: Sellier, 2009, p. 195-210.

Sabin 1991
Sabin, N.D., 'Member State Exemptions from Article 100A Harmonizing Measures: A Possible, European Court Approach', *Boston College International and Comparative Law Review*, 1991, Vol. 14, p. 225-236.

Saltelli 2014
Saltelli, A., 'Indicators for the Internal Market? An Unfinished Business', JRC Scientific and Policy Reports, 2014.

Sandrock & Moore Galston 1978
Sandrock, O. & Moore Galston, N., 'The Standard Terms Act 1976 of West Germany', *American Journal of Comparative Law*, 1978, Vol. 26(4), p. 551-572.

Schauer 2006
Schauer, M., 'Stuctural Elements of the Austrian Civil Code', in Grundmann, S. & Schauer, M., *The Architecture of European Codes and Contract Law*, The Hague: Kluwer Law International, 2006, p. 83-104.

Schmid 2005
Schmid, C.U., 'The Instrumental Conception of the Acquis Communautaire in Consumer Law and its Implications on a European Contract Law Code', *European Review of Contract Law*, 2005, Vol. 1(2), p. 211-227.

Schmidt-Kessel 2012
Schmidt-Kessel, M., 'European Civil Code', in Basedow, J. *et al.* (eds.), *The Max Planck Encyclopedia of European Private Law*, Oxford: Oxford University Press, 2012.

Schulte-Nölke *et al.* 2008
Schulte-Nölke, H. *et al.*, *EC Consumer Law Compendium – Comparative Analysis*, Munich: Sellier, 2008.

Schulte-Nölke 2015
Schulte-Nölke, H., 'No Market for 'Lemons': On the Reasons for a Judicial Unfairness Test for B2B Contracts', *European Review of Private Law,* 2015, Vol. 23(2), p. 195-216.

Schulze 2005
Schulze, R., 'European Private Law and Existing EC Law', *European Review of Private Law,* 2005, Vol. 13(1), p. 3-19.

Schulze & Schulte-Nölke 2003
Schulze, R. & Schulte-Nölke, H. (eds.), 'Analysis of National Fairness Laws Aimed at Protecting Consumers in Relation to Commercial Practices', study commissioned by the Directorate-General Health and Consumer Protection of the European Commission (DG SANCO), 2003.

Schulze & Stuyck 2011
Schulze, R. & Stuyck, J. (eds.), *Towards a European Contract Law,* München: Sellier, 2011.

Scotton 2001
Scotton, M., 'Directive 99/44/EC on certain aspects of the sale of consumer goods and associated guarantees', *European Review of Private Law,* 2001, Vol. 9(2-3), p. 297-307.

Sefton-Green 2006
Sefton-Green, R., 'Social Justice and European Identity in European Contract Law', *European Review of Contract Law,* 2006, Vol. 2(2), p. 275-286.

Sefton-Green 2010
Sefton-Green, R., 'Multiculturalism, Europhilia and Harmonisation: Harmony or Disharmony?', *Utrecht Law Review,* 2010, Vol. 6(3), p. 50-67.

Seita 1997
Seita, A.Y., 'Globalisation and the Convergence of Values', *Cornell International Law Journal,* 1997, Vol. 30, p. 429-491.

Semmelmann 2012
Semmelmann, C., 'The Public-Private Divide in European Union Law or an Overkill of Functionalism', MEPLI Working Paper 2012/12.

Shears 2007
Shears, P., 'Overviewing the EU Unfair Commercial Practices Directive: Concentric Circles', *European Business Law Review,* 2007, Vol. 18, p. 781-796.

Siems 2005
Siems, M.M., 'Numerical Comparative Law: Do We Need Statistical Evidence in Law in Order to Reduce Complexity', *Cardozo Journal of International and Comparative Law,* 2005, Vol. 13, p. 521-540.

Siems 2011
Siems, M., 'Measuring the Immeasurable: How to Turn Law into Numbers', in Faure, M. & Smits, J. (eds.), *Does Law Matter - On Law and Economic Growth,* Antwerp: Intersentia, 2011, p. 115-136.

Siems 2014a
Siems, M., *Comparative Law,* Cambridge University Press, 2014.

Siems 2014b
Siems, M., 'Bringing in Foreign Ideas: The Quest for 'Better Law' in Implicit Comparative Law', *Journal of Comparative Law,* 2014, Vol. 9(2), p. 119-136.

Siems 2016
Siems, M., 'Varieties of Legal Systems - Towards a New Global Taxonomy', *Journal of Institutional Economics,* 2016, p. 1-25.

Silkenat *et al.* 2009
Silkenat, J.R. *et al., The ABA Guide to International Business Negotiations: A Comparison of Cross-Cultural Issues and Successful Approaches,* Chicago: ABA Publishing, 2009.

Sîrbu & Gorghiu 2007
Sîrbu, M. & Gorghiu, A., 'Medierea, o modalitate alternativă de soluționare a conflictelor în domeniul protecției consumatorilor', *Law Annals Titu Maiorescu,* 2007, p. 136-142.

Sivesand 2007
Sivesand, H., 'The Hierarchy of Remedies under European Consumer Sales Law: Are There Any Alternative Solutions?', in Busch, D. & Schelhaas, H.N. (eds.), *VergelijkenderWijs: Opstellen aangeboden aan prof. mr. Ewoud Hondius,* Deventer: Kluwer Law International, 2007, p. 135-149.

Slater 2003
Slater, D., 'The Scope of EC Harmonising Powers: The ECJ's Tobacco Case (C-491/01) in Perspective', *German Law Journal,* 2003, Vol. 4, p. 137-147.

Smits 2000a
Smits, J., *The Good Samaritan in European Private Law; on the Perils of Principles Without a Programme and a Programme for the Future,* Inaugural lecture Maastricht University, Alphen aan den Rijn: Kluwer Law International, 2000.

Smits 2000b
Smits, J., 'Naar een nieuw Europees consumentenkooprecht - over de Europese richtlijn verkoop van en garanties voor consumentengoederen in het Nederlandse recht', *Nederlands Juristenblad,* 2000, p. 1825-1830.

Smits 2001
Smits, J., 'Nogmaals de richtlijn oneerlijke bedingen: Nederland veroordeeld wegens gebrekkige implementatie', *Weekblad voor Privaatrecht, Notariaat en Registratie,* 2001, Vol. 6461, p. 853-855.

Smits 2002a
Smits, J., *The Making of European Private Law - Towards a Ius Commune Europaeum as a Mixed Legal System,* Antwerp: Intersentia, 2002.

Smits 2002b
Smits, J., 'The Harmonisation of Private Law in Europe: Some Insights from Evolutionary Theory', *Georgia Journal of International and Comparative Law,* 2002, Vol. 31, p. 79-99.

Smits 2005a
Smits, J., 'Diversity of Contract Law and the European Internal Market', in Smits, J. (ed.), *The Need for a European Contract Law - Empirical and Legal Perspectives,* Groningen: Europa Law Publishing, 2005, p. 153-186.

Smits 2005b
Smits, J. (ed.), *The Need for a European Contract Law - Empirical and Legal Perspectives,* Groningen: Europa Law Publishing, 2005.

Smits 2006
Smits, J., 'European Private Law: A Plea For A Spontaneous Legal Order', in Curtin, D.M. *et al.* (eds.), *European Integration and Law: Four Contributions on the Interplay Between European Integration and European and National Law to Celebrate the 25th Anniversary of Maastricht University's Faculty of Law,* Antwerp-Oxford: Intersentia, 2006, p. 55-107.

Smits 2008
Smits, J.M., 'Contract Law in the European Union: Convergence or Not?', *Sammelband 4, Europäischer Juristentag,* 2008, p. 45-65.

Smits 2010a
Smits, J., 'The Draft Common Frame of Reference: How to Improve It', in Micklitz, H.-W. & Cafaggi, F. (eds.), *European Private Law After the Common Frame of Reference,* Cheltenham: Edward Elgar Publishing, 2010, p. 89-100.

Smits 2010b
Smits, J., 'Full Harmonisation of Consumer Law? A Critique of the Draft Directive on Consumer Rights', *European Review of Private Law,* 2010, Vol. 18, p. 5-14.

Smits 2011
Smits, J., 'Rethinking the Usefulness of Mandatory Rights of Withdrawal in Consumer Contract Law: The Right to Change Your Mind', *Penn State International Law Review*, 2011, Vol. 29, p. 671-684.

Smits 2012a
Smits, J., 'Dutch Report: Coherence and Fragmentation of Private Law', *European Review of Private Law*, 2012, Vol. 20(1), p. 153-168.

Smits 2012b
Smits, J., 'The Common European Sales Law (CESL) Beyond Party Choice', *Zeitschrift für Europäisches Privatrecht*, 2012, Vol. 20, p. 904-917.

Smits 2014
Smits, J., 'Law and Interdisciplinarity: On the Inevitable Normativity of Legal Studies', *Critical Analysis of Law*, 2014, Vol. 1(1), p. 75-86.

Smits 2016
Smits, J., 'What is Legal Doctrine? On the Aims and Methods of Doctrinal Legal Research', in Van Gestel *et al.* (eds.), *Rethinking Legal Scholarship*, Cambridge: Cambridge University Press, 2016, forthcoming.

Smits *et al.* 2014
Smits, J. *et al.* (eds.), *European Private Law*, 4th edn., Nijmegen: Ars Aequi wetseditie, 2014.

Souto-Otero *et al.* 2008
Souto-Otero, M. *et al.*, 'Filling in the Gaps: European Governance, the Open Method of Coordination and the European Commission', *Journal of Education Policy*, 2008, Vol. 23(3), p. 231-249.

Spindler 2005
Spindler, G., 'Internet-Auctions versus Consumer Protection: The Case of the Distance Selling Directive', *German Law Journal*, 2005, Vol. 6(3), p. 725-733.

Staudenmayer 2000
Staudenmayer, D., 'The Directive on the Sale of Consumer Goods and Associated Guarantees - A Milestone in the European Consumer and Private Law', *European Review of Private Law*, 2000, Vol. 8(4), p. 547-564.

Staudenmayer 2002
Staudenmayer, D., 'The Commission Communication on European Contract Law: What Future for European Contract Law?', *European Review of Private Law*, 2002, Vol. 10(2), p. 249-260.

Staudenmayer 2003
Staudenmayer, D., 'The Commission Action Plan on European Contract Law', *European Review of Private Law,* 2003, Vol. 10, p. 113-127.

Stein 2003
Stein, P., *Roman Law in European History,* Cambridge: Cambridge University Press, 2003.

Steiner *et al.* 2012
Steiner, J. *et al., Steiner & Woods EU Law,* Oxford: Oxford University Press, 2012.

Stiglitz 2002
Stiglitz, J., *Globalisation and Its Discontents,* New York: W.W. Norton & Company, 2002.

Stiglitz 2006
Stiglitz, J., *Making Globalisation Work,* New York: W.W. Norton & Co, 2006.

Stratton & Werner 2013
Stratton, J.P. & Werner, M.J., 'Consumer Behavior Analysis of Fair Trade Coffee: Evidence from Field Research', *The Psychological Record,* 2013, Vol. 63(2), p. 363-374.

Streeter 2002
Streeter, D., 'Into Contract's Undiscovered Country: A Defense of Browse-Wrap Licenses', *San Diego Law Review,* 2002, Vol. 39, p. 1363-1394.

Study Group on Social Justice in European Private Law 2004
Study Group on Social Justice in European Private Law, 'Social Justice in European Contract law: A Manifesto', *European Law Journal,* 2004, Vol. 10(6), p. 653-674.

Stuyck 1978
Stuyck, J., 'Six Years of Experience with some Aspects of the Belgian Trade Practices Act 1971 as an Instrument of Consumer Protection', in Skogh, G. (ed.), *Law and Economics. Report from a Symposium in Lund, Sweden, 24-26 August 1977,* Lund: Juridiska Föreningen, 1978, p. 133-151.

Stuyck 2009
Stuyck, J., 'Unfair Terms', in Howells, G. & Schulze, R. (eds.), *Modernising and Harmonising Consumer Contract Law,* München: Sellier, 2009, p. 115-144.

Stuyck 2010
Stuyck, J., 'The Provisions on Consumer Sales', in Schulte-Nölke, H. & Tichy, L. (eds.), *Perspectives for European Consumer Law: Towards a Directive on Consumer Rights and Beyond,* Munich: Sellier, 2010, p. 23-43.

Stuyck 2011
Stuyck, J., 'Unfair Competition Law in the EU', in Schulze, R. & Schulte-Nölke, H. (eds.), *European Private Law - Current Status and Perspectives,* Munich: Sellier, 2011, p. 107-131.

Stuyck *et al.* 2006
Stuyck, J. *et al.*, 'Confidence through Fairness? The New Directiv on Unfair Business-to-Consumer Commercial Practices in the Internal Market', *Common Market Law Review,* 2006, Vol. 43, p. 107-152.

Swire 1998
Swire, P., 'Of Elephants, Mice, and Privacy: International Choice of Law and the Internet', *The International Lawyer,* 1998, Vol. 32, p. 991-1025.

Tamanaha 2008
Tamanaha, B.Z., 'Understanding Legal Pluralism: Past to Present, Local to Global', *Sydney Law Review,* 2008, Vol. 30, p. 375-411.

Tenreiro 1995
Tenreiro, M., 'The Community Directive on Unfair Terms and National Legal Systems - The Principle of Good Faith and Remedies for Unfair Terms', *European Review of Private Law,* 1995, Vol. 3, p. 273-284.

Terryn 2008
Terryn, E., 'The Right of Withdrawal, the Acquis Principles and the Draft Common Frame of Reference', in Schulze, R. (ed.), *Common Frame of Reference and Existing EC Contract Law,* Munich: Sellier, 2008, p. 146-176.

Teubner 1998
Teubner, G., 'Legal Irritants: Good Faith in British Law or How Unifying Law Ends up in New Divergences', *The Modern Law Review* 1998, Vol. 61(1), p. 11-32.

Thøgersen *et al.* 2010
Thøgersen, J. *et al.*, 'Consumer responses to ecolabels', *European Journal of Marketing,* 2010, Vol. 44(11-12), p. 1787-1810.

Tholoniat 2010
Tholoniat, L., 'The Career of the Open Method of Coordination: Lessons from a 'Soft' EU Instrument', *West European Politics,* 2010, Vol. 33(1), p. 93-117.

Thue 2000
Thue, H., 'Norwegian Private International Law at the End of the XXth century: Progress or Regress', in Symeonides, S.C. (ed.), *XVth Congress of the International Academy of Comparative Law,* The Hague: Kluwer Law International, 2000, p. 319-328.

Tomkin 2004
Tomkin, J., 'Implementing Community Legislation into National Law', *Judicial Studies Institute Journal,* 2004, Vol. 4(2), p. 130-153.

Tracy 2005
Tracy, J.J., 'Browsewrap Agreements: Register.com, Inc. v. Verio, Inc.', *Boston University Journal of Science and Technology Law,* 2005, Vol. 11, p. 164-172.

Trstenjak & Beysen 2011
Trstenjak, V. & Beysen, E., 'European Consumer Protection Law: *Curia Semper Dabit Remedium?*', *Common Market Law Review,* 2011, Vol. 48(1), p. 95-124.

Twigg-Flesner 2001
Twigg-Flesner, C., 'The EC Consumer Sales Directive: A Lot Still to Do', *Canterbury Law Review,* 2001, Vol. 8, p. 113-128.

Twigg-Flesner 2003a
Twigg-Flesner, C., 'New Remedies for Consumer Sales Transactions: A Change for the Worse?', *Journal of Obligations & Remedies,* 2003, Vol. 2, p. 5-24.

Twigg-Flesner 2003b
Twigg-Flesner, C., *Consumer Product Guarantees,* London: Ashgate Publishing, 2003.

Twigg-Flesner 2006-2007
Twigg-Flesner, C., 'The Implementation of the Unfair Contract Terms Directive in the United Kingdom', *Contemporary Issues in Law,* 2006-2007, Vol. 8(2-3), p. 235-261.

Twigg-Flesner 2007
Twigg-Flesner, C., 'UK and EU Consumer Law', in Twigg-Flesner, C. *et al., The Yearbook of Consumer Law 2008,* Aldershot: Ashgate Publishing, 2007, p. 365-376.

Twigg-Flesner 2008a
Twigg-Flesner, C., *The Europeanisation of Contract Law: Current Controversies in Law,* London: Routledge, 2008.

Twigg-Flesner 2008b
Twigg-Flesner, C., 'Pre-contractual Duties – From the *Acquis* to the Common Frame of Reference', in Schulze, R. (ed.), *Common Frame of Reference and Existing EC Contract Law,* Munich: Sellier, 2008, p. 95-124.

Twigg-Flesner 2009
Twigg-Flesner, C., 'Fit for Purpose? The Proposal on Sales', in Howells, G. & Schulze, R. (eds.), *Modernising and Harmonising Consumer Contract Law,* Munich: Sellier, 2009, p. 147-176.

Twigg-Flesner 2010
Twigg-Flesner, C., *The Cambridge Companion to European Union Private Law,* Cambridge: Cambridge University Press, 2010.

Twigg-Flesner 2011
Twigg-Flesner, C., 'Good-Bye Harmonisation by Directives, Hello Cross-Border only Regulation? - A way forward for EU Consumer Contract Law', *European Review of Contract Law,* 2011, Vol. 7(2), p. 235-256.

Twigg-Flesner 2012a
Twigg-Flesner, C., 'Comment: The Future of EU Consumer Law - The End of Harmonisation?', in Devenney, J. & Kenny, M. (eds.), *European Consumer Protection: Theory and Practice,* Cambridge: Cambridge University Press, 2012, p. 6-20.

Twigg-Flesner 2012b
Twigg-Flesner, C., 'The Acquis Principles: An Insider's Critical Reflections on the Drafting Process', in Andenas, M. & Baasch Andersen, C. (eds.), *Theory and Practice of Harmonisation,* Cheltenham: Edward Elgar Publishing, 2012, p. 474-495.

Twigg-Flesner 2012c
Twigg-Flesner, C., 'The (Non-)impact of Harmonizing Measures on English Legal Terminology', *European Review of Private Law,* 2012, Vol. 20(5-6), p. 1369-1378.

Twigg-Flesner 2015
Twigg-Flesner, C., 'CESL, Cross-Border Transactions and Domestic Law: Why a Dual Approach Could Work (Although CESL Might Not)', *European Review of Private Law,* 2015, Vol. 23(2), p. 231-249.

Twigg-Flesner & Bradgate 2000
Twigg-Flesner, C. & Bradgate, R., 'The E.C. Directive On Certain Aspects of the Sale of Consumer Goods and Associated Guarantees - All Talk and No Do?', *Web Journal of Current Legal Issues,* 2000, Vol. 2.

Twigg-Flesner & Metcalfe 2009
Twigg-Flesner, C. & Metcalfe, D., 'The Proposed Consumer Rights Directive - Less Haste, more Thought?', *European Review of Contract Law,* 2009, Vol. 5(3), p. 368-391.

Twigg-Flesner & Schulze 2010
Twigg-Flesner, C. & Schulze, R., 'Protecting Rational Choice: Information and the Right of Withdrawal', in Howells, G. *et al.* (eds.), *Handbook of Research on International Consumer Law,* Cheltenham: Edward Elgar Publishing, 2010, p. 130-157.

Träger 2008
Träger, M., 'Party Autonomy and Social Justice in Member States and EC Regulation: A Survey of Theory and Practice', in Collins, H. (ed.), *Standard Contract Terms in Europe,* The Hague: Kluwer Law International, 2008, p. 57-74.

Van Boom 2009
Van Boom, W.H., 'Harmonizing Tort Law, A Comparative Tort Law and Economics Analysis', in Faure, M. (ed.), *Tort Law and Economics,* Cheltenham: Edward Elgar Publishing, 2009, p. 435-449.

Van Boom & Kottenhagen 2006
Van Boom, W. & Kottenhagen, R., 'De Richtlijn oneerlijke bedingen en haar plaats in het Nederlandse recht', in De Ly, F. *et al.* (eds.), *Eenvormig bedrijfsrecht: realiteit of utopie?,* The Hague: Boom Juridische Uitgevers, 2006, p. 133-154.

Van den Bergh 2010
Van den Bergh, R., 'Private Law in a Globalizing World: Economic Criteria for Choosing the Optimal Regulatory Level in a Multi-level Government System', in Faure, M. & Van Der Walt, A. (eds.), *Globalisation and Private Law, The Way Forward,* Cheltenham: Edward Elgar Publishing, 2010, p. 57-96.

Van den Bergh & Visscher 2009
Van den Bergh, R. & Visscher, L., 'Consumer Sales Law from an Economic Perspective', in Ebers, M. *et al.* (eds.), *European Perspectives on Producers' Liability,* München: Sellier, 2009, p. 125-150.

Van den Bossche 2005
Van den Bossche, P., *The Law and Policy of the World Trade Organisation,* Cambridge: Cambridge University Press, 2005.

Van Eecke & Truyens 2006
Van Eecke, P. & Truyens, M., 'Benchmarking of Existing National Legal E-Business Practices. Country Report - Belgium', DG/ENTR/04/68, 2006.

Van Gerven 1997
Van Gerven, W., 'ECJ Case-law as a Means of Unification of Private Law', *European Review of Private Law,* 1997, Vol. 5(3), p. 293-308.

Van Gerven 2006
Van Gerven, W., 'Bringing (Private) Laws Closer to Each Other at the European Level', in Cafaggi, F. (ed.), *The Institutional Framework of European Private Law,* Oxford: Oxford University Press, 2006, p. 37-78.

Van Gerven 2008
Van Gerven, W., 'The Open Method of Convergence', *Juridica International,* 2008, Vo. 15, p. 32-41.

Van Gestel & Micklitz 2014
Van Gestel, R. & Micklitz, H.-W., 'Why Methods Matter in European Legal Scholarship', *European Law Journal,* 2014, Vol. 20(3), p. 292-316.

Van Zelst 2008
Van Zelst, B., *The Politics of European Sales Law: A Legal-political Inquiry Into the Drafting of the Uniform Commercial Code, the Vienna Sales Convention, the Dutch Civil Code and the European Consumer Sales Directive in the Context of the Europeanisation of Contract Law*, The Hague: Kluwer Law International, 2008.

Verkerke 2015
Verkerke, J.H.R., 'Legal Ignorance and Information-Forcing Rules', *William and Mary Law Review*, 2015, Vol. 56(3), p. 899-960.

Verschraegen 2006
Verschraegen, B., 'The Dutch Civil Code and Its Precedents (1990-1992)', in Grundmann, S. & Schauer, M. (eds.), *The Architecture of European Codes and Contract Law*, The Hague: Kluwer Law International, 2006, p. 105-116.

Vink & Chun Luk 2014
Vink, M.P. & Chun Luk, N., 'Mapping Statistics on Loss of Nationality in the EU: A New Online Database', Liberty and Security in Europe Papers, No. 76/December 2014.

Vogenauer 2008
Vogenauer, S., 'Perceptions of Civil Justice Systems in Europe and their Implications for Choice of Forum and Choice of Contract Law: A Business Survey', available at: <www.fondation-droitcontinental.org/fr/wp-content/uploads/2013/12/oxford_civil_justice_survey_-_summary_of_results_final.pdf>.

Von Bar 2002
Von Bar, C. *et al.*, 'Communication on European Contract Law: Joint Response of the Commission on European Contract Law and the Study Group on a European Civil Code', *European Review of Private Law*, 2002, Vol. 10(2), p. 183-248.

Von Bar & Swann 2003
Von Bar, C. & Swann, S., 'Response to the Action Plan on European Contract Law: A More Coherent European Contract Law (COM(2003) 63)', *European Review of Private Law*, 2003, Vol. 11(5), p. 595-622.

Von Bar & Drobnig 2004
Von Bar, C. & Drobnig, U., *The Interaction of Contract Law and Tort and Property Law in Europe: A Comparative Study*, Munich: Sellier, 2004.

Wagner 2002
Wagner, G., 'The Economics of Harmonisation: The Case of Contract Law', *Common Market Law Review*, 2002, Vol. 39, p. 995-1023.

Wagner 2005
Wagner, H., 'Economic Analysis of Cross-Border Legal Uncertainty, the Example of the European Union', in Smits, J. (ed.), *The Need for a European Contract Law – Empirical and Legal Perspectives,* Groningen: Europa Law Publishing, 2005, p. 25-51.

Wagner 2010
Wagner, G., 'Mandatory Contract Law: Functions and Principles in Light of the Proposal for a Directive on Consumer Rights', *Erasmus Law Review,* 2010, Vol. 3(1), p. 47-70.

Wagner 2012
Wagner, H., 'Is Harmonisation of Legal Rules an Appropriate Target? Lessons from the Global Financial Crisis', *European Journal of Law and Economics,* 2012, Vol. 33(3), p. 541-564.

Wagner-von Papp 2014
Wagner-von Papp, F., 'Comparative Law & Economics and the 'Egg-Laying Wool-Milk Sow'', *Journal of Comparative Law,* 2014, Vol. 9(2), p. 137-165.

Watterson 2001
Watterson, S., 'Consumer Sales Directive 1999/44/EC – The Impact on English Law', *European Review of Private Law,* 2001, Vol. 9(2-3), p. 197-221.

Weatherill 2002
Weatherill, S., 'The Commission's Options for Developing EC Consumer Protection and Contract Law: Assessing the Constitutional Basis', *European Business Law Review,* 2002, Vol. 13(6), p. 497-515.

Weatherill 2004
Weatherill, S., 'Why Object to the Harmonisation of Private Law by the EC?', *European Review of Private Law,* 2004, Vol. 12(5), p. 633-660.

Weatherill 2005
Weatherill, S., *EU Consumer Law and Policy,* Cheltenham: Edward Elgar Publishing, 2005.

Weatherill 2011a
Weatherill, S., 'The Limits of Legislative Harmonisation Ten Years after Tobacco Advertising: How the Court's Case Law has become a 'Drafting Guide'', *German Law Journal,* 2011, Vol. 12, p. 827-864.

Weatherill 2011b
Weatherill, S., 'Interpretation of the Directives: The Role of the Court', in Hartkamp, A. *et al.* (eds.), *Towards a European Civil Code,* The Hague: Kluwer Law International, 2011, p. 181-204.

Weatherill 2012
Weatherill, S., 'Consumer Protection under EU Law 'is not Absolute': Yes, but Be Careful!', *European Review of Contract Law,* 2012, Vol. 8(2), p. 221-233.

Weber 2012
Weber, F., 'Abusing Loopholes in the Legal System - Efficiency Considerations of Differentiated Law Enforcement Approaches in Misleading Advertising', *Erasmus Law Review,* 2012, Vol. 5(4), p. 289-307.

White 2000
White, J.J., 'Autistic Contracts', *Wayne Law Review,* 2000, Vol. 45, p. 1693-1731.

White 2009
White, F., 'The Buyer, the Seller, the Producer and the Law in Ireland', in Ebers, M. *et al.* (eds.), *European Perspectives on Producers' Liability,* Munich: Sellier, 2009, p. 371-390

Whittaker 2006
Whittaker, S., 'Theory and Practice of the 'General Clause' in English Law: General Norms and the Structuring of Judicial Discretion', in Grundmann, S. & Mazeaud, D. (eds.), *General Clauses and Standards in European Contract Law,* The Hague: Kluwer Law International, 2006, p. 57-76.

Whittaker 2007
Whittaker, S., 'The Interpretation of Concepts in European Private Law', in Boele-Woelki, K. & Grosheide, W. (eds.), *The Future of European Contract Law,* The Hague: Kluwer Law International, 2007, p. 333-345.

Whittaker 2009
Whittaker, S., 'Unfair Contract Terms and Consumer Guarantees: The Proposal for a Directive on Consumer Rights and the Significance of Full Harmonisation', *European Review of Contract Law,* 2009, Vol. 5(3), p. 223-247.

Whittaker & Zimmermann 2000
Whittaker, S. & Zimmermann, R., 'Good Faith in European Contract Law: Surveying the Legal Landscape', in Whittaker, S. & Zimmermann, R., *Good Faith in European Contract Law,* Cambridge: Cambridge University Press, 2000, p. 7-63.

Wiesemann & Falletti 2006
Wiesemann, H.P. & Falletti, E., 'Internet Auctions and Harmonisation. A Comparison Between Italy and Germany', *European Review of Private Law,* 2006, Vol. 14(1), p. 3-12.

Wiewiórowska-Domagalska 2013
Wiewiórowska-Domagalska, A., *Consumer Sales Guarantees in the European Union,* Sellier: Munich, 2013.

Wilhelmsson 1993
Wilhelmsson, Th., 'European Contract Law Harmonisation: Aims And Tools', *Tulane Journal of International and Comparative Law,* 1993, Vol. 1, p. 23-46.

Wilhelmsson 2001
Wilhelmsson, Th., 'Towards a (Post)modern European Contract Law', *Juridica International,* 2001, Vol. 6, p. 23-29.

Wilhelmsson 2002
Wilhelmsson, Th., 'The Legal, the Cultural and the Political - Conclusions from Different Perspectives on Harmonisation of European Contract Law', *European Business Law Review,* 2002, Vol. 13(6), p. 541-555.

Wilhelmsson 2004
Wilhelmsson, Th., 'The Abuse of the 'Confident Consumer' as a Justification for EC Consumer Law', *Journal of Consumer Policy,* 2004, Vol. 27(3), p. 317-337.

Wilhelmsson 2006
Wilhelmsson, Th., 'Misleading Practices', in Howells, G. *et al.* (eds.), *European Fair Trading Law: The Unfair Commercial Practices Directive,* Hampshire: Ashgate Publishing, 2006, p. 49-82.

Wilhelmsson 2014
Wilhelmsson, Th., 'Free Movement of Legal Sources: The Use of Foreign Sources in Private Law in Europe', in Purnhagen, K. & Rott, P. (eds.), *Varieties of European Law and Regulation,* Cham: Springer International, 2014, p. 185-206.

Willett 1997
Willett, C., 'The Directive on Unfair Terms in Consumer Contracts and its Implementation in the United Kingdom', *European Review of Private Law,* 1997, Vol. 5(2), p. 223-236.

Willett 2007
Willett, C., *Fairness in Consumer Contracts: The Case of Unfair Terms,* Aldershot: Ashgate Publishing, 2007.

Willett 2010
Willett, C., 'Fairness and Consumer Decision Making under the Unfair Commercial Practices Directive', *Journal of Consumer Policy,* 2010, Vol. 33, p. 247-273.

Willett 2012
Willett, C., 'General Clauses and the Competing Ethics of European Consumer Law in the UK', *Cambridge Law Journal,* 2012, Vol. 71(2), p. 412-440.

Williams & Hare 2010
Williams, J. & Hare, C., 'Early Experiences of the Enforcement of the Unfair Commercial Practices Directive in Scotland', *Journal of Consumer Policy,* 2010, Vol. 33, p. 377-401.

Wimmer 2014
Wimmer, M., 'The Dinghy's Rudder: General Principles of European Union Law through the Lens of Proportionality', *European Public Law,* 2014, Vol. 20(2), p. 331-354.

Winn & Bix 2006
Winn, J.K. & Bix, B.H., 'Diverging Perspectives on Electronic Contracting in the U.S. and EU', *Cleveland State Law Review,* 2006, Vol. 54, p. 175-190.

Wissink 2002
Wissink, M., 'Interpretation', in Busch, D. *et al.* (eds.), *The Principles of European Contract Law and Dutch Law,* The Hague: Kluwer Law International, 2002, p. 241-258.

Woodroffe & Lowe 2010
Woodroffe, G. & Lowe, R., *Woodroffe & Lowe's Consumer Law and Practice,* London: Sweet & Maxwell, 2010.

Youngs 1998
Youngs, R., *English, French and German Comparative Law,* London: Routledge, 1998.

Zachariasiewicz 2011
Zachariasiewicz, M., 'Recent Developments in European Private Law: The Influence of European Consumer Law on National Legal Systems – A Report from the Conference Held on 23–24 September 2010 at the University of Silesia in Katowice, Poland', *European Review of Private Law,* 2011, Vol. 19, p. 471-480.

Zimmermann 2009
Zimmermann, R., 'The Present State of European Private Law', *American Journal of Comparative Law,* 2009, Vol. 57(2), p. 479-512.

Zollers *et al.* 1999
Zollers, F.E. *et al.*, 'Consumer Protection in the European Union: An Analysis of the Directive On The Sale of Consumer Goods and Associated Guarantees', *University of Pennsylvania Journal of International Economic Law,* 1999, Vol. 20, p. 97-131.

OTHER LITERATURE

1. Surveys and Reports

Civic Consulting, 'Study on the application of Directive 2005/29/EC on Unfair Commercial Practices in the EU', Part 1 – Synthesis Report, December 2011.

Civic Consulting, 'Study on the application of Directive 2005/29/EC on Unfair Commercial Practices in the EU', Part 2 – Country Reports, December 2011.

Ch. Biquet-Mathieu, *'Les contrats du consommateur – Rapport de droit belge'*, Association Henri Capitant, September 2007, available at: <www.henricapitant.be/documents/jcolombiennes_rapport.pdf>.

Christian Twigg-Flesner *et al.*, 'An Analysis of the Application and Scope of the Unfair Commercial Practices Directive', Report for the UK Department of Trade and Industry.

Clifford Chance Survey on European Contract law, April 2005.

Department for Business, Innovation and Skills, 'Consumer Redress for Misleading and Commercial Practices. Impact Assessment: Final', August 2013, available at: <https://www.gov.uk/government/uploads/system/uploads/attachment_data/file/226641/bis-13-1110-consumer-redress-for-misleading-and-aggressive-commercial-practices-impact-assessment-final.pdf>.

Department for Business, Innovation and Skills, 'The Consumer Protection from Unfair Trading (Amendment) Regulations 2013', August 2013, available at: <https://www.gov.uk/government/uploads/system/uploads/attachment_data/file/226640/bis-13-1112-the-consumer-protection-from-unfair-trading-amendment-regulations-2013-draft-regulations.pdf>.

Department for Business Innovation & Skills, 'Enhancing consumer confidence by clarifying consumer law – Consultation on the supply of goods, services and digital content', July 2012, available at: <https://www.gov.uk/government/uploads/-system/uploads/attachment_data/file/31350/12-937-enhancing-consumer-consultation-supply-of-goods-services-digital.pdf>.

Digital Agenda Scoreboard 2012, 'Life Online'.

ECC-Net, 'Trustmark Report 2013 - Should I trust the Trustmark?', October 2013.

EOS Gallup Europe, 'Consumers survey', January 2002.

European Securities Market Expert group (ESME), 'Report on Durable Medium - Distance Marketing Directive and Markets in Financial Instruments Directive', available at: <http://ec.europa.eu/internal_market/securities/docs/esme/-durable_medium_en.pdf>.

Expert Group, 'A European contract law for consumers and businesses: Publication of the results of the feasibility study carried out by the Expert Group on European contract law for stakeholders' and legal practitioners' feedback'.

Hans Schulte-Nölke *et al.*, *EC Consumer Law Compendium*, available at:: <www.eu-consumer-law.org/consumerstudy_full_en.pdf>.

Hans-W. Micklitz *et al.*, 'Door To Door Selling - Pyramid Selling - Multilevel Marketing', A study commissioned by the European Commission, Final Report, Volumes I and II, November 1999.

Her Majesty's Government, 'Transposition Guidance: How to implement European Directives effectively', available at: <https://www.gov.uk/government/uploads/-system/uploads/attachment_data/file/229763/bis-13-775-transposition-guidance-how-to-implement-european-directives-effectively-revised.pdf>.

House of Commons, 'The Sale and Supply of Goods to Consumers Regulations 2002 - is there a two years guarantee?', Standard Note, SN/HA/5235, December 2009.

Intergovernmental Committee created by the Conference of Messina, 'Report of Heads of Delegation of the Foreign Affairs Ministries (Spaak Report)', April 1956.

Ipsos Mori for Allen&Overy, Online Consumer Research, January 2011.

Law Society of England and Wales', 'Firms Cross-Border Work' Survey, December 2010.

National Research Council (U.S.), 'Standards, conformity assessment, and trade into the 21st century' (Washington: National Academy Press, 1995).

OECD, 'Regulatory Reform in Hungary' (Paris: OECD Publishing, 2000).

OECD, 'Better Regulation in Europe: An OECD Assessment of Regulatory Capacity in the 15 Original Member States of the EU (Project Glossary)', available at: <www.oecd.org/gov/regulatory-policy/44952782.pdf>.

OECD & European Commission, 'Handbook on Constructing Composite Indicators', 2008.

Office of Fair Trading, 'Doorstep selling: A report on the market study', May 2004, available at: <www.oft.gov.uk/shared_oft/reports/consumer_protection/oft716.-pdf>.

Office of Fair Trading, Consumer Codes of Practice: The OFT's response to the Consultation, OFT344, July 2001, electronically available at: <www.oft.gov.uk/shared_oft/Approvedcodesofpractice/oft344.pdf>.

Office of Fair Trading, 'Implementing the EU Directive on Unfair Commercial Practices and Amending Existing Consumer Legislation', OFT839, March 2006, available at: <www.oft.gov.uk/shared_oft/reports/oft_response_to_consultations/oft839.pdf.

Office of Fair Trading, 'Consumer Codes Approval Scheme; Core Criteria and Guidance', OFT390, March 2008, available at: <www.oft.gov.uk/shared_oft/-Approvedcodesofpractice/oft390.pdf>.

Office of Fair Trading, 'Unfair Contract Terms Guidance – Guidance for the Unfair Terms in Consumer Contracts Regulations 1999', September 2008, available at: <www.oft.gov.uk/shared_oft/reports/unfair_contract_terms/oft311.pdf>.

Patrick Van Eecke & Maarten Truyens, 'Benchmarking of Existing National Legal E-Business Practices. Country Report – Belgium'.

Robert Bradgate et al., 'Review of the Eight EU Consumer Acquis Minimum Harmonisation Directives and Their Implementation in the UK and Analysis of the Scope for Simplification', Independent Report prepared for the Department of Trade and Industry, September 2005, available at: <www.bis.gov.uk/files/-file27200.pdf>.

Reiner Schulze & Hans Schulte-Nölke, 'Analysis of National Fairness Laws Aimed at Protecting Consumers in Relation to Commercial Practices', study commissioned by the Directorate-General Health and Consumer Protection of the European Commission (DG SANCO).

Report from the Commission on the Implementation of Council Directive 93/13/EEC of 5 April 1993 on Unfair Terms in Consumer Contracts, COM(2000) 248 final.

The European Opinion Research Group EEIG & EOS Gallup Europe, 'Public Opinion in Europe: Views On Business-To-Consumer Crossborder Trade - Report B', November 2002.

The Law Commission & Scottish Law Commission, 'Unfair Terms In Contracts: A Joint Consultation Paper', July 2002.

The Law Commission & Scottish Law Commission, 'Unfair Terms in Contracts - Report on a reference under section 3(1)(e) of the Law Commissions Act 1965', December 2004.

The Law Commission (England and Wales), 'A private right of redress for unfair commercial practices? Preliminary Advice to the Department for Business, Enterprise and Regulatory Reform on the Issues Raised', November 2008.

The Law Commission, 'Consumer Remedies For Faulty Goods', November 2009.

The Nielsen Company, 'Is Sharing the New Buying - Reputation and Trust Are Emerging as New Currencies', May 2014.

UK Department of Enterprise, Trade and Employment, 'Consumer Protection (National Consumer Agency) Bill 2006 - Screening Regulatory Impact Analysis', August 2006.

World Bank, 'Romania - Diagnostic Review of Consumer Protection and Financial Literacy', July 2009, available at: <http://siteresources.worldbank.org/-INTECAREGTOPPRVSECDEV/Resources/RO_-_CPFL_Vol_I.pdf>.

2. Presentations at Conferences

Alan Poulter *et al.*, 'The Distance Selling Directive: Consumer Champion or Complete Irrelevance?', Paper presented at IADIS e-Society Conference on E-Commerce, E-Learning and E-Government, Unpublished (2003), available at: <www.iadis.net/dl/final_uploads/200301L042.pdf>.

Daniel Halberstam & Mathias W. Reimann, 'The Unification of Law in Federal Systems', General Report for the Thematic Conference of the International Academy of Comparative Law.

Emily M. Weitzenböck, 'Good Faith and Fair Dealing in the Context of Contract Formation by Electronic Agents', Proceedings of the AISB 2002 Symposium on Intelligent Agents in Virtual Markets, 2-5 April 2002, available at: http://folk.uio.no/emilyw/documents/Good%20Faith%20-%20Contract%20-Formation%20%26%20source.pdf>.

Helmut Wagner, 'Costs of Legal Uncertainty: Is Harmonisation of Law a Good Solution?', Modern Law for Global Commerce - Proceedings of the Congress of the United Nations Commission on International Trade Law Held on the Occasion of the Fortieth Session of the Commission, Vienna, 9-12 July 2007.

Jan Smits, 'Economic Arguments in the Harmonisation Debate: The Practical Importance of Harmonisation of Commercial Contract Law', Modern Law for Global Commerce - Proceedings of the Congress of the United Nations Commission on International Trade Law Held on the Occasion of the Fortieth Session of the Commission, Vienna, 9-12 July 2007.

Jun Gu, 'Consumer Rights Protection on the Online Auction Website - Situations and Solutions: A Case Study of EBay', paper presented at the British and Irish Law, Education and Technology Association Annual Conference 2007, available at: <www.bileta.ac.uk/>.

Nordic Council of Ministers, 'Unfair Terms in Consumer Contracts in a European Perspective - Report from a Seminar in Copenhagen, 6 June 1990', *Nordiske Seminar- og Arbejdsrapporter.*

Peter Schlechtriem, 'Good Faith in German Law and in International Uniform Laws', Saggi, Conferenze e Seminari 24, Roma (February 1997), available at: <http://cisgw3.law.pace.edu/cisg/biblio/schlechtriem16.html>.

Thomas J. Rosch, 'Forces Driving (and Impeding) Convergence: What Can The FTC (and Like Agencies) Contribute?', Consumer Protection Symposium 2007, available at: <www.ftc.gov/speeches/rosch/0711056venice.pdf>.

Valériane König, 'La transposition de la directive européenne du 25 mai 1999 surcertains aspects de la vente et des garanties des biens de consommation en droit français', presentation held at the Franco-German seminar on sales law, University of Panthéon-Assas (Paris II) and Humboldt University Berlin.

3. Commentaries to Laws

Beale/Herre/Huet/Schlechtriem/Storme/Swann/Varul/Veneziano/Zoll, Draft Common Frame of Reference, 2009.

Münchener Kommentar zum Bürgerlichen Gesetzbuch/Wurmnest, 7th edition 2016.

PEL/Hondius/Heutger/Jeloschek/Sivesand/Wiewiorowska, *Sales*, 2008.

Tekst & Commentaar Burgerlijk Wetboek/Valk, 2015.

UWG Handkommentar/Harte-Bavendamm/Henning-Bodewig/Bergmann/Goldmann/Seitz, 3rd edition 2013.

UWG Handkommentar/Piper/Ohly/Sosnitza, 5th edition 2010.

4. Online Content (Blogs with Academic Content, News and Press Releases)

Aoife White, 'Apple Warranty Ads Should Be Examined in EU, Reding Says', 1 October 2012, available at: <www.bloomberg.com/news/2012-10-01/apple-warranty-ads-should-be-examined-by-eu-states-reding-says.html>.

BBC News, 'European election results: At a glance', 27 May 2014, available at: <www.bbc.com/news/world-europe-27575869>.

Charles Arthur & Juliette Garside, 'Smartphones take the lead in European phone market', 8 September 2011, available at: <www.guardian.co.uk/technology/2011/-sep/08/smartphones-take-lead-in-mobile-phone-market>.

Ciao-shopping price review website: <www.ciao-shopping.nl>.

Consumers: the European Commission asks Belgium and France to comply with EU rules on unfair practices, European Commission Press Release - IP/11/1096, 29 September 2011, available at: <http://europa.eu/rapid/press-release_IP-11-1096_en.htm?locale=en>.

European Union terminology, <http://europa.eu/abc/eurojargon/index_en.htm>.

Italian Competition Authority, '*Garanzia di conformitàdelvenditore: antitrust sanzionailgruppo Apple per complessivi 900 mila Euro*', press release, 27 December 2011, available at: <www.agcm.it/stampa/news/5829-sanzioni-per-complessivi-900mila-euro-al-gruppo-apple-per-pratiche-commerciali-scorrette.html>.

<www.apple.com/uk/legal/statutory-warranty/>.

Paul Krugman, 'The Lesser Depression', NY Times, 21 July 2011, available at: <www.nytimes.com/2011/07/22/opinion/22krugman.html>.

Jeffrey D. Sachs, 'The Endgame in Greece', 16 June 2015, available at: <www.project-syndicate.org/commentary/greece-endgame-eurozone-default-by-jeffrey-d-sachs-2015-06>.

Paul Krugman, 'Europe's Impossible Dream', 20 July 2015, available at: <http://goo.gl/xZBjRp>.

Viviane Reding, 'An ambitious Consumer Rights Directive: boosting consumers' protection and helping businesses', Press Release, 15 March 2010, available at: <http://europa.eu/>.

World Bank Doing Business, <www.doingbusiness.org/reports>.

5. Working Papers

Claudio M. Radaelli, 'The Open Method of Coordination: A new governance architecture for the European Union?', Swedish Institute for European Policy Studies, Report nr. 1 March/2003.

Giuseppe Dari-Mattiacci, 'Soft Negligence and Cause In Fact: A Comment on Ganuza and Gomez' (October 2004), George Mason University School of Law Working Papers Series, Working Paper 4.

Hans-W. Micklitz, 'The Proposal on Consumer Rights and the Opportunity for a Reform of European Unfair Terms Legislation in Consumer Contracts', EUI Working Papers LAW 2010/2.

Marco Loos, 'Full Harmonisation as a Regulatory Concept and its Consequences for the National Legal Orders: The Example of the Consumer Rights Directive', Centre for the Study of European Contract Law Working Paper Series No. 2010/03.

Marco Loos, 'Sales Law in the DCFR', Centre for the Study of European Contract Law, Working Paper Series No. 2010/04.

Simeon Djankov *et al.*, 'Courts: the Lex Mundi project', National Bureau of Economic Research WORKING PAPER SERIES, April 2002, available at: <www.lexmundi.com/images/lexmundi/PDF/courts_nber1.pdf?SnID=2>.

6. Miscellaneous

Aristotle, *Rhetoric* (Aeterna Press, 2015).

Andreas Schwab, 'Consumer Rights: Better protection for consumers', Press Release, 3 June 2010, available at: <www.eppgroup.eu/press>.

Anne De Vries, 'Maximum Harmonisation and General Clauses - Two Conflicting Concepts?', January 2011, available at: <http://ssrn.com/abstract=1703078>.

Anne Salaun, 'Transposition de la directive contrats à distance en droit belge, commentaire de l'article 20 de la loi du 25 mai 1999', Droit des nouvelles technologies, available at: <www.droit-technologie.org>.

Ben J. Schafer *et al.*, 'E-Commerce Recommendation Applications', Grouplens Paper, available at: <www.grouplens.org/papers/pdf/ECRA.pdf>.

Brigitta Jud, 'Staatshaftung für judikatives Unrecht', Ecolex 2003.

Cinzia Alcidi *et al.*, ''Grexit': Who Would Pay for It?', CEPS Policy Brief No. 272, May 2012.

Eric Clive, 'Proposal for a Common European Sales Law withdrawn', European Private Law News, 07.01.2015, available at: <www.epln.law.ed.ac.uk/2015/01/07/-proposal-for-a-common-european-sales-law-withdrawn/>.

European Council, Presidency Conclusions at the Lisbon meeting, 23-24 March 2000.

Geraint Howells & Norbert Reich, 'Extent of Harmonisation in Consumer Contract Law', note requested by the Directorate-General for Internal Policies, October 2010.

German Standards Advertising, 'Council Rules on Advertising and its Appraisal', October 2007, available at: <www.werberat.de/sites/default/files/uploads/-media/dw_general_principles_en.pdf>.

G.I.P Ottaviano et al., 'Brexit or Fixit? The trade and welfare effects of leaving the European union', CEP Policy Analysis, CEPPA016, 2014.

Institut für Europaisches Wirtschafts und Verbraucherrecht, 'Study on the Feasibility of a General Legislative Framework on Fair Trading', November 2000, electronically available at: <http://ec.europa.eu/dgs/health_consumer/library/surveys/-sur21_vol2_en.pdf>.

Jean-Jacques M. Robert, 'Rapport fait au nom de la commission des Affaires économiques et du Plan (1) sur le projet de loi relatif au code de la consommation (partie législative)' (Report made in the name of the commission of economic affairs and of the plan (1) on the bill relating to the consumer code (legislative part)), French Senate, 2nd ordinary session 1992-1993.

Kamerstuk Tweede Kamer 1987-1988 kamerstuknummer 20443 ondernummer 3, Memorie van Toelichting, Wijziging van de Colportagewet.

Kate Roberts, 'The Extent of Unfair Commercial Practices', March 2009, available at: <www.consumerfocus.org.uk/assets/1/files/2009/11/UCPDresearch.pdf>.

Natalia Kabacinska, 'Issues on the Harmonisation of European Contract Law and the Polish Presidency Proposal Concerning an Optional Instrument', June 2011, p. 7, available at: <http://en.zpc.wpia.uw.edu.pl/wp-content/uploads/2011/01/-European-Constitutionalism-paper-NKabacińska.pdf>.

Martijn W. Hesselink, 'The Values Underlying the Draft Common Frame Of Reference: What Role for Fairness and 'Social Justice'?', European Commission Legal Affairs - Internal Market and Consumer Protection, September 2008.

Martijn Hesselink & Marco Loos, 'Unfair contract terms in B2C contracts', Briefing Note for the European Parliament's Committee on Legal Affairs, June 2012.

Memorie van implementatie van de Richtlijn consumentenrechten, Kamerstukken II 2012/2013, 33520.

Marco Loos, 'Service contracts', January 2010, p. 1, available at: <http://papers.ssrn.com/sol3/papers.cfm?abstract_id=1542506>.

Omer Tene, 'Good Faith in Precontractual Negotiations: A Franco-German-American Perspective', November 2006, available at: <http://ssrn.com/abstract=943383>.

Patricia Foucher & Françoise Hébert-Wimart, 'La garantie de la conformité du bien au contrat', *Institut National de la Consommation Hebdo* no. 1367, December 2005.

Per Liljas, 'Skype Translator Will Be Able to Interpret Calls in Real Time', Time Magazine, 28 May 2014, available at: <http://time.com/121983/skype-translator-microsoft/>.

Rafał Mańko, 'Unfair contract terms in EU law', European Parliamentary Library Briefing, September 2013.

Rafał Mańko, 'Methods for unifying private law in the EU', European Parliamentary Research Service, January 2014.

Rafał Mańko, 'EU Competence in Private Law - In-Depth Analysis', European Parliamentary Research Service, January 2015.

Rafał Mańko, 'Contract law and the Digital Single Market: Towards a New Online Consumer Sales Law?', European Parliamentary Research Service, September 2015.

Ramon Mullerat, 'How Spain Implements European Law', Jean Monnet/Robert Schuman Paper Series, Vol. 10, No. 2, March 2010.

Romanian Advertising Council, The Code of Advertising Practice, available online at: <www.rac.ro/EN/cod>.

Thierry Bourgoignie, 'La transposition de la directive 93/13/CEE dans le droit belge: un processus (très) évolutif et (trop) confidentiel', available at: <http://ec.europa.eu/consumers/policy/developments/unfa_cont_term/uct04_en.pdf>.

Trading Standards Institute, 'Consumer Codes Approval Scheme - New codes approval criteria - consultation paper', 24 October 2012, available at: <https://www.recc.org.uk/images/upload/news_62_TSI-Codes-Criteria-Consultation.pdf>.

Vanessa Veriter, 'De elektronische handel: een nieuwe muze voor wetgevers', Beroep Instituut van Erkende Boekhouders en Fiscalisten, July 2001.

CURRICULUM VITAE

Catalina Goanta received her LL.B. degree from the Faculty of Law of the University of Bucharest, a study dedicated to Romanian and international law. During her studies at the University of Bucharest, Catalina successfully participated in two international moot court competitions in Hamburg, Geneva and Washington, and subsequently interned for the Bucharest-based Price Waterhouse Coopers 'David&Baias' law firm as well as for the main Credit Europe Bank branch in Romania. She proceeded to complete an LL.M. at the Faculty of Law at Maastricht University, specializing in European comparative law and international law, and further obtained an M.Sc. from the United Nations University-MERIT Maastricht Graduate School of Governance.

Catalina started her doctoral research in 2011, funded by the UM-HiiL Chair on the Internationalisation of Law at Maastricht University's Faculty of Law. This doctoral research was presented, among others, at the European Private Law workshop organised by Prof. dr. Hans Micklitz at the European University Institute in Florence (February 2015), as well as the Summer Institute for Law and Economics organised by Prof. dr. Omri Ben-Shahar and the Coase-Sandor Institute for Law and Economics at the University of Chicago Law School (July 2016).

IUS COMMUNE EUROPAEUM

A peer-reviewed book series in which the common foundations of the legal systems of the Member States of the European Union are the central focus.

The *Ius Commune Europaeum* series includes horizontal comparative legal studies as well as studies on the effect of treaties within the national legal systems. All the classic fields of law are covered. The books are published in various European languages under the auspices of METRO, the Institute for Transnational Legal Research at the Maastricht University.

Recently published:

Volume 146: *The Citizen in European Private Law: Norm-setting, Enforcement and Choice,* C. CAUFFMAN and J. SMITS (eds.)
Volume 147: *Legal Certainty in Real Estate Transactions: A Comparison of England and France,* B. DU MARAIS and D. MARRANI (eds.)
Volume 148: *Scarcity and the State I. The Allocation of Limited Rights by the Administration,* P. ADRIAANSE, F. VAN OMMEREN, W. DEN OUDEN and J. WOLSWINKEL (eds.)
Volume 149: *Optional Instruments of the European Union. A Definitional, Normative and Explanatory Study,* W.A. BULL
Volume 150: *The European Union and National Civil Procedure. A Smooth Process or a Rocky Road for Member States?,* A. NYLUND and B.H. KRANS (eds.)
Volume 151: *Different Paths Towards Sustainable Biofuels? A Comparative Study of the International, EU, and Chinese Regulation of the Sustainability of Biofuels,* T. YUE
Volume 152: *Regulation of Cross-Border Establishment in China and the EU. A Comparative Law and Economics Approach,* G. SHEN
Volume 153: *The French Contract Law Reform: a Source of Inspiration?,* S. STIJNS and S. JANSEN (eds.)

www.ingramcontent.com/pod-product-compliance
Ingram Content Group UK Ltd.
Pitfield, Milton Keynes, MK11 3LW, UK
UKHW051925100926
8556IPUK00022B/1379

9 781780 684314